DICTIONARY OF PLACE-NAMES IN THE BRITISH ISLES

DICTIONARY OF PLACE-NAMES IN THE BRITISH ISLES

ADRIAN ROOM

BLOOMSBURY

First Published 1988
Copyright © by Adrian Room 1988

Bloomsbury Publishing Limited, 2 Soho Square, London W1V 5DE

British Library Cataloguing in Publication Data

Room, Adrian
    Dictionary of place-names in the British
    Isles.
    1. Great Britain. Place names. Etymology
    I. Title
    914.1'00142

ISBN 0 7475 0170 X

Designed by Malcolm Smythe

Printed in Great Britain by
Butler & Tanner Ltd, Frome and London

CONTENTS

Always it is the names that work the most powerful magic, and nowhere more so than in Britain ... They tell us not only where we want to go but where we have come from; clues to our past and the forces that have shaped the land we live in.

Brian Jackman, *The Sunday Times Magazine*, 24 January 1988.

*I*NTRODUCTION

THE ROLE AND LORE OF PLACE-NAMES IN OUR LIVES

Place-names play an important functional role in our lives as necessary 'indicators' for the place we wish to mention or refer to. Without thinking of their further significance, we use them to denote particular locations in everyday speech: 'Are you going up to London tomorrow?', 'I hear they've moved to Glasgow', 'Yes, she still lives in Leeds', 'He used to commute from Braintree, but now he lives in Putney things are much easier'. And apart from our own use of place-names in this way (to say nothing of their role in addresses, telephone directories, tourist maps, guidebooks, and many other 'name lists' where we seek to establish a particular location), we expect to find place-names constantly present in what we see and hear in the media to tell us 'what happened where': 'London's South Bank . . .', 'An oil slick in Belfast Lough . . .', 'Westminster County Court . . .', 'A Hagley boy . . .', 'The Crawley quads . . .'.

Apart from this basic denotative function, place-names also acquire a sort of mystique of their own in the language. We tend to react to them as 'nice' or 'nasty', 'serious' or 'funny', 'upper-class' or 'common'. Popular tourist guides like to talk of 'the curiously named village' or 'the quaintly named town', and names such as Liverpool, Basingstoke, and Neasden not only have a 'resonance' of their own but a spoken quality that is frequently exploited for an incongruous or even comic effect. In the 'North–South divide' — the popular description for the polarisation of Britain, especially England, in the 1980s, with the 'haves' in the South and the 'have-nots' in the North — even the place-names appear to take on an appropriate allusive sense that somehow reflects the area of the country they represent. One thinks of some Northern names, such as Workington, Bootle, Pudsey, Worksop, Bacup, Scunthorpe, and Scarborough as being 'artisan', while Southern names, such as Bath, Wells, Maidstone, Honiton, Weston-super-Mare, and Canterbury, are regarded as 'genteel'. The North, too, has its robust comic connections in Clitheroe, Formby, and Morecambe, names associated with actual comedians, while the 'Sunny South' has the lion's share of 'holiday' names, such as Southsea, Southend-on-Sea, Brighton, and Bournemouth. (Of course, the south has Neasden as well, which is in a special class of its own . . .!)

But the question now arises: what do all these names actually *mean*? How did they originate? How did Neasden come to be called Neasden and not, say, Dinsdale? Why is York so called? Where is the black pool, if there is one, at Blackpool? Who were the maids of Maidstone? Where is the 'Northend' that corresponds to the Southend of Southend-on-Sea?

In the back of our mind, we know that place-names are more than mere location indicators, and that their popular associations or 'image' spring from a word that, at some time, must have been created by an individual or group of people, or at least had some kind of initial 'launch' before it developed to its current form.

And because we like words to be meaningful, we devise our own explanations for them. Or rather, we allow certain 'wordmongers' and enthusiasts to explain them for us. The drinker in the pub will tell you that London's Neasden, Willesden, and Harlesden originated as the haunts of medieval thieves, respectively 'Ned's den', 'Will's den', and 'Harry's den'. The Isle of Wight is so called, we are led to believe, because of its white cliffs. And Cambridge is of course so called because it arose by a bridge over the Cam. Even at a more academic level we are told the tale about how Lichfield's name means 'field of corpses', referring to a military massacre there in times gone by (we are not sure when), and are led to suppose that Guildford is named after the golden flowers that grew by the river there. And is not Edinburgh named after its founder, Edwin, the seventh-century king of Northumbria?

Place-names, like personal names, thus breed their own folklore, and the more colourful or implausible this folklore is, the more we relish it!

Even so, we have those niggling doubts. If Lichfield is named after a historic massacre, why are not other 'fields' so named? If Edinburgh is named after Edwin, why are other historic places not named after their famous founders? In short, to what extent do names tie in with our history? That is something we should now consider.

PLACE-NAMES AND HISTORY

The British Isles have had a varied history over the centuries, and the fact that we are now broadly divided into 'Celts' and 'non-Celts', that is, the Irish, Scots, Welsh, and Cornish on the one hand, and the English on the other, shows that we do not have a unified nation, but an island group of different cultural, social, and linguistic backgrounds, of which the two divisions mentioned are only the most obvious.

There have been five clearly defined successive groups of invaders or settlers in the British Isles in historic times, and each group, speaking a different language from the others, has left its place-names in our landscape and townscape. Some have had a much greater impact on names than others; moreover, some have invaded and settled more than once, or have arrived in the islands at different times. This clearly complicates the scene, but even so a fairly steady chronological flow can be delineated.

First came the *Celts*, the ancient warrior people who came to settle in not only Britain but also Spain, Gaul (modern France), and other parts of western and central Europe in pre-Roman times, reaching the height of their power in the fourth century BC. They appear to have originated from the regions of the Rhine, the Seine, the Loire, and the upper reaches of the Danube in about 1200 BC. Today, we equate the language or languages they spoke with the Celtic languages (Irish, Welsh, Gaelic, and Cornish) still spoken, to some extent, in Britain. At the same time, many of the place-names in obviously 'English' parts of Britain are also Celtic in origin, especially the earliest names, such as those of rivers and the first human settlements. And as far as the British Isles are concerned, it is the Celtic tribe of Britons, who gave the island group its name, that concerns us the most immediately. These are the familiar 'Ancient Britons' of school history days, the people who settled mainly in southern Britain but who later, under pressure from subsequent settlers and invaders, moved to those parts of Britain with which we chiefly associate them today — Wales, Scotland, and Cornwall. In Ireland, they remained more or less fully represented throughout the land. The Picts of Scotland also belong to this period.

It was the *Romans* who next came to Britain, with the Roman Conquest beginning in AD 43. By the end of the first century AD, Latin was the official language throughout southern Britain, although the language of everyday speech was still Celtic (what is now technically known as British or Brythonic, which would later be differentiated as Welsh and Cornish). The Romans were curiously unenterprising when it came to giving names, and in many cases they simply gave a British place-name a Latin form or ending, so that what may have been something like *lindo* became *Lindum* (modern Lincoln) and what was perhaps *londo* (we are uncertain still of the exact forms) became *Londinium* (London). These two names, and many (but not all) others, are examples of modern names that have thus, thanks to the Romans, preserved their Celtic original (or even pre-Celtic, for though it is certain that the Celts used these names, in some cases their own names were based on those of the people, whoever they were, who inhabited the British Isles before them).

The Romans left Britain in the early fifth century, and in the middle of that same century, the *Anglo-Saxon* invasion and settlement began. The Angles were the original English, and the people who introduced the language now known as both Anglo-Saxon and Old English. We shall be considering this in a little more detail in due course, for the Anglo-Saxons were as prolific namers as the Romans were unprolific, and very many well-known place-names in Britain are English in origin.

Unlike the Romans, the Anglo-Saxons did not return to their native continent, but were still 'in residence' when the next settlers arrived. These were the *Scandinavians*, popularly referred to as the Norsemen or Vikings, whose raids began at the beginning of the ninth century. They in turn introduced *their* language to Britain, which is now referred to as Old Norse. They gave several names, either originally or by adapting (or translating) existing English names. Their influence was strongest in the so-called Danelaw, the northern, central, and eastern parts of England where Danish laws and customs were observed, and where many of their names can be found today, usually consisting of a personal name followed by '-by', such as Grimsby and Slingsby. These are thus the 'Danish' names proper, while the Norwegian ones, from subsequent settlers, are represented today in the north and west of Scotland, as well as in the Isle of Man and on the east coast of Ireland. Scandinavian names are also found around the southwest coasts of Wales, especially for the islands there.

The fifth and most recent settlement, and the best recorded, was that made by the *Normans* in the famous year of 1066. The Normans are so named because they were themselves descended from the tenth-century Norsemen, who had conquered their part of France (Normandy). But the language they spoke when they conquered England in the eleventh century was to all intents and purposes French, for the Norsemen adopted the language and culture of the French when they settled there. French thus became the main language of the ruling class in England for about the next two centuries, and a fairly small but conspicuously French legacy of place-names still survives to remind us of these people, including such names as Beaulieu ('beautiful place') and Malpas ('bad passage'). However, probably their most characteristic 'trademark' is the large number of 'double-barrelled' names, where the name of a French family has been added to an existing (usually English) name, such as Kingston Bagpuize or Melton Mowbray. Most such names arose in the thirteenth or fourteenth centuries, although the 'manorial' connection had already been established in the eleventh century for some places, and they are recorded with names like these in the Domesday Book. We will return to this type of name later, when considering personal names generally.

There have of course been invaders and settlers (immigrants) of other races since the Normans — the Germans gained a toehold in the Channel Islands in the Second World War, and since the war sizeable numbers of West Indians, Asians, and other nationalities have come to live in Britain — but their numbers or influence have not been sufficient to involve further new naming or renaming of places, except perhaps at a local level.

The linguistic implications of all these settlements is something we shall consider shortly.

PLACE-NAMES AND GEOGRAPHY

Most place-names refer to a specific geographical location, whether a natural feature, such as a hill, island, or river, or a man-made one, such as a farm, village, or other settlement. And it follows that where there are many rivers there will be many names containing the word (in whatever language) for 'river', and that where there are mountains there will be names containing the word for 'mountain' (such as all the 'Bens' in Scotland). Place-names can tell us not only about the local topography, which is unlikely to have changed substantially (mountains do not move, although forests can be cleared), but about the economic and social way of life of their day. Once we know, for example, that a name ending in '-stock' or '-stoke' can refer either to a secondary settlement, dependent on a primary one, or to a religious site, we can identify the sites of such settlements. Similarly, once we appreciate that a name ending in '-ing' will usually denote a group of people, such as a tribe, we can look at a map and study the location of such tribal territories and reach conclusions about them. The fact that there are many such names in Sussex, for example, shows that the territories must have been quite small in that region, unlike the much larger kingdoms held by the Anglo-Saxons as Essex, Wessex, and Sussex itself. One can carry out detective work in this way. When it turns out that the name of Accrington means 'acorn farm', for instance, we can deduce that there must have been an oak forest nearby and that pigs (who feed on acorns) must have been farmed there. In another sort of way, when it turns out that the name of Rye, in East Sussex, means 'at the island' (not 'rye farm'!), we can assume, rightly, that the place arose on an island of some kind, such as higher, drier land in marshland, which was exactly what happened. Place-names are thus not only geographical and topographical 'denotators', but, by implication, historical ones as well. Stamford means 'stone ford' so there must have been such a ford over the river there in historic times, and Newcastle (obviously) means 'new castle', so an earlier one must have been there at some stage. Names like these lead one to take the process further and to consider *why* the river should have been forded at that point, and *where* such a new castle was built. It was clearly an important matter in each case. One does not build a stone ford or a new castle without good reason!

This is only the tip of the place-name iceberg, of course, and it would take a book in itself to detail all the information that place-names can and do provide. As to *how* they provide it, that is a matter for the linguists and their records, and they are the people we should consider next.

PLACE-NAMES AND LANGUAGE

It is all very well, the reader may say, to be told that Rye means 'at the island', and that Accrington means 'acorn farm', but how do you know? How do you determine the precise meaning of a name, or work out who gave his or her name to a place.

The short answer is that, as when working with any foreign language, the names have to be translated. We now know enough about the language of the Anglo-Saxons to be able to interpret the names reasonably accurately. And as this particular language (Old English) evolved into modern English, it may be helpful to take a short look at it. Our general understanding of Anglo-Saxon place-names may be the greater if we can manage to understand at least something about the language itself.

The Angles and the Saxons (and also the Jutes, who similarly came to Britain) were members of a West Germanic tribe, with their own names still represented in Germany today by Angeln, a region of northeast Schleswig-Holstein, Saxony (Sachsen), and Jutland. The language they spoke was thus something like German today, and had grammatical rules involving 'endings' on nouns and verbs that anyone who has studied modern German will be familiar with. Many Old English place-names are based on nouns, and some of these are still easily understood today and will appear in place-names in a modern English form that corresponds to the original sense. Among such words are *clif, cumb, ende, ford, lamb, land, sand, thorn*, and *wella*, which mean what they seem to mean. Other words may need some guidance, but nevertheless can be seen to be close to their modern equivalents, such as *brōc* (brook), *brōm* (broom), *cyning* (king), *dūn* (hill, down), *feld* (open land, field), *haga* (hedge), *hyll* (hill), *myln* (mill), *scēap*, (sheep), *stān* (stone), *tūn* (farm, town), and *wudu* (wood). But others are more like their modern German equivalents, such as *beorg* (hill; German *Berg*), *burg* or *burh* (fort; German *Burg*), *cirice* (church; German *Kirche*), *cniht* (knight; German *Knecht*), *eofor* (wild boar; German *Eber*), *fugol* (bird; German *Vogel*), *stīg* (path, track; German *Steig*), and *wald* (wood; German *Wald*). Others again are now different from either modern English or modern German, such as *ærn* (building), *earn* (eagle), *ēg* (island), and *ōra* (bank, border).

With the passage of time, such words will usually have been further modified: *burg* will often be '-bury', *stīg* will frequently be simply '-sty' (as in Ansty), and *ēg* will often be merely '-ey' (as in Molesey or Witney).

Once it is realised what the modern equivalents can be, allowing for several exceptions, it is possible to 'read' many names quite accurately, and even this minimum of information given here, for instance, should enable the reader to correctly interpret such names as Brompton (ignoring the 'p'), Stanfield, and Everton (clue: animal).

The Scandinavians also spoke a Germanic language, and their Old Norse words were often similar to or even identical with the Old English ones. This makes for ease of interpretation with such pairs (Old English word first) as *fugol/fugl* (bird), *hæfen/hafn* (harbour), *holt/holt* (copse), *cirice/kirkja* (church), *næss/nes* (headland), *sand/sand* (sand), *stīg/ stígr* (path), *thorn/thorn* (thorn), and *throp/thorp* (hamlet).

One does not wish to over-simplify, of course, and it is clearly necessary to command more than a few simple words, but knowing the basic meanings of words such as these can give sense to many apparently meaningless place-names.

The accents on many of these words indicate vowel length and are part of the correct form of the word. It is hoped that after a while they will be as readily accepted by the reader as the unfamiliar spellings of the non-English words themselves.

The briefest glance at a map of Wales, Scotland, or Ireland will show that Celtic names are quite different from the English and Norse Germanic ones. The meanings of some of the more frequently encountered words are given in the listing of elements that follows this Introduction, while others will become apparent from the entries themselves. Soon enough one comes to realise that all those Welsh names starting 'Llan-' are names of churches, and that all the Irish names with 'Bally-' refer either to a township or the mouth of a ford (depending which Irish word lies behind the name). There is often surprisingly little difference between, say, Irish names and Scottish; for example, Drumbeg will mean 'little ridge' in both countries. Welsh names, too, reflect the special feature of the language known as 'mutation', whereby an initial letter of a word or element may alter to another in certain circumstances. Welsh names beginning 'Llanfair-', for example, have a second element that on its own is the personal name *Mair* (Mary), so that the meaning is 'St Mary's church'. But when following the word *llan* (church) *Mair* becomes *Fair*, according to the rules of mutation, and this has to be recognised. (Word order is another feature of Celtic place-names that will need attention. The English say 'Marychurch', the Welsh say 'Churchmary'.)

Norman names often seem the easiest to interpret of the 'foreign' names, although like all names they can become distorted and abbreviated with the passage of time. Beaurepaire, for instance, can be reasonably easily recognised as representing the French for 'beautiful retreat', but when this same name is corrupted to Belper or (even worse) Bear Park one will need to consult the early records of the name to establish the true origin and meaning.

As mentioned, the Romans left very few Latin names, although a *colonia* can be seen in the name of Lincoln and a *cataracta* or 'waterfall' may lie behind the name of Catterick. It is chiefly through the Latin words adopted by the Anglo-Saxons that we see any notable Roman legacy, such as the *castra* (camp) that gave Old English *ceaster* and the names of places ending in '-caster' or '-chester', or the *via strata* ('paved way') that gave Old English *strǣt* and modern 'street', with place-names containing 'Strat-' all on or by Roman roads.

Once one becomes familiar with the basic characteristics of each language, it is a pleasant revelation to find that some pairs of names that seem different are in fact exactly the same in meaning. Keswick is thus simply a 'Scandinavianised' form (with a 'harder' pronunciation) of Chiswick, and similarly Kirkby is synonymous with Cheriton (although the two second elements of the names are different). These two pairs respectively mean 'cheese farm' and 'village with a church'.

Pairs of names in completely different languages, such as Celtic and English, can often surprise by turning out to be exactly the same in meaning. Thus Dublin and Blackpool both mean the same, as do Holyhead and Penzance ('holy headland'), Land's End and Pembroke, and Douglas and Blackwater. Sometimes, though, the difference is a slighter one, but unexplained. Both Leyton and Luton have the same basic name, meaning 'farm on the river Lea', and Haringey (or Harringay, as it formerly was) has the same meaning as Hornsey, which is 'Hæring's hedged enclosure'.

Other surprises are in store for the reader as the pages of the Dictionary are turned. But it cannot be too often emphasised that many names do *not* mean what they outwardly appear to mean, and that one needs to go back to the original, or as near to it as possible, to establish the true sense. Meanwhile, names with apparently meaningless forms acquire new meanings that are imposed on them by modern forms of the language, or by a completely different language altogether. The Beaurepaire example previously cited is a good instance of this: the 'meaningless' French words are 'translated' into the meaningful English 'Bear Park'. However, other names remain 'meaningless' in any language, such as the other corruption of Beaurepaire — Belper.

THE SOURCES OF PLACE-NAMES

So where does one go to find the earliest forms, spellings, and (importantly) meanings of place-names? There exist various early texts in the different languages that can be consulted, some more reliable than others. A few, however, stand out by their authenticity and scholarship, and three of them should be mentioned here.

The first is *The Ecclesiastical History of the English People*, written by the Venerable Bede in the early eighth century. The work is a Latin history of the English (its Latin title is *Historia Ecclesiastica Gentis Anglorum*), completed in 731, in which Bede, a monk, scholar, and historian of Jarrow, sets out events in Britain from the time of the invasion of Julius Caesar to 731, with a section of the long work describing the state of things in Britain in that particular year. Bede was obviously interested in place-names. He quotes many, and frequently explains them, translating the Anglo-Saxon names into Latin. (Some of his references to place-names are quoted in this present Dictionary.) When he does so, we thus have not only a fairly scholarly transcription of the contemporary Anglo-Saxon name, but his translation of it as a further guide to its meaning. For instance, he translates the name of Selsey as 'seal island' (*Insula vituli marini*), and in writing about Carlisle he talks of '*Lugubalium civitatem quae a populis Anglorum corrupte Luel vocatur*' ('the city of *Lugubalium* which is corruptly called by the English people *Luel*'). Bede's work is one of the most extensive records of Anglo-Saxon place-names that we have.

The next important source is *The Anglo-Saxon Chronicle*, a record (in English) of events in England from the beginning of the Christian era (the first century AD) to 1154. The first or earliest sections of the work seem to have been written some time about the ninth century, but the span and scope of the text as a whole enables many place-names to be recorded and noted in their earliest forms, which is clearly of great value to the toponymist, or student of place-names.

However, it is the great 'Domesday Book' that provides the most detailed coverage of English place-names, although one must allow for the fact that the scribes or clerks were French-speaking Normans, and so had difficulties with the unfamiliar Anglo-Saxon names.

What does the Domesday Book give us, by way of place-names? The book contains a detailed survey, ordered by William the Conqueror in 1086, of lands held by the king and his tenants in 35 shires or counties of England, identifying the tenants-in-chief (land holders) by name, as well as their tenants and sub-tenants, and detailing the extent of land and property held (especially livestock) and its monetary value at the time. The whole survey, which did not cover some of the northern counties, and even omitted some well-known cities in southern England (such as Winchester and London), was written in a special form of stylised and abbreviated eleventh-century church Latin, which makes it hard to interpret today except by a specialist. (Modern translations for each county now exist, however.) And of course the names of the actual places, the manors and villages, appear at the head of each entry.

Here is a complete typical entry, translated into modern English, to show the sort of information that was detailed. It is for East Mersea, in Essex:

Swein holds MERESAILA in lordship, which Robert son of Wymarc held before 1066 as a manor, for 6 hides. Always 2 ploughs in lordship. Then 8 ploughs, now 6. Then 9 villagers, now 8; then 12 smallholders, now 14; then 3 slaves, now none. Woodland, then 40 pigs, meadow, 5 acres; 4 fisheries. Then 1 cob, 9 cattle, 25 pigs, 107 sheep; now 3 cobs, 12 cattle, 10 pigs, 100 sheep, 1 beehive. Value £10.

Of course, most of this interesting information will be superfluous to our purposes, for what concerns us here is the place-name. The fact that it is here recorded as *Meresaila* enables us, failing any earlier record, to interpret it as 'sea island', or 'island in the sea', with an ultimate origin in Old English *mere*, 'lake', 'sea' (plus a possessive -*s*), and *ēg*, 'island', with the latter word spelt under the influence of Old French *isle* (modern *île*), 'island'. In this way, we can establish that it is the first part of the name of Mersea that means 'sea', not the second!

As mentioned, the Norman clerks had problems with some of the names. They also, like anyone else, were prone to make mistakes and miscopyings. But all in all their records of the names are remarkably consistent and accurate, and enable much valuable name interpretation to be carried out, especially where earlier records are lacking.

Here are a few random records of names, as spelt by the Norman scribes:

Domesday Book	Modern equivalent
Badequella	Bakewell
Essecestra	Exeter
Glouucestre	Gloucester
Wicumbe	High Wycombe
Wich	Nantwich
Burg	Peterborough
Prichemaresworde	Rickmansworth
Sciropescire	Shropshire
Wendlesberie	Wellingborough
Ordingas	Worthing
Ermud	Yarmouth
Euruic	York

These eleventh-century versions of the names are more significant than it might seem, and are not simply 'misspellings'. (Our own forms of the names are frequently more distorted than the Domesday Book ones!)

Three of the names are noticeably different, showing that High Wycombe was not yet 'high', that Nantwich was not yet 'Nant-', and that Peterborough was not yet 'Peter-'. We can therefore deduce that these places acquired an additional differentiating element some time after the Domesday survey was made. 'Wich' (meaning simply 'special place') is after all a common enough name, found in many other places, such as Norwich, Ipswich, Middlewich, and Northwich. 'Burg' too, meaning simply 'fortified place' or 'manor', is a name that needs an identifying addition. As it turns out, High Wycombe became 'High' both to indicate its importance and to distinguish it from other nearby Wycombes, such as West Wycombe. Nantwich became 'Nant-' (meaning 'named' or 'famous') to be distinguished from Northwich and Middlewich which were also originally simply 'Wich'. And Peterborough added the name of the saint to whom its newly built (or rebuilt) cathedral was dedicated.

Badequella is closer to the original personal name of Beadeca that forms the first part of the name than 'Bake-' is, and Wendlesberie even more clearly preserves the personal name of Wændel than Wellingborough does. Yarmouth (Isle of Wight) may be at the mouth of the river Yar (or Yare), but this Domesday record shows that the name actually derives from Old English *ēar* (gravel), so that the river got its name from the town, not the other way round. Euruic, too, goes some way towards preserving the *eofor-wīc*, or 'boar farm', that the Anglo-Saxons had understood the original name to mean, wrongly, as it happens. Essecestre, Glouucestre, Sciropescire, and Ordingas are typical Norman adjustments and 'smoothings' of awkward letters and consonants. They look more French than English even now. Shropshire was originally something like 'Scrubsburyshire' (Shrewsbury, that gave the name, was 'Scrubsbury', or 'scrubland fort'), and it is hardly surprising that they had difficulties over this barbarity. Later, they 'eased' the name even more by substituting an *l* for the *r*, as they did for Salisbury (which was originally 'Sarisbury'), and thus came to give the alternative name of Salop for the county. Prichemaresworde is simply a copying error, with an initial *P-* that should not be there.

But despite such qualifications, the Norman records of the Domesday Book are among the most copious we have when it comes to place-names, and in many instances provide the earliest record of a name's spelling, enabling an interpretation to be made where this would otherwise be very difficult.

Other sources of early place-names are the various medieval records that exist in the form of charters, deeds, and other legal documents. In a few instances, we have really early records in the works of classical writers, such as Caesar, Tacitus, and Ptolemy, dating from the second or even first century AD. These will of course be of Celtic (British) or even pre-Celtic names, in pre-Anglo-Saxon times. It is a pity that they are not more numerous.

For names that were given in post-medieval times (i.e. from the sixteenth century onwards), it is usually a relatively easy matter to trace the origin in contemporary documents. And for the creation of the most recent names of all, those of the new administrative districts set up in the mid-1970s with the reorganisation of local government, there are the local authorities themselves to consult. The same applies for the New Towns with new names (not all that many) that have arisen since the Second World War.

In addition to sources such as these, or modern translations or editions of them, there are of course a number of separate works and publications devoted exclusively to place-names and their origins. A selection of these is considered in the Guide to Further Reading at the end of this Dictionary, on p. 410.

NAMING PATTERNS

Just as stamp-collectors like to specialise in a particular area of interest, so many place-name students choose to concentrate their attention on a particular type of place-name, or a particular geographical area. The various possible permutations and combinations are considerable, but some examples of the kinds of areas that can be studied with interest and profit are given below. In the following sections of this Introduction we shall then briefly consider two especially interesting areas of this kind, personal names in place-names and river names.

Geographical area   A study of the place-names of a particular area, such as a county, can be interesting, especially when the names are compared with those in the country in general. Many people are interested in the place-names of the area in which they live, and there are sometimes local publications dealing with them. These can be scholarly and reliable, but some can be distressingly amateur, and the student of such names is strongly recommended to consult the relevant volume (if available) in the series of books published by the English Place-Name Society (see p. 410), or any equivalent work available for countries outside England.

Language area   It can be interesting to study the place-names of a particular territory by their language, whether geographically, such as the Welsh names in Wales (or the English names in Wales), or historically, such as Scandinavian names in Scotland. Some people are attracted to the Norman 'double-barrelled' names already mentioned, and like to trace back a particular Norman family to its place of origin in France. Others find fascination in tracing the distribution of Norman-French names containing the word *beau*, and so examining the whereabouts of 'beautiful' names. A comparison of such names with the actual location may still show it to be 'beautiful' today, whether one obtains the description of the place from a guide or gazetteer or (best of all) actually visits the location. A 'collection' of the names of Roman forts and cities can be equally valuable, and if this can be combined with visits to the sites, so much the better. Again, a study of the occurrences of a particular word or element in a name can give interesting results. An example might be a search for those names that contain the root word *Eccles*, meaning 'church' (such as Eccleston, Eccleshall, Ecclesfield, Eccleshill, and so on). Such names would show where there had been an early British church, and as early Christianity was introduced to Britain by the Romans, one would expect to find such 'Eccles' names near Roman roads or settlements. Naturally, the more specialised the area the greater the need for expert knowledge, and a preliminary study of writing on the subject will be essential in cases where the researcher has not undertaken such work before.

Thematic area   This ties in quite closely with the language area just considered. The researcher may like to trace names referring to a particular animal or bird, for example, whether wild or domesticated (as on a farm). Sheep are referred to in names such as Shipton, Skipton, and Shepton, and crows in names such as Crowhurst, Crawley, Cromer, and Croydon. But here, as elsewhere, it will not be enough to collect such names by simply finding them on the map; some may not be genuine 'sheep' or 'crow' names at all, and one will need to consult an authority on the subject (if only a general one), such as Eilert Ekwall's *Concise Oxford Dictionary of English Place-Names* (see p. 411). Some apparent 'crow' names derive not from Old English *crāwe* (crow) but from *crōh* (nook), and while Crowhurst near Oxted in Surrey means 'crow wood', Crowhurst near Hastings in Sussex means 'nook wood' or 'wood in a corner of land'.

Specialised area   By 'place-names' most people understand the names of obvious features, such as rivers, hills, villages, and towns. But certain areas of name study can be centred elsewhere. Street names, for example, make a special area of interest all of their own, whether of a single town or city or of several. (Street names would include the names of Roman roads, as well.) Field names are similarly absorbing and rewarding, and enable the keen researcher to make enquiries on the spot in many cases, from long-term residents who are familiar with a particular rural area. This is one instance where 'fieldwork' means precisely what it says! Again, the naming of individual houses also falls into the general area of place-name study, whether of country mansions and 'stately homes', or of individually named houses in a suburban street (the latter have so far been investigated more widely than the former). And as a sort of compromise (or blend) between field names and house names, a survey of farm names would be unusual and valuable. None so far seems to have been undertaken, except possibly at a very local level.

All the above special lines of pursuit can be followed up with the assistance of the various volumes published by the English Place-Name Society, at least in England, and for particulars of these, and for other useful source books, the reader should see the Guide to Further Reading on p. 410.

PERSONAL NAMES AND PLACE-NAMES

A surprisingly large number of place-names, especially those of Old English and Old Norse origin, contain a personal name, usually that of the original 'owner' of the place involved, or of the head or leader of a tribe or group of people, or the ancestor of a family. Most of the names will seem unfamiliar by modern standards, although the Old English and Old Norse names will sometimes ring a bell for those familiar with the names of early rulers and warriors in British history. As a few random examples of such names, we can quote Hadstock ('Hada's place'), Halnaby ('Halnath's farm'), Hargham ('Hereca's homestead'), and Heytesbury ('Hēahthryth's fortified place'). This last is an Anglo-Saxon woman's name, meaning 'chief troop'. For the majority of such names, nothing at all is known about the named person except that he or she existed in connection with the place stated. However, some personal names are recorded and known elsewhere, so they can at least be verified. This is therefore one of the most frustrating areas of place-name study and one in which further research is very difficult. Moreover, many of the names are directly meaningful (like modern Craig and Rose), so that it is difficult to tell whether a name like Whitney means 'Hwīta's island' or 'white island' (Old English *hwīt*).

A special category of names are those that derive from tribal leaders. As mentioned in the list of elements that follows this Introduction, names ending in '-ing' will often be tribal in origin, with the first part of the name the personal name of the tribe's leader. Basing thus means '(place of) Basa's people' and Goring '(place of) Godhelm's people'. For most such personal names, it is necessary to go back to the early records to establish what the name actually was, as present spellings of such names are usually distorted and abbreviated from the original. But not all names of this type end in '-ing' (or '-ings', like Hastings), and in some instances the apparent personal name is that of the tribe as a whole. For example, Hitchin refers to the people called Hicce, and both Ripon and Repton derive their names from the people called Hrype. What these tribal names themselves mean is not known. In other cases, 'group' names like this can be interpreted, and Epping, for example, refers to the Yppe people, that is the people of the upland place, the 'lookout' people. Uppingham has a similar name.

Among the best known 'people' names of this type are the familiar Saxon ones of Essex, Sussex, and Wessex, respectively the 'east Saxons', 'south Saxons', and 'west Saxons', and equally the Anglian ones of Norfolk and Suffolk, the 'north folk' and the 'south folk'. Such names are not individually personal, of course, but they are collectively personal all the same.

A different kind of personal name is the Norman 'manorial' name already mentioned, especially as it occurs in the 'double-barrelled' names. These Norman 'lords of the manor' usually took their family name from the place where they lived in Normandy, so that one has effectively a transfer of French place-name to English place-name. Such place-names are beloved by 'poetic romantics', who like to quote such southern English names as Charlton Mackrell, Huish Champflower, Marston Maisy, and Stoke d'Abernon. The last three names derive respectively from Champfleury, Maisy, and Abenon, all places in Normandy. The first name mentioned, however, is a nickname, from a French equivalent of the English 'mackerel' but which here means something like 'courtesan'. In fact names of this type are found almost as much in the north of England as the south, and Yorkshire, for example, has its Allerton Mauleverer (a nickname meaning 'poor harrier') and its Bolton Percy (who came from Percy in Normandy).

It will be noted that in many such instances, the first word of the name is a commonly occurring one (Charlton, Stoke, Bolton), so that the added personal name also serves to differentiate this particular Stoke (or wherever) from others.

A further aspect of personal names and place-names is that many of our own surnames derive from place-names, and although it is often impossible to tell that someone named Newbury, for example, came originally (or the family's remotest ancestor did) from Newbury in Berkshire, at least he will have come from *a* Newbury (for there are others), or from a 'new borough' somewhere. There can be hardly a single place-name that has not produced at least one person of the name, and one need only glance through lists of (say) well-known writers to find such names — Abercrombie, Balfour, Caxton, Douglas, Elton, Ford, Gordon, Hazlitt ('hazel copse'), Isherwood, Kingsley, Linacre ('flax field'), Merivale ('pleasant valley'), Newton, Oldham, Penn, Rowley, Southey, Thackeray, Urquhart, and Wesley — a nearly complete alphabet of surnames derived from places in England or Scotland. (Fictional characters with surnames derived from place-names have always been popular, from Charlotte Brontë's Mr Rochester and Richardson's Clarissa Harlowe to Agatha Christie's Miss Marple and P.G. Wodehouse's Bertie Wooster. Many of these are of course already surnames in their own right.)

The interconnection between personal names and place-names thus operates on different levels.

RIVER NAMES

River names, at any rate in England, are either very old or, by place-name standards, relatively modern. The oldest names are so ancient that they are pre-Celtic, and we cannot be at all sure what they mean. The Severn is such a name. It can be traced back to a form *Sabrina* in the second century AD, but no further, and it is still uncertain what the meaning is. Attempts have been made to link the name with river names in other languages, such as the Sèvre, in France, but the ultimate sense of the name remains obscure.

To judge by the ancient river names that we do know about, Severn probably means little more than 'river' or even just 'water'. The oldest river names are the most basic, and it is disappointing to make the initial discovery that Avon means simply 'river', and Exe merely 'water'. There are many British rivers named Avon, and the name can be seen to represent the actual word for 'river' in Celtic languages, such as Welsh *afon*, Irish and Gaelic *abhainn*, and Breton *auon*. Similarly, the Exe (and other rivers with similar names, to be mentioned shortly) derives its name from a basic British (Celtic) word represented by Irish and Gaelic *uisge* (water) (which itself lies behind modern 'whisk(e)y').

Why are so many rivers named simply 'river' or 'water'? Apart from the Exe there is the Esk, Axe, and Usk (although some associate this last name more with a word meaning 'fish'). Even the Ouse is probably related to this group. The answer is that rivers are usually thought of in local not regional terms. We talk of 'the river' even now without bothering to name it. To the people of a particular locality, the river is *the* river, and when anyone else arrives in the region, they also will hear of 'the river' and come to call it thus. It is possible, of course, that this is more a Celtic characteristic than a Germanic one, so that when the Anglo-Saxons heard the Celts talk of 'Avon', they actually thought this was the river's name. Even after discovering that the name was widespread, they seemed happy to adopt the Celtic designation without bestowing a name of their own. The same would apply to 'the water', referred to locally as the water that everyone would know about.

Old river names very much run in related families, with groups of similar names. It is likely, for example, that the names of all the following rivers are interrelated: Thames, Thame, Tame, Team, Tamar, Tavy, Teviot, Taff (or Taf). Exactly what the overall sense is remains uncertain, and there are currently two schools of interpretation: those who say the basic meaning is 'dark', and those who say the general sense is simply 'water'. In view of the many instances of the name, in its different variations, it seems likely that the ultimate meaning will be a general one, such as 'water', rather than a specific one, such as 'dark'. Why so many 'dark' rivers?

Such ancient river names, incidentally, sometimes lie behind the names of Roman forts and cities, and so behind their modern equivalents. Exeter, after all is on the Exe (which the Romans called the *Isca*), and Doncaster is on the Don (called *Danum* by the Romans). However, it is not true to say that such names are in the majority, although they are quite well represented.

Yet another 'family' of names can be seen in rivers that have a basic Celtic meaning 'oak', as they flowed through oak woods, or had banks lined with oaks. The Welsh word for 'oak' is *derwen*, and among rivers that have names based on the common Celtic origin of this are the Derwent, Darwen, Darent, and (very probably) Dart, found in England from the southwest (Dart) to the northeast (Derwent). No wonder the oak is England's national tree! (The same Celtic word, incidentally, lies behind the name of Ireland's Londonderry, which was originally just Derry, 'oak wood'.)

By contrast, a surprisingly large number of river names are comparatively modern, evolving in some instances only in the sixteenth century, which is indeed modern by toponymical (or hydronymical) standards. Here are some examples of such names: Chelmer, Chelt, Eden, Rother, Mole, Wandle, Ver. Such names are technically referred to as 'back formations', because the river name derives from that of the town or village through which it flows, not the other way round, which is much more common. For example, Doncaster (as mentioned) took its name from the Don. But the Cam took its name from Cambridge, not Cambridge from the Cam. The form of the place-name from which the river name derives may be the modern one or an earlier, historic one. For example, the Chelmer took its name from Chelmsford when the name of that town was 'Chelmersford', and the Ver, which modestly flows through St Albans, took its name from the Roman name for that town, which was *Verulamium*. Of the other rivers mentioned above, the Chelt took its name from Cheltenham; the Eden from Edenbridge (this is not the major Cumbria Eden, but the minor Sussex one); the Rother from Rotherbridge, the name of a Sussex hundred (again, not the Yorkshire Rother, which gave its name to Rotherham); the Mole from Molesey (or, in Devon, from North or South Molton, which are both on it); and the Wandle from Wandsworth, when its name was closer to 'Wandlesworth'.

Some names of this type are almost ridiculously short and 'puny' when compared to the full names of the places from which they have 'back-formed'. Here are some more, with the names of the places from which they derive given after them in brackets: Tun (Tunbridge), Mude (Mudeford), Rom (Romford), Wid (Widford), Og (Ogbourne St George), Teff (Teffont), Cong (Congham), Eyn (Eynford), Mun (Mundesley) Tud (Tuddenham), Chor (Chorley), and Hiz (Hitchin, which was recorded as *Hiz* in the Domesday Book).

Now, these rivers have obviously been flowing for much longer than the mere 400 years or more since their names first appeared or were recorded. They must therefore have had earlier names, and in some cases we know what the earlier name was. The Rother, for example, was the Shire, and the Mole was the Nymet. Why did they lose these names, and who was responsible for the late appearance of the many sixteenth-century names?

The answer is usually 'the antiquarians'. That is, those writers, mapmakers, and topographers who wrote about England and who often mapped the country as well. Or, to quote from the *Oxford English Dictionary*, 'a student (usually a *professed* student), or collector, of antiquities'. Put another way, an antiquarian, so far as place-names are concerned, is a sort of geographical historian-cum-littérateur, who boldly invented river names to match the places with which they felt the rivers to be associated. Such writings were popular, and such maps widely circulated, so that the names caught on. For one thing, it is much easier as well as much more logical to have a town or village sharing a name with the river that flows through it. And who knows, people will soon come to think that the river actually *gave* its name to the town. If it can happen (as it did) at Rotherham, then why not (as it did not) at Cambridge?

One of the greatest offenders in this respect was the antiquarian William Harrison (1534–93), who wrote a work called *A Description of England* (described by the *Oxford Companion to English Literature* as 'admirable'). In this, among other things, he charted the courses of rivers and invented names for several as he did so, basing them, as we have seen, on the places through which they ran. Some are still in use, but others are not, such as the Asten (after Hastings), the Fromus (after Framlingham), the Sore (after Shoreham), and the Tudo (after a place he calls 'Toddington', which is probably the Oxfordshire village of Deddington). Other antiquarians who likewise invented river names were Michael Drayton (1563–1631), in his great topographical poem on England, *The Poly-Olbion*; John Leland (?1503–52), the earliest of modern English antiquarians, in his *Itinerary*; and William Camden (1551–1623), probably the best known of all modern English antiquarians, in his *Britannia*, published in Latin in 1586.

What serves only to confuse the situation, however, is that many of these newly devised names were identical to existing river names, such as the new and old Eden and Rother already quoted above (these were both creations of Michael Drayton). No doubt the creators felt that the already existing old name would add to the authenticity of the new one!

River names that look suspiciously like the first syllable(s) of an existing place-name, therefore, will very probably turn out to be 'back formations' of this type. Some have gained official status in recent years by their adoption for the names of the newly created administrative districts of 1974, on the reorganisation of local government. Among them are Hampshire's Hart, Surrey's Mole Valley, East Sussex's Rother, and West Sussex's Adur (one of Drayton's creations, from the Roman name *Portus Adurni*, a place supposed to be on it) and Arun (the work of Harrison, derived from Arundel).

THE RANGE, AIM, AND LAYOUT OF THIS DICTIONARY

This Dictionary aims to include a very wide selection of familiar place-names in the British Isles, including Great Britain and Ireland and the 'special' areas of the Isle of Man and the Channel Islands. The prime objective is to give the origins of the names, as far as they are known, in a clear and readable manner, avoiding wherever possible the jargon that the study of place-names (toponymy) has acquired (just like any other scientific discipline). Abbreviations have been avoided, and references to particular historical documents and sources kept to a minimum. However, the dates of such source material are almost always given, as it is important to know when a particular place-name was recorded. The earlier the better is the general principle, although in its way, the record of a name in the Domesday Book (1086) can be just as significant as one on a map of Ptolemy (second century AD).

The headword gives the name of the place, and is followed by the county (of England, Wales, and Ireland) or the region (of Scotland) in which the place is located. Where the headword is the name of an extensive feature (such as a range of mountains or a river), the location includes the names of the various counties/regions in which it occurs. The names of counties and regions are located according to country (England, Wales, Scotland, Ireland).

(For the purposes of this book, 'Ireland' incorporates Northern Ireland and the Republic.) Places with identical names are considered in the same entry, whether their origins are identical or not.

The opening statement of each entry generally gives the identity of the place (town, hill, lake, administrative district, etc.) and its location with respect to a well-known nearby place or within a larger area (in the case of an administrative or other district, for example). The location may be significant topographically, as well as serving to 'pinpoint' the place reasonably accurately. Places in London, such as Ealing, Dulwich, Westminster, Woolwich, etc. are identified as 'districts' in a particular borough. In Celtic countries, places often have a Celtic name as well as an English one or a modern version of the original. In such cases, the Celtic name is also given and, if different from the present name, is explained or translated. Place-names that have their own entry in the book are printed in small capitals when referred to in other entries so that the reader can pursue associations and relationships as they arise.

In any discussion of a place-name origin, reference to one or more early records of the name is essential. In this Dictionary, only the earliest known record is usually given, with a date when known. For names recorded in the Domesday Book the date can be taken as 1086, the date of the work's compilation.

In a sense, hardly any name is unique: if you say 'What about London?' I will direct you to Londonderry, and if you say 'How about Liverpool?', I would refer you to other 'pools', such as Welshpool and Poole itself. And if you say 'Britain', I will take you on a short cross-Channel visit to Brittany . . .

But before you go there, I hope you will find an armchair tour of the British Isles of interest and pleasure, as provided by the 4000-plus names that follow in this book, whether or not you choose to accompany your journey with maps or other, more specialised toponymical aids, such as the books mentioned in the Guide to Further Reading on p. 410.

PLACE-NAME ELEMENTS

The following pages list a selection of elements commonly found as either the first or the last part of a place-name, particularly of the names that occur in this Dictionary. The elements are given in the form in which they commonly occur today, such as the 'Bally-' that is frequently found as the first element in Irish names, or the '-ton' or '-ham' that is familiar as the end element of many English names.

Two points should be borne in mind when consulting the lists. The first is that some place-names have elements that are not what they seem, so that a '-ham', for example, is actually a '-hill', or a '-ton' is really a '-don'. The second is that in many cases a detailed study of the historic name forms is needed to establish whether a place contains a *burg* (fort) or a *berg* (hill), a *hām* (homestead) or a *hamm* (enclosure). It is unfortunate that such important Old English words, of different meanings, are so similar, especially as both *burg* and *berg* can now be a '-bury', and both *hām* and *hamm* are usually a '-ham'. Such fine differences of origin and meaning are indicated wherever possible. But it should not be assumed, for instance, that because one place is or was a clearing and has a name ending in '-ley' (Old English *lēah*), all places with this element originated likewise. Not only may the apparent '-ley' have developed from some other, different element, such as *ēg*, ('island' — as for Medley, 'middle island'), but *lēah* itself could mean both 'woodland' and (its virtual opposite) 'clearing in woodland'. Thus, do not apply the sense of one element to all other names that contain it, or appear to contain it. Also, remember that any one element could have more than one meaning, both simultaneously and, as the language developed, historically. The '-bury' of Newbury is thus not the same '-bury' in meaning as that of Banbury, for the Berkshire town developed later than the Oxfordshire one, and so its '-bury' is better understood as 'market town' rather than 'fortified place', as is more common for such names.

It will be noticed that most of the 'first-part' elements occur in Celtic names, and most of the 'last-part' ones in English and Scandinavian names. This is because of the way the respective languages work. Where English says 'red house', for example, Celtic says 'house red', with the generic before the specific. Examples of names containing the elements are given in SMALL CAPITALS; these all have their own entries in the Dictionary.

Elements commonly found as the first part of a place-name
The letters in brackets refer to the part of the British Isles where the element is most commonly found: E = England; I = Ireland; M = Isle of Man; S = Scotland; W = Wales.

Abbey- (I) abbey, monastery; translating Irish *mainistir* and usually referring to an establishment of the twelfth century or later, i.e. one founded by the Anglo-Normans. ABBEYFEALE, ABBEYLEIX.
Aber- (S,W) estuary, river-mouth; either on coast or at confluence. ABERAERON, ABERDARE, ABERDEEN, ABERPORTH, ABERYSTWYTH. *Compare* Inver-; *see also* Bel(la)-.

Ard- (I,S) height. ARDGLASS, ARDMORE, ARDNAMURCHAN, ARDROSSAN, ARDS PENINSULA.

Auchter- (S) upper. AUCHTERARDER, AUCHTERMUCHTY.

Ballin(a)- (I) 1 town of the; rendering Irish *baile na* (see Bally-). 2 ford-mouth of the; rendering Irish *béal átha na*. BALLINA, BALLINASLOE, BALLINEEN.

Bally- (I) homestead, townland, town; rendering Irish *baile*. BALLYBOFEY, BALLYBUNION, BALLYCASTLE, BALLYJAMESDUFF, BALLYNAHINCH. Occasionally represents other Irish words (see individual entries for exceptions).

Bel(la)- (I) 1 estuary, river-mouth; rendering Irish *béal*, often followed by *átha* (of the ford) to give overall sense of ford-mouth, approach to a ford. 2 town; representing Irish *baile* (*see* Bally-). BELCOO, BELFAST.

Ben (I,S) mountain, peak; rendering Irish *beann*, Gaelic *beinn*. BEN MORE, BEN NEVIS.

Blaen- (W) head, source, highland. BLAENAU FFESTINIOG, BLAENAVON.

Bryn- (W) hill. BRYNMAWR.

Caer- (W) fort, fortified place. CAERLEON, CAERNARVON, CAERPHILLY, CAERWENT.

Carrick- (I) rock; rendering Irish *carraig*. CARRICKFERGUS, CARRICKMACROSS, CARRICK-ON-SHANNON.

Castle- (E,I,S) castle; translating Irish *caislean*, Gaelic *caisteal*, and often denoting a medieval castle or a later mansion, whether fortified or not. CASTLEBAR, CASTLEBAY, CASTLEBLAYNEY, CASTLE CARY, CASTLE DOUGLAS, CASTLEWELLAN.

Clon- (I) meadow; rendering Irish *cluain*. CLONAKILTY, CLONDALKIN, CLONES, CLONMEL, CLONTARF.

Dun- (E,I,S) 1 hill; in England, rendering Old English *dūn*. 2 fort; in Ireland and Scotland, rendering Irish *dún*, Gaelic *dùn*. Often senses 1 and 2 blend and overlap, as forts were often built on hills. DUNBAR, DUNFERMLINE, DUNGANNON, DUNMOW, DUNOON.

Eccles(s)- (E,S) church; ultimately rendering Latin *ecclesia*. ECCLEFECHAN, ECCLES, ECCLESTON.

Ennis- (I) island; rendering Irish *inis* and often referring to dry or raised land in a marsh or by water. ENNISCORTHY, ENNISKILLEN, ENNISTYMON.

Glen- (I,S) valley, glen; rendering Irish and Gaelic *gleann*. GLEN AFFRIC, GLENCOE, GLENDALOUGH, GLENELG, GLENFINNAN. *Compare* Strath-.

Inver- (S) river-mouth, confluence; rendering Gaelic *inbhir*. INVERARAY, INVERESK, INVERGOWRIE, INVERKEITHING, INVERNESS. *Compare* Aber-.

Kil(l)- (I,S) 1 church; rendering Irish and Gaelic *cill* (*compare* English 'cell' in monastic sense). 2 wood; rendering Irish *coill*, Gaelic *coille*. If sense 1 the reference is usually to an early church. KILCULLEN, KILKEEL, KILLARNEY, KILLIECRANKIE, KILLYBEGS, KILMARNOCK, KILSYTH.

Kirk- (E,S) church; rendering Old English *cirice*, Old Norse *kirkja*, with latter giving most Scottish names and actual word 'kirk'. KIRKBY, KIRKCALDY, KIRKCUDBRIGHT, KIRKLEES, KIRKWALL.

Lis- (E,I,S) enclosure, circular fort, palace, hall; rendering basic Celtic element *lis-* (Irish and Gaelic *lios*). LISBURN, LISDOONVARNA, LISKEARD, LISMORE, LISS, LISTOWEL (also LIZARD).

Llan- (W) church. LLANBERIS, LLANDAFF, LLANDEILO, LLANDUDNO, LLANFAIRFECHAN, LLANGOLLEN. Word following element is often name of saint to whom church is dedicated.

Loch- (S) lake. LOCHINVAR, LOCHMABEN, LOCHNAGAR.

New- (E) new; i.e. by comparison with what was (or was not) on site before, so it may denote place that is now historically old. NEW BRIGHTON, NEWCASTLE, NEW FOREST, NEWHAVEN, NEWMARKET, NEWPORT, NEWTON ABBOT. Element is found in all parts of British Isles, chiefly in England.

Pen- (E,S,W) hill, head, top; rendering basic Celtic element *penno-* (and especially Welsh *pen*). PENARTH, PENDLE HILL, PENICUIK, PENMAENMAWR, PENZANCE (also PEMBROKE).

Pont- (E,W) bridge; rendering ultimately Latin *pons*, genitive *pontis*, often via French *pont*. PONTARDAWE, PONTEFRACT, PONTYPOOL, PONTYPRIDD.

Port- (E,I,M,S,W)1 port, harbour; from Latin *portus* (harbour). 2 town, market; from Latin *portus* or *porta* (gate). 3 gate, entrance; from Latin *porta*. Sometimes meanings blend, as a town can have a port, and a port can have an entrance. PORTADOWN, PORT CHARLOTTE, PORTHCAWL, PORTISHEAD, PORTRUSH, PORT TALBOT; note group of such names based on PORTSMOUTH — PORTCHESTER, PORTLAND, PORTSEA.

Rath- (I) ring-fort; often denoting early ecclesiastical site. RÁTH LUIRC, RATHMINES, RATHMULLAN.

Rhos- *see* Ros(s)-.

Ros(s)- (E,I,S) headland, heath, wood; rendering basic Celtic *ros* (modern Irish and Gaelic *ros*, Welsh *rhos*, latter giving Welsh names in RHOS-). ROSCOMMON, ROSS, ROSSLARE, ROSS-ON-WYE (plus Welsh RHOSLLANERCHRUGOG, RHOS-ON-SEA.)

St (E,W) saint; referring to dedication of church; common in Cornwall. ST ALBANS, ST AUSTELL, ST BUDEAUX, ST HELENS, ST IVES, ST MARY'S, ST PANCRAS (*not* ST AGNES, ST KILDA).

Stock- (E) place; rendering Old English *stoc*, often with sense religious place, secondary settlement. STOCKPORT, STOCKTON-ON-TEES (*not* STOCKBRIDGE, which is different). *See also* Stoke.

Stoke (E) place; as Stock-. STOKE-BY-NAYLAND, STOKE NEWINGTON, STOKE-ON-TRENT, STOKE POGES.

Strath- (S) valley; rendering Gaelic *srath*, denoting a much broader valley than Glen-. Element is usually followed by name of river that flows through valley. STRATHAVEN, STRATHCLYDE, STRATHMIGLO, STRATHMORE, STRATHPEFFER.

Tre- (W) homestead, village, town; rendering Welsh *tref*. TREDEGAR, TREFRIW, TREMADOC BAY.

Elements commonly found as the last part of a place-name
All elements are English or Scandinavian, and relate mostly to England.

-borough (also **-brough, -burgh, -bury**)1 fortified place, fort; Old English *burh* or *burg*, modern 'borough', Scottish 'burgh'; often a former Roman camp or prehistoric site, such as an Iron Age fort; first element is often a personal name. Later names can mean fortified house, manor. ALDEBURGH, AMESBURY, CANTERBURY, CHIPPING SODBURY, EDINBURGH, MIDDLESBROUGH, PETERBOROUGH, SALISBURY. 2 mound, hill, burial mound; Old English *beorg*, modern 'barrow'. FARNBOROUGH, PRINCES RISBOROUGH.

-bourne (also **-borne**) stream; Old English *burna*, modern 'burn'. EASTBOURNE, FISHBOURNE, PANGBOURNE, SHERBORNE, WIMBORNE MINSTER.

-bridge bridge; Old English *brycg*. BOROUGHBRIDGE, CAMBRIDGE, HIGHBRIDGE, TONBRIDGE, TROWBRIDGE, WADEBRIDGE, WEYBRIDGE, WOODBRIDGE.

-bury see -borough.

-by farmstead, village; Old Norse *bý*, modern 'by-law'. Found mainly in Danelaw, i.e. in eastern and northern England. CORBY, DERBY, FORMBY, RUGBY, SELBY, SPILSBY, WHITBY.

-caster (also **-cester, -chester**) old fortification, especially a Roman camp, fort, or city; Old English *ceaster*, modern 'castle', ultimately from Latin *castra* (camp). Most *-caster* names are in the north of England, and most *-chester* ones in the south. ALCESTER, CHESTER,

CHICHESTER, CIRENCESTER, COLCHESTER, DONCASTER, EXETER, GLOUCESTER, LANCASTER, MANCHESTER, PORTCHESTER, ROCHESTER, TADCASTER, WINCHESTER, WORCESTER, WROXETER (*not* UTTOXETER).

-cester *see* **-caster**.

-chester *see* **-caster**.

-church church; Old English *cirice*. CHRISTCHURCH, DYMCHURCH, HORNCHURCH, WHITCHURCH.

-combe narrow valley, usually one shorter and broader than that of -den (sense 1); Old English *cumb*, modern 'coomb'. Common in the West Country. BABBACOMBE, ILFRACOMBE, WIDECOMBE IN THE MOOR.

-cot cottage, shelter, hut; Old English *cot*, modern 'cottage'. Many places ending in this element are still small and 'rural' today. ASCOT, DIDCOT, KELMSCOT, PRESCOT.

-dale valley; Old English *dæl*, Old Norse *dalr*, modern 'dale'. Original Old English word meant more 'pit', 'hollow' before it was influenced by Old Norse word; common in north of England. BORROWDALE, LANGDALE, SKELMERSDALE.

-den 1 valley, especially a narrow wooded one; Old English *denu*, modern 'dean' or 'dene'. Not as broad or short as a *cumb* (*see* -combe). HEBDEN BRIDGE, HUGHENDEN MANOR, POLESDEN LACEY, RUSHDEN, TODMORDEN. 2 pasture, especially a woodland pasture for pigs; Old English *denn*. A common element of names in Kent and East Sussex: TENTERDEN. This element (senses 1 and 2) can appear disguised as -don or -ton.

-don hill, whether a sharp steep one or a slight slope; Old English *dūn*, modern 'down'. CLEVEDON, FARINGDON, HENDON, SWINDON. This element can appear disguised as -den or -ton.

-ey 1 island or area of dry or higher land surrounded by marsh or well-watered land; Old English *ēg*, represented by first syllable of modern 'island'. Often difficult to distinguish from -ey (sense 2). BARDSEY ISLAND, BERMONDSEY, HACKNEY, ROMSEY, THORNEY ISLAND. 2 water, stream, river; Old English *ēa*, indirectly related to French *eau*. Common element of river names; often difficult to distinguish from -ey (sense 1). MERSEY, PEVENSEY, ROMNEY MARSH, WAVENEY. This element (senses 1 and 2) should not be mistaken for -ley.

-field open land, especially cleared area in forestland, extensive tract without trees, hills, marshes, etc.; can mean arable land; Old English *feld*, modern 'field', South African 'veld', the latter giving much truer idea of proper sense. HATFIELD, LICHFIELD, MACCLESFIELD, PETERSFIELD, WAKEFIELD, WEDNESFIELD.

-ford ford; Old English *ford*. First element of names ending in '-ford' is rarely the name of the river involved, except to distinguish between similar or identical names. BRENTFORD, BURFORD, CAMELFORD, CHINGFORD, GUILDFORD, KNUTSFORD, OXFORD, STAFFORD, STAMFORD, STRATFORD, THETFORD.

-gate 1 pass, gap, especially one leading through hills or cliffs to a specially significant place; Old English *geat*, 'modern gate'. Often not easy to distinguish from sense 2. MARGATE, RAMSGATE, REIGATE. 2 way, road; Old Norse *gata*, related to modern 'gait'. Often not easy to distinguish from sense 1, as a result of which it is often misunderstood in street names, where it is common, so that YORK's Micklegate is 'great street' not 'great gate', and LEEDS's Briggate is 'bridge street' not 'bridge gate' (although names such as Eastgate, Westgate, Northgate, Southgate do denote gates). HARROGATE.

-ham 1 homestead, village; Old English *hām*, related to modern 'hamlet', 'home'. Often difficult to distinguish from sense 2. BLOXHAM, BURNHAM-ON-CROUCH, FAREHAM, MITCHAM, NEWNHAM, SWAFFHAM (but probably not OAKHAM and certainly not OLDHAM, among others). *See also* -ingham. 2 hemmed-in land, e.g. land surrounded by water, land in bend of river, land in valley surrounded by higher land; Old English *hamm*, probably related to modern 'hem'. Often difficult to distinguish from sense 1. CHIPPENHAM,

DYRHAM PARK, EVESHAM, EYNSHAM, FARNHAM (but *not* DURHAM, among others). *See also* -hampstead, -hampton.

-hampstead (also -hamstead) homestead, site of a dwelling; Old English *hām-stede*. BERKHAMSTED, HAMPSTEAD, HEMEL HEMPSTEAD, WHEATHAMPSTEAD.

-hampton 1 home farm, main village (as distinguished from an outlying one); Old English *hām-tūn*. 2 settlement in enclosure, farmstead by river; Old English *hamm-tūn*. Often difficult to distinguish between senses 1 and 2. HAMPTON, LITTLEHAMPTON, NORTHAMPTON, SOUTHAMPTON (but *not* OKEHAMPTON, WOLVERHAMPTON, among others).

-head head, headland, hill; Old English *hēafod*. It can literally refer to animal's head, hence a place of sacrifice. BIRKENHEAD, GATESHEAD, MINEHEAD, PORTISHEAD.

-hurst hillock, wooded hill; Old English *hyrst*. Common in Surrey and Sussex. BROCKENHURST, LYNDHURST, MIDHURST, SANDHURST.

-ing (occasionally also -ings) people of (named person), referring to group or tribe descended from, dependent on, or in some way associated with a particular person, whose name usually forms first element of place-name; Old English suffix *-ingas*. There are some instances where '-ing' simply means 'place' (e.g. Leeming, 'village by the gleaming river'). BARKING, EPPING, GODALMING, HASTINGS, READING, SPALDING, WOKING. *See also* -ingham, -ington.

-ingham homestead of the people of , i.e. -ham (usually sense 1) added to -ing; Old English *-ingahām*. First element of name will often be a personal name. BIRMINGHAM, BUCKINGHAM, GILLINGHAM, UPPINGHAM, WHIPPINGHAM.

-ington farm or village associated with (named person); i.e. -ton added to -ing; Old English *-ingtūn*. First element of name will often be a personal name. BRIDLINGTON, KENSINGTON, PADDINGTON, WILMINGTON, WORKINGTON.

-land open land, estate, new arable land; Old English *land*. Common element to names in West Yorkshire and Norfolk. COPELAND FOREST, CUMBERLAND, HOLLAND, LEYLAND.

-ley (also -leigh, -le) woodland, glade, clearing, also pasture, meadow; Old English *lēah*, modern 'lea'. BARNSLEY, BLETCHLEY, BURNLEY, HADLEIGH, MORLEY, SHIPLEY, STANLEY, YIEWSLEY.

-mere (also -mer) pond, lake; Old English *mere*, poetic 'mere', related to French *mer* (sea). Ranges in size from southern duck pond to large lakes of Lake District. BUTTERMERE, CROMER, ELLESMERE PORT, GRASMERE, WINDERMERE. Can sometimes be disguised as -more.

-minster monastery, church; Old English *mynster*. First element of name may be personal name of founder, but many such places are named after river where located. AXMINSTER, CHARMINSTER, KIDDERMINSTER, WARMINSTER, WESTMINSTER.

-more (also -moor) moor, wasteland, often in sense 'barren upland' in North, 'marshland' in Midlands and South; Old English *mōr*. DARTMOOR, EXMOOR, SPENNYMOOR. Can sometimes be disguised form of -mere, as in STANMORE.

-mouth river-mouth; Old English *mūtha*. AVONMOUTH, DARTMOUTH, EXMOUTH, PORTSMOUTH (not a river, however), TEIGNMOUTH, WEYMOUTH.

-port port, town, market, gate; Old English *port*, deriving from either Latin *portus* (harbour) or *porta* (gate). *See* Port- in list of first elements. BRIDPORT, GOSPORT, LANGPORT, NEWPORT, SOUTHPORT.

-shot (also -shott) angle of land, projecting piece of land, especially one with trees; Old English *scēat*, related to modern 'shoot' in sense of 'sprouting'. ALDERSHOT, BAGSHOT, OXSHOTT.

-stead (also -stede) place, site, often a religious site; Old English *stede*. Fairly common in southeast England. ASHTEAD, BANSTEAD, PLUMSTEAD, STANSTED. *See also* -hampstead.

-stock (also **-stoke**) place, especially a religious site or a secondary settlement, such as an outlying farm; Old English *stoc*, related to modern 'stock' in sense 'stem', 'origin'. Sense of a secondary settlement can often be seen when first element of name is same as that of another place nearby, even when this is now smaller or less important, e.g. BASINGSTOKE and Basing. CALSTOCK, TAVISTOCK, WOODSTOCK.

-ston (also **-stone**) stone, whether a boundary stone, a Roman milestone, or a natural or built stone or rock, the latter often serving as a place of assembly for a hundred; Old English *stān*. FOLKESTONE, INGATESTONE, MAIDSTONE. Should not be confused with -ton after personal name and possessive 's'.

-stow place, especially place of assembly or holy place; Old English *stōw*, related to modern 'bestow' and so to 'stow' in sense of 'to place', 'to put'. CHEPSTOW, FELIXSTOWE, PADSTOW, WALTHAMSTOW (also BRISTOL, which is really 'Bridgestow').

-thorpe secondary settlement; Old English *throp, thorp*, Old Norse *thorp*. Most places with the element are in the Danelaw, i.e. in eastern or northern England, especially in Lincolnshire and Humberside, and most are still hamlets, as they originally were, hence their small representation in this Dictionary, with the notable exception of SCUNTHORPE.

-ton farm, village; Old English *tūn*, modern 'town'. Easily the most common of all last elements, with a wide range of first elements, from personal names to descriptive words. ACTON, CREDITON, ETON, HONITON, MELTON MOWBRAY, MILTON KEYNES, NEWTON ABBOT, SOMERTON, SURBITON, SUTTON, WESTON-SUPER-MARE. *See also* -ington.

-tree (also **-try**) tree, meaning not only living tree but post, cross, crucifix; Old English *trēow*. Often denotes a boundary marker or the meeting-place of a hundred; in latter case, first element of name is often a personal name, possibly that of the 'hundred man' or 'law officer' of the assembly. AINTREE, BRAINTREE, COVENTRY, DAVENTRY, MANNINGTREE, OSWESTRY, WAVERTREE.

-ville modern settlement, resort; modern French *ville* (town), related to 'villa'. Found in recent names, especially those of planned sites, e.g. for industrial employees. BOURNVILLE, CLIFTONVILLE, COALVILLE, WATERLOOVILLE. In a few cases -ville actually means -field, as for Enville — 'level open land'.

-wardine *see* **worth**.

-well stream, well; Old English *wella*. BAKEWELL, CRANWELL, HOLYWELL, MOTHERWELL, SOUTHWELL, WOMBWELL.

-wich (also **-wick**) dwelling, premises, especially ones used for a special trade or purpose, such as a dairy farm, a place for storing or loading animals or goods, or for preparing and selling food; Old English *wīc*. First element of name sometimes states occupation carried on or describes commodity; places with this element by a river or on the coast will obviously be ports. ALNWICK, BERWICK-UPON-TWEED, CHISWICK, DROITWICH, GREENWICH, IPSWICH, KESWICK, NANTWICH, NORWICH, SANDWICH, WARWICK, WOOLWICH. In some names, -wick is derived from the Old Norse *vík* (bay), especially in Scotland, e.g. LERWICK and WICK.

-wood wood; Old English *wudu*. Many places with this element have remained small, but exceptions include: BRENTWOOD, GOODWOOD, HEYWOOD, NORWOOD, SHERWOOD FOREST.

-worth enclosure, homestead; Old English *worth*. About three places out of four ending in this element have a personal name for the first element. ISLEWORTH, LETCHWORTH, TAMWORTH, WANDSWORTH. The equivalent element for many names in the West of England is -worthy (Old English *worthig*), e.g. Woolfardisworthy — Wulfheard's enclosure. The alternative Old English *worthign* is also found in the West Midlands as **-wardine**, e.g. Leintwardine — enclosure by river Lent.

PLACE-NAMES IN THE BRITISH ISLES

A

Abbeyfeale (Limerick)
A small market town, southeast of
LISTOWEL, whose Irish name is Mainistir
na Féile, 'abbey of the Feale', the latter
being the river on which the town stands.
The Cistercian abbey here was founded by
Brian O Brien in 1188.

Abbeyleix (Laois)
A town, south of PORT LAOISE, that has a
name meaning simply 'abbey of LAOIS',
referring to the county. The original
Cistercian abbey, named De Lege Dei ('of
the law of God') and founded by Conor O
More in 1184, has long disappeared.

Abbots Bromley (Staffordshire)
The basic name of this village, west of
UTTOXETER, means 'broom clearing' or
'clearing where broom grows', from Old
English *brōm* (broom) and *lēah* (wood,
clearing). The first word denotes that the
manor here was granted to the Abbot of
Burton Abbey. The name of King's
Bromley, a smaller village southeast of
Abbots Bromley, indicates the subsequent
separation of the manor from the monastic
holding, and the granting of it to the king, as
happened for KINGS LANGLEY. The name
was recorded as *Bromleage* in a document
of 1002, and as *Bromleigh Abbatis* in 1304.
Compare ABBOTS LANGLEY.

Abbotsford (Borders)
A mansion on the TWEED west of
MELROSE, built by Sir Walter Scott
between 1817 and 1824. The name
indicates that the house was built by a ford
on land held by an abbot, in this case the
Abbot of Melrose. Scott lived here until his
death in 1832.

Abbots Langley (Hertfordshire)
A town, now a suburb of WATFORD, with a
name similar to ABBOTS BROMLEY insofar

as its 'pair', KINGS LANGLEY, arose round
a manor granted to a king. Langley means
'long clearing' or 'long grove', from Old
English *lang* and *lēah* (wood, clearing). The
first part indicates that the manor was
granted to the Abbot of ST ALBANS. The
name was recorded as *Langalege* in about
1060, and as *Lengele Regis* in a document of
1428.

Aberaeron (Dyfed)
A small town at the mouth of the River
Aeron, southwest of ABERYSTWYTH,
whose name indicates its location — Old
Welsh *aber* (river-mouth). The river's
name, which means basically 'battle' (Old
Welsh *aer*), refers to the goddess who was
believed to live in its waters. The name was
recorded in medieval Latin as *ad ostium
Ayron* in a text of 1184, with this denoting
not the present town but simply the estuary.
The town of Aberaeron only became significant as a port in the early years of the
nineteenth century, when a local minister,
the Rev. Alban Thomas Jones Gwynne,
had breakwaters built to form a harbour.

Aberavon (West Glamorgan)
A district of PORT TALBOT. As its Welsh
name, Aberafan, shows, it is located at the
mouth (Old Welsh *aber*) of the River Afan.
The river name, which may be derived
from a personal name, became altered to
'Avon' under the influence of the common
English river AVON. Welsh speakers, who
naturally use the Welsh version of the
name, colloquially call the place 'Byrafan'.
See also AFAN.

Aberdare (Mid Glamorgan)
A town in south Wales lying at the
confluence (Old Welsh *aber*) of the rivers
Dâr and Cynon. The former river's name
probably derives from Old Welsh *dâr* (oak)
(*compare* Irish DERRY), and so means a
river where oak trees grow. Another Welsh
town that similarly stands at a confluence is
ABERTILLERY. Aberdare's Welsh name is
Aberdâr, as might be expected, with this
recorded as *Aberdar* in a document of 1203.

Aberdeen (Grampian)

Just as for Welsh place-names, the 'Aber-' of this city in northeast Scotland means 'mouth', although the word is not Old Welsh but the Celtic (Brythonic) *aber* found in Scotland in regions formerly inhabited by the Picts. The river involved is the DON. It may be objected that Aberdeen stands on the DEE, which is now certainly the case, but the reference is a historic one and relates to the original settlement here, or what is now the district of Old Aberdeen to the north of the city centre, where the Don indeed flows into the North Sea. The name was recorded as *Aberdon* in about 1187 and as *Aberden* in about 1214, showing the emergence of the present 'e' of the name. The Gaelic name of the city is Abaireadhain. The county name Aberdeenshire developed in medieval times, as it did for other Scottish (and English) counties.

Aberdour (Fife)

Like ABERDEEN, the first part of the name is the Celtic (Brythonic) word for 'river-mouth', and the river here is the Dour, on whose estuary the town stands on the Firth of Forth. The river's name means simply 'waters', from the same root as in names such as ANDOVER and DOVER. The name of this small town and resort on the FIRTH OF FORTH was recorded as *Abirdaur* in a document of 1226.

Aberdovey (Gwynedd)

The Welsh name of this town is Aberdyfi, showing its location at the mouth (Old Welsh *aber*) of the River Dyfi, or Dovey (as it is usually known in English), in west Wales. As with ABERAERON, the name originally applied to the estuary. The river name is explained under DOVEY.

Aberfeldy (Tayside)

One might expect a River 'Feldy' here, if the other 'Aber-' names are anything to go by. But the town, in central Scotland, is actually on the Urlar Burn near its confluence with the TAY. Although the 'Aber-' means 'confluence', as it does for ABERDARE and other place-names, the second part refers to 'Peallaith', the name of a water spirit (or *uruisg*) believed to live in the water at this confluence.

Abergavenny (Gwent)

A market town in southeast Wales, known in Welsh as either Abergafenni or simply Y Fenni. It stands at the confluence (Old Welsh *aber*) of the River Gavenny and the USK. Gavenny probably means 'the smith' (modern Welsh *gof*), this doubtless being a sort of personal nickname for it. The Romans called the site here *Gobannium*, reflecting the same name. The Welsh name, Y Fenni, has simply lost the first syllable of the river name.

Abergele (Clwyd)

The name of this resort comprises the Old Welsh *aber* (river-mouth) and the name of the river, the Gele, on which it stands. The river's name probably comes from Old Welsh *gelau* (blade, spear), denoting the brightness and straightness of the river here, as if it was a 'sword' cutting its path directly to the North Wales coast.

Aberlour (Grampian)

A small distillery town in eastern Scotland standing where the Lour Burn flows into the SPEY. The 'Aber-' means 'confluence', as in ABERDARE, for example. The stream's own name comes from a Celtic root *labaro-*, meaning 'talkative', in the modern sense of a 'babbling brook'. The town's formal name is Charlestown of Aberlour, after Charles Grant, the man who laid out the original village in 1812. The site, however, is quite old, and was formerly known as Skirdustan, meaning 'Drostan's slice', after the original owner. Drostan's Well still stands in the grounds of the distillery.

Abernethy (Tayside)

As with so many Scottish and Welsh names, 'Aber-' denotes a location at a river-mouth or confluence. Here the village is on the River Nethy in eastern Scotland, at the point where it flows into the TAY. The river's own name comes from a Celtic root word *nectona* meaning 'pure'. The name was recorded as *Aburnethige* in a document of about 970. The type of hard biscuit called an 'Abernethy biscuit' was named after a Dr John Abernethy, not this village!

Aberporth (Dyfed)
A fishing village in southwest Wales whose name simply means 'mouth of the port', from the Old Welsh *aber* (mouth) and *porth* (port); the latter appears in Cornish form in names like PERRANPORTH and PORTHCURNO. *Compare* PORTSMOUTH.

Abersoch (Gwynedd)
A small but popular resort standing at the mouth (Old Welsh *aber*) of the River Soch on the Lleyn Peninsula in northwest Wales. The river name means 'drain' or 'ditch', and its waters are often muddy as if to bear this out.

Abertillery (Gwent)
A town in southeast Wales, Welsh spelling Abertyleri, standing at the confluence (Old Welsh *aber*) of the little Teleri Brook and the River Ebwy Fach ('Little Ebwy', *see* EBBW VALE). The stream's name is based on the personal name, Eleri (a fifth-century female saint). A text of 1332 has the name as *Teleri*.

Aberystwyth (Dyfed)
One would expect this west Wales coastal resort to be at the mouth (Old Welsh *aber*) of the River Ystwyth. But it is actually at the mouth of the Rheidol! The situation is rather similar to the development of ABERDEEN. The original site of the town was a Norman castle built in 1110 in the valley of the River Ystwyth, about a mile and a half south of the present town. A second castle was then built in 1211 at the mouth of the Rheidol, where the town stands today (the castle's ruins are still there). The name thus refers to the original site and is a misnomer for the modern town. The name Ystwyth means 'winding', describing the river's course as it flows to the sea. The name of Aberystwyth was recorded as *Aberestuuth* in a document dated 1232.

Abingdon (Oxfordshire)
A Thames-side town south of Oxford. In a charter of King Edgar dated 968 to the monks of the abbey here, the name appeared as *Abbandune*. This means 'Æbba's hill', the second half of the name deriving from Old English *dūn* (modern 'down'). Yet the monastery stood on flat ground by the River THAMES, as does the present town. So the name must have originally referred to the higher ground to the north of the town. Perhaps the monastery was originally on this hill, and kept its name when it transferred to its riverside site. Or perhaps the monks believed that it had been founded there, and recorded the name in their history of the establishment accordingly.

Aboyne (Grampian)
A village in northeast Scotland, famous for its annual Highland Games. It is actually on the DEE, but takes its name from a small stream (and loch) to the north. The name means literally 'white cow river', from the Gaelic *abh* (river; as in AVON), *bo* (cow), and *fionn* (white), this being either a descriptive name or a 'mystic' one, for white cows were regarded as bringers of good luck. The village has the formal name of Charleston of Aboyne, after Charles Gordon, 1st Earl of Aboyne, who in 1670 obtained a charter permitting him to erect a so-called 'burgh of barony' close to his castle. (The latter was referred to in Latin in thirteenth-century records as *castrum de Obeyn*.) A document of 1260 records the name as *Obyne*.

Accrington (Lancashire)
A town east of Blackburn. This is not an '-ington' name like BEDLINGTON or PADDINGTON, for example, which have a

personal name as their first element; there is no known personal name that could have given the 'Accr-'. The name was recorded in the twelfth century as *Akarinton*, and this can be interpreted as 'acorn farm', from old English *æcern* (acorn) and *tūn* (farm). Although this word has not been found in any other place-name, it suits Accrington very well, for the place was originally on the edge of ROSSENDALE Forest, and acorns from there would have been important for feeding pigs.

Acharacle (Highland)
This historic village in northern Scotland is associated with Bonnie Prince Charlie and has a name that translates as 'Torquil's ford', based on the Gaelic *ath* (ford) with a personal name, Thorcuil. It is not known who Torquil was. (*Compare* the Irish name ATHLONE.) Acharacle lies at the western end of Loch Shiel where the River Shiel flows out of it and where the ford would have been located.

Acocks Green (West Midlands)
A district of BIRMINGHAM that arose as a small village centred on a green belonging to a Richard Acock, who lived here in the seventeenth century.

Acton (Greater London)
A district of EALING whose name is fairly common elsewhere. It means 'oak farm' or 'farm by oak trees', from the Old English *āc* (oak) and *tūn* (farm). The name was recorded in its present form in a document of 1181.

Adare (Limerick)
A village southwest of LIMERICK whose name means 'ford of oaks', from the Irish *áth* (ford) and *doire* (oak tree, oak grove) (as in DERRY). There are still oak trees here by the River Maigue. The Irish form of the name is Áth Dara.

Addington (Greater London)
A district of CROYDON whose name is found elsewhere in Britain. This particular one was recorded in Domesday Book as

Eddintone, meaning 'settlement associated with Eadda', the latter being a personal name. The name is typical of the formula 'personal name' plus '-ington', the latter denoting a place associated with (but not necessarily owned by) the person named. The same personal name, possibly that of the same person, occurs in ADDISCOMBE.

Addiscombe (Greater London)
Like ADDINGTON, Addiscombe is also a district of CROYDON, and it is possible that the same person, Eadda, may be involved here. This name thus means 'Eadda's field', with the second half of the name representing the Old English *camp*, derived from the Latin *campus* and related to modern 'camp'. It implies an enclosed area of land, just as 'field' does today. The name of Addiscombe was recorded in 1229 as *Edescamp*, showing that the suggestion of 'combe' in the modern name is misleading.

Adlington (Lancashire)
A town northwest of BOLTON, whose name is similar to that of ADDINGTON, except that here the personal name is Eadwulf ('happy wolf'). The name as a whole thus means 'place associated with Eadwulf'; it is found in a document of 1190 in the form *Edeluinton*.

Adur (West Sussex)
A river in southern England that gives its name to an administrative district. The name was somewhat artificially derived from a place known as 'Portus Adurni', which a seventeenth-century antiquarian wrongly identified as the mouth of the river. In fact it was a Roman name for the harbour at PORTSMOUTH (or possibly for the Roman fort at PORTCHESTER). It is possible that the antiquarian was Michael Drayton, since he quotes the name in his *Poly-Olbion* of 1612, and it has not been found in earlier sources.

Afan (West Glamorgan)
An administrative district in south Wales that takes its name from the river flowing through it. Although suggesting AVON, the

river name is probably a personal name of some kind. It also occurs in ABERAVON.

Affleck Castle (Tayside)
A fifteenth-century castle, five miles northwest of CARNOUSTIE, whose name is simply a variant of AUCHINLECK.

Affric (Highland)
A river in northern Scotland that gives its name to the picturesque valley of GLEN AFFRIC, and also to Affric Forest. It derives from two Gaelic words *àth breac*. This literally means 'dappled ford', with the first word serving here as a sort of intensive to emphasise the second. 'Dappled' implies a river of different coloured stones and rocks.

Afton Water (Strathclyde)
A rimer in southern Scotland whose name may derive from the Gaelic *abhainn donn* (brown river), hence descriptive of its colour.

Ailsa Craig (Strathclyde)
A bleak rocky island west of GIRVAN whose name suggests a person, and indeed it was partly adopted as a stage name by the actor Gordon Craig, the illegitimate son of the actress Ellen Terry (who is on record as commenting 'Ailsa Craig, what a magnificent name for an actress!'). But the island's name actually means 'fairy rock', from the Gaelic *aillse* (fairy) and *creag* (rock), presumably for its associations with legendary tales of fairies or ghosts.

Aintree (Merseyside)
A suburb of LIVERPOOL with a famous racecourse where the Grand National is run. Its name simply means 'one tree' — at one time there would have been an isolated or 'lonely' tree here. The name is Old Norse in origin, and was recorded in about 1220 as *Ayntre*.

Airdrie (Strathclyde)
The name of this Scottish town, lying to the east of Glasgow, has had various suggested explanations over the years. It may have derived from the Gaelic *àrd* (high) and *ruighe* (slope), with this referring to the western spur of the PENTLAND HILLS on which the original settlement developed.

Aire (North Yorkshire/Humberside)
The name of this river, which flows roughly southeastwards into the OUSE, is found in a document dated 959 as simply *Yr*. This may come from an old Celtic root related to the Greek *hieros* (sacred, great), and so may have a similar meaning.

Alcester (Warwickshire)
A name like this tells us to expect two things: that it was a Roman settlement (indicated by the second part of the name) and that it is on a river (represented by the first part). This is a common pattern for names ending in '-cester' or '-caster' (such as DONCASTER). The river here is the Alne, whose Celtic name probably means 'white', referring to its waters (*compare* modern Welsh *gwyn*, 'white'). Alcester was a Roman settlement, and a Roman road runs through the town, now the A435 northwards to REDDITCH (the road is known as Icknield Street, not to be confused with the ICKNIELD WAY). To the east of the town, the FOSS WAY runs almost parallel with this road. The Romans seem to have called the settlement here *Alauna*, based on the river name.

Alconbury (Cambridgeshire)
This village, on the A1 northwest of HUNTINGDON, has a name that means 'Ealhmund's fortified place', the latter represented by the Old English *burg*. The personal name means 'temple protection'. It is the *h* of the man's name that produced the *c* of the place-name, with the original *m* dropping out altogether. The Domesday Book recorded the name as *Acumesberie*. *Compare* AMERSHAM.

Aldeburgh (Suffolk)
The name of this seaside town north of IPSWICH is Old English for 'old fort' (*ald*

and *burg*). Aldeburgh is near the mouth of the River Alde, which gets its name from the town as a 'back formation'. The Domesday Book records the name as *Aldeburc*.

Alderley Edge (Cheshire)
A town south of WILMSLOW, that gets its name from the wooded escarpment lying to the east. Its name in turn means 'Aldred's woodland' (or possibly 'Aldred's clearing', as *lēah* can mean either), with 'Edge' added to denote the escarpment. As a personal name, Aldred means 'great counsel'.

Aldermaston (Berkshire)
A village, famous for its nearby Atomic Energy Research Establishment, whose name was recorded in the Domesday Book as *Ældremanestone*. This means 'alderman's settlement' (Old English *ealdormann* and *tūn*). An alderman in this sense was the chief officer of a shire. Aldermaston is only eight miles from NEWBURY, which has long been an important town, although today the county town is READING.

Alderney (Channel Islands)
The third largest of the Channel Islands, whose French name is *Aurigny*; its Roman name was *Riduna*. All three names probably have a single, albeit uncertain, origin. The Roman name suggests a Celtic root meaning 'red' (as the modern Welsh *rhudd*), perhaps referring to the colour of the fertile soil. The present English name suggests 'alder island', from the Old English *alor* and *ēg*. However, the name is likely to be not Old English but Old Norse. If so, it could be interpreted to have the same sense, from the Old Norse *ǫlr* (alder) and *ey* (island). *Compare* JEREY.

Aldershot (Hampshire)
The name of this town west of GUILDFORD means 'piece of projecting land where alder trees grow', and is derived from the two Old English words *alor* (alder) and *scēat* (projecting piece of land, angle). Aldershot's name was recorded in a

document of 1248 as *Alreshete*, and it is one of a number of names in east Hampshire and west Surrey containing '-shot' or a similar element, such as Bramshott, Grayshott, BAGSHOT, and, in isolated form, Sheet, a village near PETERSFIELD.

Aldgate (Greater London)
Part of central London lying east of the City. The name does not mean 'old gate' but 'ale gate', from the Old English *ealu* (ale) and *geat* (gate). An 'ale gate' was a gate where ale was dispensed as a 'dole' to passing travellers. Here, the gate led into the City of London. The name was recorded in 1108 as *Alegate*. Before this, however, it was known as *Æst Geat*, that is, 'east gate'.

Aldridge (West Midlands)
This town, northeast of WALSALL, has a misleading name; its Domesday Book record, *Alrewic*, shows its true meaning, namely 'alder-tree settlement', from the Old English *alor* (alder) and *wīc* (farm, settlement). The sense is a place that was surrounded by, or close to, alder trees.

Aldwych (Greater London)
A district of central LONDON whose name means 'old farm', that is, one unused for some time. It derives from two Old English words: *eald* (old) and *wīc* (farm, settlement). Strictly speaking, it was the street that here gave its name to the district, rather than the name coming direct from the original farm. A text dated 1211 records the name as *Aldewich*.

Alexandria (Strathclyde)
A town near DUMBARTON with a modern name, derived from a local Member of Parliament in the eighteenth century, Alexander Smollett of Bonhill, who died in 1799. The town arose when bleaching and dyeing works were built here in the middle of that century. For a further connection with the Smollett family, *see* RENTON.

Alford (Grampian, Lincolnshire)
Either of two small towns, one in eastern
Scotland, the other in eastern England.
Although there is some room for
ambiguity, both names probably mean the
same, that is, 'alder-tree ford', from the
Old English *alor* (alder) and *ford* (ford).
The Scottish town is on the DON, although
the Lincolnshire town is not on a river of
note, so its name must relate to a stream,
perhaps the one flowing from the Holywell
spring, long favoured for its medicinal
properties. The Lincolnshire town appears
as *Alforde* in the Domesday Book.

Alfreton (Derbyshire)
The name of this town, south of
CHESTERFIELD, means 'village of
Ælfred's people'. The Domesday Book
records it in rather a distorted form as
Elstretune. The Norman clerk seems to
have confused *f* with *s* (the two letters were
more alike then than they are now). The
personal name means 'elf army', and also
occurs in NORTHALLERTON. *Compare*
ALLERTON.

Allan Water (Tayside/Central)
This Scottish river has a name that
corresponds to that of the Welsh River
ALUN, and means 'holy' or 'mighty'. For
the root of the name *see* ALNWICK.
Compare ALLENDALE TOWN.

Allendale Town (Northumberland)
A town, southwest of HEXHAM, that takes
its name from the river on which it stands,
the East Allen. This in turn has a name
identical to that of the Allan in Scotland
(*see* ALLAN WATER) and the ALUN in
Wales; the root of the name is described
under ALNWICK. It is of Celtic origin and
means 'holy' or 'strong'. The name was
recorded in a document of 1245 as
Alewenton.

Allerton (Merseyside, West Yorkshire)
The name of a district in both LIVERPOOL
and BRADFORD. It means 'alder-tree
farm', from the Old English *alor* (alder)

and *tūn* (farm). The same name is found in
NORTHALLERTON, but with a different
meaning. The Domesday Book recorded
the names of both places as *Alretune*.

Alloa (Central)
The name of this town, east of STIRLING,
was recorded as *Alveth* in 1357, from a
Gaelic compound word *allmhagh*, meaning
'rock plain', from which comes also the
name of nearby ALVA, as well as
ALLOWAY. The name is apt for Alloa,
which lies on level ground on the north
bank of the River FORTH.

Alloway (Strathclyde)
The village that is Burns's birthplace,
south of AYR, whose name, like ALLOA and
ALVA, comes from the Gaelic *allmhagh*
(rock plain). The final 'way' of the name is
thus misleading. Alloway lies on level
ground on the lower course of the River
Doon, which is spanned here by the bridge
called the Auld Brig o' Doon, famously
cited in Burns's poem *Tam o' Shanter*. The
name was recorded as *Auleway* in a text of
1324.

Alness (Highland)
A small town west of INVERGORDON,
which has recently expanded with the
development of the North Sea oil industry
here. It has the same name as the river on
which it stands. This was recorded in 1227
as *Alune*, and has the same origin as the
name of the River Allan of ALLAN WATER
and the East Allen of ALLENDALE TOWN,
among other places. It means 'holy' or
'mighty'.

Alnmouth (Northumberland)
A small resort at the mouth of the River
Aln, from which it takes its name. For the
meaning of the river name *see* ALNWICK.

Alnwick (Northumberland)
A town in northeast England whose name
is pronounced 'Annick', situated on the
River Aln only five miles from ALNMOUTH
at the river's mouth. It thus takes its name

from the river name, which derives from the Celtic root word *alaun*, meaning 'holy' or 'mighty'. The same derivation applies to several other place-names, including ALLAN WATER, ALLENDALE TOWN, and the Welsh River ALUN. The 'wick' of the name means 'farm', in particular one outlying from a main settlement. The river name may be related to the Roman name *Alauna*, which was given to several places, including the Roman fort at Ardoch, Tayside, which is actually on the ALLAN WATER. The Romans also used the name for the River Aln itself, as well as for their fort at MARYPORT at the mouth of the River Ellen. The earliest known record of the River Aln is in the Venerable Bede's *Ecclesiastical History of the English People*, written in Latin and dated 731; it appears there as *fluuium Alne*.

Alperton (Greater London)
This district of BRENT had its name recorded in a document of 1199 as *Alprinton*, and experts in Old English personal names have deduced that this means 'settlement associated with Ealhbeorht' — the initial 'Alpr-' represents the personal name, while the rest of the word corresponds to modern '-ington', which means 'farm or village associated with —'. The personal name means 'temple bright'.

Alresford (Hampshire)
A town northwest of PETERSFIELD and officially known as New Alresford as distinct from the village of Old Alresford to the north of it. It lies on the River Alre but the river took its name from the town, as a 'back formation'. Alresford means 'alder-tree ford', from the Old English *alor* (alder) and *ford* (ford). The name was recorded exactly as now in a text of 701.

Alston (Cumbria)
The name of this small market town east of PENRITH is found elsewhere, sometimes with an added *-e*. However, the meanings of each are not identical, and the personal

name that forms the first half of the name can vary from one Alston to another. Here it is probably Aldhūn, so the overall name means 'Aldhūn's farm'. A record of 1164 has the name as *Aldeneby*, with Old Norse *bý* giving the 'farm', as distinct from the present Old English *tūn*.

Alton (Hampshire)
This name does not begin with a personal name, as ALSTON does. It is a compound of two Old English words: *æwiell* 'stream', or more precisely 'source of a stream' (the word is related to modern English 'well') and *tūn* (settlement). It follows that many places named Alton are near the source of a river or stream. This Hampshire Alton, southeast of BASINGSTOKE, is near the source of the River WEY, while the group of Wiltshire 'Altons' (including Alton Barnes and Alton Priors) are near the source of the Piddle (*see* PUDDLETOWN). The Wey lies to the west of Alton, and enters the town through flood meadows.

Altrincham (Greater Manchester)
The name of this town, southwest of MANCHESTER, was *Aldringeham* in a text of 1290, hence it is an '-ingham' name like WOKINGHAM and many others (the soft *g* led to the *ch*). The first part of the name is a personal name, in this case Aldhere, meaning 'great army' (literally 'old army'). The name as a whole therefore means 'settlement of the people of Aldhere'. These may have been either his followers or members of his family, in the broadest sense.

Alum Bay (Isle of Wight)
This popular bay, well known for its variegated sands, is named after the alum that was quarried from the rocks here in the sixteenth century.

Alun (Dyfed, Clwyd)
Either of two Welsh rivers, one rising not far from ST DAVID'S, the other springing from the mountainside north of LLANGOLLEN. The origin for both is the

same, namely the Celtic root word meaning 'holy' or 'mighty', a derivation shared by the Scottish River Allan (*see* ALLAN WATER) and the Aln of ALNWICK, among others.

Alva (Central)
A town three miles north of ALLOA, whose name has the same origin as its neighbour, that is, the Gaelic *allmhagh*, meaning 'rock plain'. The same origin applies to the name of ALLOWAY. Alva lies at the base of the OCHILL HILLS.

Alyth (Tayside)
The name of this small town, northeast of BLAIRGOWRIE, derives from that of the nearby Hill of Alyth, at whose foot it stands. This name is based on the Gaelic *aill* (rugged bank, steep place), so is descriptive. The whole area to the north of the town is hilly or mountainous.

Amble (Northumberland)
The name of this small town on the COQUET southeast of ALNWICK means 'Anna's promontory', as historic records of the name show (for example, *Anebell* in 1256). This means that the second part of the name is the same as the 'Bill' of PORTLAND Bill. Amble is a coastal town, and the promontory here runs out into the North Sea opposite Coquet Island. Despite its similarity, Amble has nothing in common with AMBLESIDE.

Ambleside (Cumbria)
A town in the Lake District, northwest of WINDERMERE. Its name is pure Old Norse, and comprises the three words *á* (river), *melr* (sandbank), and *sǽtr* ('shieling', i.e. summer pasture). The name as a whole thus illustrates the rural practice of transhumance, or the transfer of flocks to mountain or hill pastures in the summer months, where temporary shelters would be set up. This particular pasture was one by a river with a sandbank, where the animals could drink. The third part of the name is thus related to the English

'shelter', but not to 'side'. The name was recorded as *Ameleseta* in a document of about 1095, and as *Amylside* in about 1400. The origins of the name are thus quite different from AMBLE in Northumberland.

Amersham (Buckinghamshire)
A town south of CHESHAM, whose name means 'Ealhmund's village', with the personal name the same as that found in ALCONBURY. Ealhmund may not have actually founded the original settlement, but he would have held a position of authority there in its early years. Although the Old English *hām* suggests 'hamlet', it denoted a place that was larger than a *tūn*, despite the fact that the latter word gave us the modern English 'town'. Hence the use of 'village' here rather than simply 'settlement'. Amersham's name was recorded in 1066 as *Agmodesham*, with the *g* representing the *h* of the personal name.

Amesbury (Wiltshire)
A town, north of SALISBURY, whose name was recorded in about 880 as *Ambresbyrig*, which means 'Ambr's fortified place' (Old English *burg*). The 'fort' would have been that of the nearby Iron Age hill-fort known as Vespasian's Camp. The personal name seems to have been blended with that of Aurelius Ambrosius, a fifth-century Romano-British ruler who is traditionally said to have founded his capital here.

Amlwch (Gwynedd)
This ANGLESEY port has, as might be expected, a Welsh name meaning 'near the swamp' (*am llwch*). The 'swamp' may have been the small bay here that was constructed as a proper harbour when the nearby copper mines of Parys Mountain were first fully exploited in the eighteenth century.

Ammanford (Dyfed)
The name of this town means what it says, namely 'a ford over the River Amman'. The river's name comes from the Welsh *banw* (pig), and denotes a river that 'roots'

its way through the ground like a pig. The town, adjacent to the South Wales coalfield, arose in the nineteenth century so the name is quite recent. The Welsh name is Rhydaman, translating the English.

Ampleforth (North Yorkshire)

A village east of THIRSK with a famous Roman Catholic public school. Its name comes from the two Old English words *ampre* (sorrel) and *ford* (ford), and so denotes a ford over the stream here (a tributary of the River Rye) by which sorrel grew. The Domesday Book records the name clearly as *Ampreforde*. Ampleforth College was founded here in 1802, having transferred from France at the time of the French Revolution.

Ampthill (Bedfordshire)

A town, south of BEDFORD, whose name, unexpectedly, means 'ant hill', from the Old English *ǣmette* and *hyll*, combining as *ǣmethyll*. The first word gave the dialect word for an ant, 'emmet', as well as 'ant' itself. The name was recorded as *Ammetelle* in the Domesday Book.

Ancaster (Lincolnshire)

A village west of SLEAFORD. It has a 'Roman camp' name, from the Old English *ceaster*, and has been traditionally identified as the site of the encampment known as *Causennis*. However, recent researches suggest that this was not at Ancaster but possibly at the little village of Saltersford, to the west of ERMINE STREET, on which Ancaster lies. The name Ancaster means 'Anna's encampment', and does not follow the common pattern of 'river name' plus Old English '*ceaster*' to denote a Roman station, since there is no river. There is, however, a river at Saltersford. Ancaster was recorded as *Anecastre* in the late twelfth century.

Andover (Hampshire)

Andover was originally the name of the river, now called the Anton, on which the present town stands. The name is of Celtic origin, meaning 'ash-tree stream', from the root words *onno* and *dubro* (the latter of these gave the name of DOVER). The river was thus known as the *Andever* until at least the sixteenth century. Some time after this, an antiquarian, coming across the river name *Trisanton* in a text by Tacitus, misread this as *Anton* and assumed it referred to the river at Andover, although it actually referred to the TRENT. Hence the modern river name of Anton. Andover's name (as that of the river) was recorded in a document of 955 as *Andeferas*.

Anfield (Merseyside)

A district of LIVERPOOL whose name was recorded in a document of 1642 as *Hongfield*, suggesting that the derivation lies in the Middle English *hange* (slope) and the Old English *feld* (field), so that the name as a whole means something like 'sloping piece of ground'. The ground certainly rises here as one goes northeast from the city centre. The Ordnance Survey map of 1840 shows a house here called Anfield House. No doubt the district developed around this, with the house taking its name from a piece of ground, such as a field.

Anglesey (Gwynedd)

The name of this well-known island off the northwest Wales coast has been influenced by the word 'Angle', so that it has come to be connected with the Angles, who gave their name to ENGLAND. This link is old but false; as early as the twelfth century William of Malmesbury explained the name (in Latin) as meaning *Anglorum insula*, 'island of the Angles'. But many names of islands round the Welsh coast are Scandinavian in origin, and a thirteenth-century record of the name as *Ongulsey* leads to the conclusion that the first part of the name is a personal name, so that the whole means 'Ongull's island'. The Welsh name for Anglesey is *Môn*, meaning simply 'hill' or 'mountain', with this in turn related to the name of the Isle of MAN. Anglesey does not obviously appear mountainous, so the reference must certainly be to Holyhead Mountain (Welsh *Mynydd Twr*). This is a prominent granite hill at the northwest corner of HOLY ISLAND, where it would have been an excellent landmark for approaching ships. The Roman name of Anglesey, taken direct from the Celtic, was *Mona*. *See also* CAERNARVON; *compare* ANGLESEY ABBEY.

Anglesey Abbey (Cambridgeshire)
A stately home at the village of Lode, northeast of CAMBRIDGE, built in the early seventeenth century on the site of a medieval Augustinian monastery, itself in existence from the twelfth century. The name has been recorded in a document of 1242 as *Angleseia*, suggesting that it means 'island of the Angles' (unlike ANGLESEY). 'Island' here can be understood as 'raised land', so the Old English name can tentatively be interpreted as 'area of raised land inhabited by Angles', implying that they were a sort of 'pocket' here in a region mostly inhabited by another people. But it is not clear who comprised this enclave, and it is not even certain if this is the correct interpretation.

Angmering (West Sussex)
A largely residential area northeast of LITTLEHAMPTON. Its name is typical of the many '-ing' names in this part of Sussex, such as Ferring, Patching, Poling, Goring, and WORTHING. All such names have a personal name for their first element; here it is Angemær. The name as a whole thus means 'place of Angemær's people', and it is found in the Domesday Book as *Angemare* (without the Old English '-ing' suffix, which is really *-ingas*, meaning 'people of'). The resort of Angmering-on-Sea takes its name from this older Angmering, so that the name has generally 'spread' to the coast.

Angus (Tayside)
An administrative district in eastern Scotland whose name was formerly a Scottish county name, after Angus, king of the Picts in the eighth century. The Christian name Angus means 'unique choice' (in its Gaelic form, *Aonghas*). The place-name therefore implies a region associated with this King Angus, and was recorded in the twelfth century as *Enegus*.

Annan (Dumfries and Galloway)
A town southeast of DUMFRIES and near the mouth of the River Annan, from which it takes its name, or more precisely from its valley, Annandale. This last has had its name recorded in different ways over the centuries — *Anava* in the seventh century; *Estrahanent* in 1124; *vallum de Anant* in 1147; and *Annandesdale* in 1179, among others. The second of these has a Celtic word for 'valley' directly related to the Welsh *ystrad*. The river name itself is thus very old, and of uncertain meaning. It may be based on an early Celtic root word meaning simply 'water', hence 'place by (or in) the valley of the river', which is hardly original.

Annick Water (Strathclyde)
A river in southwest Scotland, which has given its name to a district of IRVINE New Town, through which it flows. The name itself is obscure, and may have evolved from some Gaelic word, such as *èan* (water).

Ansdell (Lancashire)
A district of LYTHAM ST ANNE'S, north of the city centre, named after the painter Richard Ansdell (1815–1885), who built a large house here called 'Star Hills'. It is now a Methodist old people's home.

Anstruther (Fife)
The name of this attractive resort and fishing port on the FIRTH OF FORTH was recorded in about 1205 as *Anestrothir*. The name is pure Gaelic, and derives from *an sruthair*, 'the little stream'. A small river, the Dreel, enters the sea here between the two adjacent towns of Anstruther Easter and Anstruther Wester, which royal burghs comprise the town as a whole.

Antonine Wall (Strathclyde/Lothian)
A Roman fortification that extends for
some 37 miles from a point west of
GLASGOW to a point south of BO'NESS west
of EDINBURGH (i.e. from the CLYDE to the
FORTH). The wall dates from the first
century AD and is named after the Roman
emperor Antoninus Pius (AD 86–161),
although the wall was actually built by
order of the Governor of Britain at that
time, Lollius Urbicus. The objective was to
keep out raiding northern tribes. However,
the wall was abandoned before the end of
the second century, and today very little is
left, unlike its more southerly equivalent,
HADRIAN'S WALL.

Antrim (Antrim)
A Northern Ireland town that has given its
name to the county. The settlement
probably developed in a region that was
known in Irish as 'one house', that is, *aon*
(one) and *treabh* (house). In other words,
an isolated family dwelling formed the
basis for the present town, whose Irish
name is Aontroim.

An Uaimh (Meath)
The Irish name of the town more
commonly known as NAVAN.

Appin (Strathclyde/Highland)
A mountainous area in western Scotland
bounded by Loch LINNHE to the west and
the GRAMPIANS to the east. The name
means 'abbey lands' (Gaelic *apainn*),
referring to the land that was owned here in
medieval times by Ligmore Abbey. The
same Gaelic root also occurs in Port Appin,
a village on the shores of Loch Linnhe, and
in the Strath of Appin, a valley in the
southwest of the region.

Appleby (Cumbria)
This small town southeast of PENRITH has
a Scandinavian name meaning 'apple
farm', but possibly with the Old Norse *epli*
(apple) replaced by the Old English *æppel*.
The name occurs elsewhere, although it is
more common in its English form of

Appleton. A document of 1130 has the
name as *Aplebi*.

Appledore (Devon)
A large village north of BIDEFORD with a
name similar to that of APPLEBY. Here it is
Old English, not Old Norse, however, and
means simply 'apple tree', from the word
apuldor, where the second part of the word
is not 'door' but an Old English suffix used
when forming the names of trees. The
name was recorded in a document of 1335
as *le Apildore*.

Aran Islands (Galway)
Both the Aran Islands, in Galway Bay off
the west coast of Ireland, and Aran Island
(Donegal) have names of common origin
and meaning, from the Irish *ára*, dative
árainn (loin, kidney). This implies 'arched
back' or 'ridge', referring to the contour of
the islands. The Galway Aran Islands are
individually named Inishmore ('great
island'), Inishman ('middle island'), and
Inisheer ('eastern island'). It is possible
that the name of ARRAN, the Scottish
island, may be related.

Arbroath (Tayside)
An industrial town and coastal resort in
eastern Scotland, famous for its 'Arbroath
smokies', or smoked haddock. Its name
means 'mouth of the Brothock', with the
first part representing the more common
'Aber-', as in ABERDEEN. The Brothock is
the name of the stream (burn) here,
derived from the Gaelic *brothach* (boiling,
seething), referring to its waters. In
modern terms, the name is thus really
'Aberbrothock', and this is precisely the
name used for the town by Southey in his
famous poem *The Inchcape Rock*:

> And then they knew the perilous rock,
> And blest the Abbot of Aberbrothok.

This spelling of the name was recorded in
the twelfth century. Today a district of the
town is known by the parallel name of
Inverbrothock, with 'Inver-' meaning

'mouth' just as 'Aber-' does (*compare* INVERNESS). Arbroath's Gaelic name is Obar Brothaig, which has the same sense.

Ardee (Louth)
A town, southwest of DUNDALK, known in Irish as Baile Átha Fhirdia, which has been much shortened and 'smoothed down' in the English version. It means 'town of Ferdia's ford'. Ferdia was a warrior said to have been killed here in the first century AD when he was attempting to prevent the forces of Queen Maeve from entering Ulster. There is a plaque on the bridge over the River Dee here marking this event.

Ardglass (Down)
An attractive coastal village southeast of DOWNPATRICK whose Irish name, Árd Ghlais, means 'green height'; it is located on a slope that runs down to a small bay here.

Ardmore (Waterford)
A resort on Ardmore Bay whose name occurs several times elsewhere in Ireland and also in Scotland. It is Irish for 'great height', from *árd* (height) and *mór* (great), and invariably refers to a headland. Here in Waterford, the headland is Ram Head.

Ardnamurchan (Highland)
A large peninsula to the west of Loch SHIEL, where it culminates in Ardnamurchan Point, the most westerly point in Britain. Despite its obvious Gaelic nature, the name remains difficult to interpret satisfactorily. As early as the eighth century it was recorded as *Art Muirchol*, which suggests a combination of *ard* (height), *muir* (sea), and *chol* (sin), seeming to imply a historic link with pirates. But the present form of the name equally suggests *muirchon*, literally 'sea-dogs', in other words otters; this seems more plausible since such names usually refer to natural features.

Ardrishaig (Strathclyde)
This town on the shore of Loch Gilp in western Scotland seems to have a name that means 'height of the brambles', from the Gaelic *ard* and *dris*, 'bramble', 'blackberry'.

Ardrossan (Strathclyde)
The name of this port on the Firth of CLYDE means literally 'height of the little headland', from the Gaelic *ard* (height) and *ros* (headland), with the suffix *-an* indicating a diminutive. The reference is to the lower ground where SALTCOATS now stands to the east of the main part of the town.

Ards Peninsula (Down)
The name of this well-known peninsula running south between STRANGFORD Lough and the sea means simply 'peninsula', 'headland', with an English plural *s* added to the Irish *árd* (as in ARDMORE).

Arfon (Gwynedd)
An administrative district in northwest Wales. Its name indicates its location 'opposite Anglesey' — *ar Fôn*, with *ar* meaning 'over' and *Fôn* the grammatical form of *Môn*, the Welsh name of ANGLESEY. 'Arfon' also gives rise to the name of CAERNARVON.

Argyll (Strathclyde)
The name of this former Scottish county means 'land of the Gaels'. The 'Gaels' were originally an Irish race, known as the Dalriada, who came into the region through KINTYRE to the south and settled as a Scots kingdom in what was then Pictish territory (*compare* GALLOWAY). Today Argyll has combined with BUTE (apart from the island of ARRAN) to form the administrative district of Argyll and Bute. The name was recorded as *Arregaithel* in a document of about 970.

Arisaig (Highland)
A village, popular with tourists on Scotland's western coast, whose name disguises the fact that it really ends in the Old Norse word *vík*, meaning 'bay', as

found in LERWICK, for example. The first part of the name is also Scandinavian, meaning 'river-mouth', corresponding to the name of the Danish town, Aarhus. Arisaig thus means 'bay at the mouth of the river', although the 'river' here is only a small stream that flows into Loch nan Ceall. The Old Norse elements of the name are *á* (river; the *r* denotes a genitive), *ós* (mouth), and *vík*.

Arklow (Wicklow)

The town and resort south of WICKLOW has a name of Scandinavian origin, meaning 'Arnkel's meadow', with the last part of the name representing the Old Norse *ló* (meadow) and the first part a personal name. Arklow's Irish name is An tInbhear Mór, meaning 'the big estuary', referring to that of the AVOCA. A document of 1177 records the name as *Herketelou*. Arnkel himself remains unidentified.

Armadale (Lothian)

The name of this town, southwest of LINLITHGOW, owes its origin to the landowner here, William Honeyman, Lord Armadale. He took his title from Armadale in SUTHERLAND and gave it to the property he inherited from his mother, here in the parish of BATHGATE. The name appears on a map dated 1818, and the present town developed from the mid-nineteenth century when chemical works were established. The name itself is Scandinavian in origin and means something like 'arm-shaped valley'. This, therefore, is the origin of the name of Armadale on the Isle of Skye, and also, of course, that of the Sutherland village (now in Highland) that gave Lord Armadale's title.

Armagh (Armagh)

The name of this Northern Ireland town means literally 'height of Macha', from the Irish *árd* (height) and the personal name Macha. In Irish legendary history, Macha was a queen who (according to one popular account) founded Emain Macha or Navan Fort on the hill to the west of the town some time in the third century BC. But the legends are blurred, and there are tales of more than one queen or goddess of the name. Perhaps for this reason, some prefer to interpret the name as 'height of the plain', taking the second half of the word as the Irish *machaire* (plain). Either way, the 'height' would be the ancient fort, which was formerly the palace of the Ulster kings. The county name comes from that of the town.

Arnold (Nottinghamshire)

Somewhat unexpectedly, the name means 'eagles' corner', deriving from the Old English *earn* (eagle) and *halh* (corner of land). Arnold is now a northeast suburb of NOTTINGHAM, but at one time it could have had a 'corner of land', such as the valley of the stream here, where eagles nested. It is unusual for Old English *halh* to have produced the '-old' of this name; normally the modern equivalent is 'hall' or 'hale', as in HALE.

Arnside (Cumbria)

This town, north of CARNFORTH, had its name recorded in a document of 1208 as *Arnuluesheued*, showing that the present '-side' is misleading. The name is therefore a combination of a personal name, Earnwulf ('eagle wolf'), and the Old English *hēafod* (headland). Arnside is a resort on the tidal estuary of the River Kent, and 'Earnwulf's headland' must have been a feature on the coast here.

Arran (Strathclyde)

There may be a connection between the names of the Irish ARAN ISLANDS and this island on the west side of the Firth of CLYDE. That of the former implies an 'arched ridge', but this is not a true description of Arran, which has spiky mountain peaks, not a ridge. So it would make more sense to find a root word related to the Irish *árd* (height). The definitive explanation for the name has yet to be made.

Arun (West Sussex)
A river and an administrative district, the
latter taken from the former. The river's
name derives as a 'back formation' from
ARUNDEL.

Arundel (West Sussex)
A town and castle, north of
LITTLEHAMPTON. Its name, according to
folk etymology, has an origin in the French
hirondelle (swallow). Support for this
explanation is said to lie in the fact that this
particular bird is depicted on the town's
coat of arms, or that Hirondelle was the
name of the horse of the legendary Bevis of
Hampton (i.e. Southampton) who lived in
the castle in Norman times. But the true
source of the name, which was recorded in
the Domesday Book as *Harundel*, is the
Old English *hārhūne dell* (hoarhound
valley). Hoarhound is a plant belonging to
the nettle family, and at one time it must
have grown in abundance by the River
ARUN below the present town. The river
takes its name from that of the town. Its
earlier name was the Tarrant, which is
almost certainly related to that of the
TRENT and therefore to the Roman name
of both rivers — *Trisantona*. This was
based on a British (Celtic) root word *sent*,
which meant either 'wanderer' (that is, a
meandering river) or 'flooding'. The latter
sense would apply to the Arun, which is
subject to flooding in the region of
Amberley, north of Arundel. *See also*
ANDOVER.

Ascot (Berkshire)
This village with its famous racecourse,
southwest of WINDSOR, has a name
meaning simply 'eastern cottage' or
'eastern shelter', the latter being for
animals rather than humans. This sense
can be seen clearly in the record of the
name for 1177, which was as *Estcota*. Old
English *cot* is commonly found with a
compass direction like this, so that one
similarly finds places called Westcott,
Northcott, and Southcott, as well as the
more obvious Eastcott.

Ashbourne (Derbyshire, Meath)
Either of two places: a town northwest of
DERBY and a village northwest of DUBLIN.
The name means 'stream where ash trees
grow', 'bourne' being a stream, as in
BOURNEMOUTH. The Derbyshire town is
now on the River Henmore, which was
originally the Ashbourne, hence the town
takes its name from this. The Irish
Ashbourne has the same sense as its
English counterpart, although the village's
Irish name is quite different — it is Cill
Dhéagláin, 'St Declan's Church'. The
English Ashbourne was *Esseburne* in the
Domesday Book.

Ashburton (Devon)
A market town, west of NEWTON ABBOT,
with a name that essentially means
'Ashbourne Town', i.e. similar to
ASHBOURNE, which means 'ash-tree
stream'. The river here, now the YEO, was
formerly the Ashbourne; the Old English
tūn (settlement) was added (as the modern
'-ton') to give Ashburton. In the Domesday
Book, Ashburton's name appears as
Essebretone.

Ashby de la Zouch (Leicestershire)
A market town northwest of LEICESTER.
There are several Ashbys in the Midlands,
particularly in Leicestershire and
Lincolnshire. There was thus a need to
distinguish between them, hence the
addition in this case of 'de la Zouch' (and in
Lincolnshire, of the medieval Church
Latin 'Puerorum', referring to the singing
boys of Lincoln Cathedral). Ashby means
'ash-tree farm', from the Old Norse *askr*
(ash) and the common *bý* (farm,
settlement). The second half of the name
denotes the Norman 'lord of the manor' in
the thirteenth century, Roger de la Zuche.
(His surname, which means 'tree-stump',
gave the English surname Such.) It is
possible that some places now called Ashby
simply had their names altered by the
Danes from the Old English equivalent of
Ashton, although there is no evidence to
show that this happened in the case of

Ashby de la Zouch. The name was recorded as *Ascebi* in the Domesday Book, and as *Esseby la Zouche* in a document of 1241.

Ashdown Forest (East Sussex)

If the name suggests downs covered by ash woods, the suggestion is correct! The forest is now mainly heathland, but there are still some ash trees to be found in the region, roughly the triangle formed by UCKFIELD in the south and EAST GRINSTEAD and TUNBRIDGE WELLS in the west and east. FOREST ROW gets its name from Ashdown Forest. The name was recorded as *Essendon* in a document of 1165.

Ashford (Kent)

This industrial and market town southwest of CANTERBURY has a name that means 'ford by ash trees'. But early records of the name, such as *Essetesford* (1046) show that an element has dropped out. The *-set-* of this name may thus represent the Old English *scēat*, 'corner of land' (like the last part of ALDERSHOT), so that the name fully means 'ford by a corner of land where ash trees grow'. The ford would here have been over either the Great Stour or the East Stour, possibly the latter. *See* STOUR.

Ashington (Northumberland)

The name of this town, east of MORPETH, appears in a document of 1205 as *Essenden*, showing that the present '-ington' is misleading. The name thus means 'ash-tree valley', from the Old English *æscen-denu*. The valley would have been that of the River Wansbeck, to the south of the town.

Ashtead (Surrey)

A residential district northeast of LEATHERHEAD with a name meaning simply 'ash-tree place', from the Old English *æsc* (ash) and *stede* (place, location).

Ashton-in-Makerfield (Greater Manchester)

A town west of MANCHESTER. Ashton means 'ash-tree settlement', while the second part of the name here means 'wall' or 'ruin', plus the Old English *feld*, 'open land' (rather than 'field'). The 'Maker-' element is actually Celtic, and ultimately derives from the Latin *maceria* (masonry), so is thus indirectly related to the English 'masonry'. The 'open land with a ruin' may therefore have referred to the dilapidated Roman fort at WIGAN, which is only four miles from the town of Ashton-in-Makerfield.

Ashton-under-Lyne (Greater Manchester)

This town, east of MANCHESTER, has acquired an addition to distinguish it from other Ashtons, as ASHTON-IN-MAKERFIELD has done. Ashton means 'ash-tree settlement', and the 'Lyne' was the name of a large forest area near here ('under' means 'near'), which extended virtually from MANCHESTER to MARKET DRAYTON (in Shropshire). 'Lyne' itself is a British (i.e. Celtic) name meaning 'elm tree' (the Welsh word for this tree is *llwyf*), so it here implies a forest of elms. The name was recorded as simply *Ashton* in a document of 1255. *Compare* NEWCASTLE-UNDER-LYME.

Askern (South Yorkshire)

A town, north of DONCASTER, whose name was recorded in 1195 exactly as now. It probably derives from the Old English *æsc* (ash tree) and *hyrne* (angle, corner), and so means 'corner where ash trees grow'. However, the spelling of the name suggests that the Old Norse *askr* has replaced the Old English word for the tree.

Aspatria (Cumbria)

This small town, northeast of MARYPORT, has a Scandinavian name: *askr* (ash tree) followed by the name Patrick. The meaning is thus 'place by Patrick's ash tree'. Although Old Norse in origin, the word order is Celtic, with the personal name following the common noun, as for example in CASTLE DOUGLAS or KILMARNOCK. This is because the Norse settlers in this part of Britain spoke a dialect that reflected the language of Ireland, from where they had come. The name was recorded as *Askpatrik* in a document of 1291.

Aspull (Greater Manchester)
This town's name is Old English, a combination of *æspe* (aspen tree) and *hyll* (hill). Aspull stands on high land northeast of WIGAN, but there are few aspens today. The name was recorded as *Aspul* in a document of 1212.

Athboy (Meath)
A market town west of NAVAN with a name meaning 'yellow ford', describing the river bed at this point. The town's Irish name is thus Baile Átha Buí, 'town of the yellow ford'. The river here is also the Athboy, deriving from the name of the town.

Athelney (Somerset)
The hamlet, west of LANGPORT, where King Alfred hid in 878. Its name means literally 'island of the princes', from the Old English *ætheling* (prince, nobleman) and *ēg* (island). This implies that members of a noble Anglo-Saxon family lived here on the 'island' — in this case simply a place higher than the surrounding marshes. The association with King Alfred is coincidental. The Domesday Book recorded the name as *Adelingi*.

Athenry (Galway)
A town east of GALWAY whose name can be translated from the Irish (Baile Átha an Rí) as 'ford of the king'. It seems likely that the place was originally named after an English king, referring to its Anglo-Norman castle, and that it may at one time have been called Kingstown (or the medieval equivalent). This could then have been turned into Irish.

Atherstone (Warwickshire)
A town northwest of NUNEATON with a name meaning 'Æthelred's farm'. The personal name (meaning 'noble counsel') is followed by the Old English *tun* (farm).

The Domesday Book recorded the name as *Aderestone*. The suggestion of 'stone' in the modern name is thus misleading.

Atherton (Greater Manchester)
This town, southwest of BOLTON, has a name meaning 'Æthelhere's farm', with the personal name (meaning 'noble army') followed by the Old English *tūn* (farm). A document of 1212 recorded the name as *Aderton*.

Athlone (Westmeath)
North of BIRR, this town has the Irish name Baile Átha Luain, 'town of the ford of Luan'. The river here is the SHANNON, and Luan must have been the name of the man who held authority at this point. The river crossing was frequently the scene of battles in historic times.

Atholl (Tayside)
A mountainous area at the southern end of the GRAMPIANS. *See* BLAIR ATHOLL.

Athy (Kildare)
A market town east of PORT LAOISE whose name means 'town of the ford of Ae'. Ae was a MUNSTER chief killed in a battle here in the eleventh century. The ford was over the River Barrow. The current Irish name is Áth Í.

Attercliffe (South Yorkshire)
A district of SHEFFIELD whose name seems to derive from the Old English *æt thæt clife*, meaning '(place) at the cliff', with the final *t* of the second word for some reason turned into *r*. Attercliffe is about two miles northeast of the city centre, where the ground indeed rises to the point known as Attercliffe Hill Top. The name appears in the Domesday Book as *Ateclive*.

Attleborough (Norfolk)
This small town southwest of NORWICH has a name meaning 'Ætla's fortified place', with the personal name followed by the Old English *burg*. The Domesday Book recorded the name as *Atleburc*.

Auchinleck (Strathclyde)
A colliery town, northwest of CUMNOCK, whose name means 'field of the flat stones', from the Gaelic *achadh* (field) and *leac* (flat stone, slab of rock). The name was recorded in a document of 1239 as *Auechinlec. Compare* AFFLECK CASTLE.

Auchterarder (Tayside)
This small town, southeast of CRIEFF, has a Gaelic name meaning 'upland of high water', from, respectively, the three words *uachdar* (upper), *ard* (high), and *dobhar* (water). This last Gaelic word (represented in the name by the final '-der') is related to the name DOVER. The name exactly describes the location of the town, which lies on high ground to the north of the OCHILL HILLS on the River Ruthen.

Auchtermuchty (Fife)
The name of this town, south of NEWBURGH, is similar to that of AUCHTERARDER inasmuch as the first half of it means 'upper'. The remainder means 'pig place' (Gaelic *muccatu*), showing that pigs must have been reared here. A document of about 1210 gives the name as *Vchtermuckethin*.

Auckland
See BISHOP AUCKLAND.

Audenshaw (Greater Manchester)
A town east of MANCHESTER. The second half of the name means 'copse', from the Old English *sceaga*, found fairly commonly as the 'Shaw' that begins many place-names. Less commonly it follows a personal name, as here. 'Auden' thus represents the name of Aldwine ('old friend'), so that the name as a whole means 'Aldwine's copse'. A document of the mid-thirteenth century records the name in the form *Aldenshagh*.

Audley End (Essex)
A small village near SAFFRON WALDEN that takes its name from the Jacobean mansion of Audley End here, which was originally a house built by Lord Howard de Walden, 1st Earl of Suffolk, in the early seventeenth century. The house takes its name from the estate (on which the Abbey of Walden had stood) granted to Sir Thomas Audley (1488–1544) by Henry VIII after the Dissolution of the Monasteries in 1539. The earliest records we have of the name are *Audeley* in 1539 and *Audleyend* in 1555. 'End' means 'defined area' or 'limited territory', much as in London's WEST END.

Augher (Tyrone)
A picturesque village at the junction of the A4 and A28 southwest of DUNGANNON. Its name represents Irish *eochair* (border), reflecting its location only three miles from the county border with MONAGHAN.

Avebury (Wiltshire)
A village west of MARLBOROUGH, that is a popular tourist attraction, with its megalithic stone circle and nearby ancient SILBURY HILL. Its name was recorded in the Domesday Book as *Avreberie*, which is an Old English name meaning 'Afa's fortified place', perhaps with reference to the Bronze Age burial ground here rather than a defensive site. The second half of the name is the common Old English *burg*.

Aveley (Essex)
This town, northwest of GRAYS, had its name recorded in the Domesday Book as *Aluithelea*. The meaning is 'Ælfgȳth's clearing' or 'Ælfgȳth's grove', the latter part of this being the Old English *lēah*. Ælfgȳth is a woman's name.

Aviemore (Highland)
This famous skiing centre northeast of KINGUSSIE has a name apt for the surrounding mountains, deriving from the Gaelic *aghaid mór* (big hill-face). The name of the resort is today usually stressed on the first syllable (*A*viemore), though in Gaelic the stress would logically fall on the adjective (Avie*more*), as there are various kinds of hill-face, but this is a notably *large* one.

Avoca, Vale of (Wicklow)
A tourist area northeast of ARKLOW, with its Meeting of the Waters (the confluence of the Avonmore and Avonbeg rivers). Its name is a modern rendering of Ptolemy's ancient name *Oboka* for the River Avonmore here, found on his map of Britain, dating from the second century AD. The name *Oboka* is itself of unknown origin. The two rivers have names meaning respectively 'big river' and 'little river', from the Irish Abhainn Mhor and Abhainn Bheag (*compare* AVON). The Avonmore may formerly have been called the Dea ('goddess'). *See* DEE.

Avon (various)
Avon is the most common river name in the British Isles, occurring in all four countries (England, Scotland, Wales, Ireland). One of the best-known southern English Avons, the so-called 'Bristol Avon', gives the name of the southwestern county, formed mainly from SOMERSET in 1974 to include the cities of BRISTOL and BATH and the surrounding area. The name is Celtic, and means simply 'river'. It may be objected that this is hardly a name, but the inhabitants of a local region would refer to their local river without actually naming it, much as now we say 'the river's running high', etc. In Welsh the modern word for 'river' is *afon*, in Gaelic it is *abhainn*, and in Irish it is also *abhainn* (pronounced roughly 'owin'). *Compare* Loch AWE. *See also* AVOCA, VALE OF; AVONMOUTH.

Avonmouth (Avon)
The main port for BRISTOL, which developed as such in the nineteenth century. The name originally applied to the mouth of the River AVON here. It is thus a modern development with an ancient name, recorded as long ago as 918 as *Afene muthan*. *Compare* BOURNEMOUTH.

Awe, Loch (Strathclyde)
A loch in ARGYLL that takes its name from the river flowing from it. The River Awe in turn has a name that means simply 'river', as it is a variant of AVON. The river's name was recorded in an early document of 700 as *Aba*.

Axbridge (Somerset)
A village on the River AXE west of CHEDDAR. Its name means, not surprisingly, 'bridge over the River Axe', and has existed at least since the early tenth century, when it was recorded as *Axanbrycg*. The village lies about halfway along the course of the river as it flows west to the Bristol Channel from its source under the MENDIPS.

Axe (Somerset, Dorset/Devon)
Any of various rivers. Two of the best known occur in the West Country, one rising under the MENDIPS and flowing through AXBRIDGE to the Bristol Channel near WESTON-SUPER-MARE, the other rising near BEAMINSTER and flowing west, then southwest to enter Lyme Bay (*see* LYME REGIS) near SEATON. The latter river gives its name to AXMINSTER and AXMOUTH. Axe is similar to AVON in that it means simply 'river', 'water', from a British (Celtic) root word *isca*, which also gives the names of the ESK, the EXE (and therefore EXETER), and probably the USK in Wales. The earliest record we have of the name is in the eighth-century *Cartularium Saxonicum*, where it is referred to, in the Latin of the day, as *fluuium Aesce*.

Axminster (Devon)
A town northwest of LYME REGIS lying on the River AXE. The second half of the name refers to the ancient monastery that was once here, although today the town is better known for its carpets. The town's name was recorded in a document of about 900 as *Ascanamynster*, with the latter half of this deriving from the Old English *mynster* added to the Celtic river name. Axminster was a West Saxon settlement as early as the seventh century.

Axmouth (Devon)
A resort northeast of SEATON lying near the mouth of the River AXE, hence the name. The name dates from at least the ninth century, when it was recorded as *Axanmutha*.

Aycliffe (Durham)
The name of the village north of DARLINGTON that adjoins the Aycliffe Industrial Estate in the New Town of NEWTON AYCLIFFE; the latter is frequently called simply 'Aycliffe'.

Aylesbury (Buckinghamshire)
A market town, northwest of LONDON, whose name means 'Ægel's fortified place', with the personal name followed by the Old English word (*burg*); the latter basically denoted a fortified site but could also apply to an ancient fortification, such as an Iron Age hill-fort, or occasionally a Roman fort. There must have been an Anglo-Saxon fort here some time before the sixth century, which is when we have the earliest reference to Aylesbury (in the *Anglo-Saxon Chronicle*) as *Ægelesburg*. The same personal name (but almost certainly not the same person) is found in Aylesford, a village in Kent; Aylestone, a district of LEICESTER; and Ailsworth, a village west of PETERBOROUGH, Cambridgeshire. *See also* AYLSHAM.

Aylsham (Norfolk)
A market town, north of NORWICH, whose name incorporates the same personal name as that in AYLESBURY and other places. Aylsham means 'Ægel's village', the latter part of the name being the Old English *hām*. The Domesday Book records the name as both *Ailesham* and *Eilessam*.

Ayot St Lawrence (Hertfordshire)
A village west of WELWYN that has become a tourist attraction thanks to 'Shaw's Corner', the former home here of playwright George Bernard Shaw. The first word means 'Æga's gap', comprising the personal name plus the Old English *geat* (the latter appears in MARGATE and RAMSGATE, for example, whereas in HARROGATE the word is different and means 'road'). The 'gap' here is probably the lower area between Ayot St Lawrence and Ayot St Peter, which stand on low hills less than two miles apart. The additions for both names are the dedications of their respective parish churches, and serve to differentiate the places. The name does not derive from a word meaning 'island', as for Chiswick Eyot on the THAMES, as has been wrongly proposed.

Ayr (Strathclyde)
A town and resort southwest of KILMARNOCK that takes its name from the river at whose mouth it stands on the Firth of CLYDE. The river name, an ancient one, means basically 'river', from a British (Celtic) root word, or even from a pre-Celtic word. The same word can be traced in the names of certain other rivers in Britain, such as the Oare in Somerset, and also behind some continental rivers, such as the Aar in Switzerland and the Ahr in West Germany, both tributaries of the Rhine. Ayr in Gaelic is Inbhir-àir, that is, the equivalent of 'Inverayr' (like INVERNESS), denoting its location at the mouth of the river.

Babbacombe (Devon)

The district of TORQUAY that gave its name to Babbacombe Bay. Its name means 'Babba's valley', with the Old English *cumb* forming the second part. Babbacombe lies to the east of the town centre, at a point where the ground slopes fairly steeply down to the beach.

Babergh (Suffolk)

This old name was adopted for the administrative district set up in south Suffolk in 1974. It is that of an old hundred here, and means 'Babba's mound', the latter part of the name representing the Old English *berg* (hill, mound).

Bacup (Lancashire)

The name of this industrial town, south of BURNLEY, derives from the two Old English words *bæc*, 'ridge' (as in modern English 'back') and *hop* (valley). The 'valley by a ridge' is thus a description of the site of the town, which is in the Irwell Valley with high ground to the west. In 1324 the name was recorded as *Bacop*. But some hundred years earlier, a document of about 1200 has the name as *Fulebachope*, where the first element is the Old English *fūl* (dirty, foul). The valley must therefore have been noticeably muddy at that time.

Badminton (Avon)

A village, country house, and estate east of CHIPPING SODBURY and the seat of the Duke of Beaufort. Badminton House gave its name to the sport of badminton, which was first played here some time in the nineteenth century (the *Oxford English Dictionary* dates the term from 1874). The name of the village, which is properly Great Badminton, derives from the personal name Beadumund, together with the Old English '-ington' ending that means 'settlement of the people of'. The name was recorded in 972 as *Badimynctun*, although the Domesday Book gets it slightly wrong (perhaps due to a mishearing rather than a miscopying) as *Madmintune*.

Bagenalstown (Carlow)

A market town south of CARLOW, now usually known by its Irish name of MUINE BHEAG.

Baglan (West Glamorgan)

The name of this town, northwest of PORT TALBOT, is really a short form of Llanfaglan, meaning 'church of St Baglan'; St Baglan was the patron saint of the former parish church here (now disused). Little is known about the saint apart from his name. He may have lived some time in the sixth century.

Bagshot (Surrey)

A town northeast of CAMBERLEY. As mentioned in the entry for ALDERSHOT, the second half of the name is found fairly widely in west Surrey and east Hampshire. It comes from the Old English *scēat*, 'projecting piece of land', so that Bagshot's name as a whole can be interpreted as 'projecting corner of woodland where badgers live'. The first half of the name thus represents the Old English *bagga*, as found also in the more common place-name Bagley ('badgers' wood'). The town's name was recorded in 1165 as *Bagshete*.

Baildon (West Yorkshire)

A northern suburb of BRADFORD that takes its name from Baildon Hill here; the latter half of the name is the Old English *dūn*, 'hill' (modern English 'down'). The first part of the name is uncertain, but a record dated about 1030 has the name with a *g* (as *Bægeltun*), and this could represent the Old English *bealg* (rounded), despite the different order of the letters. Hills frequently have a descriptive word for the first part of their name, and 'rounded hill' would suit Baildon.

Bailieborough (Cavan)
A town, southwest of CARRICKMACROSS, whose name includes the personal name Bailie, which would have been that of the Anglo-Norman proprietor here. (The surname Bailey is of French origin, and relates to 'bailiff'.) The town's Irish name is Coill an Chollaigh, 'wood of the boar', a descriptive name for the location. There are still woods here, even if no boars, and the town is not far from Dun a'Ri Forest Park, as well as having its own forest and lakes.

Bakewell (Derbyshire)
Perhaps by association with 'Bakewell tart', the name of this market town northwest of MATLOCK suggests 'bake well'. But the Domesday Book records the name as *Badequella*, showing that the actual meaning is 'Beadeca's spring'. The same personal name can be seen in the Warwickshire village of Baginton. Bakewell is on the River WYE, and the warm springs here are well known — they remain at a constant temperature and the waters are swum in for curative purposes in the Bath House.

Bala (Gwynedd)
A market town northeast of DOLGELLAU that stands close to Bala Lake but does not take its name from it. The Welsh word *bala* means 'outlet', denoting the site of the town at the point where the River DEE leaves the lake. The true (Welsh) name of the lake is Llyn Tegid, meaning 'Tegid's lake', the first word being a personal name.

Balbriggan (Dublin)
The Irish name of this seaside resort north of DUBLIN is Baile Brigín, meaning 'Brigín's town'. The first element 'Bal-' is commonly found in both Irish and Scottish place-names (see below), and in Irish place-names is particularly common in the form 'Bally-'. The derivation of the element is from the Irish *baile* (town, homestead).

Baldock (Hertfordshire)
One of Britain's more unusual names, as it represents Baghdad! The town, north of STEVENAGE, was founded in the twelfth century by Knights Templars, who named it after the Arabian city, then known to them as 'Baldac', an early French form of the name. A twelfth-century record gives the name as *Baldoce*.

Balerno (Lothian)
Balerno, southwest of EDINBURGH, is well known for the attractive gardens of Malleny House. By coincidence, the name has a kind of 'garden' origin, as it derives from the two Gaelic words *baile* (homestead) and *airneach* (sloe tree). The name was recorded in 1280 as *Balhernoch*, and since then has become smoothed to its present form.

Balham (Greater London)
The name of this district of WANDSWORTH could mean either 'Bealga's riverside land' or simply 'rounded riverside land'. The second half of the name is Old English *hamm*, not *hām*, this often referring to land in a bend of the river. As far as Balham is concerned, this means land between the two arms of Falcon Brook, streams of which join up near CLAPHAM Common and then flow west to the THAMES. The first part of the name may be a personal name, or it may come from the Old English *bealg*, 'rounded' (*compare* BAILDON). Balham's name was recorded in 957 as *Bælgenham*.

Ballachulish (Highland)
A village on the shore of Loch LEVEN. Its name means 'homestead on the narrows', from the Gaelic *baile* (homestead, village) and *caolas* (narrows). It is this latter word that gives the 'Kyle' of KYLE OF LOCHALSH. A glance at the map will show that Ballachulish is indeed at the point where the loch narrows markedly (to the west) as it flows into Loch LINNHE.

Ballantrae (Strathclyde)

A small fishing port on the bay of the same name, southwest of GIRVAN. Its name simply means 'village on the shore', from the Gaelic *baile* and *traigh* (shore). This is not the place that features in Stevenson's novel *The Master of Ballantrae*, however, although Stevenson took the name from here. The novel is actually set in the village of Borgue, southwest of KIRKCUDBRIGHT.

Ballater (Grampian)

A village and resort east of BRAEMAR on the River DEE has a name that originally applied to the pass here where the Ballater Burn flows through the mountains. The name was recorded as *Balader* in 1704 and as *Ballader* in 1716, suggesting that the origin is in Gaelic *bealach*, 'pass' and *dobhar*, 'water', therefore meaning simply 'water pass', 'place where river flows through mountains'.

Ballina (Mayo)

This cathedral town north of CASTLEBAR is the largest centre of population in the county. Its name means '(place at the) mouth of the ford', which perfectly suits its location at the head of the River Moy estuary. The name is found in many other locations in Ireland, and derives from *béal an átha*, with the first of these words meaning 'mouth' and the last 'ford'.

Ballinasloe (Galway)

This town, famous for its annual October livestock fair, stands at a crossing over the River Suck, southwest of ATHLONE. Its name means 'ford-mouth of the gathering', the latter part of the name representing the Irish *slua* (crowd, host). This seems to refer to some kind of historic and doubtless regular gathering of people and animals, almost certainly the forerunner of the present livestock market, which developed out of the previous horse fairs here.

Ballindaloch (Grampian)

Ballindaloch Castle is a baronial edifice on the right bank of the River AVON near the point where it joins the SPEY southwest of ABERLOUR. The land is low-lying here, as is implied by the Gaelic name, which derives from *baile dalach* (homestead of the field).

Ballineen (Cork)

An attractive village on the River BANDON west of Bandon, whose Irish name is Béal Átha Fhínín, meaning 'ford-mouth of Fínín', the latter being a personal name.

Ballybofey (Donegal)

The Irish name of this small town, which stands on the River Finn west of STRABANE, is Bealach Féich, showing that the first part of the name is not the usual 'homestead' (*baile*). Irish *bealach* is 'road', and the name as a whole thus means 'Fiach's road', from a personal name. Ballybofey is located at the junction of two important roads, now the T18 running up the valley of the Finn, and the T59, which leads northwards to LETTERKENNY. The former is almost certainly the road implied by the name, as the valley route leads to STRABANE, LONDONDERRY, and Lough FOYLE.

Ballybunion (Kerry)

A popular Atlantic coastal resort northwest of LISTOWEL. It has the Irish name of Baile an Bhuinneánaigh, meaning 'Bunion's homestead'; the first part of this is a personal name.

Ballycastle (Antrim, Mayo)

Any of several places in Ireland. The two best known are the coastal resort in ANTRIM and the smaller seaside resort in MAYO. The names are not quite the same, however. The Antrim Ballycastle is called Baile an Chaistil, meaning 'homestead by the castle' (the castle, no longer here, was located at The Diamond, in Ballycastle Old Town). The Mayo resort, on the other hand, has the Irish name of Baile an Chaisil, 'homestead by the stone fort', with the Irish word *caiseal* becoming the English 'castle'. *See also* CASHEL.

Ballyclare (Antrim)

This town, north of BELFAST, is famous for its annual fair. The name means 'road of the plain', the 'road' here being the A57 from ANTRIM to LARNE on the coast. Like BALLYBOFEY the first element of the name is not the usual 'homestead'. Ballyclare's Irish name is Bealach Cláir. The town stands on level fairly low-lying ground at the southern end of the ANTRIM Plateau.

Ballyjamesduff (Cavan)

Names like this seem strange to those unfamiliar with the reversed order of Celtic place-name elements, and with the 'agglutination' or 'running together' of the various parts of an Irish name (as also, for instance, in NEWTOWNSTEWART). But the word order is normal for Celtic languages, where the general precedes the specific. The name of this small town southeast of CAVAN is also familiar from the popular song, 'Come Back Paddy Reilly to Ballyjamesduff', which implies a reference to James Duff, an English officer who fought in Ireland in the Rising of 1798. The Irish version of the place-name is Baile Shéamais Dhuibh.

Ballymena (Antrim)

A town, north of ANTRIM, that stands at the meeting point of a number of main roads, notably the A26, A42, and A36. This gives rise to its name, which means 'the middle town' (in Irish, An Baile Meánach).

Ballymoney (Antrim)

The name of this market town southeast of COLERAINE is found elsewhere in Ireland, and could mean either 'homestead of the moor' (Irish, Baile Monaidh) or 'homestead of the thicket' (Baile Muine). Both Irish names have been recorded for it, and either would be suitable for its location and the terrain here.

Ballynahinch (Down)

This name is found in different parts of Ireland, and literally means 'homestead of the island', as is indicated by the Irish version of the name — Baile na hInse. 'Island' can mean dry land surrounded by a marsh, or higher land surrounded by a plain, as well as the common 'water-girt' sense. For the town of this name south of BELFAST, the original 'island' was probably the area between the river (the Annacloy), the lake (now drained, and laid out as playing fields), and a stream that ran from the lake into the river.

Ballyshannon (Donegal)

The name of this town, south of DONEGAL, indicates its location on a hill overlooking the River Erne. It thus means 'ford-mouth of the hillside' (in Irish, Béal Átha Seanaidh), and the town is sited at the final point where the river can be crossed (now by the T18) as it widens to the west to flow into DONEGAL Bay.

Balmoral (Grampian)

Balmoral Castle, the famous royal residence east of BRAEMAR, has a name that means 'homestead in the big clearing', comprising the Gaelic *baile* (homestead), Gaelic *mór* (big), and British (Celtic) *ial* (clearing, open space). This name is not unique, occurring also in Ireland; for example, the former village that is now a southwest suburb of BELFAST. But here the name means 'townland of the big cliff', rather than 'of the clearing'.

Baltimore (Cork)

Better known as a US city, the name of the country house and estate south of BANTRY by the south coast means 'townland of the big house', or in its Irish version, Baile na Tighe Mór. The US Baltimore acquired its name through the Calvert family, whose hereditary title (Lord Baltimore) came from the family seat in Cork. The Irish name of the settlement here is Dún na Séad, literally 'fort of the jewels', with the latter word implying something precious, not necessarily jewellery.

Baltinglass (Wicklow)
The English name of this town on the River Slaney northeast of CARLOW is a corruption of its Irish original, Bealach Conglais, meaning 'road of Cúglas'. The latter word is a personal name, meaning 'grey hound' (*Cú Ghlas*). The 'road' would be the one that follows the course of the Slaney, eventually down to ENNISCORTHY and WEXFORD, now the N81 at Baltinglass (and the N80 further south).

Bamburgh (Northumberland)
A coastal village, opposite FARNE Island, that is today well known as the place where St Aidan died and Grace Darling is buried. Its ancient name means 'Bebba's stronghold', combining the personal name and the Old English *burg* (fortified place). For once, we know the identity of the named person: Bebba was the wife of King Æthelfrith of Northumbria, who ruled between 593 and 617. An early eighth-century Latin text refers to the place: *in urbe quae Bebbanburge dicitur* ('in the city which is called Bamburgh'). It is the Venerable Bede's *Ecclesiastical History of the English People* that identifies Bebba for us, for the place was *in urbe regia quae a regina quondam uocabulo Bebba cognominatur* ('in a royal city which is known by the name of Bebba, formerly the queen').

Bampton (Devon)
This market town north of TIVERTON had its name recorded in the Domesday Book as *Badentone*. Both this and the present name are 'smoother' versions of the Old English original, *Bæthǣmatūn*. In effect this is 'Bathampton' (like the village near BATH), and means 'settlement of the people by the bath', that is, people who lived near a warm spring. Bampton is on the River Batherm, which is named after it (in one of its earlier spellings). Also near here is the village of Morebath ('moorland bath'), and it is doubtless these particular springs that gave rise to the town name. The Bampton southwest of WITNEY in

Oxfordshire has a name with a different origin: it was a 'beam town', or a settlement where beams of timber were used, perhaps to build a footbridge over a stream here.

Banagher (Londonderry, Offaly)
The name means 'place of pointed hills', and in the case of the town northwest of BIRR in Offaly, the reference is said to be to the sharp rocks in the River SHANNON. Irish *beann* (point) can denote a peak or point of almost any size (it is the basic Celtic word that gives rise to Scottish mountain names, such as BEN NEVIS).

Banbridge (Down)
The name of this town, north of NEWRY, means what it says: 'bridge on the River Bann'. It is possible that the river's name may mean 'goddess' (related to the Irish *bean*, 'woman') and thus have a common element with the name of the River BANDON.

Banbury (Oxfordshire)
The name of this town north of OXFORD means 'Bana's fortified place', with the Old English *burg* forming the latter half. The reference could be to an Iron Age hill-fort, although no such fort is known here. The Domesday Book gave the name of Banbury as *Banesberie*.

Banchory (Grampian)
The name of this small town on the River DEE northwest of STONEHAVEN is Beannachar in its Gaelic form, meaning 'place of the peaks'. Banchory is in a valley but surrounded by hills and mountains. *Compare* BANAGHER.

Bandon (Cork)
A town southwest of CORK, that takes its name from the river on which it lies. The river name may mean 'goddess' and be related to that of the Bann (*see* BANBRIDGE).

Banff (Grampian)

Rather unexpectedly, the name of this coastal town, east of ELGIN, derives from the Gaelic *banbh* (little pig). This seems to have been the name, or nickname, of the river here, which is now known as the Deveron. Celtic rivers are known to have been called after animals, and the parallel here may be with the name of AMMANFORD, where the river was regarded as 'rooting' its way pig-like to the coast. The county name followed from that of the town, and is now incorporated in the title of the administrative district, Banff and BUCHAN. In a mid-twelfth-century document, the name of Banff was given as *Banb*.

Bangor (Gwynedd, Down)

Either of two towns, one in Wales and one in Ireland. Both arose as monastic establishments, with the Irish Bangor (east of BELFAST) being a daughter foundation of the Welsh one and borrowing its name. It is officially known as Bangor Mór ('big Bangor') to distinguish it from the Welsh town west of CHESTER, and was founded in the sixth century shortly after its namesake. The Welsh name means 'upper row of rods in a wattle fence' (*bangor*), this probably referring to the original wattled construction of the monastic cells, or to the fence that enclosed them. The Welsh Bangor was recorded in the seventh century as *Benchoer*.

Bannockburn (Central)

A village southeast of STIRLING that gave its name to the famous battle of 1314, in which the Scots (under Robert the Bruce) routed the English (under Edward II). It takes its own name from the stream here, the Bannock Burn. This in turn means 'white stream' (Celtic *ban oc*). There is no connection between the stream name and the 'bannock' — a type of flat oatmeal cake.

Banstead (Surrey)

A town, south of SUTTON, whose name means 'bean place', from the Old English *bēan* (bean) and *stede* (place). It was recorded in the Domesday Book as *Benestede*.

Bantry (Cork)

A town on the bay of the same name, west of BANDON, known in Irish as Beanntrai. This means '(place of) Beann's people'; Beann is said to be a son of Conor Mac Nessa, a first-century king of Ulster. Another version of the Irish name is Beanntraighe, 'hill shore', from the Irish *beann* (hill, headland) and *traigh* (shore), and this appears to be appropriate as Bantry is set among hills by the coast here.

Bardsey Island (Gwynedd)

A Welsh island lying off the tip of the LLEYN PENINSULA. Like many islands off the Welsh coast it has a name of Scandinavian origin, meaning here 'Bardr's island': the Norse personal name is followed by the Old Norse *ey* (island). Despite the fact that Bardsey is known for its bird life, the name does *not* mean 'birds' island', as some like to suggest.

Bargeddie (Strathclyde)

This town southwest of COATBRIDGE is in a slightly elevated region, and its name may be based on the Gaelic *barr* (height), with the second part of the name of uncertain meaning.

Bargoed (Mid Glamorgan)

The name of this town north of CAERPHILLY is that of the river on which it stands; the river's own name apparently derives from the Welsh *bargod* (boundary). The river forms the boundary even now between Mid Glamorgan and GWENT.

Barking (Greater London)

The name of this town east of central LONDON means '(place of) Berica's people', and was recorded in the eighth century as *Bercingum*; the Domesday Book version of the name is *Berchinges*. The Old English suffix *-ingas* meant 'people of'.

Barkingside (Greater London)
Part of the borough of Redbridge north of
ILFORD, previously in the parish of Ilford.
It developed as a place that was 'beside'
BARKING, i.e. to the north of it. The name
is relatively recent, and was recorded in a
text of 1538 in its present form.

Barmouth (Gwynedd)
One would expect the name of this resort
west of DOLGELLAU to mean 'at the mouth
of a river named 'Bar''. But this is not the
case, for the town is at the mouth of the
Mawddach! The name is actually a jumble
of English and Celtic. The river name
probably derives from a Celtic personal
name, Mawdd. This was then assimilated
to the English 'mouth'. The 'Bar-' is a sort
of anglicisation of the common Celtic
element 'Aber-', meaning 'mouth'. The
true name of the place should thus be
something like 'Abermawdd', and early
records confirm this: a late thirteenth-
century document gives it as *Abermau*.
The present Welsh name, Abermo, reflects
this. But the latter also appears,
wrongly, as Y Bermo: Abermo is
mistakenly divided as 'A-bermo', and the
initial vowel taken to be the Welsh definite
article *y*.

Barnard Castle (Durham)
This town, west of DARLINGTON, arose
round the twelfth-century castle here,
which was owned and probably built by a
Norman baron, Bernard de Balliol, who
died c1167. The name therefore derives
from his own name. A mid-twelfth-century
text refers to the castle as *Castellum Bern'*.
Remains survive of his castle, in particular
the Round Tower.

Barnehurst (Greater London)
Now in the borough of Bexley, north of
CRAYFORD, Barnehurst probably has a
name that means 'wood cleared by
burning', with its Old English components
as *berned* (burnt) and *hyrst* (wooded hill). If
this is so, its name is similar to BARNET
and BRENTWOOD.

Barnes (Greater London)
A district of RICHMOND whose name really
means what it says, i.e. a settlement that
arose by a barn or barns. The earliest
records of the name are in the singular, as
the Domesday Book entry of *Berne* shows.
Later, the *s* was added; a text of 1222 gives
the name as *Bernes*. No doubt one barn did
become many as the place grew over the
years.

Barnet (Greater London)
Although this borough of north LONDON
has a similar name to BARNES, the origin is
quite different. Barnet means 'burnt place',
that is, it denotes a settlement that arose on
a site cleared by burning. There is a whole
cluster of 'Barnet' names in the region,
including (from north to south) New
Barnet, East Barnet, and Friern Barnet, all
to the east of Barnet itself. Probably the
name originally applied to more or less the
whole of this area, between what is now the
A1000 to the west and the A111 to the east.
It would have been woodlands that were
cleared by burning, as the many places
ending in '-ley' here testify, such as
HADLEY WOOD, Arkley, and, further
north, Cuffley. New Barnet and East
Barnet have self-explanatory names, while
Friern Barnet means 'Barnet of the
brethren', and refers to the Knights of St
John of Jerusalem who held it. Barnet's
name was recorded in about 1070 as
Barneto, and its direct Old English origin is
the word *bærnet* (burnt place). *Compare*
BRENTWOOD.

Barnoldswick (Lancashire)
This industrial town, north of COLNE, was
recorded in the Domesday Book as
Bernulfeswic, showing that the name means
'Beornwulf's farm'. The Old English *wīc*
implied a farm used for special purposes,
as was the case at CHISWICK, for example.
The personal name means 'warrior wolf'.
Compare BARNSLEY.

Barnsley (South Yorkshire)
A town, north of SHEFFIELD, whose name

means 'Beorn's woodland clearing'; the common Old English element *lēah* is frequently found with places that arose in or near such a clearing. As it stands, Beorn's name means just 'warrior', but it may have been a longer name originally, as in BARNOLDSWICK. In the Domesday Book, Barnsley appears as *Berneslai*.

Barnstaple (Devon)

A market town at the head of the River Taw estuary, northwest of EXETER. The name is similar to DUNSTABLE and WHITSTABLE; in these the second half of the name is the Old English *stapol*, 'post' (the same word that gave modern English 'staple'). For Barnstaple the meaning is thus 'bearded post', which takes a little imagination to explain. Perhaps there was a post here with a 'beard' of twigs, like a besom. It could have served either as a meeting place for the local 'hundred', or, in view of the location of the town, was probably a landmark for approaching or mooring ships. The Domesday Book records the name virtually as it is now: *Barnestaple*.

Barra (Western Isles)

Island names are often basically descriptive, as are names of rivers. The name of this hilly Scottish island south of UIST is no different, and 'hilly island' is precisely what it means. The name is a combination of a Celtic root word *barro* (as for BARRHEAD) and the Old Norse *ey* (island). The name was recorded in the late eleventh century as *Barru*. *Compare* BARROW-IN-FURNESS.

Barrhead (Strathclyde)

The name of this industrial town south of PAISLEY is really a tautology, as it comprises the Gaelic *barr* (top, headland) and the modern English 'head'. No doubt the latter was added when the former was no longer understood. Either way, the name is apt, Barrhead lying on Levern Water at the foot of lofty moorland.

Barrow-in-Furness (Cumbria)

There are two names to deal with here, for this port on the Irish Sea northwest of LANCASTER. Barrow means 'headland island', with exactly the same origin as BARRA; that is, a Celtic root word *barro* (headland, hill) combined with the Old Norse *ey* (island). A record of 1190 shows this more clearly, when the name was given as *Barrai*. Barrow was thus the name of an island here, although it has now become joined to the mainland. Furness is the name of the peninsula on which Barrow is located, and the name is a combination of the Old Norse words *futh* (buttock) and *nes* (headland). Futh was also the name of an island, today called Peel Island, which still lies at the tip of the peninsula. Its former name graphically refers to the 'slit' or long depression that runs from the north of the island to the south. 'Futh Ness' (or *Futharness*, as it was actually known) was therefore the 'ness' or headland opposite this island, and from the headland the name then spread to the whole peninsula. Doubtless it was thought necessary to add '-in-Furness' to 'Barrow' in order to distinguish it from other places of the same name.

Barry (South Glamorgan)

The name of the present resort and port southwest of CARDIFF has hardly changed over the centuries, being recorded in 1176 as *Barry*, in 1186 as *Barri*, and in 1610 as *Barrye Island*. The basic origin is thus in the Old Welsh *barr* (hill), referring more to the island than to the town behind it, the latter being a relatively recent development. However, the town is on hilly ground, and any settlement here would equally have merited the name. So Barry means little more than 'hill site'.

Barton-upon-Humber (Humberside)

There are so many places called Barton that it is often necessary to add a distinguishing description, as here. Barton means 'barley farm', with the Old English *tūn* (giving the modern 'town') often used of a farm that was subsidiary to a larger or more important place, such as a manor or a monastery. Several Bartons were thus the granges of monasteries, and there is still a current English word 'barton' to denote a farmyard. The name of the Humberside Barton, southwest of HULL, was recorded as *Bertone* in the Domesday Book. *See also* HUMBER.

Basford (Nottinghamshire)

This district of NOTTINGHAM has a name that means 'Basa's ford', with the Domesday Book record of it as *Baseford*. The ford would have been over the River Leen.

Basildon (Essex, Berkshire)

The Essex Basildon is both the name of a New Town (designated in 1949), east of LONDON, and that of an administrative district. However, the name itself is old, as is that of Basildon in Berkshire, a village northwest of PANGBOURNE. But the names are not the same in origin, and indeed have had a variety of forms in the past. The Essex Basildon has thus appeared as *Berlesdune* in the Domesday Book, *Bartelisdon* in 1247, *Bastelden* in 1510, and *Basseldon* in 1594; the Berkshire Basildon was recorded as *Bastedene* in the Domesday Book, *Bastlesden* in 1175 (and again in 1212), *Baselesden* in 1199, and *Bestlesdene* in 1242. The final element of the Essex Basildon is certainly the Old English *dūn* (hill), as the town is on raised ground. And for the Berkshire village, beside the THAMES, it is the Old English *denu* (valley). But the first part of each name is a problem. It is clearly a personal name, but has undergone various spelling changes in each instance. Probably the Essex Basildon means 'Beorhtel's hill', with the first *e* of this name becoming *a* as a result of the Essex dialect. The Berkshire Basildon would then seem to be 'Bessel's valley'. No doubt the final form of both names owes something to the modern name 'Basil'.

Basingstoke (Hampshire)

The Old English *stoc* (stoke) meant 'place', but frequently implied a place that was a secondary settlement dependent on another place. In the case of Basingstoke, the town northeast of WINCHESTER, this primary place (although of lesser importance) would have been the settlement of Basing, itself now an eastern extension of Basingstoke. Basing, in its turn, means '(place belonging to) the people of Basa', so that the name is the personal name Basa plus the ending '-ing' (originally Old English *-ingas*) meaning 'people of'. Basingstoke's name is recorded in a late tenth-century document as *Basinga stoc*.

Bassenthwaite (Cumbria)

Both a lake (the northernmost) in the Lake District and a village at its northern end. The lake took its name from the village, whose name was recorded in a document of 1225 as *Bastunthuait*. This means 'Bastun's clearing', with '-thwaite' representing the Old Norse *thveit*. The lake was originally known as Bastunwater, which gave it a similarity to other lake names roundabout, such as DERWENT WATER, HAWESWATER, and ULLSWATER. Today, as Lake Bassenthwaite, it is the only one in the Lake District to have the title 'Lake'.

Bassetlaw (Nottinghamshire)

A modern administrative district that contains the original Bassetlaw, which was a wapentake in north Nottinghamshire. Its name probably means 'hill of the dwellers at the burnt place', comprising the Old English *bærnet* (burnt place; as in BARNET), *sæte* (dwellers; as in DORSET), and *hlāw* (hill, mound; as in LEWES).

Bath (Avon)

A city and spa southeast of BRISTOL. The name means precisely what it says, referring to the Roman baths here. Somewhat surprisingly, it contains no element to indicate its Roman origin (for example, no '-chester'), but this is probably because the name is pure English, not Celtic. A ninth-century document refers to the Roman baths here, in a passage that is a mixture of Latin and Old English: *in illa famosa urbe þæt is æt þæm hatum baþum* ('in that famous town that is at the hot baths'). The Roman name of Bath was originally *Aquae Calidae* ('hot waters'), then *Aquae Sulis* ('waters of Sulis'). The latter refers to the name of a pagan god (*Sulis* is not the genitive of a name 'Sul', as is sometimes translated). An alternative Anglo-Saxon name for Bath was Akemanchester, with this apparently derived from the latin *Aquae*, and the Roman road of Akeman Street, which ran generally eastwards from Bath across to ST ALBANS and WATLING STREET. Many villages round Bath have names that refer to it and so emphasise its importance, such as Batheaston, Bathford, Bathwick, and Bathampton.

Bathgate (Lothian)
The name of this iron- and coal-mining town south of LINLITHGOW does not mean what it seems. It is of Celtic origin (British, rather than Gaelic), and is composed of two Cumbric root words meaning 'boar wood'. (*Compare* modern Welsh *baedd*, 'boar' and *coed*, 'wood'. *Compare* also BETWS-Y-COED.) Bathgate's name was recorded in a document of about 1160 as *Batket*.

Batley (West Yorkshire)
The name of this textile and engineering town, southwest of LEEDS, which was recorded in the Domesday Book as *Bathelie*, means 'Bata's wood' or 'Bata's clearing' (Old English *lēah* could mean either). This part of Yorkshire must have been heavily wooded at one time, as there are several names here ending in both '-ley' and '-wood', among them Ardsley, MORLEY, PUDSEY, Bromley, Stanningley, Oakwood, Monkswood, Outwood, and Whitwood, all in the LEEDS and BRADFORD area.

Battersea (Greater London)
The name of this district of WANDSWORTH has nothing to do with either 'batter' or 'sea', even though Battersea lies beside the THAMES. The earliest record of the name is the late seventh-century one, *Batrices ege*. This means 'Beaduric's island', with the personal name followed by an Old English word (*ēg*); this latter usually translates as 'island' but often denoted, as here, higher land by lower marshland. Occasionally a version of the name has been recorded beginning with *P*, not *B*, such as *Patriceseia* in 1067, tempting some people to see St Patrick's name in it. There is no etymological foundation for this. The personal name means 'battle ruler'.

Batterstown (Meath)
This village northwest of DUBLIN has a name that represents its Irish original, Baile an Bhóthair, 'townland of the road', with the English 'town' translating the Irish *baile*. Today the 'road' is the L4 to TRIM.

Battle (East Sussex)
A rare example of a place-name meaning exactly what it says. All one needs to know is *which* battle is commemorated here. The geographical location should give a clue, and the abbey here, six miles northwest of HASTINGS, was in fact founded by William I to mark the site of the famous Battle of Hastings (1066). We have a record of the place in the Domesday Book only twenty years later as *La batailge*, this showing the Norman French version of the original name. 'Battle of Hastings' is thus strictly speaking a misnomer, for Battle is some distance from Hastings.

Bawtry (South Yorkshire)
This small town southeast of DONCASTER had its name recorded in a document of 1199 as *Baltry*. This means 'Balda's tree' (or possibly 'Bealda's tree'). The personal name is a conjectural one.

Bayswater (Greater London)
Today one hardly associates the district of Bayswater, in the City of WESTMINSTER, with water, but the association is correct, for at one time the River Westbourne crossed the main road to OXFORD here, that is, the present Bayswater Road (the A40), the extension to Oxford Street. A document dated 1380 records the name in a way that reveals its meaning: *Aqua vocata Bayards Watering Place*. Historic maps of LONDON show that the area was not really settled until the beginning of the nineteenth century. The Westbourne itself was dammed up in 1730 on the suggestion of Queen Caroline, wife of George II, thus forming the Serpentine in Hyde Park. What is left of the river is now the Ranelagh Sewer, flowing south from the Serpentine.

Beachy Head (East Sussex)
The famous chalk headland on the coast southwest of EASTBOURNE has a name that suggests 'beach'. In origin, however, it is Old French *beau chef* (fine headland), with the English 'Head' added when the former was no longer understood. The name was thus given by the Normans, who must have regarded the white cliffs as an excellent landmark when approaching the English coast across the Channel.

Beaconsfield (Buckinghamshire)
The name of the town southeast of HIGH WYCOMBE means more or less what it says, bearing in mind that the Old English *feld* implied a stretch of open country rather than a modern 'field'. But where was the beacon, and for what purpose was it lit? It was almost certainly a signal fire to warn of an approaching enemy. A raised location is obviously most likely, which the town of Beaconsfield (to be precise, Old Beaconsfield, down by the railway) is clearly not. The Ordnance Survey map shows a hill called Beacon Hill at Penn. This is about three miles from Beaconsfield, but could well have been the site. The name was recorded in 1185 as

Bekenesfeld. There are other Beacon Hills in the south of England, one of the best known (also known as Ivinghoe Beacon) again being in Buckinghamshire, at Ivinghoe, east of AYLESBURY.

Beaminster (Dorset)
The name of the small town north of BRIDPORT has been recorded as early as the mid-ninth century, when it was given as *Bebingmynster*. This means either 'Bebbe's church' or, in view of the '-ing', 'church of the people of Bebbe'. No doubt the old minster was on the site of the present fifteenth-century parish church. Bebbe was a woman's name. There are a number of 'minster' names in Dorset, others including Charminster, Yetminster, STURMINSTER NEWTON, Sturminster Marshall (some distance from it), Iwerne Minster, and (just over the border in Devon) AXMINSTER.

Bearsden (Strathclyde)
This mainly residential town northwest of GLASGOW has a deceptively difficult name to interpret, and many 'place-name books' omit it altogether! According to one account, it was named after a house built near the railway station in 1863. If this is so, it *might* be possible to interpret it as a whimsical 'bear's den', perhaps with a punning reference to the name of the owner of the house. It does not seem to be related to other place-names beginning 'Bear-' (which in some instances is actually French *beau*, 'beautiful').

Beattock (Dumfries and Galloway)
A village south of MOFFAT well known for Beattock Summit, the highest point of the LONDON to GLASGOW railway. The origin of the village name lies in that of the hill, although this is not certain: Gaelic *biodach* (sharp-topped) has been suggested.

Beaufort (Gwent)
The name of this town, north of EBBW VALE, is a modern one, deriving from the title of the landowner here in the late

eighteenth century, the Duke of Beaufort. The Welsh name of the town is Cendl, a Welsh rendering of the surname of Edward Kendall, the ironmaster who was granted a lease of this site in 1780. The name Beaufort ('fine fortress') is a real asset for any place, implying a blend of 'strength with beauty'. The Duke's own title comes from the French town of Beaufort-en-Vallée, in the *département* of Maine-et-Loire.

Beaulieu (Hampshire)
The name is French for 'beautiful place', a description still apt for the village northeast of LYMINGTON at the head of the River Beaulieu estuary. The name was recorded in Latin form in a document of 1205 as *Bellus Locus Regis*. The name was adopted for Bewley Castle, Cumbria, when one of the abbots of the Hampshire Beaulieu, Hugh, became Bishop of Carlisle and took up residence at the castle. Today, the name has an anglicised pronunciation like that of the castle ('Bewley'). Vintage motor cars in the Motor Museum here may be regarded as some of the village's modern 'beauties'. *Compare* BEAULY; BEWDLEY.

Beauly (Highland)
The name of this Scottish town on the river of the same name derives from the French *beau lieu* (beautiful place), like the southern English BEAULIEU. The name was recorded in 1230 as *Prioratus de bello loco*, 'priory of the lovely spot'. Beauly is indeed in a picturesque setting, near the east coast west of INVERNESS and surrounded by mountains. The name is pronounced 'Bewley'.

Beaumaris (Gwynedd)
The Norman French name of this ANGLESEY resort means 'beautiful marsh', *beau marais*, describing its attractive low-lying site by the Menai Straits, four miles northeast of MENAI BRIDGE. The name was recorded in Latin form in a document of 1284 as *Bello Marisco*, and a sixteenth-century text has the name as *Duwmares*, with the initial 'Beau-' altered, consciously

or not, to the Welsh *Duw* (God). The present Welsh version is Biwmares, which also indicates the pronunciation.

Bebington (Merseyside)
The name of this town, south of BIRKENHEAD, is very similar in origin to that of BEAMINSTER, with the Old English *tūn* instead of *mynster*. The meaning is thus 'farmstead associated with Bebbe', the latter being a woman's name. The name was recorded in about 1100, in exactly the modern spelling.

Beccles (Suffolk)
An attractive town west of LOWESTOFT lying on the River WAVENEY. The origin is in the Old English *bæce* (stream, hence 'beck') and *læs* (pasture, meadowland). The Domesday Book version of the name, *Becles*, was little different from today's.

Beckenham (Greater London)
A former KENT town in the borough of BROMLEY whose name means 'Beohha's village', the latter part of the name being the common Old English *hām*. The Domesday Book distorted the name slightly as *Bacheham*. The personal name also occurs in BECONTREE.

Becontree (Greater London)
A district of BARKING whose name means 'Beohha's tree', the personal name being the same as that in BECKENHAM. The 'possession' of such a tree would have had significance, for it would have served as an assembly point for a 'hundred'. (Many old hundred names end in '-tree' or the equivalent for this reason.) The name appeared in the Domesday Book as *Beuentreu*; much later, a map dated 1805 has the name as *Beacon Tree Heath*, showing that this was supposed to be the origin of the name. It is likely that there actually was a beacon or signal fire here on 'Beacon Tree Heath', which is now called Becontree Heath — the site of playing fields just west of the Wood Lane Sports Centre.

Bedale (North Yorkshire)
This small town, southwest of
NORTHALLERTON, had its name recorded
in the Domesday Book exactly as now. It
means 'Beda's corner of land'. The Old
English *halh*, which gives the latter part
of the name (not 'dale'!), often implied
land by the bend of a river, and this is
exactly what one finds at Bedale, which lies
at the curve of Bedale Beck. (Bedales
School, at the village of Steep, near
PETERSFIELD, Hampshire, was
transferred there from a district of
HAYWARDS HEATH named Bedales, in
turn named after one Thomas le Budel,
who held land there.)

Beddgelert (Gwynedd)
This popular tourist site, southeast of
CAERNARVON, is the supposed grave
(Welsh *bedd*) of the hound named Gelert,
wrongly killed by its master, Prince
Llewellyn, who thought it had killed his
baby son. The animal had actually
protected the child and killed a wolf that
threatened the boy. This story is not
peculiar to Wales, and it seems likely that
an eighteenth-century innsman here,
David Prichard, enterprisingly invented
the story to attract custom. However, the
name of the place was not all that different
in early records; a document of 1281
records the name as *Bedkelert*. This means
'Celert's grave', with the personal name
that of some local person of note.

Bedford (Bedfordshire)
The name of this town, north of LONDON,
was recorded in 880 as *Bedanford*, which
means 'Beda's ford'. It is clear that Bedford
has long been an important place, the site
where many roads converge to cross the
River OUSE (today they are the A6, A428,
A603, A600, A418, and A428). It is
therefore rather surprising that the name is
not more 'towny', with an ending such as
'-ton' or at least '-ham' instead of simply
'-ford', for this is the usual pattern when a
significant settlement develops based on a
personal name like this. (OXFORD is

different, as no personal name is involved.)
The county name developed from that of
the town, and is recorded in a text of 1011
as *Bedanfordscir*.

Bedlington (Northumberland)
A town southeast of MORPETH that is
associated both with coal-mining and with
the Bedlington terrier, bred here for
badger-baiting. Its own name means 'farm
associated with a man named Bēdla', so is
similar to DARLINGTON. Records of the
name show little difference from its present
form; one dated 1104, for example, gives
Betlingtun.

Bedwas (Mid Glamorgan)
The name of this coal-mining town,
northeast of CAERPHILLY, comes from the
Old Welsh *betguas*, 'birch-tree grove'
(modern Welsh *bedw*, 'birch'). As with
many towns here, industrial development
is comparatively recent.

Bedworth (Warwickshire)
A town north of COVENTRY in a coal-
mining district. Its name means 'Beda's
enclosure', the latter half being the Old
English *worth*. The Domesday Book entry
for the name is not much different, as
Bedeword.

Beer (Devon)
This little resort west of SEATON has a
name that promises one thing while
actually delivering another, for it means
simply 'grove', from Old English *bearu*. In
the Domesday Book the name appears as
Bera. Compare BERE REGIS.

Beeston (Nottinghamshire)
A manufacturing town, immediately
southwest of NOTTINGHAM, whose name
means 'settlement where bent grows', from
the Old English (conjectural) *bēos* (bent-
grass) and the common *tūn* (settlement).
Bent-grass has a practical use for both
pasture and thatching, and this no doubt
explains why the word occurs in 'pockets'
in the country. Apart from here, there are

several instances in Norfolk (including the villages Beeston, Beeston Regis, and Beeston St Lawrence). The same plant name is recognised more readily in the many places named BENTLEY. This Nottinghamshire Beeston was recorded in the Domesday Book as *Bestone*.

Beith (Strathclyde)
The name of this industrial town, southwest of PAISLEY, is a direct rendering of the Gaelic *beither* (birch tree), so that the name simply means 'place where birches grow'.

Belcoo (Fermanagh)
A pleasant village west of ENNISKILLEN, located on the main road (T17) where it crosses an isthmus of land between the Upper and Lower Loughs Macnean. Its name describes this location, as it derives from Irish *béal* (mouth) and *caol* (narrowing). The present Irish version of the name, Béal Cú, actually translates as 'mouth of the dog'. No doubt *caol* became *cú* because a dog and its mouth are closely associated.

Belfast (Antrim)
The Irish name of the Northern Ireland capital is Béal Feirste, which is 'mouth of the sandbank' (Irish *béal* and *fearsad*). The sandbank concerned is the one that formed at the point where the small River Farset (whose own name comes from the same word) flows into the Lagan, a short distance below Queen's Bridge. Another small river, the Owenvarna (or Blackstaff) joined the Lagan at a point further upstream, and the tongue of land between the two was extended in the direction of the opposite shore, on the Co. Down side. At low tide, it was possible to ford the Lagan here, and it was by this ford (or 'ford-mouth', as *béal* implies) that the present town arose. The crossing was an important one, and only fell out of use when Long Bridge was built.

Belford (Northumberland)
This sizeable village, southeast of BERWICK-UPON-TWEED, will be familiar to anyone who has driven up the A1 trunk road. Its name is more complicated than it looks. Although it appears to mean something like 'Bella's ford', no one of this name has ever been recorded. Perhaps there is no personal name involved at all, and the 'Bel-' represents some other word, although it is difficult to see what it could be. It can hardly be the Old English *belle* (bell), and it is certainly not the French *bel*, which occurs in names such as BELVOIR. The ford is over a small stream here that joins the Elwick Burn about a mile away, almost at the coast. Belford's name was recorded in 1242 as *Beleford*.

Belgravia (Greater London)
This prestigious district of southwest LONDON takes its name from Belgrave Square here, in turn named after the estate of Belgrave in Cheshire. This was the property of the Dukes of Westminster, who owned much of what is now Belgravia. The buildings were largely constructed in the early nineteenth century by Thomas Cubitt (whose brother gave his name to Cubitt Town, in the Isle of DOGS), and it has been recorded that a letter to Mr Cubitt addressed 'Belgravia' was sent by the Post Office to Hungary. The Cheshire estate has a name of unusual origin. It was recorded in the Domesday Book as *Merdegrave*, which was taken to be of French origin and to mean 'dung grove', although it actually represented the Old English *mearth*, 'marten' (the weasel-like animal). For reasons of supposed propriety, therefore, the 'undesirable' name was changed to an acceptable opposite, so that 'Belgrave' was taken to mean 'beautiful grove'. The second part of the name remained as the Old English *grāf* (grove).

Belle Isle (Cumbria)
This popular island on WINDERMERE has a French name that means what it says, 'beautiful island'. However, the name was given in 1781 by one Isabella Curwen, who may have been incorporating something of her own name in it (as Peter the Great did

when he founded St Petersburg, for example). The island's earlier name was simply The Holme, otherwise 'the island'.

Bellingham (Northumberland)
A small town northwest of HEXHAM whose name is similar to that of BELFORD inasmuch as there is uncertainty as to what the initial 'Bell-' is. It may be a personal name, as it is for the district of Bellingham in LEWISHAM, Greater London, although the two names are different. The town's name was recorded in a document of about 1170 as *Bainlingham*, and is today sometimes pronounced with a 'j' sound (as if 'Bellinjam') which adds to the difficulty.

Belper (Derbyshire)
The present form of the town's name conceals its Norman French origin, which is *bel repaire*, or 'beautiful retreat'. 'Grand' names like this (another is BEAULIEU) were given by Norman barons to their country seats, so are really more like modern English house names (compare 'Belle Vue'). An unexpected distortion of this same name occurs in the Durham village of Bearpark, although this too means 'beautiful retreat'. Belper was recorded in 1231 as *Beurepeir*, and Bearpark in 1267 as *Beaurepayre*. One has to admit that the location of Belper (north of DERBY) is an attractive one, on the River DERWENT, even if now the industrial town does not feature prominently in the guide books. *Compare* BELVEDERE.

Belvedere (Greater London)
A district of Bexley whose Norman French name means 'beautiful view' (a combination of *bel* and *vedeir*, the latter from the Latin *videre*, 'to see'). The actual 'beautiful view' here is the one from Lessness Heath, where a fine house named Belvedere (no longer standing) was built in the first half of the eighteenth century to enjoy an attractive prospect over the THAMES. Lower Belvedere is still sometimes known here by its old Norman

French name of Picardy. *Compare* BELVOIR, VALE OF.

Belvoir, Vale of (Leicestershire)
Famous for its beauty, its hunting, and its coalmines, the Vale of Belvoir west of GRANTHAM has a name that certainly reflects the first of these aspects, for the origin is in Norman French meaning 'beautiful view'. The name was recorded in 1130 as *Belveder*, thus corresponding exactly to BELVEDERE.

Bembridge (Isle of Wight)
A resort and yachting centre southeast of RYDE whose name is recorded in a document of 1316 as *Bynnebrygg*. This represents the Old English *binnan* (within) and *brycg* (bridge). Bembridge thus arose as a place that was 'within the bridge'. The town is on a peninsula that once must have been reached only by a bridge across the entrance to what is now Bembridge Harbour (with a ferry providing the link with the northern headland known as The Duver).

Benbecula (Western Isles)
A low-lying island between North and South UIST. Its name appears to mean 'hill of the fords', from the Gaelic *beinn-na-fhaodla* (the first part of this is the familiar 'Ben' of BEN NEVIS, etc.). The island contains many lochs and streams, and fords would certainly be common. The name occurs in a document of 1449 as *Beanbeacla*.

Benfleet (Essex)
Either of two places to the west of SOUTHEND-ON-SEA. South Benfleet is a town at the head of Benfleet Creek, while North Benfleet is a village about three miles to the north. Both places get their name from the creek (Old English *flēot*, 'stream'), which is thus called literally 'beam stream'. The first part is the Old English *bēam* (plank), meaning that the stream had a wooden footbridge. The name was recorded in the late ninth century as *Beamfleot*.

Benllech (Gwynedd)
The name of this coastal resort on
ANGLESEY is a straight Welsh compound
of *ben* (cart) and *llech* (flat stone), implying
a place where a slab of rock could enable a
cart to cross a stream or marshy area of
land.

Ben More (Central, Strathclyde)
Either of two mountains, one west of
CRIEFF, the second on the island of MULL.
The Gaelic name simply means 'big
mountain', and is common for a noticeably
prominent peak — both mountains are
over 3000 feet high. The basic Gaelic words
are *beinn* (mountain) and *mór* (big, great).

Ben Nevis (Highland)
Scotland's best-known mountain and the
highest in Britain. Its name derives, as so
often, from that of the nearby river. The
first word is the Gaelic *beinn* (mountain),
and the river name represents the Gaelic
nemess (spiteful). Both the river and its
valley (Glen Nevis, running down to Loch
LINNHE at FORT WILLIAM) have an evil or
'malicious' reputation in local folklore.

Bentley (West Yorkshire)
The name is by no means confined to the
northern district of LEEDS; DONCASTER
has a northern suburb of Bentley, and
WALSALL a western district of the same
name, among several others. The name
means 'clearing where bents grow', from
the Old English *beonet* (bent-grass) and the
frequently found *lēah* (clearing in a wood).
As mentioned for BEESTON, whose name
also refers to the plant, bents were useful
for both feeding livestock and thatching.
The well-known surname Bentley comes
from this place-name, meaning a person
who dwelt in or near such a clearing.

Bere Regis (Dorset)
This village northwest of WAREHAM was
recorded in the Domesday Book as simply
Bere. This probably represents the Old
English *bearu* (wood, grove), so the name is
basically identical with BEER. In a

document of 1280 the royal reference is
incorporated, with the name appearing as
Kingesbere (*compare* similar names
beginning 'King' or 'Kings', such as
KINGS LANGLEY). Later, the 'Kings-'
became latinised as 'Regis'. The addition of
the word means that the place was a crown
demesne (i.e. a manor and estate held by
the king) in Norman times.

Berkeley (Gloucestershire)
A name familiar from Berkeley Castle in
the village of Berkeley near the SEVERN
Estuary, and from the Vale of Berkeley
here. The Old English name means 'birch-
tree wood' or 'clearing in a birch wood',
from *beorc* (birch) and the common *lēah*
(wood, clearing). *Compare*
BERKHAMSTED.

Berkhamsted (Hertfordshire)
The name of this town, northwest of
LONDON, 'translates' straightforwardly
from the Old English, in which it meant
'homestead by a hill', from *beorg* (hill) and
hāmstede (homestead — as in HAMPSTEAD
and many other names). Berkhamsted's
location fits the description, lying in a gap
in the CHILTERN HILLS. Its name was
recorded in about 1100 as *Beorhhamstede*.

Berkshire (England)
A county in central southern England
whose name is unusual in that it does not
derive from one of its important towns (as
Nottinghamshire does from
NOTTINGHAM, Lincolnshire from
LINCOLN, etc.). There must have existed a
place of some kind to give the present
'Berk-', to which 'shire' has been added.
According to the ninth-century monk
Asser, who wrote a life of King Alfred, the
name comes from what he calls *Berroc silva*
('Berroc wood'), which he describes in his
writings as a place *ubi buxus abundantissime
nascitur* ('where box grows in great
abundance'). This suggests that the wood
was itself named after a hill, because
'Berroc' resembles the Celtic root word
barro- meaning 'hill' (as in BARRHEAD, for

example). Local research has determined that such a hill was probably near HUNGERFORD. So 'Berroc' (or 'Barroc', to give the correct vowel) was the hill that gave the name of Berkshire. It is worth noting that the present *e* of the name is still pronounced like an *a*. Berkshire was recorded in 860 as *Bearrucscir*.

Bermondsey (Greater London)
A district by the THAMES in the borough of SOUTHWARK. Its name means 'Beornmund's island', with the 'island' (Old English *ēg*) referring to the area of higher drier ground here beside the lower marshy bank of the river. The name is thus similar to that of BATTERSEA and CHERTSEY, which are also 'islands' of this kind. Bermondsey's name was recorded in the Domesday Book as *Bermundesye*. By 1617 it had been 'smoothed' to *Barmsey*, but local people later reintroduced a form of the original name. The personal name means 'warrior protection'.

Berrylands (Greater London)
A district of KINGSTON UPON THAMES whose name misleadingly suggests an area of berries. It is actually a combination of the Old English *beorg* (hill) and *land* (tract of land), and was originally given to a farm here. In a sense, therefore, the name corresponds to the modern 'Hill Farm'. The Old English word for 'land' invariably implied a stretch of land put to agricultural use.

Berwick-upon-Tweed (Northumberland)
Berwick is a common name, but it is unusual to find it used for a town since most places called Berwick are villages. Literally it means 'barley farm', from the Old English *berewīc*; such a farm was one outlying from a more important settlement or place, such as a manor. The town's name was recorded in 1167 without the distinguishing river name, as simply *Berewich*, but by 1229 it had become (in the Latin of the day) *Berewicum super Twedam*. From its humble origin, this

particular Berwick, northwest of NEWCASTLE, has become an important border town, and, in recent times, has given its name to an administrative district here. Berwick has passed to and fro between Scotland and England over the centuries, symbolising the constant warring between the two countries, until in 1551 it was declared neutral territory. In 1885, however, Queen Victoria again included it in England, where it has since remained.

Bessbrook (Armagh)
A pleasant village just northwest of NEWRY. The name comes from that of the house, Bess Brook, built here in the early nineteenth century by John Pollock, who founded a linen manufacturing business here. He named his house partly after his wife Elizabeth, née Carlile, and partly after the 'brook' by which it stood, the River Camlough. Bessbrook served as a model for the English garden settlement of BOURNVILLE.

Bethesda (Gwynedd)
This North Wales slate-quarrying town, southeast of BANGOR, has a name of biblical origin, and is typical of several 'chapel' names of this type found in Wales. The town arose round a Calvinistic Methodist Bethesda Chapel, itself established in 1820 on a site called Y Wern Uchaf, 'the upper marshland'. Most places with such names remain villages or hamlets, but Bethesda is an exception, and owes its growth to the slate quarries. In the Bible, Bethesda (meaning 'house of mercy') is the name of the pool in Jerusalem where Jesus healed the sick (John 5:1–10). There are other places called Bethesda in Wales; examples of similar 'chapel' names are Berea, Bethania, Bethel, Bethlehem, Beulah, Carmel, and Nebo.

Bethnal Green (Greater London)
A district of central east LONDON. The 'green' was the village green here, so that

the name proper is Bethnal. This means 'Blitha's corner of land', with the Old English *halh* giving the second half of the name. Although Blitha seems to be a personal name here, it could have been a river or stream name (*see* BLYTH). The original 'green' was part of CAMBRIDGE HEATH, now built over, as is Bethnal Green. The name was recorded in the thirteenth century as simply *Blithehale*, and only in the fifteenth century as *Blethenalegrene*.

Bettystown (Meath)
This seaside resort east of DROGHEDA did not arise as a 'town' belonging to a lady named Betty! Its name is an anglicisation of the Irish name, Baile an Bhaitaigh, 'Betagh's homestead'; the Irish *baile* has been translated as 'town'.

Betws-y-Coed (Gwynedd)
A popular tourist centre and village, south of COLWYN BAY, well known for the Swallow Falls amid woods and streams. The name is interpreted as a blend of English and Welsh to mean 'prayer house in the wood'. The first word is a Welsh version of the Middle English *bed-hūs*, literally 'bead-house', that is, an oratory or prayer house. (Originally, 'bead' meant 'prayer', and acquired its modern English meaning through 'telling one's beads', or saying one's prayers.) Welsh *coed* means 'wood'. The name was recorded in 1254 as simply *Betus*, later adding various other personal names and words by way of distinguishing this prayer house from others, until the present form of the name became established in about the eighteenth century.

Beverley (Humberside)
This town north of HULL and well known for its fine minster, has a name meaning 'beaver stream', from the Old English *beofor* and a conjectural word *lecc*, meaning 'stream'. These words form the basis of early records of the name, such as *Beferlic* in about 1100. But by the twelfth century

the rare word *lecc*, known only in this place-name, had become confused with the much more common *lēah* (clearing), which is why the name today ends in '-ley'. The town lies near the River Hull, but this is not necessarily the 'stream' of the original. The name has been given to the famous Beverly Hills of Los Angeles, and has been adopted as a first name, mostly through the surname.

Bewdley (Hereford and Worcester)
The name of this town on the River SEVERN west of KIDDERMINSTER has the same origin as that of BEAULIEU — the Norman French meaning 'beautiful place'. A document of 1275 gives it as *Beuleu* and a later text of 1308 as (in medieval Latin) *Bellum Locum*. Invariably, places named after a form of the Old French *beau lieu* are on or near a river.

Bexhill (East Sussex)
The name of this residential seaside town west of HASTINGS is misleading, for there is no hill here by the coast. Early forms of the name thus show the true origin, such as the record of 722 as *Bexlea*. This means 'box wood' or 'woodland where box grows', from the Old English conjectural *byxe* and *lēah* (woodland, clearing). The Domesday Book recorded the name as *Bexelei*, and no doubt it was such a spelling that caused the final letters of the name to be understood as the Old English *hyll* instead of *lēah*. BEXLEYHEATH has it right!

Bexleyheath (Greater London)
Like the name of BEXHILL, that of Bexleyheath means 'box wood'. The 'heath' was added when the district became greater in size than that of the village of Bexley, and to distinguish the two. Until the late nineteenth century, Bexley Heath (as two words) was thought of as a survival of the great heath that formerly existed to the north of Bexley, where it was crossed by the main road from DOVER to LONDON. The first built-up area here was known as Bexley New Town for a while in the early

nineteenth century, before the
development took the name of the heath.
The latter is today represented by some of
the sports grounds and playing fields
beside the A207 (which is a survival of the
main road, formerly the old Roman
WATLING STREET).

Bicester (Oxfordshire)

A town northeast of OXFORD. The second
half of the name shows that it was formerly
a Roman settlement, deriving from the Old
English *ceaster*, which was in turn
borrowed from the Latin *castra* (camp).
The first part of the name is not that of a
river, as is often the case, nor is it even
Celtic. It is the Old English *byrgen* (burial
place, tumulus). The Domesday Book
recorded the name as *Bernecestre*.

Bickley (Greater London)

A district of BROMLEY, Bickley has a name
that probably means 'Bica's wood', with
the second half of the name the frequently
occurring Old English *lēah* (wood,
clearing). A late-thirteenth-century text has
the name as *Byckeleye*.

Biddulph (Staffordshire)

As it stands, the name of this town, north
of STOKE-ON-TRENT, appears to have no
obvious meaning, and even the Domesday
Book version of it, *Bidolf*, masks the actual
origin. This is in the Old English *bī* (by)
and a conjectural form *dylf*, meaning
'diggings' (compare the modern English
'delve'). In other words, the place arose as
a settlement by some diggings, and these
were almost certainly stone quarries, which
still exist in the neighbourhood.

Bideford (Devon)

A town and port on the River TORRIDGE
northwest of EXETER. Its name probably
means 'Byda's ford', the latter being over
the aforementioned river. Qualification is
necessary, however, as the exact form of
the personal name is uncertain. It could
also have been Bīeda. The Domesday Book
gives the name as *Bedeford*.

Bigbury-on-Sea (Devon)

The small resort west of KINGSBRIDGE
whose name is recorded in the Domesday
Book as *Bicheberie*. This means 'Bica's
fortified place', the latter half of the name
being the Old English *burg*. Like many
coastal resorts, the town added '-on-Sea' in
recent times, mainly as a way of
commercial enticement.

Biggar (Strathclyde)

The name of this town, west of PEEBLES,
is probably Scandinavian in origin, deriving
from the Old Norse *bygg* (barley) and *geiri*
(triangular plot of ground). A record of
1170 has the name as *Bigir*. Although one
finds many Scandinavian names in the
north of Scotland, the Viking settlers
equally came to live in the southwest and
southeast of the country, leaving names
such as the one here.

Biggleswade (Bedfordshire)

The Domesday Book recorded the name of
this town, southeast of BEDFORD, as
Pichelesuuade. The initial *P* for *B* may be
an error, but the remainder of the name
gives a truer idea of its original than does
the present spelling. It means 'Biccel's
ford'. The substitution of *g* for *c* took place
from the fifteenth century. The word that
gives 'ford' is not the Old English *ford* but
wæd, that is, a place where people and
animals can walk or wade through the stream
or river. The river here is the Ivel (*see*
YEOVIL).

Billericay (Essex)

The name of this town, east of
BRENTWOOD, has long proved a puzzle, as
it seemed to be neither Old English nor
Celtic in origin. Only in 1983 did a
member of the English Place-Name Society
propose a likely origin. He claimed that the
name relates to a conjectural Latin word
bellerica, found in the botanical name
Terminalia bellerica, for the myrtolan, a
fruit that grows in the Far East. When
dried, this was used for tanning and
dyeing. The place-name, therefore, could

mean something like 'tannery' or 'dyehouse', and as such would have occurred in medieval Latin texts. The name is not unique, there being a Bellerica Farm at Upton Noble, Somerset, for example.

Billinge (Merseyside)

This coal-mining town northeast of ST HELENS derives its name from that of a hill here, whose own name could be based on the Old English *bill* (sword), denoting a hill with a sharp 'edge'. If this is so, the name as a whole would mean 'people of Billinge Hill'. But names ending in '-ing' are often based on a personal name; here this could be Billa, giving '(place of) Billa's people'. Either explanation could suit Billinge; there is certainly a prominent hill here rising to nearly 600 feet. *Compare* BILLINGHAM; BILLINGSHURST.

Billingham (Cleveland)

The name of this industrial town, northeast of STOCKTON-ON-TEES, poses the same problem as that of BILLINGE, since it could equally derive from a hill name or a personal name. A hill name, based on the Old English *bill* (sword), seems unlikely as there is no prominent hill nearby. Therefore an origin in the personal name Billa seems more plausible, giving the name's full meaning as 'village of the people of Billa', with the name ending in the Old English *hām* (homestead, village). A record of about 1050 has the name spelt exactly as now. *See also* BILLINGSHURST.

Billingshurst (West Sussex)

This small town, southwest of HORSHAM, has a name that means 'wooded hill in the territory of Billa's people', with the final element of the name the Old English *hyrst* (wooded hill). The personal name is derived from the Old English *bill* (sword), and was a nickname for a Saxon warrior. The place-name has been recorded in spellings little different from today's, such as *Bellingesherst* in 1203. *Compare* BILLINGE; BILLINGHAM.

Bilston (West Midlands)

A district of WOLVERHAMPTON whose name means 'settlement of the people of Bil'. The present name is an abbreviated form of the original, which was recorded in 996 as *Bilsetnatun*. This represents the Old English *tūn* added to *Bilsætan*, itself comprising the Old English *sætan* (settlers) added to the name Bil. However, it is hard to know what this refers to. There is no local place-name that could give it, unless it was the former name of the hill near Bilston. If this is so, the name derives from *bill* (sword), like BILLINGE, BILLINGHAM, and BILLINGSHURST.

Bingley (West Yorkshire)

Bingley means 'forest clearing of Bynna's people', and the name of the present town, northwest of BRADFORD, was recorded in the Domesday Book as *Bingelei*. There are thus three elements to the name. These are the personal name Bynna, the Old English element *-ingas* (people of), and *lēah* (clearing). Usually names of this type end in '-ham', but sometimes, as here, other endings are found.

Birchington (Kent)

The western district of MARGATE, and a seaside resort in its own right. It has a straightforward Old English name meaning 'birch hill farmstead', from, respectively, *birce*, *hyll*, and *tūn*. The name was recorded in 1240 as *Birchilton*'.

Birkenhead (Merseyside)

An industrial town and port southwest of LIVERPOOL on the WIRRAL peninsula. Its name means 'headland on which birch trees grow'. Precisely which headland is meant is uncertain, but it could have been the one now known as Woodside Ferry (with this name therefore significant). Although the name is Old English, it has become 'Birkenhead' rather than 'Birchen-head' due to Scandinavian influence; there are records with both *ch* and *k*, with the latter spelling prevailing. Examples are *Birchened* in 1325 and *Birkenhed* in 1278.

Birmingham (West Midlands)
Although it is Britain's second largest city, Birmingham's name is typical of a number of small villages. It means 'village of Beorma's people', and was recorded in the Domesday Book virtually as now, in the form *Bermingeham*. The personal name is a shortened version of Beornmund, as found in the name BERMONDSEY. A text dated 1537 has the name as *Brymedgham*, showing a typical example of the colloquial form of the name as 'Brummagem'.

Birr (Offaly)
A former garrison town south of ATHLONE on the River Camcor. Its Irish name Biorra indicates this location, translating as 'watery place'. Birr was earlier known as Parsonstown, after Sir Thomas Parsons of Leicestershire, to whom it was assigned by James I in 1620.

Bishop Auckland (Durham)
The first word of the name of this town southwest of DURHAM refers to the bishops of Durham, who had their residence here from the twelfth century. The second word is Celtic, and was recorded in the eleventh century as *Alclit*. This means 'cliff on the CLYDE', with the first element as in ALLOA. But the river here is actually the Gaunless, whose name means 'useless', that is, for practical purposes. The Clyde name would have been borrowed from the Scottish river. Thus what was effectively 'Alclyde' developed into 'Auckland', no doubt because the Norsemen here associated it with the Old Norse *aukland* (additional land). The name is thus rather complex. For a parallel *see* DUMBARTON.

Bishopbriggs (Strathclyde)
A northern suburb of GLASGOW whose name seems to be straightforward, that is, 'bishop's bridge', although some claim that the second half of the name is actually the plural of 'rigg', a Scottish word for a field. But there is no waterway of significance here that could have had a bridge over it, and the derivation therefore remains

uncertain. The name appears in a text of 1665 as *Bishop Bridge*. The reference, as for BISHOPTON, is to the Bishop of Glasgow.

Bishop's Castle (Shropshire)
This small town northwest of CRAVEN ARMS has a name that means exactly what it says. The town was founded in about 1154 by the Bishop of HEREFORD, although only scanty remains are left of his castle. The name was recorded in 1269 as *Bissopes Castell*.

Bishop's Stortford (Hertfordshire)
The basic name of this town, north of HARLOW on the River Stort, is Stortford, which means literally 'tail ford'. The Old English *steort*, which gives the first half of this, meant 'tail' or 'tail of land', in many cases this applying to a 'tongue' of land between streams, as here. To cross this land, with its streams, a ford (or fords) would have been needed. (The same Old English word lies behind the name of the redstart, a bird with a red tail.) The river name Stort is technically a 'back formation', deriving from the town name. The first word of the present name refers to the fact that the settlement here was held by the bishops of LONDON. Bishop's Stortford was recorded in the Domesday Book as simply *Storteford*. *Compare* BISHOP'S WALTHAM.

Bishop's Waltham (Hampshire)
As with BISHOP'S STORTFORD, the basic name of this small town, north of FAREHAM, is Waltham, and it was recorded exactly in this spelling in a document of 904. The name means 'homestead by a wood', and comprises the two Old English words *weald*, 'woodland' (as in The WEALD of Kent) and the commonly found *hām* (homestead). The first word of the name indicates that in medieval times the place was held by the bishops of WINCHESTER.

Bishopton (Strathclyde)
This village, northeast of GLASGOW, is less

than a dozen miles, as the crow flies, from
BISHOPBRIGGS, and the similarity of the
names is not coincidental. Here, as there,
the reference is to the Bishop of Glasgow.
The name dates from about the fourteenth
century.

Blaby (Leicestershire)

A southern suburb of LEICESTER and an
administrative district. It is a typical Old
Norse name, meaning 'Bla's farm', the
latter part of the name being the common
Norse ending *by* (farm, settlement). The
Domesday Book records the name slightly
incorrectly, as *Bladi*. The personal name is
more a nickname, and means 'dark', that
is, dark-complexioned or dark-haired.
(The literal sense is 'blue', as applied to
dark-blue water.)

Blackburn (Lancashire)

This industrial town northwest of
MANCHESTER has an easy, straightforward
name — 'black burn', that is, a place
that arose by a dark stream. To help
things even more, the stream here is
called the Blackwater. The Domesday
Book version of the name was
Blacheburne.

Blackheath (Greater London)

A district of LEWISHAM whose name
means what it says — 'black heath'. The
former heathland here was dark-coloured
because of the peat that overlay the sand. A
section of the heath remains as the public
gardens south of GREENWICH Park. A text
of 1166 records the name as *Blachehedfeld*,
comprising the Old English *feld* 'stretch of
open land' (modern 'field') added to the
basic name.

Black Mountains (Powys/Gwent)

A South Wales range of hills, which extend
over the border into England. They are so
named not from the dark colour of the
soil, which is Old Red Sandstone, but
because they generally appear dark when
viewed from the eastern and southern
side.

Blackpool (Lancashire)

A well-known coastal resort and conference
centre west of PRESTON with an ostensibly
uninviting name. The original settlement
here, recorded in about 1260 simply as *Pul*,
arose by a peaty-coloured pool of water
about half a mile from the sea. By the end
of the eighteenth century this spot had
been turned into meadowland, and the
stream that flowed from the pool is now the
town's main sewer. The present name was
established by the seventeenth century,
and a document dated 1637 refers to the
settlement as *Lepoole, commonly called
Black-poole*.

Blackrock (Dublin)

Despite its gloomy and even forbidding
name, Blackrock has been a fashionable
and popular seaside resort south of
DUBLIN since the eighteenth century. The
name is fairly common in Ireland for a
coastal site that has arisen by some dark-
coloured rocks, as here. The Irish name is
similarly descriptive, An Charraigh
Dhubh, 'the black rock'.

Blackrod (Greater Manchester)

A coal-mining and textile town west of
BOLTON. Its name does not mean quite
what it says, but has the sense of 'black
clearing'. The Old English conjectural *rod*
denoted a clearing in a wood, and occurs in
some place-names in the form '-royd', such
as Ackroyd ('oak-tree clearing') and
Murgatroyd ('Margaret's clearing'). These
two places gave the corresponding
surnames, although the original Yorkshire
place called Murgatroyd no longer exists,
and is known only from historical
documents. Blackrod's name was recorded
in the early thirteenth century as
Blakerode. 'Black' refers to the darkness of
the clearing due to overgrowth of the trees
and bushes rather than to the colour of the
soil.

Blackwater (Hampshire/Berkshire)

A river rising near ALDERSHOT that joins
the LODDON south of READING. It has a

straightforward name referring to the darkness of its waters. An almost parallel river that flows into it before it joins the Loddon is called the Whitewater, after its contrasting appearance. Any village or district with the name is found to have arisen by an identically named river or stream. Scotland in particular has many rivers named Black Water. *Compare* BLACKBURN. *See also* DOUGLAS.

Blackwood (Gwent)
This South Wales town north of CAERPHILLY has a name that describes the dark-coloured wood by which it arose, here in the valley of the River Sirhowy. Its Welsh name, with the same meaning, is Coed-duon.

Blaenau Ffestiniog (Gwynedd)
This slate-quarrying town southeast of CAERNARVON has a duplex name referring to another place. The Welsh *blaenau* (the plural of *blaen*) means 'heights', 'headwaters of a stream'. Other places incorporate the word, such as BLAENAVON and the administrative district of GWENT named Blaunau Gwent. The word occurs on its own in an anglicised form as Blaina, the coal-mining village south of BRYNMAWR. Blaenau Ffestiniog is located some three miles north of Ffestiniog, near the source of the River Dwyryd that flows through both places. Ffestiniog's name means 'defensive position', from the Welsh *ffestin* plus the adjectival ending *-iog*. The original village occupied a good strategic site on a hill between the rivers Dwyryd and Cynfal, with its name recorded in 1419 as *Festynyok*.

Blaenavon (Gwent)
A coal-mining and steel-manufacturing town north of PONTYPOOL with a name meaning 'head of the river', from the Welsh *blaen* (height, headstream) (*compare* BLAENAU FFESTINIOG) and *afon* (river). The river involved here is the Afon Lwyd, which flows down the valley from Blaenavon to Pontypool. The Welsh

spelling of the name is little different, as Blaenafon.

Blair Atholl (Tayside)
A village, northwest of PITLOCHRY, that is well known for the large mansion of Blair Castle here, the seat of the Dukes of Atholl. The first word of the name means 'plain', from the Gaelic *blàr*. The second word, somewhat unexpectedly, means 'Ireland again', from the Gaelic *ath* (again) and *Fotla*, a poetic name for Ireland, linked with the name of Fodla, an Irish goddess. Atholl is thus really 'New Ireland', and was the name chosen by the Gaels (the original 'Scots') when they came from Ireland to settle in Scotland in the fifth century. Atholl is itself a mountainous area of around 450 square miles, while Blair Atholl, located where many glens and rivers meet, is the most extensively cultivated settlement. The original Blair ('plain') added the district name ('Atholl') to distinguish it from BLAIRGOWRIE, only 24 miles away. The name was recorded as *Athochlach* in about 970.

Blairgowrie (Tayside)
Just as BLAIR ATHOLL added the name of the district (Atholl) to the name of the settlement (Blair), so the present town of Blairgowrie, northwest of DUNDEE, arose as a settlement also named Blair, and added the name of the district, Gowrie, to distinguish itself from nearby Blair Atholl. The name means 'plain of the territory of Gabran'. Gabran was a sixth-century Gaelic king who held the territory here. The name was recorded in the thirteenth century simply as *Blare*, and in the early seventeenth century as *Blair in Gowrie*; Gowrie itself was recorded in a document of 1165 as *Gouerin*.

Blakeney (Norfolk)
A coastal village and yachting centre northwest of HOLT. The name means either 'Blaca's island' or 'black island', with the 'island' being not the shingle spit that leaves the coast here but an area of

higher ground in the marshes at this point. The name was recorded in 1242 as *Blakenye*, making it hard to determine whether the first part of the name is the personal name or the Old English *blæc* (black, dark-coloured). Until at least the thirteenth century the place was also known as Snitterley, recorded in the Domesday Book as *Snuterlea*. This earlier name means 'Snytra's clearing'. The reason for the change of name is uncertain, and it is unusual for a 'clearing' (Old English *lēah*) to become an 'island' (*ēg*).

Blanchardstown (Dublin)

A village northwest of DUBLIN on the N3 road to NAVAN. Blanchard was the name of the Anglo-Norman family who held the settlement here in medieval times, with the name recorded in 1249 as *Villa Blanchard*. The Irish version of the name translates 'town' but simply renders the Norman name phonetically, as Baile Bhlainsear.

Blandford Forum (Dorset)

A town on the River STOUR northwest of BOURNEMOUTH, usually known simply as Blandford. The 'Forum' is a reminder that Blandford is an ancient market town, for this is the meaning of the medieval Latin word. Blandford itself probably means 'gudgeon ford', from the Old English *blæge* and the common *ford*. Today, the gudgeon is chiefly used by anglers for bait, but it is a tasty dish in its own right, and it is noteworthy that even now Blandford is famous for its good angling and for the restaurants here that serve fish (not necessarily gudgeon) caught in the river. 'Forum' was added to distinguish this place from others nearby of the same name, such as Blandford St Mary (a mile away) and Langton Long Blandford (at a similar distance and also on the Stour). The name with 'Forum' is first recorded in a late-thirteenth-century document as *Blaneford forum*. Interestingly, Thomas Hardy's name for Blandford in his novels was Shottsford Forum. He may have based this name on that of Shottesbrooke, a Berkshire

village perhaps known to him. This name itself means 'trout brook', from the Old English *sceota* (trout). Hardy may have been aware of the meaning, and so created a fictional name that was similarly 'fishy', Shottsford Forum meaning in effect 'Troutsford Forum'. The trout is also readily obtainable in the river here.

Blantyre (Strathclyde)

The name of this town, immediately northwest of HAMILTON, has a first element of uncertain origin. Some have proposed a word related to the Welsh *blaen* (fore, front, top) (as for BLAENAU FFESTINIOG). The latter half of the name is probably from the Gaelic *tir* (land, territory). But Blantyre is not in noticeably elevated country. If the interpretation is correct, perhaps it means 'edge land' or 'territory at the foot of higher ground', as would suit Blantyre.

Blarney (Cork)

This village northwest of CORK is famous for its Blarney Stone but has an unremarkable name meaning simply 'the small field', as the Irish original, An Bhlarna, shows.

Blaydon (Tyne and Wear)

This manufacturing town on the River TYNE west of GATESHEAD has had its name interpreted as meaning 'black hill' — a combination of the Old Norse *blár* (black) and the Old English *dūn* (hill). But Scandinavian names are uncommon in this part of the country, and there is no obvious hill here, although there is one at Winlaton to the southwest. However, a small stream, the Barlow Burn, rises at the village of Barlow about two miles away; near its source is a place named Blaydon Burn, suggesting that Barlow Burn was itself once known by this name. If this is so, the stream name could have given that of the town, despite the fact that the Tyne is the major waterway here. Such an instance occurred in Oxfordshire, where Bladon was the former name of the River Evenlode and gave its name to the village of Bladon in that county. Unfortunately, the origin of Bladon is unknown.

Blenheim Palace (Oxfordshire)
A stately home south of WOODSTOCK, built over the period 1705–22 for the Duke of Marlborough as a gift from Queen Anne to commemorate his victory at the Battle of Blenheim in 1704. The house was thus named after the battle, which took place at the Bavarian village known to the French and English as Blenheim, but now known in German as Blindheim (although the Germans now refer to the battle as *die Schlacht bei Höchstädt*, using the second half of the village's full name of Blindheim Höchstädt). It is perhaps fortuitous that the palace name contains the element *heim* (home) — appropriate for a 'house name'.

Blessington (Wicklow)
This town southeast of NAAS owes its present English name to a mistranslation. The Irish name is Baile Coimin, 'Comyn's townland', and the original English name was based on this — Ballycomin. This, however, was wrongly understood as representing the Irish *baile comaoine* (townland of favour), with *comaoin* meaning 'Holy Communion', 'divine favour'. For this reason, the English name was altered to Blessington, to be understood as 'town of blessing'.

Bletchley (Buckinghamshire)
The name of this town, at the south end of MILTON KEYNES, was recorded in the early twelfth century as *Blechelai* and means 'Blecca's clearing', with the Old English *lēah* as the second element. Bletchley is near Whaddon Chase, a former hunting forest and a heavily wooded area, where there would have been more than one clearing to establish new settlements. The name is thus similar to BARNSLEY, which is also based on a personal name.

Bloomsbury (Greater London)
The name of this district of CAMDEN

suggests 'blooms', perhaps partly due to its (modern) literary associations. But it actually means '(fortified) manor house held by de Blémund'. The Anglo-Norman family who held this manor may well have come from Blémont, in the *département* of Vienne. The name was recorded in 1242 as *Soca Blemund*, and in 1274 as *Manerium de Blemund*. The Old English *burg* is better translated as 'manor house' in this instance, rather than the more common 'fortified place'.

Bloxham (Oxfordshire)
A village southwest of BANBURY, famous for its public school. The name means 'Blocc's village'. The unusual personal name is found only in places beginning 'Blox-', others being Bloxholm in Lincolnshire, Bloxwich as a district of WALSALL, and Bloxworth in Dorset. Bloxham's name was recorded in the Domesday Book as *Blochesham*.

Blyth (Northumberland)
The North Sea port and resort north of TYNEMOUTH is situated at the mouth of the River Blyth, and takes its name from it. The river's own name corresponds more or less to the modern 'blithe' (cheerful), referring to its more fast-flowing upper reaches. There are other rivers of the name in England. This one was recorded in a text of about 1137 as *Blitha*.

Boat of Garten (Highland)
The somewhat unusual name of this village on the River SPEY, northeast of AVIEMORE, means 'ferrying place by the field of corn'. The English 'boat' translates the Gaelic *coit* (small boat), while 'Garten' represents the second half of the Gaelic name of the place, *Coit Ghairtean*. The 'of' is frequently found in Scottish river names, especially of smaller rivers, such as Burn of Maitland.

Bodiam Castle (East Sussex)
The castle here takes its name from the village of Bodiam southwest of

Sandhurst, with this meaning 'Boda's riverside land'. The name was recorded in the Domesday Book as *Bodeham*, although the latter element is not the common *hām* (settlement) but *hamm*. This Old English word was frequently applied to land in a bend of a river, in the case of Bodiam the River ROTHER. The village is in the river valley, but the moated castle is on rising ground above it.

Bodmin (Cornwall)

This agreeable Cornish town, west of PLYMOUTH, has a Cornish name which translates as 'house of the monks', from *bod* (house) and *meneich*, the plural of *manach* (monk). King Athelstan is said to have founded a monastery here in the tenth century. The Domesday Book record of the name is *Bodmine*, by which time the final *-ch* of the original name had disappeared. *See also* PADSTOW.

Bognor Regis (West Sussex)

The first and chief part of the name of this seaside resort, southeast of CHICHESTER, means 'Bucge's shore', from the personal name (that of a woman) and the Old English *ōra* (shore, landing place). This latter word is related to the Latin *os*, genitive *oris* (mouth), which itself developed to produce the word for 'shore' (Latin *ora*). The Old English word is found only in the south of England. The royal affix 'Regis' was bestowed by George V after convalescing at Craigwell House in the village of Aldwick near Bognor in 1929. The present town began to develop at the end of the eighteenth century, when Sir Richard Hotham, a London hatter, bought 1600 acres of land on the site with the aim of developing a resort to equal BRIGHTON. He renamed his development 'Hothampton', but the name fell out of use after his death in 1790, although the town's main public park is still Hotham Park. Bognor was recorded as early as 680 in the form *Bucgan ora*. Bucga herself would have been a Saxon woman who owned a landing place here.

Boldon (Tyne and Wear)

This coal-mining town, between SOUTH SHIELDS and SUNDERLAND, has a name meaning 'hill with a homestead'. The first part of the name is the Old English *bōthl* (*compare* BOLTON). The latter part is the common *dūn* (hill). Boldon's name has changed little over the centuries, and in a text of 1291 appears exactly as now.

Bolingbroke Castle (Lincolnshire)

Only earthworks now remain at the village of Old Bolingbroke to mark the site of the Norman castle, but the name has become familiar through the surname Bolingbroke given to Henry IV, who was born here. The place-name means 'brook of Bula's people', with the final part of the name representing the Old English *brōc* (brook, stream). The Domesday Book recorded the name as *Bolinbroc*. The village, west of SPILSBY, is now called Old Bolingbroke to differentiate it from New Bolingbroke, a nineteenth-century village developed five miles away on a site within the parish.

Bollington (Cheshire)

A town, northeast of MACCLESFIELD, named after the nearby River Bollin, although itself standing on the River Dean. There is also a village of the same name 14 miles to the northwest of the town, but right by the River Bollin. The origin of the river name is uncertain.

Bolsover (Derbyshire)

This mainly industrial town, east of CHESTERFIELD, was recorded in the Domesday Book as *Belesovre*. The latter half of this is the Old English *ofer* (slope, ridge), but the first part remains uncertain; it may well be a personal name. The 'ridge' is a hillside spur to the east of the town, which may have been used for defence. Bolsover has given its name to the administrative district here.

Bolton (Greater Manchester)

The name of this town, northwest of MANCHESTER, is shared by a number of other places in northern England, such as Bolton Priory in North Yorkshire and the town of Bolton-le-Sands in Lancashire. The origin lies in the Old English *bōthl* (building) plus the common *tūn* (settlement, village). It is thought that such a 'village with buildings' was the main residential part of a settlement, as distinct from subsidiary or outlying farms. Bolton-le-Sands has a distinguishing addition, indicating its location by the sandy coast on MORECAMBE Bay. The Old English *bōthl* occurs on its own in the name of BOOTLE.

Bo'ness (Central)

The more or less official abbreviation for Borrowstounness, the town west of EDINBURGH on the FIRTH OF FORTH. The full name means 'promontory of Beornweard's farm'. The original name was recorded in a text of about 1335 as *Berwardeston*, without the Old English *næss* (headland), and this might well have developed into a form such as 'Bernardston'. But the name was understood as 'burrowstown', a Scottish term for a town that is a burgh. The personal name means 'warrior guardian'. The abbreviated form of the name has at least retained an apostrophe to indicate the missing nine letters!

Bonhill (Strathclyde)

A town on the River LEVEN north of DUMBARTON. Its name was recorded in a document of 1225 as *Buchlul*, and the present version appears to be a corruption of the Gaelic *both an ùidh*, 'house by the stream'.

Bonnybridge (Central)

An industrial development west of FALKIRK on the Bonny Water. The name means what it says, for there certainly is a bridge over the small river here. The name is fairly recent, dating from the seventeenth century. The meaning of the river name is uncertain; it was recorded in 1682 as *aquae de Boine*.

Bonnyrigg (Lothian)

The name of this town, southwest of DALKEITH, is quite different from that of BONNYBRIDGE. It was recorded in a text of 1773 as *Bannockrig*, which means 'bannock-shaped ridge'. A bannock is a round, flat oatmeal cake, a characteristically Scottish product, and it would have been quite natural for the shape of the cake to have been used to describe a ridge or field. In England, 'Pancake' has been recorded as the name of a field in Lancashire, for similar reasons. The Scottish name later became assimilated to 'Bonny', as in Bonnybridge, Bonnybank, Bonnyton, and so on.

Boothferry (Humberside)

An administrative district in the west of the county. Its name comes from Boothferry Bridge, at the small village of Booth; the bridge today carries the A614 over the River OUSE. The bridge name refers to when a crossing could be made only by ferry. The name is recorded as *Booth's Ferry* in 1651, with Booth presumably being the name of the owner of the land here, if not of the actual crossing.

Bootle (Merseyside)

A town immediately north of LIVERPOOL. Like BOLTON, Bootle has a name that represents the Old English word for 'building'. Here it occurs in the form *bōtl*, and must have indicated a special or unusually large or prominent building. This may not necessarily have been a residence, as for Bolton, but may have been an outlying building. The town shares its name with a village in Cumbria, northwest of MILLOM. The Domesday Book recorded the Merseyside town as *Boltelai*, with an apparent duplication of the *l* in error.

Borders (Scotland)

An administrative region of southeast Scotland with a name aptly describing its situation by the border with England. Although the region was officially formed only in 1975, 'The Borders' (or 'The Border') has long been a term to describe the district straddling the border between the two countries. The designation almost certainly originated in Scotland, as this is the only Scottish border, i.e. *the* border. For this reason the name has been more common among the Scots than the English, who tend to think of the Borders more as the CHEVIOT HILLS.

Borehamwood (Hertfordshire)

The Old English *bor* is a conjectural word that probably meant 'hill'. The name of this residential suburb, north of EDGWARE, therefore means 'wood of the hill settlement', with the wood's own name in turn used for the housing development here. The name was regularly two words (Boreham Wood) until the twentieth century.

Boroughbridge (North Yorkshire)

The name of this small town, on the banks of the River URE southeast of RIPON, might well have turned into 'Pontborough' or something similar; it was recorded in 1155 as *pons de Burgo*, in 1169 as *Ponteburc*, and in 1194 as *Puntdeburc* (*compare* PONTEFRACT). As it is, the Old French *pont* was translated into the Old English *brycg*, so that the name means 'bridge of the fortified place'. The bridge was over the Ure, and the 'fortified place' (Old English *burg*) was that of nearby Aldborough ('old fortified place') — the Roman settlement of *Isurium Brigantum*. The first word of this Roman name refers to the River Ure; the latter denotes that the Roman camp was the capital of the tribe of Brigantes (the Celts who were here before the Romans).

Borrowdale (Cumbria)

The valley of the River DERWENT above DERWENTWATER in the Lake District. Why is it not then 'Derwentdale'? The answer is that the upper Derwent was called 'Borgará' (stream by a fort), from the Old Norse *borg* (fort; genitive *borgar*) and *á* (stream). This name gave rise to the

modern 'Borrow'. There was probably a Romano-British hill-fort here at the site now called Castle Crag.

Borstal (Kent)

Now a southern district of ROCHESTER but formerly a clearly identified village, with a name that literally meant 'security place', from the Old English *borg* (security) and *steall* (place). This implied a place where refuge could be sought when fleeing in battle, and 'borstal' itself developed as a local dialect word to mean a steep and narrow path up the side of a hill, in which a person could 'lose' himself. It is a curious coincidence that the original meaning of the name should be appropriate for the modern 'borstal' — a place of detention for young offenders. This was so named because the first such reformatory was established at Borstal in 1901 in a converted prison. The village was recorded in the Domesday Book as *Borcstele*.

Borth-y-gest (Gwynedd)

A small Welsh resort, south of PORTHMADOG, whose name translates literally as 'port of the belly', from *porth* (port, ferry), *y* (the), and *cest* (belly, paunch). The village, in effect a southern extension of Porthmadog, lies near a mountain named Moel y Gest, 'bare hill of the belly', alluding to its shape, and took its name from it. The ferry would formerly have been over the Traeth Bach here, the estuary of the rivers Dwyryd and Glaslyn. Another resort on CARDIGAN Bay in Dyfed is simply called Borth.

Boscastle (Cornwall)

This coastal village north of CAMELFORD does not have a Cornish name but a combined Norman and English one. The first part of the name represents that of William de Botereus, who held the castle here in the fourteenth century. The name as a whole was thus recorded in a document of 1302 as *Boterelscastel*, with *castel* here being Middle English for 'castle'. The remains of the castle are still here at the end of the village street.

Boscobel House (Shropshire)
This seventeenth-century country house, where Charles II hid after his defeat at the Battle of WORCESTER, lies in attractive countryside northeast of SHIFNAL. According to the *Dictionary of National Biography*, this was not the original Boscobel House, which had been 'built by the Giffards [of Chillington] about 1580, partly as a hunting lodge and partly as an asylum for recusant priests [. . .] in the thickest part of the forest of Brewood'. (The *DNB* entry is for Richard Penderel, who occupied Boscobel House at the time when Charles II took refuge there.) This particular location, in a wood, seems to suggest that the name Boscobel is a form of the Latin *boscus bellus*, 'beautiful wood', or an italianised version of this as *Boscobello*.

Bosham (West Sussex)
A yachting centre at the head of CHICHESTER Harbour. The name is pronounced 'Bozzum', which recognisably preserves the original personal name of Bosa, on which the place-name is based. The '-ham' could be either the Old English *hām* (homestead, village) or *hamm* (waterside place). Certainly, the location suggests the latter, and the village is on a stretch of Chichester Harbour called Bosham Channel. The name of 'Bosa's water meadow' was recorded in the Domesday Book as *Boseham*. It was at Bosham that King Canute (Cnut) is traditionally said to have attempted to control the incoming tide.

Boston (Lincolnshire)
A coastal town southeast of LINCOLN, famous for its 'Boston Stump', the tower of St Botolph's church. The name was recorded in a document of 1130 as *Botuluestan*, which means 'Botwulf's stone'. This person has been assumed to be St Botolph, to whom the church is dedicated, with the 'stone' the one at which

he once preached here. But historical evidence has not established his identity, and Botwulf (whose name probably means 'commanding wolf') may simply have been a landowner here, with the 'stone' either a boundary marker of his estate or a point of assembly. Boston gave its name to the US city of Massachusetts, which was founded in 1630 by Puritans from the Lincolnshire town.

Bosworth Field (Leicestershire)
The site, two miles south of MARKET BOSWORTH, of the battle in which Richard III was defeated in the Wars of the Roses in 1485. *See* MARKET BOSWORTH.

Bothwell (Strathclyde)
This historic Scottish town northwest of HAMILTON and known for its ruined castle, has an English name that derives from the Middle English *bothe* (booth, temporary shelter) and the Old English *wella* (well, spring). Bothwell is on the River CLYDE, and the 'well' was doubtless one that ran into it, and was perhaps a site for fishing. The name was recorded in about 1242 as *Botheuill*.

Botley (Hampshire)
A small town on the River Hamble east of SOUTHAMPTON with a name that probably means 'Bota's clearing', comprising the personal name followed by the Old English *lēah*. It was recorded in the Domesday Book as *Botelie*.

Bourne (Lincolnshire)
A small town west of SPALDING. It is near the source of a stream, which is called the Bourne Eau after it, and its Old English name is shared by other places that are likewise situated by a stream. The source word is the Old English *burna* (as the Scottish 'burn'). This particular Bourne was recorded in a document of about 960 as *Brunne*. The Old English word is equally found as the second element in many names, such as ASHBOURNE, PANGBOURNE, and SITTINGBOURNE.

Compare BOURNE END; BOURNEMOUTH; BOURNVILLE. *See also* BURNHAM BEECHES; BURNHAM-ON-CROUCH; BURNHAM-ON-SEA; BURNLEY.

Bourne End (Buckinghamshire)

A residential district and resort on the THAMES east of MARLOW, located at a point where the stream called the Wooburn enters the river. It is thus an 'end' or defined location by this stream (for the origin of the stream name *see* WOBURN ABBEY). There are several other places named Bourne End in a similar location, such as the small village of Bourne End to the west of HEMEL HEMPSTEAD, which is by the stream called the Bulbourne. Note how both Wooburn and Bulborne themselves contain the element 'burn' or 'bourne'.

Bournemouth (Dorset)

This large and fashionable seaside resort, southwest of SOUTHAMPTON, arose only in the nineteenth century. The name is much older, however; in a text dated 1407 there is reference to a whale (in the original, *magnus piscis, anglice a whale*) that was washed up *iuxta litus maris prope la Bournemouthe* ('next to the sea-shore near the Bournmouth'). The name thus means simply 'mouth of the stream', and the small river here can still be seen running down to the English Channel through the Pleasure Gardens. It is simply called the Bourne.

Bournville (West Midlands)

A district of southwest BIRMINGHAM laid out in 1879 as a model estate for the employees of George Cadbury's chocolate factory. The original name proposed for the development was Bournbrook, after a mansion here named Bournbrook Hall; however, the more stylish and 'residential' Bournville was eventually selected. The latter '-ville' element was popular in nineteenth-century developments (*compare* CLIFTONVILLE, WATERLOOVILLE), and it suggested both the English 'villa' and the French *ville* (town), while at the same time

indicating a new kind of English 'village' or settlement. The first part of the name refers to the stream here, called the Bourne or Bournbrook; Bournbrook is now itself a district here, as well as Bournville. The estate name became familiar as the brand name of Cadbury's cocoa or chocolate drink. (For the reverse, i.e. a brand name producing a place-name, *see* PORT SUNLIGHT.)

Bourton-on-the-Water (Gloucestershire)

A small town southwest of STOW-ON-THE-WOLD. The first and main part of the name corresponds to the 'Burton' of BURTON-UPON-TRENT and means 'farm by a fortified place', i.e. a combination of the Old English *burg* (fortified place) and *tūn* (farm, settlement). The 'on the water' refers to its location by the River WINDRUSH. The name 'Bourton' or 'Burton' is so common that in many instances there are distinguishing additions, such as in Bourton-on-the-Hill, Black Bourton, Burton Constable, and BURTON LATIMER.

Bovey Tracey (Devon)

This small town northwest of NEWTON ABBOT is on the River Bovey, which explains the first half of the name, although the river's own name is still unexplained. The latter part refers to Eva de Tracy, the Anglo-Norman lady who held the manor here in the early thirteenth century. Her own name probably comes from the French village of Tracy-Bocage, near Caen, or possibly Tracy-sur-Mer, near Bayeux. (The forename Tracy is a form of Teresa, and does not derive from this French Tracy; the latter remains as a British surname.) Bovey Tracey was recorded in the Domesday Book simply as *Bovi*, and first occurred in its present form in a document of 1276 as *Bovy Tracy*. The addition of 'Tracey' distinguishes the town from North Bovey, some six miles northwest of it.

Bow (Greater London)
This district of TOWER HAMLETS has a
name that crops up elsewhere. It refers to
an arched bridge, from the Old English
boga (bow, arch). This particular Bow was
formerly known as Stratford-le-Bow or
Stratford-at-Bow, with the addition of
'Bow' distinguishing it from the nearby
STRATFORD in Essex (now in Greater
LONDON). The arched bridge at Bow was
built in the first half of the twelfth century
over the River Lea, on which Stratford, to
the north, also stands. Bow was thus
recorded in 1203 as *Strafford*, and in
Chaucer's *Canterbury Tales* it is mentioned
as *Stratford atte Bowe*.

Bowes (Durham)
A small town southwest of BARNARD
CASTLE on the site of the Roman
settlement of *Lavatris*. Its name represents
the plural of the Old English *boga* (bow,
arch), this referring to a former arched
bridge over the River Greta (*see* GRETA
BRIDGE). Its name was recorded in 1148 as
Bogas. The Roman name is quite different;
it suggests a connection with the Latin
lavare (to wash) and *lavatorium* (wash-
house, bath-house) (and so indirectly with
the English 'lavatory'). But it seems odd to
name a place after a wash-house, which
was a regular feature in Roman forts,
although the word *balneum* (bath-house) is
found in some names on the continent
(such as French places named *Bains*). It
therefore seems likely that the Roman
name was a 'latinisation' of the original
Celtic river name, which could have been
something like *Lautra*, and related to the
modern Irish *leaba* (river-bed).

Bowland, Forest of (Lancashire)
A region of wild moorland between the
rivers LUNE and RIBBLE. Its name means
more or less what it says, for much of the
area lies in a bend ('bow') of the Ribble,
hence it is the 'bow-land' here.

Bowling (West Yorkshire)
A southeastern district of BRADFORD that
gave its name to 'Bowling Tide', the
Bradford annual holiday. The name was
recorded in the Domesday Book as *Bollinc*,
which seems to suggest that the ending
'-ing' is not the usual Old English suffix *-ing*
or *-ingas*. The name may thus be a
combination of the Old English *bolla*
(bowl) and *hlinc* (bank, edge). This could
describe a stretch of land with depressions
or bowl-like 'dips'. The older form of the
name survives here in that of Bolling Hall,
an old house that dates back to the early
fifteenth century.

Box Hill (Surrey)
A steep chalk hill northeast of DORKING
whose name simply means 'hill where box
grows'. The name has not been recorded
earlier than 1629, however, and may have
been adopted from a nearby farm called
something like 'Box Hill Farm'. Box still
grows on Box Hill.

Boyle (Roscommon)
A town, west of CARRICK-ON-SHANNON,
that takes its name from the river on which
it stands; the river name is still of uncertain
origin. The Irish name of the town is
Mainistir na Búille, 'monastery of the
Boyle'.

Boyne (Kildare/Offaly/Meath)
A river flowing to the eastern Irish coast
that has become well known from the
Battle of the Boyne, fought on its banks
west of DROGHEDA in 1690. Here William
III of England defeated the deposed James
II. The name is traditionally said to derive
from that of Boand, the river goddess, but
the true origin is probably in the Irish *bo
bhán* (white cow), this being a legendary
symbol of good fortune.

Brackley (Northamptonshire)
The name of this town east of BANBURY
means 'Bracca's clearing', and was
recorded in the Domesday Book as
Brachelai. The final '-ley' is the Old
English *lēah*, 'clearing in woodland'.
Compare BRACKNELL.

Bracknell (Berkshire)
Now well known as a New Town (designated in 1949) east of WOKINGHAM, Bracknell has an ancient name dating back to at least 942, when it was recorded as *Braccan heal*. This means 'Bracca's corner of land', the latter half of the name representing the Old English *halh* (nook, corner of land). The personal name is Bracca, as for BRACKLEY.

Bradford (West Yorkshire)
Britain has many Bradfords, of which the industrial city west of LEEDS is the best known. The name means simply 'broad ford', from the Old English *brād* (broad) and *ford* (ford). The actual ford here would probably have been at a point in the centre of the present city, over the little Bradford Beck. Bradford is unusual in being an important industrial (and cathedral and university) city that is not on a river of any size. All Bradfords will have developed on or near a stream or river. *Compare* BRADFORD-ON-AVON.

Bradford-on-Avon (Wiltshire)
As for BRADFORD, the name means 'broad ford', in this case over the River AVON, this name being added for distinguishing purposes. The picturesque town, northwest of TROWBRIDGE, appears in early records with this addition: the *Anglo-Saxon Chronicle* (dating from 652) refers to it as a place *æt Bradanforda be Afne*.

Bradwell-on-Sea (Essex)
A coastal village and tourist resort northeast of BURNHAM-ON-CROUCH, also known as Bradwell juxta Mare, the two Latin words meaning 'on-Sea'. Bradwell means 'broad stream', from the Old English *brād* (as for BRADFORD) and *wella* (well, spring, stream). Bradwell is on the River Blackwater. In the Domesday Book, Bradwell is given quite another name — *Effecestra*. This seems to be a later development of the name of the nearby Roman fort, which was known as *Othona*. It is uncertain what this meant. Most Roman names were based on Celtic names, but the sound *th* did not exist in Celtic. Perhaps the spelling was originally with *tt*. Either way, its original sense is obscure.

Braemar (Grampian)
A village west of BALLATER famous for its annual Highland Games, known as the 'Braemar Gathering'. The first part of the name does not represent the Scottish 'brae' (which is Scandinavian in origin) but the Gaelic *braigh* (upper). The second part of the name is a personal name, so that the overall meaning is 'upper part of Marr'. The name was recorded in 1560 as *the Bray of Marre*.

Braintree (Essex)
The second half of this name means, quite reasonably, 'tree'. The first half is not 'brain', however, but the personal name Branuc. 'Branuc's tree' would have been either a prominent tree on land owned by Branuc, or perhaps a 'built' tree in the form of a cross, which the Old English *trēow* also meant. Either could have served as a meeting place for an assembly of some kind. The combination of a personal name and the word 'tree' (or a related element) is found in other names, such as COVENTRY, DAVENTRY, and OSWESTRY. Braintree, northeast of CHELMSFORD, is on the River Brain, which took its name from the settlement, not vice versa (*compare* the Stort at BISHOP'S STORTFORD). The town's name was recorded in the Domesday Book as *Branchetreu*.

Bramhall (Greater Manchester)
This town, south of STOCKPORT, has a name that straightforwardly translates as 'corner of land where broom grows'. The two parts of the name are the Old English *brōm* (here in the form 'Bram-') and *halh* (nook). Bramhall appeared in the Domesday Book as *Bramale*. *Compare* BRAMPTON; BROMLEY; BROMPTON; BROMSGROVE; BROMYARD.

Brampton (Cumbria)
A small town northeast of CARLISLE whose
name is found elsewhere. It means 'village
where broom grows', with the two Old
English components as *brōm* (broom;
changed here as for BRAMHALL) and the
common *tūn* (village). In a document of
1252 the name was recorded as *Braunton*
(*compare* BRAUNTON).

Brandon (Durham, Suffolk)
Any of various places in Britain, notably a
town southwest of DURHAM City, and a
town west of THETFORD. In most cases the
name means 'broom hill' or 'hill where
broom grows', from the Old English *brōm*
(broom) and *dūn* (hill). The Durham town
was recorded in the late twelfth century as
Bromdune, and that of the Suffolk town in
the Domesday Book as *Brandona*. It is
possible that the name of the village of
Brandon north of GRANTHAM in
Lincolnshire may be different, however, as
it is on the River Brant, and this may
therefore lie behind the name. *Compare*
BRANDON MOUNTAIN.

Brandon Mountain (Kerry)
An Irish mountain north of DINGLE whose
name means St Brendan's Hill. St Brendan
had his retreat here in the sixth century,
and remains of his cell and oratory can be
seen on top of the hill. The Irish name,
with the same meaning, is Cnoc Bréanain.

Brands Hatch (Kent)
A famous motor-racing circuit south of
GRAVESEND. Its name, somewhat
inappropriately, means literally 'brink
gate', that is, a gate (hatch) that leads
to land on a slope (brink); Brands Hatch
is situated on a fairly steep slope.
The name dates back to at least the
thirteenth century, and in 1292 was
recorded as *Bronkeshach*'. A 'hatch' (Old
English *hæcc*) was a wicket gate or hatch
gate that allowed entrance to a forest or
wooded area, such as a park. The same
word is found as the final element of
STEVENAGE.

Braunstone (Leicestershire)
There are two places of the name in
Leicestershire, one with a final *-e* (the
southwest suburb of LEICESTER) and one
without (the village southwest of OAKHAM,
which was formerly in RUTLAND). Both
mean the same, and are the equivalent of
Branston, i.e. 'Brant's settlement', with the
personal name followed by the very
common Old English *tūn*. The Leicester
Braunstone was recorded in the Domesday
Book as *Brantestone*, and the former
Rutland one as *Branteston* in a document of
1167. There is no reason to assume that
both places were named after the same
man, despite their relative proximity to
each other.

Braunton (Devon)
A town near the coast northwest of
BARNSTAPLE whose name corresponds to
BRAMPTON, i.e. 'broom hill'. The town
was recorded in the Domesday Book as
Brantona.

Bray (Berkshire, Wicklow)
A village southeast of MAIDENHEAD and a
well-known resort south of DUBLIN. Both
have names that coincidentally mean the
same thing, although they derive from
different languages. The name of the
Berkshire village was recorded in the
Domesday Book as *Brai*, which comes
from the Old English *brēg* (brow, i.e. 'brow
of a hill'). The Irish resort has an Irish
name, with *bri* meaning 'hill'. (Neither
word is related to the modern Scottish
'brae', which although meaning 'steep
bank' is of Scandinavian origin.) In the
case of the Irish resort, the reference is to
nearby Bray Hill, which rises to almost 800
feet. The English Bray is on ground rising
from the THAMES.

Brechin (Tayside)
The name of this manufacturing and
market town west of MONTROSE is based
on the same personal name that occurs in
BRECON, which is the British (Celtic) name
Brychan. The name thus means 'Brychan's

place'. A document dated about 1145 records the name in exactly the same spelling as now.

Breckland (Norfolk)
Both an administrative district of central and southern Norfolk and a large area of sandy heath on the borders of Norfolk and Suffolk, where it is mostly planted with conifers. The name means literally 'broken land', from the Old English *bræc*, 'broken land', 'land that is difficult to cultivate'. In the present century the Forestry Commission has embarked on a vast tree-planting programme here. Earlier, the area was simply barren heathland.

Brecknock (Powys)
An administrative district in the new county, and formerly an alternative anglicised form of BRECON.

Brecon (Powys)
The name of this market town north of MERTHYR TYDFIL derives from the personal name Brychan, so it can be understood as 'Brychan's place'. Brychan was a fifth-century Welsh prince. A development of the name was the Welsh *Brycheinioc*, recorded in the fifteenth century. This is the same name with the 'territorial' suffix *-ioc*, and it was this form that came to be anglicised as BRECKNOCK. However, the town's current Welsh name is Aberhonddu, meaning '(place at the) mouth of the Honddu'. *Aber-* means 'mouth' as in many other names of coastal places or places at the confluence of two rivers, while Honddu means 'pleasant', 'easy', and is related to the modern Welsh *hawdd*. Brecon is thus at the confluence of the Honddu and the USK. *See also* BRECON BEACONS.

Brecon Beacons (Powys)
A range of mountains to the south and southwest of BRECON. They are called 'Beacons' because they were used as sites for signal fires in medieval times (*compare* BEACONSFIELD, DUNKERY BEACON).

The Welsh name is Bannau Brycheiniog, 'peaks of the Brechin district'. The two highest peaks are Pen-y-Fan ('head of the peaks') and Corn Du ('black top'). The mountains have given their name to the Brecon Beacons National Park, designated in 1957, although this covers a wider area, extending from the Black Mountain in the west to the BLACK MOUNTAINS in the east.

Brent (Greater London)
A borough of northwest LONDON that contains the districts of WEMBLEY and WILLESDEN. It takes its name from the River Brent that flows through it. The river name means 'holy one', 'mighty one', and is of British (Celtic) origin, relating to the tribal name Brigantes, the ancient people of northern Britain who had their capital at what is now Aldborough (*see* BOROUGHBRIDGE). The river's name can be thought of as the name of its pagan goddess. It was recorded in a document of about 974 as *Brægentan*. *Compare* BRENTFORD.

Brentford (Greater London)
A district of the borough of HOUNSLOW whose name means 'ford over the River Brent' (*see* BRENT). This was recorded in the early eighth century as *Bregunt ford*. The actual ford was probably at a point where the present Commerce Road runs down to join the High Street (A315), in the west of the town.

Brentwood (Essex)
This town, southwest of CHELMSFORD, has a name that means 'burnt wood' (so it is not related to BRENTFORD). The earliest record of it is in a document of 1176, where it appears in medieval Latin as *Boscus Arsus*. In 1227 the name appears in Norman French as *Bois Ars*, which suggests that it was meaningful until at least the thirteenth century and that it arose after the Norman Conquest (of 1066). The inference is that the remains of the fire that destroyed the wood, formerly between

LONDON and CHELMSFORD along what is now the A12, were visible for many years.

Bressay (Shetland)

An island, lying east of MAINLAND, whose name may mean 'breast-shaped island', deriving from the two Old Norse words *brjóst* (breast) and *ey* (island). This description would certainly fit the island's highest eminence, the conical hill called the Ward of Bressay, although there are other rounded hills in its vicinity.

Bridgend (Mid Glamorgan)

A name found widely in Britain applying to a settlement that arose by a bridge over a river or stream, with '-end' implying that the location was that portion of an estate that was close to the bridge. The best-known Bridgend is the town on the River OGMORE west of CARDIFF. Its name was recorded in 1535 as *Byrge End*, and the site here was that of a Norman castle used to protect the river crossing. Today the town is traditionally divided into Newcastle, on the west bank of the river, and Oldcastle, on the east bank. There is no trace of the 'old' castle, while the ruins of the 'new' one, which dates from the twelfth century, stand on a spur of a nearby hill. The town's corresponding Welsh name is Pen-y-bont ar Ogwr, 'head of the bridge over the Ogmore'.

Bridge of Allan (Central)

This residential town north of STIRLING has a name of a type found elsewhere in Scotland, with the last word the name of the river crossed by the particular bridge. The word order ('Bridge of X' rather than 'X Bridge') reflects that of the Gaelic original, and is found in other names not relating to bridges, such as BOAT OF GARTEN. (It is found in other Celtic languages, too, such as Wales's PONTYPOOL and PONTYPRIDD, and the many 'Port-' names in Ireland, such as PORTADOWN and PORTAFERRY, where the generic word precedes the particular.) The town is south of the Strath Allan, or

valley of the ALLAN WATER. *Compare* BRIDGE OF WEIR.

Bridge of Weir (Strathclyde)

A small town west of PAISLEY on the River Gryfe, so it does not take its name from that of the river, as is often the case in names of this type, but from that of the weir here.

Bridgewater Canal (Greater Manchester/Cheshire)

Although a suitable name for a canal with bridges, the reference is actually to the title of the Dukes of Bridgewater, who were responsible for planning and building this canal, which links the LEEDS and LIVERPOOL Canal at LEIGH (Greater MANCHESTER) with the TRENT and MERSEY Canal at Preston Brook in Cheshire. It was the third Duke, Francis Egerton, who financed the construction of the canal in the seven-year period from 1759 to 1765. The Dukes took their title from BRIDGWATER in Somerset.

Bridgnorth (Shropshire)

A town west of WOLVERHAMPTON, and the administrative district in which it is situated. They are named after a bridge over the River SEVERN here, which was sited further north than the earlier bridge over the river at Quatford, two miles southeast of Bridgnorth. The name was recorded simply as *Brug* in 1156 and as *Brugg Norht* in 1282.

Bridgwater (Somerset)

A town northeast of TAUNTON on the River Parrett, although this is not the 'water' of the name. The Domesday Book records the name as *Brugie*, and the place was originally known simply as 'The Bridge', as many such settlements were by bridges (*compare* BRIDGNORTH). A later text of 1194 gives the name as *Brigewaltire*, showing that the true sense of the name is 'Walter's bridge'. The personal name was that of the Norman owner of the bridge, Walter de Dowai. The addition of a personal name to distinguish places of the same name was quite common. Usually, however, it was an owner's surname (as at MELTON MOWBRAY), not a Christian name.

Bridlington (Humberside)

The name of this seaside resort and port north of HULL means 'settlement of Beorhtel's people', and was recorded in the Domesday Book as *Bretlinton*. The personal name is based on the Old English *beorht* (bright), and so is similar to that of the man after whom BRIGHTON is named.

Bridport (Dorset)

A market town west of DORCHESTER near the English Channel coast. The name means 'Bredy port', with Bredy the name of a former borough here, itself named after the River Bride. This river rises at the village of Little Bredy (which preserves the borough name) and flows south to enter the sea to the east of Bridport. 'Bredy' is of Celtic origin and means something like 'boiling one' (*compare* the modern Welsh *brydio* — to boil, to throb), with reference to its rapid current. Bridport itself is on the River Brit, however, and this river's name derives from that of the town (i.e. as a 'back formation').

Brierfield (Lancashire)

A textile town immediately southwest of NELSON whose name seems to mean what it says, 'field of briars', although the name is not found in early documents and is not even on a local map of 1786. No doubt it was given partly under the influence of nearby Briercliffe, southeast of Nelson, whose name is much older (recorded in the late twelfth century) and which has the similar meaning of 'cliff where briars grow'.

Brigg (Humberside)

An agricultural town east of SCUNTHORPE, originally known as Glanford Brigg, which means 'bridge by a ford where sports are held'. This unexpected meaning derives from the Old English *glēam* (revelry,

merrymaking), to which has been added the familiar *ford*, with Brigg representing the Old English *brycg* (bridge). The small river here is the Ancholme. The town's name has thus been recorded as *Glannford Brigg* in a document of 1235, and this version is found in texts down to at least the nineteenth century (there is an entry for *Glanford Brigg* and *Glamford Bridge* in *Cassell's Gazetteer of Great Britain and Ireland* of 1896). The administrative district in this part of the country is now officially known as GLANFORD.

Brighouse (West Yorkshire)

The name of this town, north of HUDDERSFIELD on the River CALDER, means almost what it says: 'houses by the bridge'. The plural form of the name can be seen in a document of 1240, which gives it as *Brighuses*. The river crossing here is an old one, and even now six different roads meet at Brighouse, including the main A641 HUDDERSFIELD to BRADFORD road. The pronunciation of 'bridge' here is influenced by the Old Norse word for it, which was *bryggja*.

Brightlingsea (Essex)

A yachting and boat-building town southeast of COLCHESTER near the mouth of the River Colne. Its name seems to suggest 'bright sea', but in fact means 'Beorhtric's island', with the Old English personal name (meaning 'bright ruler') followed by *ēg* (island), as for BATTERSEA. The original name can be deduced more clearly from the Domesday Book rendering of it, which was *Brictriceseia*. This does not incorporate the '-ling-', however, which may have been added to the personal name as a sort of 'pet' ending (in the same way that 'dear' became 'darling'). A text of 1212 thus gives the name as *Brihtlenggesseya*. The name could well have come to be abbreviated, in the way that BRIGHTON was.

Brighton (East Sussex)

The well-known seaside resort has a name that suggests 'bright' in the same way that

BRIGHTLINGSEA does. The original name meant 'Beorhthelm's enclosure', with the personal name meaning 'bright helmet' (implying good protection). This was recorded in the Domesday Book as *Bristelmestune*, and the long form of the name was in use as recently as the nineteenth century (as *Brighthelmstone*). The pronunciation by then was as now, however, and the name was shortened accordingly. In a sense, therefore, the suggestion of 'bright' is an accurate one, although from a man's name, not the sea.

Bristol (Avon)

A famous city and port whose name in essence means 'bridge place', since it derives from the Old English *brycg* (bridge) and *stōw* (place). In place-names, 'stow' normally implied either an assembly place or a holy place; here, the former meaning seems more likely, as the latter use occurs mostly in names that begin with a saint's name, such as PADSTOW. The original bridge of the assembly place may have been where Bristol Bridge is now, at the point where the modern A4 crosses the Floating Harbour. The final *l* of the name arose through Norman French influence (*compare* the modern French *beau* and *bel* as forms of the same word). Many Bristol people still sound a final *l* on words ending in a vowel; for example, Monica can become 'Monical', and Russia 'Russial'. An eleventh-century document gives the name simply as *Brycg stowe*, and the Domesday Book has it as *Bristou*. Later, the *l* came in, as in the spelling of 1200 as *Bristoll*.

Britain

The name of the island of Britain derives from that of her inhabitants, the Britons, whose own name was recorded by the Greeks in the fourth century BC as *Prettanoi*. This has traditionally been explained as meaning 'figured folk', 'tattooed people', from their habit of decorating their bodies (as some do still). The ancient Indo-European root word that gave their name is thus probably related to the Latin *curtus* (cut), with the initial *Pr*- appearing through Celtic influence. The Latin translation of the tribal name was *Picti*, giving the people we now know as the Picts, with this word more closely related to 'picture'. (It is likely, though, that the Picts themselves had some other name, which by coincidence is represented in the initial 'Pit-', probably meaning 'share', of such names as PITLOCHRY and PITTENWEEM.) The modern spelling of the name Britain came to us through Norman French, with this in turn being an adaptation of the Latin *Britannia*, the noun formed from the *Britannici*, the tribal name that was itself an adaptation of the Greek *Prettanoi* (but with *B*- replacing the *P*-). The same origin lies behind the name of Brittany (French *Bretagne*), to which many Britons fled when the Anglo-Saxons invaded mainland Britain. The medieval Latin name of Brittany was thus *Britannia Minor*, 'Little Britain', as distinct from *Britannia Major*, 'Great Britain'. This interpretation gave the current official name of the country as Great Britain, therefore, with this English version of the name recorded in a document of 1338, for instance, as *Bretaygne the grete*. The modern Welsh name of Britain is *Prydain*, retaining the Celtic *Pr*-.

Brittas Bay (Wicklow)

A popular stretch of sandy beach between WICKLOW and ARKLOW. Its name is based on the settlement of Brittas here, whose own name represents the Irish *briotás* (brattice) — a brattice was a type of wooden tower used in siege operations, or a covered gallery on the wall of a castle. There would have been a need for a defensive position here along the coast road. The Irish name of the place is Cuan an Bhriotáis, 'harbour of the brattice'.

Brixham (Devon)

This coastal town south of TORQUAY had its name recorded in the Domesday Book as *Briseham*. The name could mean either

'Beorhtsige's village' or 'Brioc's village';
the former personal name is an Old English
one (meaning 'bright victory'), also found
in BRIXTON (and the Devon village of
Brixton east of PLYMOUTH); the latter is a
Celtic one, also occurring in France in the
Breton village St Brieuc (where the name is
that of a sixth-century Breton saint).
Although one can assume that the final
element is the Old English *hām*
(homestead, village), a possible alternative
is *hamm* (enclosure, land by a river). The
interpretation of the name thus cannot be
conclusive.

Brixton (Greater London)
As mentioned in the entry for BRIXHAM,
this name contains the Old English
personal name Beorhtsige, and so means
'Beorhtsige's stone'. Now a district in the
borough of LAMBETH, Brixton was
recorded in a document of 1062 as *Brixges
stan*, showing that the second half of the
name is not '-ton' (meaning 'farm',
'village') but refers to a stone, probably a
natural rock used as a landmark or as a
meeting point for an assembly. As the
name was also that of a hundred here, the
latter seems more likely, although there is
little evidence to show where the stone was
located.

Broadford (Highland)
The main village on the Isle of SKYE. The
English name is a translation of the Gaelic
an t-Ath leathan, 'the broad ford', referring
to the ford over the river here, now called
the Broadford.

Broads, The (Norfolk)
A series of narrow lakes connected by
channels and rivers and surrounded by
marshes, well known as a habitat for
wildfowl. (One lake, OULTON BROAD, is
over the border in Suffolk.) The name
refers to the wider waters of the lakes, by
contrast with the 'narrows' of the rivers,
channels, and various 'cuts' here. The
name seems to have come into use some
time in the eighteenth century.

Broadstairs (Kent)
The name of this coastal resort, north of
RAMSGATE, means more or less what it
says, and refers to a 'broad stairway' that
was apparently built in the cliffs here to
gain access to the sea some time in the
fifteenth century. The earliest known
record of the name is one of 1434 which
speaks of *Brodsteyr Lynch*. The second
word represents the Old English *hlinc*
(ridge, bank), and although this could
mean a natural bank, it was probably part
of the original man-made 'stair', unless it
was the original ledge on which this was
cut.

Broadway (Hereford and Worcester)
A town, below the COTSWOLDS southeast
of EVESHAM, whose name means 'broad
road', that is, the one by which the
settlement originally arose. This is not
the town's present main road (the A44) but
the older, now more minor one, that runs
from north to south up the valley to the
small village of Snowshill. The town's
name was recorded in 972 as *Bradanuuege*.

Brockenhurst (Hampshire)
A village south of LYNDHURST on the
south edge of the NEW FOREST. Its name
almost certainly means 'Broca's wooded
hill', rather than 'broken wooded hill', as
has also been proposed. The name in the
Domesday Book is *Broceste*.

Brockworth (Gloucestershire)
This town, southeast of GLOUCESTER, has
a descriptive name that means 'brook
enclosure', from the Old English *brōc*
(brook, stream) and *worth* (also occurring
as *worthig* and *worthign*) meaning
'enclosure'. The Domesday Book has the
name as *Brocowardinge*.

Brodick (Strathclyde)
A port and resort on Brodick Bay in the
Isle of ARRAN. It has an Old Norse name
meaning simply 'broad bay', comprising
breithr (broad) and *vík* (creek, inlet, bay).
The Gaelic name of Brodick is Traigh a'

Chaisteil, 'beach of the castle'. This refers to Brodick Castle, which dates back to at least the fourteenth century.

Bromley (Greater London)
A borough in southeast London, whose name is found elsewhere in the country and means 'broom clearing' or 'forest clearing where broom grows'. The London Bromley was recorded in 862 as *Bromleag*, representing the two Old English words *brōm* (broom) and *lēah* (clearing). *Compare* BROMPTON; BROMYARD. *See also* BRAMPTON; BRAUNTON.

Brompton (North Yorkshire)
A suburb of NORTHALLERTON whose name is found elsewhere in the country and means 'broom farm' or 'farm where broom grows'. This particular Brompton was recorded in the Domesday Book as *Bruntone*. *Compare* BROMLEY.

Bromsgrove (Hereford and Worcester)
The name of the town, southwest of BIRMINGHAM, does not mean 'grove where broom grows', as might be supposed from similar names such as BROMPTON and BROMYARD. This is shown by a text of 804 recording the name as *Bremesgrefan*, which means 'Breme's grove', from an Old English personal name and the word *grǣfe* (grove, thicket). Bromsgrove is now also the name of an administrative district here.

Bromyard (Hereford and Worcester)
An old market town west of WORCESTER whose name means 'broom enclosure', like BROMLEY and BROMPTON. The Old English word giving the second half of the name is *geard*, related to the modern 'yard' and 'garden'. Bromyard was recorded as *Bromgeard* in a document of about 840, and as *Bromgerde* in the Domesday Book.

Brooklands (Surrey)
A former motor-racing circuit, now an industrial site north of BYFLEET. The name simply means 'land by the brook',

and occurs elsewhere in Britain, as in districts of MANCHESTER and SALE.

Brora (Highland)
This Scottish east-coast village northeast of GOLSPIE takes its name from the river at whose mouth it lies. The river name is of Old Norse origin, and simply means 'river of the bridge', from the Old Norse *brú*, genitive *brúar* (bridge) and *á* (river). Normally a bridge will be named after the river it crosses, but here the reverse is true because the particular bridge was for long the only bridge in SUTHERLAND. The village name can thus be understood as 'place by the river that has a bridge'. A document of 1499 gives the name as *Strabroray*, with the first half of this referring to Sutherland.

Broseley (Shropshire)
An urban area south of IRONBRIDGE with a name meaning 'Burgheard's clearing', from an Old English personal name (meaning 'fort protection') and the common word *lēah* (clearing in a forest). A text dated 1194 has the name as *Burgardeslega*. *See also* BURSLEM.

Brough (Derbyshire, Humberside, Nottinghamshire)
A hamlet west of Hathersage (Derbyshire); a community on the north bank of the HUMBER west of HULL; and a hamlet on the FOSS WAY northeast of NEWARK-ON-TRENT. All three are on the sites of Roman camps, respectively: *Navio* (from the river here, the Noe, whose name means 'fast-flowing water'); *Petuaria* (from the Celtic word for 'fourth', denoting one of four tribal districts here); and *Crococalana* (perhaps meaning 'tumulus settlement'). There are other Broughs, too, with all their names deriving from the Old English *burg* (fort), and every fort being a Roman camp.

Broughty Ferry (Tayside)
A district of DUNDEE that arose at a point on the River TAY where a ferry crossed from a bank (Gaelic *bruach*) to where

TAYPORT now stands on the south side of the Firth of Tay. The Gaelic word thus provides the first part of the name, and the English 'ferry' the second. The name was recorded in 1595 as *Brochty*.

Brownhills (West Midlands)
This town, in a coal-mining area northeast of WALSALL, has a self-explanatory name, referring to the brown-coloured hills here south of CANNOCK CHASE.

Brownsea Island (Dorset)
The largest island in POOLE Harbour and now a nature reserve. Its earlier name was Branksea Island; this was recorded in 1276, for example, as *Brunkeseye*. The latter part of this is certainly the Old English *īeg* (island); the first part may be a personal name, such as Brunoc, or perhaps an early conjectural word related to the modern 'brink'. If the latter, the reference could be to the several steep slopes on the island. The original name of Branksea was 'smoothed' to Brownsea which is more meaningful (although wrongly so).

Brown Willy (Cornwall)
A granite tor on BODMIN Moor southeast of CAMELFORD, and the highest point in the county. It is a corruption of the two Cornish words *bron*, 'hill' (literally 'breast') and the plural *guennol*, 'swallows'. So the overall sense is 'breast-shaped hill of the swallows'.

Broxbourne (Hertfordshire)
Both a southern suburb of HODDESDON and an administrative district. The name means 'badger stream' or 'stream where badgers are found', from the Old English *brocc* (badger; *compare* the popular name 'Brock') and *burna* (stream). The name was recorded in the Domesday Book as *Brochesborne*. *Compare* BROXBURN.

Broxburn (Lothian)
A town west of EDINBURGH whose name is the counterpart of BROXBOURNE, i.e. 'badger stream'. It was recorded in 1638 as *Broxburne*. The Broxburn is itself the name of a stream near the town.

Broxtowe (Nottinghamshire)
An administrative district in the southwest of the county that has the name of a former hundred here, recorded in the Domesday Book as *Brochelestou*, meaning 'Brocwulf's place'. In local use, Broxtowe is also a northwest suburb of NOTTINGHAM.

Bruton (Somerset)
A small town southeast of SHEPTON MALLET on the River Brue. It is named after the river, being recorded in the Domesday Book as *Briwetone*. The river name, meaning 'fast-flowing' or 'vigorous', is Celtic, and is related to the modern Welsh *bryw* (lively, brisk).

Bryher (Isles of Scilly)
The smallest of the five populated islands in the group. Its name derives from a conjectural Cornish word *bre*, 'hill' (*compare* BRAY in Ireland), with the plural ending *-yer*; the meaning as a whole is thus 'place of hills'. The hills referred to were probably those of both Bryher and an adjoining island that is now submerged. The name was recorded in 1319 as *Braer*.

Brynmawr (Gwent)
An industrial town, west of ABERGAVENNY, that developed in the nineteenth century and has a Welsh name meaning 'big hill'. The name was recorded in 1832 as *Bryn-mawr*, but previous to this the site was known as *Gwaun-helygen*, 'moorland of the willow tree'. It seems that this was changed deliberately to give a simpler and 'grander' name to the new development. Brynmawr does indeed command an elevated location, on the southern edge of the BRECON BEACONS National Park.

Buchan (Grampian)
A stretch of countryside in the northeast of the district, extending roughly from the BANFF to TURRIFF road (the A947)

eastwards to the coast. The name means 'place of cows' (Old Welsh *buwch* with the suffix *-an*), and was recorded in a document of about 1150 exactly as now.

Buckfastleigh (Devon)

A market and manufacturing town northwest of TOTNES. The name means 'forest clearing of Buckfast', this latter being the name of a village to the north. Buckfast itself means 'buck's stronghold', from the Old English *bucc* (male deer) and *fæsten* (stronghold, i.e. 'fastness'). Buckfastleigh was recorded in the thirteenth century as *Leghe Bucfestre*. A 'stronghold' would have been an area of more or less inaccessible land, such as an 'island' of firm land in a marsh or swamp. Buckfast is in an area of moorland at the southern edge of DARTMOOR Forest.

Buckhaven (Fife)

The town and port on the north coast of the FIRTH OF FORTH, northeast of KIRKCALDY, has a name that seems to mean what it says — 'harbour where bucks are found'. The town was founded only in about 1550, and its name was recorded in 1605 as *Buckheven*.

Buckhurst Hill (Essex)

An extensive residential area to the south of EPPING Forest that derives its name from a hill here, itself named after its beech trees (Old English *bōc-hyrst*, 'beech grove').

Buckie (Grampian)

A fishing town and resort on SPEY Bay east of ELGIN. It has a name based on the Gaelic *boc* (buck), with this apparently taken from the stream on which it stands — the Burn of Buckie. The name was recorded in a document of 1362 as *Buky*.

Buckingham (Buckinghamshire)

The name of this town, west of BLETCHLEY, can be understood as 'land in a bend of the river that belongs to Bucca's people'. The '-ing-' of the name indicates the people who were in some way

associated with Bucca, and the final '-ham' represents the Old English *hamm*, 'land in a river bend' (as distinct from *hām*, 'homestead', 'village'). The town lies in a bend of the River OUSE. The name was recorded in 918 as *Buccingahamme*; the county name appears in a document of 1016 as *Buccingahamscir*.

Buckley (Clwyd)

A Welsh town north of WREXHAM whose name appears to mean simply 'beech clearing' or 'clearing in a beech forest', from the Old English *boc* (beech) and *lēah* (forest, clearing). The Welsh name is Bwcle, apparently influenced by the Welsh *bwcl* (buckle).

Bude (Cornwall)

A north-coast resort northwest of LAUNCESTON on the stream called the Bude. The town takes its name from the stream name, which may mean 'turbulent', from a Celtic root word probably also behind the name of the River Boyd in Avon. The town's name was recorded in a text of 1400 exactly as now. *See also* STRATTON.

Budleigh Salterton (Devon)

The south-coast resort east of EXMOUTH has a name that means 'salt works at Budleigh'. Salterton thus derives from a combination of the Old English *sealt* (salt) and *ærn* (building), with a final '-ton' that should not really be there. Budleigh means 'Budda's clearing', from the Old English personal name with the common *lēah* (clearing), here found as '-leigh' rather than '-ley'. The name as a whole was recorded in 1210 as *Saltre*, showing that there must have been salt pans here at the mouth of the River Otter in medieval times. In 1405 the name was noted as *Salterne in the manor of Buddeleghe*.

Buildwas (Shropshire)

The name of this village, northeast of MUCH WENLOCK, looks Welsh but is in fact English, from the two words *byld* (conjectural) 'building' and *wæsse* (conjectural) 'wet place', 'marsh'. The overall meaning is thus 'marshy place with a building', and indeed the ground is low-lying here beside the River SEVERN. The village was recorded in the Domesday Book as *Beldewes*.

Builth Wells (Powys)

'Builth' is an English rendering of the Welsh *buellt* (cow pasture), with this word comprising *bu* (cow) and *gellt* (later, *gwellt*; grass, pasture). 'Wells' was added in the nineteenth century when it was found that the chalybeate springs here attracted visitors from England, so the word was both descriptive and of commercial value. The Welsh name of the town (north of BRECON) is Llanfair-ym-Muallt, 'St Mary's in the cow pasture', with this originally the designation of the parish church. (The last word of the Welsh name represents the first word of the English equivalent. It seems likely that the spelling of the Welsh word may have been influenced by *allt*, 'hill'.) The earliest record we have of the name is a tenth-century one, as *Buelt*.

Buncrana (Donegal)

A town standing on the eastern shore of Lough SWILLY at the mouth of the River Crana. Its name describes this location, deriving from the Irish Bun Cranncha, 'mouth of the Crana'. The river's name means 'tree-lined', from the Irish *crann* (tree). The first element of the name — Irish *bun* (end, river-mouth) — also occurs in BUNDORAN.

Bundoran (Donegal)

A resort on DONEGAL Bay at the mouth of the River Dobhrán; its Irish name denotes this — Bun Dobhráin, 'mouth of the Dobhrán'. The river's name means 'otter' (Irish *dobhrán*). Compare the River Otter in Devon (*see* OTTERY ST MARY).

Bungay (Suffolk)

A town southeast of NORWICH whose name probably means 'island of Buna's people', with 'island' referring to the location of Bungay in a loop of the River WAVENEY. The Domesday Book recorded the name as both *Bongeia* and *Bunghea*. The final element of the name is Old English *ēg* (island), while the single letter g represents the Old English element *-ing*, meaning 'people of'.

Buntingford (Hertfordshire)

A small town north of WARE with a straightforward name that means precisely what it says — 'ford where buntings are found'. The ford here would have been over the little River Rib. Buntingford's name was recorded in a document of 1185 more or less as now, *Buntingeford*.

Burford (Oxfordshire)

This attractive COTSWOLD town west of WITNEY was recorded in the *Anglo-Saxon Chronicle* of 752 as *Beorgfeord*, showing its derivation from the Old English *beorgford*, 'hill ford'. Burford is set in a hilly location, and the ford would have been over the River WINDRUSH here.

Burgess Hill (West Sussex)

The town of Burgess Hill north of BRIGHTON is a fairly modern development, which arose here after the opening of the Brighton Railway in the mid-nineteenth century. The name thus originally referred to a hill at this location, which itself was associated with a family named Burgess or Burgeys. Records of the thirteenth and fourteenth centuries show that a family named Burgeys lived at the village of Clayton, south of Burgess Hill; they could have been the ones indicated by the present name.

Burgh-by-Sands (Cumbria)

A village northwest of CARLISLE, sited on what was almost certainly the line of HADRIAN'S WALL. Its name indicates this defensive structure, as it derives from the Old English *burg* (fort), with the second part of the name added to distinguish it from other places named Burgh. The 'Sands' are the sandy soil here near the SOLWAY FIRTH. The name was recorded as simply *Burgh* in about 1220, then as *Burgh on the Sands* in a document of 1247. Places named Burgh frequently denote a Roman fort or defensive position, such as Burgh-on-Bain and Burgh-le-Marsh, both in Lincolnshire. This Cumbria Burgh is pronounced 'Bruff' (*compare* BROUGH).

Burnham Beeches (Buckinghamshire)
An area of beech woodland northwest of SLOUGH and a nearby suburb of Slough, formerly a distinct village. Burnham almost always means 'homestead by a stream', from the Old English *burna* (stream) and *hām* (homestead, village). The name is common and frequently has a distinguishing addition, as for BURNHAM-ON-CROUCH and BURNHAM-ON-SEA. Here, the second word is really the generic one, itself distinguished by the first. The settlement name was recorded in about 880 in exactly the same spelling as now, although in the Domesday Book it was *Burneham*. The beeches here have long been recognised as some of the finest and oldest specimens in the country.

Burnham-on-Crouch (Essex)
A town and yachting centre on the estuary of the River CROUCH southeast of MALDON. Like most other Burnhams, its name means 'homestead by a stream'. The 'stream' here is not the river, which is really an inlet of the sea at this point, but the stream to the north of the present town. The Ordnance Survey map of 1840 shows two distinct Burnhams here about three-quarters of a mile apart, with the northern one right by the stream. It seems that the riverside Burnham borrowed its neigh-bour's name, added '-on-Crouch' to be dis-tinguished from it, and eventually merged with it. *See also* BURNHAM BEECHES.

Burnham-on-Sea (Somerset)
A small resort north of BRIDGWATER whose name means 'riverland by a stream',

unlike that of BURNHAM BEECHES and BURNHAM-ON-CROUCH. The name was recorded in a document of about 880 as *Burnhamm*, showing that the second element is not the Old English *hām* (homestead), but *hamm* (riverside land). The 'stream' would be the River Brue (*see* BRUTON), which enters the BRISTOL Channel just south of the town. The addition '-on-Sea' was probably made in quite recent times, more for commercial reasons than for distinguishing the town from other Burnhams.

Burnley (Lancashire)
An industrial town north of MANCHESTER lying at the confluence of the rivers Brun and CALDER. Its name refers to the former of these, meaning 'clearing by the River Brun'. The second part of the name is the Old English *lēah* (forest clearing). The river name means 'brown one', referring to the colour of its waters. Burnley's name was recorded in 1124 as *Brunlaia*. The change from 'Brun-' to 'Burn-' may have come about by association with other names that begin with the latter element, such as the BURNHAMS.

Burntisland (Fife)
A shipbuilding town southwest of KIRKCALDY whose name seems to mean what it says: 'burnt island'. The reference may be to a fire on a small island to the west of the present town where some fishermen's huts were destroyed some time in the early sixteenth century. On the other hand, the name was recorded in 1543 as *Brunteland*, which could be interpreted simply as 'burnt land', and denote land here that was deliberately cleared for cultivation by burning.

Burry Port (Dyfed)
This small town and port west of LLANELLI has a name that derives from the sand dunes here, locally known as 'burrows', with this word itself a development of the Old English *beorg* (mound, hill).

Burslem (Staffordshire)
One of the 'Five Towns' that comprise
STOKE-ON-TRENT. Its name means
'Burgheard's territory in Lyme Forest',
with the first part of the name a contraction
of the personal name (with the possessive *s*)
and the latter half the name of the great
forest, also found in the names of
ASHTON-UNDER-LYNE and NEWCASTLE-
UNDER-LYME. The forest name itself
means literally 'elm place', and the
personal name is the same as that
in BROSELEY. In the Domesday
Book, Burslem appears as
Barcardeslim.

Burton Latimer (Northamptonshire)
Burton is a very common place-name meaning 'farm of the fortified place', from the Old
English *burg* (fort) and *tūn* (farm,
settlement). As the name is found so frequently, it often takes an additional word for
purposes of distinction. In the case of Burton
Latimer, the town southeast of KETTERING,
the second word represents the name of
William le Latymer, who is recorded as
having held the manor here in 1323. His
Norman surname means 'interpreter'
(literally 'latiner', i.e. 'one who can
translate Latin'). The town's name was
recorded in the Domesday Book simply as
Burtone. Compare BURTON-UPON-TRENT.
See also BOURTON-ON-THE-WATER.

Burton-upon-Trent (Staffordshire)
As mentioned in the entry for BURTON
LATIMER, the common name Burton
almost always means 'farm of the fortified
place'. This is therefore the sense here,
with the distinguishing addition referring
to the River TRENT, on which the
industrial town is located southwest of
DERBY. The name was recorded in a
document of 1002 as *Byrtun*, where the first
half of the name represents the genitive
(*byrh*) of the Old English *burg* (fort).

Burtonwood (Cheshire)
A town northwest of WARRINGTON whose
name can be understood as 'wood by

Burton', although where the original
Burton was has not been established. The
name was recorded in 1228 as
Burtoneswood.

Bury (Greater Manchester)
A town north of MANCHESTER whose
name ultimately derives from the Old
English *burg* (fort), as in the BURTON
names. Grammatically, it is actually the
dative of this (*byrig*), which had the
meaning 'at the fort', meaning a place by a
fort; the name appears in a document dated
1194 as *Biri. Compare* BURY ST EDMUNDS.

Bury St Edmunds (Suffolk)
Bury is a fairly common name, and so is
frequently found with a distinguishing
addition, as here. As noted in the entry for
BURY, the basic meaning is 'place by a
fort', although in the case of Bury St
Edmunds, the town northwest of IPSWICH,
the Old English *burg* had come to mean
'town' rather than 'fort' when used for the
name here. The latter part of the name
refers to St Edmund, who was killed in 869
by Viking invaders and who soon came to
be revered as a saint and martyr. His
remains were interred at Bury, which at the
time was called *Beadriceswyrth* ('Beaduric's
enclosure'), and a small monastic
community was established there to
safeguard them. In the eleventh century,
when the much larger Benedictine
monastery had been founded and the place
had become an important religious centre,
the original name was superseded by the
present one, to commemorate St Edmund.
It was thus recorded in 1038 as *Sancte
Eadmundes Byrig* (a name revived for the
administrative district of ST
EDMUNDSBURY); subsequently, the word
order was reversed. For another example of
burg meaning 'town' rather than 'fort', *see*
NEWBURY.

Bushey (Hertfordshire)
A residential town southeast of WATFORD
whose name probably means 'enclosed
place by a thicket' — literally 'bush hedge',

with the two Old English components being *bysc* (bush, thicket) and *hæg* (hedge). Although the two words can be reasonably supposed to combine in this way, the resulting sense is not very clear, since a thicket hardly requires a neighbouring hedged-in place. The Domesday Book recorded the name as *Bissei*. An alternative name for Bushey in medieval times was 'Hartshead' (recorded as *Hertesheved* in the fourteenth century), and some texts call the place by a combination of both names, as does one of 1346, which has *Bissheyehertesheved*. For the sense of 'Hartshead', see the similarly named GATESHEAD.

Bushmills (Antrim)
A small town east of PORTRUSH. The Irish name is Muileann na Buaise, meaning 'mill of the Bush', which refers to the river on which it stands and to the mill here, around which the town arose.

Bute (Strathclyde)
An island in the Firth of CLYDE, separated from the mainland by the KYLES OF BUTE. Its name is said to derive from the Gaelic *bochd* (fire), probably referring to signal fires lit here. The name was recorded in 1093 as *Bot*.

Butetown (South Glamorgan)
A dockland region of CARDIFF whose name derives from that of the second Marquis of Bute (John Crichton-Stuart), who in the nineteenth century developed several local industrial enterprises, including the docks.

Buttermere (Cumbria)
One of the lakes in the Lake District, southwest of DERWENT WATER. Its name means what it says: 'butter lake', i.e. a lake with neighbouring rich pastures for grazing, where cows will produce

good milk to make butter. In a text of 1343 the name appears as *Water of Buttermere*.

Buttevant (Cork)
The name of this town, north of MALLOW, has been popularly held to derive from the French war-cry of the de Barrys, *Boutez en avant*, 'press forward'. The true source is much more likely to be the Norman French *botavant*, a term for the defensive outwork of a fortification. The Irish name is quite different: Cill na Mallach, 'church of the summits'.

Buxton (Derbyshire)
An inland spa southeast of MANCHESTER with a name meaning literally 'rocking stone', from the Old English *būgan* (to bend — which gave the modern 'buxom') and *stān* (stone). There must once have been such a stone near here, but it has not been traced or identified. Buxton was recorded in a document of about 1105 as *Buchestanes*, showing that the latter half of the name is not the usual '-ton' but effectively 'stone'. The name gives no indication that Buxton arose on the site of a Roman spa, known as *Aquae Arnemetiae*, 'waters of Arnemetia'; the latter is the name of a Roman goddess, meaning 'before the sacred grove' (*compare* the *Aquae Sulis* of BATH). The goddess's name is derived from British (Celtic) root elements.

Byfleet (Surrey)
A suburb northeast of WOKING whose name means 'place by a fleet', that is, by a stream (*compare* FLEET). The 'fleet' here is the River WEY, which also lies (directly) behind the name of WEYBRIDGE and (indirectly) that of GUILDFORD. Byfleet was recorded in the Domesday Book as *Biflet*.

Cadbury Castle (Somerset)
An Iron Age camp southeast of Sparkford. Its name means 'Cada's fort', with the personal name followed by the Old English *burg* (fortified place). There is another Cadbury Castle, also an Iron Age fort, northeast of the village of Cadbury in Devon. Its name has exactly the same origin. Named after the Somerset fort are also the nearby villages of North Cadbury and South Cadbury.

Cader Idris (Gwynedd)
A precipitous ridge southwest of DOLGELLAU. Its name means 'seat of Idris', the latter perhaps being a descendant of the Celtic chief Cunedda, whose name lies behind that of GWYNEDD, in which the mountain is situated. The 'seat' is thus fancifully his 'chair' here, as a kind of lofty throne. The central peak of the ridge is Pen y Gadair, 'head of the chair'. 'Cader' represents the Old Welsh conjectural *cadeir* (modern *cadair*), 'chair'. The personal name Idris has been explained as meaning 'impulsive lord', from *iud* (lord) and *ris* (ardent). Popular folklore explains Idris as a giant and magician, not a historical character.

Caerleon (Gwent)
A town northeast of NEWPORT on the River USK. It is the site of the Roman camp of *Isca*, whose name is directly related to that of the river. The full Roman name (although there are alternatives) was *Isca Legionis*, 'Isca of the legion', and this is represented by the present name of the town, which is half Welsh (*caer*, 'fort') and half Latin (*legionis*, 'of the legion'). The reference is to the Second Legion, who were stationed here when they moved from *Glevum* (GLOUCESTER) in AD 75. Another version of the fort's name was *Isca Silurum*, 'Isca of the Silures', the latter

being a tribe whose name is similarly recorded for an early version of the name of CAERWENT. *Compare* EXETER.

Caernarvon (Gwynedd)
A town and port near the southwest end of the Menai Strait (*see* MENAI BRIDGE); the name was formerly anglicised as Carnarvon, and is now properly the Welsh *Caernarfon*. Caernarvon arose round the Roman camp of *Segontium*, whose own name reflects that of the river here, the Seiont. The town's name means 'fort in ARFON', that is, a fort facing ANGLESEY. The river's name (which in its correct modern Welsh form is Saint) means 'vigorous one'. The first element of the town's name is the Welsh *caer* (fort), as for CAERLEON, CAERPHILLY, CAERSWS, and CAERWENT. *Compare* CAHIR.

Caerphilly (Mid Glamorgan)
A town north of CARDIFF. The first part of the name is the Welsh *caer* (fort), giving the overall meaning 'Ffili's fort'. It is not known who Ffili was. The Welsh form of the name is Caerffili, showing that the English version is a distorted reflection of the original; perhaps the spelling was influenced by 'Phillip'.

Caersws (Powys)
A large village west of NEWTOWN whose name means 'fort of Sws', with the Welsh *caer* (fort) as the first part of the name. Popular legend links the second part of the name with a Queen Susan, who is said to have had her administrative centre here. But the personal name remains unidentified. It may somehow link up with the Roman fort here, of which only slight traces remain.

Caerwent (Gwent)
A village southwest of CHEPSTOW whose name means 'fort of the favoured place', comprising the Welsh *caer* (fort) and a pre-Celtic root element *ven-*. The latter is apparent in both GWENT and WINCHESTER, and in the first word of the

name of the Roman camp here, which was *Venta Silurum*. The best parallel is with WINCHESTER, as both the Welsh *caer* and English *ceaster* (giving the '-chester') derive from the Latin *castra*. The Welsh name has the 'fort' element as a prefix, in the Celtic manner, while the English name has the same element after the name, as typical of English. The Roman name relates to the tribe known as the Silures, who had their capital here.

Cahir (Tipperary)
This town south of CASHEL has the Irish name of An Chathair, 'the stone fort', based on the Irish *cathair*, 'fort' (usually implying a stone fort). Its full name was *Cathair-duna-iascaigh*, 'fort of the fortification abounding in fish', with the 'fortification' (Irish *dún*) a rocky island in the River Suir here.

Cairngorms (Highland/Grampian)
A granite mountain mass between AVIEMORE and BRAEMAR. The name is pluralised from the highest peak, Cairn Gorm, whose name means 'blue rock', from the Gaelic *carn* (rock) and *gorm* (blue). The current English pronunciation of the name stresses the wrong syllable; in Gaelic it is the *gorm* (i.e. the colour) that is emphasised.

Caister-on-Sea (Norfolk)
The coastal resort north of YARMOUTH has a name representing the Old English *ceaster* (fort), implying a Roman fort (*compare* CAISTOR). The individual name of the Roman fort (*castra*) here is not known, and the settlement was called simply *Castra* in a record of about 1045. In the nineteenth century the resort was commonly known as *Caistor-next-Yarmouth*, so that the '-on-Sea' is a recent commercial addition.

Caistor (Lincolnshire)
As for CAISTER-ON-SEA, the name of this small town north of MARKET RASEN derives from the Old English *ceaster* (Roman fort), in turn from the Latin *castra*

(camp). The Roman fort might have been the one known as *Bannovalium* ('strong horn'), although an equally good claim to the name is held by HORNCASTLE (not least because of the 'horn' in both names).

Caithness (Highland)
A former Scottish county and now an administrative district in the northeast of the region. The name means 'promontory of the Cat people', with the Old Norse *nes* (headland, promontory) added to the Celtic tribal name. Little is known about these people, or why they were called (or called themselves) 'cats'. The name was recorded in about 970 as *Kathenessia*.

Calder (Highland, Lancashire, West Yorkshire, Cumbria)
Any of at least half a dozen rivers of the name in Britain, including two in Lancashire. In each instance, the Celtic name derives from two root words meaning 'violent' (modern Welsh *caled*, *see* CALEDONIAN CANAL) and 'water' (modern Welsh *dwfr*, *see* DOVER). So the rivers are 'rapid streams' or 'turbulent waters'. The Cumbrian river Calder gives the name of Calder Hall, the atomic power station north of Seascale, past which it flows. *See also* CALLANDER.

Caldicot (Gwent)
A town southwest of CHEPSTOW whose name derives from the Old English *calde cot*, literally 'cold hut'. The reference is to an exposed shelter for humans or animals. The Domesday Book version of the name was *Caldecote*.

Caldy Island (Dyfed)
An island at the southwest end of CARMARTHEN Bay. It has a Scandinavian name, as do many islands off the Welsh coast. It means, understandably enough, 'cold island', from the Old Norse *kald* (cold) and *ey* (island). Caldy is certainly exposed to the southwest winds and gales, which sweep across it unchecked. The Welsh name is Ynys Byr, 'Pyr's island'.

Pyr or Pyro was a sixth-century saint who established a religious community here; a Trappist monastery is still present. The island's name was recorded in a document dated about 1120 as *Caldea*. *See also* MANORBIER.

Caledon (Tyrone)

A historic village west of ARMAGH that derives its present name from the Earls of Caledon, who had their family seat here. The village's earlier name was Kenard, an anglicisation of the Irish name, Cionn Aird, meaning 'high head'.

Caledonian Canal (Highland)

A canal extending across Scotland from the North Sea (at the MORAY Firth) to the Atlantic (at Loch LINNHE). Its construction began in the early nineteenth century, and its name derives from the Roman name of Scotland, *Caledonia*, which is now more commonly applied to the Highlands (north of a line joining the Firths of CLYDE and FORTH). *Cal-* is a Celtic root meaning 'strong', 'turbulent', 'hard' (*compare* CALDER), and was a tribal name meaning 'hard men'. One thinks of hardy Highlanders and their 'hooches' and the name seems very apt. *Compare also* CALLANDER.

Calf of Man (Isle of Man)

A small island off the southwest extremity of the Isle of MAN. The name may suggest the calf of a leg, especially in view of the 'three-legged' symbol of the Isle of Man, but it actually means 'calf of a cow', denoting the smaller island's dependence on the larger, like a calf on its mother. The name is similarly found for other smaller islands, such as the Calf of Eday off Eday in the ORKNEYS, or the Calf of Mull off MULL. The word is Old Norse (*kalfr*) in origin, not English.

Calke Abbey (Derbyshire)

An eighteenth-century country house on the site of a former abbey, north of ASHBY DE LA ZOUCH. It takes its name from the nearby village of Calke, whose own name means 'chalk' or 'limestone' (referring to the soil), from the Old English *calc*.

Callander (Central)

A town and tourist centre northwest of STIRLING. Its name is related to that of the River CALDER and, less directly, to Caledonia. It denotes a place by a 'turbulent stream' (for the origin of the Celtic roots, *see* CALDER). In the case of Callander, this would refer to the River Teith on which it stands. The name of the town was recorded in 1504 as *Kalentare*.

Callington (Cornwall)

The Old Cornish name of Callington, a town northwest of SALTASH, was *Kellewik*, meaning 'forest grove', from *kelli* (grove) and a conjectural *gwyk* (forest) (*compare* GWEEK). To this, the Old English *tūn* (settlement) was added, while the *wik* of the original name became a misleading '-ing-'. The Domesday Book recorded the town's name as *Caluuitona*.

Calne (Wiltshire)

A town, east of CHIPPENHAM, named after the river on which it stands, now called the Marden Brook. The meaning is something like 'noisy stream', and the name is probably related to that of the CALDER, or at least the first part of this. The same origin lies behind the name of COLNE. The river's name was recorded as *Calne* in 955.

Calstock (Cornwall)

A former port on the TAMAR east of CALLINGTON. It is to the latter place that the name relates, for it means 'secondary settlement belonging to Callington', with the Old English *stoc* added to the first element of the former name of Callington, *Kellewik* (compare the similar relationship between BASINGSTOKE and Basing). The Domesday Book recorded Calstock as *Calestoch*.

Camber (East Sussex)

The seaside resort east of RYE has a Norman French name derived from *cambre* (chamber, room), apparently applied to the restricted area of the harbour here. The name was recorded in 1375 as *Camere* and in 1397 as *Portus Camera*.

Camberley (Surrey)

A residential and military town south of BRACKNELL that arose only in the early nineteenth century, when it was originally known as Cambridge Town, after the then Commander-in-Chief of the British Army, George William Frederick Charles, second Duke of Cambridge. When a railway station was opened here in 1877, however, the name was changed to Camberley to avoid confusion with CAMBRIDGE. The new name partly reflected the former name, while blending with other names ending in '-ley' in the region, such as the villages of Frimley, Eversley, and Yatesley. However, Camberley is still confused by many with CAMBERWELL.

Camberwell (Greater London)

A district in the Borough of SOUTHWARK whose name seems to mean 'spring at the crane stream', from the Old English *cran* (crane), *burna* (stream), and *wella* (spring, well). The Domesday Book gave the name as *Cambrewelle*.

Camborne (Cornwall)

A town west of TRURO. The latter half of the name is not the '-bourne' or '-burn' of such names as EASTBOURNE and BLACKBURN, which contain the Old English *burna* (stream). It is an entirely Cornish name, based on *cam* (crooked) and *bron* (hill; literally 'breast'). The name can thus be understood as 'place by a curving slope', and this is almost certainly a reference to Camborne Beacon, to the south of the town.

Cambrian Mountains (Wales)

Mountains extending from CADER IDRIS in the northwest to the BRECON BEACONS in the southeast. The name is based on *Cambria*, the Roman name for Wales, itself derived from the Welsh people's name for themselves, in modern Welsh *Cymry*. *Compare* CUMBERLAND; CUMBRIA.

Cambridge (Cambridgeshire)

A famous university town whose name tempts the popular misinterpretation as 'bridge over the Cam', for the river here is indeed the Cam. But the river's name derives as a 'back formation' from that of the town, so another origin must be sought for. In the eighth century, the Venerable Bede recorded the name of the place as *Grantacaestir*, meaning 'Roman camp on the River Granta', with the Old English *ceaster* (denoting the camp) added to the Celtic river name, which means 'marshy river'. (The river here is still known also as the Granta.) This name could have developed to GRANTCHESTER, but instead the original 'Grantabridge', recorded in the same eighth century as *Grontabricc*, developed into the modern 'Cambridge'. The change in pronunciation and spelling is due to the Normans, who found it difficult to pronounce *Gr-* so changed it first to *Cr-* then simply to *C-*. At the same time, they simplified the consonants *-ntbr-* in such versions of the name as *Cantbrige* to *-nbr-*, subsequently altering the *n* to *m* for further ease of pronunciation before *b*. The Domesday Book records the name halfway through its metamorphosis as *Cantebrigie*. The '-chester' of Bede's name implies a Roman camp here, and this was known as *Duroliponte*. The suggestion of the Latin *pons* (bridge; genitive *pontis*) here is coincidental, although undoubtedly the Romans did have a bridge over the river. The name basically means 'marshy land', from an Indo-European root element that eventually gave the English 'liquid', with this preceded by the Celtic *Duro-* element seen in other Roman place-names and meaning 'fort', 'walled town'. The overall sense is thus 'walled town in a marshy place', which certainly suits the location of Cambridge, on low-lying ground at the edge of the FENS. The county name was recorded in 1010 as *Grantabrycgscir*, showing the original form of the town's name. *See also* GODMANCHESTER.

Cambridge Heath (Greater London)
The railway traveller departing from Liverpool Street Station for CAMBRIDGE will probably notice that he passes through Cambridge Heath station on his way out of LONDON. However, early records of the name show that it has nothing to do with its position *en route* for Cambridge; a text of 1275, for example, gives the name as *Camprichthesheth*. The first part of this may be a personal name, such as Cantbeorht; the latter part is certainly the Old English *hæth* (heath). Hence, the name *may* mean something like 'Cantbeorht's heathland'.

Cambuslang (Strathclyde)
A town on the River CLYDE southeast of Glasgow. It has a name appropriate for its location and meaning 'river bend of the ship', from the Gaelic *camas* (bay, creek, crooked channel) (itself based on *cam* (bend); *compare* CAMBORNE), and *long* (ship) (not the Scots *lang*, 'long'). The name was recorded in 1296 as *Camboslanc*.

Camden Town (Greater London)
A district of LONDON, north of MARYLEBONE, that was laid out on the property of the Earl of Camden (Charles Pratt) towards the end of the eighteenth century; it is named after him. The Earl's own title comes from Camden Place, CHISLEHURST (formerly in KENT), which was in turn named after the sixteenth-century antiquarian (and writer on place-names) William Camden, whose surname came from CHIPPING CAMPDEN. The Earl had his seat at Bayham Abbey, East Sussex (near the Kent border), and its name is now a street name (Bayham Street) in Camden Town, as is the maiden name of his wife Elizabeth (Jeffreys Street), his own surname (Pratt Street), and his title (Camden Street). The borough of Camden here was named after Camden Town.

Camelford (Cornwall)
A small town north of BODMIN on the River Camel, after which it is named. The river's name means 'crooked stream', from the Cornish *cam* (crooked, bent) (*compare* CAMBORNE) and *pol* (pool, stream) (*compare* POLRUAN). The river name was recorded in a medieval Latin text of 1147 as *flumen Cambula*.

Campbeltown (Strathclyde)
Campbeltown, south of TARBERT, is the chief town and port of KINTYRE. It is named after Archibald Campbell, Earl of Argyle, who was granted the site here (formerly called Lochhead, 'head of the loch') in 1667, for the erection of a so-called 'burgh of barony' to be named after him. The loch here is now called Campbeltown Loch. This Campbeltown should not be confused with the smaller Campbelltown (now usually known as Ardersier) in Highland.

Campsie Fells (Central/Strathclyde)
A range of hills, to the north of GLASGOW, that takes its name from one of its individual hills, called Campsie; this name means 'crooked fairy hill', from the Gaelic *cam* (crooked) (*compare* CAMBORNE) and *sith* (fairy). 'Fells' comes from an Old Norse word *fjall* (hill). The *p* of the name may have arisen through a suggestion of 'camp', as sometimes found in hill names, especially those of historic sites such as Iron Age or Roman camps or forts.

Canning Town (Greater London)
The name of this region of NEWHAM, in what is now the recent development of LONDON'S Docklands, almost certainly derives from that of Sir Samuel Canning, of the India Rubber, Gutta Percha and Telegraph Works Company, which was based here in the nineteenth century. This company's managing director was Colonel Silver, who gave his name to SILVERTOWN.

Cannock (Staffordshire)
A coal-mining town northeast of
WOLVERHAMPTON whose name derives
from the Old English *cnocc* (hill), with the
particular reference doubtless to Shoal
Hill, west of the town. For ease of
pronunciation, the Normans inserted a
vowel between the initial *c* and the *n*, much
in the same way that King Cnut came to be
called Canute (similarly the French *canif*
(pen-knife) is related to the English
'knife'). Without this modification, the
town's name today would probably be
'Knock'. For similar 'easings' *see*
CAMBRIDGE, NOTTINGHAM, SALISBURY,
and SHREWSBURY. Cannock's name was
recorded in 1156 as *Cnot*.

Cannock Chase (Staffordshire)
An administrative district in the south of
the county, and also an elevated wooded
region to the north of CANNOCK, from
which the name derives. Cannock Chase
was formerly an enclosed royal hunting
ground, hence 'Chase'. *Compare*
CRANBORNE CHASE.

Canonbury (Greater London)
This district of ISLINGTON has a name
meaning 'manor of the canons', the latter
being the Augustinian canons at
Smithfield, to whom land was granted in
the thirteenth century. The Old English
burg, which usually translates as 'fort',
could also mean 'manor' in later names, as
here and in the name of FINSBURY.
Canonbury's name was recorded in a
document of 1373 as *Canonesbury*.

Canterbury (Kent)
The name of this famous cathedral city is
directly linked to that of the county in
which it is located, for its name means
'fortified place of the men of KENT'. The
name was recorded in about 900 as
Cantwaraburg. The first part of this denotes
the *Cantware*, 'people of Kent'; what is
now the county name is followed by the
Old English element -*ware*, meaning
'people of', 'inhabitants' (*compare*

TENTERDEN); in the modern name this
element has been smoothed to '-er'. The
Roman name was *Durovernum*, meaning
'walled town by an alder marsh', from the
Celtic root words *duro-* (walled town) and a
conjectural *uerno-* (alder, 'swamp where
alders grow') (compare the modern Welsh
gwern). If the Roman name had been
adopted or adapted by the Anglo-Saxons,
we might thus have had a 'Dorchester' here
today. Until about the end of the ninth
century, both *Dorubernia* and
Cantwaraburg were used for the settlement;
the latter version of the name later
prevailed.

Canvey Island (Essex)
An island on the north side of the THAMES
estuary whose name perhaps means 'Cana's
island'. The final part of the name is
certainly the Old English *ēg* (island), but
interpretation of the first part is made
difficult by the presence of the *v*. This
could represent an element '-ing-',
meaning 'people of', but it is too corrupt to
be certain. The name was recorded in 1255
as *Canaeveye*.

Capel Curig (Gwynedd)
A village west of BETWS-Y-COED, popular
with tourists. Its name means 'Curig's
chapel'. Curig was the son of Ilid, a
seventh-century Welsh saint, and the
church here is dedicated to him. Many
Welsh names with Capel as their basis have
a distinguishing addition, either a saint's
name or a descriptive word of some kind
(such as Capel Goch, 'red chapel', or the
commonly found Capel Dewi, 'David's
chapel').

Cape Wrath (Highland)
A headland at the northwest point of
SUTHERLAND whose name seems
appropriate for the stormy seas often
encountered here. But the name in fact
derives from the Old Norse *hvarf* (turning
point). The cape marks the point where
ships would alter course to follow the coast,
for example, turning south to enter The

MINCH if sailing westwards. The name was recorded in 1583 as *Wraith*.

Cappoquin (Waterford)
A market town west of DUNGARVAN, whose Irish name, Ceapach Coinn, translates as 'Conn's plot' and gave rise to the English version. It is not known who Conn was.

Caradon (Cornwall)
An administrative district in the east of the county that takes its name from Caradon Hill, on the southeast edge of BODMIN Moor. The hill's own name means 'tor hill', from the Cornish *carn* (rock-pile, tor), to which the Old English *dūn* (hill) has been added, possibly with the sense 'hill of Carn' when Carn itself became a district name. Either way, the present name of the hill is tautologous, containing a Cornish, Old English, and Modern English word for 'hill'! (For an identical analogy, *see* PENDLE HILL.)

Cardiff (South Glamorgan)
The capital city of Wales, whose name is the anglicisation of the Welsh Caerdydd, meaning 'fort on the TAFF', from the Welsh *caer* (fort) and the name of the river on which Cardiff stands. The name was recorded in 1106 as *Kairdiff*. A directly related name is LLANDAFF, the name of a district of Cardiff and the name of the cathedral.

Cardigan (Dyfed)
A town southwest of ABERYSTWYTH on the estuary of the River Teifi. Its name means 'Ceredig's land', otherwise CEREDIGION. This was the name of the district around the town after which, rather unusually, the town itself took its name. The Welsh name for Cardigan is Aberteifi, denoting the town's position at the mouth of the Teifi (*compare* similar Aber-names, such as ABERYSTWYTH). The town's name was recorded as *Kerdigan* in a document of 1194. *See* CEREDIGION.

Carisbrooke (Isle of Wight)
The village southwest of NEWPORT is famous for its castle, in which Charles I was imprisoned. The name may mean 'brook of Cary', referring to the name of the river or stream here, although no such name now exists. The latter half of the name is certainly the Old English *brōc* (brook). The name was recorded in about 1175 as *Karesbroc*. Any such river name would probably have had the same meaning as that which gave its name to CASTLE CARY. The present name of the brook at Carisbrooke is the Lukely Brook, which presumably was its original name before 'Cary'.

Carlingford (Louth)
A resort, southeast of NEWRY, that takes its name from Carlingford Lough, on which it lies. The last element of the name is not the English 'ford' but the Old Norse *fjórthr* (sea-inlet) (*compare* modern 'fjord'), while the first part of the name represents the Old Norse *kerling* (hag), with probable reference to the three mountain peaks here (now known as The Three Nuns, not 'The Three Hags'), which could have served as landmarks for ships entering the lough. The lough's earlier Irish name was *Snámh Each*, 'swimming-crossing of the horses'. Carlingford was itself a Viking trading centre.

Carlisle (Cumbria)
A cathedral city and industrial town west of NEWCASTLE UPON TYNE. Its name begins with the same Celtic *cair* (fort) found in several Welsh names, such as CAERNARVON and CARMARTHEN. The second half of the name represents the name of the Roman fort here, which was *Luguvalium*; this in turn derives from a Celtic personal name, Luguvallos, meaning 'strong as Lugus' (Lugus was the name of a Celtic god). The Roman name became smoothed and abbreviated to such an extent that by the eleventh century it was simply *Luel* (a text of about 1106 refers to the settlement as *Luel, quod nunc Carleol*

appellatur: 'Luel, which is now called Carleol'). The present spelling of the name is due to the influence of the Normans, who doubtless associated the latter half of the name with *isle* (modern French *île*), 'island'. The presence of a 'Car-' name so far north in Britain is a reminder of the extensive territory occupied by the Britons; this included virtually all western Britain south of the present Scottish border, including the more 'obvious' Celtic regions of Wales and Cornwall.

Carlow (Carlow)

A cathedral town and county capital south of ATHY. It is known as Ceatharlach in Irish, meaning 'four lakes'. There is no trace of the lakes now, but they may have been at the site where the rivers Burren and Barrow now meet. The region is very low-lying here, and drainage work has been carried out in the present century on the Barrow.

Carlton Towers (North Yorkshire)

The historic house west of GOOLE takes its name from the village of Carlton here. There are at least four villages of the name in the county, besides many others elsewhere in the country. The spelling Carlton or Carleton is usually found in the north of England and Midlands, and Charlton in the south. It means 'farm of the churls', the latter being one of the lower classes of peasant, above a serf but lower than a noble or thane. (Their boorish manners and way of life gave rise to the modern sense of 'churlish'.) Carlton is the Scandinavian form of the Old English combination *ceorla-tūn*, the first word of which is grammatically the genitive plural of *ceorl*.

Carluke (Strathclyde)

A Scottish town northwest of LANARK. The first half of the name is probably the Gaelic *carn* (cairn) (*compare* CARADON), although it could also be the Celtic 'Car-' (modern Welsh *caer*), 'fort', found in such names as CARMARTHEN and CARLISLE.

The second half of the name remains obscure, and could be a personal name or a place-name in its own right. The name as a whole was recorded in 1315 as *Carneluk*.

Carmarthen (Dyfed)

A town northwest of SWANSEA on the River TOWY. The first element of the name is the Old Welsh *cair* (modern *caer*), 'fort'. The rest of the name represents the British (Celtic) name *Maridunum*, meaning 'seaside fort', from the elements *mari-* (maritime) and *duno-* (fort) — Carmarthen is only ten miles from the sea (Carmarthen Bay). The original Celtic name gave the name of the Roman camp here, which was *Moridunum*, and it also lies behind the modern Welsh name of the town, which is Caerfyrddin (with *m* becoming *f* after *r*, as happens in Welsh). The name is thus really a tautology, with the word 'fort' occurring twice. By about the twelfth century the name had come to be misinterpreted as *caer* (fort) plus *Myrddin*, the latter taken to be a personal name and believed to be (or invented to be) that of a sixth-century warrior, who performed many wonderful deeds. The twelfth-century Benedictine monk, Geoffrey of Monmouth, then latinised this as *Merlinus* and incorporated the character into his account of the legends of King Arthur. Thus Merlin the magician was born!

Carnforth (Lancashire)

A town north of LANCASTER whose name was recorded in the Domesday Book as *Chreneford*, showing it to be in essence the same as the common place-name Cranford, which means 'cranes' ford' or 'ford where cranes are seen'. The ford would have been over the River Keer near here.

Carnoustie (Tayside)

This coastal resort southwest of ARBROATH has a name that still defies explanation. The first element could be the Gaelic *cathair* (walled town, fort; hence literally 'chair'), or *carragh* (rock), or even *carn* (cairn, rounded hill); the rest of the name has still not been satisfactorily deciphered. The *t* of the name seems to have appeared only in the sixteenth century. A document of 1493 refers to the place as *Donaldus Carnusy*.

Carrantuohill (Kerry)
The dominant mountain of MACGILLYCUDDY'S REEKS and the highest mountain in Ireland. Its Irish name is Corrán Tuathail, 'reversed reaping hook', with the second word, *tuathail*, applied to something that is 'wrong' or reversed from its normal direction. The name describes the appearance of the mountain when seen from the KILLARNEY side: its 'edge' is not concave, as on a reaping hook or billhook, but convex.

Carrick (Strathclyde, Cornwall, Donegal)
A Celtic name found with an identical meaning in three different countries of the British Isles. The Scottish Carrick is a district south of the River Doon south of AYR. The Cornish Carrick is the name of an administrative district with TRURO as its centre. The Irish Carrick is a coastal village in the west of Donegal. Many other places bear the name (*see also* CARRICKFERGUS; CARRICKMACROSS; CARRICK-ON-SHANNON; CARRICK-ON-SUIR). The name itself means 'rock', respectively from the Old Gaelic *carrec*, the Cornish *karrek*, and the Irish *carraig*. The Cornish Carrick takes its name directly from the Carrick Roads, the name given to the estuary of the River Fal (*see* FALMOUTH), in the middle of which is Black Rock, formerly *n garrak ruen*, 'the rock of seals'.

Carrickfergus (Antrim)
A historic port and town northeast of NEWTOWNABBEY, whose Irish name, Carraig Fhearghais, means 'Fergus's rock'. Fergus was a kinglet of the Dál Ríada, who brought Irish settlements in Scotland under his rule. The name properly applies to the rocky peninsula beside BELFAST Lough on which the Norman castle stands.

Carrickmacross (Monaghan)
The name of this market town west of DUNDALK means 'rock of the plain of Ross', as shown also by its Irish name, Carraig Mhachaire Rois. Ross is the name of a lough to the north of the town.

Carrick-on-Shannon (Leitrim)
A town east of BOYLE whose English name indicates its location — on the River SHANNON. The town's Irish name, however, shows that the place is not a true 'Carrick' at all. It is Cora Droma Rúisc, 'weir of the ridge of the bark', from the Irish *cora* (weir), *droim* (ridge), and *rúsc* (tree-bark). The name implies that a weir was built across the river here and that tree-bark was used in its construction. A former anglicised version of this Irish name was 'Carrickdrumrusk'. No doubt the present English name was patterned on a name such as CARRICK-ON-SUIR.

Carrick-on-Suir (Tipperary)
A town west of CLONMEL with a name meaning 'rock of the (river) Suir', referring to a large rock that remains in the river-bed here. The Irish name is similar: Carraig na Siúire.

Carron (Highland, Central)
Any of three rivers, comprising two in Highland and one in Central. The name derives from a basic Celtic root *kar-*, meaning 'stony', 'rocky'. The Carron that rises in ROSS and CROMARTY district was recorded in a text of the mid-tenth century as *Cære*.

Carshalton (Greater London)
A district of SUTTON whose name, perhaps unexpectedly, turns out to mean 'cress-growing Alton', with the latter name meaning 'farm by a spring'. The Old English root words here are thus *cærse* (cress), *æwiell* (well, spring), and *tūn* (farm, estate). The reference is to the source of the River Wandle (*see* WANDSWORTH) here. Watercress has been grown here since the Middle Ages, and it is

no coincidence that ALTON in Hampshire has also long been a producer of watercress, since its name has the same sense as this Alton. The town's name was originally simply Alton (in a text of 675, *Æuueltone*), and only subsequently was its 'speciality' of watercress added (*Kersaulton*, in a text dated about 1150).

Carstairs (Strathclyde)

A village and railway junction east of LANARK. The first part of the name is actually the Middle English *castel* (castle), with the second half the personal name Tarres. The sense is more obvious in early records of the name; a text of 1170 records it as *Casteltarres*. It is not known who Tarres was.

Cartmel (Cumbria)

This attractive village west of GRANGE-OVER-SANDS has a similarly 'sandy' name meaning 'sandbank by rocky ground', from the Old Norse conjectural *kartr* (rocky ground) and *melr* (sandbank). The village is on elevated ground above MORECAMBE Bay, with a ridge of high land running east to Fell End. The name was recorded in the twelfth century as *Ceartmel*, which suggests an influence of the Old English *ceart*, 'rough ground' (as in names common in KENT with 'Chart', such as Chart Sutton). Similar origins can be traced for the name of Cartmel Fell, the upland bordering the eastern shore of WINDERMERE.

Cashel (Tipperary)

The name of this town east of TIPPERARY is a rendering of the Irish name Caiseal, which means 'circular stone fort'; this can be seen here as the famous Rock of Cashel, the chief stronghold of the kings of MUNSTER for nine hundred years. The name is found elsewhere in Ireland, particularly in Galway.

Castlebar (Mayo)

A town east of WESTPORT whose name refers not to a 'bar' of some kind but in fact means 'Barry's castle' (Irish, Caisleán an Bharraigh), after the Barry family who held the castle after the invasion of the English. The town itself was not founded until the early seventeenth century.

Castlebay (Western Isles)

It always comes as something of a surprise to find such an English name on such a very Gaelic island. The small town of Castlebay, on BARRA, takes its name from the bay here (Castle Bay) on which the town arose as a fishing port in the nineteenth century. The castle of the name is thus the one in the bay, which is the medieval fortress of Kiessimul Castle, built on a rocky outcrop in the water. The town's Gaelic name is Baile MhicNéill, 'town of the MacNeils'. The MacNeils held Barra from the fifteenth century, and the castle was their ancestral home.

Castleblayney (Monaghan)

This town, southeast of MONAGHAN, stands on land granted by James I to Edward Blayney, governor of Monaghan, and the castle that he built here took his name. The town's Irish name is quite different: Baile na Lorgan, 'town of the strip of land'. The 'strip of land' is the sloping western shore of Lough Muckno, where the town now stands.

Castle Bromwich (West Midlands)

An eastern suburb of BIRMINGHAM. The castle of the name survives here as a twelfth-century 'motte and bailey' defence to the north of the church of St Mary and St Margaret, next to the M6 motorway. 'Bromwich' means 'broom farm' or 'farm where broom grows', from the Old English *brōm* (broom) and *wīc* (farm). The name of the present suburb was recorded in 1168 as simply *Bramewice*. When the castle had been built, the Middle English word *castel* was added; a record of the thirteenth century gives it as *Castelbromwic*. *See also* WEST BROMWICH.

Castle Cary (Somerset)

A small town southwest of BRUTON whose name refers to its castle and to the river on which it stands, and which rises nearby, the Cary. Only the foundations of the Norman castle remain, on the hillside. The river's name probably means 'pleasant stream', deriving from a Celtic root word seen in the modern Welsh *cariad*, 'love' (and thus in the Welsh forename Ceri). The name was recorded in a document of 1237 as *Castelkary*. *See also* CARISBROOKE.

Castle Combe (Wiltshire)

A picturesque village northwest of CHIPPENHAM that stands in a winding valley or 'combe' (that of the By Brook), which explains the second word of the name. The original castle here was destroyed by the Danes in the ninth century, and even the Norman replacement has not survived. The village was recorded in the Domesday Book simply as *Come*.

Castle Donington (Leicestershire)

A village northwest of LOUGHBOROUGH, well known for its nearby airport and motor-racing circuit. 'Donington' means 'place of Dunn's people', with this recorded in the Domesday Book as *Dunintone*. Slight traces of the Norman castle remain. The 'Castle' of the name distinguishes this Donington from Donington le Heath, south of COALVILLE.

Castle Douglas (Dumfries and Galloway)

This market town at the northern end of Carlingwark Loch bears the surname of Sir William Douglas, the merchant who bought the village of Carlingwark (as it was then called) in 1789 and who developed it into a burgh of barony. The earlier name, and still that of the loch, is apparently from the Old Norse *kerling* (hag; *compare* CARLINGFORD) and *verk* (work), alluding to some local legend. An even earlier name of the village, however, was Causewayend, referring to its location by the loch at the end of a causeway. Sir William Douglas was also the founder of NEWTON STEWART. The castle at Castle Douglas was the seat of the Douglas family.

Castleford (West Yorkshire)

A historic town southeast of LEEDS on the River AIRE at its confluence with the CALDER. The name implies a ford (over the Aire) by a Roman fort, since although the first half of the word suggests the modern English 'castle', it actually derives from the northern form (*cæster*) of the Old English *ceaster* (as in CHESTER), which indicates a Roman settlement. There was indeed a Roman fort here, where the road called Roman Ridge crosses the river. It was called *Lagentium*, a name apparently unconnected with the name Aire and therefore of some other origin. A word related to the modern Welsh *llafn* (blade) has been suggested, so that the fort name could mean something like 'fort of the swordsmen'. The name of the town was recorded in 948 as *Ceasterford*.

Castle Howard (North Yorkshire)

An impressive baroque mansion west of MALTON, built in the 1730s for the Howard family to replace Henderskelfe Castle, which had burnt down in 1693. It was Charles Howard, third Earl of CARLISLE, who requested Vanbrugh to design the present house. The name of the earlier house is Scandinavian in origin, meaning 'Hildr's shelf', that is, a ledge of land belonging to Hildr (a woman's name). Henderskelfe was recorded in the Domesday Book as *Hildreschelf*, and the name continued in local use down to the present century.

Castlemilk (Strathclyde)

A district of RUTHERGLEN, south of GLASGOW, named after the little Milk Water here, whose own name simply refers to the 'milky' waters of the stream. The castle here has a tower of the fifteenth or sixteenth century, but that dates back earlier than this. There is another

Castlemilk near LOCKERBIE, with a name of the same origin.

Castle Point (Essex)
An administrative district in southern Essex, although the name exists elsewhere in the country to denote a headland with a castle. The Essex name was devised (as the result of a public competition) to refer to two prominent features here: the Norman HADLEIGH Castle and Canvey Point, a Site of Special Scientific Interest on CANVEY ISLAND. The district was established in 1974.

Castle Rising (Norfolk)
A village with the remains of a Norman castle, located northeast of KING'S LYNN. The name does not refer to the rising ground here, but means either 'place of the people who live by the brushwood' (from the Old English hrīs, 'shrubs', 'brushwood') or 'place of Risa's people'. The earliest known record of the name is the Domesday Book one of Risinga, and without any earlier Old English spellings it is hard to give a precise sense, or to be sure of the spelling of the personal name, if that is what it is.

Castletown (Isle of Man)
A town in the south of the island whose name means 'settlement by a castle'; it was recorded in a text of about 1370 as villa castelli. The present castle was built in the fourteenth century on the site of one erected in the eleventh century.

Castlewellan (Down)
This attractive village northwest of NEWCASTLE has the Irish name of Caisleán Uidhilín, 'Uidhilín's castle', with the personal name (Wellan) an Anglo-Norman one.

Caterham (Surrey)
This town south of CROYDON has a name that means literally 'settlement by the hill called Cadeir', the latter being a Celtic name directly related to that of CADER

IDRIS and so meaning 'chair'. It is not clear which hill the name refers to, although the ground south of the town rises to White Hill and Gravelly Hill. Caterham was recorded in 1179 as Catheham, and this spelling serves as a reminder that the hill name is itself also related to the Latin cathedra, and so indirectly to the English 'cathedral'. See also CHADDERTON.

Catford (Greater London)
A district of LEWISHAM whose name actually means what it says: 'ford where wild cats are seen'. Formerly it would not have been unusual to see wild cats in the wooded countryside by the River Ravensbourne here; today the vestiges of these open spaces are used for recreation grounds and sports fields. The name was recorded exactly as now in 1254. Compare CATHAYS.

Cathays (South Glamorgan)
A district of CARDIFF, with Cathays Park containing the city's main administrative and public offices. The name was recorded in a document of 1699 as Catt Hays. It almost certainly dates from much earlier than this, however, and could well derive from the Old English cat (cat) and haga (enclosure, literally 'hedge'), so meaning 'enclosure where wild cats are seen'. The current pronunciation of the name is 'Katays' (second syllable stressed), apparently supporting this.

Cathcart (Strathclyde)
This district of GLASGOW has a name meaning 'fort on the River Cart', from the Cumbric (Old Welsh) cair (modern Welsh caer) meaning 'fort', and the name of the river here, which may derive from the same Celtic root element kar- (stony), as seen for CARRON. Cathcart was recorded as Kerkert in 1158.

Catterick (North Yorkshire)
A village southeast of RICHMOND, well known for its army camp. The name is believed to be somewhat unusual, deriving

from the Latin *cataracta* (cataract), so referring to the waterfalls or rapids on the River SWALE near here. The place has long had military links, for there was a Roman fort here called *Cataractonium*, a name of the same origin. Some toponymists have reservations about this origin, as *cataracta* was not a common spoken word and was, moreover, taken into the language from Greek. They therefore propose a name of Celtic origin, as is commonly found for Roman camps. It is difficult, though, to deduce what this could have been, but some word related to the modern Welsh *cadr* (powerful) may lie behind the name. In the second century AD, Ptolemy recorded the name as *Catouraktonion*, which happens to suggest the British (Celtic) root word *catu-* (war). This could therefore equally well be the origin.

Cavan (Cavan)

The chief town in the county of the same name, the latter deriving from the former. The town, south of CLONES, lies in a hollow, with a round grassy hill rising above it. The Irish word *cabhán*, which could denote either feature, is the origin of the name. The town's current Irish name is An Cabhán, 'the hollow' (or 'the grassy hill').

Caversham (Berkshire)

A northern district of READING, across the THAMES. Its name seems to derive from a personal name, such as Cafa, itself perhaps originating as a nickname based on the Old English *cāf* (bold, active). The name as a whole thus probably means 'Cafa's settlement'. It was recorded in the Domesday Book as *Cavesham*.

Cawdor (Highland)

A village southwest of NAIRN, famous for its castle and its Shakespearean reference (Macbeth was 'Thane of Cawdor'). The name probably derives from the Gaelic *call dobhar*, 'hazel stream', although some have related it to the same origin as CALDER.

Ceannanus Mór (Meath)

The Irish name for the town of KELLS.

Cemaes Bay (Gwynedd)

A wide bay on the north coast of ANGLESEY and also a fishing village and resort on its southern shore. The origin of the name lies in the Celtic root element *cam-* (crooked, bending), and refers to the curving coastline here. *Compare* CAMBORNE; CAMBUSLANG.

Central (Scotland)

A rather obvious name for the administrative region set up in 1975 in central Scotland, roughly between Loch LOMOND to the west and the FIRTH OF FORTH to the east. It comprises the former counties of CLACKMANNAN and STIRLING, together with the southwestern part of PERTH.

Ceredigion (Dyfed)

The old name of the county of CARDIGAN, reintroduced for the administrative district established in northwest DYFED in 1974. As explained under CARDIGAN, the name means 'Ceredig's land'. Ceredig, whose own name means 'amiable', 'lovable' (*compare* the modern forename Ceri), was one of the sons of Cunedda in the fifth century. Cunedda gave his name to the present county of GWYNEDD.

Cerne Abbas (Dorset)

A picturesque village north of DORCHESTER, famous for the Romano-British figure known as the Cerne Giant, which is cut into the chalk of a nearby hill. It takes its name from the River Cerne here, which itself means 'stony' from the Celtic root *kar-*, seen in such names as CARADON, CARRICK, and CARRON. One would have expected 'Charn' or 'Chern', but the present spelling and pronunciation are due to Norman influence. 'Abbas' denotes the Benedictine abbey that was here from the tenth to the sixteenth century. The river name was recorded as *aqua de Cerne* in 1244, and the village is referred to as *Cerne*

Abbatis in a text of 1291. This same river gave the name of CHARMINSTER. *Compare also* CHARMOUTH.

Chadderton (Greater Manchester)

A textile town northeast of MANCHESTER with a name meaning 'farm by the hill called *Cadeir*', the latter being exactly the same name with the same origin as that which gave the name of CATERHAM. In the case of Chadderton, the hill was probably the nearby one (in ROYTON) known as Hanging Chadder. The town was recorded in about 1200 as *Chaderton*.

Chagford (Devon)

This small town on the eastern edge of DARTMOOR has a name that means exactly what it says, that is, 'place by a ford where chag grows'. 'Chag', from the Old English *ceacge*, is a dialect word for broom or gorse. The river here is the Teign (*see* TEIGNMOUTH). Chagford was recorded in the Domesday Book as *Cagefort*.

Chalfont St Giles (Buckinghamshire)

The name of this town southeast of AMERSHAM, needs to be considered along with that of CHALFONT ST PETER (below). The first word of each name means 'calves' spring', 'spring where calves come to drink', from the two Old English words *cealf* (calf) and *funta* (spring) (related to the modern English 'fountain' and 'font', and itself 'loaned', via Celtic, from the Latin *fons, fontis*). The towns are only two miles apart, and therefore add the names of their parochial saints to distinguish each from the other. Chalfont St Giles was in the Domesday Book as *Celfunte*, with the present name recorded in a document of 1242 as *Chaufonte Sancti Egidii* (*Egidius* was the Latin equivalent of modern Giles).

Chalfont St Peter (Buckinghamshire)

A town northwest of UXBRIDGE. For the meaning of the first part of the name, *see* CHALFONT ST GILES. A document of 1242 (cited in the previous entry) gives this town's name as *Chaufunte Sancti Petri*.

Chalk Farm (Greater London)

A district of Camden whose name suggests there was formerly a farm here on chalky land. But no trace of such a farm has been found, and the name appears to be a corruption of early forms of 'Chalcot', meaning 'cold shelter'. The gradual metamorphosis of the name can be seen in the following records: *Chaldecote* (1253); *Caldecote* (about 1400); *Chalcot* (1593); *Chalk* (1746). 'Chalcot' probably came to be associated with 'chalk' when the original Old English *ceald* (cold) had itself passed out of use, and when the *d* had disappeared from the name. There is still a Chalcot Road here, however. Any farm hereabouts was probably known as 'Chalcot Farm', with this in turn giving the name of a residence called 'Chalcot Manor'.

Chanctonbury Ring (West Sussex)

The site of an Iron Age fort on the northern edge of the South Downs, north of WORTHING. The 'Ring' refers to the circle of stones here, while 'Chanctonbury' consists of the Old English *burg* (fort) added to the name of a nearby farm, Chancton, which apparently means 'farm of Ceawa's people'. The farm name was recorded in the Domesday Book as *Cengeltune*, and Chanctonbury's name is found as *Changebury* in a text of 1351. It seems strange that the name has not been smoothed or abbreviated further since then, to something such as 'Changbury Ring'. With an inhabited site this would surely have happened.

Chapel-en-le-Frith (Derbyshire)

There are many places named directly after a chapel, often in the form of common combinations, such as Chapel End, Chapel Hill, or Chapeltown. This manufacturing town north of BUXTON has a distinctive addition, showing it to be a 'chapel in the forest', that is, in Peak Forest here. The middle '-en-le-' is Norman French in origin, and in many other names of this type has been reduced to simply '-le-', as in CHESTER-LE-STREET. 'Frith' is the Old

English *fyrhth* (wood). The chapel here was built in the thirteenth century, and rather unusually is dedicated to St Thomas Becket (who was murdered in 1170). The name of the place is first recorded in a document of 1219 as *Ecclesia de Alto Peccho,* a medieval Latin rendering of 'church of the high peak', referring to the forest.

Chapelizod (Dublin)
The name of this village, on the road from DUBLIN to LUCAN, is said to derive from Yseult, the Irish king's daughter who was the tragic heroine of the tale *Tristram and Yseult,* although in the Arthurian legend, Yseult (or Iseult) was the daughter of a king of Brittany. The Irish name preserves this reference, being Seipeal Iosoid, 'Yseult's chapel'.

Chard (Somerset)
The present name of this town southeast of TAUNTON has been abbreviated from two Old English words, *ceart* (rough ground) and *renn* (house; an older form of *ærn*). The name thus originally meant 'house on rough common land', and was recorded in 1065 as *Cerdren.* The second element was subsequently dropped.

Charing Cross (Greater London)
Folklorists like to derive the name of this district of central LONDON from the French *chère reine,* 'dear queen', said to be Edward I's endearing tribute to his wife, Queen Eleanor. But truth has blended with more than an equal measure of fiction here. The name as a whole can be understood as meaning 'cross at the place by the bend', with the first word deriving from the Old English *cierring* (turn, bend). This could be either a bend in the River THAMES here or, more likely, a bend in the road from London to the West of England. The cross commemorated Queen Eleanor on the route taken by her coffin from LINCOLN to London following her death in 1290 at Harby in Nottinghamshire. Charing was the last resting-place of her coffin, and the king had a cross erected, as at each of the

previous resting points (they were at LINCOLN, GRANTHAM, STAMFORD, Geddington, NORTHAMPTON, STONY STRATFORD, WOBURN, DUNSTABLE, ST ALBANS, Waltham (now WALTHAM CROSS, in the same manner as Charing Cross), and West Cheap (now CHEAPSIDE). A modern replica of the Charing cross stands in the forecourt of Charing Cross railway station on the Strand. The name of the place was recorded in about 1000 as *Cyrringe* and in 1360 as *La Charryngcros.* Three of the original 'Eleanor crosses' survive — at Geddington (northeast of KETTERING), Northampton, and (although much restored) Waltham Cross.

Charlbury (Oxfordshire)
A small town southeast of CHIPPING NORTON that came to have a name meaning 'the fortified place of Ceorl's people'. Although the Old English *ceorl* was used as a common noun ('churl', *see* CARLTON TOWERS), it was also a personal name. Charlbury was recorded in about 1000 as *Ceorlingburh,* showing the now lost '-ing' element that meant 'people of'.

Charlestown of Aberlour (Grampian)
The full name of the town more usually known as ABERLOUR.

Charleville (Cork)
The former name of RáTH LUIRC.

Charminster (Dorset)
A village north of DORCHESTER that takes its name from the River Cerne, on which it lies (for the origin of the river name *see* CERNE ABBAS). The minster or church was one here in Anglo-Saxon times, as the Domesday Book record of the name (*Cerminstre*) shows.

Charmouth (Dorset)
A small resort northeast of LYME REGIS at the mouth of the River Char, as its name indicates. The river's own name is a variant of Cerne (*see* CERNE ABBAS). Charmouth

was recorded in the Domesday Book as *Cernemude*.

Charnwood Forest (Leicestershire)
A region and former hunting ground southwest of LOUGHBOROUGH. The meaning of Charnwood is 'wood in rocky countryside', with the first part of the name the Celtic root word *carn*, found in CARADON and CARRON. The present name is something of a tautology, although 'Forest' denotes a wider area than 'wood'. The name was recorded in a text of 1276 as *Charnewode*.

Chartwell (Kent)
A country house south of WESTERHAM and the former home of Sir Winston Churchill. It takes its name from the locality, whose name means 'spring in rough ground', from the Old English *ceart* (rough ground) and *wella* (spring, well). There are several places named 'Chart' in Kent, others being Chart Corner, near MAIDSTONE; Great Chart, near ASHFORD; Chart Sutton, near Maidstone; and Chartham, near CANTERBURY.

Chatham (Kent)
This historic naval and military base, east of LONDON on the MEDWAY, has a name that means 'settlement by a wood'. It comprises the British (Celtic) root word *ceto-* (wood) (also discernible in LICHFIELD and, more obviously, in BETWS-Y-COED), and the common Old English *hām* (farm, settlement). The countryside to the south of Chatham is still well wooded. Chatham was recorded in the tenth century as *Cætham*. *See also* CHATTERIS; CHEADLE.

Chatsworth (Derbyshire)
A mansion west of CHESTERFIELD and the seat of the Dukes of Devonshire. The location here was recorded in the Domesday Book as *Chetesuorde*, meaning 'Ceatt's enclosure' from the Old English personal name and *worth* (enclosure). The house dates from the seventeenth century.

Chatteris (Cambridgeshire)
A small town south of MARCH, sometimes said to have a name of the same origin as CATTERICK, although there is little to support the assertion. The name was recorded in 974 as *Cæateric* and in the Domesday Book as *Cetriz*. This suggests a combination of the British (Celtic) *ceto-* (wood) and perhaps the Old English conjectural *ric* (stream, strip of land), so that the name could mean something like 'stream by a wood' or 'narrow road by a wood'. Alternatively, the first part of the name could be a personal name, such as Ceatta, with the second part regarded more as 'ridge'. Early one-inch Ordnance Survey maps do actually show a narrow ridge running alongside the road that extends northwest of Chatteris.

Cheadle (Greater Manchester, Staffordshire)
Either of two towns, one west of STOCKPORT, the other east of STOKE-ON-TRENT. Both names have the same origin and meaning. The name is similar to CHATHAM, in that the Celtic word for 'wood' (*ceto-*) has had an Old English word added to it. The interesting thing here, however, is that the second word also means 'wood' (old English *lēah*)! Probably the second word was added when the meaning of the first had teen forgotten, thus resulting in the present tautology. The neighbour of Stockport is recorded in the Domesday Book as *Cedde*, without the second element (today represented by the final '-le'). The Staffordshire town was recorded in a document of 1197 as *Chedele*. *See also* CHEADLE HULME.

Cheadle Hulme (Greater Manchester)
A southern district of CHEADLE. The first word of the name is identical in origin to that of the town. The second word is Scandinavian in origin and means literally 'island' (Old Norse *holmr*). Here it can be understood as meaning 'promontory', 'raised ground'. Cheadle Hulme lies higher than the main part of the town.

Cheam (Greater London)

A district of SUTTON whose name is more complex than it seems. It was recorded in 675 as *Cegeham*, in the Domesday Book as *Ceiham*, and even as recently as 1722 as *Cheham*, showing that there are two elements. The second is undoubtedly the Old English *hām* (settlement, village), and the first appears to be the conjectural Old English *ceg* (tree-stump). The meaning is thus 'village by the tree-stumps'.

Cheapside (City of London)

Cheapside is now regarded simply as the street that runs eastward from the rear of St Paul's Cathedral towards the Bank of England. The original Cheapside was a more extensive area, being the chief market place of medieval LONDON. The name thus derived from the Old English *cēap*, 'market' (the word gives modern English 'cheap'), with 'side' denoting that the original street ran along the side of the market. The names of nearby streets still preserve the trades and crafts of the people who lived and worked here: Bread Street for the bakers; Milk Street for the dairymen; Poultry for the poulterers; and so on. The name of both the market and the street is thus found as *Chepe* in medieval documents, including the writings of Chaucer. The present street name occurs in a text of 1436 as *Chapeside*. Cheapside was also sometimes known as West Cheap to distinguish it from Eastcheap (now a street running eastward from London Bridge), where the medieval meat market was. (*Compare* the various CHIPPING entries, and also the MARKET entries.)

Cheddar (Somerset)

A famous cheese-making town northwest of WELLS that derives its name from the Old English *ceod* (bag, pouch). The word is used (in some transferred sense) to refer to the nearby caves, now best known for their stalagmites and stalactites. The name appeared in the Domesday Book as *Cedre*.

Chelmsford (Essex)

A cathedral city northeast of LONDON that appears in the Domesday Book as *Celmeresfort*; this means 'Cēolmær's ford', the latter being over the River Chelmer here. The river's name comes from that of the town, and must have done so at a fairly early stage in its development when the settlement name was more like 'Chelmersford'. The ford would have been an important one, since many main roads converge here to cross the river. The earlier name of the river has been recorded as *Beaduwan*. The meaning of this is uncertain, but it gave the names of Great Baddow and Little Baddow to the south of the town. Chelmsford is on the site of a Roman town, which was called *Caesaromagus*, 'Caesar's market'. The latter half of this name is a British (Celtic) conjectural word *magos*, also found in the Roman names of CHICHESTER and CRAYFORD, which were both called *Noviomagus*.

Chelsea (Greater London)

A well-known district of southwest central LONDON. As with BATTERSEA, the final '-sea' of the name is misleading. The name means 'chalk landing place', from the Old English *cealc* (chalk) and *hȳth* (landing place) (as exemplified in HYTHE). Early records of the name confirm this meaning, such as the text of 789 which has it as *Celchyth*. The name implies that chalk was either shipped from here or was unloaded here on the THAMES.

Cheltenham Spa (Gloucestershire)

A residential town and former spa east of GLOUCESTER. It was recorded in a text of 803 as *Celtanhomme*. The latter part of this is certainly the Old English *hamm* (river meadow), which describes the site of the original settlement here by the River Chelt (whose own name comes from that of the town). There has been some dispute concerning the first part of the name, which has been related to that of the CHILTERN HILLS. Current research gives the meaning 'hill' to the element common to both names, with the root element perhaps being a pre-British *celt-* almost certainly not related to 'Celt' itself. In the case of Cheltenham, the hill would thus be Cleeve Hill, which overlooks the town to the northwest ('Cleeve' simply means 'cliff'). Overall, we thus have a name that means 'well-watered meadow by a cliff-like hill', which is a good description of the town's original site. The 'Spa' of the name developed from the early eighteenth century.

Chepstow (Gwent)

A Welsh town east of NEWPORT with an English name meaning literally 'market place', from the Old English *cēap* (market) (*compare* CHEAPSIDE) and *stōw* (place) (as in PADSTOW). The implication is a place of assembly that was a market. (A sort of inversion of this occurs in STOWMARKET.) Chepstow was recorded in a text of 1224 as *Strigull*, which seems to be quite a different name of unexplained origin. The town also has a Welsh name, Cas-Gwent, meaning 'castle in GWENT'. *See also* the CHIPPING entries.

Chequers (Buckinghamshire)

The British Prime Minister's country residence, northeast of PRINCES RISBOROUGH. The full name of the house is Chequers Court, and the present building developed on the site of a thirteenth-century one owned by a Laurence de Scaccario, who probably owed his surname to the fact that he was an official of the medieval Court of Exchequer, the court of law that dealt with matters of revenue. The surname Scaccario was thus translated as 'Exchequer' and shortened as 'Chequer'. Chequers was given to the nation by Lord Lee of Fareham in 1921, 'as a place of rest and recreation for her prime ministers for ever'.

Chertsey (Surrey)

A town south of STAINES on the THAMES. Its name probably means 'Cerot's island',

with the personal name followed by the Old English *ēg* (island); Cerot is a British (Celtic) name. The Venerable Bede referred to the place in his eighth-century *Ecclesiastical History of the English People* as *Cerotaesi*, that is, *Ceroti insula*, 'island of Cerotus' (as his name was in Latin). The 'island' was probably not one in the river but the higher ground where the present town stands, on a site between streams (such as The Bourne and the Abbey River) that flow down to the river. There was probably once a monastery here.

Cherwell (Oxfordshire)

An administrative district in the north of the county that takes its name from the River Cherwell, which flows into the THAMES at OXFORD. The name was recorded in 681 as *Ceruelle*, of which the second element is almost certainly the Old English *wella* (stream, well). The first part of the name may be the Old English *cierr* (turn, bend) (*compare* CHARING CROSS), so that the name as a whole means 'winding river'.

Chesham (Buckinghamshire)

The name of the town northwest of LONDON was recorded in a document dated 1012 as *Cæstæleshamme*, which shows its ultimate origin in the Old English *ceastel* (heap of stone) and *hamm* (river meadow, well-watered valley). The river here is the Chess, which takes its name as a 'back formation' from that of the town. In the Domesday Book, Chesham appears as *Cestreham*, so that the name seems to derive from the Old English *ceaster* (as in CHESTER), and so denote a former Roman camp. But the true reference is to the circle of stones on which the church was built.

Cheshire (England)

A county in the northwest that derives its name from that of its chief town, CHESTER, as if it were really 'Chestershire' (the name actually appears in this form in a text of 1326). The oldest record of the name is one of 980, in which the region is referred to as

Legeceaster scir. The first word here represents the original, longer name of CHESTER itself. For a similar 'smoothed' and shortened county name *compare* LANCASHIRE.

Cheshunt (Hertfordshire)
The name of this town north of LONDON is usually interpreted as 'spring by a Roman camp', with the two Old English elements *ceaster* (Roman camp) and *funta* (spring, well; from the Latin *fons, fontis*). But there are two difficulties. The first is that no Roman camp or other remains are known here, although Cheshunt is actually on ERMINE STREET. The second is that no early forms of the name contain the necessary *f* that enables us to quote *funta* with confidence. The records include *Cestrehunt* (in the Domesday Book), *Cesterhunte* (in 1198), and *Chesthunte* (in 1292), almost as if the second half of the name were 'hunter' rather than 'fount'. But the present interpretation is the most likely without further evidence; certainly, the *f* has similarly disappeared in other places containing *funta*, such as Tolleshunt Major in Essex, or Boarhunt in Hampshire (where the false 'hunting' association has even influenced the first half of the name, which is really the Old English *burg* or *burh*, 'fortified place').

Chesil Beach (Dorset)
A shingle bank, also known as Chesil Bank, that extends southeast for some ten miles from the village of Abbotsbury, to the Isle of PORTLAND. Its name actually means 'shingle', from the Old English *ceosol*. The Beach was recorded in about 1540 as *The chisil*.

Chessington (Greater London)
This district of KINGSTON UPON THAMES looks as if it has an '-ington' name like PADDINGTON or KENSINGTON. But as earlier records of the name show, this is not so. In the Domesday Book, for instance, Chessington appears as *Cisendone*, and in 1255 as *Chessendone*. Here, the final element represents the Old English *dūn* (hill), preceded by the personal name Cissa (as in the origin of CHICHESTER). Chessington, or 'Cissa's hill', is on high ground, as any visitor to Chessington Zoo will discover.

Chester (Cheshire)
A cathedral city and the county town of CHESHIRE. Its name clearly shows it to have been a Roman town, deriving from the Old English *ceaster* (Roman fort). It is thus similar to such names as MANCHESTER, CHICHESTER, and WINCHESTER, but unlike these, no longer has its initial element, distinguishing it from other 'Chesters'. The modern shortened form of the name is first recorded in the Domesday Book, as *Cestre*. In the eighth century, however, the Venerable Bede refers to the town as *Legacæstir*, where the first part of the name represents the Latin *Legionum*, 'of the legions'. Bede's full reference to the place is interesting: ... *ad civitatem Legionum, quae a gente Anglorum Legacaestir, a Brettonibus autem rectius Carlegion appellatur* ('to the city of the Legions, which the Angles call Legacaestir, and the Britons also more correctly Carlegion'). If this last name had continued in use, it might have prevailed to produce an almost exact equivalent of the modern CAERLEON. But even before this, the settlement was recorded by Ptolemy in the second century AD as *Deva*, a name that properly refers to the River DEE, on which Chester stands. The Roman name of the station here was also *Deva*.

Chesterfield (Derbyshire)
This market town south of SHEFFIELD has a straightforward name that consists of the Old English *ceaster* (Roman fort) and *feld* (modern 'field', i.e. open land). A Roman fort has recently been found at Chesterfield, but its name is unknown; it seems to have been less important than the ones at CHESTER and CHESTER-LE-STREET, for example. Chesterfield was

recorded in a text of the mid-tenth century as *Chesterfelda*, much as now.

Chester-le-Street (Durham)

The name of this town, north of DURHAM on the former Roman station of *Concangis*, is in a sense doubly Roman, containing the Old English words (*ceaster* and *strǣt*) that themselves derive from Latin, respectively *castra* (camp) and *via strata* (paved way). Chester-le-Street is thus the 'Roman camp by the Roman road', with the latter half of the name added to distinguish this place from CHESTER itself. The Roman *Concangis* is difficult to explain, although a Celtic tribal name meaning 'horse people' may lie behind it, according to one authority. This old name is still partly seen in a record of the town's name of about 1050, where it is *Cunceceastre*, and even today the town is on the small stream called the Cong Burn, which also appears to be based on the ancient Celtic name. *See also* CONSETT.

Chesterton (Cambridgeshire)

There are two places of the name in Cambridgeshire and others elsewhere in the country. The meaning is basically 'village by a Roman station', with the Old English *tūn* (farm, estate) added to the Old English *ceaster* (Roman fort). The village of Chesterton southwest of PETERBOROUGH had the Roman name of *Durobrivae*, the same as the Roman station at ROCHESTER (which see for its origin). The northeast district of CAMBRIDGE called Chesterton has a name that refers to one or other of the Roman developments here, or to the Roman road that passed through the Roman station where it forded the River Cam (Granta).

Cheviot Hills (England/Scotland)

A range of hills extending along the border of England and Scotland. It takes its name from the single mountain here called The Cheviot (or Great Cheviot). This was recorded in 1181 as *Chiuiet*, a name still unexplained. It is almost certainly of pre-Celtic origin.

Chevy Chase (Northumberland)

The name has gone down in history as that of the Battle of Chevy Chase, in which the Scots defeated Henry Percy ('Hotspur') at Otterburn, north of HEXHAM, in 1388. 'Chevy' is a hill-name that may relate to CHEVIOT, while 'Chase' refers to a former hunting ground here. Otterburn is only fifteen miles from the Cheviots.

Chichester (West Sussex)

This cathedral city east of HAVANT has a name that proclaims it to have arisen on a former Roman station (Old English *ceaster*). The name as a whole means 'Cissa's Roman fort', and Cissa himself is mentioned in the *Anglo-Saxon Chronicle* as being one of the sons of Ælle, the first king of the South Saxons (who gave their name to SUSSEX). The settlement's name was recorded in 895 as *Cisseceastre*. The name of the Roman station itself was *Noviomagus*, meaning 'new market', a name found elsewhere in Britain (at CRAYFORD) and also on the continent; it is still recognisable in the present-day name of Nijmegen in Holland. The name comprises two Celtic elements, the first related to the Latin *novus* (new) and the latter to the Irish *machaire* (plain) (as in MAGHERA). There are still plenty of visible Roman remains in Chichester, and two of the city's churches, St Andrew's and St Olave's, are built on Roman foundations. *See also* CISSBURY RING.

Chigwell (Essex)

In the Domesday Book, the name of this town northeast of LONDON was recorded as *Cingheuella*, showing the derivation to be a conjectured Middle English word for 'shingle' (*chingel*) and the Old English *wella* (stream, well). The name thus means 'shingly stream'. There is no obvious stream here now, although the River Roding (*see* RODINGS, THE) runs to the west of the town, separating it from the similarly named CHINGFORD.

Chiltern Hills (Oxfordshire/Hertfordshire)
A range of hills extending northeastwards
from READING to beyond TRING. The
name almost certainly derives from a pre-
British (i.e. pre-Celtic) conjectured
element *cilt-* meaning simply 'hill', found
also in the name of CHELTENHAM. A
document of 1006 has a reference to
Cilternes efese, meaning 'precipice of
Chiltern', this relating to the steeper,
western side of the hills.

Chingford (Greater London)
A town to the north of central LONDON,
west of the similarly named CHIGWELL.
The name begins with the conjectured
Middle English *chingel* (shingle), so the
name overall means 'shingly ford'; it was
recorded in 1050 as *Cingeford*. The ford
would have been over the river now named
the Ching, after the town. Its original name
was simply the Bourne.

Chippenham (Wiltshire)
A town northeast of BATH on the River
AVON. The name means 'Cippa's riverside
land', with the personal name followed by
the Old English *hamm*, frequently applied
to land in the bend of a river, as here.
Chippenham was recorded as *Cypeham* in a
text of about 1080, and the name is almost
identical to SYDENHAM. There is also a
village of Chippenham near NEWMARKET
in Cambridgeshire.

Chipping Campden (Gloucestershire)
The name of this town southeast of
EVESHAM has a first word that, like other
'Chipping' place-names, represents the
Old English *cēping* (market place) (from
cēap, 'market', as in CHEAPSIDE). This
word was added to an earlier name when a
particular place gained a market. Here,
'Campden' means 'valley enclosure', from
the Old English *camp* (modern 'camp', but
itself from the Latin *campus*, 'field')
meaning 'enclosed field', and *denu* (valley).
Chipping Campden was thus originally
recorded in the Domesday Book as simply
Campedene, but in a document of 1315 the

name appears in full as *Cheping
Caumpedene*. It was Chipping Campden
that ultimately, at several 'removes', gave
the name of CAMDEN TOWN.

Chipping Norton (Oxfordshire)
A COTSWOLD town northwest of OXFORD.
Like the other 'Chipping' places, it was
originally known just by its second name,
so that it was one of a number of 'northern
homesteads' (Old English *north* and *tūn*).
After acquiring a market, it gained its
present name, recorded in Anglo-Latin
form in a document of 1246 as *Norton
Mercatoria* (*compare* modern 'merchant'),
then as *Chepyngnorton* in 1280.

Chipping Ongar (Essex)
As mentioned under CHIPPING CAMPDEN,
'Chipping' was added to an earlier name
when the place concerned gained a regular
market. For this small town northwest of
BRENTWOOD, the original was *Angra* in
the Domesday Book, deriving from the
Old English conjectural *anger* (pasture
land). A later text dated 1388 gives the
name in its present form as *Chepyng
Hangre*. The same origin lies behind the
name of nearby High Ongar.

Chipping Sodbury (Avon)
This town northeast of BRISTOL was
recorded in the Domesday Book as
Sopeberie, meaning 'Soppa's fortified
place'. When the market became
established here, the name appeared in its
present form, as in a text of 1316, where it
is *Sodbury Mercata* (*compare* CHIPPING
NORTON).

Chirk (Clwyd)
A small town north of OSWESTRY above
the River Ceiriog, from which it takes its
name in anglicised form. The river's name
means something like 'favoured', from a
derivative of the Celtic root element *car-*,
'love' (as in the River Cary that gave its
name to CASTLE CARY). The Welsh name
of Chirk is Y Waun, 'the moorland', from
the Welsh *gwaun* (moor, mountain).

Chislehurst (Greater London)
A district of BROMLEY whose name simply
means 'gravel hill', from the Old English
ceosol (gravel, shingle) (*compare* CHESIL
BEACH) and *hyrst* (wooded hill). The name
was recorded in 973 as *Cyselhyrst*.

Chiswick (Greater London)
A district of HOUNSLOW north of the
THAMES, whose name means basically
'cheese farm', from the Old English *ciese*
(cheese) and the common *wīc*, denoting a
specialised farm of some kind (another
example is WOOLWICH). Compare the
northern variant of the same name in
KESWICK. Chiswick was recorded in about
1000 as *Ceswican*.

Chorley (Lancashire)
The name is found in several places in
England, and its meaning is 'clearing of the
churls', the latter being free peasants (*see*
CARLTON TOWERS for the Old English
origin and its sense). The Lancashire town
northwest of BOLTON has given its own
name to an administrative district, and was
recorded in a document of 1246 as *Cherleg*.
Compare CHORLEYWOOD; CHORLTON
CUM HARDY.

Chorleywood (Hertfordshire)
The name of this residential town is
basically identical to that of CHORLEY,
with 'wood' added in relatively recent
times to name first a wood, then the present
settlement that arose by it. The name is
recorded in a document of 1524 as
Charlewood, and the Ordnance Survey one-
inch map of 1822 marks the embryo
development here northwest of
RICKMANSWORTH as a group of houses
around *Charley Wood Common*.

Chorlton cum Hardy (Greater Manchester)
A district of MANCHESTER named after
two former distinct villages linked by the
medieval Latin *cum* (with). Chorlton is
related to the names of CHORLEY and
CHORLEYWOOD and means 'farm of the
churls'. Hardy, which was recorded in a

text of 1555 as *Hardey*, probably has a
personal name as the first element of the
word, with the second being the Old
English *ēg* (island). Chorlton cum Hardy is
southwest of the city centre. There is
another district to the southeast called
Chorlton on Medlock, the latter being the
name of the river here ('meadow stream').

Christchurch (Dorset)
When an Augustinian priory was founded
here, east of BOURNEMOUTH, in the mid-
twelfth century, it was given a name
('church dedicated to Christ') that replaced
the earlier name of the settlement. This was
Twynham, meaning 'between the rivers',
referring to the location of the place
between the STOUR and the AVON. The old
name is recorded in the *Anglo-Saxon
Chronicle* of the early tenth century as *æt
Tweoxneam*, representing the Old English
æt 'at' (with 'place' understood) followed
by *betweoxn* 'between' (compare 'betwixt
and between') and *ēam*, the dative plural of
ēa (river), with this case required
grammatically after the preposition
betweoxn. The first known record of the
name Christchurch dates from 1177, when
it appears as *Cristescherche*, although a text
of 1242 records both the old and the new
name — *Cristechurch Twynham*. The old
name is still preserved in the town — in
Twynham Avenue and Twynham
Comprehensive School.

Chudleigh (Devon)
This small town north of NEWTON ABBOT
has a name that means 'Ciedda's clearing',
with the personal name (a West Saxon form
of Cedda) followed by the Old English *lēah*
(forest clearing). Nearby Chudleigh
Knighton has a name based on that of the
town, with the first word added to
Knighton for distinguishing purposes. The
town's name was recorded in 1259 as
Cheddeleghe, and the village was recorded
in the Domesday Book two centuries
earlier as *Chenistetone*, showing the clerk's
efforts to render the difficult Anglo-Saxon
name based on the Old English *cniht*

(knight), with his *s* representing the special sound of *h* in this word.

Chulmleigh (Devon)

The name of this small town, south of SOUTH MOLTON, was recorded in the Domesday Book as *Calmonleuge*, which not very accurately represents its meaning as 'Cēolmund's clearing'. The place-name is identical in origin to that of Cholmondeley Castle in Cheshire, which itself gave the surname Cholmondeley (and its variants), often pronounced 'Chumley', just as the name of the Devon town is. The personal name involved here means literally 'throat protection', with this doubtless taken figuratively as well to mean 'defence of the gorge'.

Church (Lancashire)

A simple self-explanatory name for this textile town west of ACCRINGTON. The name was recorded in 1202 as *Chirche*, and probably refers to a church that stood either on or close to the site of the present St James's Church, which is still sometimes known locally as 'Church Kirk'.

Church Stretton (Shropshire)

Any place named Stretton or Stratton is likely to be on or near a Roman road, with the name deriving from the Old English *strǣt* (Roman road) and *tūn* (settlement). This is certainly true of the town of Church Stretton, although the road branches off to the northeast at All Stretton. The name appears as *Chirchestretton* in 1337, and the church referred to is the part-Norman one of St Lawrence, which dates from the twelfth century. 'Church' would have been added to distinguish this Stretton, south of SHREWSBURY, from All Stretton to the north and Little Stretton to the south.

Cinderford (Gloucestershire)

A colliery town west of GLOUCESTER with a name that appropriately relates to its main present-day industry. The first half of the name thus directly indicates 'cinder' (Old English *sinder*) and the name as a whole may have denoted a place where slag and the waste products of smelting were carried across the river to be dumped, or where a trackway to the ford was built up from cinders or slag. The ford would not have been over the nearby SEVERN but over the small stream here that flows through the FOREST OF DEAN towards the greater river. Cinderford's name was recorded in 1258 as *Sinderford*, showing the long connection with smelting and coal-mining locally.

Cinque Ports, The (Kent/East Sussex)

Five ports (Old French, *cink porz*) that combined for defence of the English Channel from the twelfth century. The original five were HASTINGS, Romney (*see* NEW ROMNEY), HYTHE, DOVER, and SANDWICH, with WINCHELSEA and RYE added later. These towns were granted special privileges in return for providing men and ships for the navy, although such privileges were mostly revoked in the late seventeenth century. The *Oxford English Dictionary* quotes a Latin text of 1191 mentioning them: *ne* [. . .] *aliter quam Barones de Hastingiis et de quinque portibus placitant* ('not [. . .] otherwise than the barons of Hastings and the five ports are most pleasing'). The Supreme Court of the Cinque Ports was at SHEPWAY. The present spelling and pronunciation of the name owe more to the Latin than the original French (compare the name of the plant cinquefoil, pronounced 'sinkfoil').

Cirencester (Gloucestershire)

The second part of the name of this country town northwest of SWINDON indicates the former Roman station here, as it represents the Old English *ceaster* (Roman camp). The first part of the name is a remnant of the name of the station, which was *Corinium*. The precise origin of the latter is still uncertain, as no early forms of the name have been recorded, and there are no similarly named places for comparison. Cirencester was recorded in the late ninth century as *Cirenceaster*. Either *Corinium* or the present name gave the name of the River Churn, on which the town stands. The river name at least preserves the *ch* sound of the Old English *ceaster*; this became softened to an *s* sound under the Normans. The Domesday Book spelt the name *Cirecestre*, which may have led to a fifteenth-century spelling as *Cisetur*; this caused the actual pronunciation of the name to be 'Sissiter' until quite recently.

Cissbury Ring (West Sussex)
An Iron Age fort on the South Downs north of WORTHING. Its name has been derived from Cissa, the man who gave his name to CHICHESTER, but this association, probably the work of antiquarians, has been made only since the end of the sixteenth century, when the name was first recorded. Before that, the fort was known simply as Bury, from the Old English *burg* (fortified place).

Clackmannan (Central)
The name of this town east of ALLOA means literally 'stone of Manau', the latter being the name of the district here. The stone (compare Welsh *clog* 'rock') is a glacial rock in the middle of the town, where it stands (as the Stone of Manau) next to the Town Cross and the Tolbooth. The town's name was recorded in a document of 1147 as *Clacmanan*. The former county of Clackmannanshire was named after the town, as was usual.

Clacton-on-Sea (Essex)
A coastal resort southeast of COLCHESTER. The name was recorded in a text of about 1000 as *Claccingtun*, showing it to have been an '-ington' name, like PADDINGTON. The meaning is thus 'estate connected with Clacc'; the personal name means 'hill dweller'. The suffix '-on-Sea' is partly commercial, but also distinguishes this Clacton from nearby Great Clacton and Little Clacton. The first of these, formerly a separate village, is now a northern district of Clacton itself.

Clapham (Greater London)
The two Old English words that comprise this name are the conjectural *clop* (hillock) (compare modern 'clump') and the common *hām* (village). The implication is that the original settlement was on or near rising ground. Clapham is on such terrain south of the THAMES, where the ground rises to the south and east of Clapham Common. The district's name was recorded in the Domesday Book as *Clopeham*.

Clare (Suffolk, Clare)
Although the English town and the Irish county share the same name, the origin of each is quite different. The SUFFOLK Clare, northwest of SUDBURY, is on the River STOUR, to which its name refers, deriving from a Celtic root word related to the modern Welsh *claear* (mild), so meaning something like 'pleasant water'. (Some scholars, however, have related the name to the modern Welsh *claer* 'bright', 'shining'.) The Irish county, in the west of the country, has a name deriving from the word *clar*, literally ('board', 'plank'), taken figuratively here to mean 'level place'. The settlement that gave its name to the county is now known as Clarecastle, a small town south of ENNIS. The Latin form of the English Clare, *Clarentia*, gave the name Clarence, the title of nobility. The first duke to use it was Lionel of Antwerp, the third son of Edward III, who was granted the title in 1362. His wife, Elizabeth de Burgh, whom he had married in 1352 (when he was 14 and she was 19), had inherited the lordship of the town of Clare from her grandmother, Elizabeth of Clare, and Lionel's title was thus taken from that of his wife. The year 1362 was selected as this was the one in which the king, Lionel's father, celebrated his fiftieth birthday.

Clay Cross (Derbyshire)
A town south of CHESTERFIELD that has developed in fairly recent times thanks to its collieries and ironworks. It apparently owes its name to a clayey crossing over the

stream here, which flows north from Clay Cross to join the ROTHER at Chesterfield.

Clayton-le-Moors (Lancashire)

The first word of the name of this town northwest of ACCRINGTON means 'clayey settlement' or 'village on clayey soil', from the Old English *clǣg* (clay) and the frequently found *tūn* (estate, village). The distinguishing addition '-le-Moors' refers to the high ground between Accrington and Great Harwood. The town's name was recorded simply as *Clayton* in 1263, and then in 1284 as *Clayton super Moras*. Other Claytons in the vicinity are Clayton-le-Dale and Clayton-le-Woods, with self-descriptive additions.

Cleator (Cumbria)

This mining village north of EGREMONT seems to have an Old Norse name comprising *klettr* (cliff, rock) and *erg* (hill pasture, shieling). The sense 'hill pasture by a cliff' can be deduced from a record of the name in a document of about 1200 as *Cletergh*. The second word of the name implies that there was a smallish dairy settlement here for use only in the summer months.

Cleckheaton (West Yorkshire)

The second half of the name of this town, northwest of DEWSBURY, is the fairly common 'Heaton', meaning simply 'high town' or, in the Old English original, 'farm on high ground', from *hēah* (high) and *tūn* (farm, village). As such, the name appeared in the Domesday Book as *Hetun*. Like many other places of the name, it then added a distinguishing word, which here is the Old Norse *klakkr*, literally 'lump', meaning a small hill. A few miles south of Cleckheaton is the village of Kirkheaton, 'church Heaton'.

Cleethorpes (Humberside)

A town and resort immediately east of GRIMSBY at the mouth of the HUMBER. Its name means 'the Clee hamlets', with the second half of the name representing the Old Norse *thorp* (outlying farm, hamlet). The first part of the name, which in itself means 'clayey place', is that of the ancient settlement of Clee, a short distance inland. The collective name was used for the administrative group of hamlets here (Hole, Clee and Itterby). All three (with Clee now called Old Clee) have now been swallowed up by the combined development of Grimsby and Cleethorpes itself. The name of Cleethorpes has not been found in any documents earlier than the seventeenth century, when it was spelt as now.

Clerkenwell (Greater London)

The name of this district of northeast LONDON suggests 'well of the clerks', and this is really what it means, allowing for the fact that in medieval times a 'clerk' was a student. One can thus imagine a scene on a summer evening when students gathered round a spring here north of the THAMES. A mid-twelfth-century text records the name spelt exactly as now. 'Clerken-' represents the former plural of 'clerk' (as in 'oxen'). The 'student' sense of 'clerk' is familiar from Chaucer's *Canterbury Tales*, where the *Prologue* has the lines:

> A Clerk ther was of Oxenford also
> That vn to logyk hadde longe ygo

Nevill Coghill's modern translation preserves the old word thus:

> An *Oxford Cleric*, still a student though,
> One who had taken logic long ago.

Chaucer's original here, incidentally, gives the name of OXFORD as it was in the late fourteenth century.

Clevedon (Avon)

A residential town and resort northeast of WESTON-SUPER-MARE on the SEVERN estuary. It has a straightforward name meaning 'cliffs hill', that is, a hilly place with cliffs, from the Old English *clif* (cliff) and the common *dūn* (hill). The name was recorded in the Domesday Book as *Clivedon*. Clevedon has a number of hills, and the cliffs behind the town rise to a considerable height.

Cleveland (England)

The present northeastern county, formed in 1974, takes its name from the Cleveland Hills that cross its southeastern portion; their own name means 'land of cliffs' or 'hilly district'. Cleveland has coastal cliffs to the east of SALTBURN-BY-THE-SEA. The name is an old one, and was recorded in a document of about 1110 as *Clivelanda*.

Cleveleys (Lancashire)

A coastal town to the north of BLACKPOOL whose name literally means 'clearing by a cliff', from the Old English *clif* (cliff) and *lēah* (forest clearing). But this is quite inappropriate for the flat coast here, and the true origin seems to be in a surname. According to Ralph Smedley and Fred Anton, *Thornton Cleveleys in Old Picture Postcards* (1984), there was an innkeeper here named Mr Cleveley or Cleveleys.

Cley-next-the-Sea (Norfolk)

The first word of the name of this village northwest of HOLT is from the Old English *clæg* (clay). The Domesday Book recorded the village as *Cleia*. Cley is indeed in a clayey location on the River Glaven by some marshes near the low-lying coast. The latter part of the name has been added for commercial (or distinguishing) reasons.

Clifden (Galway)

This attractive market town in western CONNEMARA has a name that appears to be a distortion of its Irish name, An Clochán, 'the stepping stones'. Although there are hills and mountains to the east of the town, Clifden itself is low-lying at the mouth of the River Owenglin. It would have been across this river that the stepping stones lay by way of a ford.

Clifton (Avon)

There are many Cliftons in Britain, all having names that denote a 'hillside settlement' or a settlement by a hill. The district of BRISTOL called Clifton is a good illustration: it is a residential district on a steep hill to the west of the city but to the east of the deep AVON Gorge, which is crossed by the Clifton Suspension Bridge. Its name was recorded in the Domesday Book as *Clistone*, where the clerk may have made an error in rendering *f* as *s*. Perhaps he misheard the name.

Cliftonville (Kent)

The district of MARGATE called Cliftonville got its name from a hotel here in the nineteenth century, the Cliftonville Hotel. This derived its own name apparently from a Clifton Street, adding the then fashionable '-ville'. The name may have been partly suggested by the already existing suburb of BRIGHTON called Cliftonville, further west along the south coast.

Clitheroe (Lancashire)

This industrial town northeast of BLACKBURN has a name interpreted by some as 'hill of loose stones', and by others as 'thrush hill'. The second element of the name is generally agreed to be the Old Norse *haugr* (hill), although this could equally be the Old English *hōh* (spur), of similar meaning. The first part of the name thus represents either a conjectural Old English *clȳder* (loose stones), referring to the crumbling limestone on which the twelfth-century castle was built, or the Old Norse *klithra* (thrush), denoting a hill where thrushes gathered. The latter interpretation, with both parts of the name thereby Old Norse in origin, seems more logical, but the former explanation cannot be ruled out. The name was recorded in 1102 as *Cliderhou*.

Cliveden (Buckinghamshire)

Cliveden House, north of TAPLOW, dates from the seventeenth century and takes its name from the locality here. Cliveden means 'valley by the cliff', from the Old English *clif* (cliff, hill-slope) and *denu* (valley). The 'cliff' here is an escarpment by the THAMES, over which there is a fine view from the house and its grounds. The name was recorded in 1195 as *Cliueden*.

Clogher (Tyrone)
This former cathedral town southeast of
OMAGH has a name that means simply
'stony place', referring to the ground or to
an ancient stone building, such as a fort.
The Irish name is An Clochár, from *cloch*
(stone).

Clonakilty (Cork)
The name of this small market town
southwest of BANDON is a rendering of its
original Irish name, Cloich na Coillte,
literally 'stone of the woods', meaning that
the place arose round a stone fort by some
woods.

Clondalkin (Dublin)
A fairly modern industrial complex to the
west of DUBLIN. Its Irish name is Cluain
Dolcáin, which means 'Dolcán's meadow'.
It is not known who Dolcán was.

Clones (Monaghan)
This town north of CAVAN grew round a
monastery founded here in the sixth
century. Its Irish name is Cluain Eois,
'meadow of Eos'. The English version is
still pronounced as two syllables.

Clonmel (Tipperary)
A market town west of CARRICK-ON-SUIR
on the River Suir. Its attractive name
means 'meadow of honey', as shown by the
Irish original, Cluain Meala. This probably
denoted a meadow where wild bees nested,
rather than one with beehives.

Clontarf (Dublin)
The fashionable northeast DUBLIN suburb
has a name with an unexpected meaning:
'pasture of bulls', from Cluain Tarbh, its
Irish original. There is a tract of land here
still known as North Bull, now serving as a
bird sanctuary.

Cloud, The (Cheshire/Staffordshire)
A hill on the county border east of
CONGLETON, famous for its fine views. Its
name does not relate to the clouds above,
but comes from the Old English *clūd* (rock,

mass of rock; or simply 'hill' in general).
This certainly describes The Cloud. *Clūd*
came to acquire the modern meaning of
'cloud' in the thirteenth century, probably
at first due to the 'hilly' appearance of
cumulus clouds. This word thus
superseded the former word for cloud,
which was 'welkin'.

Clovelly (Devon)
A coastal village west of BIDEFORD, built
on a steep cliffside. Its name combines the
Old English *clof* (something cut, cleft) and
the place-name Velly, the latter being a
nearby hill, whose own name comes from
the Old English *felg* (felly), that is, the rim
of a wheel. The hill is thus semi-circular in
shape, suggesting the rim of a wheel, and
Clovelly is in a 'cleft' or V-shaped
indentation in it. The Domesday Book
gives the name as *Clovelie*, more or less as
now.

Clun (Mid Glamorgan, Shropshire)
The river name in both counties simply
means 'water', from a British (Celtic)
conjectural root word *colauno-* which also
gave the name of the River Colne on which
COLCHESTER stands. The name appears as
an element in several place-names, such as
the Mid Glamorgan village of Pontyclun
('bridge over the Clun') and the Shropshire
village of Clun itself.

Clwyd (Wales)
The ancient name was revived for the new
north Wales county formed in 1974. It
comes from the River Clwyd here, whose
own name means basically 'hurdle' (Welsh
clwyd), perhaps as hurdles were used to
ford it or to build a causeway across it. If
so, the name has an exact parallel in that of
Baile Átha Cliath, the Irish name of
DUBLIN. The Welsh river's name appears
in a text of 1191 as *Cloid fluvium*.

Clydach (West Glamorgan)
A town northeast of SWANSEA that takes its
name from the river on which it stands,
with this in turn deriving from the same

Celtic root word that gave the name CLYDE, meaning 'cleansing one'. It was recorded in a document of 1208 as *Cleudach*.

Clyde (Strathclyde)
A famous Scottish river whose name means 'cleansing one', from a British (Celtic) conjectural root element *clouta-*, seen also in CLYDACH. The Clyde was recorded in the second century AD as *Clota*, this being the Roman name of the river. The same root element thus lies behind the Latin word *cloaca* (sewer). *See also* CLYDEBANK; STRATHCLYDE.

Clydebank (Strathclyde)
An industrial town whose name describes its location on the north bank of the River CLYDE; the name is also that of the administrative district here.

Coalbrookdale (Shropshire)
This village immediately northwest of IRONBRIDGE seems to have an apt 'industrial' name for a place that is the 'cradle of the iron industry'. However, the name does not derive from 'coal'! It means 'valley of the Coalbrook', this being the small river here, whose own name means merely 'cold brook'. This sense can be confirmed by early records of the name, such as the one of 1250 that gives it as *Caldebrok*. *Compare* COALVILLE.

Coalville (Leicestershire)
The name of this coal-mining town northwest of LEICESTER is a modern one, given to the mining settlement that developed here round a house called Coalville House in the 1820s and '30s. The original hamlet comprised a few straggling cottages known as Long Lane. The '-ville' of the name is a typical nineteenth-century 'habitation' element, found also in the names of BOURNVILLE, CLIFTONVILLE, and WATERLOOVILLE, among others.

Coatbridge (Strathclyde)
The name of this mining settlement east of GLASGOW means more or less what it says,

that is, 'bridge by a place called Coats'. The latter name, which derives ultimately from the Old English *cot* (shelter), refers to the cottages here by the Monkland Canal (*see* MONKLANDS). The name was recorded in a text dated 1584 simply as *Coittis*.

Cóbh (Cork)
Normally in Ireland an English spelling of a name will derive from an Irish original. Here the reverse has happened, the Irish *An Cóbh* representing the English 'the cove'. The port east of CORK is renowned for its fine harbour (Cork Harbour) — the 'cove' of the name. From 1849 to 1922 the town was known as Queenstown, in honour of Queen Victoria, who paid an official visit here in 1849. For a matching Kingstown, *see* DUN LAOGHAIRE. Before the queen's visit, the port was usually known as Cove, with the English spelling.

Cobham (Surrey)
A residential town (more an enlarged village) northwest of LEATHERHEAD whose name means 'Cofa's village', with the personal name followed by the common Old English *hām* (homestead, village). The Domesday Book gave the name as *Covenham*, and the present spelling with a *b* seems to have arisen due to the influence of the name of Chobham, a village about nine miles west of the town.

Cockenzie (Lothian)
The name of this town northeast of MUSSELBURGH is usually coupled with that of PORT SETON, but here it is considered separately for convenience. Its meaning is obscure, although a personal name is probably involved. It was recorded in 1590 as *Cowkany*, and a local pronunciation of the name is still 'Cockenny'.

Cockermouth (Cumbria)
A town east of WORKINGTON lying at the confluence of the rivers Cocker and DERWENT. It takes its name from the former, whose own name means 'crooked

one', from a Celtic root that gave the modern Welsh *crwca* (crooked) and is indirectly linked to the English word.

Cockfosters (Greater London)

This northern district of LONDON arose at the edge of ENFIELD Chase, and ts name is associated with this former hunting ground. It thus means 'place of the chief forester', with 'cock' as in 'cock of the walk', and 'foster' representing 'forester', as the surname Foster often does. The name was recorded in 1524 as *Cokfosters*.

Colchester (Essex)

This ancient town, the first Roman capital of Britain, has the required '-chester' in its name to denote its former Roman station. The first part of the name represents that of the River Colne on which it stands, with the river name itself meaning simply 'water' and related to that of the CLUN. The name of the Roman town here was *Camulodunum*, deriving from the name of the Celtic war-god, Camulos, whose name lay behind that of the Iron Age fort formerly here. The '-dunum' of the Roman name means 'fort' (*see* DINAS POWYS). The name of Colchester has been popularly associated with Old King Cole, and folklorists like to claim that he gave the name of the town. A more reasonable suggestion, but just as groundless, is that the first part of the name derives from the Roman *colonia* (colony), especially as the Roman name of the town was recorded by Tacitus as *Colonia Camulodunum*. But this is pure coincidence, and the river name is the true source. However, compare the Roman name of LINCOLN.

Coldstream (Borders)

A small town northeast of KELSO on the River TWEED. Its name probably refers to the cold waters of this river, although the smaller Leet Water, which flows into the Tweed here, may have been the original source.

Coleford (Gloucestershire)

A town in the FOREST OF DEAN whose name means roughly 'coal ford', but with the first part referring to charcoal not coal. There is only a small stream here that the ford could have crossed. Presumably charcoal was made near it. The name was recorded in 1534 as *Colford*.

Coleraine (Londonderry)

The name of this town northeast of LONDONDERRY is a corruption of its Irish name, Cúil Rathain, 'recess of ferns'. Variations on this spelling are found for other places in Ireland, such as Cooleraine in Limerick and Coolrainy in Wexford.

Coleshill (Warwickshire)

This town, on hilly ground east of BIRMINGHAM, has a fairly straightforward name, recorded in 799 as *Colles hyl*. Coleshill is on the River Cole, whose name is Celtic meaning 'hazel' or 'river where hazel nuts grow' (*compare* the modern Welsh *collen*, 'hazel'). To this is added the Old English *hyll* (hill).

Colindale (Greater London)

A district of BARNET that takes its name from a family called Collin, who are on record as having lived here in the sixteenth century. A document of 1550 gives the name as *Collyndene*, 'Collin's valley'. Subsequently the final '-dene' was changed to '-dale', which retains the basic sense of 'valley', however. The 'valley' is that of the Silk Stream here, which flows south through Colindeep Open Space and the area known as The Hyde into the Brent Reservoir.

Colinton (Lothian)

This southwest district of EDINBURGH was recorded in a document of 1319 as *Colbanestoun*, showing the original personal name to be Colban, not Colin, as it now appears. The overall sense is thus 'Colban's estate'. Records of the sixteenth and seventeenth century spell the name as *Colingtoun* and *Collingtoun*, as if the name contained the '-ington' ending that means 'place associated with'.

Colintraive (Strathclyde)
Travellers to the island of BUTE will know that the ferry operates from Colintraive, on the shore of the KYLES OF BUTE. The name of the village represents the Gaelic *caol an t-snaimh*, 'straits of the swimming place', referring to the point where drovers crossed the Kyles of Bute with their cattle bound for market on the mainland.

Coll (Strathclyde)
An island in the Inner HEBRIDES with a name probably derived from Old Norse *kollr*, 'bald head', i.e. 'barren place'. *Compare* ROCKALL.

Collyweston (Northamptonshire)
Famous for its roof tiles, this village southwest of STAMFORD has a name that means 'western estate owned by Nicholas', with 'Colly' a short form of this Christian name. The name is Norman, first recorded in its present form in a document of 1309 as *Colynweston* (but in the earlier Domesday Book simply as *Westone*). The individual referred to was Nicholas de Segrave, who died in 1322. The Christian name Colin is itself derived from Nicholas.

Colne (Lancashire)
A town northeast of BURNLEY on the Colne Water, after which small river it takes its name. Although now identical in spelling to the River Colne that gave the name of COLCHESTER, the derivation of Colne Water is the same as that of the river after which CALNE is named. Its meaning is thus 'noisy one', from a British (Celtic) conjectural root element *calaun-*. The Lancashire town was recorded in a text of 1124 as *Calna*, showing the original *a* of the British word and its close similarity to the present name of the Wiltshire town.

Colonsay (Strathclyde)
An island northwest of JURA in the Inner HEBRIDES. It has an Old Norse name translating as 'Kolbein's island', the last element being the Old Norse *ey* (island), as in the name of its smaller southern neighbour, ORONSAY. The name was recorded in a fourteenth-century document as *Coluynsay*.

Colwyn Bay (Clwyd)
This North Wales coastal town and resort west of RHYL arose only in the 1860s, and added 'Bay' to be distinguished from the original village of Colwyn to the east, itself now called Old Colwyn and a suburb of the resort. This earlier Colwyn takes its name from the small stream here, which directly comes from the Welsh *colwyn* (puppy), alluding to its small size. The village's name was recorded in 1334 as *Coloyne*. The larger resort is on Colwyn Bay, named after it.

Colyton (Devon)
This small town north of SEATON, like the village of Colyford south of it, is on the River Coly and takes its name from it. The river's name is British (Celtic) in origin, and means 'narrow'. Compare the name of the KYLES OF BUTE for the strait there. Colyton was recorded in 940 as *Culintona*, 'farm on the Coly'.

Compton Wynyates (Warwickshire)
A famous Tudor country house whose name can be literally interpreted as 'estate in a valley where there is a windy pass'. 'Compton' derives from the common Old English *cumb* (narrow valley) (as in CASTLE COMBE) and *tūn* (farm, estate). The second word of the name corresponds to the name Wingate, literally 'wind gate', from the Old English *wind-geat*, and denotes a windswept pass. The house is situated in a valley surrounded by low hills. The name was attached to the settlement here (east of SHIPSTON ON STOUR) long before the house was built in the late fifteenth century, and was recorded as *Cumpton Wintace* in a document of 1242. The second word was added to distinguish this Compton from the many others, and in the

Domesday Book Compton Wynyates was recorded simply as *Contone*.

Comrie (Tayside)

A village and resort west of CRIEFF situated at the junction of Glen Artney (the valley of Ruchill Water), Glen Lednock (of the River Lednock), and Strathearn (of the River Earn). It is therefore hardly surprising that its name means 'confluence', from the Gaelic *comar*. The name was recorded in 1268 as *Comry*.

Congleton (Cheshire)

A mainly industrial town north of STOKE-ON-TRENT in the valley of the River Dane. There are a number of hills nearby (including MOW COP less than four miles to the south), and one of these must have been known as Conkhill, meaning 'round-topped hill', giving its name thus to the town. The Old English *hyll* and *tūn* combine with the conjectural *canc* (steep round hill). Congleton was recorded in the Domesday Book as *Cogleton*.

Conisbrough (South Yorkshire)

This town southwest of DONCASTER has a name meaning 'king's manor', from the Old Norse *konungr* (king) and the Old English *burg* (fortified place, manor). The name was recorded in 1002 as *Cunungesburh*. *Compare* CONISTON WATER.

Coniston Water (Cumbria)

One of the lakes in the Lake District, named after the village of Coniston at its northern end. The village's name means 'king's farm', with the Old Norse *konungr* (king) followed by the common Old English *tūn* (farm, estate). *Compare* CONISBROUGH.

Connah's Quay (Clwyd)

An industrial town and port west of CHESTER on the DEE. It was originally known as New Quay when a channel was cut in the river estuary here in the early eighteenth century. The personal name

Connah is first recorded later in the same century; Connah was said to be an Irish merchant, although of uncertain identity. The presence of the Irish here is attested by such street names as Cork Row and Dublin Row. According to the *Liverpool Daily Post* (24 May 1949) Irish immigrants here 'can be traced to the middle of the 18th cent. when an Irish Colliery Company employing Irish labour worked the mines in the neighbourhood' (quoted in E. Davies, *Flintshire Place-Names*, 1959).

Connaught (Ireland)

Connaught (usually spelt Connacht by the Irish) is the name of the most westerly of the five historic provinces of Ireland, the others being LEINSTER, MEATH, MUNSTER, and ULSTER. It is from the name of the Connachta tribe, in turn said to be derived from the Irish *connadh* (fuel, firewood).

Connemara (Galway)

The western, coastal region of the county that derives its name ultimately from Conmac, the son of the ULSTER warrior Fergus MacRoy (Fergus mac roich) who married the legendary Queen Maeve (Medb). The first part of the name is based on Conmac's own name; the latter part derives from the name of his territory, itself derived from the Irish *muir* (sea). Overall, Connemara means 'maritime territory of the people of Conmac'. The name has been recorded in a historical document as *Conmaicne-mara*.

Consett (Durham)

This industrial town west of CHESTER-LE-STREET had its name recorded in a document of 1183 as *Covekesheued* and in one of 1228 as *Conekesheued*. These are very similar, and if one allows that the *v* of the former name is a copying error for *n* (as in the present name), it is possible to interpret it as meaning 'headland of *Cunuc*', with the Old English *hēafod* (head, hill) added to the name of the hill. *Cunuc* (in its Old English form of *Conek* here) is probably a pre-British (Celtic) root word meaning simply 'hill', also perhaps discernible in such names as Conock (Wiltshire) and CONGLETON. Consett is on a prominent hill, so the name is appropriate. Some recent toponymical research has similarly related the root word to the Roman name of Chester-le-Street, which was *Concangis*.

Conwy (Gwynedd)

A resort and small port south of LLANDUDNO whose name, formerly spelt Conway, derives from the river at the mouth of which it stands. The river name is from a conjectural British (Celtic) root element *can-* meaning 'famous'. This root is also seen in the name of *Canovium*, the Roman fort that stood on the River Conwy at the village now known as Caerhun, south of Conwy town. The former name of Conwy was *Aberconwy*, denoting its location at the mouth (Welsh *aber*) of the river, and Aberconwy was revived as the name of the administrative district formed here in 1974.

Cookham (Berkshire)

This riverside resort north of MAIDENHEAD on the THAMES has a name that means 'hillock homestead', from the conjectural Old English *cocc* (heap) (as in modern 'haycock') and *hamm* (land in the bend of a river). A record of 798 gives the name as *Cocham*, and a later document of 1220 records a hill here called *Cocdun*. Perhaps this was where the nearby Cookham Rise is today, on higher land to the west of the resort.

Cookstown (Tyrone)

A market town with a long main street, on the road from DUNGANNON to MAGHERA. It was laid out at the beginning of the seventeenth century by Alan Cook, and takes its name from him. Its Irish name is quite different: An Chorr Chríochach, 'the boundary hill'. Cookstown is close to the county boundary between Tyrone and Londonderry.

Cootehill (Cavan)

The name of this town southeast of CLONES includes the surname of the Coote family, who held lands here in the seventeenth century. Cootehill's Irish name is Muinchille, 'sleeve', indicating the outline of some former territory here. Compare the French use of *La Manche* to denote the sleeve-like shape of the English Channel.

Copeland Forest (Cumbria)

An area of fells north of WAST WATER. The name is Scandinavian in origin, and comes from the Old Norse *kaupa-land*, 'purchased land'. This was the Viking designation for land that had been bought, as distinct from what they called *othalsjorth*, which was land acquired by law. The name of the forest was recorded in the early twelfth century as *Couplanda*.

Coquet (Northumberland)

A river flowing from the CHEVIOT HILLS to the North Sea at WARKWORTH. Its name was recorded in about 721 as *Coquedi fluminis*. It is probably of pre-British (Celtic) origin, and its meaning is still uncertain.

Corbridge (Northumberland)

This small town east of HEXHAM has a name that seems to indicate a bridge over a river called 'Cor'. But the river here is the TYNE. The name of the former Roman station here, *Corstopitum*, has been shortened to its first syllable, with the Old English *brycg* (bridge) added. The meaning of the Roman name, which may itself be a corruption of something like *Coriosopitum*, has not yet been deciphered. The name Corbridge does not suggest a Roman station, but that of Corchester does — this is the local name of the actual site of the camp, a mile to the west of Corbridge.

Corby (Northamptonshire)

A steel-manufacturing town north of KETTERING with a Danish name meaning 'Kóri's village'. It dates from the late ninth century, when the Danes took possession of large areas of northeast England. The element '-by' is common here to represent the Old Norse *bý* (village). Corby is not too far from the village of Corby Glen, Lincolnshire, north of STAMFORD, and it is possible that the same man may have given the name of both places. Corby was recorded in the Domesday Book as *Corbei*.

Corfe Castle (Dorset)

This village with its well-known Norman castle, southeast of WAREHAM, is in a gap in the PURBECK Hills on the River Corfe, and took its name from this. The river's name derives from a conjectural Old English word *corf* that means 'cutting', 'pass', so relates directly to the gap in the hills here. (The word is itself related to the modern English 'carve'.) The name was recorded in 955, before the castle was built, simply as *Corf*.

Cork (Cork)

A city and county in southeast Ireland. The name of the city derives directly from the Irish *corcach* (marsh), referring to the marshland here by which a monastery was founded in the sixth century. Muddy streams crossed the town as late as the eighteenth century, and the present St Patrick's Street and Grand Parade were built over deep stretches of water where boats formerly loaded and unloaded. Waterways and quaysides still abound in the city, with the River Lee dividing into two channels as it flows eastwards through the city to Lough Mahon and Cork Harbour. Cork's present Irish name is Corcaigh. The county took its name from the town.

Cornwall (England)

The county lying at the southwesternmost tip of mainland Britain. Its name is based on a tribal name, that of the Cornovii, who lived both here and in the West Midlands and Scotland in pre-English times. Their name means simply 'promontory people'. To the tribal name, the Anglo-Saxons

added the Old English *walh* (foreigner), implying someone who spoke a Celtic language, unlike themselves. This same word is more obvious in the origin of WALES, where the Welsh were also Celtic speakers. Cornwall was recorded in the sixth century as *Cornubia*.

Corrib, Lough (Galway/Mayo)

A lough in western Ireland whose name derives from that of Orbsen or Oirbsean, a legendary hero. The present spelling of the name is a rendering of the Irish An Choirb, 'Oirbsean's lake', where the original personal name has been abbreviated and corrupted.

Corringham (Essex)

A town south of BASILDON whose name means 'homestead of Curra's people'. The personal name can be deduced from the early spellings of the name with *u*, not *o*, as in the *Currincham* of the Domesday Book.

Corrour Forest (Highland)

A forest to the east of Loch Ossian whose name is found elsewhere in the Highlands. It represents the Gaelic *coire* (cup, cauldron), describing a hollow or a depression in the ground. The forest has more than one such hollow. (The same basic word can be seen in the Gaelic version of 'Polly, put the kettle on', which is *Phoileag, cur an choire air*. The 'kettle' of the rhyme is thus more a cauldron or pot, without the modern spout, lid, and handle!)

Corsham (Wiltshire)

A small town southwest of CHIPPENHAM, well known for the local mansion, Corsham Court. The name means 'Cosa's village'; the *r* appears to have been added under late Norman influence. In the Domesday Book it was recorded as *Cosseham*, which should have produced a modern name identical with COSHAM.

Corwen (Clwyd)

A market town on the River DEE west of

LLANGOLLEN. The name was earlier recorded as *Corfaen*, meaning 'sacred stone', the latter element being the Welsh *maen* (stone). This is presumably the ancient stone known as the 'Carrig-y-Big' ('pointed stone') that is built into the porch wall of the church, and that was probably once a free-standing monolith.

Coseley (West Midlands)
A northern district of DUDLEY whose name means 'charcoal burner's wood', from the conjectural Old English *colere* (charcoal burner) (*compare* the modern English 'collier') and the frequently occurring *lēah* (wood, clearing).

Cosham (Hampshire)
A town, now a district of PORTSMOUTH, whose name shares its origin with CORSHAM and means 'Cosa's village'; the personal name is followed by the Old English *hām* (homestead, village). Like Corsham, it was recorded in the Domesday Book as *Cosseham*, and even in the present century was pronounced 'Cossam' (without the 'sh' sound) to preserve the identity of the personal name.

Cotswold Hills (Gloucestershire)
A range of hills extending northeastwards from BATH to BANBURY. The name means 'Cōd's weald', that is, 'high open ground belonging to Cōd' (pronounced 'Code'). The name was recorded in the twelfth century as *Codesuualt*. For explanation of the second half of the name *see* WEALD, THE. The Cotswold village of Cutsdean was named after the same man, with '-dean' a corruption of '-ton'.

Cottingham (Humberside)
A town northwest of HULL whose name means 'homestead of Cotta's people', and was recorded in the Domesday Book as *Cotingeham*.

Coulsdon (Greater London)
A district of CROYDON with a name meaning 'Cuthred's hill'; the personal name is followed by the Old English *dūn* (hill). The original *r* of the name, recorded in 675 as *Curedesdone*, became *l* under the influence of the Normans, as happened also with SALISBURY. The Domesday Book thus gave the name with its letter change as *Colesdone*.

Coupar Angus (Tayside)
This small town southeast of BLAIRGOWRIE may have a name derived from the Gaelic *comh-phairt* (community, common sharing), although this is uncertain. The second word identifies it as the town in the (former) county of ANGUS, as distinct from CUPAR (Fife).

Coventry (West Midlands)
The name of this industrial city east of BIRMINGHAM means 'Cōfa's tree', making it similar to BRAINTREE, MANNINGTREE, and OSWESTRY, all of which have a personal name followed by a form of 'tree' (Old English *trēow*). Many such places used the tree as the meeting place of the 'hundred', or local assembly, although Coventry was not the centre of a hundred and the tree may therefore have had some other function or significance. The name was recorded in 1043 as *Couentre*.

Coverack (Cornwall)
The name of this village southeast of HELSTON, on the east coast of the LIZARD peninsula, was recorded in a text of 1262 as *Porthcovrec*. The Cornish *porth* means 'harbour', but the remainder (representing all of the modern name) is a place-name of unknown meaning. A personal name may be involved.

Cowbridge (South Glamorgan)
A market town west of CARDIFF whose name means what it says: 'cows' bridge', 'bridge used by cows (when they go to market)'. The town is on the site of the Roman station of *Bovium*, which name derives from the Latin *bos*, genitive *bovis* (cow, ox), showing that the connection

with cattle is an old one. The town's Welsh name does not preserve this link, however, for it is Y Bont-faen, 'the stone bridge'.

Cowcaddens (Strathclyde)

A district of GLASGOW whose name is a corruption of the Gaelic *cuil calldainn*, 'nook of hazels' (*compare* COCKENZIE). The present form of the name may well have been influenced by the fact that cows passed through here on their way to pasture. A document of 1510 gives the name as *Kowcawdennis*. The local pronunciation of the name is 'Cucaddens'.

Cowdenbeath (Fife)

The name of this town northeast of DUNFERMLINE has been derived from the Gaelic *cul duin*, 'back of the hill'. However, there are no early records of the name, and a document of 1626 refers to the place as *terris de Baithe-Moubray alias Cowdounes-baithe*, suggesting that the first part of the name is a personal name, possibly Cowden. The latter part is certainly the Gaelic *beith* (birch), so that the overall name may mean 'Cowden's land by the birches'.

Cowes (Isle of Wight)

A well-known resort and yachting centre north of NEWPORT. The name comes from two sandbanks off the mouth of the River MEDINA here that were called 'The Cows' (*compare* the CALF OF MAN); this name was transferred to the settlement that arose on the shore. The sandbanks were individually named in a document of 1413 as *Estcowe* and *Westcowe*, and were later known jointly as either 'The Cow' or 'The Cows'.

Cowley (Oxfordshire)

A southeast district of OXFORD, famous for its car factory. The name is fairly common, being found elsewhere in the country, and probably means 'Cufa's clearing', with the personal name followed by the Old English *lēah* (forest, clearing). This particular Cowley was recorded in the Domesday

Book as *Covelie*. (However, not all Cowleys have this meaning; the Gloucestershire village south of CIRENCESTER has a name meaning simply 'cow pasture', as early forms of the name show.)

Craigavon (Armagh)

A New Town designated in 1965 and sited southwest of BELFAST. It is named after the first prime minister of Northern Ireland in that year, James Craig, Viscount Craigavon.

Craigellachie (Grampian)

A distillery village south of ROTHES with a pure Gaelic name meaning 'crag of the rocky place', comprising *carraig* (a diminutive of *carr*, 'crag') and *eileach*, 'rocky place' (in modern Gaelic this is the word for 'dam'). *Compare* CRAIL.

Craiglockhart (Lothian)

A district of EDINBURGH whose name is referred to in a text of 1278 as *Crag quam Stephanus Locard miles tenuit*, showing that those who like to derive the name from *loch ard* (high loch) are incorrect. The Latin here means 'The rock which Stephen Lockhart, soldier, held'.

Crail (Fife)

This attractive small fishing town and resort has a name that has 'telescoped' two Gaelic words for 'rock': *carr* and *all*, the latter of which is no longer current in modern Gaelic. Crail has been recorded in historical documents as *Caraile*, showing the two elements of the name. The coast is noticeably craggy here southwest of FIFE Ness.

Cramlington (Northumberland)

It has been suggested that the first part of the name of this town north of NEWCASTLE UPON TYNE may derive from the Old English *cran-wella* (cranes' spring), like the name of CRANWELL. With the Old English *-ingtūn* added the overall meaning is 'place associated with (the people who live by the) cranes' spring'. The name was

recorded in a document of about 1130 as
Cramlingtuna.

Cranborne Chase (Dorset/Wiltshire)
A hilly, partly wooded region, southeast of
SHAFTESBURY, that was formerly a forest
and hunting preserve, as the 'Chase'
indicates. The first word of the name
means 'cranes' stream' or 'stream where
cranes live', from the Old English *cran*
(crane) and *burna* (stream). The original
Cranborne here is the village northwest of
RINGWOOD. *Compare* CRANBROOK.

Cranbrook (Kent)
A small town west of TENTERDEN whose
name means 'cranes' stream', from the Old
English *cran* (crane) and *brōc* (stream). The
name is thus identical in meaning to
Cranbourne (*see* CRANBORNE CHASE). A
stream near Cranbrook is called the Crane
Brook.

Cranford (Greater London)
A district of HOUNSLOW with a name
meaning 'ford frequented by cranes'; this is
the sense of the name wherever else it
occurs.

Cranleigh (Surrey)
A town with its public school of the same
name southeast of GUILDFORD. The name
means 'wood where cranes live', from the
Old English *cran* (crane) and *lēah* (wood,
forest clearing).

Cranwell (Lincolnshire)
A village northwest of SLEAFORD, well
known for its RAF college and airfield.
The name means 'cranes' spring' or 'spring
where cranes come regularly'. The Old
English components are *cran* (crane) and
wella (spring, well). The name was
recorded in the Domesday Book as
Craneuuele.

Craven (North Yorkshire)
An administrative district in the west of the
county. It is a historic name, recorded in
the Domesday Book as *Crave*, and may

have British (Celtic) origins related directly
to the Welsh *craf* (garlic).

Craven Arms (Shropshire)
A small town northwest of LUDLOW that
owes its name to an inn here, the Craven
Arms, erected in the early nineteenth
century as a 'rival' to an existing nearby
New Inn. The inn itself was named after
the Earls of CRAVEN, who held the manor
of Stokesay near here in the early
seventeenth century. A road junction came
to be called after the Craven Arms, and the
name was subsequently adopted in the
mid-nineteenth century for the railway
station built here. The present town
developed around the station. It remains as
an important railway junction where the
line from SHREWSBURY branches off from
the main HEREFORD line to serve many
Welsh stations to SWANSEA.

Crawfordsburn (Down)
A village east of BELFAST situated at the
head of the glen from which it takes its
name. The small river flowing through is
named after a local landowner called
Crawford, so the complete name (in Irish,
Sruth Chráfard) means simply 'Crawford's
stream'.

Crawley (West Sussex)
This town south of LONDON, designated a
New Town in 1947, has a name that means
'crows' wood' or 'wood where crows
congregate', from the Old English *crāwe*
(crow) and *lēah* (wood, clearing). A
document of 1203 has the name as
Crauleia. The name is found elsewhere in
the country.

Crayford (Greater London)
A district of Bexley that takes its name
from the River Cray, in whose valley it lies.
The river's name is probably derived from
a British (Celtic) root element meaning
'clean' (*compare* modern Welsh *crai*,
'clean', 'fresh'). The settlement's name was
recorded in 1199 as *Creiford*, and the
original ford may have been where the

High Street now branches off from
Crayford Road (a section of WATLING
STREET, the old Roman road from
CANTERBURY to LONDON, now the A226
here). It is unusual for '-ford' to be added
to a river name; this is to distinguish
between the particular ford and one of a
nearby river, in this case DARTFORD, two
miles to the east, where the ford crosses the
River Darent. The name of the River Cray
is well in evidence near Crayford, for
example in the places known as North
Cray, Foots Cray, St Paul's Cray and St
Mary Cray, the two latter being church
dedications. Foots Cray is named after the
Norman lord of the manor here in the
eleventh century, Godwine Fōt. His
surname would have been a nickname, and
gave the modern surname Foot(e).

Crediton (Devon)

An ancient small town northwest of
EXETER on the River Creedy, after which
it takes its name. The river's name is
British (Celtic) in origin and means
'winding one'. The overall name thus
means 'farm on the Creedy', with the Old
English *tūn* added to the river name.
Crediton was recorded in a document of
930 as *Cridiantune*.

Crewe (Cheshire)

This town northwest of STOKE-ON-TRENT,
with its famous railway junction, is near
enough to the Welsh border to have a name
of Welsh origin. It has the literal meaning
'creel', from the Welsh *cryw*; a creel is a
fish basket. However, the word came to
acquire the meaning 'stepping stones',
probably because such stones would have
been laid alongside a wickerwork fence
placed across a river to trap fish. This is
therefore the best sense here — no doubt
there were stepping stones across one of the
small streams here. The town's name was
recorded in the Domesday Book as *Crew*.

Crewkerne (Somerset)

The name of this town southwest of
YEOVIL consists of a conjectural British

(Celtic) element *crouco-*, meaning 'hill',
followed by the Old English *ærn* (house,
building). The overall meaning is thus
'building by a hill called *Cruc*'. The
Domesday Book records Crewkerne
simply as *Cruche*, without the second word.
The town lies in a hollow surrounded by
hills, and one of these would have been the
original *Cruc*. The same British element is
similarly found in the name of the village of
Cricket St Thomas, four miles west of
Crewkerne, and also occurs (in Welsh
form) in CRICCIETH.

Criccieth (Gwynedd)

This seaside resort south of CAERNARVON
has a name of Welsh origin (better spelt
Cricieth) meaning literally 'mound of the
captives', from *crug* (mound, hill) (*compare*
CREWKERNE) and *caith*, the plural of *caeth*
(captive, bondsman). The reference is to
the (now ruined) Norman castle here, for
long a defensive post. Criccieth Castle was
built in 1230 on a headland (the 'mound')
to the south of the town. The name was
recorded in 1273 as *Crukeith*. *See also*
CRICKHOWELL.

Crickhowell (Powys)

A village northwest of ABERGAVENNY
whose name is based on *crug* (mound), also
evident in the names CRICCIETH and,
possibly, CRICKLADE. Crickhowell thus
means 'Hywel's mound', with the two
Welsh words anglicised in their traditional
manner. The Welsh name is Crucywell,
closer to the original. 'Hywel's mound'
(called locally Crug Hywel, or sometimes
the 'Table Mountain') is the Iron Age fort
about a mile and a half north of the village.

Cricklade (Wiltshire)

The name of this village on the THAMES
northwest of SWINDON was recorded in the
early-tenth-century *Anglo-Saxon Chronicle*
as *Crecca gelād*, showing that the first part
of the name is possibly (but not certainly)
the same British root word (meaning 'hill')
discernible in the above three place-names.
The second part of the name is certainly the

Old English *gelād* (river crossing). The name as a whole could thus mean 'place by a river crossing near a hill'. If the first half of the name does indeed mean 'hill', the reference would probably be to the nearby Horsey Down.

Cricklewood (Greater London)
A district of BRENT whose name means virtually what it says, implying a 'crickled wood', that is, a wood with a 'crimped' or uneven edge. 'Crickle' is a dialect word probably related to 'crinkle', if not to similar words such as 'crimp' and 'crank'. The name was recorded in 1294 as *Crikeldwode*. The wood would have been a western extension of the present HAMPSTEAD Heath.

Crieff (Tayside)
A town and resort west of PERTH whose name derives directly from the Gaelic *craobh* (tree), and so means 'place among the trees'. An early (undated) record of the name shows it as *Craoibh*. Crieff overlooks the River Earn in a location that is still surrounded by trees.

Cromarty (Highland)
A small town northeast of INVERNESS at the entrance to Cromarty Firth. The coastline here is very irregular, and this may be the source of the name, which means 'crooked place', based on an Old Gaelic word that produced the modern Gaelic *crom* (crooked). The name was recorded in 1264 as *Crumbathyn*; the second part of this is indirectly related to the English 'bay'. The town's name was given to the (former) county of ROSS and Cromarty; this was one main territory (Ross) containing 'enclaves' (Cromarty).

Cromer (Norfolk)
The name of this seaside resort north of NORWICH simply means 'crows' lake' or 'pond where crows are frequently seen', from the Old English *crāwe* (crow) and *mere* (lake, pond). Although Cromer is by the sea, the 'mere' (in modern terms)

would have been inland from it. The name was recorded in the thirteenth century as *Crowemere*, showing the elements more clearly.

Crompton (Greater Manchester)
An urban area north of OLDHAM, formerly a town, which has a name deriving from the Old English *crumb* (crooked) — characteristically of a bend in a river or stream — and *tūn* (farm, village). Crompton is thus a 'settlement on a bend of the river', although there is only a stream here. The name was recorded in a document of 1246 with the spelling as now. *Compare* CROOK.

Crook (Durham)
This coal-mining and engineering town northwest of BISHOP AUCKLAND has a more or less self-explanatory name meaning 'place in the bend (crook) of a river'. The small river here is a tributary of the WEAR. The town's name was originally 'Crookton', as shown in a document of 1267, which gives it as *Cruketona*. Other places named Crook could take their name not from a 'crook' in this sense but from the Celtic root word for 'hill', as in CRICCIETH.

Crosby (Merseyside)
This town at the mouth of the MERSEY has a fairly common name meaning 'village with a cross', from the two Old Norse words *cros* (cross) and *bý* (village). Most places of the name are thus in northern England, where most of the Scandinavian names are found. The village of Little Crosby, north of Crosby, still has six original Viking stone crosses.

Crossmaglen (Armagh)
A border town southwest of NEWRY whose original Irish name is Crois Mhic Lionnáin, meaning 'cross of the son of Lionnán'. The Irish *cros* could mean 'crossroads' as well as 'cross', and this may well have been the sense here — Crossmaglen is at a crossroads.

Crouch (Essex)

The river on which BURNHAM-ON-CROUCH is located. The name probably arose as a 'back formation' from the name of Creeksea, on its left bank, with the 'creek' of this name being the Crouch itself. (The latter half of Creeksea is not 'sea' but probably the Old English *hȳth*, 'landing place'.) However, some authorities prefer a derivation from 'cross', as for CROUCH END.

Crouch End (Greater London)

This district of HARINGEY proclaims itself to have been originally a 'district' ('end') 'by a cross', as early records show (*Crutche Ende* in 1553). The first word of the name thus represents the Middle English *crouche*, from the Old English *crūc*. (It was this form of the word that gave the name of the London street called Crutched Friars, after the monks here who wore a cross on their habit as an emblem of their Friary of the Holy Cross.) In the case of Crouch End, the cross would probably have been a wayside crucifix at a crossroads, perhaps as a type of visual pun on the two senses of 'cross' as crucifix and crossroads (*see also* CROSSMAGLEN). There is still an important road junction at Crouch End, where Crouch End Hill, Crouch Hill, Park Road, and Tottenham Lane all meet at The Broad.

Crowborough (East Sussex)

This town's name means 'crow hill' or 'hill where crows gather', from the Old English *crāwe* (crow) and *berg* (mound, hill). Crowborough was recorded in 1390 as *Crowbergh*, and the town is itself on an elevated site to the east of ASHDOWN Forest.

Crowland (Lincolnshire)

A small fenland town (*see* FENS) northeast of PETERBOROUGH whose name was recorded in the first half of the eighth century as *Crugland*; this has been tentatively derived from an unrecorded Old English word *crūw* meaning 'bend', so that the place-name means 'land by a bend', with the reference to a former bend (now obscured because of land reclamation) by the River WELLAND here.

Crowthorne (Berkshire)

This town, southwest of BRACKNELL and famous for its school (Wellington College) and its psychiatric hospital (Broadmoor), arose only in the latter half of the nineteenth century after the establishment of these two institutions. The earliest known record of the name is exactly as now on a map of 1607 and refers to an isolated tree at a road junction. This was a 'thorn tree where crows gather', as the name indicates. Perhaps significantly the junction was at the point where a former Roman road crosses what is now the A3095 main road to Bracknell. For the origin of the school's name *see* WELLINGTON.

Croxteth Hall (Merseyside)

A country house and estate east of LIVERPOOL city centre just within the city boundary. It takes its name from the former village here, with the meaning 'Krókr's landing place'. The name is Scandinavian, and comprises the personal name followed by the Old Norse *stǫth* (landing place, jetty) (*compare* TOXTETH). Croxteth was recorded in 1257 as *Crocstad*.

Croydon (Greater London)

This town east of SUTTON has a name that is more interesting than it might appear. It means 'saffron valley', from the Old English *croh* (saffron) (*compare* modern 'crocus') and *denu* (valley). The name was recorded in 809 as *Crogedene*. Saffron was a herb used for dyeing and for medicinal purposes in ancient times. For a name that reflects its use more obviously *see* SAFFRON WALDEN.

Crumlin (Antrim)

The name is fairly common in Ireland and means 'crooked glen' or 'winding valley' from the Irish *crom* (crooked) (*compare* CROMPTON) and *gleann* (glen, valley). This particular village, east of Lough NEAGH, is the one to which BELFAST's Crumlin Road leads.

Cuckfield (West Sussex)
This small town west of HAYWARDS HEATH has a name that means not 'cuckoo field' but 'Cuca's open land', with the Old English personal name Cuca followed by *feld* (modern 'field') meaning 'open land'. However, the place-name has almost certainly been influenced by 'cuckoo', even though the bird's name is not Old English but Old French (*cucu*). (The Old English word for 'cuckoo' was *gēac*, giving the modern Scottish and dialect 'gowk'.) Cuckfield was recorded in 1114 as *Kukufeld*.

Cudworth (South Yorkshire)
A colliery town northeast of BARNSLEY whose name means 'Cutha's enclosure', with the personal name followed by the Old English *worth* (enclosure). The name was recorded in the late twelfth century as *Cudeuurdia*.

Cullen (Grampian)
A fishing village on the bay of the same name east of BUCKIE. It was originally known as Invercullen, indicating its location at the mouth of a small river here. The former site of the village was around Cullen House, now about half a mile to the southwest. Cullen may derive from the Gaelic *cuilan* (little nook), and is a fairly common place-name in Scotland; it gave the identical surname.

Culloden (Highland)
Culloden Moor, east of INVERNESS, gave its name to the famous battle of 1746 in which the army of Prince Charles Edward Stuart (the 'Young Pretender') was destroyed by the Duke of Cumberland. The moor's name is said to derive from the Gaelic *cul lodain*, 'back of the little pool'. This must have originally referred to a particular location in the area. A text of 1238 records the name as *Cullodyn*.

Cullompton (Devon)
A small town southeast of TIVERTON on the River Culm, after which it takes its name: the name is in effect 'Culmtown', that is, 'village on the Culm'. The river's name is Celtic in origin and means 'winding one' (*compare* the modern Welsh *clwm*, 'knot', 'tie'); the reference is to a river with 'loops'. The town's name was recorded in the late ninth century as *Columtun*, but in the Domesday Book as the somewhat truncated *Colunp*. No doubt the cluster of consonants proved too much for the Norman clerk. The river does have a number of loops or bends here as it flows south to join the EXE near EXETER.

Culross (Fife)
A small town on the north side of the FORTH west of DUNFERMLINE whose name apparently derives from the Gaelic *cuileann ros*, 'holly wood'. It was recorded in the early twelfth century as *Culenross*.

Cults (Grampian)
A southwestern suburb of ABERDEEN with a Gaelic name representing *coillte* (woods), with the English plural *s* added. The name appears in a mid-fifteenth-century document as *Qhylt*.

Cumberland (England)
A former county (now represented by CUMBRIA) whose name means 'land of the Welsh', that is, the Cymry ('fellow countrymen'), this being the name the Britons used for themselves. The Britons originally occupied a far wider area than the present territories of Scotland, Wales, and Cornwall. The Cymry inhabited an area that reached into southern Scotland, up to and including modern STRATHCLYDE. The actual county of Cumberland is first referred to in a document of 1117, much later than the southern counties of England. The name itself, though, was recorded in the tenth-century *Anglo-Saxon Chronicle* as *Cumbra land. Compare* CAMBRIAN MOUNTAINS; CUMBRAE.

Cumbernauld (Strathclyde)
A town northeast of GLASGOW whose name
is quite unrelated to CUMBERLAND; it
derives from the Gaelic *comar-an-allt*,
'meeting of the streams', otherwise
'confluence'. Although now a New Town
(designated as such in 1955), the name was
recorded as *Cumbrenald* in a late-
thirteenth-century document. A stream
still flows through the original village of
Cumbernauld here, to join another nearby.

Cumbrae (Strathclyde)
Either of two islands in the Firth of CLYDE,
Great Cumbrae and the smaller Little
Cumbrae to the south. The name means
'island of the Welsh', with the Old Norse
ey (island) added to the tribal name *Cymry*
(*see* CUMBERLAND). The name is
associated with the former Welsh (or
Cumbrian) inhabitants of southern
Scotland, and was recorded in a document
of 1264 as *Cumberays*.

Cumbria (England)
A county formed in 1974 and covering an
area somewhat smaller than the original
CUMBERLAND in northwest England. The
name itself is much older than this,
however, and was recorded in exactly the
same form as now in documents of the
eighth century. *See* CUMBERLAND.
Compare CAMBRIAN MOUNTAINS;
CUMBRAE.

Cumnock (Strathclyde)
The name of this town east of AYR has
never been satisfactorily explained, despite
suggestions of the Gaelic *cumhann* (strait),
among others. It was recorded in 1297 as
Comnocke and a year later as *Comenok*.

Cupar (Fife)
This market town northeast of
GLENROTHES probably has a pre-Gaelic
name, whose meaning has still not been
satisfactorily determined. It appears in a
document of 1183 as *Cupre*. *See also*
COUPAR ANGUS.

Curragh, The (Kildare)
The plain east of KILDARE that has become
world famous as the home of Irish horse-
racing. Its Irish name, An Currach, means
simply 'the racecourse' (the basic word is
cuirreach).

Currie (Lothian)
A southwestern suburb of EDINBURGH
whose name means 'wet place', 'marsh',
from the Gaelic *currach*. Currie is
on low-lying ground by the Water of
LEITH. Its name was recorded in 1368 as
Corry.

Cushendall (Antrim)
An attractive village at the mouth of the
River Dall south of CUSHENDUN. Its name
derives from a former Irish name, Cois
Abhann Dalla, 'foot of the River Dall',
although its current name is Bun Abhann
Dalla, 'mouth of the River Dall'. The Irish
cois occurs in place-names to denote the
location of one place by another, in this
case of the settlement by the river. *Compare*
CUSHENDUN.

Cushendun (Antrim)
A village located at the mouth of the River
Dun north of CUSHENDALL. Its name
indicates this location, deriving from the
Irish Cois Abhann Duinne, 'foot of the
River Dun' (*see* CUSHENDALL for the sense
of the Irish *cois*). The current Irish name of
the village is Bun Abhann Duinne, 'mouth
of the River Dun'.

Cwmbran (Gwent)
A New Town (in Welsh correctly
Cwmbrân) designated in 1945. It originally
arose as an industrial town in the
nineteenth century, with the development
of the coal and steel industry in the area. It
takes its name from the river here, north of
NEWPORT, and means 'valley of the Brân',
based on the Welsh *cwm* (valley). The
river's own name means 'raven' (Welsh
brân), referring to its dark waters. The
valley name was recorded in a text of 1707
exactly as now.

Dacorum (Hertfordshire)
An administrative district formed in 1974 in the west of the county. The name is that of a former hundred here, and in its present form is Latin for 'of the Danes', as in a document of 1196, *de hundredo Dacorum*. The name referred to a hundred located on the English side of the Danelaw boundary, that is, one in an Anglo-Saxon region but with a Danish overlord. The Danelaw was the area of eastern and northern England where Danish law and customs had been introduced. Its western boundary, WATLING STREET, runs generally northwest through the western portion of Hertfordshire, leaving Dacorum to the west of it. The Domesday Book recorded the name of the hundred as *Danais*.

Dagenham (Greater London)
A district of eastern LONDON whose name was recorded in a document of 692 as *Dæccanhaam*. This means 'Dæcca's homestead', with the name ending in the Old English *hām*.

Daingean (Offaly)
This village, on the Grand Canal east of TULLAMORE, has an Irish name, An Daingean, that means simply 'the fortress'. The fortress referred to is the medieval one formerly here. From 1556 to 1920 the name of the village was Philipstown, after the husband of Queen Mary, Philip II of Spain, who ascended the throne in 1556. For another former name referring to him *see* OFFALY.

Dalbeattie (Dumfries and Galloway)
A small town southwest of DUMFRIES whose Gaelic name translates as 'field by the birch trees', from *dail* (field) and *beith* (birch). The name was recorded in 1469 as *Dalbaty. Compare* DALKEITH.

Dalkeith (Lothian)
The name of this town southeast of EDINBURGH is Gaelic, translating as 'field by a wood', from the British (Celtic) *dol* (field) and the root word *coed-* (wood); the latter also occurs in disguised form in the name of LICHFIELD (*compare also* KEITH). The area round the town is still well wooded. The name was recorded in a document of 1144 as *Dolchet*.

Dalkey (Dublin)
A seaside resort, now a residential area of DUN LAOGHAIRE, that has a Scandinavian name meaning 'thorn island', from the Old Norse *dalkr* (thorn) and *ey* (island). The first of these words is similar to the Irish word *dealg*, which has the same meaning. Hence the present Irish name of Deilginis, with *inis* as 'island'. The name refers to an island off the coast here, after which the resort was named.

Dalry (Strathclyde)
The name of this town northeast of ARDROSSAN probably means 'field of heather', from the Gaelic *dail* (field) and *fraoch* (heather).

Dalston (Greater London)
A district of HACKNEY with a name meaning 'Dēorlāf's farm', exactly as for DARLASTON (this does not of course mean that the person named was the same man!). Dalston was recorded in 1294 as *Derleston*, showing the *r* that has now disappeared. The personal name means 'remains of a deer', which was presumably a nickname.

Dalton-in-Furness (Cumbria)
Dalton is a fairly common name in northern England. It means 'valley village' (almost 'dale town'), from the Old English *dæl* (valley) and *tūn* (village). This town has the distinguishing addition '-in-Furness' to denote its location in this region. For the meaning of Furness *see* BARROW-IN-FURNESS. Dalton is only four miles from Barrow.

Dalwhinnie (Highland)
A village southwest of KINGUSSIE that has a Gaelic name meaning 'field of the champions', from *dail* (field) and *cuingid* (champion). This may refer to some historic contest.

Darlaston (West Midlands)
A southwest district of WALSALL whose name has exactly the same meaning as that of DALSTON, hence is 'Dēorlāf's village'. The Darlaston near STONE in Staffordshire also has this meaning. The Walsall Darlaston was recorded in 1262 as *Derlaveston*.

Darlington (Durham)
This industrial town south of NEWCASTLE UPON TYNE has a name meaning 'estate associated with Dēornoth'. The *n* of this personal name has become *l* under the influence of the Normans, just as Boulogne (in France) was originally *Bononia*. Darlington was thus recorded in 1106 as *Dearnington*.

Dartford (Kent)
This industrial town east of LONDON is not on the River 'Dart' but the Darent, and the name thus refers to a former ford across it here. As mentioned for CRAYFORD, it is unusual for a ford to be named after the river it crosses, and where it does occur the name will distinguish between two neighbouring fords. The Cray is a tributary of the Darent, and the two places are not far apart. 'Darent' means 'oak river' or 'river where oaks grow', from the same British (Celtic) root word that gave the name of the DERWENT and the Dart of DARTMOOR and DARTMOUTH. Dartford's name was recorded in the Domesday Book as *Tarentefort*.

Dartmoor (Devon)
An extensive upland area in southwest England with rocky peaks and tors (*see* YES TOR). It is named after the River Dart, which rises here and flows in a southeasterly direction to the sea at DARTMOUTH. As mentioned in the entry for DARTFORD, the name of the river means 'oak stream'. Dartmoor appears in a document of 1182 as *Dertemora*.

Dartmouth (Devon)
A small port and resort southeast of TOTNES, with its Royal Naval College on a hill overlooking the town. Its name indicates its location on the estuary of the River Dart. The river's name means 'oak stream' (*see* DARTFORD). Dartmouth was recorded in 1049 as *Dertamutha*.

Darvel (Strathclyde)
This town east of KILMARNOCK on the River IRVINE has a difficult name that may possibly be based on the Gaelic *dobhar* (oak wood). An early version of the name has been recorded as *Darnevaill*.

Darwen (Lancashire)
An industrial town south of BLACKBURN that takes its name from the River Darwen on which it stands. The river's name means 'oak stream', so is based on the same Celtic root word that gave the names of the Darent (*see* DARTFORD), the Dart (*see* DARTMOOR, DARTMOUTH), and the DERWENT. The name was recorded in 1208 as *Derewent*.

Datchet (Berkshire)
A town east of WINDSOR on the THAMES with a name of British (Celtic) origin that has been related to the Latin *decus* (ornament) (as on pound coins); thus the meaning is something like 'special place', 'favoured place'. The name was recorded in a tenth-century text as *Deccet* and in the Domesday Book as *Daceta*.

Daventry (Northamptonshire)
The final element of the name of this town west of NORTHAMPTON is the same as that in COVENTRY and OSWESTRY, meaning 'tree' (Old English *trēow*). The name as a whole thus means 'Dafa's tree', and was recorded in the Domesday Book as *Daventrei*. Such a tree was often the

meeting place of a 'hundred', or local assembly. But Daventry was not the centre of the hundred here (that of Fawsley), so the 'tree' may have been a cross or even a crucifix erected by Dafa.

Davidson's Mains (Lothian)
A northwestern district of EDINBURGH whose name refers to the former location here of the 'mains' (home farm) of a family named Davidson, in this case the Davidsons of Muirhouse, a member of which was Randall Thomas Davidson (Lord Davidson), the Archbishop of Canterbury who died in 1930. A former name of Davidson's Mains was Muttonhole, said to be a corruption of the Gaelic *meadhonach coill* (middle hill). 'Mains' is related to 'demesne' and 'domain'.

Dawley (Shropshire)
A town forming the central area of TELFORD. Its name was recorded in a document of 1185 as *Dalilega*, showing it to be really 'Dallingley', and so to mean 'clearing of Dealla's people', with the Old English *-ingas* (here shortened to *-ing*, as often the case) meaning 'people of', and *lēah* (clearing) added to the personal name, which itself means 'proud one'. The name appeared in the Domesday Book as *Daleli*.

Dawlish (Devon)
A seaside resort south of EXETER named after the river here, the Dawlish Water, whose own name means 'black stream', from the British (Celtic) *dubo-* (black) (as in DUBLIN) and a conjectural word *glassio* (stream). The derivation is thus similar to that of DOUGLAS. Dawlish was referred to in a document of 1044 as *Doflisc, on doflisc ford*. This means that the town could have been called 'Dawlishford' (or some shorter form of this), if the final '-ford' had not been dropped from the name.

Deal (Kent)
A coastal resort northeast of DOVER (and one of the original CINQUE PORTS) whose

name directly represents the Old English *dæl* (valley), as if today it were simply 'Dale'. This seems an unlikely description of modern Deal, however, as the terrain here is flat. There may have been a change in the local topography that has erased some former hollow or depression here. The name was recorded in the Domesday Book as *Addelam*. The first part of this represents the Old English word for 'at', with the appropriate grammatical ending on the following noun to give the final *-am* of the name. *Compare* RYE.

Dedham (Essex)
A village northeast of COLCHESTER on the River STOUR, famous for its depiction in the paintings of John Constable. Its name means 'Dydda's homestead', with the Old English personal name followed by the common *hām* (homestead, manor). The Domesday Book recorded the name as *Delham*, apparently with a miscopying of *l* for *d*.

Dee (Gwynedd/Cheshire/Merseyside; Grampian)
Any of at least four rivers in Britain. One of the best known, the Anglo-Welsh Dee, is famous for its wide estuary west of the WIRRAL Peninsula. It has the Welsh name of Dyfrdwy, meaning simply 'River Dee' or 'waters of the Dee', with the first part of this name also behind that of DOVER. Another famous Dee flows through eastern Scotland to enter the North Sea at ABERDEEN. Dee itself is a name of British (Celtic) origin, deriving from *deva*, meaning 'goddess' (*compare* the Roman name of CHESTER on the river then called the *Deva*). Ptolemy recorded the name of both rivers in the second century AD as *Deova*. *See also* GLYNDŵR.

Delabole (Cornwall)
A village west of CAMELFORD. The name's final element is the Cornish *pol* (pool), but the first part is still uncertain; it may be a personal name.

Delyn (Clwyd)
An administrative district in the north of the county formed in 1974. Unlike many district names, this is not a revived ancient name but a modern blend of the names of two rivers in the district, the DEE and the ALUN. The latter's name was adjusted to the spelling occurring in the neighbouring district of Alyn and Deeside. By a fortunate coincidence, *delyn* happens to be the (mutated) form of *telyn* (harp), the musical instrument associated with Wales.

Denbigh (Clwyd)
The name of this town south of RHYL on the River Clwyd means 'little fortress', from the Welsh *din* (fortress) and *bach* (little). The fortress referred to would have stood where the ruins of the twelfth-century castle now lie, on Castle Hill south of the town. The Welsh name of Denbigh is Dinbych, and this exact form of the name is found in a document of 1269. The name of TENBY is identical in meaning.

Dennistoun (Strathclyde)
This eastern district of GLASGOW appears to have a name that refers to the 'toun' or settlement of a family named Dennis or Denny or Daniel.

Denny (Central)
A town west of FALKIRK whose name represents the Old English *denu* (valley) and *ēg* (island), and so can be interpreted as 'well-watered land in a valley'. This suits the location of Denny on the River Carron. The name was recorded in 1510 as *Litill Dany*.

Dent (Cumbria)
This small town southeast of SEDBERGH is in the valley of the River DEE, which is here known as Dentdale after the town. The town is named after the nearby hill, Dent Crag. Its name derives from a British (Celtic) word meaning simply 'hill', itself corresponding to the Old English *dūn*. The town's name was recorded in a document of about 1200 as *Denet*.

Denton (Greater Manchester)
A town northeast of STOCKPORT whose name is found widely elsewhere in the country and means 'valley village', from the Old English *denu* (valley) and the common *tūn* (village). This particular Denton is in the valley of the River Tame. Its name was recorded in 1255 spelt exactly as now.

Deptford (Greater London)
A district of LEWISHAM whose name means 'deep ford'. Deptford is situated at the confluence of the Ravensbourne and the THAMES, and the ford would have been across the former, smaller river, perhaps at a point where Deptford Bridge now is. The Old English components of the name are *dēop* (deep) and *ford* (ford). The name was recorded in 1334 as *Depford*.

Derby (Derbyshire)
This industrial city and county town southwest of NOTTINGHAM has a Scandinavian name meaning 'deer village', from the Old Norse *djúr* and *bý*. When the Danes came to settle here in the ninth century, they changed the English name of Northworthy ('north enclosure') to the present name, which presumably was more meaningful to them. (A corresponding 'Southworthy', which one would expect, has still not been identified.) The northern district of Derby known as Darley Abbey has a name that also refers to the deer here, although this name is Old English, deriving from *dēor* (deer) and *lēah* (clearing). The city's name was thus recorded as *Northworthige* in a document of about 1000, and nine years later as *Dyreby*. The county name is recorded in a text of 1049 as *Deorbyscir*.

Derg, Lough (Clare/Galway/Tipperary)
The present name of this lough in central Ireland represents its Irish name, Loch Deirgeirt, 'lake of the red eye'. A legend tells how a king gave his eye to a wandering poet and then washed his face in the lough, whose waters ran red with his blood. The

true reference is probably to the reddish colour of a whirlpool seen at some point in the lough, perhaps where the SHANNON flows into it.

Derry (Londonderry)
The shorter (and original) name of the city still officially known as LONDONDERRY.

Derwent (Derbyshire)
Any of several rivers in England. The Derbyshire Derwent rises in the PEAK DISTRICT and flows roughly southeastwards to the TRENT. The name means 'oak river' or 'river that flows among oak trees', from the British (Celtic) root word *deruenta-* that also gave the names of the rivers Darent (*see* DARTFORD) and Dart (*see* DARTMOOR, DARTMOUTH), and the river on which DARWEN stands. All these names point to the abundance of oak forests in ancient Britain. *See also* DERWENT WATER.

Derwent Water (Cumbria)
One of the lakes in the Lake District that takes its name from the River DERWENT that flows from the BORROWDALE Fells to the Irish Sea through Derwent Water and BASSENTHWAITE Lake. The meaning of the name is 'oak river'.

Desborough (Northamptonshire)
A small manufacturing town northwest of KETTERING whose name means 'Dēor's fortified place'. The *r* of the personal name has been dropped by the process known as dissimilation, that is, it has come to be represented by the second *r* of the name. The name was recorded in a document of 1088 as *Dereburg*. The personal name means 'animal', 'deer'.

Devenish Island (Fermanagh)
An island in Lough ERNE whose name derives from its Irish equivalent, which is Daimhinis, 'ox island', from *damh* (ox) and *inis* (island). The English 'island' was added to this when the Irish name ceased to be meaningful. Devenish is not the origin

of the English surname, which means 'from Devon'.

Devil's Dyke (West Sussex)
There are a number of 'devilish' names around the country, all more or less fancifully attached to different legends, mainly involving the Devil (Satan) himself. The Devil's Dyke is a steep declivity in the South Downs, below a large Iron Age fort. The particular legend here tells how the Devil, horrified by the large number of churches in this part of Sussex, dug a deep chasm with the aim of letting in the sea to inundate them all. However, he was thwarted by an old woman who observed him working at night and who held up a candle at her cottage window to obtain a better sight of his activity. The Devil saw the candle, thought it was the sun rising, and fled, never to return. The dyke here is an ancient earthwork, as is the Devil's Dyke (also known as the Devil's Ditch) in Cambridgeshire. Such names usually date from medieval times.

Devizes (Wiltshire)
The attractive name of this attractive town southeast of CHIPPENHAM represents the Old French *devises* (boundaries), itself from the Latin *divisae*. Like many important towns in England, Devizes is at the boundary between two former hundreds, in this case that of POTTERNE (which was held by the king) and that of Cannings (which was held by the Bishops of SALISBURY). The boundaries of the two hundreds passed through the former Devizes Castle. The name occurs in a document of 1139 as *Divisas*, and some of the older local people still talk of the town as 'The Vize' or as simply 'Vize'.

Devon (England)
This southwestern county, also known as Devonshire, traces its name back to the British (Celtic) tribe here known as the *Dumnonii*, with their own name meaning 'deep ones' or deriving from that of their god Dumnonos. In its present form, the county

name was recorded in a text of about 1000 as *Defnascir*. The village of Denbury, southwest of NEWTON ABBOT, also refers to the tribe; its name means 'fortified place of the Devon men'. *Compare* the Roman name of EXETER, the tribe's capital. *See also* DEVONPORT.

Devonport (Devon)

A district of PLYMOUTH originally known as Plymouth Dock when it arose around the dockyard established here in the late seventeenth century by William III. When the docks were enlarged in the 1820s, the name was changed to Devonport, this suggesting that it was to be one of the leading ports and dockyards in the county.

Dewsbury (West Yorkshire)

A manufacturing town southwest of LEEDS whose name means 'Dewi's fortified place', comprising the Old English *burg* following the personal name. The Domesday Book recorded the name as *Deusberia*.

Didcot (Oxfordshire)

The name of this town south of OXFORD was recorded in a document of 1206 as *Dudecota*, showing the meaning to be 'Dudda's cottage'. The *u* of the personal name later became *i*. The Old English *cot* usually means 'cottage', 'humble dwelling' when preceded by a personal name like this, though in other names it can mean merely 'shelter', especially in the name Caldecote, where it means 'shelter from the cold for travellers'.

Dinas Powys (South Glamorgan)

A western suburb of PENARTH, with the site of an ancient hill-fort to the north of it. The Welsh *din* means 'fort', and here refers to the hill-fort. The second word of the name is identical to the county name POWYS, and probably has the same basic meaning of 'province'. The place-name as a whole was recorded in 1187 as *Dinaspowis*.

Dinefwr (Dyfed)

An administrative district in the southeast of the county, formed in 1974. The name is a revival of an ancient name, originally that of the castle at LLANDEILO, and means 'fort of the yew', from *din* (fort) and *efwr* (yew, cow parsnip).

Dingle (Kerry)

This small town and the peninsula on which it is located to the west of TRALEE take their name from the Irish *daingean* (fortress). Dingle was important as a stronghold long before the Norman occupation. The second *n* of the Irish word has become assimilated to *l* in the English rendering of the name.

Dingwall (Highland)

The chief town of the ROSS and CROMARTY district at the head of the Cromarty Firth northwest of INVERNESS. The Scandinavian name means 'parliament field', from the Old Norse *thing-vǫllr*, referring to the regular assembly held here to administer justice and discuss matters of public importance. (The modern English 'thing' derives directly from this earlier meaning of 'assembly', 'parliament'.) An exact parallel to the name can be seen in the Tynwald, the parliament of the Isle of MAN (*see* TYNWALD HILL). The name of Dingwall was recorded in 1227 as *Dingwell*. For the Gaelic name of Dingwall *see* STRATHPEFFER.

Disley (Cheshire)

A town southeast of MARPLE whose name ends in the Old English *lēah* (clearing); the first half is believed to be a personal name. The name has been recorded as *Desteleg'* in about 1251, *Distilegh* in 1274, and in similar spellings down to at least the sixteenth century (*Distley Deyn* in 1535). This prompted one researcher to suggest, in the mid-1970s, that the first half of the name represents a conjectural Old English word *dystels*, meaning 'mound', itself related to a Middle English verb *dust* (not related to modern 'dust'), meaning 'throw', 'fling'. This is now the generally accepted origin of the name, which thus means 'clearing by a mound'.

Diss (Norfolk)
This small market town southwest of NORWICH has a straightforward name that derives directly from the Old English *dīc* (ditch), with the *ch* of the pronunciation softened to *s* under the influence of the Normans. There must have been an ancient ditch or dyke somewhere here. Diss is in low-lying land on the River WAVENEY.

Ditchling (East Sussex)
A large village southeast of BURGESS HILL, famous for its hill-fort and viewpoint of Ditchling Beacon nearby. The name means 'place associated with Diccel's people'; it was recorded in the late ninth century as *æt Diccelingum* and in the Domesday Book as *Dicelinges*.

Dodworth (South Yorkshire)
A colliery town west of BARNSLEY whose name means 'Dudda's enclosure', with the personal name followed by the Old English *worth* (enclosure). The personal name is the same as that for DIDCOT. Dodworth was recorded in the Domesday Book as *Dodeswrde*.

Dogs, Isle of (Greater London)
A peninsula (not an island) at the centre of London's new Docklands region, where it is bounded on three sides by the THAMES. The name was recorded as *Isle of Doges ferm* in 1593, before which time the region was generally known here as STEPNEY Marsh. The name has not been conclusively explained; it may be a corruption of some other name ('Isle of Ducks' has been suggested) or a reference either to dead dogs deposited by the tide on the shore here, or to a former kennels here. The name was almost certainly a derogatory one in the first place.

Dolgellau (Gwynedd)
A small market town southwest of BALA whose name derives from the Welsh *dôl*

(loop, bend) (later, 'water meadow') and *cellau*, the plural of *cell* (cell). The reference is probably to monastic cells formerly here. The town is located at the confluence of the rivers Aran and Wnion. Its name was recorded in 1254 as *Dolkelew* and was until comparatively recently spelt 'Dolgelly' or 'Dolgelley' in English, this coming from sixteenth-century versions of the name.

Dollar (Central)
A small town northeast of ALLOA whose name probably derives from the British (Celtic) *dol* (field) and *ar* (ploughed land), thus meaning simply '(place by a) ploughed field'. It is a name that lends itself to folk etymologies and punsters. The former include a derivation from the French *douleur* (sorrow), with reference to nearby Castle Gloom; the latter like to point out the proximity of the place to STIRLING.

Don (South Yorkshire/Humberside; Lancashire; Grampian)
Any of three rivers in Britain. The two English Dons denote simply 'river' (*compare* AVON), from a British (Celtic) root word that is also seen on the continent in the names of the Russian River Don and the Danube; the Yorkshire river gave the name of DONCASTER. The Scottish Don, however, has its origin in the British *Deuona* (goddess), with this related to the name of the DEE. It was this Don that gave the name of ABERDEEN.

Donabate (Dublin)
A small town between BALBRIGGAN and DUBLIN having the Irish name of Domhnach Bat, 'church of the boat'. However, the original version of the name is unreliable, and this may not be the true interpretation.

Donaghadee (Down)
This pleasant town and port east of BANGOR is called Domhnach Daoi in Irish, meaning 'church of Diach'. Although the first element of the name almost certainly represents the Irish *domhnach* (church), the

latter part is uncertain; if it is a personal name, the spelling is conjectural.

Doncaster (South Yorkshire)

The name of this town northeast of SHEFFIELD proclaims it to be a former Roman station on the River DON, with '-caster' representing the northern form of the Old English *ceaster* (Roman fort), as found in the Danelaw. The Roman fort was called *Danum*, deriving directly from the name of the river, which as explained in its own entry means simply 'river'. The settlement here was recorded as *Donecastre* in a document of 1002.

Donegal (Donegal)

This market town southwest of BALLYBOFEY has an Irish name, Dún na nGall, which translates as 'fort of the foreigners', from the Irish *dún* (fort) and *gall* (stranger, foreigner). The 'foreigners' were the Danes, who took possession of a primitive fort here in the tenth century. The Irish word is related to the tribal name of the Gauls, who inhabited what is now France, and it is also indirectly connected with the word 'Welsh' or the name of WALES, as well as (more directly) with that of GALLOWAY (but not GALWAY). The county of Donegal took its name from the town.

Donnybrook (Dublin)

A southeastern suburb of DUBLIN known in Irish as Domhnach Broc, meaning 'church of St Broc'. Nothing is known about this saint.

Dorchester (Dorset, Oxfordshire)

The county town of DORSET, north of WEYMOUTH, has a name that declares it (because of the '-chester') to have arisen by a former Roman station. The latter's name was *Durnovaria*, now represented simply by the initial abbreviated 'Dor-' of the current name. The Roman name is based on the British (Celtic) conjectural root word *durno-*, meaning 'fist', found also

behind the name of DORNOCH. This could imply a place covered with fist-sized stones or pebbles, or else refer to fist-fights, that is, boxing contests, held here. The former supposition seems more likely. The second element of the Roman name is of obscure origin, but was probably associated by the Anglo-Saxons with the Old English *-ware* (settlers), as occurs in the earlier names of CANTERBURY. Dorchester is thus recorded as *Dornuuaranaceaster* in a document of 847 and as *Dorecestre* in the Domesday Book.

The Oxfordshire village of Dorchester northwest of WALLINGFORD has a name of different origin. It was referred to by the Venerable Bede in his *Ecclesastical History of the English People* of 731 *as ciuitatem quae vocatur Dorcic*, 'a town which is called Dorcic'. This is believed to derive from a conjectural British (Celtic) word *derk* meaning 'splendid', 'good-looking', as in the modern Welsh *drych* (mirror, spectacle). The latter half of the name denotes a former Roman fort here near the THAMES, but although Roman remains and relics have been found, between the village and the river, its name is still unknown. It was not *Dorocina*, despite the fact that this is the name popularly given to it (in both tourist guides and 'school' books, such as R.R. Sellman's *Roman Britain*, published in 1956). This name is a fanciful one devised by the so-called monk 'Richard of Cirencester' (actually the pseudonym of the eighteenth-century literary forger, Charles Bertram).

Dore (South Yorkshire)

A district of SHEFFIELD whose name means 'door', that is, 'pass'. Dore is in a pass about five miles southwest of the city centre at a point on the former boundary between the kingdoms of Northumbria and Mercia; even today it is virtually on the South Yorkshire/Derbyshire border. Its name was recorded by the Domesday Book exactly as now. The Old English word for 'door' was *dor*.

Dorking (Surrey)

The name of this town east of GUILDFORD means 'place of Deorc's people', with the Old English suffix *-ing* (originally *-ingas*; 'people of') added to the personal name. In the Domesday Book Dorking was recorded as *Dorchinges*.

Dornoch (Highland)

A small town of GOLSPIE in the SUTHERLAND District whose name literally means 'place of fist-stones', that is, of pebbles that could be thrown as missiles. The root word behind the name is the Gaelic *dorn* (compare Welsh *dwrn*) (*see also* DORCHESTER, Dorset). Dornoch was recorded in 1145 as *Durnach*.

Dorset (England)

A county in southern England whose name can be understood as 'settlers of *Dorn*', with the Old English *sǣte* (settlers) following the basic original name of DORCHESTER. Dorset was recorded in the late ninth century as *Thornsaeta* and as *Dorseteschire* in about 944. Today, the name is not usually suffixed with '-shire', although there is a good precedent for doing so. For a similar name *see* SOMERSET.

Douglas (Isle of Man, Strathclyde)

For both the capital of the Isle of MAN and the Scottish town south of LANARK, the Celtic origin of the name is the same: it means 'black stream' and refers to the stream or river on which each is situated. (For the Scottish town, this is the Douglas Water.) The root words are thus those represented by the modern Welsh *du* (black) and *glas* (stream), or Gaelic *dubh* and *glais*. The name of the Manx town was recorded in about 1257 as *Dufglas*. There are also places of the name in Ireland, where the meaning will be identical and refers to the dark waters of the stream. *See also* DAWLISH. *Compare* the English BLACKWATER.

Dove (Derbyshire, South Yorkshire, North Yorkshire, Suffolk)

All four rivers have a name of British (Celtic) origin meaning 'black', 'dark' (*see* DOUGLAS). A stretch of the valley of the Derbyshire Dove is named Dove Dale, and is famous as a scenic area in the PEAK DISTRICT, where the river flows between steep cliffs, with woods on either side.

Dover (Kent)

This Channel port southeast of CANTERBURY has a British (Celtic) name related directly to the modern Welsh *dwfr* (water). It was recorded in the fourth century in its plural form of *Dubris*, and this was preserved by the Anglo-Saxons in the seventh century as *Dofras*. The name refers not to the sea but to the stream or streams that entered the sea here. One of these today is still called the Dour. Dover had a Roman fort, but like other similar places in Kent (such as RECULVER and RICHBOROUGH) has no '-chester' on the name to indicate this. The Roman fort had the same name as that of the River Dour, which was the *Dubris* already mentioned. The fort itself was where Dover Castle now stands.

Dovercourt (Essex)

A district of HARWICH whose name has become associated with that of DOVER, if only because both towns are well-known ports. The connection is partly correct, as a small stream flows into the sea north of Dovercourt, and this could be referred to by the Celtic word that gave the name of Dover itself, meaning simply 'stream'. But the 'court' of the name is harder to explain. It seems to derive from a rare Old English word, perhaps *cort*, that denotes a short piece of land, with the word thus related to 'curt', French *court*, Latin *curtus*, and so on. The best that can be proposed for Dovercourt is thus 'short piece of land by a stream'. Its name was recorded in about 1000 as *Douorcortae*.

Dovey (Gwynedd/Powys)
A Welsh river that gives the name of
ABERDOVEY and may derive its own name
from either Welsh *du* (black), like the
River DOVE; or else *dwfn* (deep). The
Welsh version of the name is Dyfi, which
also suggests a possible link with the name
of the TAFF (as in CARDIFF). A single firm
origin has not yet been obtained.

Down (Ireland)
A county in Northern Ireland whose name
relates to the fort (Irish *dún*) that forms the
basis of the name of its county town,
DOWNPATRICK, which was itself originally
known simply as 'Down'.

Downham Market (Norfolk)
A market town south of KING'S LYNN.
'Downham' means 'hill farm', from the
Old English *dūn* (hill) and *hām* (farm). The
distinguishing 'Market' was added later
when it became a market town. Downham
Market was thus recorded in the
Domesday Book simply as *Dunham*; as
Forum de Dunham in a document of about
1110 (*compare* BLANDFORD FORUM); and
as *Mercatus de Dunham* in 1130.

Downpatrick (Down)
The first part of the name is the Irish *dún*
(fort), which probably stood on the site of
the present Church of Ireland cathedral.
The original name of the town, southeast of
BELFAST, was thus simply Down. A
number of relics were discovered here in
the late twelfth century, including ones
alleged to be of St Patrick, and the name
was modified to *Dún Pádraig*, 'Patrick's
fort', giving, in anglicised form,
Downpatrick. For the county name *see*
DOWN.

Downside Abbey (Somerset)
A Benedictine abbey and Roman Catholic
public school (Downside School) at
Stratton-on-the-Fosse (*see* STRATTON)
southwest of RADSTOCK. The name
indicates its location near the hamlet of
Downside, itself named for its location

beside a hill (Old English *dūn*, modern
'down'). There is another small village of
the name a further four miles southwest,
just north of SHEPTON MALLET. The
region here is at the eastern end of the
MENDIP HILLS. The abbey and school
settled here only in the nineteenth century.

Drake's Island (Devon)
An island in PLYMOUTH Sound named
after the famous navigator, Sir Francis
Drake, who took refuge from the Catholics
on the island with his father in 1548 and
who anchored his vessel, the *Golden Hind*,
near it in 1580 on his return to Plymouth.
The earlier name of the island was 'St
Nicholas' Island', recorded as *isle of St.
Nicholas* in 1396, after the chapel dedicated
to this saint here, demolished in 1548. The
island was renamed in about 1590. The
significance of the island is summed up by
Drake's own comment that 'he who holds
the island, holds the town [of Plymouth]'.

Drogheda (Louth)
An industrial town, north of DUBLIN on
the River BOYNE, that has the Irish name
Droichead Átha, 'bridge of the ford',
represented by the abbreviated English
name. The reference is to a bridge that was
built to replace a ford; a bridge crossed the
river here as early as the twelfth century.
Compare DROICHEAD NUA.

Droichead Nua (Kildare)
This town southwest of NAAS on the River
LIFFEY has been known in the past by the
English name of Newbridge, which
translates its present Irish name. The
original 'new' bridge would have been a
medieval one.

Droitwich (Hereford and Worcester)
The name of this town northeast of
WORCESTER was recorded in a late-ninth-
century document as *Saltwic*, reflecting
the name of the former Roman station
here, which was *Salinae*. The reference is
to the salt works that were once here. This
special nature of the place is today

indicated by the second element of the name, with '-wich' (Old English *wīc*) especially associated with salt works, as also at NANTWICH and NORTHWICH. The first part of the name represents the Old English *drit* (dirt, mud), so that the overall meaning is 'muddy place where there are salt workings'. The Domesday Book recorded the name simply as *Wich*, but the 'dirt' element appeared subsequently, as in *Drihtwych*, found in a text of 1347. Droitwich, on the River Salwarpe, has long been well known for its saline springs and was a spa until quite recently. *See also* WYCHAVON.

Dromore (Down)

A town between BANBRIDGE and LISBURN whose name occurs elsewhere in Ireland. In all cases it means 'big ridge' (Irish *droim mór*), referring to a nearby long low hill. This particular town has also been known in Irish as *Druim Mocholmog*, after its sixth-century founder, Mo-Cholmóg, better known as St Colmán. A stone inscribed with a cross in the wall of the present cathedral is known as St Colmán's Pillow and is said to be a relic of the original monastery built by him. The current Irish name of the town is Droim Mór.

Dronfield (Derbyshire)

A town north of CHESTERFIELD whose name means 'drones' field', that is, an open space (Old English *feld*) infested by drones (Old English *drān*), these being male honey-bees. The rather unusual name was recorded in the Domesday Book as *Dranefeld*. The bees would have been wild ones.

Droylsden (Greater Manchester)

An eastern suburb of MANCHESTER whose name probably means 'valley of the dry stream', from the Old English *drȳge* (dry, dried up) and the common *denu* (valley). One has to qualify this interpretation as early records of it are open to some doubt. A mid-thirteenth-century document, for example, has the name as *Drilisden*, and it

is assumed that the central element here, in addition to the two mentioned, is the Old English *wella* (stream, well).

Drumcondra (Dublin)

The Irish name of this DUBLIN suburb is Droim Conrach, translating as 'Contra's ridge'. It is not known who Contra was.

Dryburgh Abbey (Borders)

The name of this abbey, founded southeast of MELROSE in the mid-twelfth century, is taken from the village of Dryburgh. Its own name, despite its proximity to the River TWEED, means 'dry fortress', from the Old English *drȳge* (dry) (*compare* DROYLSDEN) and *burg* (fort). The name was recorded in a document of about 1160 as *Drieburh*. There was presumably once a stream here.

Dublin (Dublin)

The Irish capital city has a name that (coincidentally) matches that of BLACKPOOL across the Irish Sea, for it comprises the Irish *dubh* (black) and *linn* (pool). The reference is to the section of the River LIFFEY, with its dark waters, where the settlement originally arose. Ptolemy recorded the Celtic name in the second century AD as *Eblana*, and this is now used as a name for Dublin in literary imprints. The city's current Irish name, however, is Baile Átha Cliath, meaning 'town of the hurdle ford', from the Irish *baile* (town), *áth* (ford), and *cliath* (woven withy, hurdle). This name also relates to the Liffey but is more historical than geographical, describing the material (hurdles) used for fording the river in ancient times. Had this been the sole name, it might have been anglicised as 'Ballyclee', since this approximates to the pronunciation of the Irish name. It is interesting that the Irish have preferred the historical name, commemorating their feat in fording the river, while the English have preserved the descriptive name, which is also easier to say. The original 'hurdle ford' may have been where the nineteenth-century

Father Matthew Bridge now spans the river, to the west of the city centre.

Dudley (West Midlands)

The name of this industrial town west of BIRMINGHAM means 'Dudda's woodland clearing'. It was recorded in the Domesday Book as *Dudelei*, the latter element of which represents the Old English *lēah* (forest, clearing). The many names ending in '-ley' locally (others are SEDGLEY, WARLEY, Hagley, Cradley, and Brierley Hill) point to the local importance of timber when the area's iron and steel industry was developing. The personal name Dudda also occurs in the names of DIDCOT and DODWORTH.

Dufftown (Grampian)

A small town southeast of ELGIN founded in 1817 by James Duff, fourth Earl of FIFE, and named after him. *Compare* MACDUFF.

Dukinfield (Greater Manchester)

The name of this town, east of MANCHESTER, literally means 'ducks' field', from the Old English *dūce*, 'duck' (genitive plural *dūcena*) and *feld*, 'open space' (modern 'field'). The reference may have been to domestic ducks, but most names of this type (another is DRONFIELD) relate to wild animals. The name was recorded in the twelfth century as *Dokenfeld*. The town is on the River TAME, so the ducks would have had a congenial habitat here.

Dulverton (Somerset)

A small town north of TIVERTON on the River Barle. Its name relates to the river, as it means 'village at the hidden ford', from the Old English *digol* (hidden), *ford* (ford), and *tūn* (village). The second element has become obscured in the present form of the name, where it is represented by the middle '-ver-'. Dulverton is on the edge of EXMOOR, and it is easy to imagine how a ford could have become 'hidden' here. The name was recorded in the Domesday Book as *Dolvertune*.

Dulwich (Greater London)

This large district of SOUTHWARK has a name that differs from the majority of those ending in '-wich'. Here, this element comes from the Old English *wisce* (marshy meadow), and the first part of the name represents the old English *dile* (dill). The name thus means 'marshy land where dill grows'. The herb dill has been cultivated for medicinal use since the earliest times, and parts of Dulwich are still low-lying and potentially marshy, with ponds and lakes. The sense of the name can be deduced from early records of it, such as *Dilwihs* in 967 and *Dilewysshe* in 1277.

Dumbarton (Strathclyde)

The name of this town northwest of GLASGOW means 'fort (Gaelic *dùn*) of the Britons' — the neighbouring Gaels' reference to the stronghold occupied by the British here from the fifth century. From that time until the eleventh century Dumbarton was the capital of the kingdom of Strathclyde, and the fort itself stood where Dumbarton Rock now stands with the remains of later fortifications. The Britons called their fortress here *Alclut*, meaning 'fort by the CLYDE' (this name is an exact parallel to the 'Auckland' of BISHOP AUCKLAND). The Gaelic name was recorded in the late thirteenth century as *Dumbrethan*, with the latter half of this representing *Breatann*, 'of the Britons'. For the county name *see* DUNBARTONSHIRE.

Dumfries (Dumfries and Galloway)

This manufacturing town southeast of GLASGOW has a name that describes it as a 'woodland stronghold', from the Gaelic *dùn* (fort) and *preas* (copse, thicket). The fort probably stood in the centre of the oldest part of the town (in the bend of the River NITH), now known as Mid Steeple. The surrounding countryside is still well wooded. The name was recorded in a document of the late twelfth century as *Dunfres*. The county of Dumfries-shire then developed from the town.

Dunbar (Lothian)

A coastal resort east of EDINBURGH whose name means 'fort on the height', from the Gaelic *dùn* (fort) (or an earlier British equivalent to this) and *barr* (height). The 'height' where the fort stood is the rocky headland above the harbour where the ruins of Dunbar Castle now are. The name was recorded in the early eighth century as *Dynbaer*.

Dunbartonshire (Scotland)

The former county that had DUMBARTON for its county town. The alteration of the naturally developing *m* of this name to *n* took place in relatively recent times, and seems somewhat pointless. The final '-shire' would have ensured that there was no confusion between the name of the town and that of the county.

Dunblane (Central)

A small town north of STIRLING on ALLAN WATER whose name means 'hill of Blaan', the latter being the name of the bishop who had his monastery here, on the site above the river where the cathedral now stands. The name was recorded in about 1200 as *Dumblann*. The bishop (now usually referred to as St Blane) lived in the sixth century and was born in BUTE.

Duncansby Head (Highland)

The headland in the extreme northeast of mainland Scotland, east of JOHN O'GROAT'S. Its name means 'Dungad's farm', with the Scandinavian personal name followed by the Old Norse *bý* (or *býr*; farm). The name was recorded in a document of about 1225 as *Dungaelsbaer*.

Dundalk (Louth)

The Irish name of this town south of NEWRY is Dún Dealgan, meaning 'Dealga's fort'. The fort referred to was the one on Castletown Hill, to the west of the present town. Dealga is said to have been the chief who built it in ancient times.

Dundee (Tayside)

An industrial city and port on the TAY whose name means 'Daig's fort', recorded in about 1180 as *Dunde*. The fort would have been where the long-destroyed Dundee Castle once stood, by the present High Street. It is not known who Daig was but his name may have meant 'fire' (Gaelic *daig*), this being a nickname.

Dundonald (Down)

This industrial village east of BELFAST has a name that means 'Donall's fort', as its Irish name of Dún Dónaill indicates. The fort would have been on the site of the present Anglo-Norman motte near the Church of Ireland parish church.

Dundrum (Down)

An attractive fishing village northeast of the MOURNE MOUNTAINS whose name simply means 'fort of the ridge' (Irish Dún Droma), a name found in many other parts of Ireland. The original fort would have been on the site of the present castle remains, with a fine view over Dundrum Bay.

Dunfermline (Fife)

It is disappointing to record that the second part of the name of this famous town, northwest of the FORTH road bridge, has never been satisfactorily explained. The initial 'Dun-', as in most names of this type, means 'fort' or 'hill' (Gaelic *dùn*), but the rest of the name remains obscure. Historic documents give the name as *Dumfermelyn* in the eleventh century and as *Dumferlin* in 1124, with similar versions found subsequently. Some toponymists consider that there is a difference between *-fermelyn* and *-ferlin*, which could be significant, but this seems on the whole to be unlikely. The fort would have been in Pittencrieff Park, by the winding Tower Burn.

Dungannon (Tyrone)

The Irish name of this town south of COOKSTOWN is Dún Geanainn,

'Geanann's fort'. There are no records of the precise location of the original fort; it may not have been on the site now occupied by the remains called O'Neill's Castle.

Dungarvan (Waterford)
The Irish name of Dungarvan, the town northeast of YOUGHAL, is Dún Garbháin, meaning 'Garbhán's fort'. The original fort was almost certainly on the site by the estuary of the River Colligan where the remains of the castle and the old town walls now stand.

Dungeness (Kent)
A headland southeast of LYDD whose name declares it to be a promontory (Old English *næss*, modern 'ness') of nearby Denge Marsh. 'Denge' thus means 'valley district', from the Old English *denu* (valley), with the rarish Old English conjectural word *gē* (district), related to German *Gau* (as in Oberammergau). Dungeness is thus a 'headland by the valley district'. There is no obvious valley in Denge Marsh, so the meaning of the Old English word must perhaps be modified to mean 'plain'. Denge Marsh appears in a document of 774 as *Dengemerse*. *Compare* SURREY.

Dunkeld (Tayside)
A small cathedral town west of BLAIRGOWRIE whose name means 'fort of the Caledonians', referring to the Picts who occupied the region here. The name was recorded in the tenth century as *Duncalden*. The fort may have been the one whose prehistoric remains can be found in the grounds of Dunkeld House, to the west of the town.

Dunkery Beacon (Somerset)
The highest point of EXMOOR, on Dunkery Hill southwest of MINEHEAD. The name is undoubtedly based on the British (Celtic) root word for 'hill' or 'fort' (*duno*), also found in many other place-names beginning with 'Dun-'. The second part of the name may be related to the modern Welsh *craig* (rock) and so to the English 'crag'. The hill's name was recorded in the thirteenth century as *Duncrey*.

Dun Laoghaire (Dublin)
This port on DUBLIN Bay has an obviously Irish name that means 'Laoghaire's fort'. The identity of Laoghaire is still uncertain; according to some accounts he was a fifth-century high king of Ireland and a disciple of St Patrick. From 1821 to 1920 Dun Laoghaire was known as Kingstown, after George IV, who passed through the port in 1821 on his return to England after a state visit to Dublin. Before that, the name was usually rendered in English as 'Dunleary', its approximate pronunciation today. The fort may have been where Monkstown Castle now stands.

Dunmow (Essex)
A town east of BISHOP'S STORTFORD, officially known as Great Dunmow, as distinct from the village of Little Dunmow east of the town. Dunmow has a name that means 'hill meadow', from the Old English *dūn* (hill) and the conjectural *māwe* (meadow), from the Old English verb *māwan* (to mow). The name was recorded in the mid-tenth century as *Dunemowe*, and in the Domesday Book as *Dommauua* (where the 'double *u*' represents *w*). In the thirteenth century, Great Dunmow and Little Dunmow were known as *Dunmawe Magna* and *Dunmawe Parva*.

Dunoon (Strathclyde)
The name of this town and resort west of GOUROCK means 'fort of the river', from the Gaelic *dùn* (fort) and *abh* (river) (*compare* AVON). The present form of the name thus directly represents the Gaelic *dun obhainn*, the latter an adjectival word. The name was recorded in a document of about 1240 as *Dunnon*, and in 1270 as *Dunhoven*. The fort would have stood where the castle remains now lie, above the steamer pier overlooking the Firth of

CLYDE, and the 'river' would have been the Clyde itself.

Duns (Borders)

The former county town of Berwickshire west of BERWICK-UPON-TWEED, now little more than a village. Its name is simply the Gaelic *dùn* (hill), with the English plural *s* added. The most obvious of the 'hills' here is Duns Law, at whose foot the small town stands. The English word 'dunce' derives indirectly from the village, as it is here that (according to some accounts) the thirteenth-century controversial theologian John Duns Scotus is said to have been born. His followers were regarded as pedants or 'blockheads'.

Dunstable (Bedfordshire)

The name of this town west of LUTON means 'Dunna's post', with the personal name followed by the Old English *stapol* (post, pillar) (as in BARNSTAPLE). This was probably a distinctive landmark or 'waypost' here, for Dunstable stands at the intersection of the Roman roads WATLING STREET and the ICKNIELD WAY. Not surprisingly, therefore, there was a Roman camp here, known as *Durocobrivis*, which on the evidence of other Roman names (such as the one for ROCHESTER) ought to mean 'fort with joined bridges'. But there is no bridge at Dunstable, and no river, so the name must have some other origin. Possibly it meant 'fort with a bridge-like structure', referring to a sort of portico made of planks. The English name was recorded in a document of 1123 as *Dunestapele*.

Dunster (Somerset)

An ancient village below EXMOOR southeast of MINEHEAD whose name originally meant simply 'tor', recorded as such (*Torre*) in the Domesday Book. This is therefore the latter half of the present name. The first half represents the personal name Dunn. 'Dunn's tor' was probably the nearby hill on which the eleventh-century castle stands.

Dunwich (Suffolk)

A former coastal village southwest of SOUTHWOLD, and once a thriving port before erosion of the cliffs gradually destroyed the buildings. Its name means 'deepwater place' (there was thus no original 'dun' and no '-wich' as one might expect from similar names). The name is in fact British (Celtic) in origin, not English, and an eighth-century record of it as *Domnoc* shows the root word, which also underlies the tribal name *Dumnonii*, 'deep ones', after whom DEVON is named. The second part of the name was taken to be '-wich' by the Anglo-Saxons, and indeed there are plenty of such names on or near the east coast here, from HARWICH and IPSWICH in the south to NORWICH in the north.

Durham (Durham)

The name of this cathedral city south of NEWCASTLE UPON TYNE refers to its location on a hill in a bend of the River WEAR, deriving from the Old English *dūn* (hill) and from the Old Norse *holmr* (island). The latter refers to the riverside location rather than an island in the common sense. The name was thus recorded as *Dunholm* in about 1000, and it is this earlier form of the name that gave the abbreviation 'Dunelm' for the university and the signature of the Bishop of Durham. The *n* of the name became *r* under the influence of the Normans, just as, for example, in the name of DARLINGTON. The county name never took '-shire'.

Dursley (Gloucestershire)

This COTSWOLD town southwest of STROUD was recorded in the Domesday Book as *Dersilege*, this representing 'Dēorsige's clearing', with the personal name followed by the Old English *lēah* (woodland, clearing).

Dwyfor (Gwynedd)

An administrative district in the west of the county that takes its name from the river that flows through it, this probably meaning 'great water' (literally 'two waters').

Dyfed (Wales)

A county formed in 1974 and covering the southwestern region of the principality. The name is a revival of an ancient name, ultimately deriving from the tribe known as the *Demetae*, who inhabited this part of Wales during the Roman occupation. The origin of their name is unknown, and there are no similar names for comparison. The name *Demetae* was recorded in the second century A D by Ptolemy.

Dymchurch (Kent)

A small coastal town southwest of HYTHE whose name was recorded in about 1100 as *Deman circe*, suggesting an origin in the Old English *dēma* (judge) and *cirice* (church). The latter element is certainly correct, but the first part of the name may derive from a man called Diuma, who was bishop of Mercia in the seventh century. (His name was sometimes recorded in the form Dionia, leading to a belief that he was a woman!) So the name of Dymchurch may mean either 'judge's church' or 'Diuma's church'. The town's parish church is dedicated to St Peter and St Paul.

Dyrham Park (Avon)

This eighteenth-century country house south of CHIPPING SODBURY has a name that means 'well-watered valley where deer are found', from the Old English *dēor* (deer) and *hamm* (riverside land). One of the specialised senses of *hamm* is 'valley bottom hemmed in by higher ground'. This could well apply to such places as CHELTENHAM and CHESHAM, and to Dyrham Park; it perfectly describes the latter, for the deer are still here in the grounds, and anyone who has visited the house will have noted the steep descent to the valley bottom. The name of the original site (Dyrham) was recorded in the mid-tenth century as *Deorham*.

E

Ealing (Greater London)
This town and borough in west LONDON
had its name recorded in about 700 as
Gillingas, showing the personal name Gilla
with the Old English suffix *-ingas*, meaning
'people of'. The overall sense of the name is
thus '(place of) the people associated with
Gilla'. It is possible that in more recent
times the name has come to be wrongly
associated with 'eel', because of its
proximity (and even more, that of Little
Ealing) to the THAMES. The name appears
in a document of 1553 as *Elyng*. *Compare*
ELY (which is correctly associated with
eels).

Earls Court (Greater London)
A district of KENSINGTON and CHELSEA
whose name refers to a manor house
(which is what 'court' formerly implied)
owned by the Earls of OXFORD here until
the sixteenth century. The district
developed around the house, which was on
the site between Barkston Gardens and
Bramham Gardens, almost opposite Earls
Court Underground Station, next to Earls
Court Road.

Earlston (Borders)
A small town northeast of MELROSE with a
misleading name suggesting 'earls'. But as
early records of the name show (*Erchildon*
in about 1144; *Ercildune* in about 1180),
the true origin is in the personal name
Earcil, followed by the Old English *dūn*
(hill). Earlston is in Lauderdale (*see*
LAUDER) surrounded by hills.

Earn, Loch (Tayside)
As in most cases, this loch, to the west of
COMRIE, is named after the river that flows
from it. The river's name derives from an
Old Celtic root word *ara*, meaning simply
'flowing one'. The name was recorded in a
document of 1190 as *Erne*.

Easington (Durham)
This coal-mining town northwest of
PETERLEE has a name that was recorded in
a text of 1242 as *Yesington*. This suggests
that the stream here may have had a name
related to that of the OUSE, and thus
meaning simply 'water'. The name as a
whole will therefore mean 'place of the
people who live by the stream', and little
more. *Compare* JESMOND, which is on a
river called the Ouseburn.

East Bergholt (Suffolk)
A village northeast of COLCHESTER and
famous as the birthplace of the painter,
John Constable. 'Bergholt' means 'hill
wood', from the Old English *beorg*
(occurring in East Anglia as *berg*; hill) and
holt (wood). The overall sense is thus
'eastern settlement on a hill by a wood', as
distinct from West Bergholt, which is
almost ten miles away, northwest of
Colchester. Both villages were recorded in
the Domesday Book as *Bercolt*.

Eastbourne (East Sussex)
This well-known seaside resort east of
BRIGHTON has a name that shows it to
have an 'eastern stream', by contrast with
some other place on a 'western stream'; the
second half of the name is the Old English
burna (stream) (as for BOURNEMOUTH).
The place on a 'western stream' is actually
the village of Westbourne, east of HAVANT
some fifty miles from Eastbourne.
Originally, both were known locally as
'Bourne', a colloquial name used for each
place until as recently as the 1930s. The
particular stream that gave Eastbourne its
name rises near St Mary's Parish Church,
in the old part of the town. Both
Eastbourne and Westbourne were
recorded in the Domesday Book simply as
Burne with the places differentiated from
the thirteenth century (*Estburn* in 1279,
Westburne in 1302). The 'bourne' of
Westbourne would have been the River
Ems (*see* EMSWORTH), which marks the
boundary between Hampshire and Sussex
here.

East Dereham (Norfolk)
A town west of NORWICH and over twenty miles northeast of the small village of West Dereham, which lies east of DOWNHAM MARKET. 'Dereham' means 'deer pasture', from the Old English *dēor* (deer) and *hamm* (meadow, riverside land). East Dereham was simply *Derham* in the Domesday Book, and 'East' and 'West' were added to the two places for purposes of differentiation from the thirteenth century.

East Grinstead (West Sussex)
A town east of CRAWLEY. 'Grinstead' means 'green place', that is, 'location in grassy country'. The name was recorded as *Grenestede* in a document of 1121, and by the thirteenth century had added 'East' (*Estgrenested* in 1271) to distinguish the settlement from West Grinstead, a small village almost twenty miles southwest of it, south of HORSHAM. The meaning differs slightly from that of the Wiltshire place-names East Grimstead and West Grimstead, villages only a mile apart southeast of SALISBURY. Early records of these names show 'Grimstead' to mean 'green homestead' (Old English *hǣmstede*) rather than simply 'green site' (Old English *stede*).

East Ham (Greater London)
The town of East Ham (originally 'Ham', or *Hamme* in a document of 958) has a name that means 'eastern riverside land', derived from the Old English *hamm*, which frequently denotes a place in a river bend. East Ham, in the borough of NEWHAM, is not in a bend of the THAMES, but could be said to be in an angle formed by the Thames to the south and the River Roding (*see* RODINGS, THE) to the east. *See also* WEST HAM.

East Kilbride (Strathclyde)
A town lying some seven miles south of GLASGOW. 'Kilbride' means 'Brigid's church', from the Gaelic *cill* (church) and the name of St Brigid. There were several saints of this name, the best known being Brigid of KILDARE, who died in 525. The town's name was recorded as *Kellebride* in 1180, and later added 'East' to distinguish it from WEST KILBRIDE, almost thirty miles west of it near the coast. East Kilbride was designated a New Town in 1947.

Eastleigh (Hampshire)
The present town of Eastleigh, northeast of SOUTHAMPTON, developed only in the nineteenth century with the coming of the railway. However, the Domesday Book records a location here named *Estleie*, meaning 'eastern clearing', from the Old English *lēah* (wood, clearing); this shows that it was already regarded as 'east' of another identically named place nine hundred years ago. It is still uncertain where the 'Westleigh' was.

East Linton (Lothian)
A small town on the River TYNE west of DUNBAR. 'Linton' means 'flax enclosure', from the Old English *līn* (flax) (compare 'linen') and the common *tūn* (enclosure, village). In a document of 1127 its name appears simply as *Lintun*, with 'East' added later to distinguish it from West Linton, a village over thirty miles southwest of it, southwest of PENICUIK (in the Borders region).

East Molesey (Surrey)
East Molesey and West Molesey are neighbouring urban locations west of KINGSTON beside the River Mole, which takes its name from them as a 'back formation'. 'Molesey' means 'Mūl's island', with the personal name followed by the Old English *ēg* (island). The name was recorded in about 670 as *Muleseg*. Later, 'East' and 'West' were added to differentiate the two places. East Molesey is regarded as the more important of the two, at least postally, so that West Molesey's official postal designation is 'West Molesey, East Molesey, Surrey'. The river gave its name to the administrative district of MOLE VALLEY.

Eastwood (Nottinghamshire)

The name of this town northwest of
NOTTINGHAM is found in many places
elsewhere in the country, to denote an
'eastern wood', by contrast with one to the
west. However, this particular Eastwood is
a rather more subtle name, as early records
show. The Domesday Book recorded it as
Estewic, and a document of 1165 as
Estweit. The second half of this is not
'wood' but the Old Norse *thveit*
(corresponding to the English 'thwaite' in
such names as BASSENTHWAITE). This
meant 'forest clearing', and later 'meadow',
so this is the sense here. No doubt the
presence of many names ending in '-ley'
locally (representing the Old English *lēah*,
'wood', 'clearing') led to the substitution of
the English 'wood' for the Old Norse word.
A text of 1575 thus has the name as
Estwood, and one of 1608 as *Eastwait alias
Eastwood*. It is not clear where the 'western
clearing' was, and the name could simply
have indicated that Eastwood was east of
the River EREWASH. There are several
Scandinavian names in the area, another
being KIRKBY IN ASHFIELD. The 'east' of
Eastwood's name is the Old English *ēast*,
however, not Old Norse.

Ebbw Vale (Gwent)

This coal-mining and steel-manufacturing
town north of CARDIFF has the Welsh
name of Glynebwy, which means 'valley of
the (River) Ebwy' and which translates the
English name. This was a nineteenth-
century designation selected for the town
that developed around the ironworks here.
The river's name, recorded in the early
twelfth century as *Eboth*, may mean 'horse
river', from a Celtic word related to the
modern Welsh *ebol* (colt). The river may
have been associated in some special way
with horses, who drank or worked here, or
who forded the river here.

Ecclefechan (Dumfries and Galloway)

This small town north of ANNAN has a
name of British (Celtic) origin meaning
'little church', with the first half of the
name related to the Latin *ecclesia* (itself
from Greek) and so to the French *église*
and the English 'ecclesiastic'. The second
half of the name is related to the modern
Welsh *bach* (little). *Compare* ECCLES;
ECCLESTON.

Eccles (Greater Manchester)

A town west of MANCHESTER whose name
means simply 'church', from the same
British root word (conjectural *egles*) that
gave the names of ECCLEFECHAN and
ECCLESTON. The name was recorded in a
late-twelfth-century document exactly as
now, showing that the original church was
an ancient one. The Anglo-Saxons
borrowed the word for 'church' from the
Romans; being pagans, they had no word
of their own for the Christian place of
worship.

Eccleston (Lancashire)

Like ECCLEFECHAN and ECCLES, this
town west of CHORLEY has a name based
on the British word for 'church', to which
the Old English *tūn* (farm, village) has been
added. The name was recorded in a
document of 1094 as *Aycleton*. There are
several 'Eccles' names in Lancashire,
including Eccleshill near DARWEN and
Great and Little Eccleston near POULTON-
LE-FYLDE. They all refer to an ancient
church.

Eden (Cumbria)

Any of various rivers. The river in
northern England rises near KIRKBY
STEPHEN and flows northwestwards to the
SOLWAY FIRTH. Its name means 'gushing
one', from a British (Celtic) root word
ituna; it was recorded by Ptolemy in the
second century AD as *Itouna*. The Eden in
Kent takes its name from EDENBRIDGE.

Edenbridge (Kent)

The name of this town west of TONBRIDGE
was recorded in about 1100 as
Eadelmesbrege, meaning 'Eadhelm's
bridge', showing that the River Eden was
named after the town, not vice versa. The

personal name means 'rich protection' (literally 'happy helmet'). The name as a whole is Old English, with the personal name followed by *brycg* (bridge).

Edenderry (Offaly)

The Irish name of this market town west of DUBLIN is Éadan Doire, meaning 'hill-brow of the oak grove', from the Irish *éadan* (front, face, brow) and *doire* (oak wood) (as in LONDONDERRY). The hill of the name could be either the one to the south of the town, on which Blundell's Castle stands, or possibly Carrick Hill to the north.

Edgbaston (West Midlands)

This district of BIRMINGHAM was recorded in the Domesday Book as *Celboldestone*, which somewhat disguises its true origin, which is 'Ecgbald's farm'. The Old English personal name means 'bold sword'.

Edge Hill (Warwickshire)

The Civil War Battle of Edge Hill took place in 1642 on this escarpment northwest of BANBURY. It forms an extension of the COTSWOLD HILLS, and its name means literally 'hill with an edge'.

Edgeworthstown (Longford)

The obviously English name of this Irish town southeast of LONGFORD derives from the English Edgeworth family, who settled here in the sixteenth century, making their home at Edgeworthstown House. Novelist Maria Edgeworth, author of *Castle Rackrent*, was a member of this family, whose surname comes from the village of Edgeworth in Gloucestershire. The Irish name of the town is Meathas Troim, meaning 'frontier of the elder tree', with this name appearing in anglicised form as Mostrim. The 'frontier' is the boundary between the counties of Longford and Westmeath.

Edgware (Greater London)

The name of this district of BARNET has nothing to do with 'edge'; in an early record of about 975 it appears as *Æcges Wer*, showing it to mean 'Ecgi's weir'. The Old English *wer* often implied a fishing enclosure in a river, as probably here, in what is now known as Edgware Brook. This small stream is crossed by Edgware High Street here, which itself is a section of WATLING STREET.

Edinburgh (Lothian)

The historic city, Scotland's capital, is often popularly believed to be named after Edwin, the seventh-century king of Northumbria who was overlord of all England except Kent, and who is stated to have built the original fort here on the site of the present medieval Edinburgh Castle. But the place-name was recorded before his time (as *Eidyn* and *Din Eidyn* in about 600), so the name cannot simply mean 'Edwin's fort'. There is still uncertainty about the precise meaning of *Eidyn*, but it could have the sense 'fort on a slope' (the present Castle is on Castle Rock), and it could thus be British (Celtic) in origin. *Din Eidyn* gave the name of Dunedin in New Zealand, which was founded by Scottish Presbyterians in 1848 and named after their native Edinburgh. The '-burgh' of the capital's name is the Old English *burg* (fort).

Edmonton (Greater London)

A town in the Borough of ENFIELD, recorded in the Domesday Book as *Adelmetone*, and in a later document of 1216 as *Edelmeston*, showing the origin to be 'Ēadhelm's estate'. The Old English personal name is the same as that in EDENBRIDGE, but is here followed by *tūn* (estate).

Egham (Surrey)

This residential town west of STAINES has a name that means 'Ecga's homestead', with this found in a mid-tenth-century text as *Egeham*. The Old English personal name is followed by the common *hām* (homestead, village).

Egremont (Cumbria)

The small industrial town southwest of WHITEHAVEN has a purely Norman name meaning 'steep hill', apparently imported from the Normandy village of Aigremont. The name was recorded in a document of about 1125 exactly as now. There is no obvious 'steep hill' here, but perhaps the reference is to the site of the (long-ruined) Norman castle. It is possible, too, that the name may have been at least partly suggested by that of the river here, the Ehen, which was formerly known as the *Egne* (*see* ENNERDALE WATER).

Eigg (Highland)

An island southeast of RUM in the Inner HEBRIDES. It has a 'gap' between its high plateau to the north and its rocky moorland to the south, and the name may therefore represent the Gaelic *eag* (nick, notch, gap). It was recorded in 1654 as *Egg*.

Elgin (Grampian)

A town and cathedral city south of LOSSIEMOUTH whose name means 'little Ireland', from *Ealg*, one of the early Gaelic names for Ireland, with the diminutive suffix *-in*. Such a name would have been given by Scots who emigrated from Ireland, to commemorate their mother country. *Compare* such names as BLAIR ATHOLL and, especially, GLENELG. (In modern times, English and Scottish settlers overseas have similarly 'exported' names from their homeland, and there are now places named Elgin in North America, for example.) The town's name was recorded in a document of 1136 exactly as now.

Elie (Fife)

A resort west of ANSTRUTHER on the FIRTH OF FORTH. Its name suggests the Gaelic *ealeach* (rock, mound, bank) (*see* CRAIL), but such a link is only conjectural. It is hardly a duplicate of the English ELY, although a document of 1491 refers to it as *port and havin of the Elye*.

Elland (West Yorkshire)

A town on the River CALDER northwest of HUDDERSFIELD whose name refers to its location here, and derives from the Old English *ēa-land* (riverside land), with the 'land' here probably referring to a tract that had been recently cultivated. The name was recorded in the Domesday Book as *Elant*. For a similar name *see* PONTELAND.

Ellesmere (Shropshire)

This small town northeast of OSWESTRY has a name meaning 'Elli's lake', the lake in question being the one to the east of the town known as The Mere, now used mainly for pleasure boating. Ellesmere's name was recorded in the Domesday Book as *Ellesmeles*. The town indirectly gave its name to ELLESMERE PORT.

Ellesmere Port (Cheshire)

A town north of CHESTER that arose at the point where the Ellesmere Canal joined the estuary of the MERSEY, taking its name from the former. The canal itself thus ran from ELLESMERE as an arm of the Shropshire Union Canal. The town's name was in use in the eighteenth century, although at first the preferred name was Whitby Wharf or Whitby Locks; the railway station was called by the latter name when it opened here in 1863. (The local name Whitby still remains as a district of Ellesmere Port, southwest of the town centre.) For a somewhat similar name *see* STOURPORT.

Ellon (Grampian)

This small town is on the River Ythan north of ABERDEEN, not far from the sea. Its name has been derived from the Gaelic *eilean* (island), but this origin has not been substantiated, even though it suits the locality of the place, and the mid-twelfth-century record of the name as *Eilan* does appear to support it.

Elmbridge (Surrey)

An administrative district in northeast Surrey. The name is deceptive, being a former hundred name meaning 'Emel bridge'. Emel was the former name of the River Mole (*see* MOLE VALLEY), itself perhaps meaning 'misty'. The bridge in question may have crossed the Mole between ESHER and HERSHAM, where Albany Bridge (on the Esher Road, A244) is today.

Elswick (Tyne and Wear)
A southwestern district of NEWCASTLE UPON TYNE whose name was recorded in 1204 as *Alsiswic*, meaning 'Ælfsige's farm'. The name is normally pronounced 'Elzick'.

Eltham (Greater London)
A district of GREENWICH, recorded in the Domesday Book as *Elteham*. This means 'Elta's village'. As so often in such cases, the identity of the person named is unknown.

Ely (Cambridgeshire)
This cathedral city northeast of CAMBRIDGE has a name that correctly suggests 'eels'. The name was cited in the Venerable Bede's *Ecclesiastical History of the English People* (731) as a place *in regione quae uocatur Elge* ('in a region that is called Elge'). This early record of the name shows it to be a combination of the Old English *æl* (eel) and the rather uncommon *gē* (district), which also occurs in DUNGENESS and SURREY. Bede's text makes specific the reference to 'region', and this would have been one of the administrative districts of Anglo-Saxon England, before the division into counties. Later records of the name, such as *Eli* in about 1100, show that the second element has been taken to be the Old English *īeg* (island), which would certainly suit the city's fenland location on the River OUSE. Bede, too, adds that Ely got its name from the great number of eels caught in the FENS here; eels continued to be of local economic importance long after Anglo-Saxon times.

Emsworth (Hampshire)
A town east of HAVANT whose name means 'Æmele's enclosure', recorded in 1224 as *Emeleswurth*. Emsworth is on the River Ems, which took its name from the town.

Enfield (Greater London)
A town and borough in north London whose name means 'Eana's open land'; it was recorded in the Domesday Book as *Enefeld*. The Old English *feld* (which gave the modern 'field') must be taken to imply a large clearing in woodland, since neighbouring place-names, such as HADLEY WOOD, COCKFOSTERS, and BARNET, indicate that Enfield was in a forest region. Enfield is not far from EPPING Forest.

England (Great Britain)
Part of the island of BRITAIN, with a name clearly referring to the Angles, who, with the Saxons and the Jutes, came from what is now northern Germany to settle in southern Britain in the fifth and sixth centuries AD. Their own name is preserved in that of Angeln, a district in Schleswig, this in turn describing the 'angle' shape of the region just south of the present border with Denmark. The name of England was recorded in the late ninth century as *Englaland*, and it is quite possible that the Angles themselves associated the name with their word *angel* (hook), perhaps descriptive of some stretches of the southern coast, with its many headlands. It is even possible that this gave the name the advantage over a name based on that of the Saxons, although they did leave their inheritance in the well-known names of ESSEX, MIDDLESEX, SUSSEX, and WESSEX.

Ennerdale Water (Cumbria)
The westernmost lake in the Lake District, that takes its name from the valley here, whose Old Norse name meant 'Anundr's valley'. This was recorded in the late twelfth century as *Ananderdala*. A document of 1321 has the name as

Eghnerdale; this is based on the name of the river here, the Ehen (*compare* EGREMONT). The river's name is British (Celtic) in origin, and may mean 'cold', 'icy', from a word related to the modern Welsh *iâ* (ice).

Ennis (Clare)

A market town northwest of LIMERICK whose name is simply the Irish *inis* (island), which forms the basis for the following three names. Ennis is on the River Fergus, which itself has several small islands. But the name can equally well mean 'riverside land', and this interpretation will suit the location just as well.

Enniscorthy (Wexford)

A town north of WEXFORD on the steep west bank of the River SLANEY; this 'island' location accounts for the first part of the name (*compare* ENNIS). The Irish name of Enniscorthy is Inis Corthaidh. The latter part of this remains of uncertain origin; it is not likely to represent the Irish *corthair* (border, fringe), as Enniscorthy is not near any border or boundary of note.

Enniskillen (Fermanagh)

A county town southwest of OMAGH with the Irish name Inis Ceithleann, meaning 'Cethlenn's island'. The town is indeed on an island in the River ERNE. The personal name is that of the semi-legendary wife of Balor of the Great Blows, the Fomorian pirate. The British army regiment known as the Inniskilling Fusiliers take their name from this town, which is where they were raised in 1689.

Ennistymon (Clare)

This small market town northwest of ENNIS has the Irish name of Inis Díomáin, meaning 'Díomán's riverside land'. Ennistymon is situated on the River Cullenagh. *Compare* ENNIS; ENNISCORTHY; ENNISKILLEN.

Epping (Essex)

A town northeast of LONDON, at the northern end of Epping Forest, whose name is similar to that of UPPINGHAM and has a similar meaning. This is 'people of the lookout site', from the Old English *yppe* (lookout place), related to *upp* (up). The '-ing' of the name thus represents the Old English suffix *-ingas* (people of), with the name as a whole recorded in the Domesday Book as *Eppinges*. The actual 'lookout place' of the name may have been the ancient hill-fort called Ambersbury Banks in the surviving portion of the original Epping Forest to the south of the town, by the Epping Road (B1398). The name of the administrative district here is Epping Forest.

Epsom (Surreye

A town south of KINGSTON whose name means 'Ebbe's homestead', with the original Old English *hām* resulting in the present final '-om' of the name. Epsom was recorded in about 973 as *Ebbesham*, and as recently as 1718 as *Ebisham alias Epsom*.

Epworth (Humberside)

A small town southwest of SCUNTHORPE, recorded in the Domesday Book as *Epeurde*. This not very clearly represents the original sense, which is 'Eoppa's enclosure', with the personal name followed by the Old English *worth* (enclosure).

Erdington (West Midlands)

A district of BIRMINGHAM whose name means 'farm of Eorēd's people'. The Domesday Book recorded the name as *Hardintone*, with an erroneous initial *H*.

Erewash (Derbyshire)

An administrative district in the southeast of the county that takes its name from the river that flows through it. The river name, recorded in about 1145 as *Irewys*, means 'wandering marshland', from the Old English *irre* (wandering; compare modern 'err') and *wisce*, literally 'marshy meadow' but here better translated as 'river'. For much of its meandering course, the Erewash forms the county boundary between Derbyshire and Nottinghamshire. The second half of its name came to be associated with the common stream name and river name, Wash (as in Washbourne, Washford, etc.).

Eriskay (Western Isles)
The name of this small island between UIST and BARRA probably means 'Erik's island', with the Old Norse *ey* added to the personal name. But some prefer a derivation from the Gaelic word *uruisg*, the term for an evil water spirit or 'brownie'. The island's name was recorded in 1549 as *Eriskeray*.

Erith (Greater London)
A district of Bexley whose name was recorded in the mid-tenth century as *Earhyth*. This appears to represent the Old English *ēar* (gravel; related to modern 'earth') and *hȳth* (landing place). Erith is on the south bank of the THAMES, so the name could mean either 'gravel landing place' or 'landing place for gravel', or even both. The second half of the name is also found for other Thames-side places in LONDON, such as PUTNEY, CHELSEA, LAMBETH, ROTHERHITHE, and STEPNEY, although the original word is well disguised in most of these.

Ermine Street (England)
The Roman road that ran from a point near PEVENSEY, East Sussex, to YORK, passing through LONDON and LINCOLN. Another road of the same name also ran from GLOUCESTER to SILCHESTER, north of BASINGSTOKE. Like WATLING STREET, it took its name from that of the people through whose territory it passed. These were the *Earningas*, the 'people associated with Earna'. No other place now bears their name, whereas the people who gave their name to Watling Street (*see* ST ALBANS) have left a richer legacy. The road's name appears in a document of the mid-tenth century as *Earninga stræt*. The present form of the name has apparently been influenced by the quite unrelated

word 'ermine', as if associated with this fur (or the animal that provides it).

Erne, Lough (Fermanagh)
A lough in western Northern Ireland, whose name refers to the people known as the Erni or Ernai, who were said to be an ancient race living here on a plain that existed before the lake covered it. The Irish name of the lough is Loch Éirne.

Errigal, Mount (Donegal)
The Irish name of this mountain, east of GWEEDORE, is An Earagail, 'the oratory'. No doubt there was once an oratory or hermitage on it, in common with many other mountains in Ireland.

Erskine (Strathclyde)
The name of this town by the CLYDE, northwest of RENFREW, remains of uncertain origin, although some authorities relate it to the Welsh *ir* (green) and *ysgîn* (mantle), suggesting a grassy slope. This could suit the site but is not supported by early records of the name, such as *Erskin* in 1225 and *Yrskin* in 1227.

Esher (Surrey)
A residential town southwest of KINGSTON whose name appears in a document of 1005 as *Æscæron*, showing its origin to be the Old English *æsc* (ash) and *scearu* (share, district) (not related to modern 'shire', however). The overall sense is thus 'ash-tree district'.

Esk (Cumbria, North Yorkshire, Dumfries and Galloway, Lothian)
Any of at least four rivers in Britain, whose names have the same meaning: 'water', from the conjectural British (Celtic) root element *isca-*, which also gave the name of the EXE (but probably not that of the similarly spelt USK).

Essex (England)
A county in southeast England. Its name, together with that of SUSSEX, the former MIDDLESEX, and the ancient kingdom of

WESSEX, derive from the tribal name of the Saxons, here the East Saxons, whose kingdom included not only the present county of Essex but also that of Middlesex and a good deal of Hertfordshire. The name was recorded in the late ninth century as *East Seaxe*.

Eton (Berkshire)

This town with its famous college beside the THAMES has a name that describes its location — 'well-watered land by a river', from the Old English *ēg* (literally 'island') and the common *tūn* (farm, village). The name is found widely elsewhere, often in the spelling Eaton, and in a number of cases is based on the Old English *ēa* (river), rather than on the similar *ēg*. To determine which is the derivation, it is necessary to examine early records of the name and to study the topography of the place; sometimes only the latter is helpful. This is the case with Eton, whose name was recorded in the Domesday Book as *Ettone*. But the low-lying terrain of Eton, its location in a bend of the river, and the presence of many islands on the river itself nearby, suggest the above origin of the name rather than simply 'village by a river'. Eton lies directly across the river from WINDSOR.

Etruria (Staffordshire)

A district of STOKE-ON-TRENT that has a relatively modern name, referring to the Etrurian (i.e. Etruscan) style of pottery that was produced here by Josiah Wedgwood from the second half of the eighteenth century. The actual source of the name was that of Wedgwood's house, which he built here in the 1760s under the name of Etruria Hall. Etruria itself was an ancient country of central Italy, more or less corresponding to modern Tuscany (the name is similar to Etruscan). This was famous for its elegant vases, friezes, and lifesize sculptures found here in the eighth century BC.

Ettrick (Borders)

Any of several places in Scotland, such as the river of Ettrick Water, the village of Ettrick, the Ettrick Forest through which the river flows, and the mountain of Ettrick Pen, on the border between the regions of Dumfries and Galloway and Borders. An administrative district in the latter region is named Ettrick and Lauderdale (*see* LAUDER). Unfortunately, the precise origin of the name is unknown, and it may well be not only pre-Celtic but even pre-Indo-European, or at least non-Indo-European. It was recorded in a document of 1235 as *Ethric*.

Euston (Greater London)

A district in the Borough of Camden (*see* CAMDEN TOWN), whose name is also given to Euston Station, Euston Road, Euston Square, and other places in the area. The name derives from the title of the Earls of Euston, who owned the land here. The title itself comes from the village of Euston, Suffolk, southeast of THETFORD, whose own name means 'Eof's village', recorded in the Domesday Book as *Euestona*.

Evanton (Highland)

A village near the shore of the CROMARTY Firth, northeast of DINGWALL, that derives its name from Evan Fraser of Balconie, who founded it in the early years of the nineteenth century. Evanton can thus be interpreted as 'Evan's town'.

Everton (Merseyside)

The district of LIVERPOOL, like other Evertons elsewhere, derives its name from the Old English *eofor* (wild boar) and the frequent *tūn* (farm, village). Many places with a name beginning 'Ever-', such as Evercreech, Everley, Eversden, Eversholt, Eversley, and so on will also derive from *eofor*. *See also* YORK.

Evesham (Hereford and Worcester)

This town southeast of WORCESTER is in a bend of the River AVON, and this particular kind of location is indicated by the name, whose second part represents the Old English *hamm*, often meaning 'land in a bend of a river' (as also at BUCKINGHAM and CHIPPENHAM). The first part of the name is the personal name Eof, as in EUSTON (the original Suffolk village). Evesham was recorded in 709 as both *Homme* and *Eveshomme*. As so often, the identity of Eof is not known.

Evington (Leicestershire)
A district of LEICESTER whose name translates as 'farm associated with Eafa', with the name recorded in the Domesday Book as *Avintone*.

Ewell (Surrey)
A town southeast of KINGSTON whose name correctly suggests 'well'; it actually derives from the Old English *æwell* (river-source), this word being a compound of *ēa* (river) and *wella* (spring, source, well). The stream called the Hogsmill River rises at Ewell, flowing first north and then west from it to enter the THAMES at Kingston. The name was recorded in a document of 933 as *Euuelle*.

Exe (Somerset/Devon)
A river that rises on EXMOOR and flows south to enter the English Channel south of EXETER. The river's name simply means 'water' (*compare* AVON), representing the conjectural British (Celtic) *isca*. The Exe has given its name to a number of places in Devon, among them Exeter (whose Roman name was *Isca Dumnoniorum*), Exmoor, EXMOUTH, and EXWICK. In his second-century map of Britain, Ptolemy marked the river as the *Iska*. *See also* ESK.

Exeter (Devon)
The cathedral city southwest of BRISTOL derives its name from the River EXE, on which it stands. The name as a whole thus represents a 'smoothed' form of what amounts to 'Exchester', the latter half of the name indicating the presence of a former Roman camp here. This was called *Isca Dumnoniorum*, with the first word of

this representing the name of the Exe, and the latter being the name of the *Dumnonii*, the people who gave DEVON its name. Exeter was their capital. The name of the city was recorded in 894 as *Exanceaster*, and in the Domesday Book as *Essecestra*. The present form of the name is thus due to the influence of the Normans, who found clusters of consonants difficult to pronounce (*see* SHREWSBURY for another name they simplified). For another Roman *Isca see* CAERLEON and also USK.

Exmoor (Somerset/Devon)
The high moorland area bordering the Bristol Channel in southwest ENGLAND, officially known as Exmoor Forest. It takes its name from the River EXE that rises on it. The overall name was recorded in a document of 1204 as *Exemora*. *Compare* DARTMOOR.

Exmouth (Devon)
As its name indicates, this seaside resort nine miles southeast of EXETER lies at the mouth of the River EXE; the name was recorded in a text of 1001 as *Exanmuthan*.

Exwick (Devon)
A village beside the River EXE immediately northwest of EXETER city centre. The second half of its name represents the Old English *wīc*, basically meaning 'farm', especially one associated with a particular product or activity, such as CHISWICK (cheese). Here, as at ALNWICK, the first part of the name is that of the river on which it stands. Exwick was recorded in the Domesday Book as *Essoic*.

Eye (Suffolk)
A small town southeast of DISS whose name simply represents the Old English *ēg* (island, area of higher ground in a marshy district). Eye is situated by the River Dove among a network of streams that flow north to the WAVENEY. The name was recorded in the Domesday Book as *Eia*.

Eyemouth (Borders)

As its name implies, this fishing town and resort northwest of BERWICK-UPON-TWEED is at the mouth of the Eye Water. The river's own name derives from the Old English *ēa* (river).

Eynsham (Oxfordshire)

This town's name was recorded in a document of 571 as *Egonesham*, meaning either 'Egon's homestead' or 'Egon's river meadow'. If the first, the final element represents the Old English *hām*; if the second, *hamm*. The latter seems more likely, in view of the town's location, northwest of OXFORD near both the THAMES and the Evenlode. (Some authorities even link the town's name with that of the latter river, although it is usually regarded as being a 'back formation' from the village of Evenlode in Gloucestershire, near which it rises.

F

Failsworth (Greater Manchester)
This town northeast of MANCHESTER has a name that has been rather tentatively interpreted as 'fenced enclosure', from an unrecorded Old English word *fēgels*, derived from the verb *fēgan* (to join), with the more certain *worth*(enclosure). This conjecture is based not so much on early records of the name, such as *Fayleswrthe* in 1212, but on the known occurrence of *worth* with a first element denoting a particular type of enclosure, such as for LETCHWORTH ('locked enclosure') and Shuttleworth ('bolted enclosure').

Fairford (Gloucestershire)
A small town east of CIRENCESTER whose name virtually means what it says — 'fair ford' — with the Old English *fæger* (that gave the modern 'fair') having the sense 'clean', 'free from blemish'. A place called Fairford would thus be the opposite of a place called Fulford ('foul ford', i.e. a muddy one). Fairford is on the River Coln. The town was recorded in 872 as *Fagranforda*.

Fair Isle (Shetland)
The name suggests an attractive island, or one with good weather, but it actually means 'sheep island', from the Old Norse *faar* (sheep). Hence the modern association of the island with wool and Fair Isle knitwear. The name of Fair Isle is thus an exact parallel to that of the Faroes ('sheep islands'), which were also settled by the Scandinavians (who imported sheep there). Fair Isle lies midway between ORKNEY and SHETLAND.

Fairlie (Strathclyde)
This resort south of LARGS on the Firth of CLYDE may have a name of Old English origin, meaning 'beautiful clearing', from *fæger* (*see* FAIRFORD) and *lēah* (clearing).

Fakenham (Norfolk)
A town northwest of NORWICH whose name means 'Facca's homestead'. It was recorded in the Domesday Book as *Fachenham*.

Falkirk (Central)
The name of this industrial town west of EDINBURGH translates as 'speckled church', that is, one built with speckled or mottled stone. The two words that comprise the name are the Old English *fāg* (variegated, multi-coloured) and *cirice* (church). The authenticity of this is proved by versions of the town's name in other languages, such as *Egglesbreth* in 1065 (from the Gaelic *eaglais* 'church' and *breac* 'mottled'); the Latin *varia capella* in 1166; and the French *vaire chapelle* in the late thirteenth century. The English version of the name was recorded as *Faukirke* in a document of 1298. The present parish church stands on the site of the original church, one or two parts of which remain.

Falkland (Fife)
A small town north of GLENROTHES whose name has been said to mean 'falcons' land', and so to refer to a place where falconry or hawking was practised. But early records of the name, such as *Falleland* in about 1128 and *Falecklen* in 1160, suggest that this is probably not the true origin, which remains uncertain. The seventeenth-century Viscount Falkland gave his name to the Falkland Islands, in the South Atlantic.

Fallowfield (Greater Manchester)
A district of MANCHESTER whose name could mean what it says, 'fallow field', referring to newly cultivated land, or 'fallow-coloured field', describing a tract of yellowish-coloured land. The two words are identical now, but in Old English they were respectively *fealg* (ploughed land) and *fealu* (fallow-coloured). The latter seems more likely. The name was recorded in 1317 as *Fallufeld*.

Falmouth (Cornwall)

The port southeast of R E D R U T H obviously takes its name from the River Fal, at whose mouth it lies. The river's name remains of uncertain meaning, and there is no known word with which it can be connected. It does not appear to be Cornish, and the letter *f* is rare in Celtic languages (except in modern words borrowed from other languages); there are hardly any river names beginning with *F*-. Falmouth was recorded in 1235 as *Falemuth*, and the river name as *Fæle* in a document of 969.

Fareham (Hampshire)

A town northwest of P O R T S M O U T H whose name means 'fern homestead', that is, 'dwelling-place among ferns'. The name, recorded in the Domesday Book as *Fernham*, is thus a virtual doublet of F A R N H A M, and a near cousin of F A R I N G D O N.

Faringdon (Oxfordshire)

A small town northeast of S W I N D O N whose name means 'fern hill'. The middle '-ing-' of the name is misleading, as the name's early records show: *Fearndun* in a document of 924, for instance. The two elements of the name are thus the Old English *fearn* (fern) and *dūn* (hill). Faringdon is still surrounded by fern-covered hills. *Compare* F A R E H A M; F A R N B O R O U G H; F A R N H A M.

Farnborough (Hampshire)

A town north of A L D E R S H O T, whose name means 'fern hill', exactly the same as F A R I N G D O N, although the two elements of the name are not identical. Here the Old English *fearn* (fern) is followed by *beorg* (hill), as the record of the name in the Domesday Book shows — *Ferneberga*. The particular hill involved here may be the lowish one that has Farnborough Park at its southern end, north of the town centre.

Farne Islands (Northumberland)

A group of about thirty islands off the Northumbrian coast opposite B A M B U R G H.

Their name was recorded in a text of about 730 as *Farne*, and appears to mean 'fern islands', although the islands are noted more for their seals and seabirds. Perhaps the grouping of the islands was thought to resemble the fronds of a fern. Most places with names based on the Old English *fearn* (fern) denote the plant itself (*see* other F A R N- entries).

Farnham (Surrey)

The name of this town west of G U I L D F O R D means either 'fern homestead' (from the Old English *hām*) or 'fern meadow' (from *hamm*). The latter seems more likely, partly because the name was recorded in 894 as *Fearnhamme*, and partly because Farnham is on the River W E Y and the Old English *hamm* often indicates meadowland beside a river. Many Farnham place-names, however, will simply mean 'fern homestead', particularly when the place is not near water.

Farnworth (Greater Manchester)

A town southeast of B O L T O N whose name means 'ferny enclosure', from the Old English *fearn* (fern) and *worth* (enclosure). Farnworth was recorded in 1185 as *Farnewurd*. *See* other F A R N- entries.

Faversham (Kent)

This market town and small port west of W H I T S T A B L E has a name that means 'smith's village'. The first part of the name represents an Old English word conjectured to be *fæfer*, derived from the Latin *faber* (smith). Metal workings are believed to have existed in this area since Roman times. Some think, however, that the first half of the name may represent a personal name. The name itself was recorded in a document of 811 as *Fefresham*.

Fazakerley (Merseyside)

This district of L I V E R P O O L has a name that comprises three Old English words: *fæs* (fringe, border); *æcer* (plot of cultivated land; modern 'acre'); and *lēah* (forest, clearing). The overall sense is thus 'clearing by the newly cultivated borderland'. The name was recorded in a document of 1325 as *Fasacrelegh*.

Felixstowe (Suffolk)
A seaside resort and port southeast of IPSWICH whose name would appear to mean 'St Felix's holy place', with the first part referring to St Felix, the first Bishop of East Anglia, and the second part the Old English *stōw*, which although meaning basically 'place' often denoted a holy place following the name of a saint, as here (*compare* PADSTOW). But the name was recorded in 1254 as *Filchestou*, with no evidence of Felix but rather a person named Filica. What probably happened was that this earlier name became assimilated to that of the bishop when the town's association with St Felix became widely known. Even so, the seat of his bishopric was not at Felixstowe but at DUNWICH, further up the Suffolk coast.

Feltham (Greater London)
A district of HOUNSLOW whose name may mean simply 'open land village', from the Old English *feld* (open land; modern 'field') and *hām* (village). However, early records of the name, such as the Domesday Book's *Felteha'*, suggest that the first part of the name may not be *feld* but the Old English *felte* (wild marjoram or mullein). If this is so, the name would mean 'village where wild marjoram grows'. But conclusive evidence for this sense is still lacking, and 'village on open land' seems a safer interpretation. The name suitably describes Feltham as it was even as recently as the early nineteenth century.

Fens, The (England)
A flat low-lying tract of land with rivers, streams, and man-made channels that drain into The WASH. It comprises a large circular region of east and south Lincolnshire, north and east Cambridgeshire, and northwest Norfolk. The word is the Old English *fen* (fen,

marsh), occuring in many place-names, such as Fenton, Fenwick, Fenstanton, Fen Ditton, and so on, and less obviously in such names as Venton, Swinfen, Bulphan, and the like, most of these places being in The Fens.

Fermanagh (Ireland)
A county in the southwest corner of Northern Ireland. The name is a tribal one, representing the Irish Fear Manach, 'men of Monach', the latter being the name of their leader. They came and settled here from their native LEINSTER after murdering the son of its king; their territory occupied a larger area (including part of County DOWN) than that of the present county. Fermanagh is one of the few Irish counties not to be named after its county town (which is ENNISKILLEN) or after some other populated location. *Compare* FERMOY.

Fermoy (Cork)
A town northeast of CORK whose name represents the Irish Mainistir Fhear Maí, 'monastery of the men of the plain'. The two elements of the present name are forms of the Irish *fir* (men) and *machaire* (plain).

Ferns (Wexford)
The name of this cathedral town, northeast of ENNISCORTHY and the former royal seat of LEINSTER, could mislead the English speaker! It does not relate to 'ferns' but represents the Irish Fearna, 'elder trees', with the English plural *s* added to the Irish noun, itself already plural (the singular is *fearn*).

Ferryhill (Durham)
The name of this town south of DURHAM City represents the Old English *fiergen* (wooded hill), and it was recorded in the tenth century as *Feregenne*. This became shortened to *Ferye*, and the present '-hill' (originally 'on the Hill') was added, although the meaning 'hill' is implicit in the original name. No doubt the addition was made to distinguish this place from

Ferrybridge in West Yorkshire, whose name was also *Ferie* at one stage (but referring to a ferry crossing over the River AIRE). Both places were on the Great North Road, hence the potential confusion.

Ffestiniog *See* Blaenau Ffestiniog.

Fife (Scotland)
The modern administrative region, former county, and ancient kingdom share a name that traditionally derives from Fib, 'one of the seven sons of Cruithe, legendary father of the Picts' (James B. Johnston, *Place-Names of Scotland*). But this personal name dates from later than the territory associated with it, so some earlier but unidentified name must be involved. Fife was recorded in the mid-twelfth century as *Fib*, and as *Fif* in 1165.

Filey (North Yorkshire)
The North Sea resort southeast of SCARBOROUGH included in the Domesday Book as *Fiuelac*. Its name means 'five clearings', from the Old English *fīf* (five) and the common final element *lēah* (clearing). 'Number' names like this are not uncommon: *compare* SEVENOAKS and (less obviously) PIDDLETRENTHIDE.

Filton (Avon)
A suburb of BRISTOL with a name meaning 'hay farm', from the Old English *filethe* (hay) and *tūn* (farm). The name was recorded in a document of 1187 exactly as now.

Finchley (Greater London)
A district of BARNET whose name means more or less what is says: 'wood where finches live', from the Old English *finc* (finch) and *lēah* (wood). Finchley was recorded in a document of about 1208 as *Finchelee*.

Fingal's Cave (Strathclyde)
A large cave on the island of STAFFA, perhaps even more famous than the island itself, and said to be named after the legendary Celtic giant, Fionn MacCaul (commonly known as Finn mac Cool). He is supposed to have built the GIANT'S CAUSEWAY in Ireland and to have lived in this cave. The Gaelic name of the cave is An Uamh Binn, 'the melodious cave', referring to the strange sounds made by the sea among the cave's basalt pillars. Was Mendelssohn aware of this 'musical' association when he composed his 'Fingal's Cave Overture' after visiting Staffa in 1829?

Finsbury (Greater London)
A district of ISLINGTON, with its well-known Finsbury Park (although this is itself in the borough of HARINGEY). Its name means 'Fin's manor'; the personal name is Anglo-Scandinavian, while the final part is the Old English *burg* (fortified place, manor). The complete name was recorded in 1231 as *Vinisburh'*.

Firth of Forth (Fife/Lothian)
A large sea inlet in eastern Scotland, at the mouth of the River FORTH. There are several 'Firths' in Scotland, but this is probably the best known, partly because of its road and rail bridges, and partly, no doubt, because of the alliteration in the name. 'Firth' itself is used commonly in Scottish names for an estuary or river mouth, with the word directly related to 'fjord' and thus less directly to 'ford'. Other well known estuaries of the name are the Firth of CLYDE and Firth of TAY.

Fishbourne (West Sussex)
A village with the remains of a Roman palace west of CHICHESTER. It has a straightforward name meaning 'fish stream' or 'stream abounding in fish', with the second half of the name the Old English *burna* (as in EASTBOURNE). The Domesday Book recorded the name as *Fiseborne*.

Fishguard (Dyfed)
A small town north of HAVERFORDWEST, with its port of Fishguard Harbour. Its

name means 'fish yard' — an enclosure for catching fish or for keeping them in when caught. The name is from the Old Norse *fiskr* (fish) and *garthr* (yard). No doubt the present English look of the name arose from the fact that Fishguard is in an English-speaking part of Wales (this region of former Pembrokeshire has been called 'Little England Beyond Wales'). Also, the English words 'fish' and 'yard' (or 'guard') closely resemble their Scandinavian equivalents, and are indeed related to them. The Welsh name of Fishguard is Abergwaun, 'mouth of the Gwaun', with the river's name directly derived from the Welsh *gwaun* (marsh, moor). Other Scandinavian names around this stretch of coast include CALDY, SKOKHOLM, SKOMER, and GRASSHOLM — all islands.

Fivemiletown (Tyrone)

This small Irish town east of ENNISKILLEN is said to be so named because it is roughly five miles equidistant from Clabby, Clogher, and Colesbrooke. Its Irish name is Baile na Lorga, 'town of the shank', this relating perhaps to a 'shin' of land here.

Flamborough Head (Humberside)

A headland on the North Sea coast northeast of BRIDLINGTON that takes its name from the nearby village of Flamborough, whose own name means 'Flein's fort', with the Scandinavian personal name followed by the Old English *burg* (fortified place). The Domesday Book gave the name as *Flaneburg*.

Fleet (Hampshire)

This town west of FARNBOROUGH takes its name from the Old English *flēot* (stream) (compare related words, such as 'flow', 'flood', 'float', and 'fleet' itself), as do other places of the name, such as LONDON's Fleet Street over the small River Fleet that flows into the THAMES. The Hampshire town has such a stream, and the name was recorded in 1506 as *Le Flete*.

Fleetwood (Lancashire)

The name of this port north of BLACKPOOL is a recent one, derived from the surname of Sir Peter Hesketh Fleetwood, of Rossall Hall (now Rossall School), who founded it in the 1830s. The name happens to be suitable for a port at the mouth of a river, with 'fleet' suggesting water, ships, etc., and 'wood' a rural location, or at least the town's parks and gardens. The surname Fleetwood itself derives from a location named after a wood by a stream, although no such name is listed in the Ordnance Survey *Gazetteer of Great Britain* (1987).

Flint (Clwyd)

This town of northwest of CHESTER on the estuary of the River DEE has a name that means exactly what it says, referring to the hard rock here on which Flint Castle was built. ('Flint' here has a more general sense than it has today, however, and means more 'hard stone' than its current sense of 'a type of quartz'.) The Welsh name of the town is Y Fflint, meaning the same. A document of 1277 has the name in a French form, as *Le Chaylou* (Modern French *le caillou*, 'the pebble'). A seventeenth-century Welsh version of the name, *Caer Gallestr* ('flint fort') did not catch on. The town gave its name to the former county of Flintshire.

Florence Court (Fermanagh)

A Georgian mansion southwest of ENNISKILLEN named after its original owner in the eighteenth century, Lord Mount Florence, created Earl of Enniskillen in 1784. Its Irish name is Mullach na Seangán, 'height of the ants'. It is now the family seat of the Earls of Enniskillen.

Fochabers (Grampian)

A village by the River SPEY east of ELGIN. The name probably contains an early Gaelic word represented by the modern Gaelic *abar* (marsh), with the first part of the name perhaps equivalent to the modern Gaelic *fothach* (lake). The final *s* seems to have been an English addition, and records of the name down to the sixteenth century (such as *Fouchabre* in 1325) do not have it.

Folkestone (Kent)

A town and Channel port east of ASHFORD. For some time toponymists have debated whether the first part of the name represents the Old English *folc* (people; modern 'folk') or the personal name Folca. The latter half is certainly *stān* (stone), and this is likely to have been a meeting-place, which supports either interpretation: 'people's meeting-place' (a sort of 'assembly point') or 'Folca's stone'. Early records of the name, such as *Folcanstan* in a document of 696, seem to suggest the latter. Either way, Folkestone is known to have been the centre of its hundred. Other names comprising a personal name plus 'stone' include BRIXTON. The stone was probably located some way inland rather than by the coast.

Fordingbridge (Hampshire)

The name of this town on the River AVON north of RINGWOOD means not 'bridge where fording was possible' but 'bridge of the people who live at Ford'. Fordingbridge was thus recorded as *Forde* in the Domesday Book, and the '-ing-' section of the name represents the Old English suffix *-ingas* (people of). No doubt it was these 'people', or their descendants, who built the bridge to replace the original ford. The Domesday Book records the name of the hundred here in the present form, as *Fordingebrige*. The present seven-arched stone bridge is medieval in origin and probably not that of the name. The original bridge was the meeting-place of the hundred here.

Forest of Bowland

See Bowland, Forest of

Forest of Dean (Gloucestershire)

This heavily wooded area, between the rivers SEVERN and WYE, was formerly a royal hunting ground. The 'Dean' of the name simply represents the Old English *denu* (valley), although the word also occurs in the names of local places, such as Little Dean and Mitcheldean, on the edge of the Forest, and West Dean, well inside the Forest. The name was recorded in a document of 1130 simply as *Dena*.

Forest Row (East Sussex)

A village southeast of EAST GRINSTEAD that was recorded in 1467 as *Forstrowe*. The 'Forest' of the name is ASHDOWN FOREST, and the 'Row' would probably have been a row of houses or cottages built here below what is now the northern edge of the Forest. The village is on the upper reach of the River MEDWAY, which no doubt was an important factor for the builders of the original dwellings here as a water supply was guaranteed.

Forfar (Tayside)

This jute-manufacturing town north of DUNDEE has a Gaelic name which probably means 'ridge wood', from the Old Gaelic *fothir faire*, although some consider the Gaelic *faire* to be another (identical) word meaning 'watching', so that the sense is perhaps 'wood of watching' — a kind of lookout place. However, Forfar itself is on level ground, and an unlikely place for a lookout, unless the reference is to one of the nearby hills, such as the Hill of Finhaven to the northeast of the town. This is today well known as a local viewpoint. The name was recorded as *Forfare* in a document of about 1200. The town gave its name to the former county of Forfarshire, which was also known as ANGUS.

Formby (Merseyside)

This residential town north of LIVERPOOL has a Scandinavian name, meaning 'Forni's village', with the personal name followed by the Old Norse *bý* (village). The name was recorded in the Domesday Book as *Fornebei*.

Forres (Grampian)

This town west of ELGIN has a Gaelic name

meaning literally 'below the shrubs', from *fo* (below, under) and *ras* (shrub, underwood). A late-twelfth-century document gives the name as *Forais*.

Fort Augustus (Highland)

A village at the southwest end of Loch NESS at the entrance to the CALEDONIAN CANAL. It grew up around the fort, which was enlarged (but not originally built) in the 1730s by General Wade. The fort was named after William Augustus, Duke of Cumberland, who set up a camp here after the suppression of the Jacobite rising of 1745 and who defeated Charles Edward Stuart (The 'Young Pretender') at the Battle of CULLODEN the following year.

Forth (Central)

This well-known Scottish river rises north of the CAMPSIE FELLS in central Scotland and enters the North Sea at the FIRTH OF FORTH. It derives its name from an Old Celtic root word meaning 'silent one', referring to its slow current. The Roman writer Tacitus recorded the name in the second century AD as *Bodotria*. A reflection of this can be seen in the modern Irish *bodhaire* (deafness).

Fortrose (Highland)

A small town and resort in the ROSS and CROMARTY district. Its name has nothing to do with 'fort', and still less with 'rose'; it represents the Gaelic *foterros* (subsidiary cape), from the preposition *fo* (under, below) and *ros* (peninsula, cape) (*compare* FORRES). (A roadsign on the A9 near KINGUSSIE bears the single word 'Phones'. This is not the sign for a telephone but the name of a locality, which represents the Gaelic *fo-innis*, 'under the meadow'.) Fortrose was recorded in a document of 1455 exactly as now.

Fort William (Highland)

The town near the head of Loch LINNHE derives its name from the fortress here, originally built in 1655 by General Monck, but rebuilt as a garrison in 1690 and named after the reigning monarch, William III. It had earlier been known as *Gordonsburgh* after the Duke of Gordon, on whose land it was originally built, and for a while as *Maryburgh*, after Queen Mary, wife of William III.

Foss Way (England)

This ancient trackway, also spelt Fosse Way, runs from near SIDMOUTH in Devon up to the HUMBER, passing through ILCHESTER, LEICESTER, and LINCOLN, after which it coincides with ERMINE STEET. It was adapted and used by the Romans, and its line is still followed today by important trunk roads, such as the A37, A429, and A46. Although not found as such in Old English, the word *foss* at some time entered the English language, either from the Latin *fossa* (ditch) or from a modern Celtic equivalent, such as the Welsh *ffos*; it meant an artificial ditch or channel. The Foss Way was so called because it had a ditch on one side, or even both. The road was recorded in a document of 956 as *strata publica de Fosse*.

Fotheringhay (Northamptonshire)

This village northeast of OUNDLE, is known from history books as the site of the castle where Mary, Queen of Scots, was executed in 1587. The name means 'island of the people of Forthhere'. The three elements are thus the Old English personal name Forthhere (meaning 'army leader', from *forth* 'in front' and *here* 'army'), the suffix *-ingas* (people of), and *ēg* (island, land between streams). Fotheringhay has water on three sides, with the River NENE to the south and east and Willow Brook to the north. The name was recorded in about 1060 as *Fodringeya*. The former castle is now marked by a mound.

Foula (Shetland)

An island west of SCALLOWAY noted for its sea birds. And this is exactly what its name means: 'bird island', from the Old Norse *fugl* (bird; compare the English 'fowl') and *ey* (island). *Compare* FOULNESS.

Foulness (Essex)
An island northeast of SOUTHEND-ON-
SEA, well known for its wildlife, especially
its wildfowl. It has an Old English name
that is therefore apt, deriving from *fugol*
(bird) and *næss* (promontory) (*compare*
FOULA). Foulness is often known today as
Foulness Island, but it was originally
simply a promontory or peninsula; it is still
connected with the mainland by a road at
its southwest end. The name was recorded
in a document of 1215 as *Fughelnesse*.

Fountains Abbey (North Yorkshire)
A medieval abbey whose remains are now a
tourist attraction southwest of RIPON. The
name refers not so much to fountains here
but to springs. As it stands now, the name
represents the Old French *fontein* (fountain, spring), itself from the Latin *fons*,
plural *fontes*. The name is believed to have
been given to the springs discovered by the
monks of St. Mary's, YORK, when they
began building the Cistercian monastery
and abbey on the site in the first part of the
twelfth century. Contemporary records
refer to it as *Sancta Maria de Fontibus*.

Fowey (Cornwall)
A town south of LOSTWITHIEL on the
south coast at the mouth of the River
Fowey, after which it is named. The river's
name derives from the conjectural Old
Cornish *faw* (beech trees) (compare the
Latin *Fagus* for the botanical genus of
beech), and so means 'river where beech
trees grow'. The '-ey' of the name is a
Celtic element found in many river names
in Wales and southwest England, such as
Teifi, Tywi, Wylye (*see* WILTON), Bovey
(*see* BOVEY TRACEY), Cary (*see* CASTLE
CARY), and Tavy (*see* TAVISTOCK); it
probably means simply 'water' (compare
the Roman name *Isca* for EXETER and the
USK). Fowey was recorded in a document
of about 1200 as *Fawe*.

Foyle, Lough (Donegal/Londonderry)
A sea lough in the north of Ireland, that
takes its name from that of the river flowing
into it; the River Foyle is formed by the
confluence of the Finn and the Mourne at
LIFFORD. The name is found elsewhere as
a river name, and represents the Irish *faill*
(cliff), denoting the source of many
streams.

Fraserburgh (Grampian)
A fishing town and port northwest of
PETERHEAD whose name is first recorded,
in a latinised text of 1592, as *burgum de
Fraser*. This refers to Sir Alexander Fraser,
who constructed a harbour here and
founded what was virtually a new town on
the site of the former settlement called
Faithlie (a text of 1597 tells of *the toun and
burghe of Faythlie, now callit Fraserburghe*).
The '-burgh' of the name is the Old
English *burg*, here in its sense of 'chartered
town'.

Fratton (Hampshire)
This district of PORTSMOUTH, familiar to
train travellers as a railway junction, has a
name that was recorded in a text of 982 as
Frodingtun, which means 'place of the
people of Frōd'. The personal name appears
in some other place-names, such as
FRODSHAM and the district of
SCUNTHORPE known as Frodingham.

Freshford (Kilkenny)
An attractive village northwest of
KILKENNY whose name arose as a
mistranslation of the original Irish name.
This was (and is) Achadh Úr, 'fresh field',
a name implying clean land. The Irish
achadh (field) was taken to be *áth* (ford),
itself a common element in Irish place-
names (*see* ATHLONE, for example).
Moreover, 'ford' would suit the location, as
Freshford is on a stream (the Clashacrow).

Freshwater (Isle of Wight)
A resort east of Totland (*see* TOTLAND
BAY) whose name virtually means what it
says, and describes the clear water of the
River Yare on which it lies. Freshwater was
actually the former name of the river,
which takes its present name from

YARMOUTH, also on it. The Domesday Book records Freshwater as *Frescwatre*.

Friern Barnet (Greater London)
See Barnet.

Frimley (Surrey)
This town, immediately south of CAMBERLEY, has a name that means 'Fremi's clearing', with the personal name followed by the Old English *lēah* (clearing in a forest). The name was recorded in a document of about 933 as *Fremeley*.

Frinton-on-Sea (Essex)
A resort northeast of CLACTON-ON-SEA whose name probably means 'Fritha's village'; it was recorded in the Domesday Book as *Frientuna*. The suffix '-on-Sea' is purely for commercial reasons, since there is no other Frinton with which the town could be confused. The present resort developed only in the late nineteenth century.

Frodsham (Cheshire)
The name of this town south of RUNCORN means 'Frōd's farm', recorded in the Domesday Book as *Frotesham*. The personal name also occurs in FRATTON, although it is hardly likely to be the same person!

Frome (Somerset)
A town south of BATH that takes its name from the river on which it stands. The river's name in turn is British (Celtic) in origin and comes from a conjectural root element *fram-* meaning 'fair', 'fine', 'brisk'.

Other rivers of the same name, such as the one that flows through BROMYARD, will have the same meaning. The name of both town and river is pronounced 'Froom', and was recorded in a document of 705 as such (*Froom*).

Fulham (Greater London)
A district north of the THAMES whose name means 'Fulla's riverside meadow', with the personal name followed by the Old English *hamm*, the word frequently used of a place in the bend of a river, as here (and also at BUCKINGHAM, CHIPPENHAM, and EVESHAM). Perhaps something of the original waterside meadows is represented in modern Fulham by Bishop's Park and Hurlingham Park. Fulham was recorded in a document of about 704 as *Fulanham*.

Fylde (Lancashire)
An administrative district of the county with an old name meaning simply 'plain' (Old English *filde*, related to *feld*, 'open land', and so to modern 'field'). The region here east of BLACKPOOL is still known as The Fylde, with the word similarly occurring in the name of POULTON-LE-FYLDE, the local town. The name was recorded in 1246 as *Filde*.

Fyne, Loch (Strathclyde)
Like many lochs, Loch Fyne, in ARGYLL, is named after the river that flows into it. The river's name is related to the modern Gaelic *fion* (wine), perhaps referring to the supposed healing or medicinal powers of its waters, or to its holy nature.

G

Gainsborough (Lincolnshire)
An inland port northwest of LINCOLN on
the River TRENT. Its name means 'Gegn's
fort', with the personal name followed by
the Old English *burg* (fortified place). The
Old English personal name is a short form
of a longer name, such as Gænbeald or
Geanburh. The name of the town was
recorded in 1013 as *Gegnesburgh*.

Gairloch (Highland)
The village at the head of Gair Loch takes
its name from the loch, whose own Gaelic
name means 'short lake' (from *geàrr* 'short'
and *loch* 'lake'). The name was recorded in
1275 as *Gerloth*.

Galashiels (Borders)
The first half of the name of this town north
of HAWICK comes from that of the river on
which it stands, the Gala Water, whose
own name may mean 'gallows stream'. The
second half of the name is the same as that
of NORTH SHIELDS and SOUTH SHIELDS,
and means 'huts' or 'shelters', from the
Middle English *schele* (shed), a term
applied to a temporary hut used by
shepherds on a summer pasture (compare
modern 'shieling'). Galashiels has long
been a centre of woollen manufacture,
showing that it was sheep who grazed here
in the summer. The name was recorded in
1237 as *Galuschel*.

Galloway (Dumfries and Galloway)
The former district of Galloway in
southwest Scotland comprised the two
former counties of KIRKCUDBRIGHT and
WIGTOWN, and its name is now preserved
in the present region of DUMFRIES and
Galloway and the town of NEW
GALLOWAY. The name is a tribal one,
representing the *Gall-Ghóidil*, the 'stranger
Gaels' of mixed Irish and Norse descent
who settled here from the ninth century.

They were so named by the Scots as they
were regarded as foreigners. The same
'Gael' element (*Ghóidil*) occurs in the name
ARGYLL, while *gall* is present in the name
DONEGAL. Galloway was recorded in a
document of about 970 as *Galweya*. The
name of GALWAY is quite different in
origin. *See also* GALSTON.

Galston (Strathclyde)
A town east of KILMARNOCK whose name
means 'village of the strangers', from the
Gaelic *gall* (stranger) (*compare* GALLOWAY)
and the Old English *tūn* (village). The
reference would have been to invaders or
'immigrants' of a different race or
background to the native Scottish (Gaelic)
dwellers. The name was recorded in 1260
as *Gaulston*.

Galtee Mountains (Tipperary/Limerick)
A range of mountains to the south of
TIPPERARY also known as the Galty
Mountains. The name represents the Irish
Na Gaibhlte, '(mountains) of the woods'.

Galway (Galway)
A county town (which gave its name to the
county) in western Ireland. It has a
descriptive name meaning basically 'stony'
(modern Irish *gall* is 'stone'), referring to
its rocky location and to the stony bed of
the River CORRIB at whose mouth it
stands. The current Irish name of Galway
is Gaillimh.

Garforth (West Yorkshire)
This town east of LEEDS was recorded in
the Domesday Book as *Gereford*, which
seems to mean 'Gæra's ford'. The personal
name would be a short form of such a name
as Gærburh or Gærwine.

Gatehouse of Fleet (Dumfries and Galloway)
The site of the present small town,
northwest of KIRKCUDBRIGHT near the
mouth of the Water of Fleet, appears on a
map of 1759 simply as a single house by a
road. This was the 'gate house', with 'gate'
meaning 'road' or 'way', as it does in many

place-names in northern England and Scotland (such as HARROGATE). The town grew up around it and took the second part of its name from the river at whose mouth it lies. The river's name represents either the Old Norse *fljót* or the Old English *fléot*, 'river'.

Gateshead (Tyne and Wear)
An industrial town on the south bank of the TYNE opposite NEWCASTLE UPON TYNE. Its name was referred to by the Venerable Bede in his *Ecclesiastical History of the English People* as (in Latin) *Ad Caprae Caput*, 'at the (place) of the goat's head'. The name thus means either that goats were found on a headland here, or that there was a special site here where the head of a goat was displayed for some religious reason, probably in connection with sacrificial rites. Similar names consisting of an animal's name followed by 'head' are found elsewhere; BUSHEY, for example, had an earlier name of 'Hartshead', probably for the same totemic or pagan religious reason as Gateshead. (It is possible in such cases that the animal's head may have been merely a representation, and not a real head.) The two basic elements of Gateshead are the Old English *gāt* (goat) and *hēafod* (head, headland).

Gatwick (West Sussex)
The well-known airport south of HORLEY has a name that means 'goat farm', from the Old English *gāt* (goat) (*compare* GATESHEAD and *wīc* (farm). Early Ordnance Survey one-inch maps show that there was a farm here in the nineteenth century, called Gatwick Farm.

Gedling (Nottinghamshire)
This administrative district in the centre of the county takes its name from that of a former hundred here, recorded in the Domesday book as *Ghellinge*. The name probably means '(place of) the people of Gedel'.

Gerrards Cross (Buckinghamshire)
The suburban district northwest of UXBRIDGE takes its name from a family named Gerrard (Gerard) or Garrard, who lived here in the fourteenth or fifteenth century. The name of the present place was recorded in a document of 1692 as *Gerards Cross*. The original cross may have been a boundary marker or one by a crossroads, such as the one on Gerrards Cross Common where a smaller road crosses the A40 from BEACONSFIELD to UXBRIDGE.

Giant's Causeway (Antrim)
The famous promontory on the north coast of Northern Ireland, with its thousands of basalt columns, has been given a 'folk' name to match the legends associated with it. The main one concerns the legendary hero Finn mac Cool (Finn mac Comaill), who is said to have built a bridge from the promontory across to Scotland in order to vanquish a mighty enemy. It was thus his 'causeway' (i.e. road to the bridge). A former Irish name of the place was *Clochán na bhFórmorach*, 'stepping stones of the Fomorians', the legendary giant sea rovers who used the columns as their causeway. The Fomorians were a race of demons said to have had their base on TORY ISLAND. Their name may derive from the Irish *fo* (under) and a word meaning something like 'devil'. The current Irish name of the Giant's Causeway is Clochán an Aifir, 'stepping stones of the giant'. *See also* FINGAL'S CAVE.

Gidea Park (Greater London)
A district of ROMFORD whose name probably means something like 'park of the giddy hall', with the first word of the name representing the Old English *gydig* (giddy). This could refer either to a foolishly built place, rather like a folly, or a building that was constructed carelessly or unsteadily. The earliest record we have of the name is one in a document of 1258 as *La Gidiehall*.

Gillingham (Dorset, Kent)

Either of two towns. The Dorset Gillingham is pronounced with a hard 'g' (as in 'guilt') and the Kent town with a soft one (as in 'jilt'). The name of each is exactly the same in origin and meaning, which is 'homestead of the people of Gylla'. It is hardly likely that the same man is involved, as the places are quite far apart. The Dorset Gillingham, northwest of SHAFTESBURY, was recorded in 1016 as *Gillingaham*, and the Kent one, immediately east of CHATHAM, occurs in the Domesday Book as *Gillingeham*. There is also a village of the same name near BECCLES in Norfolk, with the same origin (and pronounced with a hard 'g').

Girton (Cambridgeshire)

A suburb of CAMBRIDGE, with its well-known women's college, has a name that means 'gravel village' or 'settlement built on gravel', from the Old English *grēot* (gravel; modern 'grit'), and *tūn* (farm, estate, village). The name was recorded in 1060 as *Gretton*.

Girvan (Strathclyde)

A fishing town and resort southwest of AYR at the mouth of the Water of Girvan, after which it takes its name. The river's name may be based on the Gaelic *geàrr* (short) and *abhainn* (river), making it distinct from the longer River Stinchar to the south of it. The name was recorded in 1275 as *Girven*.

Glamis (Tayside)

This village, north of DUNDEE at the northeastern end of the SIDLAW HILLS, is famous for Glamis Castle, the birthplace of Princess Margaret. The name represents the Gaelic *glamhus* (wide gap, open country), referring to the local terrain. The name was recorded in a document of 1187 as *Glames*.

Glamorgan (Wales)

A former county of South Wales, now subdivided into Mid, South, and West Glamorgan. Its name means 'Morgan's shore', with the Welsh *glan* (bank, shore) forming the 'Gla-' preceding the personal name Morgan, who was a seventh-century prince of GWENT. His name probably means 'bright one', although popularly thought to mean 'sea-born', from two root words seen in modern Welsh: *môr* (sea) and *geni* (to be born). (This derivation is reflected in the name of the fourth-century heretic Pelagius, whose name means 'sea-born', from the Greek *pelagos* (sea), and whose original Celtic name was said to be Morgan!) The Welsh name of the former county was Morgannwg, where the final element represents the word for 'land', 'territory'.

Glanford (Humberside)

The name of this administrative district in the south of the county is that of the former name of BRIGG.

Glasgow (Strathclyde)

This famous Scottish city and port has a name that essentially means 'green hollow', from early British (Celtic) root words represented today by the modern Welsh *glas* (green, greenish grey) and *cau* (hollow). The name was recorded in 1136 as *Glasgu*. The original 'green hollow' would have been a natural feature here long before the settlement.

Glasnevin (Dublin)

A northern district of DUBLIN whose name appears to mean 'stream of the infants', from the Irish *glaise* (stream) and *naoidhin*, the genitive plural of *naoidhe* (infant, young child, girl). It is hard to see what this could mean, unless it refers to a stream where children played or could cross easily (*compare* MAIDENHEAD). The current Irish name, supporting this translation, is Glas Naíon.

Glastonbury (Somerset)

A town east of BRIDGWATER famous as an ancient centre of Christian culture and for its earlier pagan and mystical associations. The name is of pagan origin, ultimately deriving from a Celtic word meaning 'woad' (compare the modern Welsh *glaslys*, 'woad'); originally it was something like 'Glastonia'. This can be understood as meaning 'place where woad grows', referring to the original British settlement here. Woad is a plant of the cabbage family that yields a blue dye, used by the 'Ancient Britons' for decoration of the body. Old English *burg* (fortified place) was then added to the original name. A Welsh record of the name dating from 601 is *Ineswytrin*, literally 'glass island', with the word for 'glass' (modern Welsh *gwydr*) related to the Latin *vitrum*, which meant both 'glass' and 'woad' (the English 'glass' is thus indirectly linked with the name of Glastonbury). 'Island' is explained by the fact that the town lies on land in low marshy terrain. Texts of the eighth century record the name as both *Glastingaea* and *Glestingaburg*.

Glen Affric (Highland)

This popular tourist region in INVERNESS district is named after the valley of the River Affric, whose own name means 'dappled one', from the Gaelic *ath* (a so-called 'intensive', used to emphasize a word) and *breac* (dappled, speckled) (*compare* FALKIRK). The initial 'Glen' of this name (and of the Scottish and Irish entries below) means 'valley'; it is usually followed by the name of the river in that valley.

Glencoe (Highland)

The name of the valley of the River Coe, east of BALLACHULISH, is usually associated with the notorious massacre that took place here in 1692. The river's name is of unknown origin, but was recorded in its earliest forms as *Comhann*. The village of Glencoe is at the foot of Glencoe.

Glendalough (Wicklow)

A picturesque glen west of WICKLOW popular with tourists. Its name means 'valley of the two lakes', these being the straightforwardly named Upper Lake and Lower Lake. The Irish form of the name is Gleann Dá Loch (*da* is 'two').

Gleneagles (Tayside)

A locality south of AUCHTERARDER, well known for the Gleneagles Hotel and its famous golf courses. The 'eagles' of the name has nothing to do with birds (and even less with the golfing term), but represents the Gaelic *eaglais* (church) (*compare* ECCLES). This is one 'Glen' name that does not derive from that of its river, which here is the Ruthven. The name was recorded in a document of about 1165 as *Gleninglese*.

Glenelg (Highland)

A village in the LOCHABER district whose name means 'valley of Ireland', referring to the Irish settlers who came to live here in early times; *Ealg* was one of their names for their homeland (*compare* ELGIN, also named for their motherland). Popular guidebooks additionally like to point out that the place-name is palindromic; although adding little to the name's interpretation this may add to the toponymist's pleasure. Glenelg appears in late-thirteenth-century documents as spelt now.

Glenfinnan (Highland)

A village west of FORT WILLIAM in Glen Finnan. Both village and glen are named after the River Finnan. The river is held by some to be named after Fingon, a fourteenth-century Abbot of IONA, but most river names are much older than this.

Glengarnock (Strathclyde)

A steel-manufacturing village southeast of KILBIRNIE. It derives its name from the river here, the Garnock. The origin of its name is uncertain, although some have derived it from the Gaelic *gearanach* (plaintive, groaning one), with apparent reference to the sound made by its waters.

Glengarriff (Cork)

An attractive coastal village south of KENMARE at the northern head of BANTRY

Bay. Its name represents the Irish An Gleann Garbh, 'the rough valley', referring to the craggy glen here, which directly gave its name to the river on which the village stands.

Glenrothes (Fife)

A New Town designated in 1948 and located northeast of the FORTH road bridge. Its name was devised to blend with the genuine 'Glen' names of Scotland. There is no obvious glen (valley) here, but doubtless the 'Glen-' part was intended to refer to the River Leven, which flows past the north of the town from Loch LEVEN to the sea. The second part of the name refers to the Earls of ROTHES, who have long been connected with the region and who had an estate here. A more natural name would have been 'Glenleven', especially as this name did not already exist for the region or a settlement here.

Glossop (Derbyshire)

This town east of MANCHESTER was recorded in the Domesday Book as *Glosop*. This conceals its true origin, which is in 'Glott's valley'. The personal name is followed by the Old English *hop*, a word used for a small enclosed valley, especially one that overhangs the main valley. (The word also appears in the name of BACUP.) The town is in such a narrow valley on the edge of the PEAK DISTRICT National Park. Glott may be a nickname meaning 'starer', related to the modern English 'gloat'.

Gloucester (Gloucestershire)

An industrial and cathedral city west of CHELTENHAM. The latter half of the name ('-cester') declares it to be a former Roman camp. The first half of the name represents the old Roman name, *Glevum*. Rather unusually, this latter does not derive from the river here, which is the SEVERN, but from the original British (Celtic) conjectural root element *glev-* describing the river and meaning simply 'bright', 'shining'. (Compare the modern Welsh *gloyw*, 'bright', 'clear', 'shining'.) No

doubt the Anglo-Saxons associated this name with Old English words such as *glēow* (play, sport), or even (coincidentally) *glōwan* (to glow). The present name was well established by the time the Domesday Book recorded it as *Glouuecestre*. The county name was recorded in a document of 1016 as *Gleawcestrescir*.

Glyndebourne (East Sussex)

An Elizabethan house east of LEWES, famous for its annual summer opera season. It takes its name from the Glynde Reach river here, itself named after the nearby village of Glynde. The village's name probably derives from the Old English conjectural *glind* (fence, enclosure). The river name appears in a document of 1288 as *Burne juxta Glynde*, while the village name was recorded exactly as now in a text of 1210.

Glyndŵr (Clwyd)

An administrative district in the centre and south of the county. The name is a historic personal one, that of the fourteenth-century Welsh rebel, better known (to English speakers) as Owen Glendower, whose own name was taken from that of the district of which he was lord. The name's ultimate origin is thus in the historic region of *Glyndyfrdwy*, 'valley of the Dyfrdwy', the latter being the Welsh name of the DEE.

Godalming (Surrey)

The name of this old town southwest of GUILDFORD means '(place) of the people of Godhelm'; and this is recorded in a document of the late ninth century as *æt Godelmingum*, with the final syllable representing the grammatical ending required after the Old English *æt* (at). The personal name means 'God's defence' (literally 'God's helmet').

Godmanchester (Cambridgeshire)

The name of this small town immediately south of HUNTINGDON suggests an uneasy combination of 'God' and 'Manchester'. In fact it divides in the middle as 'Godman/chester', showing it to be the site of a former Roman town. The meaning is thus 'Roman station associated with Godmund', whose personal name means 'God's protection'. The name of the Roman settlement here was probably *Durovigutum*, which consists of a word meaning 'fort' followed by what may be an unrecorded personal name (although no instance of 'Duro-' being followed by a personal name is known). Some authorities, however, give the name of the Roman camp not as *Durovigutum* but as *Duroliponte* (*see* CAMBRIDGE). Godmanchester is at an important site, where ERMINE STREET crossed the River OUSE, and where it is joined (now as the A14) by two other main roads from Cambridge and SANDY. Godmanchester was recorded as *Godmundcestre* in the Domesday Book.

Godstone (Surrey)
A village east of REDHILL whose name probably means 'God's village'; it was recorded in a document of 1248 as *Godeston*. Its earlier name was Walkingstead, meaning 'Wolcen's place'. The 'God' of the present name could be simply a short form of a personal name, such as Godmann, rather than the name of the Deity.

Golders Green (Greater London)
This district of BARNET derives its name from a family called Golder or Godyere (modern Goodyear) who lived by (or owned) the green here some time before the seventeenth century. The name was recorded as *Golders Greene* in a document of 1612.

Goldthorpe (South Yorkhire)
A town west of DONCASTER whose name simply means 'Golda's thorp', with a 'thorp' being the Old Norse word for a secondary settlement, dependent on another. The name was recorded in the Domesday Book as *Goldetorp*.

Golspie (Highland)
A small fishing town and holiday resort northeast of DORNOCH in the SUTHERLAND District. Further south its name could perhaps have been 'Goldsby', as it is Scandinavian in origin, and means 'Gold's farm', with the second element of the name as the Old Norse *bý* (farm). It appears in a document of 1330 as *Goldespy*.

Gomersal (West Yorkshire)
The worsted and wool-spinning district east of CLECKHEATON has a name that probably means 'Gōdmær's corner of land', with the personal name followed by the Old English *halh* (modern 'haugh'), meaning 'nook', but also referring to an area of land by a river, as Gomersal is. In the Domesday Book, the name of Gomersal appears as *Gomershale*.

Goodwick (Dyfed)
This suburb of FISHGUARD probably has a name of Scandinavian origin, representing the Old Norse *góthr* (good) and *vík* (bay), although the second element could equally be the Old English *wīc* (port) (as in GREENWICH). The Welsh name of Goodwick is Wdig, representing the original, whichever it was.

Goodwin Sands (Kent)
It is quite possible that the name of the notorious shoals in the Straits of DOVER was devised in a medieval attempt to 'placate' any evil spirit that lived in the waters here, for the original Old English name corresponding to modern Godwin or Goodwin meant 'good friend'. But equally, the reference may be a historic one, to Earl Godwine of Kent, who held the island here that was subsequently drowned by the sea to become the present sands. This event is said to have occured in 1097. The name is recorded in a document of 1371 as *Godewynesonde*.

Goodwood (West Sussex)
A famous racecourse northeast of CHICHESTER that takes its name from the

nearby Goodwood Park, part of the estate of Goodwood House, whose own name derives from the original location, called 'Gōdgifu's wood'. Gōdgifu (meaning 'God-given') was an Old English woman's name, and was the 'correct' name of Lady Godiva. The name of Goodwood was recorded in a document of about 1200 as *Godiuawuda*. 'Godiva' is a latinised form of the Old English personal name.

Goole (Humberside)

An inland port on the River OUSE west of HULL. Its name refers to its location, and derives from the Middle English word *goule* (ditch, channel) (compare the modern English 'gully' and 'gullet'). It is possible that the present canal called Dutch River may represent the (straightened) course of the original stream or channel here that gave Goole its name. The name appears in a document of 1356 as *gulla in Merskland*, meaning 'channel in marshland' (*compare* MARSKE-BY-THE-SEA).

Gorbals (Strathclyde)

A former slum area of GLASGOW whose name is difficult to interpret satisfactorily. It appears in a document of 1521 simply as *Baldis*.

Gordon (Grampian)

An administrative district in the centre and east of the region, that takes its name from the clan or family of Gordon, many of whose members were or are associated with places in the district, notably HUNTLY and ABERDEEN. The clan name derives from the village of Gordon, northwest of KELSO in the BORDERS District.

Gordonstoun (Grampian)

This well-known coeducational public school west of LOSSIEMOUTH takes its name from Sir Robert Gordon, who acquired the estate here, formerly known as Bog of Plewlands, in 1638.

Gorebridge (Lothian)

This town south of DALKEITH is said to

take its name from the bridge by which it arose at a 'gore', or triangular piece of land (Old English *gāra*); the river here, the Water of Gore, then took its name from this. If this is so, the name is similar to that of KENSINGTON Gore in LONDON, the present street of the name having been built along one side of a triangle of land.

Gorey (Wexford)

A market town southwest of ARKLOW that has the Irish name Guaire, which means 'sandbank'. But Gorey is only on a small stream and is some distance from the coast. An origin in the Irish *guaireach* (wooded) would suit its locality much better.

Goring-by-Sea (West Sussex)

This district of WORTHING was recorded as *Garinges* in the Domesday Book, with this meaning '(place of) the people of Gora'.

Gorleston-on-Sea (Norfolk)

A district of Great YARMOUTH that was recorded in the Domesday Book as *Gorlestuna*, which means 'Gurla's village'. The personal name is a rare one.

Gormanston (Meath)

A small but attractive village northwest of BALBRIGGAN with the Irish name Baile Mhic Gormáin, 'homestead of Mac Gormáin' (or of the sons of Gormán). The English '-ton' represents the Irish Baile.

Gorseinon (West Glamorgan)

This town northwest of SWANSEA has a name that probably means 'Einion's marsh', with the first element of the name representing the Welsh *cors* (marsh). It is not clear which person of the name is referred to. The personal name itself means 'anvil'.

Gort (Galway)

A market town southeast of GALWAY whose name is simply the Irish for 'field'; it is found as an element of many other names, such as Gorteen ('little field') and Gortmore ('big field'). Gort's current Irish name is An Gort, 'the field'.

Gosforth (Tyne and Wear)

This town immediately north of NEWCASTLE UPON TYNE has a name that means 'goose ford'; it is a northern variant of the common name Gosford, found further south. A 'goose ford' would probably be one where geese could be driven across, although it could also denote a place on a river where wild geese were commonly found. There are two small streams here, one north of the town and one south, either of which could have been the original 'goose ford'. The name was recorded in the Domesday Book as *Goseford*.

Gospel Oak (Greater London)

A district of CAMDEN whose name describes a particular oak tree where a church procession would halt for the gospel to be read at Rogationtide, during the ceremony of 'beating the bounds'. Gospel Oak is on the border of the parishes of HAMPSTEAD and ST PANCRAS. The actual oak tree here is mentioned in documents of 1761 and 1819, after which it was cut down. Where the name occurs elsewhere in the country, the origin will be the same. The Ordnance Survey *Gazetteer of Great Britain* (1987) lists five other Gospel Oaks besides this one.

Gosport (Hampshire)

A town west of PORTSMOUTH whose name probably indicates it was a former 'goose port', that is, a market town where geese were regularly sold. Here 'port' has the sense of 'market town' (derived from the Latin *porta*, 'gate') rather than 'harbour' (from the Latin *portus*), although the issue in this instance is complicated by the fact that Gosport is also a sea port, and is moreover just across the water from Portsmouth. But its name almost certainly developed independently from that of the neighbouring city. Local guidebooks like to give the derivation of the name as 'God's Port', after a French Bishop who found refuge from a storm here in the twelfth century. But although theoretically possible, this derivation is most unlikely here. Gosport was recorded in a document of 1250 as *Goseport*.

Gourock (Strathclyde)

A resort and boat terminus on the River CLYDE west of GREENOCK. It has a Gaelic name that is said to derive from the word for 'pimple' (*guirean*), with metaphorical reference to a small hill here. The name of the locality was referred to in a document of 1661 as *Ouir et Nether Gowrockis*.

Govan (Strathclyde)

This district of GLASGOW may have a name that means 'dear rock', from two Celtic words related to the Welsh *cu* (dear) and the mutated (*m* to *f*) form of *maen* (stone). But what or where the particular 'dear rock' was is not known. The name was recorded in about 1150 as *Gvuan*.

Gower Peninsula (West Glamorgan)

A peninsula that juts out to the west of SWANSEA into the BRISTOL Channel. The name derives from the Welsh *gŵyr* (crooked, sloping). Its current Welsh name is simply Gŵyr. *See also* GOWERTON.

Gowerton (West Glamorgan)

A town northwest of SWANSEA that takes its name from the GOWER PENINSULA, on which it is situated. Its original name was Gower Road, after its location on the main road leading to the Peninsula. With its increase in size and importance, however, it was felt that a new 'town' name would be more appropriate, and the change of name was thus made in 1885. Gowerton's Welsh name, with the same meaning, is Tre-Gŵyr.

Gracehill (Antrim)

This village west of BALLYMENA arose as a Moravian settlement in 1746, and was given a name that would reflect the religious nature of its foundation, although there is no actual hill here. Other Moravian settlements include Fulneck in West Yorkshire, named after the Moravians' original home in Silesia (earlier names for this English settlement were Lamb's Hill and Grace Hall); and Gnadenhutten in Ohio, USA, with the German *Gnade* (grace) added to the second half of the Moravians' native German town of Herrnhut. Until at least the nineteenth century, Gracehill was also regularly known as Ballykennedy, an anglicisation of its Irish name, Baile Uí Chinnéide, 'homestead of the people of Kennedy'.

Grain, Isle of (Kent)

This peninsula to the west of the mouth of the River MEDWAY has a name that misleadingly suggests stocks or stores of grain. 'Grain' here represents the Old English *grēon* (gravel; related to *grēot* that gave the name of GIRTON), referring to the gravelly or gritty shore of the peninsula, which was once an island. The name was recorded in about 1100 as *Grean*.

Grampians (Scotland)

The great mountain system forming the Central Highlands, south of the 'Great Glen'. Its name remains of uncertain origin despite attempts to equate it with that of *Mons Graupius* mentioned by Tacitus, who wrote that *Agricola ad montem Graupium pervenit* ('Agricola reached Mount Graupius') in his campaign. It is now known that 'Mons Graupius' was actually Bennachie, the upland area to the west of INVERURIE, which is not even in the Grampians. But it is possible that sixteenth-century antiquarians introduced the name 'Grampian', based on 'Graupius', to replace the earlier name of *The Mounth* for the district. This name derives from the Gaelic *monadh* (hilly district), and is preserved today in the Cairn o'Mount road between BANCHORY and FETTERCAIRN, and also in the name of the plateau known as the White Mounth, southeast of BRAEMAR. Grampian is the modern administrative district here.

Grand Union Canal (England)

A canal that connects the THAMES at LONDON with the River Soar south of LEICESTER, and so with the TRENT at Trent Junction north of Kegworth, Leicestershire. The name formerly applied only to the northern part of the canal, with the southern section, extending from its union with the Oxford Canal southeast of RUGBY, known as the Grand Junction Canal. Both the Grand Union Canal and the Grand Junction Canal were constructed in the early years of the nineteenth century.

Grangemouth (Central)

A container port east of FALKIRK on the south side of the FIRTH OF FORTH. It lies at the mouth of a small river called the Grange Burn, itself named after the grange of Newbattle Abbey nearby. The town was founded in 1777 in connection with the construction of the FORTH and CLYDE Canal.

Grange-over-Sands (Cumbria)

A resort north of MORECAMBE, across Morecambe Bay, that was originally known simply as *Grange* (so recorded in 1491), this being the name of a farm (later known as Grange Farm) that was owned by Cartmel Priory. The resort that developed here took the name of the farm, and added '-over-sands' to refer to its location at the end of a (sometimes treacherous) route across the sands of Morecambe Bay. It was thus a place called 'Grange' over (i.e. above) these sands.

Grantchester (Cambridgeshire)

The name of this village is, perhaps fittingly enough, interwoven with that of CAMBRIDGE, two miles northeast of it. Its final '-chester' would appear at first sight to denote a former Roman fort here (Old English *ceaster*), as at WINCHESTER, CHICHESTER, and other similarly named places. But this element is actually a development of the Old English *sǣte* (settlers), as in the names of DORSET and SOMERSET. The name thus properly means 'settlers on the River Granta'. The river's own name means 'fenny one', from a conjectural British (Celtic) root element *grant-*. However this river name gave the name of Cambridge, which in turn, by a back formation, gave the modern name of the same river, the Cam. (Compare the alternative name of ISIS for the THAMES at OXFORD.) The present form, Grantchester, was influenced by the Venerable Bede's reference to Cambridge as *Grantacaestir*. But the Domesday Book recorded Grantchester as *Granteseta*, showing the true second element of the name.

Grantham (Lincolnshire)

A town on the River WITHAM east of NOTTINGHAM whose name was recorded in the Domesday Book spelt exactly as now. The meaning is either 'Granta's village' or possibly 'village built on gravel'. If the latter, the Old English words behind the name will be the conjectural *grand* (gravel; related to modern 'grind') and *hām* (village).

Granton (Lothian)

This district of EDINBURGH had its name recorded in a document of about 1200 as *Grendun*, suggesting that the origin might be in the Old English *grēne* (green) and *dūn* (hill), as for the village of Grendon in Northamptonshire (and elsewhere). Granton, however, with its harbour on the FIRTH OF FORTH, is not a noticeably hilly district, and there may be some other explanation for the name.

Grantown-on-Spey (Highland)

A market town and resort south of FORRES that arose as a model village planned, in 1765 by James Grant on a site about a mile from his home, Castle Grant. It is thus named after him. The latter part of the name indicates its situation by the River SPEY.

Grasmere (Cumbria)

One of the central lakes of the Lake District, just to the west of RYDAL WATER.

Its name means 'grassy lake', probably with reference to its grassy shores, or possibly indicating the grass-like vegetation of its waters. The name was recorded in 1375 as *Grissemere*, suggesting that 'mere', meaning 'lake', had been added to an earlier name that was something like *Grisse*. This could well represent the two Old Norse words *gres* (grass) and *sǽr* (lake, sea), which would have given the full sense in themselves.

Grassholm (Dyfed)

A small island west of SKOMER which, like its neighbour, has a Scandinavian name, meaning simply 'grassy island'. It was referred to in a fifteenth-century text as *Insula Grasholm*, but the first word is redundant, as is the English 'Island' added to 'Grassholm' on some maps today.

Gravesend (Kent)

This industrial town on the THAMES northwest of ROCHESTER has a name that wrongly suggests 'graves' when it should suggest 'groves'. The name means 'place at the end of the grove', with the original grove of the name perhaps located to the east of the present town where the Fort Gardens are today. The 'grave' is present because the Old English word for 'grove' was *grāf*. The name was recorded in the Domesday Book as *Gravesham*, a version revived for the administrative distict here.

Gravesham (Kent)

An administrative district in the northwest of the county, formed in 1974 and adopted from the Domesday Book record of the name of GRAVESEND.

Grays (Essex)

This town northwest of TILBURY is formally known as Grays Thurrock, with the latter part of the name its older element. 'Thurrock' derives from the Old English *thurruc*, which somewhat surprisingly turns out to mean 'bilge (of a ship)'. (The word is related to the modern English 'through'.) The reference here would have been to soggy or marshy land, and Grays is a THAMES-side town east of Thurrock Marshes. 'Grays' represents the name of the Norman family, de Grai, who held the manor here from the end of the twelfth century, although the first known record of the place-name incorporating their family name is dated only 1248, as *Turrokgreys*. The Domesday Book records the settlement simply as *Turruc*. Henry de Grai took his name from Graye, in Normandy. *See also* THURROCK.

Great Driffield (Humberside)
A town southwest of BRIDLINGTON whose name declares it to be not a 'dry field', but a 'dirty field', or more precisely a muddy stretch of open land. The two Old English components of 'Driffield' are thus *drit* (dirt) and *feld* (open land; modern 'field'). The name was recorded in the Domesday Book as *Drifelt*. 'Great' distinguishes the town from Little Driffield, a village located one mile to the west.

Great Missenden (Buckinghamshire)
Great Missenden and Little Missenden are villages two miles apart northwest of AMERSHAM. The basic name of each derives from the river on which they are located, the Misbourne, whose own name is based on the Old English *mos* (moss), and so means 'mossy one', perhaps referring to water plants actually in the river rather than moss growing beside it. Probably something like 'Mysse' was the river's original name, to which 'bourne' has been added, much as we add 'River' to 'Thames' when talking about it. The final element of the name Missenden is the Old English *denu* (valley). The basic name was recorded in the Domesday Book as *Missedene*.

Great Ormes Head (Gwynedd)
Great Ormes Head and Little Ormes Head are peninsulas respectively west and east of LLANDUDNO, the former being the larger, as its name implies. The name is a Scandinavian one, and means 'snake's

head' from the Old Norse *ormr* (snake, worm) and *hofuth* (head). A 'snake's head' would have been a distinctive landmark on the coast here for approaching ships. A fifteenth-century document refers to the larger headland as *Ormeshede insula*. An exact Old English parallel to the name is found at the southern end of Wales, in the WORMS HEAD. The Old Norse and Old English words for 'serpent' are mutually related, and so also relate to the modern English 'worm', which itself originally meant 'snake'.

Greatstone-on-Sea (Kent)
A seaside resort southeast of NEW ROMNEY that takes its name from a rocky headland here called Great Stone. The resort of Littlestone-on-Sea, about one mile distant, takes its name similarly from a smaller 'matching' headland called Little Stone. Despite its name, the latter resort is now larger than the former, no doubt because it developed as an extension of the established town of New Romney, whereas Greatstone-on-Sea arose much later, and had to develop 'from scratch'. This is one example, therefore, of names that denote the opposite of what they seem to imply.

Great Tew (Oxfordshire)
Great Tew and Little Tew are smallish villages about a mile apart to the east of CHIPPING NORTON. The name 'Tew' is a difficult one, recorded in a document of 1004 as *æt Tiwan* and in the Domesday Book as *Tewe*. The origin may lie in the Old English *tīg* (meeting-place), referring to a place of assembly. The nearby village of Duns Tew took its name from the other Tews and means 'Tew owned by Dunn'.

Great Yarmouth (Norfolk)
See Yarmouth.

Greenford (Greater London)
This district of EALING has a straightforward name that means what is

says, and denotes a settlement that arose by a 'green ford'. 'Green' probably means that the ford was on a minor route, so was more grassy and less obviously an important crossing place. The name was recorded in a document of 845 as *Grenan Forda*. The name is not as common as might be supposed, and the Ordnance Survey *Gazetteer of Great Britain* (1987) lists only three other Greenfords, all in Scotland. *See also* PERIVALE.

Greenham Common (Berkshire)

The name has been in the news so much in the 1980s that it should perhaps be included here. It became prominent because of Greenham Common Airfield, which was built on the common (a tract of open land used in common by all local residents) of the nearby village of Greenham, now a southern suburb of NEWBURY. The airfield lies southeast of Greenham, on a tract of ground marked on the earliest one-inch Ordnance Survey maps (early nineteenth century) as *Greenham Heath*, which was renamed Greenham Common subsequently, no doubt for 'aesthetic' reasons. ('Common' now implies public land where there are facilities for walkers and strollers, while 'heath' still has the implication of rough and barren land.) The name Greenham, found elsewhere in Britain, here means 'green riverside meadow', incorporating the Old English *hamm* (riverside land) not *hām* (homestead, village). The river here is the KENNET. The village was recorded in the Domesday Book as *Greneham*.

Greenhithe (Kent)

A locality on the THAMES east of DARTFORD whose name means 'grassy landing place', from the Old English *grēne* (green) and *hȳth* (landing-place). The grounds of Ingress Abbey and the Thames Nautical Training College are still 'green' here, and there are still 'landing places' in the form of jetties and piers.

The name was recorded in 1264 as *Grenethe*.

Greenock (Strathclyde)

An industrial town and port on the south side of the Firth of CLYDE whose name denotes not 'green' but 'sunny', from the Gaelic *grianaig* '(place at the) sunny hillock'. The terrain here rises from flat land by the river to higher ground, and this would have been the original 'sunny hillock'. The name was recorded at the end of the fourteenth century as *Grenok*.

Greenwich (Greater London)

A town and borough on the south bank of the THAMES whose name means 'green harbour'. The Old English *wīc* is used here in its 'specialising' sense of 'port', as found, for example, in IPSWICH and NORWICH. It is probable that river or sea ports called '-wich', like Greenwich, were more important than ones called '-hythe', like GREENHITHE or ROTHERHITHE, although such differences may no longer be apparent. Greenwich was recorded in a document of 964 as *Grenewic*.

Gresford (Clwyd)

A colliery town north of WREXHAM whose name probably derives from the Welsh *croesffordd* (crossroads), as its Welsh name of Gresffordd indicates. The reference would be to the minor road that leads across the River ALUN here from the main road (now the A483) to CHESTER. This could have been a more important crossing point than it might now seem.

Greta Bridge (Durham)

This village on the River Greta southeast of BARNARD CASTLE takes its name from the river that the bridge here crosses, now superseded by the adjacent A66 bridge. The river's name is of Old Norse origin and means 'stony stream', from *grjót* (gravel, stones) and *á* (river, stream). There was a Roman station here whose name is uncertain. although it may have been *Morbium*, itself of unknown meaning.

Gretna Green (Dumfries and Galloway)
This village east of ANNAN, once famous as the scene of marriages between runaway sweethearts, takes its name from the nearby village of Gretna. This is close enough to the English border to have a name of Old English origin, meaning 'place by the gravel hill', from the (conjectural) *grēote* (gravel) and *hōh* (height, hill). The *n* of the name developed from the grammatical ending on the word that means 'gravelly place'. Gretna was recorded in a document of 1223 as *Gretenho*.

Greyabbey (Down)
This village by STRANGFORD Lough, southeast of NEWTOWNARDS, takes its name from the grey stone of the Cistercian abbey here, which remains one of the most complete in Ireland. The Irish name of the village, with the same meaning, is An Mhainistir Liath. The abbey was built at the end of the twelfth century.

Greystones (Wicklow)
The village and seaside resort south of BRAY has a name that refers to the few grey-stoned buildings, such as fishermen's cottages, that were originally here before the railway was built in the nineteenth century. The earliest record of the name is in a document of 1760 as *Gray Stones*. The Irish name is Na Chlocha Liatha, 'the grey stones'.

Grimes Graves (Norfolk)
These Neolithic flint mines northeast of BRANDON have a name similar to those of other ancient sites in Britain, such as Grim's Bank near ALDERMASTON, Grims Ditch, southwest of SALISBURY, and Grims Dyke north of FORDINGBRIDGE, among others. These all relate, as possibly does the name of GRIMSBY, to a nickname, meaning 'masked one', of the Norse god Odin. This nickname implies an 'unknown' and therefore terrible person; the English 'grimace' and (less directly)

'grim' are related words. These 'graves' or flint mines are still mysterious and somewhat 'grim' today.

Grimsby (Humberside)
A port at the mouth of the HUMBER with a Scandinavian (Danish) name, meaning 'Grim's village'. There are many names ending in '-by' (Old Norse *bý*, 'village') in this area of eastern England, but most of them are of inland villages, not important places on the coast. There are also several names with 'Grim-' in the region, such as Grimesthorpe, Grimsthorpe, and Grimston, all named after the same Grim. Although this was a Scandinavian personal name in its own right, it was also familiar as one of the names of Odin (*see* GRIMES GRAVES), and this association may have been in the mind of the Danes when they occupied this part of Britain. Odin was known as Woden to the Anglo-Saxons, and his name appears similarly in WANSDYKE, WEDNESBURY, and WEDNESFIELD (and in 'Wednesday'). In the Domesday Book, Grimsby appears as *Grimesbi*. The name of the administrative district in this part of the county is New Grimsby.

Groombridge (East Sussex/Kent)
A village lying on the county border west of TUNBRIDGE WELLS. Its name means 'bridge of the grooms', with the older sense of 'groom' as 'servant'. Perhaps the bridge here was one where servants crossed or gathered. Some '-bridge' names are connected with specific groups of people, as in KNIGHTSBRIDGE. The river here is the MEDWAY. The village name was recorded in 1318 as *Gromenebregge*.

Groomsport (Down)
A seaside village northeast of BANGOR with the Irish name of Port an Ghiolla Ghruama, traditionally translated as 'port of the gloomy individual'. This may relate to a personal name, or at least to a nickname; the English name is simply a corruption of the Irish, so that no 'groom' is involved.

Guernsey (Channel Islands)

The second largest of the Channel Islands (after JERSEY). The name is probably Old Norse in origin, and means 'Gærn's island'; a much less likely alternative is 'green island', from the Old Norse *grænn* (green) and *ey* (island). If the latter origin is correct, it is reflected in the greater 'greenness' that Guernsey has even today by comparison with Jersey. Not for nothing does it have hundreds of greenhouses for its tomatoes and flowers! Its name was recorded in about 1170 as *Guernesi* and in 1219 as *Gernereye*.

Gugh (Isles of Scilly)

An island joined to ST AGNES by a bar of sand and rock at low tide. Its name is locally pronounced 'Hugh', showing it to be basically the same as that of HUGH TOWN on ST MARY'S, and so to derive from the Old English *hōh* (height); this word is also found in the names of HOUGHTON-LE-SPRING and LUTON HOO, among many others.

Guildford (Surrey)

For long the name of this town on the River WEY was thought to derive from the 'golden' flowers that grew by the original 'ford' here. Recent local research has shown, however, that although the reference is to 'gold', it is not to golden flowers but to golden sand. The ford of the name would not have been where the present main bridge of Bridge Street crosses the river, for the current here would have been too strong, at least for most of the year. The original ford was thus probably at a more suitable point to the south of the town, in the district known as St Catherine's, where the PILGRIMS WAY crosses the river. Moreover, approaching St Catherine's from the east, either along the Pilgrims Way or from Pewley Down, one can still see the golden sandy soil on the escarpment below St Catherine's. And as if to clinch the matter, the village of Shalford ('shallow ford') lies just to the south here, showing that the river was

regarded as easily 'fordable' in this region. Hence the original 'golden ford' that gave Guildford its name. The town's name was recorded in a document of about 875 as *Gyldeforda*.

Guisborough (Cleveland)

A town south of REDCAR whose name means 'Gigr's fort', this being a Scandinavian personal name followed by the Old English *burg* (fortified place). The Domesday Book recorded the name as *Ghigesburg*.

Guiseley (West Yorkshire)

A town northwest of LEEDS whose name means 'Gīslica's clearing'. The Old English personal name is a diminutive (affectionate form) of a name such as Gīsla. A document of about 872 has the name as *Gislicleh*, and in the Domesday Book it is simply *Gisele*. The latter half of the name is the Old English *lēah* (clearing).

Gweedore (Donegal)

An attractive village in the area of the same name near the northwest coast of Ireland. It is on the River Clady but takes its name from the stream here that flows into Gweedore Bay, the latter giving its name to the stream. Gweedore thus refers to the bay and means simply 'water inlet', from the Irish *gaoth* (inlet) and *dobhair* (of water).

Gweek (Cornwall)

The name of this village, east of HELFORD, represents the conjectural Cornish *gwyk* (village), deriving from the Latin *vicus* (community) (which also gave the Old English *wīc*, 'outlying farm', 'village'). At some stage, however, the Cornish word came to mean 'forest' (compare modern Welsh *gwig* with this meaning). In fact, both meanings suit Gweek, which can be regarded as a 'village by a wood', so possibly the original Cornish word had a sort of intermediate sense shown here by this village. A document of 1337 gives the name as *Wike*.

Gwent (Wales)

A county of south Wales formed in 1974 and given an ancient name of pre-British origin, meaning simply 'place', that is '*the* place', as if especially favourable in some way. The conjectural root element is *venta*, which also gave the first element of WINCHESTER and the second element of CAERWENT.

Gwynedd (Wales)

Like GWENT, the county of Gwynedd was formed in 1974 (in northwest Wales) and derives from an ancient name. It represents the personal name Cunedda, a fifth-century ruler who had a kingdom here. Ceredig, one of the sons of Cunedda, gave his name to CEREDIGION, and so to CARDIGAN. Cunedda's own name means 'good quality', from *cynneddf* (quality) and *dda* (good).

H

Hackney (Greater London)
A town and borough in northeast LONDON whose name means 'Haca's island', with 'island' referring to dry land among marshes. The name was recorded in 1198 as *Hakeneia*, showing the personal name followed by the Old English *ēg* (island). Hackney carriages were originally drawn by hackneys, horses who came from Hackney marshes.

Haddington (Lothian)
This historic town on the TYNE has a name that means 'farm associated with Hada'; it comprises the personal name followed by the Old English *-ingtūn* element that meant 'place associated with'. The name was recorded in 1098 as *Hadynton*, and the former county of Haddingtonshire, an alternative name for East LOTHIAN, was recorded from the twelfth century.

Hadleigh (Essex, Suffolk)
Either of two towns with names of the same origin, meaning 'heather clearing' or 'forest clearing where heather abounds', from the Old English *hǣth* (heather; modern 'heath') and *lēah* (forest clearing). The Essex town, west of SOUTHEND-ON-SEA, was recorded in about 1000 as *Hǣthlege*; the Suffolk one, west of IPSWICH, was in the Domesday Book as *Hetlega*. *Compare* HADLEY WOOD; HATFIELD.

Hadley Wood (Greater London)
A district of ENFIELD whose name has a first word derived exactly like HADLEIGH. The name as a whole thus means 'wood by a place called Hadley'; the latter name means 'clearing abounding in heather'. The name was recorded in a document of 1248 as *Hadlegh*. There is still woodland at Hadley Wood, both on Hadley Common and in adjoining Enfield Chase. BARNET,

immediately southwest of Hadley Wood, has a similarly 'silvan' name.

Hadrian's Wall (Cumbria/Northumberland/Tyne and Wear)
A famous Roman fortification of the second century AD, named after the Roman emperor Hadrian (or Adrian), who visited Britain in AD 122. The wall, which extends across the North of England, was built to provide a defensive barrier against the then unconquered tribes of Caledonia (Scotland). The line of the wall was from WALLSEND in the east to Bowness-on-Solway, northwest of CARLISLE, in the west. Many places along the course of the wall still have 'wall' names, such as Benwell ('inside the wall', now a district of NEWCASTLE UPON TYNE, Walbottle (*compare* BOOTLE), Heddon on the Wall, Wall Houses, Wall, Walwick, Walltown, Thirlwall ('gap in the wall'), and Walton.

Haileybury (Hertfordshire)
The public school northwest of HODDESDON takes its name from a location here entered in the Domesday Book simply as *Hailet*. This seems to represent the Old English *hēg* (hay) and *hlēt* (share, lot), to which '-bury', meaning 'manor', was added later. The complete name thus means 'manor by the hay allotment'.

Hailsham (East Sussex)
This town north of EASTBOURNE appeared in the Domesday Book as *Hamelesham*, which menas 'Hægel's homestead'. The same personal name is found in HAYLING ISLAND.

Hainault (Greater London)
This district of REDBRIDGE, with its French-seeming name (Hainaut is actually a Belgian province), was recorded in a document of 1221 as *Henehout*; this represents the Old English *hīgna* (household) and *holt* (wood). The 'household' was a monastic community here, belonging to BARKING Abbey.

Possibly the present spelling of the name was influenced by that of Philippa of Hainaut, wife of Edward III in the fourteenth century; her title came from the Belgian Hainaut mentioned. Hainault Forest, northeast of Hainault, is a wooded area with a tautological name, as Hainault actually means 'wood that belongs to a monastic community'.

Hale (Greater Manchester)
The name of this town immediately south of ALTRINCHAM is found elsewhere in the country and derives from the Old English *halh* (nook, corner of land), often implying land in a hollow or land that is low-lying by the bend of a river. Hale corresponds to the latter, with the River Bollin forming its southern boundary. The name was recorded in the Domesday Book spelt exactly as now. *See also* HALESOWEN.

Halesowen (West Midlands)
A town west of BIRMINGHAM whose name literally means 'Owen's nooks of land', with the first half of the name the same in origin as that of HALE. Here, however, the reference will be more to 'hollows' or slight valleys. Owen was a Welsh prince who married a sister of Henry II and became Lord of Hales in the early thirteenth century. The name was recorded in 1272 as *Hales Owayn*.

Halesworth (Suffolk)
A town northeast of IPSWICH with a name that means 'Hæle's enclosure',with the personal name followed by the Old English *worth* (enclosure), as in ISLEWORTH, for example. The town's name was recorded in the Domesday Book as *Healesuurda*.

Halifax (West Yorkshire)
This industrial town southwest of BRADFORD has a difficult name which has caused much discussion and speculation. It probably means 'rough grassland in a nook of land', or 'rough grassland by a rocky slope'. The first part of the name is either the Old English *halh* (nook), as for HALE,

or *hall* (rock, stone). The second part is derived from the Old English word for 'hair', which was *feax* (as in the surname Fairfax—'fair hair'), here used metaphorically to apply to rough 'hairy' grass. For many years, the name of Halifax was interpreted as 'holy hair', giving rise to many legends about beheaded virgin martyrs and the like. A document of 1095 has the spelling of Halifax exactly as now.

Halstead (Essex)
The town northeast of BRAINTREE derives its name from a combination of the Old English *hald* (protection; as in modern 'hold') and *stede* (place). Halstead was thus originally a place of refuge or shelter. The location of the town no doubt has something to do with this, as Halstead is by the River COLNE around the base of a hill. The river would thus protect on one side, and the hill on the other. The hill now has the parish church of the town on its summit. The name was recorded in the Domesday Book as *Haltesteda*.

Haltwhistle (Northumberland)
The name of this market town west of HEXHAM lends itself all too readily to obvious puns about railway trains. The name is interesting: the first half is the Old French *haut* (high), and the latter half is the Old English *twisla* (confluence), a term usually found in North Country names (OSWALDTWISTLE is another). The name of Haltwhistle thus means 'confluence of streams by a high place'. The 'high place' is Castle Hill here. The name was recorded in a document of 1240 as *Hautwisel*.

Hambleton (North Yorkshire)
An administrative district in the centre and north of the county. It takes its name from the Hambleton Hills here, lying southwest of the CLEVELAND Hills. Hambleton is a compound of the Old English *hamel* (crooked, broken; literally 'maimed') and *dūn* (hill), and it was doubtless one single hill (almost certainly Hambleton Hill) that gave its name to the

whole group. *Compare* HAMILTON;
HEMEL HEMPSTEAD.

Hamilton (Strathclyde)

This town southeast of GLASGOW is
sometimes said to have taken its name from
the Hamilton family who settled here from
England. A much more likely derivation is
from the Old English *hamel* (broken) and
tūn (farm), thus meaning 'farm in broken
country'. The name was recorded in 1291
as *Hamelton*.

Hammersmith (Greater London)

A district of west LONDON whose
name means precisely what it says:
'hammer smithy', with the Old English
smiththe meaning 'smithy', 'metalworker's
shop', also seen in the name of
SMETHWICK. The 'Hammer-' of the name
emphasizes the fact that the smithy was a
forge. The name was recorded in 1294 as
Hamersmyth'. It is not known where the
original smithy was, but the situation of
Hammersmith on an important road
leading out of London would have made
it a place worth noting for travellers by
horse.

Hampshire (England)

This southern county takes its name
from the town on which it has long
been historically based, SOUTHAMPTON
(which was itself originally just
'Hampton'). Hampshire is thus a 'smoothed'
form of 'Hamptonshire'. The traditional
abbreviated form of the name,
'Hants', comes from the Norman
rendering of the county name as
Hantescire, which occurs in the Domesday
Book. The Normans found *-nt-* easier to
pronounce than the awkward collection of
consonants found in the *Anglo-Saxon
Chronicle* version of the name, which was
Hamtunscir. Local-government offices in
the county reproduce the county crest on
official notices, and this bears the wording
COM: SOUTHTON (*comitatus
Southantoniensis*, Latin for 'county of
Southampton').

Hampstead (Greater London)

This district of CAMDEN has a commonly
found name — the Old English *hām-stede*,
meaning simply 'homestead'. A
'homestead' would have been a very small
settlement, perhaps even a single dwelling,
such as a farm. For other names containing
the Old English term *compare*
BERKHAMSTEAD, WHEATHAMPSTEAD,
and HEMEL HEMPSTEAD. Hampstead was
recorded in the mid-tenth century as
Hemstede and in the Domesday Book as
Hamestede.

Hampton (Greater London)

A village west of KINGSTON UPON
THAMES, famous for Hampton Court
Palace. The riverside location, especially
the great bend of the Thames here, makes
it more than likely that the first element of
the name is the Old English *hamm* (land in
the bend of a river), rather than *hām*
(homestead). The name of Hampton Court
itself was recorded in a document of 1476
as *Hampton Courte*, 'Court' here meaning
'manor house'. Note that this name
predates the present palace, which was
built by Cardinal Wolsey in the sixteenth
century. The original settlement of
Hampton appears in the Domesday Book
as *Hammtone*.

Handsworth (South Yorkshire, West Midlands)

The coal-mining district of SHEFFIELD has
a name with a different origin to the
Handsworth that is a district of
BIRMINGHAM. The former appears in the
Domesday Book as *Handeswrde*, meaning
'Hand's enclosure'. The latter Handsworth
was recorded in this same book as
Honesworde, which means 'Hūn's
enclosure'. The difference is thus in the
respective personal names.

Hanley (Staffordshire)

One of the 'Five Towns' that comprise
STOKE-ON-TRENT. Its name means
'(place) at the high clearing', from the Old
English *hēah* (high; here in its dative form

of *hēan*, to denote 'at') and *lēah* (clearing). The name appears in a document of 1212 as *Henle*. Hanley is quite obviously situated on a hill. The name Handley, where it occurs, will have the same origin.

Hanwell (Greater London)
A district of EALING whose name means, perhaps unexpectedly, 'spring where wild birds are found', from the Old English *hana* (cock; the masculine equivalent of *henn*, modern 'hen') and *wealla* (spring, well). No doubt the original spring was not far from the River BRENT here. Hanwell's name appears in the mid-tenth century as *Hanewelle*.

Hardwick Hall (Derbyshire)
An Elizabethan mansion northwest of MANSFIELD that takes its name from the locality here, with Hardwick meaning literally 'herd farm' (Old English *heorde-wīc*), and probably used as a term to denote the part of a manor that was devoted to livestock, rather than the *bere-wīc* (in modern terms, BERWICK) that would have been devoted to arable farming. The name is found in many parts of Britain.

Harewood (West Yorkshire)
A name found in various parts of Britain, but particularly associated with Harewood House, the eighteenth-century mansion north of LEEDS. As it implies, the name means 'hare wood' or 'wood where hares are found', and was recorded as *æt Harawuda* in a document of the tenth century. The present pronunciation, 'Harwood', disguises the association with hares. In some cases, the name can mean 'grey wood', with the first element representing the Old English *hār* (grey) (compare 'hoary').

Haringey (Greater London)
The name of this borough in north LONDON has two versions, Haringey and Harringay, of which the former is now predominant. The name means 'Hæring's woodland enclosure', with the personal name followed by the Old English *gehæg* (enclosure, fenced-in land) (compare 'hedge'). Strictly speaking, the name really applies to HORNSEY, which is now a district of Haringey; the two names are thus actually one and the same. The present version of the (original) name seems to have been revitalised by the owner of a house here in the late eighteenth century; he called the property Haringay House. The earliest existing record of the name dates from 1201, as *Haringeie*. The spelling 'Harringay' is still in use for Harringay Stadium and Harringay West (both railway stations) and for Harringay Greyhound Track (which is the 'Stadium' of the first name), as well as for various streets, such as Harringay Road.

Harlech (Gwynedd)
This small but historic town north of BARMOUTH, famous for its castle, has a name that actually refers to the site of the castle and means 'beautiful rock', from the Welsh *hardd* (beautiful, handsome) and *llech* (slab, smooth rock). Harlech Castle was built in the thirteenth century on the craggy hilltop here. But the site was already noted before this, featuring in the *Mabinogion*, the twelfth-century collection of Welsh legends. The name was recorded in the late thirteenth century as *Hardelagh* — an attempted English rendering of the Welsh component elements.

Harlesden (Greater London)
This district of BRENT has a name that is probably exactly the same as that of HARLESTON, meaning 'Heoruwulf's farm'. There is some doubt, however, as to whether the final element is the Old English *tūn* (farm, village) or *dūn* (hill), or even *denu* (valley). Previous records of the name show all three endings: *Herulvestune* in the Domesday Book; *Herleston* in 1195; *Herlesdon* in 1291; *Harleston* in 1365; and as now in 1606. It is possible that it is really a '-ton' name, but the final element became '-den' under the influence of nearby NEASDEN and WILLESDEN.

Harleston (Norfolk)

A small town east of DISS whose name means 'Heoruwulf's farm', a meaning almost certainly identical with HARLESDEN. Harleston was recorded in the Domesday Book as *Heroluestuna*.

Harlington (Greater London)

A district of HILLINGDON whose name means 'farm associated with Hygerēd', with the personal name followed by the fairly common Old English suffix *-ingtun*, denoting a farm or estate (*tūn*) associated with the person named. Harlington was recorded in a document of 831 as *Hygereding tun*, and in the Domesday Book as *Herdintone*. The present form of the name should really be more like 'Hardington' to reflect the true origin, but the *d* of the personal name has been replaced by *l*.

Harlow (Essex)

There was a Harlow here, northeast of LONDON, long before the New Town, designated in 1947. The name means 'army mound', from the Old English *here* (army) (as in HEREFORD) and *hlāw* (mound) (as in LEWES). Such an 'army mound' would have been both an administrative centre and a meeting-place, the latter also for the original Hundred of Harlow. The site in question was that of the Roman temple, today in Harlow Old Town just west of Harlow Mill railway station. The town's name was recorded in a document of 1045 as *Herlawe*.

Harold Wood (Greater London)

This district of HAVERING has a historic name which refers to the wood here held by King Harold until his death in 1066 at the Battle of HASTINGS. The place-name was recorded in about 1237 as *Horalds Wood*. The fairly recent loss of the *-s* helps to disguise the famous association.

Harpenden (Hertfordshire)

For many years it was supposed that the name of this residential town north of ST ALBANS meant 'harper's town', deriving from the Old English *hearpere* (harper), and indicating a place where the harp was regularly played. But such an origin is contrary to the much more topographical nature of most place-names, and a more favoured interpretation is now 'valley of the military road', from the Old English *here-pæth* (military road; literally 'army way') and *denu* (valley). Apart from the better general sense, the description fits Harpenden very well, as WATLING STREET runs along the slight valley here; this could well have been used by the Anglo-Saxon armies and those of the Danes after the Romans had initially exploited it. Harpenden was recorded in a document of about 1060 as *Herpedene*. For other 'army' names *see* HARLOW; HEREFORD.

Harris (Western Isles)

The southern and more mountainous region of the Isle of LEWIS, in the Outer HEBRIDES. Its topography is described by its name, which derives from the Gaelic *na-h-earaidh*, 'that which is higher', with possibly a further influence of the Old Norse *hár* (high). Many names in this part of Scotland are Scandinavian in origin, such as UIST, immediately south of Harris.

Harrogate (North Yorkshire)

A spa town and conference centre north of LEEDS. Its name means literally 'cairn way', representing the Old Norse *hǫrg* (heap of stones, cairn) and *gata* (road, way) (as in the many street names in '-gate' of northern towns, such as Briggate in LEEDS). However, it was probably not the cairn itself that was particularly significant, but some other place to which the road led. This is indicated by the later meaning of *gata*—'pasturage'. Harrogate's name thus means precisely '(place by the) road that leads to the pastureland'. This definition has fairly recently replaced the former incorrect one, which derived the first element of the name from the Old English *here* (army) (as for HARLOW). The name of the town was recorded in 1333 as *Harougat*.

Harrow (Greater London)

A borough of northwest LONDON, famous for its public school. Its name comes from the Old English *hearg* (heathen temple). There must have been such a noted Saxon shrine here, and almost certainly it was on the summit of the hill (Harrow-on-the-Hill, in the literal sense) where St Mary's Church stands prominently today. There has long been a Christian church on this site, and Pope Gregory the Great specifically urged Christian missionaries to convert heathen temples into Christian churches wherever they could. Harrow's name was recorded in a document of 767 as *Gumeninga Hergae*. The first word of this denotes a tribe called the Gumenings, about whom nothing else is known. The Domesday Book gives Harrow as *Herges*, and the full '-on-the-Hill' version of the name dates back to at least the fourteenth century: *Harowe atte Hille* is found in a document of 1398.

Hart (Hampshire)

An administrative district in the northeast of the county. It takes its name from the River Hart that flows through it. The river's name is a 'back formation' from that of Hartfordbridge, which stands on it. It also reflects the name of nearby HARTLEY WINTNEY, whose rural district council combined with that of FLEET urban district council to form the new administrative district in 1974. The new name thus equally commemorates these villages and other places similarly named here with 'Hart'.

Hartland Point (Devon)

A headland west of BIDEFORD, originally known as something like 'Harty', representing the Old English *heorot-īeg* (stag island, hart peninsula), indicating that stags were found here. This later became 'Harton' (*Hertitone* in the Domesday Book), i.e. 'hart island village', and then Hartland (*Hertilanda*, or 'hart island land', in 1130). The 'island' element of the name is no longer present. The *tūn*

and *land* names apply specifically to the village of Hartland on the peninsula. *Compare* HARTLEPOOL.

Hartlepool (Cleveland)

This industrial town and port on the bay of the same name north of MIDDLESBROUGH has a name that actually refers to this bay as 'Hart Island pool', for 'Hart Island' (or simply 'Hart') was the original name of the headland on which the old town stands today (as distinct from the modern, larger town of West Hartlepool). The Venerable Bede, in the eighth century, referred to the headland as *insula cervi*, 'island of the stag', alluding to the stags that lived on the headland, not to the shape of the headland. The present middle '-le-' of the name seems to represent the original 'island' element, the Old English *ēg*. The eighth-century name was *Hereteu*, while the present form of the name is found in a document of about 1180, as *Herterpol*.

Hartley Wintney (Hampshire)

This village northeast of HOOK has a name whose first word means 'stag clearing', from the Old English *heort* (stag) and *lēah* (clearing). The second part of the name means 'Winta's island', referring to dry land among rivers and streams that belonged to a man named Winta. (The main river here is the HART.) The Prioress of Wintney (no longer a separate place) held the manor of Hartley in 1228, and this name was added soon after to distinguish the place from Hartley Wespall, to the west of it. The name thus appears as *Hurtlege* in a twelfth-century document, and as *Hertleye Wynteneye* a century later.

Harwich (Essex)

A town and port east of COLCHESTER whose name means 'military settlement', from the Old English *here-wīc* (*compare* HARLOW; HARPENDEN). There was a sizeable Danish military camp here in the ninth century. The name was recorded in a document of 1238 as *Herwyz*.

Haslemere (Surrey)

A town southwest of GODALMING whose name means 'hazel mere' or lake among hazel-trees here. There is no lake now, but it may have been on a site between the High Street and Derby Road. The name was recorded in a document of 1221 as *Heselmere*. The lake or pool was doubtless important to the original settlers here, and would have provided their water supply.

Haslingden (Lancashire)

A town southeast of ACCRINGTON whose name is similar to HASLEMERE and means 'valley where hazel-trees grow'. It derives from the two Old English words *hæslen* (growing with hazels) and *denu* (valley). (The '-ing-' of the name is thus misleading.) The town is in a valley surrounded by high moorland. Its name was recorded in a document of 1242 as *Heselingedon*. The surname Heseltine probably derives from Haslingden, or from a similarly named place.

Hassocks (West Sussex)

A residential district south of BURGESS HILL that developed only in the mid-nineteenth century with the coming of the railway to BRIGHTON. Hassocks was originally the name of a field here, so called for its rough tussocks of grass. (The Old English word for such grass, *hassuc*, gave the modern 'hassock', or kneeling mat.) The name still exists as a field-name elsewhere in the country, and there is one such Hassocks near MARSDEN, West Yorkshire. No doubt this particular name was chosen for the settlement in order to blend in with the markedly 'rural' names of the older places in the region, such as CUCKFIELD, HENFIELD, and HAYWARDS HEATH.

Hastings (East Sussex)

This seaside resort has a name that retains almost the whole of the Old English suffix *-ingas* (people of), which usually loses the final *-s*. The name thus means '(territory of) the people of Hæsta', whose own name was probably a nickname meaning 'violent one' (related to modern 'hasty'). This territory would have been much more extensive than that of the modern town. A document of 1050 records the name as *Hæstingceaster*, as if it were 'Hastingchester', suggesting that there was a former Roman station here. There probably was, but its name is not known.

Hatch End (Greater London)

A district of HARROW whose name means 'district by a gate', with the Old English *ende* used to denote the end of something, such as the extremity of a parish or village. This particular 'end' was by a 'hatch' (Old English *hæcc*), that is, a hatch-gate that gives entrance to a park or forest. Probably this gate led into PINNER Park, to the south of Hatch End. The name appears in a text of 1448 as *Le Hacchehend*.

Hatfield (Hertfordshire, South Yorkshire)

Both towns have names of identical origin, and both were recorded identically in the Venerable Bede's *Ecclesiastical History of the English People* of the eighth century as *Haethfelth*. The meaning is 'heather-covered open land', from the Old English *hæth* (heather) and *feld* (open land). This particular name also occurs in the spelling Hadfield (*compare* HADLEIGH) and, even more obviously, in HEATHFIELD. Heather still grows in Hatfield Park, to the east of the Hertfordshire town, and is even more abundant in Hatfield Chase, the area of fenland east of the South Yorkshire town.

Havant (Hampshire)

The present spelling of the name of this town northeast of PORTSMOUTH disguises both its elements. The first part of the name represents the personal name Hama, while the latter half is the Old English *funta* (spring) (compare 'fountain'). Early records of the name show the origin more clearly, such as the early-tenth-century spelling as *Hamanfunta*. What subsequently happened was that the *m* of the personal name became 'blended' with the *f* of *funta*. In many similar names this latter word appears as '-hunt', as with CHESHUNT and Boarhunt; the latter, a village six miles from Havant, is really 'spring by the fortified place' (Old English *burg*).

Haverfordwest (Dyfed)

A town northwest of PEMBROKE whose name leads one to expect a 'Haverfordeast'. The original name of the place was 'Haverford' (*Haverfordia* in a document of 1191), which means 'goat ford', 'ford (over the Western Cleddau) where goats can cross'. Later spellings such as the *Hareford* recorded in 1283, wrongly suggested HEREFORD. 'West' was therefore added to distinguish the settlement from Hereford. The Welsh name of Haverfordwest is Hwlffordd, which is simply a rendering of the English, not a translation. (To a modern Welshman, this could even suggest 'sail road', from *hwyl*, 'sail' and *ffordd*, 'road', 'way'. The association is quite wrong, of course, but on the other hand Haverfordwest is on the main road to MILFORD HAVEN, only seven miles south of it.)

Haverhill (Suffolk)

This industrial town southeast of CAMBRIDGE has a name that means 'oat hill' or 'hill where oats are grown', from the Old Norse *hafri* (oats) (originally carried in a *haver*sack) and the Old English *hyll* (hill). The name of Haverhill (pronounced 'Hayvril') appeared in the Domesday Book as *Hauerhella. Compare* MARKET HARBOROUGH.

Havering (Greater London)

The borough of Havering, in the extreme east of Greater LONDON, has a name that means '(place of the) people of Hæfer', with this name recorded in the Domesday Book as *Haueringas*. Within the borough is the village of Havering-atte-Bower, with the latter part of this name meaning 'by the residence' (Old English *būr*, 'dwelling', giving modern 'bower' and the related

'byre'). The reference is to the Royal Liberty which was created here in 1465. This encompassed the parishes of Havering, ROMFORD, and HORNCHURCH, so was thus virtually identical in extent to the modern borough.

Hawarden (Clwyd)

A town south of QUEENSFERRY, famous for Hawarden Castle, the former home of W E Gladstone. The name means 'high enclosure', from the Old English *hēah* (high) and *worthign* (enclosure) (a Midlands equivalent to *worth*). The town is on rising ground above the River DEE. Hawarden was recorded in the Domesday Book as *Haordine*. Its Welsh name is Penarlag, probably representing *pennardd*, 'height' with some personal name, such as Alaog, or else a word related to *alaw* (lily). In southern English terms the name Hawarden corresponds to that of HIGHWORTH.

Hawes (North Yorkshire)

A small town in WENSLEYDALE whose name represents the Old English or Old Norse *hals* (neck), referring to a 'neck of land', as here by the River URE, where the 'neck' is a pass between the hills (what is known in the North of England as a 'hause'). The name was recorded in a text of 1614 as now.

Haweswater (Cumbria)

One of the central lakes of the Lake District lying southeast of ULLSWATER and now converted into a reservoir. Its name is not related to HAWES, but means 'Hafr's lake', from the Old Norse personal name that was probably a nickname meaning 'he-goat' (*compare* HAVERFORDWEST). The lake's name was recorded in 1199 as *Havereswater*.

Hawick (Borders)

This town on the River TEVIOT is close enough to the English border to have an English name. It means 'hedge village' or 'village enclosed by a hedge', from the Old

English *haga* (hedge) and *wīc* (outlying farm, village). Its name was recorded in about 1165 as *Hawic*. There may have been a dairy farm here originally to represent the '-wick'.

Haworth (West Yorkshire)
The name of this town southwest of KEIGHLEY is similar to that of HAWICK, and probably means 'hedge enclosure', from the Old English *haga* (hedge) and *worth* (enclosure). Specifically, the Old English *haga* also meant 'haw' (the fruit of the hawthorn), so that the enclosure may have been one of hawthorn. The name was *Hauewrth* in a text of 1209.

Haydock (Merseyside)
A town east of ST HELENS, lying close enough to Wales to have a name of Welsh (or at least Celtic) origin. It means 'barley place' (compare the modern Welsh *haidd*, 'barley'), so in a sense it corresponds to English names, such as BERWICK and BARTON. The name was recorded in a document of 1169 as *Hedoc*.

Haydon Bridge (Northumberland)
A small town bridging the South TYNE west of HEXHAM, 'Haydon' means 'hay valley', from the Old English *hēg* (hay, mowing grass) and *denu* (valley). The location, plus an early record of the name as *Haden* (in 1236), confirms that the final element is 'valley' and not 'hill' (Old English *dūn*).

Hayes (Greater London)
This district of HILLINGDON has a name that represents the conjectural Old English word *hǣse* or *hǣs*, meaning 'brushwood'; hence the original settlement would have been overgrown with rough bushes. Hayes appeared in the Domesday Book as *Hesa*. The other Hayes in Greater London, in the Borough of BROMLEY, has a name of exactly the same origin.

Hayfield (Derbyshire)
What could be more obvious than the name of this town south of GLOSSOP? But the fact that it was recorded in the Domesday Book as *Hedfeld* suggests that the first part of the name *may* be a Scandinavian form of the Old English *hǣth* (heather), in which case the name will mean the same as HATFIELD. It should be borne in mind, too, that '-field' here represents the Old English word (*feld*) that meant 'open land' rather than just 'field'.

Hayle (Cornwall)
This industrial town with its harbour on ST IVES Bay has an appropriate name to describe its location on the estuary of the River Hayle, for it means simply 'estuary', from the Cornish conjectural *heyl*. The river's name is the ultimate source of the sense, so that the town is named directly after it. The name was recorded in a text of 1265 as *Heyl*.

Hayling Island (Hampshire)
An island south of HAVANT, now joined to the mainland by a bridge. Hayling means '(place of) the people of Hægel'; the same personal name is involved in the name of HAILSHAM. The name as a whole was recorded in a document of about 1140 as *Hailinges island*.

Hay-on-Wye (Powys)
A small market town northeast of BRECON on the River WYE. As its name indicates, it originated as a fenced enclosure (Old English *gehæg*), this doubtless being an area of the forest here that was fenced in as a hunting ground. Its name was recorded in a document of 1144 as *Haya*, and it has a parallel in that of The Hague, the Dutch city that arose round a hunting lodge in a wood. The Welsh name of Hay-on-Wye is Y Gelli, or, in full, Y Gelli Gandryll, literally 'the broken grove', implying the same fencing off ('breaking') of the woodland.

Haywards Heath (West Sussex)
A residential town north of BRIGHTON whose name was originally simply 'Heyworth' (spelt as such in a document of

1261), this meaning 'hedge enclosure', 'enclosure surrounded by a hedge'. 'Heath' was subsequently added (*Haywards Hoth* in 1544), giving the overall sense of 'heathland by a hedged enclosure'. The site here was actually open heathland until the railway line to BRIGHTON was built across it in the mid-nineteenth century, when the present town developed. As it stands now, the name suggests that the 'Heath' was owned by a man named Hayward, and indeed a local legend tells how a highwayman of the name carried out robberies on the heath. This particular association with a surname may have been prompted by the names of neighbouring places, such as BURGESS HILL and the villages of Whitemans Green (to the west) and Jeffreysgreen (south of the town).

Hazel Grove (Greater Manchester)

This town southwest of STOCKPORT has a name that means what it says; there must have been a grove of hazels here at some time.

Headford (Galway)

A market village north of GALWAY whose Irish name, Áth Cinn, translates as 'ford of the peak'. There is no peak here, however, so presumably this translates literally the surname Head, giving the meaning 'Head's ford'. Families of this particular surname have been associated with the county since the seventeenth century.

Headingley (West Yorkshire)

A district of LEEDS, famous for its cricket ground, whose name means 'clearing of the people of Hedde'. The personal name is followed by '-ing', representing the Old English suffix *-ingas* (people of), and *lēah* (clearing). The Domesday Book records the name as *Hedingeleia*.

Headington (Oxfordshire)

This northern district of OXFORD appears in an early-eleventh-century document as *Hedenedune*, showing that the meaning is probably 'Hedena's hill'. Headington,

which is certainly on a hill, is thus really a '-don' name, not a '-ton' one; i.e. from the Old English *dūn* (hill) not *tūn* (farm).

Heanor (Derbyshire)

This coal-mining town northwest of ILKESTON is on a hill, as its name indicates, deriving from the Old English *æt hēan-ofre*, '(place) at the high hill'. The second element (*hēan*) is the dative case (required after *æt* 'at') of the adjective *hēah* (high). For another name containing the basic word for 'hill', 'ridge' (*ofer* or *ufer*) *compare* MICKLEOVER. Heanor was recorded in the Domesday Book as *Hainoure*.

Heathfield (East Sussex)

The name of this small town south of TUNBRIDGE WELLS means more or less what it says — 'open land covered by heather'. It was recorded in a document of 1234 as *Hadfeld'*, showing that it has exactly the same origin as HATFIELD.

Heathrow (Greater London)

LONDON's major airport, in the Borough of HILLINGDON, has a name indicating its humble origin as a 'heath row', that is, a row of cottages by (or on) a heath. This would have been HOUNSLOW Heath. The name is recorded in an early-fifteenth-century document as *La Hetherewe*. The place was merely a hamlet (also known as Heath Row) down to the twentieth century.

Heaton (Tyne and Wear, West Yorkshire)

This name occurs fairly frequently in the North of England. The district of NEWCASTLE UPON TYNE and another of BRADFORD are just two instances. The name simply means 'high farm', from the Old English *hēah* (high) and *tūn* (farm).

Heavitree (Devon)

An eastern district of EXETER whose name does not mean 'heavy tree' but 'Hefa's tree'. This must have been a meeting point of some kind, unless it was a cross or crucifix; it was not the name of a hundred here. The name itself was recorded in a document of about 1130 as *Hefatriwe*.

Hebburn (Tyne and Wear)
An industrial town east of GATESHEAD on the south bank of the TYNE. Its name means 'high burial place', from the Old English *hēah* (high) and *byrgen* (burial place, tumulus). In an early-twelfth-century text the name appears in the form *Heabyrm*. It is not certain where the original burial place was.

Hebden Bridge (West Yorkshire)
A town at the confluence of Hebden Water and the CALDER. It takes its name from the former river, whose own name means 'hip valley' or 'valley where the wild rose grows', from the Old English *hēope* (hip) and *denu* (valley). The original settlement here was simply Hebden (*Hebedene* in the Domesday Book), with 'Bridge' added later (*Hepden Bridge* in 1508).

Hebrides (Scotland)
A group of islands off the west coast of Scotland. The name remains of uncertain origin, although there have been several attempts at interpretation. The Roman name for them was *Ebudae* or *Ebudes*, and the present spelling of the name is due to a misreading of the latter version, with the *u* written as *ri*. Originally the name applied to the Inner Hebrides only, but excluding SKYE. The name itself is probably pre-Celtic in origin. *See* SUTHERLAND for the Norse name of the Hebrides.

Heckmondwike (West Yorkshire)
A town northwest of DEWSBURY whose name means 'Hēahmund's farm', with the personal name (meaning 'high protection') followed by the Old English *wīc*, often used to denote an outlying or special farm. The town's name appears in a document of 1166 as *Hedmundewic*.

Hednesford (Staffordshire)
A town in CANNOCK Chase district whose

name may mean 'Heddīn's ford'. It was recorded in the thirteenth century as *Hedenesford*. The personal name is probably a diminutive of the name Headda.

Hedon (Humberside)
A town east of HULL whose name probably means 'heather-covered hill', from the Old English *hǣth* (heather) and *dūn* (hill). However, there is not much of a hill at Hedon. A document of 1115 gives the name as *Heldone*. The name is pronounced 'Heddon'.

Helen's Bay (Down)
This resort and bay west of BANGOR commemorate the name of Helen Sheridan, Countess of Dufferin, the wife of the fourth Baron Dufferin and Clandeboye, who lived here at Clandeboye in the nineteenth century.

Helensburgh (Strathclyde)
A residential town on the north shore of the Firth of CLYDE. It takes its name from Lady Helen Sutherland, the wife of Sir James Colquhoun, who founded the settlement here in 1776 and who named it after her.

Helford (Cornwall)
A village on the River Helford east of HELSTON. Its name means '(place at the) ford of the River Hayle', with HAYLE being the former name of the River Helston. The village name was recorded in 1230 as *Helleford*, and in a document of 1318 as Hayleford.

Helmsley (North Yorkshire)
This small town east of THIRSK has a name that means 'Helm's clearing', with the Old English personal name followed by *lēah* (clearing). The name appeared in the Domesday Book as *Elmeslac*.

Helston (Cornwall)
Although Helston is close to the source of the River HELFORD, southwest of TRURO,

the name of the town and that of the river are not related. Helston's name is a compound of the conjectural Cornish *hen-lys* 'ancient court', 'ruins' (from *hen* 'old' and *lys* 'court'; *compare* LISS and LIZARD) and the Old English *tūn* (farm, village). In the Domesday Book, the name of Helston was recorded as *Henlistone*. The town is actually on the Lizard Peninsula.

Helvellyn (Cumbria)

This Lake District mountain appears to have a Celtic name, but its precise meaning is uncertain. It was recorded as *Helvillon* in a document of 1577, and no earlier forms of the name have been found. A recent tentative meaning for the name is 'yellow moor', of Cumbric origin.

Hemel Hempstead (Hertfordshire)

We have a double name to deal with here. 'Hemel' translates literally as 'maimed', from the Old English *hamol* (*compare* HAMBLETON), referring to 'broken' land. There is evidence that this was the name of the district around the town, and indeed this description fits the topography locally, with the many hills and valleys to the east of the CHILTERN HILLS. 'Hempstead' is exactly the same as HAMPSTEAD, and so means 'homestead'. The overall meaning is thus 'homestead in the broken country'. The Domesday Book gave the name as *Hamelamestede*, combining the two words, and this remained as the spelling, with minor variations, until the sixteenth century. Subsequent versions of the name became shorter, such as *Hemlamsted* in 1339 and then just *Hempsted* in 1544. The present form of the name thus seems to be a clear reconstruction of the original.

Hemsworth (West Yorkshire)

A coal-mining town south of PONTEFRACT whose name means 'Hymel's enclosure', with the Old English *worth* (enclosure) following the personal name. Hemsworth appears in the Domesday Book as *Hamelesuurde* and also as *Hilmeuuord*.

Hendon (Greater London)

This district of BARNET grew up round St Mary's Church, which, like many churches, is on a hill. The name 'Hendon' describes this location and means '(place) at the high hill', with the Old English *hēan* (high) as the first part of the name, and *dūn* (hill) as the second. (*Hēan* is the grammatical form of *hēah* (high) required after a word like 'at' or 'on'.) The name appeared in a text of 959 as *Hendun*.

Henfield (West Sussex)

A town north of SHOREHAM-BY-SEA whose name probably means 'rocky open land', from the Old English *hān* (stone) (compare modern 'hone') and *feld* (open land; modern 'field'). The name was recorded in the late eighth century as *Hanefeld*.

Hengistbury Head (Dorset)

The headland at the western end of CHRISTCHURCH Bay. Its name seems to comprise the Old English *hengest* (horse, stallion) and probably *beorg* (hill) or *bearu* (wood) (the latter is often found after the names of animals) rather than *burg* (fortified place). On the other hand, if the first part of the name is the personal name Hengist, then 'fort' would be a more suitable word to follow it. The site could have thus been either a 'stallion hill' or 'Hengist's fort'. There are some remains of an ancient fortification here, and the terrain is not wooded, which seems to rule out *bearu*.

Henley-in-Arden (Warwickshire)

A village northwest of STRATFORD-ON-AVON. The first word meaning 'high clearing' (Old English *hēan* as for HENDON, and *lēah* 'clearing'). 'Arden' probably means 'steep place', from a British (Celtic) root word meaning 'high', which is also found in such names as ARDMORE and the ARDS PENINSULA. It in turn relates to the name of the Ardennes, the forested plateau in southeast Belgium and Luxembourg. The name of Arden was recorded in a document of 1088 as *Eardene*, and that of Henley in a text of 1285 as *Hanleye*. The addition of '-in-Arden' was made to distinguish this Henley from others. *Compare* HENLEY-ON-THAMES.

Henley-on-Thames (Oxfordshire)
This town, famous for its annual regatta, has a name that shares its origin with HENLEY-IN-ARDEN. However, Henley-on-Thames is not on high ground, so that 'high' here may have had a figurative sense of 'important' (as the modern 'High Street' is the most important street in a town). Its name was recorded in 1186 as *Heanlea*. For the river name *see* THAMES.

Hereford (Hereford and Worcester)
A cathedral town on the River WYE whose name means 'army ford', from the Old English *here* (army) (*compare* HARLOW) and the obvious *ford* (ford). An 'army ford' was probably one where an army of men could cross in broad ranks, without breaking formation. A Roman road crosses the river at Hereford, and the ford would have been here. The town's name was recorded in a document of 958 with the spelling exactly as now, and in fact the two original Old English words have been accurately preserved. The former county of Herefordshire was referred to as *Herefordscir* in a text of about 1038. *See also* HAVERFORDWEST.

Herm (Channel Islands)
An island in the bailiwick of GUERNSEY. It has a Celtic or pre-Celtic name of uncertain origin. It is almost certainly not related, as has been suggested, to the Greek *eremos* (solitary), and so to the English 'hermit'. Its Roman name was probably *Sarmia* (sometimes misquoted as *Sarnia*).

Herne Bay (Kent)
This resort on the north coast of the county takes its name from the Old English *hyrne* (angle, corner), with the original settlement here (giving its name to the bay) arising in a corner of land. A reference to the site appears in a text of the eleventh century, which tells of a monastery *æt hyrnan*, 'at the angle'.

Herstmonceux (East Sussex)
A village northeast of HAILSHAM, with a distinctive name and the Royal Observatory based at its castle. It arose as a manor held by the Monceux family (from Monceaux, Normandy), sited by a wooded hill (Old English *hyrst*). Ownership by this Norman family dates from the twelfth century, and a text of 1243 refers to the manor as *Hurst quod fuit Willelmi de Munceus* ('Hurst, which belonged to William of Monceaux'). Herstmonceux Castle was built in the first half of the fifteenth century by Sir Roger de Fiennes, whose ancestor, Sir John de Fiennes, had married Maud de Monceux, the heiress to the estate, in 1320.

Hertford (Hertfordshire)
This town on the River Lea has a name that means what it says: 'hart ford' or 'ford where harts regularly cross or gather' (*compare* OXFORD). The name was recorded in the mid-eighth century as *Herutford*. Hertingfordbury, just north of Hertford, has an unusual name, not for its meaning, which is 'manor of the Hertford people', but for the order of its elements: one would have expected 'Hertfordingbury', but the Old English *-ingas* (here as just '-ing-') has somehow come to split the original name. The county name appears in a document of 1011 as *Heortfordscir*. *Compare* HARTLAND POINT; HARTLEPOOL; HARTLEY WINTNEY.

Hertsmere (Hertfordshire)
An administrative district in the south of the county, formed in 1974. It was given an artificially devised name consisting of a combination of *Herts*, the abbreviated county name, and *mere*, 'boundary' (from the Old English *gemǣre*). The boundary referred to is that between Hertsmere itself and Greater LONDON.

Hessle (Humberside)
The town on the HUMBER immediately
west of HULL has a name that represents
the Old Norse *hesli* (hazel). There must
have been a grove of hazel trees here at one
time. The name was recorded in the
Domesday Book as *Hase. Compare*
HASLEMERE; HASLINGDEN.

Hetton-le-Hole (Tyne and Wear)
A coal-mining town northeast of DURHAM
with a compound name that refers in two
different ways to the hill at whose foot it
stands. The first part of the name, found
elsewhere, means 'hip hill' or 'hill on
which the wild rose grows', from the Old
English *hēope* (hip) and *dūn* (hill). The
latter part of the name, added to
distinguish this Hetton from other places of
the name, means 'hollow', 'valley',
indicating that Hetton is not actually on the
hill but below it, in the valley. Its name was
recorded in 1180 as *Heppedun*.

Hever (Kent)
The village with its castle (a moated manor
house) lies southeast of EDENBRIDGE and
has a name that means '(place) at the high
bank', which in the original Old English
would have been *æt thæm hēan ȳfre*. The *n*
of the original name, representing the
grammatical ending of *hēan* (high), has
since dropped out, but it was still present
when the name was recorded in 814 as
Heanyfre. The village is above the castle,
which is itself above the River Eden. The
present pronunciation of the name,
'Heever', does something to preserve the
long vowel of the original Old English.

Hexham (Northumberland)
This market town on the TYNE west of
NEWCASTLE UPON TYNE has a name that
perhaps unexpectedly turns out to mean
'bachelor's homestead'. The 'bachelor' of
the name was the Old English *hagustald*,
who was a younger son of the family
entitled to have his own holding outside the
main village, as a sort of medieval
independent 'bachelor pad'. (*Hagustald*

itself derives from the words for 'enclosure'
gehæg, and the verb 'to occupy', *stealdan*.)
The name was recorded in 685 as
Hagustaldes ham, and in 1188 as
Hexteldesham, since when it has been
further shortened to the present spelling.

Heysham (Lancashire)
A coastal town southwest of MORECAMBE
whose name means 'brushwood
settlement', from the Old English *hǣs*
(brushwood, open land covered with rough
bushes) (as for HAYES) and *hām*
(homestead, village). The Domesday Book
gives the name as *Hessam*, and the local
pronunciation of the name as 'Heessum' to
some extent reflects this and similar early
spellings.

Heywood (Greater Manchester)
A town west of BURY whose name means
'high wood', from the Old English *hēah*
(high) and *wudu* (wood); it was recorded in
a document of 1246 as *Heghwode*.
Heywood is not noticeably elevated in its
location, but perhaps it was regarded as
'high' by comparison with nearby Bury,
which is on lower ground.

Higham Ferrers (Northamptonshire)
Higham is a common name meaning
simply 'high homestead' (Old English *hēah*
and *hām*). Not surprisingly, therefore,
many places of the name added a
distinguishing word. For this town east of
WELLINGBOROUGH it is Ferrers, deriving
from the name of a Norman family. A
certain Comes ('Count') de Ferariis is
recorded as holding the manor here in
1166. Twenty years later, the Domesday
Book gave the name as *Hecham*.

Highbridge (Somerset)
This industrial town southeast of
BURNHAM-ON-SEA stands near the mouth
of the River Brue (*see* BRUTON), over
which there must have been a medieval
'high bridge'. Rather than 'elevated',
'high' could have simply meant 'important'
(*compare* HENLEY-ON-THAMES). The

name was recorded in a document of 1324 with the spelling exactly as now.

Highcliffe-on-Sea (Dorset)
This seaside district east of CHRISTCHURCH has a relatively modern name, deriving not directly from any 'high cliffs' here but from a Gothic-style house of the name. A document of 1759 has the name as *High Clift*. The 'seaside suffix' '-on-Sea' was added much later.

Highgate (Greater London)
A district in the Borough of HARINGEY whose name means what it says: 'high' refers in a literal sense to the former tollgate here on the Great North Road, over 400 feet above sea level. The name was recorded in 1354 as *Le Heighgate*.

Highland (Scotland)
The northernmost region of mainland Scotland derives its name directly from the Highlands, the general name for this mountainous part of the country (as distinct from the Lowlands, further south). Traditionally, the Highlands are the essentially 'Celtic' region of Scotland. The Highland region was formed, like the other Scottish regions, in 1975.

Highworth (Wiltshire)
This town northeast of SWINDON was originally called just 'Worth', that is, 'enclosure'; this name is in the Domesday Book as *Wrde*. Later, 'High' was added to distinguish such a standard designation from any other. A document of 1252 thus has the name as *Hegworth*. Highworth is located in an obviously elevated position near the VALE OF (THE) WHITE HORSE, and has good views over three counties (Wiltshire, Berkshire, Gloucestershire).

High Wycombe (Buckinghamshire)
A town on the south side of the CHILTERN HILLS. 'Wycombe' does not contain 'combe', as in ILFRACOMBE and many other names, but derives from the grammatical form (dative plural) of the Old English word *wīc* (outlying farm) required after the word *æt* (at)—*wīcum*. The sense of Wycombe here is thus '(place) at the outlying farms', and the name was recorded in the late tenth century as *æt Wicumun*. 'High' differentiates this Wycombe from nearby West Wycombe, formerly an individual village but now a district of northwest High Wycombe itself. The adjective probably meant 'important' rather than literally 'high'; the town is not on a noticeably elevated site.

Hillhead (Strathclyde)
A district of northwest GLASGOW, immediately north of the University. The ground rises to one or two hundred feet above sea level to the north of the city, and that is where many of its 'hill' names are, such as this one, which means simply 'top of the hill' (as distinct from the foot of a hill).

Hillingdon (Greater London)
A district on the western outskirts of LONDON. The name *does* refer to a hill (or rising ground), but it is the last part of the name that does so, not the first. The name as a whole means 'Hilda's hill'. The first half of the name thus represents the Old English man's name, 'Hilda', which was itself the short or 'pet' form of a full name, such as Hildrīc ('war ruler') or Hildwulf ('war wolf'). The final element of the name is the Old English *dūn* (hill). The name was recorded in the Domesday Book as *Hillendone*, and the '-ing-' of the name is thus misleading.

Hillsborough (Down)
A town southwest of BELFAST named after Sir Moyses Hill, the army officer who obtained lands here in the early seventeenth century. The Irish name of Hillsborough is Cromhghlinn, meaning 'winding valley', like CRUMLIN.

Hinckley (Leicestershire)
A town southwest of LEICESTER whose name means 'Hynca's clearing', with the

personal name followed by the Old English *lēah* (clearing), as in many names of this type. The name was recorded in the Domesday Book as *Hinchelie*.

Hindhead (Surrey)

A town northwest of H A S L E M E R E that arose as a residential district only in the early twentieth century. Before this, the name was simply that of a 'hill ridge and common', as *Cassell's Gazetteer* of 1896 describes it. Although no record of the name earlier than 1571 has been found, when it was given as *Hyndehed*, it is almost certainly a much older name, meaning 'hill where does are found'.

Hindley (Greater Manchester)

This town southeast of W I G A N has a name that means 'hinds' wood', 'wood where does are found'. The two Old English components are *hind* (hind) and *lēah*. The latter word can mean both 'clearing' and 'woodland', among other things, but here 'woodland' seems right for the does, especially as Hindley is south of H O R W I C H Forest. A document of 1212 gives the name as *Hindele*. Compare H I N C K L E Y.

Hitchin (Hertfordshire)

This town northeast of L U T O N has a name that represents the Old English *Hiccum*, the dative plural of the tribal name, Hicce. The overall meaning is thus '(territory) of the Hicce tribe'. Nothing is known about them apart from this record of their name. The Domesday Book recorded the town's name as simply *Hiz*, and this name was adopted in recent times for the river on which Hitchin stands. Its earlier name is uncertain.

Hoddesdon (Hertfordshire)

A town south of W A R E whose name means 'Hod's hill'; it was recorded in the Domesday Book as *Hodesduna*. The last part of the name is thus the familiar Old English *dūn* (hill). The modern town lies to the east of the hill of the name.

Hog's Back (Surrey)

A chalk ridge that runs west from G U I L D F O R D, today taking the A31 road. It was recorded as *Geldedon* in a document of 1195, then as *Gildowne* in 1495, and *Gill Down* in 1744. Its original name was thus a form of 'Guildown', which suggests 'Guildford Down'. The present name is not found earlier than 1823, and must have been a local descriptive nickname for the ridge, which resembles a pig's broad back when seen from below. The name is linguistically appropriate, as the standard Old English word for 'back' was *hrycg*, modern 'ridge'.

Holbeach (Lincolnshire)

This small town east of S P A L D I N G is only seven miles from the sea (The W A S H), but its name does not derive from 'beach'. It may mean 'hollow stream', with 'hollow' referring to a deep stream. But this does not suit the locality here, and an alternative derivation of the name has been recently proposed in 'hollow ridge', taking the second half of the name to be the Old English *bæc* (ridge) and not *bæce* (stream) (as in modern Scottish 'beck'). The name of Holbeach could thus be understood as denoting a slight ridge, and the one-inch Ordnance Survey map does show a number of small streams draining away from its location. The name was recorded in the Domesday Book as *Holebech*.

Holborn (Greater London)

This district at the south end of the Borough of C A M D E N has a name that means 'stream in a hollow', from the Old English *hol* (hollow) and *burna* (stream). Holborn was also the name of the stream itself, a tributary of the F L E E T. The 'hollow' of the name can still be seen in the form of a dip in a section of Farringdon Road. The name was recorded in the Domesday Book as *Holeburne* and in 1551 as *Howeborne*. The latter spelling lacks the *l* of the name, as does the common pronunciation of Holborn today as 'Ho'burn'.

Holderness (Humberside)

An administrative district of Humberside that takes its name from the low flat peninsula here that extends southeast of HULL to terminate in SPURN HEAD. Its name means 'promontory ruled by a *hold*', the latter being the title of a high-ranking yeoman in the Danelaw (the word is related to the German *Held*, 'hero'). 'Ness' is the promontory, as in many similar names, such as CAITHNESS and FOULNESS. The Domesday Book recorded the name as *Heldernesse*. The actual Old Norse name for the title was *holder*

Holkham Hall (Norfolk)

The famous eighteenth-century house west of WELLS-NEXT-THE-SEA takes its name from the hamlet of Holkham here, whose own name means 'hollow homestead'. The 'hollow' may have been a lake in the park here. The Domesday Book recorded the hamlet's name as *Holcham*.

Holland (Lincolnshire)

Holland was formerly one of the three administrative divisions of Lincolnshire, called the 'Parts of Holland', the others being KESTEVEN and LINDSEY. It is now represented by the administrative district of South Holland (there is no 'North Holland'). The basic name probably means literally 'heel land', that is, a district (Old English *land*) with a number of hill spurs (Old English *hōh*). However, hill-spurs are hardly an obvious feature of this fenland region of southeast Lincolnshire. Holland is popularly associated with the European country, if only because both have similar low-lying and well-watered landscapes, and both are well known for their tulips.

Holloway (Greater London)

This district of ISLINGTON has a name that means what it says: 'hollow way', applying to a road (now a section of the A1) that runs through a valley here, between the counternamed Highbury (to the south) and HIGHGATE (to the north). The name was recorded in a document of 1307 as *Le Holeweye in Iseldon*, this latter place being Islington.

Holmfirth (West Yorkshire)

A town on the River Holme south of HUDDERSFIELD whose name means 'woodland by Holme', the latter being a village three miles to the southwest. Holm means 'raised ground in moorland', from the Old Norse *holmr* (island). 'Firth' represents the Old English *fyrhth*. The name was recorded as *Holnesfrith* in 1274. For another name containing the 'island' element *compare* DURHAM.

Holsworthy (Devon)

This town east of BUDE has a name meaning 'Heald's enclosure', with the Old English personal name (a nickname, meaning 'bent one') followed by *worthig*, a common equivalent to *worth* in southwest England. The name appeared in the Domesday Book as *Haldeword*.

Holt (Norfolk)

A small town west of CROMER with a straightforward name meaning simply 'wood', Old English *holt*. The word *holt* is all too easily recognised here, whereas it is well camouflaged in the name of WORMWOOD SCRUBS. Holt was recorded in its present spelling in the Domesday Book.

Holyhead (Gwynedd)

The name of this port and industrial town on HOLY ISLAND, ANGLESEY, relates directly to the island and means 'holy headland'. Holyhead has a long history as a Christian centre, and missionaries came to settle on many of the islands off the west Welsh coast in the sixth century. The real 'head' of the name is Holyhead Mountain, to the west of the town. The Welsh name of Holyhead is Caergybi, 'Cybi's fort', with Cybi being the saint to whom the town's parish church is dedicated. The English name has its exact equivalent in the Cornish name of PENZANCE. Holyhead was recorded as *Halihefed* in 1315.

Holy Island (Gwynedd, Northumberland, Strathclyde)

All three 'Holy Islands' (of Wales, England, and Scotland) have ancient Christian links, which explains their name. Holy Island, ANGLESEY, is the island on which HOLYHEAD is located. Its Welsh name is Ynys Gybi, 'Cybi's island', after the sixth-century saint who founded a monastery here. Holy Island, NORTHUMBERLAND, was the site of a famous abbey, and its name was recorded in the mid-twelfth century as *Healand*. It is also known as LINDISFARNE, a much more interesting name. The Scottish Holy Island lies off the east coast of ARRAN, in the Firth of CLYDE. Its main historic Christian link is with St Molaise (Mol As), who had a cell here in the sixth century.

Holy Loch (Strathclyde)

A sea inlet, shorter than most lochs, north of DUNOON. According to tradition, its name refers to a ship from the Holy Land that was stranded here while transporting a load of earth to lay beneath the foundations of GLASGOW Cathedral, when building was underway in the twelfth century. But the name almost certainly refers to an earlier period, and is probably associated with St Columba or his followers, who were active in this part of Scotland in the sixth century.

Holyroodhouse (Lothian)

Scotland's main royal residence, at the end of the Royal Mile in EDINBURGH, was built in the mid-sixteenth century by James IV, who based the new palace on the existing guesthouse of thirteenth-century Holyrood Abbey. The palace thus takes its name from this abbey, whose own name declares its dedication to the Holy Rood, otherwise the Holy Cross, the cross on which Christ was crucified.

Holywell (Clwyd)

This manufacturing town near the River DEE northwest of CHESTER has a name that refers to the sacred well or spring of St Winefride, who founded a nunnery here in the seventh century. The well is still a centre of pilgrimage and is contained in the Roman Catholic church of St Winifred. The Welsh name of Holywell is Treffynnon, 'village of the well'. The English name of the town was recorded in 1093 as *Haliwel*.

Holywood (Down)

A residential town on the east side of BELFAST Lough whose name probably refers to the seventh-century church of St Lasrén here. The Normans referred to the place as *Sanctus Boscus*. Holywood's Irish name is quite different — Ard Mhic Nasca, 'height of Nasca's sons'. The place has also been known as Ballyderry, 'townland of the oak wood' (*compare* LONDONDERRY).

Honiton (Devon)

The name of this town east of EXETER is usually pronounced 'Hunniton'. But there the association with honey ends; the name actually means 'Hūna's farm', and was recorded in the Domesday Book as *Honetone*. However, there is a district of SOUTH MOLTON, also in Devon, called Honiton Barton, and there the association *is* with honey: the name means 'farm where honey is produced'. Honiton Barton was in the Domesday Book as *Hunitona*, showing the difference of meaning between the two places. (For the meaning of Barton *see* BARTON-UPON-HUMBER).

Honor Oak (Greater London)

A document of 1609 mentions an *Oke of Honor* here, which served as a boundary marker between CAMBERWELL and LEWISHAM. This is probably all that lies behind the name, although there have been several colourful stories about Queen Elizabeth paying a special visit here in the early years of the seventeenth century. It is not clear what exactly she did: one account says she dined in the shade of the tree, another says she 'went hither a-maying'. Probably these are later stories designed to explain or at least embellish the origin of the name. The tree itself has long since gone. The spelling of 'honor' in this way (not 'honour') was common down to the seventeenth century.

Hook (Greater London)
This district of KINGSTON UPON THAMES has a name that means what it says, and refers to a hook-shaped hill or spur of land here. It is not certain precisely which hill is so designated. *Compare* LIPHOOK.

Hopeman (Grampian)
A fishing village and resort west of LOSSIEMOUTH that has a deceptive name, suggesting a surname or an individual. It is actually a distortion of the name of a former estate here, called Haudmont, designed to represent the French for 'high hill'. The village was founded in the early nineteenth century by a local landowner, William Young of Inverugie.

Horbury (West Yorkshire)
This manufacturing town southwest of WAKEFIELD had its name recorded in the Domesday Book as *Horberie*. It is difficult, however, to see what the first half of the name represents. It could perhaps be the Old English *horu* (dirt, filth), and so give a name meaning 'dirty fort', 'fortified place on muddy land'. The town is close to the River CALDER.

Horley (Surrey)
A town north of CRAWLEY whose name means 'clearing in a horn-shaped area of land', from the Old English *horn* (used of land between two streams, among other meanings) and *lēah* (clearing). *Compare* other 'HORN-' entries below.

Horncastle (Lincolnshire)
The name of this town east of LINCOLN appeared in the Domesday Book as *Hornecastre*. This might have been preserved as something like 'Horncaster', and indicates that a Roman station (Old English *ceaster*) was here. But the possible '-caster' became '-castle' instead. The name is similar to that of HORLEY in that it refers

to a 'horn' of land, in this case land between two rivers. Here, the precise reference is to the land between the rivers Bain and Waring. The name of the Roman camp here was *Bannovalium*. The first part of this probably relates to the name of the River Bain, which may possibly mean 'straight', from the Old Norse *beinn*. But it also represents a conjectural Celtic root word *banna*, meaning 'peak', 'horn' (giving the familiar 'Ben' of such names as BEN NEVIS), and this could refer to the same 'horn of land' as the English word. The rest of the Roman name is also Celtic in origin and means 'strong', as in the Roman name of CARLISLE, which was *Luguvalium*. So to sum up: the older, Roman name means '(place) at the strong spur of land'; the subsequent English one means 'Roman station on the tongue of land'.

Hornchurch (Greater London)
This former ESSEX town, southeast of ROMFORD, has an intriguing name which really does seem to mean 'church with horns', as it says. This would have been some sort of medieval embellishment or decoration, although it is no longer in evidence. More recently, a representation of a bull's head with horns was fixed to the eastern end of the church roof. But this eighteenth-century adornment was probably more an attempt to 'illustrate' the name of the town than to re-create the original adornment, whatever it was. A similar device occurs in some town shields, where the name will be shown punningly. (An example is the ox over wavy lines on the city shield of OXFORD. In heraldry, this is known as 'canting'.) The name of Hornchurch appears in a document of 1163 as *Ecclesia de Haweringis*. A later Latin rendering of the name, dated 1222, was *Monasterium Cornutum*.

Horndean (Hampshire)
A town north of HAVANT whose name probably means 'valley by a horn-shaped hill'. There are many names in this part of Hampshire derived from the Old English

denu (valley), such as Finchdean ('finch valley'), Denmead ('valley meadow'), and so on; others just over the border in West Sussex include East Dean and West Dean. Horndean is at the western end of the South Downs, and lies below both Horndean Down and Windmill Hill, with probably the former as the actual 'horn-shaped hill'.

Hornsea (Humberside)
This coastal resort northeast of HULL takes its name from Hornsea Mere, a large lake to the west of the town. The lake has an irregular shape, with a 'horn' of land projecting into it; it got its own name from the Old Norse *horn* (horn), *nes* (promontory), and *sær* (sea, lake). The Domesday Book recorded the name as *Hornesse*.

Hornsey (Greater London)
A district whose name is identical in origin to that of HARINGEY, the borough in which it is located. This particular variant of the original is first recorded in a document of 1564, in the present spelling, and another document about twenty years later refers to both names as *Haringey al. Hornesey* ('al.' being 'alias').

Horsham (West Sussex)
A town southwest of CRAWLEY whose name means 'horse village', from the Old English *hors* (horse) and *hām* (village). A document of 947 records the name in the same spelling as now. Horses would have been bred here.

Horwich (Greater Manchester)
This town west of BOLTON has a name that was originally that of a forest here, which was recorded in a document of 1254 as *Horewych*, showing more clearly that the origin is in the Old English *hār* (grey) (compare 'hoary') and *wice* (wych-elm). The forest was thus one of grey wych-elms.

Houghton-le-Spring (Tyne and Wear)
This town southwest of SUNDERLAND has a fairly common name meaning 'farm on a hill-spur', from the Old English *hōh* (hill-spur) and the common *tūn* (farm). The town is on a spur of land below the high hill called Warden Law. The addition '-le-Spring' was made to distinguish this Houghton from the many others. The reference is popularly supposed to refer to local springs, but it is more likely to be a personal name. One Henry Spring is mentioned here in a document of the early thirteenth century. 'Houghton' was recorded as *Hoctun* in this same document (of about 1220).

Hounslow (Greater London)
A west LONDON borough whose name means 'Hund's mound', with the personal name followed by the Old English *hlǣw* (mound, barrow) (as in BASSETLAW). The 'mound' could perhaps have been the burial place of the man named. The place-name appears in the Domesday Book as *Honeslaw*.

Housesteads (Northumberland)
The site of the finest Roman fort on HADRIAN'S WALL, north of HAYDON BRIDGE. 'Housestead' is a standard English word (compare 'homestead') for a place where houses stand, from the Old English *hūs-stede*. In this instance, however, the 'houses' are the remains of the Roman fort itself. The name of the fort was *Vercovicium* (not *Borcovicium* as misquoted until quite recently). This effectively means '(fort of the) working fighters', with the first half of the name of Celtic origin, but related indirectly to English 'work' itself. The latter half is also Celtic, but represented by English 'victor'. A 'working' fighter is a strong and capable one.

Hove (East Sussex)
A residential town and seaside resort immediately west of BRIGHTON whose name ultimately derives from the Old English *hūfe* (hood), a word that has not been confirmed in any other place-names. It is used metaphorically here to denote

some natural feature that acted as a 'hood' or place of shelter. It is difficult to be sure what this was, and to know whether it was a shelter for the people who lived here or ones who came here by boat. Perhaps there is some remote link between the Old English word and modern 'haven', which may indicate the latter sense rather than the former? Hove was recorded in a document of 1288 as *La Houue*.

Howden (Humberside)

A document of the mid-tenth century records the name of this town, north of GOOLE, as *æt Heaffuddæne*, with this representing the Old English *hēafod* (head) and *denu* (valley). There is hardly a valley at Howden in the accepted sense of the word, but perhaps the reference is more to a delimited area, of which this was the most important. (A suggestion has been made that the name may contain a reference to what is now known as the Vale of YORK.) The present form of the name is due to Scandinavian influence, with the Old English word replaced by the Old Norse *hǫfuth* (*compare* HOWTH).

Howth (Dublin)

A residential district and resort on a rocky promontory east of DUBLIN. Its name directly represents the Old Norse *hǫfuth* (headland). The Irish name is Binn Éadair, 'Éadar's peak': Éadar is a legendary hero associated with this headland.

Hoxton (Greater London)

A district of HACKNEY whose name means 'Hoc's farm', recorded in the Domesday Book as *Hochestone*.

Hoy (Orkney)

The second largest of the ORKNEY Islands (after MAINLAND), with a name of Scandinavian origin, meaning 'high island', from the Old Norse *hár* (high) and *ey* (island). It is well known for the massive column of rock at its northwest corner, known as the Old Man of Hoy, rising to 450 feet (137 metres).

Hoylake (Merseyside)

This coastal resort west of BIRKENHEAD developed from the end of the eighteenth century. Its name refers to the former tidal lake, now silted up, that existed between the mainland and a sandbank known as Hile or Hoyle, this name deriving from the Old English *hygel* (hill). The lake became known as both Hoyle Lake and High Lake, the latter name resulting as a wrong division of the two words. The earliest known record of the name is one of 1687, as *Hyle Lake*.

Hucknall (Nottinghamshire)

A town north of NOTTINGHAM whose name means 'Hucca's nook of land', with the personal name followed by the Old English *halh* (nook). This may originally have been the name of a district by the River Leen here, and Hucknall is close to the border with Derbyshire. The name appeared in the Domesday Book as *Hochenale*.

Huddersfield (West Yorkshire)

An industrial town south of BRADFORD whose name means 'Hudræd's open land', with the Old English *feld* (open land; modern 'field') following the personal name. The Domesday Book recorded the name as *Oderesfelt*.

Hughenden Manor (Buckinghamshire)

The late-eighteenth-century house where Disraeli lived for much of his life takes its name from the adjacent small village of Hughenden, north of HIGH WYCOMBE. The name means 'Hucca's valley', and the village is itself now known tautologically as Hughenden Valley. The name was recorded in the Domesday book as *Huchedene*, showing the Old English *denu* after the personal name (which is the same as for HUCKNALL).

Hugh Town (Isles of Scilly)

The 'capital' of the Scilly Isles, on the main island of ST MARY'S. Its name describes its location, on a spur of land (Old English *hōh*) at the foot of the hill on which Star Castle stands. The many personal names in the islands, especially those of saints, no doubt led to the present form of the name. It was recorded in a document of 1593 as *Hew Hill*.

Hull (Humberside)

A city and port at the confluence of the HUMBER and the River Hull, taking its name from the latter. The river's name was long regarded as being Scandinavian in origin, meaning 'deep one', from the Old Norse *holr* (deep, running in a deep hollow). But there are two good reasons why this an unlikely origin. First, the River Hull is not in a deep valley here, but flows across flat land. Second, the name was recorded in the copy of an early manuscript that contained no Scandinavian names at all (even DERBY is given by its former name of Northworthy). So the name must predate the Vikings. It may not even be Anglo-Saxon, but is more likely to be Celtic, and to derive from a British (Celtic) root element, such as *hul-* (muddy). This certainly suits the fenland location of the river. The official name of Hull is Kingston-upon-Hull; the first word came into use after 1292, when Edward I exchanged lands elsewhere for the port here. Hull was also known as Wyke in the twelfth and thirteenth centuries, this either representing the Old English *wīc* (special settlement, port) (here the latter, as for NORWICH or WOOLWICH), or the Old Norse *vík* (creek, inlet, bay) (as for WICK). Perhaps the former is more likely. The name has thus been recorded in three different ways over the centuries; three examples are: *thare ea Hul* (Old English, 'the river Hull') in about 1025; *Wyk'* in about 1160; and *Kyngeston super Hul* in 1299.

Humber (Humberside)

The estuarial river formed by the TRENT and OUSE probably has a name of British (Celtic) origin, from a conjectural element *bro-* (river) preceded by an element such as *su-* or *hu-* meaning 'good'. A 'good river' would probably have been one with favourable conditions for fishing and trading, but the name could also have been given deliberately with the aim of appeasing a 'bad' or destructive river god. The name was recorded in the late ninth century as *Humbre*.

Humberside (England)

A county in northeast England, formed in 1974. Like other 'riverside' names, 'Humberside' is also an older designation for land beside the HUMBER. Almost all rivers of note or importance have produced a similar name to denote the land along their banks, such as 'Thames-side', 'Tyneside', 'Teesside', and MERSEYSIDE.

Humberstone (Leicestershire)

This district of LEICESTER has a name, recorded in the Domesday Book as *Humerstane*, that means 'Hūnbeorht's stone'. It is not known where the stone was, or what its purpose was. It was probably a boundary stone of some kind.

Hungerford (Berkshire)

This town west of NEWBURY has a name that means exactly what it says: 'hunger ford', 'ford by barren ground'. The ford here would have led across the River KENNET to land that did not yield well, so that people went hungry. The name was recorded in the early twelfth century as *Hungreford*.

Hunslet (West Yorkshire)

A southern district of LEEDS whose name means 'Hūn's stream', with the personal name followed by the Old English *flēot* (stream). The name appeared in the Domesday Book with the same spelling as now.

Hunstanton (Norfolk)

A coastal resort on The WASH, recorded in the Domesday Book as *Hunestanestuna*, which gives its meaning as 'Hūnstān's farm'.

Hunter's Quay (Strathclyde)
This village and resort north of DUNOON, with its landing stage on the Firth of CLYDE, takes its name from the Hunter family of Hafton House, northwest of the village. The well-known yacht club here was founded in 1856, and the clubhouse was a gift from the family in 1872. The 'quay' is the landing stage and its facilities.

Huntingdon (Cambridgeshire)
A town on the OUSE northwest of CAMBRIDGE whose name probably means 'huntsman's hill', that is, a hill (Old English *dūn*, modern 'down') favoured by huntsmen. The hill referred to is the low broad one on which the town is located overlooking the river. The name was recorded in a document of 973 as *Huntandun*. The former county of Huntingdonshire ('Hunts') was recorded in a document of 1011 as *Huntadunscir*. The actual Old English word for 'huntsman' was *hunta*.

Huntly (Grampian)
A town founded at the confluence of the rivers Deveron and Bogie in 1769. It takes its name from the founder, Alexander Gordon, fourth Duke of Gordon and Earl of Huntly. The Duke's second title derives from the lost village of Huntly in what was then Berwickshire (i.e. the extreme south-east district of Scotland, now in BORDERS).

Hurstpierpoint (West Sussex)
This town southwest of BURGESS HILL was originally known as simply as Hurst (*Herst* in the Domesday Book). This means 'wooded hill'. The rest of the name represents the Norman lord of the manor here at this time (late eleventh century), Robert de Pierpoint. The addition would have been made to distinguish this Hurst from the many others, as well as to denote the ownership of the place.

Huyton (Merseyside)
A town east of LIVERPOOL whose name means 'estate by a landing-place'. The first half of the name represents the Old English *hȳth* (landing-place) (as in HYTHE), while the second is the common *tūn* (farm, estate). The reference would have been to a stage on either the River Alt or on Ditton Brook. The Domesday Book gave the name as *Hitune*.

Hyde (Greater Manchester)
A town northeast of STOCKPORT whose name shows it to have originally been an estate assessed as one hide (Old English *hīd*), this being the amount of land that could support one household. It was usually about 120 acres in size, but the actual extent varied from one region to another, and depended on the productivity of the land. A hide was the standard unit for taxation purposes, and the Domesday Book usually stated the number of hides assessed for a particular estate. In place-names, the word 'hide' (in its Old English form or a variant of this) accompanies a numeral, such as the fairly common Fifehead or Fifield ('five hides'), Tinhead ('ten hides'), or the much more impressive PIDDLETRENTHIDE. The mention of Hyde on its own means just one hide.

Hyndburn (Lancashire)
An administrative district in the east central region of the county. Its name was artificially devised when the district was formed in 1974. It was felt that none of the town names would serve as a basis for the new name, so the name of the small River Hyndburn that flows through the district was selected instead.

Hythe (Kent)
A resort west of FOLKESTONE and one of the original CINQUE PORTS, whose name simply means 'landing-place' (Old English *hȳth.*) In names containing this word, the reference is always to a landing-stage on a river, such as at PUTNEY, CHELSEA, LAMBETH, and STEPNEY, all on the

THAMES (and with the original *hȳth* mostly well disguised). In the case of Hythe, therefore, the landing-place would have been not on the coast but a short distance inland. Coastal changes have been so great in this region of Kent over the centuries, that it is now difficult or impossible to say which river was used for the original landing-stage.

I

Ickenham (Greater London)
A district of HILLINGDON whose name means 'Ticca's village'. The Domesday Book recorded the name as *Ticheham*, showing the initial *T*. This was then dropped, when it was thought to be the final letter of *æt* (at), a preposition that frequently occurred as the first element of a written place-name. For an example where this same *T*- was added in error *see* ILKESTON.

Icknield Way (England)
An ancient trackway that originally ran from The WASH down to the south coast, with sections of it adapted for use by the Romans. The meaning of the name is unknown, and is probably pre-British (Celtic) in origin. Any attempt to link the name with that of the Iceni tribe remains unfounded, even though this British tribe had their capital at what is now Caistor St Edmund (Roman *Venta Icenorum*) in Norfolk, in an area where the Icknield Way begins. Its name was recorded in a document of 903 as *Icenhylte*, with no 'Way' or even 'Street', as for ERMINE STREET, for example. It may be significant that two villages named Ickleford and Ickleton are on the Icknield Way, the former in Hertfordshire, north of HITCHIN, the latter in Cambridgeshire, south of CAMBRIDGE. Their names have been interpreted as the respective 'ford' and 'farm' of 'Icel's people'.

Iffley (Oxfordshire)
A southern district of OXFORD whose name has been interpreted as 'plovers' clearing', 'forest clearing where plovers are found', from a conjectural Old English word *gifete* (plover) (compare modern German *Kiebitz*, 'plover', which in its colloquial sense 'busybody' gave the modern 'kibitzer'). The Domesday Book recorded the name as *Givetelei*.

Ilchester (Somerset)
The village northwest of YEOVIL is on the Roman road known as the FOSS WAY. Moreover, it has the '-chester' ending that states it to be on the site of a former Roman camp. It derives the first part of its name from the River YEO on which it stands; the former name of this river was the Gyfle. The name of the Roman fort was *Lindinis*, based on a Celtic word meaning 'river', 'pool' that also lies behind such names as LINCOLN and DUBLIN. The Domesday Book records Ilchester as *Givelcestre*.

Ilford (Greater London)
This former ESSEX town in the borough of REDBRIDGE takes its name from the Hyle, which was the former name of the River Roding (*see* RODINGS, THE) on which it stands. The old river name means 'trickling one', from a conjectural British (Celtic) root *sil-*. The ford itself may have been where the bridge linking Romford Road and High Road crosses the river. Ilford was recorded in the Domesday Book as *Ilefort*.

Ilfracombe (Devon)
A coastal resort north of BARNSTAPLE, recorded in the Domesday Book as *Alfreincombe*, which represents the original sense of 'valley of Ilfred's people', with the personal name being a West Saxon form of Ælfred. The 'valley' (Old English *cumb*) is the one up which the steep High Street runs in a westerly direction from the harbour to Holy Trinity Church.

Ilkeston (Derbyshire)
The various records of the name of this town (northeast of DERBY) need to be examined and compared to establish the true meaning. The Domesday Book, for example, recorded it as *Tilchestune*. But the initial *T*- here is simply the final letter of a preceding *æt* (at), so must be ignored. Then in the early eleventh century a record shows the name as *Elkesdone*, and another

of about 1160 gives it as *Helchesdun*. These show the name as ending in '-don', not '-ton', and such spellings predominate. The true meaning of the name is thus 'Ealac's hill', with the personal name followed by the Old English *dūn* (hill), not *tūn* (farm).

Ilkley (West Yorkshire)

The name of this town and resort north of BRADFORD is familiar from the song about nearby Ilkley Moor. The latter half of the name is almost certainly the Old English *lēah* (clearing). The first half of the name remains a mystery, however: it has long been traditionally linked with with name *Olicana* which occurs in the writings of Ptolemy in the second century AD. But recent research has shown that this name resulted as an error on Ptolemy's part (it should have been *Olenacum*), therefore *Olicana* was not the name of the Roman station here. It was probably not even *Olenacum*, but was perhaps *Verbeia*, as this was what the Romans called the River WHARFE, on which the town stands. So all one can do is consider the remaining early records of Ilkley's name, among them *Hillicleg* in about 972 and *Illiclei* in the Domesday Book.

Ilminster (Somerset)

Although this town southeast of TAUNTON is not far from ILCHESTER, and has a similar name, it is of different origin. The first part of the name relates to the River Isle, on which it stands, with this name probably meaning 'swift one', from a conjectural British (Celtic) root element *il-*. The 'minster' was the original church or monastery here, where St Mary's Parish church now stands. The name was recorded in a text of 995 as *Illemynister*.

Immingham (Humberside)

This town with its well-known docks north of GRIMSBY has a name meaning 'homestead of Imma's people'; the Old English *hām* (homestead) follows the personal name plus *-ingas* (now '-ing-'), meaning 'people of'. The Domesday Book's record of the name is *Imungeham*.

Ince-in-Makerfield (Greater Manchester)

A town southeast of WIGAN whose basic name 'Ince' means simply 'island', from a Celtic word related to the Welsh *ynys* and Irish *inis* (*compare* ENNISKILLEN). It was recorded in the Domesday Book as *Inise*. For the origin of the second part of the name *see* ASHTON-IN-MAKERFIELD.

Ingatestone (Essex)

A town northeast of BRENTWOOD whose name can be analysed as 'Ing (place) at the stone', that is, a place by a stone in the district called 'Ing'. This last is the name of a tribe, and can be interpreted as meaning 'Giga's people'. It is not clear what exactly the stone was. It may have been a Roman milestone, but the district would have had several of these, and it is unlikely that one was singled out without any further exact indication. Possibly there was a rock here, that served as a meeting-place. The name was recorded in a text of 1254 as *Ginges at Petram*, the last word here being the Latin (*petra*) for 'rock'. There are other names locally with the 'Ing' element, such as Ingrave, a suburb of Brentwood, and the River Ingrebourne, which rises near this town.

Innerleithen (Borders)

This small town is at the confluence of the Leithan Water and the River TWEED, showing that the 'Inner-' of the name is really 'Inver-', meaning 'river-mouth', 'confluence', as in many of the following entries. The Gaelic word that gives this element is *inbhir*, which corresponds to the Old Welsh *aber* (in names such as ABERYSTWYTH) and the identical Pictish word in Scottish names (such as ABERDEEN). The river name Leithen probably derives from a conjectural Celtic root element *lik-to-* meaning something like 'ooze', 'drip', related to the modern Welsh *llaith* (damp). The town's name was recorded in a document of about 1160 as *Innerlethan*.

Innisfree (Sligo)

The poet Yeats's 'Lake Isle of Innisfree' is actually in Lough Gill, but the name is a common one in Ireland, and also occurs in the spelling Inishfree. Poetically enough, it means 'island of heather', from the Irish *inis fraoigh*.

Inveraray (Strathclyde)

Inverarary, like most other 'Inver-' place-names, refers to a place at the mouth of a river or at a confluence. As with 'Aber-' names (such as ABERYSTWYTH), the second part of the name is usually that of the river on which the place stands. Inveraray is thus a small town on the shore of Loch FYNE at the mouth of the River Aray, whose name is probably related to that of the AYR and so means simply 'river'. The town's name has not been recorded earlier than the mid-eighteenth century, with the spelling as now. *See also* INNERLEITHEN.

Inverbervie (Grampian)

A small town at the mouth of Bervie Water on the east coast south of STONEHAVEN. The river's name is of uncertain origin, but is almost certainly Celtic, or even pre-Celtic. For 'Inver-' *see* INNERLEITHEN.

Inveresk (Lothian)

A southern suburb of MUSSELBURGH at the mouth of the River ESK. Its name alone does not reveal that it also stands on the site of a former Roman station. This was probably known as *Coria*, possibly meaning simply 'army', from a Celtic root word related to the modern Welsh *cor* (host, tribe) and to the Old English *here* (army), seen in such names as HEREFORD and HARLOW. For 'Inver-' *see* INNERLEITHEN.

Invergordon (Highland)

This town has a name whose second half does *not* derive from the river on which it stands. This is because it is a fairly recent name, given to the settlement here in about 1760 and named after the landowner at the time, Sir Alexander Gordon. Before that, the name of the place was Inverbreckie, with the stream here (the Breckie) having a name that means 'speckled' (*compare* the former name of FALKIRK). Invergordon is now an important port on the CROMARTY Firth, northeast of DINGWALL. For 'Inver-' *see* INNERLEITHEN.

Invergowrie (Tayside)

A western suburb of DUNDEE on the Firth of TAY. The small river here is the Gowrie, whose name is of uncertain origin, but is almost certainly Celtic or pre-Celtic. (It is also a former district name here.) For 'Inver-' *see* INNERLEITHEN.

Inverkeithing (Fife)

A town southeast of DUNFERMLINE on the bay of the same name. It takes its name from the Keithing Burn here, whose own name relates to that of KEITH and so means 'wooded stream'. The town's name was recorded in a document of the mid-eleventh century as *Hinhirkethy*. For 'Inver-' *see* INNERLEITHEN.

Inverleith (Lothian)

A district of EDINBURGH that takes its name from the Water of Leith, which gave its name to LEITH. The fact that Inverleith is not actually at the mouth of the stream, as one would expect from the 'Inver-' (*see* INNERLEITHEN, to whose name it also relates), suggests that the FIRTH OF FORTH, to the north of it, was originally much wider. The name was recorded in a text of about 1130 as *Inerlet*.

Inverness (Highland)

This well-known town takes its name from the River Ness, at whose mouth ('Inver-'; *see* INNERLEITHEN) it stands. The river's name perhaps means simply 'river', 'stream', from a conjectural pre-Celtic root element *ned-* (to flood, to wet) (probably related to the German *nass*, 'wet'). A document of 1300 records the town's name as *Invernis*. The former county of Inverness-shire took its name from the town in medieval times.

Inverurie (Grampian)

This town stands near the confluence of the rivers DON and Urie, taking its name from the latter. The river's name may mean either 'strong river' or 'holy river', and may come from the same Celtic or pre-Celtic root that gave the name of the URE. The town, northwest of ABERDEEN, was recorded in the same spelling as now in a late-twelfth-century document. For 'Inver-' *see* INNERLEITHEN.

Iona (Strathclyde)

This well-known island off the southwest coast of MULL has many historic Christian connections. The best known is with St Columba, who founded a monastery here in the sixth century. His association with the island caused it to be named as *Hiona-Columcille* in a document of about 1100, the latter word here meaning 'Columba's cell (or church)'. But the present form of its name has arisen through a less well-known connection, with the name of the biblical character, Jonah. The association came about through a miscopying. Originally, the name of the island was just *I* or *Hi*, probably deriving from a Celtic word for 'yew tree' (*compare* YOUGHAL). This element was then incorporated into various forms of the name and appeared in a document of about 700 as *Ioua insula*, 'island of the yew-tree place'. But the first word seems to have been misread as *Iona*, one of the forms of the name Jonah. The spelling with *n* then persisted, to give the name of today.

Ipswich (Suffolk)

An industrial town and port on the River ORWELL at its confluence with the little River Gipping. The town's name means 'Gip's landing-place'. The personal name is followed by the Old English *wīc* in one of its best-known specialized meanings of 'port', 'landing-place', as for NORWICH, WOOLWICH, GREENWICH, and many others. At the same time, Ipswich is really the 'Southwich' to the 'Northwich' of Norwich! The name was recorded in a document of 993 as *Gipswic*, showing the personal name clearly. The village of Gipping (near NEWMARKET), which gave its name to the river, has a name that refers to the same man, and means '(place of) the people of Gip'.

Ireland

Whereas England is named after the Angles, and Scotland after the Scots, Ireland is not directly named after the Irish. The country's name really means 'Éire-land', that is, 'land called Éire', the latter being the Irish name for the country, which itself may mean 'western'. (The modern Irish *iar-* means 'west' in compound words.)

Ireland's Eye (Dublin)

A small island to the north of DUBLIN. As one approaches the capital across the Irish Sea, it might be supposed that the name was given imaginatively to denote an island that was an 'eye' on the eastern 'face' of Ireland. But the name actually evolved as a corruption (and mistranslation) of the former Irish name of the island, which was *Inis Ereann*, 'Eria's island'. Eria is the name of a woman said to have built a church on the island in the seventh century. However, the second word of this was mistaken for the genitive of *Éire*, the Irish name of IRELAND and the Scandinavian translation of *inis* as *ey* (Old Norse for 'island') gave the present English 'Eye'. Today, moreover, the island has a quite different Irish name, Inis Mac Neasáin, 'island of the sons of Neasán'. Neasán was a prince of the royal family of LEINSTER.

Irlam (Greater Manchester)

A town southwest of MANCHESTER at the confluence of the rivers Irwell and MERSEY. It takes its name from the former, with the last two letters of the town's name representing the Old English *hām* (homestead). The river name Irwell means 'winding river', from the Old English *irre* (wandering, winding) (compare modern 'err' and the name of the EREWASH) and *wella* (spring, stream). A document of the late twelfth century records the name of Irlam as *Urwilham*.

Ironbridge (Shropshire)
A town in TELFORD, situated on the side of the River SEVERN gorge, that takes its name from the iron bridge spanning the river here. This was the first cast-iron bridge in the world, designed by Abraham Darby and built in 1778. It is still in use (but by pedestrians only). The place-name, although modern, commemorates a historic 'first'.

Irthlingborough (Northamptonshire)
This town northeast of WELLINGBOROUGH had its name recorded in a document of 780 as *Yrtlingaburg*, which probably means 'fortified place of the people of Yrtla', although the first part of this name may represent the Old English *yrthling* (ploughman), so that the name means 'fortified place of the ploughmen'. But generally the Old English *burg* (fortified place) is more often found after personal names than 'group' names like this. It is perhaps rather surprising that the name has not been 'smoothed down' to a shorter form, especially as the Normans did just that when they recorded it in the Domesday Book as *Erdinburne*.

Irvine (Strathclyde)
A port (and New Town, designated in 1965) at the mouth of the River Irvine west of KILMARNOCK. It obviously takes its name from this river, which is said to mean 'green river', from Celtic words related to the modern Welsh *ir* (fresh, green) and *afon* (river) (as for AVON). The valley here was recorded in a document of about 1130 as *Strathyrewen in Galwegia*, the latter word of which refers to GALLOWAY.

Isis (Oxfordshire)
The name for the River THAMES at OXFORD. It is said to arise from the fact that the former Latin name of the Thames, *Thamesis* (or some similar form), was wrongly split into *Thame* and *Isis*, the former thus relating to the River Thame (a tributary of the Thames west of Oxford: *see* THAME), and the latter applying to the Thames itself here. This new name (first recorded in a document of 1347 as *Isa*) was in turn associated with the goddess Isis. One would have thought that Oxford scholarship would have done better than this, despite the traditional 'inspired guesswork' of medieval linguistics!

Islay (Strathclyde)
The most southerly island of the Inner HEBRIDES. As it stands, the name appears to mean little more than 'island'. But the *s* is a relatively recent insertion in the name, apparently made under the influence of the word 'island', and early records show the name without it, for example *Ilea* in about 690, and *Ile* in 800. The origin of this is obscure (a Celtic meaning 'swelling' has been suggested), but at any rate the Old Norse *ey* seems to have been added to the base name, to give it the same 'island' ending as other islands locally, such as COLONSAY, ORONSAY, and off Islay itself, Orsay.

Isle of . . .
See the next word(s); for example, for Isle of Dogs *see* Dogs, Isle of.

Isleworth (Greater London)
A district on the left bank of the THAMES in the Borough of HOUNSLOW. Its name has nothing to do with 'isle' but means 'Gīslhere's enclosure'. The form of the personal name can be deduced from a record of the place in 695 as *Gislheresuuyrth*. The last element of the name is the Old English *worth* (enclosure). *Compare* ISLINGTON.

Islington (Greater London)
A borough east of CAMDEN TOWN with a

name somewhat similar to that of ISLEWORTH and meaning 'Gīsla's hill'. The '-ington' of the name is thus misleading, as is shown by the record of the name in a document of about 1000, as *Gislandune*, with the last element of this the Old English *dūn* (hill). The similarity of the personal name with that of Isleworth does not necessarily mean that the same person was involved.

Islwyn (Gwent)

An administrative district in the west of the county, formed in 1974, like all similar districts in Wales. It adopted the name of the mountain here, Mynydd Islwyn, whose own name means 'underbush mountain'. At the same time, the place-name commemorates the bardic name of the poet William Thomas, who was born near the mountain in 1832 and took his name from it.

Itchen (Hampshire)

A district of SOUTHAMPTON that takes its name from the River Itchen, on whose east bank it stands. The name has been associated, probably groundlessly, with that of the Iceni tribe. Its precise origin remains uncertain; it may represent the name of a Celtic river god. The name was recorded in a document of 701 as *Icene*.

Iver (Buckinghamshire)

This village east of SLOUGH was recorded in the Domesday Book as *Yfreham*, showing its basic derivation in the Old English *yfer* (slope), itself related to *ōfer* (bank). Whichever is involved here, the reference will be to higher ground of some kind, and Iver lies just by a low spur of land overlooking marshy ground, so the name must ultimately relate to this spur.

Ivybridge (Devon)

This small manufacturing town east of PLYMOUTH is not on the River 'Ivy' but the Erme. Its name was recorded in medieval Latin (in the ablative or locative case) in a document of 1280 as *Ponte Ederoso*, showing that the present name means 'ivy bridge', that is, a bridge covered with ivy. (The Latin botanic name of the ivy genus is *Hedera*.)

Jarlshof (Shetland)

This famous prehistoric site near SUMBURGH has an obvious old Norse name meaning 'jarl's temple' (*jarl* and *hof*); a jarl (related to English 'earl') was a Norse nobleman. The name may be Old Norse, but it was given to the site in relatively modern times by Sir Walter Scott. He came here in 1816 and used the name for the medieval farmhouse that features in his novel *The Pirate*, published in 1821.

Jarrow (Tyne and Wear)

An industrial town on the south bank of the TYNE. It has a tribal name, referring to the Gyrwe people who once lived here. Their name may mean 'fen people' (Old English *gyr* 'mud', 'marsh', related to modern English 'gore'). The name was recorded in the Venerable Bede's *Ecclesiastical History of the English People* of 731, where he refers to a place *qui uocatur Ingyruum* ('which is called *In Gyruum*', i.e. in the district of the *Gyruii*, or the Gyrwe).

Jedburgh (Borders)

A small town northeast of HAWICK on the Jed Water, after which it takes its name. Early records of the name, however, give the second part of the word not as '-burgh' but as '-worth', as shown by a text of 800, where is appears as *Gedwearde*. This therefore means 'enclosure by the River Ged'. The river's name probably means 'winding one', and is of Celtic origin (compare the modern Welsh *gwden*, 'withe', which two words are ultimately related, as they are to the English 'wend' and 'wind').

Jersey (Channel Islands)

The largest island in the group, whose name is traditionally said to derive from its Roman name of *Caesarea*, itself referring to Julius Caesar. But there is no evidence that this *was* the Roman name of Jersey, and recent research into the Roman names of the Channel Islands has concluded that *Caesarea* was actually the name of SARK. Jersey's name appears in early records in forms such as *Gersus* (about 1070) and *Gersui* (about 1170), strongly suggesting that the name is Scandinavian in origin and means 'Geirr's island'. The last two letters of the present name thus represent the Old Norse *ey* (island), after the personal name (with a 'possessive' *s*). The personal name is a nickname, meaning 'spear' (Old Norse *geirr*).

Jervaulx Abbey (North Yorkshire)

This twelfth-century Cistercian monastery above the River URE, northwest of MASHAM, is now a picturesque ruin. The name relates directly to the river, and means 'valley of the Ure', comprising a French adaptation of the river's name followed by the Old French *val* (valley). The name was recorded in about 1145 as *Jervalle. Compare* RIEVAULX.

Jesmond (Tyne and Wear)

This district of NEWCASTLE UPON TYNE stands on the little River Ouseburn, near the point where it enters the TYNE. Its name is a Norman adaptation of what might otherwise have become 'Ousemouth', with the river name taking a *J*- and the latter half of the name influenced by French *mond* (mount) (as in the name of RICHMOND). A document of 1205 gives the name as *Gesemue*. For the meaning of the river name *see* OUSE.

Jethou (Channel Islands)

A small island southwest of HERM, that has a name of uncertain but probably Scandinavian origin, with the final '-ou' perhaps representing the Old Norse *ey* (island). Its Roman name was *Barsa*, derived from Celtic root elements that mean 'summit place' (*compare* BARRHEAD). This well describes the topography of the island, which has a conical peak rising to 268 feet (82 metres).

Jodrell Bank (Cheshire)
The well-known radio telescope and radio astronomy laboratory of the University of MANCHESTER, west of MACCLESFIELD. It has a former field name, meaning 'Jodrell's bank', with 'bank' used of a slope or bank in an otherwise level field. The first part of the name is that of the original landowner here. (The name is Norman in origin, related to the French *chaudronnier*, 'tinker'.)

John o' Groats (Highland)
A locality in the extreme northeast of mainland Britain (although DUNCANSBY HEAD is further east). It takes its name from John o' Groat (perhaps a Dutchman, Jan de Groot) who was appointed a bailee to the earls of CAITHNESS here in the fifteenth century. The final *s* of the name is the 'possessive' that denotes the name of his house, no longer in existence here.

Johnstone (Strathclyde)
This town west of PAISLEY has a name that can be traced back to a document of 1292, where it appears as *Jonestone*. It is not known who the original John of the name was. The present apparent '-stone' is actually '-ton', that is, the Old English *tūn* (farm, settlement). The modern town developed only from the 1780s, when a large cotton mill was built here.

Joppa (Lothian)
This district of EDINBURGH has a biblical name that has been explained as deriving by way of a corruption of the Gaelic *dubh abh* (black water). But this seems too contrived, and there seems no doubt that the name derived, probably in the 1780s, from that of a farm here, the original aim being to express a religious sentiment. (Joppa was the town where Tabitha was restored to life: 'and it was known throughout all Joppa; and many believed in the Lord'; Acts 9:42.)

Jordans (Buckinghamshire)
A small village east of BEACONSFIELD, famous for being the location of an early Quaker meeting-house, attended by William Pitt, who is buried here. The name derives from that of the meeting-place itself, where the Quakers gathered in the second half of the seventeenth century. This was a yeoman's house called Old Jordan's Farm, after the original owner. A family named Jourdemayn was recorded as living here in 1301.

Joyce's Country (Galway)
This picturesque area of western GALWAY, between CONNEMARA and Lough CORRIB, takes its name from the Joyces, a family who came to this part of Ireland from Wales in the thirteenth century; some of the family's descendants still live here. The Irish name of the area is Dúiche Sheoigheach, 'Joyce's district', with the first word representing the Irish *dúthaigh* (native land, country).

Juniper Green (Lothian)
A district of EDINBURGH that derives its name from the juniper bushes that formerly grew here, with the name first recorded in 1812. Before this, the location here, southwest of the modern city centre, was called Curriemuirend, after Currie Muir ('moor of the plain': compare The CURRAGH).

Jura (Strathclyde)
The fourth largest island in the Inner HEBRIDES. Its name was recorded in a document of 678 as *Doirad Eilinn*, 'Doirad's island'. The present name is a 'smoothed' version of the personal name, although the final '-a' is popularly regarded as representing the Gaelic or even Old Norse for 'island', respectively *eilean* and *ey*.

Kanturk (Cork)
This market town northwest of MALLOW has a name that represents its Irish equivalent, Ceann Toirc, 'head of the boar'. This is probably the name of a local hill, referring to its outline like a boar's head.

Katrine, Loch (Central)
A loch to the west of The TROSSACHS whose name is probably based on the British (Celtic) root element *ceto-* (wood), with the rest of the name perhaps representing a personal name, such as Eriu. The whole name could then mean 'lake of the wood of Eriu'. It was recorded in 1463 as *Loch Ketyerne*. No doubt the present form of the name has at least partly been influenced by the woman's name Katrine, itself fairly popular in Scotland and associated with its Gaelic equivalent, Catriona.

Kearsley (Greater Manchester)
A town southeast of BOLTON whose name means 'water-cress meadow', from the two Old English words *cerse* (cress) and *lēah* (clearing). The latter word seems to have its more appropriate sense of 'meadow' here, in view of the 'watery' connection, and the River Croal flows through the town. The name was recorded in a document of 1187 as *Cherselawe*.

Keele (Staffordshire)
A village, famous for its university and lying west of NEWCASTLE-UNDER-LYME, whose name means 'cow hill', from the Old English *cu* (cow) and *hyll* (hill). The hill of the name may be the one on which Keele Hall stands, with this former country house now the nucleus of the university. The name was recorded in 1169 as *Kiel*.

Keighley (West Yorkshire)
An industrial town northwest of BRADFORD whose name was recorded in the Domesday Book as *Chichelai* (in which *ch* represents the sound of the Old English *h*, something like the *ch* in modern Scottish 'loch'). This means 'Cyhha's clearing'. The modern name is pronounced 'Keethly', in a rare attempt to preserve the original sound of the Old English *h*. In most names with '-gh-', such as LEIGH, this is silent.

Keith (Grampian)
A town southeast of ELGIN with a British (Celtic) name meaning simply 'wood', from the same basic element that gives the names of CHATHAM and LICHFIELD. The name was recorded in a document of 1203 as *Ket*. The man's name Keith derived (as a surname) from the place-name.

Kelham (Nottinghamshire)
This village northwest of NEWARK-ON-TRENT, famous for its nineteenth-century Gothic mansion, Kelham Hall, has a name that means '(place) at the ridges'. The name thus does not contain the element '-ham', but represents the dative plural (after a word such as 'at') of the Old Norse *kjǫlr* (ridge) (compare the modern English 'keel'). The Domesday Book recorded the name as *Calun*.

Kells (Kilkenny, Meath)
This name is common in Ireland, and represents the Irish *cealla*, plural of *cill* (cell, church), with an English plural *s* added. The town of Kells northwest of NAVAN is famous for the Book of Kells, which survived from its monastery (the 'cells' of the name). Its Irish name is Ceannanas Mór, meaning 'great head fort' (Irish *ceann-lios mór*). The village of Kells south of KILKENNY is also known in Irish as Ceannanas ('head fort'), but its full name is Kenlis Osraighe (*Ceannanas Osrai*), 'head fort in Ossory'. (Ossory was the name of an ancient kingdom in southwest LEINSTER.)

Kelmscot (Oxfordshire)
A village on the THAMES, famous for its old manor house that was the home of William Morris. The name means 'Cēnhelm's cottage', and it was recorded in a document of 1279 as *Kelmescote*.

Kelso (Borders)
This market town northeast of HAWICK is close enough to England to have an Old English name, meaning 'chalk hill-spur', from *cal* (chalk) and *hōh* (hill-spur). Kelso stands at the confluence of the rivers TEVIOT and TWEED, and the hill-spur referred to is the low broad one to the north of the town. Its name was recorded in a document of 1126 as *Calkou*.

Kelty (Fife)
A small town north of COWDENBEATH whose name represents the Gaelic *coilltean*, 'woods'; it was recorded in a mid-thirteenth-century document as *Quilte*.

Kelvinside (Strathclyde)
This district of GLASGOW takes its name from the River Kelvin here, whose own name is said, on rather doubtful grounds, to derive from the basic Gaelic *caol abhuinn* (narrow water). Its name was recorded in about 1200 with the spelling as now. The name of the river also lies behind other places here, such as Kelvindale, Kelvinhaugh, and Kelvingrove Park, all in Glasgow. The latter elements of these names denote, respectively, the 'valley', 'nook' (Old English *halh*), and 'wood' of or by the river.

Kempton Park (Surrey)
A well-known park and racecourse north of SUNBURY whose name was recorded in the Domesday Book as *Chenetone*, which means 'Cēna's farm'. The park is that of the eighteenth-century manor house here of the same name.

Kemp Town (East Sussex)
An eastern district of BRIGHTON named after Thomas Read Kemp, Member of Parliament for LEWES, who laid it out in the 1820s.

Kendal (Cumbria)
A town on the River Kent, north of LANCASTER. It derives its name from the river. It was previously known as Kirkby Kendal, that is, 'village with a church in Kendal', the latter being the equivalent of 'Kent-dale', i.e. the name of the river valley. Hence its original name was simply Kirkby, with 'Kendal' added to distinguish this Kirkby from others in the district, especially KIRKBY LONSDALE and KIRKBY STEPHEN (which were also originally Kirkby). So somewhat unusually the 'proper' name of the settlement has been superseded by that of the region it is in. All the elements of these names except that of the river itself are Old Norse in origin, from *kirkju-býr* (church village) and *dalr* (valley). The river name is Celtic, and has the same meaning as that of the KENNET. The Domesday Book recorded the town's name as *Cherchebi*, and the present name began to emerge shortly after this, as *Kircabikendala*, for example, in about 1095.

Kenilworth (Warwickshire)
A town southwest of COVENTRY whose name means 'Cynehild's enclosure', with the Old English personal name (that of a woman, and meaning 'royal battle') followed by *worth* (enclosure). The Domesday Book records the name as *Chinewrde*.

Kenmare (Kerry)
A town at the head of the Kenmare estuary whose name refers to this location, deriving from the Irish *ceann-mara* (sea head). Its current Irish name is Neidín, 'little nest', alluding to its 'secure' setting among the KERRY hills and mountains.

Kennet (Wiltshire)
An administrative district in the centre and east of the county. It takes its name from the River Kennet, which rises in it, and

from the Kennet and AVON Canal, which
crosses it. The river's name is of British
(Celtic) origin, deriving from a conjectural
root name *Cunetio-*, which means 'high
one'. This is not to be taken literally, as the
terrain is largely low-lying along its course,
but can be understood figuratively to
mean 'noble one', 'holy one'. The name
was recorded in the late ninth century as
Cynetan. This same Celtic root is believed
by many (but not all) to lie behind the
Roman name of MILDENHALL, which was
Cunetio.

Kennington (Greater London)
The name of this district of LAMBETH
means 'farm of Cēna's people', with the
personal name followed by the Old English
suffix *-ingtūn* that showed a particular place
to be associated with the person named.
Kennington appeared in a document of 821
as *Chenitun*.

Kennoway (Fife)
A small town northwest of LEVEN whose
name may mean 'head field', from the
Gaelic *ceann* (head) and *achadh* (field). The
name was recorded in a document of 1250
as *Kennachyn*.

Kensal Green (Greater London)
The first word of the name of this district of
BRENT means 'king's wood', from the Old
English *cyning* (king) and *holt* (wood). The
latter word was doubtless taken to be *healh*
(nook) over the centuries, and this resulted
in the present spelling of the name. But
early records show the true origin, such as
Kingisholte in 1253. The second word of the
name was recorded in the mid-sixteenth
century, with the whole name then
appearing as *Kynsale Grene*.

Kensington (Greater London)
A district (and royal borough) of west
central LONDON. Its name suggests a royal
association, from the resemblance of the
word to 'king' and the status of the
borough. But it actually means 'farm of
Cynesige's people', as early records show.

The name was recorded in the Domesday
Book as *Chenist*. (The personal name,
however, does mean 'royal victory', so the
royal association is ultimately there!)

Kent (England)
This southeastern county of England has
an ancient name, perhaps the oldest in the
country. It was recorded by Julius Caesar
as *Cantium*, which closely reflected the
Kantion of the early Greek geographers
(Strabo, in the first century BC, mentions
the name three times). The probable Celtic
root element of the name is *cant-*, meaning
'border', 'edge', referring to the coastal
situation of the region. The original name
probably first applied only to the coastal
section, or even to a single promontory
(presumably the present North Foreland of
the Isle of THANET). Caesar then extended
the territory covered by the name to
something like the present county.

Kentish Town (Greater London)
The name looks recent, but Kentish Town,
a district of Camden (*see* CAMDEN TOWN),
was recorded in a document of 1208 as
Kentisston. Presumably the original
reference was to an estate (Old English *tūn*)
held by a man called Kentish, or something
similar. His own name relates to that of
KENT.

Kenwood House (Greater London)
The eighteenth-century house at the
northern end of HAMPSTEAD Heath has a
name that can be traced back to the
sixteenth century but no earlier. In a
document of 1543 it appears as *Canewood*,
and in 1640 it occurs as *Caen Wood*. The
precise source of the name is not known; a
derivation from a surname such as
Kentwode has been suggested, but cannot
be proved.

Kerrier (Cornwall)
An administrative district in the southwest
of the county. The name was adopted in
1974, when the new districts were formed,
from that of a former hundred here,

recorded in 1201 as *Kerier*. This may be based on the conjectural Cornish word *ker* (fort, round) (compare the related Welsh *caer*, as in CAERNARVON), with the plural ending -*yer*. The sense would thus be '(place of) rounds', a 'round' being a term for a special type of circular hill-fort found in the county. This explanation is still disputed.

Kerry (Ireland)

The southwesternmost county of Ireland, having a tribal name referring to Ciar and his people. In early legend, Ciar was the son of King Fergus and Queen Maeve. His descendants are said to have taken possession of the land to the west of ABBEYFEALE, with their name passing to it. The Irish name of the county is Ciarraí, '(land of the) descendants of Ciar'.

Kesteven (Lincolnshire)

The former division of the county, representing the southwestern portion, has its name represented today in the two administrative districts of North and South Kesteven. The name itself is an unusual combination of Celtic and Scandinavian: the first half is the British (Celtic) element *ceto-* meaning 'wood'; the latter is the Old Norse *stefna* 'meeting (-place)' (*compare* STEYNING). The name as a whole can thus be understood as 'meeting-place in the wood'. The mixture of languages in the name shows that the same meeting-place must have been used by both the Danes and by the earlier Britons here. The name was recorded in about 1000 as *Chostefne*, and in the Domesday Book as *Chesteven*.

Keston (Greater London)

This district of BROMLEY has a '-stone' name, not a '-ton' one. It means 'Cyssi's stone', and was recorded in the Domesday Book as *Chestan*. An earlier record of the name, dated 862, gives it as *Cystaninga mearc*, 'boundary stone . . . (Old English *mearc*, modern 'mark') . . . of the Keston people'.

Keswick (Cumbria)

The name of this town west of PENRITH exactly corresponds with that of CHISWICK, and so means 'cheese farm', from the Old English *cēse* (cheese) and *wīc* (special type of farm). The spelling and pronunciation of the name, here in the North of England, are due to Scandinavian influence. The name was recorded in a document of 1276 as *Kesewik*.

Kettering (Northamptonshire)

This town northeast of NORTHAMPTON has a difficult name, for which no satisfactory meaning has been found. It is probably based on a personal name, with the final '-ing' meaning 'people of', as in READING; if so, it has not been identified, and no personal name has been traced that could give the first element of the name as it occurs in the earliest record — *Cytringan* (in 956).

Kew (Greater London)

A district of west LONDON, famous for its Royal Botanic Gardens by the THAMES. Its name is actually a combination of two words: the Old French *kai* (landing-place; modern 'quay') and the Old English *hōh* (spur of land). The name was recorded in a document of 1327 as *Cayho*. The 'spur' is that of the land here in the bend of the Thames.

Keymer (West Sussex)

A town south of BURGESS HILL whose name means 'cow's pool', from the Old English *cy*, genitive of *cu* (cow) and *mere* (pool). The reference was probably to one of the streams of the River ADUR here, where the cows must have had a regular watering place. The name was recorded in the Domesday Book as *Chemere*.

Keynsham (Avon)

A town on the River AVON midway between BATH and BRISTOL. Its name means 'Cǣgīn's riverside land'. The personal name is followed by the Old English *hamm* (water meadow, riverside land), here relating to Keynsham's location by the Avon. The name was recorded in about 1000 as *Cægineshamme*, showing the personal name and word in their full form.

Kidderminster (Hereford and Worcester)
An industrial town on the River STOUR west of BIRMINGHAM, whose name shows it to have had an important monastery ('-minster'). This was founded here in the eighth century, on the site now occupied by All Saints Church. The first part of the name represents the personal name Cyda. Before 'Cyda's monastery' was built, the place was known as *At Stour*, referring to the river on which it stands. The Domesday Book gave the name as *Chideminstre*.

Kidsgrove (Staffordshire)
This town northwest of STOKE-ON-TRENT has a name that may mean 'Cyda's grove'. No early forms of the name have been recorded, so a precise origin can be only speculative.

Kidwelly (Dyfed)
A small town northwest of LLANELLI whose name may mean '(place of) Cadwal', with the final syllable of the name representing a Welsh ending, *-i*, that denotes the territory of the named person. The name was recorded in the tenth century as *Cetgueli*. The Welsh form of the name is Cydweli, and the '-ll-' of the English spelling developed by association with other names, such as Llanelli. This phenomenon makes it the only Welsh town to have a 'double *l*' pronounced like a single English 'l', rather than as the distinctive Welsh sound for the double letter.

Kielder Forest (Northumberland)
A large area of conifers planted by the Forestry Commission in the northwest of the county, by the CHEVIOT Hills and the Scottish border. It takes its name, as does the reservoir called Kielder Water here, from the Kielder Burn, which rises in the Cheviots. The river's name is British (Celtic) in origin, from two root words that mean respectively 'rocky' (*compare* Welsh *caled*, 'hard') and 'stream' (*compare* Welsh *dwfr*, 'water'). A document of 1326 gives the name as *Keilder*, almost as now.

Kilbarchan (Strathclyde)
The name of this small town west of JOHNSTONE shares the initial element, 'Kil-', with many other Scottish and Irish place-names (see below). This element *may* mean 'church' (Gaelic and Irish *cill*), especially if a saint's name follows. Alternatively it can mean 'wood' (Gaelic *coille*, Irish *coill*), or even 'corner', 'nook' (Gaelic *cùil*, Irish *cúil*) or some other word. Sometimes there is no sure way of telling. For Kilbarchan we almost certainly have a saint's name, so that the name means 'St Berchan's church', this being the name of an Irish saint. The name was recorded in a document of about 1246 with the spelling as now.

Kilbirnie (Strathclyde)
A town northeast of ARDROSSAN whose name means 'St Brendan's church'. Whether this was the famous Brendan who was a friend of St Columba is difficult to say. The name was recorded in 1413 as *Kilbyrny*.

Kilburn (Greater London)
A district of BRENT whose name may mean 'cattle stream'. The second half of the name is almost certainly the Old English *burna* (stream; modern 'burn'), but there is some doubt about the first element. It may be the Old English *cu* (cow). A document of about 1130 has the name as *Cuneburna*, and one of 1181 as *Keleburna*. There is no sign of the stream here now, but Kilburn formerly had a well-known spring whose waters were drunk for their medicinal properties.

Kilcullen (Kildare)
A small town on the River LIFFEY southeast of DROICHEAD NUA. Its name may mean 'church of the slope', 'church of

St Cuilleann', 'church of the wood', or even 'church of the holly', depending which Irish word or name the initial 'Kil-' represents. The first meaning here is borne out by the topography, but the others cannot be finally ruled out.

Kildare (Kildare)

The name of this cathedral town, which gave the county its name, almost certainly means 'church of the oak', with the latter half of the name representing the Irish *doire* (oak grove, oak wood) (as for LONDONDERRY). St Brigid is said to have established a nunnery here in the fifth or sixth century on a site in a pagan oak grove. The present St Brigid's Cathedral may stand on the original site. The Irish name is Cill Dara.

Kilkee (Clare)

This attractive resort west of KILRUSH has a name that probably means 'St Caoi's church'. Its Irish name is Cill Chaoi. Little or nothing is known about the named saint.

Kilkeel (Down)

A coastal town south of the MOURNE MOUNTAINS whose name probably means 'church of the narrows', with the first element the Irish *caol* (narrow) (corresponding to the first word of the Scottish KYLE OF LOCHALSH). The description suits the location of the place, between the mountains and the sea. The Irish name is Cill Chaoil.

Kilkenny (Kilkenny)

This attractive town, which gave its name to the county, has the Irish name of Cill Chainnigh, which means 'St Kenneth's church'. St Kenneth was a sixth-century monk who worked in Scotland before founding a monastery here, very probably on the site now occupied by St Canice's Cathedral, on top of the hill here. (The cathedral's dedication is to the same saint, with the name in a spelling rather closer to the true Irish Cainneach, anglicized as Kenneth or Kenny.)

Killarney (Kerry)

This well-known town, in its fine lakeside setting east of MACGILLYCUDDY'S REEKS, has the Irish name Cill Airne, meaning 'church of the sloes', from the Irish *airne* (sloe, sloe-tree).

Killiecrankie (Tayside)

A village southeast of BLAIR ATHOLL, famous for the battle of 1689 in which the troops of William III were defeated by the Jacobites. Its name means 'wood of aspens', representing the Gaelic *coille creitheannich*. Frequently, 'Killie-' or 'Killy-' names, as distinct from 'Kil-' ones, will have the meaning 'wood', not 'church' (*see* KILBARCHAN).

Killiney (Dublin)

This resort south of DUN LAOGHAIRE has the Irish name of Cill Iníon Léinín, 'church of the daughters of Léinín', with the English name being a shorter 'smoother' version of this. Léinín is said to have been an ancestor of St Colmán, active in the sixth century.

Killybegs (Donegal)

A small fishing port west of DONEGAL whose name means 'the little churches', 'the little monastic cells', with an English plural *s* added to the Irish name, currently Na Cealla Beaga.

Killyleagh (Down)

A small town on the west shore of STRANGFORD Lough, that has the Irish name Cill Ó Laoch, traditionally translated as 'church of the descendants of the heroes', although the latter element of the name could equally be a personal name.

Kilmacolm (Strathclyde)

A town southeast of GREENOCK whose name translates as 'church of my Colm', that is, of St Columba, with 'my' (Gaelic *mo*) added to the saint's name to show a personal dedication to him, a sort of affectionate 'possession' of him. The name is sometimes wrongly associated with the personal name Malcolm, and even pronounced in a way that implies this connection.

Kilmacthomas (Waterford)

A town west of WATERFORD whose name means 'wood of the sons of little Thomas', representing the current Irish name, which is Coil Mhic Thomáisín. (The 'little' of the name renders the diminutive suffix -*ín* on the personal name, as in the word 'colleen', which is Irish *cailín*, the diminutive form of *caile*, 'girl'.)

Kilmallock (Limerick)

This old town southwest of TIPPERARY is known in Irish as Cill Mocheallóg, 'St Mocheallóg's church'. St Mocheallóg (whose name is otherwise rendered as St Molach or St Mo-Cheallóg) founded a monastery here in the seventh century. *Compare* the saint's name in KILMARNOCK.

Kilmarnock (Strathclyde)

An industrial town southwest of GLASGOW whose name means 'St Ernan's church', with the saint's name prefixed by the Gaelic *mo* 'my' (the -*m*- of the name) and suffixed by the diminutive -*oc*, so that the personal name is in effect 'my little Ernan' (*compare* KILMACOLM; KILMALLOCK). The name was recorded in a document of 1299 as *Kelmernoke*. Ernan was a sixth-century saint and a disciple of St Columba.

Kilrush (Clare)

This port and market town on the estuary of the SHANNON west of LIMERICK has the Irish name of Cill Rois, 'church of the peninsula' (or possibly originally 'wood of the peninsula', from *coill*, not *cill*). The peninsula of the name is not so much the main one here to the north of the Shannon, but the small headland to the south.

Kilsyth (Strathclyde)

A coal-mining town northwest of CUMBERNAULD whose name has been interpreted as 'St Syth's church', or as 'church of the arrows' (from the Gaelic *saighead*, genitive *saighde*). Neither derivation can be regarded as definitive. The name was recorded as now in a document of 1239, but in 1210 appears as *Kelvesyth*, and in 1217 as *Kelnasythe*, which suggests a possible connection with (or influence of) the name of the River KELVIN, which rises three miles east of Kilsyth.

Kilwinning (Strathclyde)

A town east of ARDROSSAN whose name means 'St Vinin's church', with the saint's name that of an Irish monk (also known as Finan) who is said to have founded a monastery here in the early eighth century, on the site of the present Kilwinning Abbey. The name was recorded in about 1160 as *Killvinin*.

Kimbolton (Cambridgeshire)

A village northwest of ST NEOTS whose name means 'Cynebald's farm', with the Old English *tūn* (farm) following the personal name. It was recorded in the Domesday Book as *Chenebaltone*.

Kincardine (Highland, Grampian, Tayside, Fife)

Any of various places of the name in Scotland, including the former county of Kincardineshire and the present administrative district of Kincardine and Deeside. The county took its name from the now-ruined Kincardine Castle north of Fettercairn, where a former 'town' (actually a straggling village) had been the county town until supplanted by STONEHAVEN in the seventeenth century. The present largest place of the name is the port of Kincardine-on-Forth, southeast of ALLOA. In each case the meaning of the name is the same: 'head of the thicket', from the Gaelic *cinn* (head) and a Pictish word meaning 'grove' that is related to the British (Celtic) *cardden* (thicket). Kincardine O'Neill, the village west of BANCHORY, has a name that shows it to have been a possession of the great Irish O'Neill family.

Kinder Scout (Derbyshire)
The highest summit of the High Peak in
the PEAK DISTRICT. The first word of the
name has not been interpreted satisfactorily
as yet. The second word represents the Old
Norse *skúti* (projecting cliff, overhanging
rock) (related to the English 'shoot' and
found in its own right as a dialect word for
such a cliff or rock).

Kinghorn (Fife)
This small resort on the FIRTH OF FORTH
east of *Burntisland* does not have a 'royal'
name, like many of those below, despite its
appearance. It derives from the Gaelic
cinn gronn (head of the marsh), as shown by
early records of the name, such as *Kingorn*
in about 1140 and, ten years later, *Kyngor*.
The false association with 'king' may have
been reinforced by the fact that King
Alexander III died here after falling from
his horse in 1286, and his monument
stands on the rock known as King's Crag.

Kingsbridge (Devon)
A town south of TOTNES that arose by a
bridge here at the head of the Kingsbridge
Estuary. The bridge name was recorded in a
document of 962 as *Cinges Bricge*. It is not
known which monarch gave his name to
'the king's bridge', but he was clearly an
Anglo-Saxon one.

Kingsbury (Greater London)
A district of BRENT whose name was
recorded in 1044 as *Kynges Byrig*. This
means 'king's manor', and it is known that
the manor was granted by Edward the
Confessor to WESTMINSTER Abbey shortly
before this date. *Compare* QUEENSBURY.

King's Cross (Greater London)
A district of north central LONDON, well
known for its railway terminus. Its name
can be understood with 'cross' in either of
its popular senses as 'stone monument in
the shape of a cross' or 'crossroads'. Both
can apply to the monument erected at the
crossroads here (the junction of Gray's Inn
Road, Euston Road, and Pentonville

Road) as a memorial to King George IV after
his death in 1830. It stood here until 1845,
when it was removed for the present railway
terminus to be built. The earlier name of the
location here was Battlebridge, itself a corruption of the original name of 'Bradford',
recorded as *Bradeford* in 1207; this related
to a 'broad ford' over the former Fleet
River here (*see* FLEET). The word 'bridge'
was added to this name, which then
gradually evolved to its present form
(recorded as *Battyl brydge* in 1559). This
former name is still preserved in the King's
Cross area in the names of Battlebridge
Basin, a dock on the Union Canal, and the
short Battlebridge Road, behind the station.

Kings Langley (Hertfordshire)
This village south of HEMEL HEMPSTEAD
arose around a manor house granted to the
king in the early twelfth century here, with
the manor itself having previously been in
the tenure of the Abbot of ST ALBANS. (*See*
ABBOTS LANGLEY for the earlier history of
the name and the meaning of 'Langley'.)
Kings Langley was recorded as *Lengele
Regis* in a document of 1428.

King's Lynn (Norfolk)
The name of this town and port on the
River OUSE basically means 'king's manor
in Lynn', with the king being Henry VIII.
The second word of the name is British
(Celtic) in origin and means 'pool'
(compare Welsh *llyn*, 'lake'; *see also*
LINCOLN). The 'pool' would have been the
mouth of the Ouse where the town now
stands. The name was recorded in the
Domesday Book as *Lun*.

Kingsteignton (Devon)
This small industrial town north of
NEWTON ABBOT has a name that shows the
manor here was held by the king in the
eleventh century (a fact recorded in the
Domesday Book). The basic name is thus
Teignton, recorded in about 1000 as
Tegntun, meaning 'estate by the River
Teign'. For the meaning of the river name
see TEIGNMOUTH.

Kingston-upon-Hull *See* Hull.

Kingston upon Thames (Greater London)
This former SURREY town and royal
borough was a royal possession as long ago
as the ninth century, when its name was
recorded as *Cyninges tun*, 'king's farm'.
Later, its location by the THAMES was
added to distinguish this Kingston from
the many others. The present title of 'Royal
Borough' was conferred on the town by
George V in 1927, in recognition of the fact
that Kingston had long enjoyed royal
status.

Kingswear (Devon)
A town standing on the River Dart
opposite DARTMOUTH. Its name means
what it says, referring to the 'king's weir'
here. The name appears in a document of
the late twelfth century as *Kingeswere*. The
king then was Henry II.

Kingswood (Avon)
A town and suburb of BRISTOL whose
name means what it says, 'king's wood',
and was recorded in a document of 1252 as
Kingesuuode. The king at that time was
Henry III, although this dating does not
necessarily refer to the contemporary
monarch.

Kington (Hereford and Worcester)
A town close to the Welsh border west of
LEOMINSTER whose name means 'royal
manor'. It was recorded in the Domesday
Book as *Chingtune*. The king then was of
course William the Conqueror, although
the name may well refer to an earlier
monarch.

Kingussie (Highland)
This small town and tourist centre south of
INVERNESS does not have a 'royal' name
but a Gaelic one meaning 'head of the
pinewood'. The component Gaelic words
are *cinn ghiuthsaich*. The name itself was
recorded in about 1210 as *Kinguscy*. The
pines are still very much in evidence here
in STRATHSPEY.

Kinlochleven (Highland)
A small town standing at the head of Loch
LEVEN, as its name exactly indicates,
deriving from the Gaelic *ceann* (head) and
the name of the loch. All Scottish names
beginning 'Kinloch-' will thus denote a
place at the head of a loch.

Kinross (Tayside)
A town and resort on the western side of
Loch LEVEN north of DUNFERMLINE. Its
name indicates its location at the 'head of a
promontory', deriving from the Gaelic
ceann (head) and *ros* (cape), this latter being
one that juts into the loch. East of the
promontory the town has a famous island
castle in the waters of the loch. Its name
was recorded in a text of about 1144 as
Kynros. The former county of Kinross-
shire was named after the town in medieval
times.

Kinsale (Cork)
A town south of CORK above the estuary of
the BANDON river, at a location described
by its name, which means 'head of the sea',
from the Irish *ceann* (head) and *sál*,
genitive *sáile* (sea) (the word implies salt
water). The town is thus at roughly the
highest point on the estuary that the tide
can reach. Its Irish name is Cionn tSáile.

Kintyre (Strathclyde)
A peninsula in ARGYLL, where it runs
south to the MULL OF KINTYRE. The name
is descriptive of the location, and means
'end of the land', from the Gaelic *ceann*
(head) and *tire* (land) (as in TYRONE). A
text of 807 has the name as *Ciunntire*.

Kinver (Staffordshire)
This town west of STOURBRIDGE has a
name of British (Celtic) origin that
originally applied to a forest here, now
represented by Kinver Edge, to the west of
the town. The second part of the name
means 'hill', and is related to the Welsh *bre*
(hill) (which is *fre* in its 'mutated' form).
The first part of the name is still of
uncertain origin, but may well relate to the

river name KENNET, and so mean
something like 'great'. The earliest records
of the name show it as *Cynibre* (in 736),
with similar spellings subsequently. It is
possible that the first element of this was
associated either with a personal name,
such as Cynestan or Cynehild (as in a
number of other 'Kin-' names), or that it
was understood as the Old English prefix
cyne-, meaning 'royal'. The Domesday
Book gives the name as *Chenevare*. Even
now an alternative spelling of the name is
Kinfare.

Kirkby (Merseyside)

A town northeast of LIVERPOOL whose
name occurs in other similar place-names
(see below). It is of Scandinavian origin
and means 'village with a church', from the
Old Norse *kirkju-bý*. (The basic Old Norse
word for 'church' was *kirkja*, and the
English and Norse words are related, as
more obviously is the Scots 'kirk'.) Most
places of the name added a distinguishing
word (see below). This Kirkby was
recorded in the Domesday Book as
Cherchebi.

Kirkby in Ashfield (Nottinghamshire)

The full name of this town southwest of
MANSFIELD can be interpreted as 'village
with a church in the open land with ash
trees', a combination of the Old Norse (*see*
KIRKBY) and the Old English (from *æsc*
'ash' and *feld* 'open land'). Ashfield was the
name of a former region here. *Compare*
SUTTON IN ASHFIELD, a few miles to the
north of Kirkby. The Domesday Book had
the basic name as *Chirchebi*.

Kirkby Lonsdale (Cumbria)

A small town northeast of LANCASTER.
'Kirkby' means 'village with a church' (Old
Norse *kirkju-bý*), and 'Lonsdale' is a
distinguishing addition that refers to its
location in the valley of the River LUNE,
that is, in 'Lune-dale' or Lonsdale. In the
Domesday Book the town's name is simply
Cherchebi, but barely five years later a
document records it as *Kircabilauenesdala*.

Kirkbymoorside (North Yorkshire)

A small town west of PICKERING below the
North Yorkshire Moors. Early records of
the name, however, show that the place
was regarded as being at the head or top of
the moors, as in a text of 1282, which gives
the name as *Kirkeby Moresheved*, the last
element of which represents the Old
English *hēafod* (head). 'Moorshead' thus
became 'Moorside', perhaps as the locality
of the town suggested a lower site rather
than a higher one. But the main street of
the town climbs steeply to the moors, and
the name doubtless originally applied to an
elevated site. The first part of the name is
the Scandinavian 'village with a church'
(*see* KIRKBY).

Kirkby Stephen (Cumbria)

A small town southeast of APPLEBY.
'Kirkby' is from the Scandinavian and
means 'village with a church' (*see* KIRKBY).
'Stephen' distinguishes this Kirkby from
others locally, and relates to one Stephen
who was an early owner of the manor here,
or possibly to Stephanus, the Abbot of St
Mary's Abbey, YORK, to whom the place
was given by a Norman lord, Ivo
Taillebois. The latter suggestion seems to
be supported by the fact that the town's
parish church is dedicated to St Stephen,
showing a religious link rather than a
simply manorial one. The name was
recorded in the late eleventh century as
Cherkaby Stephan.

Kirkcaldy (Fife)

This resort and port north of EDINBURGH
across the FIRTH OF FORTH does not
have a 'Kirk-' or 'church' name at all. The
first element is actually the British (Celtic)
caer (fort) (*compare* the Welsh
name CAERNARVON) followed by
Caledin, which means 'hard hill' (*caled
din*). The fort was doubtless one on the site
of the present fifteenth-century
Ravenscraig Castle. The name was
recorded in a twelfth-century text as
Kircalethyn.

Kirkconnel (Dumfries and Galloway)
A town northwest of SANQUHAR whose name means 'St Congal's church'; it was recorded in 1347 as *Kyrkconwelle*. In names like this, where one might expect the 'kirk' to come as the second element, and the personal name first (as in ORMSKIRK), it is probable that the Old Norse 'Kirk-' has replaced an earlier Gaelic 'Kil-', for the normal Gaelic word order was 'church + personal name', not 'personal name + church' (compare the 'Kil-' names above, such as KILMARNOCK). Congal (or Conghal) is an Irish name. *Compare* KIRKCUDBRIGHT.

Kirkcudbright (Dumfries and Galloway)
The name of this town on the estuary of the River DEE is similar to that of KIRKCONNEL, with the personal name following the word for 'church' instead of preceding it, as is normal in 'kirk' names. This means that the initial 'Kirk-' may originally have been the Gaelic 'Cil-'. The personal name is actually an English one, and 'Cudbright' represents St Cuthbert, the seventh-century Northumbrian monk who made many missionary journeys in GALLOWAY. The original parish church here was thus St Cuthbert's, although now only its churchyard remains. The name was recorded in a document of 1286 as *Kircuthbright*. The town was the chief one in the former county of Kirkcudbrightshire, otherwise known as STEWARTRY.

Kirkham (Lancashire)
This town west of PRESTON has a name that in the south of England would probably be 'Churcham' but here owes its present form to Scandinavian influence. It means 'village with a church', so virtually corresponds to places named KIRKBY. The town's name was recorded in the Domesday Book as *Chicheham*.

Kirkintilloch (Strathclyde)
A town northeast of GLASGOW whose name is similar to KIRKCALDY in that the first element does not mean 'church' but 'fort', from a British (Celtic) word corresponding to the modern Welsh *caer*. The remainder of the name contains the Gaelic *ceann* (head) and *tulaich*, the genitive of *tulach* (hillock). The whole name thus means 'fort at the head of the hillock'. The name refers to a Roman fort on the ANTONINE WALL here, on which the town is located. Its earlier name was something like 'Caerpentulach' (*Caerpentaloch* in a tenth-century document), with *pen-* an earlier Celtic word for 'head' (as in PENZANCE and PENMAENMAWR). Probably the final element of this early name was something like *-bre*, as in the modern Welsh *bre* (hill), with this later translated into *-taloch*. In its present form, the name appears in a text of about 1200 as *Kirkintulach*.

Kirklees (West Yorkshire)
The name of this administrative district in the southwest of the county ultimately comes from what is now Kirklees Hall, a Jacobean mansion northeast of HUDDERSFIELD, built on the site of a Cistercian nunnery and the place where traditionally Robin Hood is said to have died. The name, recorded in 1246 as *Kyrkelegh*, means 'wood belonging to a church', this being the nunnery. The second part of the name represents the Old English *lēah* (wood), so that the first half may originally also have been Old English, as *cirice* (church).

Kirk Michael (Isle of Man)
The name of this large village southwest of RAMSEY means what it says, 'St Michael's church'. The first word of the name is the Old Norse *kirkja*.

Kirkwall (Orkneys)
The chief town and port of the ORKNEY Islands. Its name does not mean 'church wall' but 'church bay', representing the Old Norse *kirkja* (church) and *vágr* (bay) (as in STORNOWAY). The bay referred to is the Bay of Kirkwall, to the north of the port, where it opens out to the Wide Firth.

The church is the twelfth-century cathedral of St Magnus. The Old Norse word for 'bay' gives the 'Voe' of other names of inlets in the Orkney and SHETLAND Islands, such as SULLOM VOE. The name was recorded in a document of about 1225 as *Kirkiuvagr*, and as *Kyrkvaw* in 1364. No doubt this last element became '-wall' in the same way that the Scots *ba'* means 'ball' and *a'* is 'all'.

Kirriemuir (Tayside)
A small town northwest of FORFAR whose name represents the Gaelic *ceathramh* (quarter) followed by *mór* (great). A 'quarter' was a measure of land considered large enough to support a single household. The 'great quarter' had its name recorded in a document of 1250 as *Kerimor*.

Kirton in Lindsey (Humberside)
This small town south of SCUNTHORPE has a name whose first word means 'church village'; it is probably a Scandinavian form of what in the south of England would have been something like 'Churchton' (*compare* CHERITON and the Wiltshire village of Chirton). Its name was recorded in the Domesday Book as *Chirchetone*. The second part of the name was added to distinguish it from other Kirtons. The town was in LINDSEY, one of the three main divisions of Lincolnshire until 1974.

Kittybrewster (Grampian)
The name of this district of ABERDEEN invites fanciful references to some lady named Kitty Brewster (a female innkeeper, so the tales tell). The '-brewster' may well refer to a brewer, but the first part of the name represents the Gaelic *cèide* (green) (i.e. a green where things were sold). So the name is really 'brewer's green'.

Knaresborough (North Yorkshire)
The name of this town northeast of HARROGATE was recorded in the Domesday Book as *Chenaresburg*, which probably represents the personal name

Cēnheard (although the *d* is missing from the recorded spelling) followed by the Old English *burg* (fortified place). On the other hand, Knaresborough Castle, which must be on the site of the original fort, is on a rugged rock above the town and the gorge of the River NIDD, and this suggests that the first part of the name may actually represent the conjectural Old English *cnearr*, Middle English *knar*, which means precisely this, 'rugged rock', as in the name of Knarsdale, a village in Northumberland, where this derivation is certain and suits the location. Possibly one version of the name affected the other, and it is significant that the *d* of the personal name appears in later records of the first interpretation mentioned here, such as *Chenardesburg* in 1130, almost suggesting that the Domesday Book spelling was influenced by the Old English word of the second interpretation, which has no *d*. Pending further evidence, 'Cēnheard's fortified place' seems the best interpretation.

Knebworth (Hertfordshire)
A town south of STEVENAGE whose name was recorded in the Domesday Book as *Chenepeworde*, and in a document of 1220 as *Knebbewrth*. The Domesday Book clerk obviously had problems with so many consonants, and the latter version of the name is more straightforward, showing the meaning to be 'Cnebba's enclosure', with the Old English *worth* following the personal name.

Knighton (Powys)
This town west of LUDLOW is near enough to the English border (right by OFFA'S DYKE) to have an English name. It means virtually what it says, 'knights' village', with 'knights' not in the modern 'grand' sense but meaning, in medieval usage, servants or personal followers of a baron or lord. The Old English word for 'knight', as here, was *cniht*, and for this particular Knighton (there are several others) the Domesday Book version was *Chenistetone*, with *Cnicheton* recorded in a later text of

1193. The Welsh name for the town is Trefyclo, which represents an earlier *Trefyclawdd*, 'farm by the dyke', from the Welsh *tref* (farm), *y* (the), and *clawdd* (dyke), the latter referring to Offa's Dyke, which runs just to the west of Knighton. *Compare* KNIGHTSBRIDGE.

Knightsbridge (Greater London)
The name of this fashionable street and area of the WEST END of LONDON seems at first sight to have a suitably 'grand' name. It means what it says, 'knights' bridge', but as for KNIGHTON the 'knights' would have been the servants of a baron or lord, not the titled noblemen they are today. So the name is best understood as something like 'bridge of the soldiers' or, a little more widely, 'bridge of the young men'. The bridge would have been where the road crossed the River Westbourne, near the site of the present Albert Gate. The name was recorded in the mid-eleventh century as *Cnightebricge*.

Knock (Mayo)
This famous pilgrimage centre east of CASTLEBAR has a name found frequently elsewhere in Ireland, meaning simply 'hill' (Irish *cnoc*). *Compare* KNOCKMEALDOWN MOUNTAINS; KNOCKTOPHER.

Knockmealdown Mountains (Waterford)
The English name of this well-known mountain range in southwest Ireland represents the Irish name, Cnoc Mhaoldonn, of the group's highest peak. The name means 'hill of Maol Duin', after a semi-legendary person associated with the mountain. His name can be interpreted as 'warrior of the fort', or, in another spelling of the name (Maoldomhnach), as 'servant of the church', the latter being a sort of Christian counterpart to the former pagan name.

Knocktopher (Kilkenny)
A small town south of KILKENNY whose name means 'hill of the causeway', representing the Irish Cnoc na Tóchair.

Traces of an ancient causeway can still be seen here in the valley.

Knottingley (West Yorkshire)
The name of this town east of WAKEFIELD means 'clearing of Cnotta's people', and was recorded in the Domesday Book as *Notingeleia*. This is therefore a name like that of BINGLEY, which is also in West Yorkshire and, like Knottingley, also on the River AIRE.

Knotty Ash (Merseyside)
A district of LIVERPOOL whose name means what it says, and originally referred to a gnarled ash tree here, around which a village developed in the late seventeenth or early eighteenth century. It was originally known simply as 'Ash'. The tree in question is said to have grown at the top of what is now Thomas Lane.

Knowle (Avon, West Midlands)
A district of BRISTOL and of SOLIHULL whose name occurs elsewhere in the country. In each case it derives from the Old English *cnoll* (modern 'knoll'), meaning either 'hill-top' or, later, 'hillock'. A survey of the local topography will show which is the better interpretation for a particular place. The Bristol Knowle was recorded by the Domesday Book as *Canole*, showing the 'smoothed' Norman spelling, while the Solihull Knowle appeared as *La Cnolle* in a document of 1251.

Knowsley (Merseyside)
An administrative district in the central region of the county that takes its name from the village of Knowsley northeast of LIVERPOOL, with its mansion of Knowsley Hall. The name means either 'Cēnwulf's clearing' or 'Cynewulf's clearing', depending how the personal name is read. The Domesday Book recorded the name as *Chenulueslei*. The last element of this, the '-ley' of the present name, is the Old English *lēah* (clearing).

Knutsford (Cheshire)

A town west of WILMSLOW whose name has been traditionally associated with King Canute (Cnut), and that has been interpreted as 'Cnūt's ford', which is probably correct. The reference is almost certainly not to King Canute, however, and the two personal names just happen to be identical (Knutsford's Canute Place is a quite recent name; in the mid-nineteenth century it was known as Market Place). The difficulty is knowing exactly where the ford was, as the town is on high ground away from any river. It has been suggested that the crossing referred to may have been a causeway over the marshy ground south of Tatton Mere, the lake that lies to the north of the town. The name was recorded in the Domesday Book as *Cunetesford*. The town formed the basis of Mrs Gaskell's novel *Cranford* (keeping the '-ford' of the original name). For the meaning of this literary name *see* CRANFORD!

Kyle of Lochalsh (Highland)

This village and port stands on the eastern side of the narrow entrance to Loch Alsh, and takes its name from this strait, as 'Kyle' represents the Gaelic *caol* (narrow). *Compare* KYLES OF BUTE.

Kyles of Bute (Strathclyde)

The narrow channel that surrounds the northern part of the island of BUTE, separating it from the mainland of ARGYLL. 'Kyles' thus refers to this channel, from the Gaelic *caol* (strait; literally 'narrow', 'thin'), to which an English plural *s* has been added.

Kynance Cove (Cornwall)

This popular cove of serpentine rock, northwest of The LIZARD, has a name that derives from the conjectural Cornish *kewnans* (ravine; literally 'hollow valley'). The name properly describes not the cove itself, but the narrow passage leading down to it in a fissure of the cliffs.

L

Lacock (Wiltshire)

This picturesque village south of
CHIPPENHAM has a name that represents
the conjectural Old English *lacuc* (small
stream; related to modern 'lake'), with the
name itself recorded in the mid-ninth
century as *Lacok*. The reference is
probably not to the River AVON here, but
to the small tributary of it on which the
village stands a short distance to the west.

Ladybank (Fife)

This small town southwest of CUPAR is said
to have a name that is an 'improved'
English rendering of the Gaelic *leathad bog*,
'moist slope', referring to the peat formerly
dug here from the thirteenth century. If so,
the present name was doubtless modelled
on existing names, such as Ladykirk and
Ladywell, which refer to the Virgin Mary
('Our Lady').

Laggan (Highland, Strathclyde)

Any of various places in Scotland, such as
the village of Laggan on the River SPEY
north of DALWHINNIE, and the River
Laggan on the island of ISLAY. The South
Laggan Forest, too, extends along both
sides of Loch LOCHY. Wherever it occurs
the name has the same meaning, a
diminutive of the Gaelic *lag* (cave, hollow).
Lag also gives the name of places called
Lagg.

Lahinch (Clare)

A resort west of ENNISTYMON with the
Irish name An Leacht, which means 'the
grave'. But it could also represent the Irish
leath-inis (peninsula; literally 'half island'),
presumably referring to the peninsula
north of Lahinch. However, a longer
version of the former name has been
recorded as *Leacht Uí Chonchúir*, 'O
Connor's grave', so this may be the correct
interpretation.

Lambeth (Greater London)

This LONDON borough, on the south side
of the THAMES, has a name that refers to
this river, since it means 'landing-place for
lambs', from the Old English *lamb* (lamb)
and *hȳth* (landing-place) (compare 'hythe'
and the names of HYTHE and
ROTHERHITHE). The two elements of the
name can be seen more clearly in early
records of it, such as *Lamhytha* in a
document of 1088 and *Lambhehithe* in
1312. For two other London names with a
disguised 'hythe' *compare* CHELSEA and
PUTNEY.

Lambourn (Berkshire)

This small town northwest of NEWBURY
takes its name from the river on which it
stands. The river's name means literally
'lambs' stream' (Old English *lamb-burna*),
that is, a stream where lambs were washed.
The name was recorded as *Lamburna* in a
document of 943.

Lammermuir (Borders)

An upland area of the region, which
includes the Lammermuir Hills, that
extends westward from ST ABB'S HEAD
southeast of EDINBURGH. The name
means what it says, 'lambs' moor',
denoting an area where lambs graze. The
Scottish-seeming name is actually Old
English in origin, from *lambra*, genitive
plural of *lamb* (lamb) and *mōr* (moor),
originally (as probably here) 'barren waste
land'. The name of the hills was recorded
in a document of 800 as *Lombormore*. The
name occurs in the title of Sir Walter
Scott's novel set in the region, *The Bride of
Lammermoor*.

Lamorna Cove (Cornwall)

The village of Lamorna, south of
PENZANCE, is beside a steep-sided valley
that runs down to the picturesque bay of
Lamorna Cove. The first element of the
name is undoubtedly the Cornish *nans*
(valley), referring to this particular one.
For the second part of the name, we need
to examine early records of it, such as

Nansmorno in 1305 and *Nansmurnou* in 1309; it is hard to say precisely what it means, but it certainly seems to be based on the Cornish *mor* (sea). A tentative meaning is thus something like 'valley that leads down to the sea'. The village took its name from the valley, as did the cove.

Lampeter (Dyfed)

This small market town northeast of CARMARTHEN has a name that represents the Welsh Llanbedr, 'St Peter's church', from *llan* (church) and the Welsh form of the name *Pedr* (Peter), as required after this first word. Thus although the town is perhaps best known for St David's College, of the University of Wales, its name is properly preserved in its (mostly rebuilt) parish church of St Peter. The full Welsh name of the town is Llanbedr Pont Steffan, 'St Peter's church at Stephen's bridge'. Stephen would have been the name of the man appointed to look after the bridge in medieval times, an important matter in those days, when a bridge was the lifeline to a place and the route by which an enemy could enter. The name was recorded in 1284 as *Lanpeter*, and in a document of 1301 as *Lampeter Pount Steune*. For further occurrences of the Welsh *pont* (bridge) *see* PONTARDAWE and its following entries.

Lanark (Strathclyde)

A market town southeast of MOTHERWELL that has a Celtic name, represented by the Welsh *llannerch* (glade), which is therefore its meaning. The name was recorded in 1188 as *Lannarc*. The former county name of Lanarkshire came from that of the town in the Middle Ages.

Lancashire (England)

The name of this northwestern county can be understood as 'LANCASTER-shire', for that is its origin, and Lancaster is still its county town. The name was recorded in a document of 1140 as *honor de Lancastre*, and in another of 1169 as *Comitatus de Lancastra*, with the present version of the name developing subsequently (*Lancastreshire* in the fourteenth century).

Lancaster (Lancashire)

This city and county town of LANCASHIRE is on the River LUNE, north of PRESTON, and the first part of its name refers to this river. The second half of the name indicates that Lancaster was a Roman station (Old English *ceaster*). Its name is traditionally said to have been *Olenacum*, but recent research has established that this is more likely to have been the name of the Roman fort at Elslack, west of SKIPTON. The name of the fort here is thus unknown, although it is likely to have been based on the name of the Lune; a Roman milestone found four miles northeast of Lancaster has been discovered with a text that ends 'L MP IIII'. This can be interpreted as 'from L— 4 miles' ('MP' stands for the Latin *milia passuum*, 'miles', literally 'thousands of paces'). One would expect the Roman name to begin with *L-* for the reasons stated. It is just a pity that we have no record of the complete name. Lancaster was recorded as *Loncastre* in the Domesday Book. *Compare* LANCHESTER.

Lanchester (Durham)

A small town northwest of DURHAM whose name proclaims it to have been a former Roman station, as does the '-caster' of LANCASTER. The first part of Lanchester is simply the Old English *lang* (long), so that the name means 'long Roman fort'. But the Roman name of the fort here, *Longovicium*, was almost certainly not based on the Latin *longus* (long), and it seems that the first element of the name was taken by the Anglo-Saxons to mean 'long' in their own language. Hence their record of the name as *Langecestr* in 1196. So the Roman name must have another origin, probably a Celtic one, as they frequently do. One possibility is a word related to the modern Welsh *llong* (ship). The name *Longovicii* could then be a kind of 'tribal' name meaning 'ship fighters' ('fighters' being represented by the *-vicium* of the Roman name, as for the

Delgovices of WETWANG). Lanchester is not on a river, but it is less than twenty miles from the sea, and the 'ship fighters' could have made their base here.

Lancing (West Sussex)

A town (officially North Lancing and South Lancing) east of WORTHING. Its name means '(place of) Wlanc's people'; the '-ing' of the name, representing the Old English *-ingas* (people of), is found in many other place-names here, suggesting that the groups of people referred to must have been quite small. Lancing appears in the Domesday Book as *Lancinges*.

Land's End (Cornwall)

The most westerly point of England (but not the most southerly, which is The LIZARD). Its name implies a place at the 'end of the mainland', as it actually is. It has its parallels in France's Finistère and Spain's Cape Finisterre. The name was recorded in the fourteenth century as *The Londis End*. The Cornish name of Land's End is PENWITH.

Langbaurgh (Cleveland)

The name of this administrative district, in the east of the county and formed in 1974, derives from that of Langbaurgh Ridge here, which runs from east to west along a basaltic dike. The derivation is thus in the Old English *lang* (long) and *beorg* (hill, mound), describing the ridge. In the south of England the equivalent name is Longbarrow.

Langdale (Cumbria)

This name is familiar from Langdale Pikes, the jagged peaks ('pikes') at the summit of Langdale Fell, west of GRASMERE, and from villages and lakes named Langdale elsewhere in the county. The name means what it says, 'long dale', with the Old English *denu* (valley) replaced by the Old Norse *dalr*.

Langholm (Dumfries and Galloway)

This woollen-manufacturing town east of LOCKERBIE stands on a strip of fertile land beside the River ESK. Its name thus describes this location, as a 'long island', or strip of land beside the river. The 'island' aspect of the name is all the more relevant in that two other rivers join the Esk here, the Ewes Water from the north, and the Wauchope Water from the west. (*Compare* the name of LONGTOWN, further south on the Esk but across the English border in CUMBRIA.) Langholm's name was recorded in 1376 as now.

Langport (Somerset)

This market town northwest of ILCHESTER is on the River Parrett, but its name does not mean that it is a 'long port' here! The sense is 'long market-place', with 'port' having the sense it has in GOSPORT. At one time there were doubtless market booths or stalls set out along the street, as still occurs on market days in some towns. (Some streets have names that reflect this 'market' sense of the word, such as LINCOLN's Newport, in the north of the city.) For Langport, therefore, the specific reference will be to Bow Street, the long straight street that climbs through the town from the river, and off which the weekly market is still held. The name was recorded on a coin of about 930 as *Longport*, and in the Domesday Book as *Lanport*. Places named Lamport, such as the village north of NORTHAMPTON, will have an identical meaning.

Lanhydrock House (Cornwall)

A fine country house southeast of BODMIN that takes its name from the parish here, Lanhydrock. This is derived from a conjectural Old Cornish word *lann*, related to the Welsh *llan* (church), plus the name of the saint, Hydroc, to whom the small church here is dedicated. Nothing is known about him apart from his name.

Laois (Ireland)

The name of this county in central Ireland, formerly anglicized as Leix, means '(place of the people of) Lugaid Laígne', the legendary ancestor of the O Mores and related families who was granted lands here after he had driven invading forces from MUNSTER. From 1556 to 1920 Laois was named Queen's County, after Queen Mary. *Compare* PORT LAOISE.

Larbert (Central)
This town northwest of FALKIRK had its name recorded in a document of 1195 as *Lethberth*, apparently from the Gaelic *leth* (portion) and Pictish *pert* (wood) (compare PERTH). Its present name, however, suggests that the first part of the name was replaced by the Gaelic *làrach* (farm). The name thus now means 'farm by the wood'.

Largo (Fife)
A town northeast of LEVEN that really consists of two separate villages, Upper Largo and Lower Largo, situated a mile apart. The name was recorded in a document of 1250 as *Largauch*, suggesting an origin in the Gaelic *leargach* 'steep (place)'. This certainly suits the topography of the place, as the ground rises steeply from the low sandy shore of Largo Bay here, culminating in the hill called Largo Law, a mile north of Upper Largo, where its height is 952 feet (290 metres). *Compare* LARGS.

Largs (Strathclyde)
A town and resort on the Firth of CLYDE sheltered by lofty hills, whose name testifies to such a topography, deriving from the Gaelic *learg* (slope), to which an English plural *s* has been added. The name was recorded in about 1140 as *Larghes*. *Compare* LARGO.

Larkhall (Strathclyde)
This town southeast of HAMILTON has a name that can hardly derive from the Gaelic *learg* (slope) (*see* LARGS), because it lies in lowish land by the AVON Water in the valley of the CLYDE. Perhaps the Gaelic *làrach* (farm) lies behind it, as may be so for LARBERT. A text of 1620 has the name as *Laverockhall*; a 'laverock' is a lark!

Larne (Antrim)
A port and resort at the mouth of Larne Lough in Northern Ireland. Its name represents the Irish Latharna, interpreted as '(territory of the) people of Lathair'. He was the son of the legendary Hugony the Great (Ugaine Mór), a pre-Christian monarch, and was granted lands here.

Lasswade (Lothian)
This town southwest of DALKEITH may have a Gaelic or English name. If the former, 'fortified place by a wood' has been suggested, from *leas*, a variant of *lios* (fort, court) (as for The LIZARD) and *bhaid*, genitive of *bad* (thicket, grove). If the latter, the name may mean 'ford by meadow-land', from the Old English *lǣs* (meadow, pasture) and *gewæd* (ford). The name was recorded in a document of about 1150 as *Laswade*. The 'ford' origin would suit the location: Lasswade lies on the North ESK river.

Lauder (Borders)
This small town is on the Leader Water north of MELROSE and takes its name from the river. The river's name may relate to that of the LOWTHER HILLS and so derive from a British (Celtic) root element *lou-* meaning 'wash', implying a river that 'washes' the soil or land through which it runs. The name was recorded in 1208 as *Louueder*. The surrounding district is named Lauderdale, after the valley of the river.

Laugharne (Dyfed)
A village on the estuary of the River TAFF and also at the mouth of a much smaller river called the Corran; it takes its name from the latter. The name thus represents the Welsh *tâl* (end) followed by the river name, which itself probably means simply 'little one', from a diminutive of *cor* (dwarf). Early records of the name show the origin more clearly, such as *Talacharn* in 1191. The same document also gives the name as *Abercoran*, 'mouth of the Corran', an 'Aber-' name like ABERYSTWYTH, for example.

Launceston (Cornwall)

A town on a hill above the valley of the River Kensey, northwest of PLYMOUTH. Its name is half Cornish, half English, deriving from the Old Cornish *lann* (enclosure) and *scawen* (elder-tree), with the Old English *tūn* (farm) added. The Domesday Book thus has the name as *Lanscavetone*. Officially, Launceston is known as 'Dunheved otherwise Launceston', with this title first recorded in a document of 1538: '*Launston* otherwys cawlled *Lostephen* yn old tyme cawlled *Dunheved*'. This last name may represent the conjectural *dyn* (hill-fort) and *haf* (summer), and so mean something like 'hill-fort that is a summer residence'. The third name, *Lostephen*, is traditionaly interpreted as meaning 'St Stephen's church', with the Cornish *lann* (as in LANHYDROCK) followed by the saint's name. If this is so, the reference would seem to be to the former village of St Stephens that is now a northern district of Launceston. It is possible that the town was the former Roman station of *Tamara*, which was probably somewhere nearby. Its name derives from that of the River TAMAR, which is about two miles east of the town.

Laurencekirk (Grampian)

This small market town northeast of BRECHIN has a straightforward name referring to the patron saint of its church, St Laurence of Canterbury. The town was founded in about 1770 by Lord Gardenstone, and was at first known as Kirkton of St Laurence. Before this, the location here was known as Conveth, perhaps deriving from the Gaelic *coinmheadh* (free quartering).

Lavenham (Suffolk)

A small town northeast of SUDBURY whose name means 'Lāfa's homestead'; it was recorded in a document of about 995 as *Lauanham*.

Laxey (Isle of Man)

A small town and resort on the east coast south of RAMSEY that takes its name from the Laxey river, on which it stands. The river's name is Old Norse for 'salmon river', from *lax* (salmon) and *á* (river). There are several rivers in Iceland named Laxa, with an identical meaning. *Compare* LEIXLIP.

Leamington Spa (Warwickshire)

A town on the River Lean south of COVENTRY; it gets its name from this river, whose own name is of Celtic origin and means 'elm river'. 'Leamington' as a whole thus means 'farm (Old English *tūn*) by the elm river', and in 1838, after visiting the town, Queen Victoria granted Leamington the full 'honorific' title of Royal Leamington Spa. The 'royal prefix' has been granted to only one other English town, TUNBRIDGE WELLS. The latter word singles out the town's importance as a centre of medicinally beneficial springs. The Domesday Book recorded the town's name as *Lamintone*. The river's name links up with that of LYMPNE.

Leatherhead (Surrey)

Until 1980, it was thought that the name of this town, on the River Mole (*see* MOLE VALLEY) south of KINGSTON UPON THAMES, meant 'people's riding path', that is 'ford over which people can ride'. This was said to derive from the Old English *lēode* (folk, people) and a conjectural word *rida* or *ride* (riding path). It was not the present name that led to this hypothesis, but a ninth-century record of it as *Leodridan*. (The Domesday Book gives it as simply *Leret*.) However, in 1980 a scholar of the English Place-Name Society established that the name was not English at all but Celtic, and that it meant 'grey ford', deriving from a word related to the Welsh *llwyd* (grey, pale) (found also in the name of LICHFIELD) and a word related to the Welsh *rhyd* (ford) (as in the name of PENRITH). The 'grey-coloured ford' would thus have been over the Mole here.

Lechlade (Gloucestershire)

A village on the River THAMES north of SWINDON whose name means 'river-crossing near the (river) Leach'. It derives from the name of this river (which joins the Thames about half a mile southeast of the town), whose name means 'muddy one', followed by the Old English *gelād* (river-passage; compare modern 'lode'). The 'river-passage' itself would have been over the Thames here. Lechlade was recorded in the Domesday Book as *Lecelade*.

Ledbury (Hereford and Worcester)

A town east of HEREFORD that takes its name from the River Leadon, on which it stands. The Old English *berg* (hill) has been added to the river name, which probably comes from the conjectural Old English *hlid* (slope). Ledbury was recorded in the Domesday Book as *Liedeberge*. The town is situated on the southern slope of the MALVERN HILLS.

Leeds (West Yorkshire)

The name of this well-known industrial city was originally that of the district here, itself deriving from that of a people who lived by what is now the River AIRE. (Compare the name of LEICESTER for a similar history.) The river must then have been called something like *Lat*, itself of British (Celtic) origin and meaning 'flooding', 'flowing'. The Venerable Bede recorded the district name in the eighth century as *Loidis*. It can thus be said that Leeds means 'place of the people who live by the River Lat'. The same original river name is seen in place-names such as Ledsham and Ledston, both villages about ten miles southeast of Leeds.

Leeds Castle (Kent)

The name of this country house in its picturesque moated setting east of MAIDSTONE is only coincidentally identical to that of the city of LEEDS. The name comes from that of the village of Leeds here, whose own name comes from that of the brook on which it stands, this in turn deriving from the conjectural Old English *hlȳde* (noisy one) (related to the modern English 'loud'). The village was thus originally known as something like *Hlydes*, 'belonging to the noisy one', and its name was recorded in the Domesday Book as *Esledes*.

Leek (Staffordshire)

A textile town northeast of STOKE-ON-TRENT whose name simply means 'brook', from the Old Norse *lékr*, the particular reference being to the stream that flows through the town as a tributary of the nearby River Churnet. Leek appears in the Domesday Book as *Lec*.

Lee-on-the-Solent (Hampshire)

A resort and residential community west of GOSPORT. 'Lee' means 'meadow', from the Old English *lēah* (which more commonly means 'forest' or 'clearing in a forest'). The second part of the name, denoting the location of the resort on the SOLENT, was added only in the late nineteenth century, partly to distinguish it from other places called Lee or Lea, but partly as a commercial enticement, at a time when the resort was being developed.

Leicester (Leicestershire)

The latter half of the name of this city denotes that it has developed on the site of a former Roman station (Old English *ceaster*). The first half of the name probably relates to the name of the river here. However, Leicester is on the Soar, which has a Celtic name (meaning 'flowing one'). This seems to rule out the river name, which has been long established, and in any case does not resemble the 'Lei-' of the city's name. It seems likely, therefore, that the river name was that of a tributary of the Soar; a suitable candidate is the small stream on which the village of Leire stands, about ten miles southwest of Leicester, with the village name coming from it. As with LEEDS, the name came to be used of the people who lived in this district, and as Leicester appears as *Ligera Ceaster* in a text of 917, we must assume that they were called something like the *Ligore*. The ultimate origin of both the river name and the folk name is still uncertain. The Roman name of the station here was *Ratae Coritanorum*, 'fortifications of the Coritani'. Again, the origin of the tribal name is unknown. The town of Leicester gave its name to that of the county of Leicestershire, recorded in a document of 1087 as *Lægreceastrescir*.

Leigh (Greater Manchester)

A town west of MANCHESTER with a very common name, deriving from the Old English *lēah* (woodland, clearing, meadow), found frequently as the final '-leigh' or '-ley' of a name. In the case of Leigh, the meaning is probably 'meadow', as the town stands on an area of low marshland (mentioned in connection with KNUTSFORD). Its name was recorded as *Leeche* in a document of 1276.

Leigh-on-Sea (Essex)

A district of SOUTHEND-ON-SEA whose name derives from one of the senses of the Old English *lēah*, as mentioned under LEIGH. Since Leigh-on-Sea is on low ground by the THAMES estuary, it seems likely that 'meadow' or 'pasture' is the most reasonable interpretation. The name was recorded in 1254 as *Leye*. The '-on-Sea' was added in the nineteenth century, mainly for commercial reasons when the place began to develop as a resort.

Leighton Buzzard (Bedfordshire)

An industrial town northwest of LUTON. 'Leighton' literally means 'leek farm', from the Old English *lēac-tūn*. This can be understood rather more generally, however, as meaning 'vegetable farm', in other words 'kitchen garden', implying that in medieval times Leighton Buzzard was a market-garden centre. The second word of the name is the name of the first prebendary here, Theobald de Busar. The Domesday Book recorded the name as *Lestone*, and the present full name

appears in a document of 1254 as *Letton Busard*.

Leinster (Ireland)

This former province in the east and southeast of the country has a name that means 'place of the Lagin people'. They were a Celtic tribe who came to Ireland, possibly in the third century BC, with their legendary leader, said to have been Labraid Longsech. Their own name may come from a word related to the modern Irish *laighean* (spear), so that they were originally the 'spear folk'. The place-name has the '-ster' element, found also in MUNSTER and ULSTER. This is a combination of the Old Norse genitive (possessive) *s* and Irish *tír* (land, district) (as in TYRONE). The Irish name of Leinster is Laighin, referring to the people alone, not their territory.

Leiston (Suffolk)

A town east of SAXMUNDHAM whose name may derive from the Old English *lēages-tūn*, 'farm in a clearing', although the Old English *lēah* rarely occurs as the first element of a name. It has been suggested that the location of the town, near the oast, could offer a more suitable alternative in the Old English *lēg*, 'fire' (with *tūn* added), implying that the site would be a good one to light a beacon. The name was recorded in the Domesday Book as *Ledestuna*, but in a document of 1168 as *Legestona*.

Leith (Lothian)

A district of EDINBURGH beside the FIRTH OF FORTH. Its name may well therefore represent a Celtic word related to the Welsh *llaith* (moist). It was re-corded as *Inverlet* in about 1130, with the first part of this the 'river-mouth' word 'Inver-' found in INVERNESS, for example. Leith is at the mouth of the Water of Leith, where it flows into the FORTH. The river name may have come from that of the settlement here, rather than vice versa.

Leitrim (Ireland)

This name is fairly common in Ireland, and means 'grey ridge', from the Irish *liath* (grey) and *droim* (ridge). The name of the northwestern county comes from the village of Leitrim northeast of CARRICK-ON-SHANNON, where the 'grey ridge' would be the rising ground to the east. The Irish name of the county is Liatroim.

Leixlip (Kildare)

This old town by the LIFFEY, west of DUBLIN, has a Scandinavian name, from the Old Norse *leax* (salmon) and *hlaup* (leap). Leixlip is thus a 'salmon leap'. The name describes the point where salmon were able to leap up the cataract on the river here, now replaced by a specially constructed fish pass. The town's name was recorded in a document of 1328 as *Lexlepe. Compare* LAXEY.

Lennoxtown (Strathclyde)

A small town north of GLASGOW that arose in the late eighteenth century with the introduction of calico printing. It took its name from the Lennox family, long associated with the district. The earls and dukes of Lennox took their title in turn from the ancient territory of Lennox, whose own name probably derives from the Gaelic *leamhanach*, 'abounding in elms', from *leamh* (elm). The original name of the village here was Clachan of Campsie, with 'clachan' a Scots word for a small village (from *clach*, 'stone'), and Campsie referring to the CAMPSIE FELLS nearby.

Leominster (Hereford and Worcester)

A town on the River Lugg north of HEREFORD whose name is a sort of semi-translation of its Welsh name, Llanllieni. This means 'church on the streams', from *llan* (church) and *llieni* (streams), so that the Welsh word for 'church' is translated by '-minster' and the initial 'Leo-' represents *llieni*. The 'streams' are really a district here, consisting of a triangle of land with Leominster at the eastern point, and the rivers Arrow and Lugg as converging boundaries, enclosing other streams in the middle. The town's name was recorded as *Leomynster* in a tenth-century document.

Lerwick (Shetland)

The chief town of MAINLAND has a Scandinavian name, as is to be expected in this northern area of Scotland. It means 'mud bay', from the Old Norse *leirr* (mud) and *vík* (inlet, bay) (as for WICK). The bay referred to is Bressay Sound, on the east coast. The town's name was recorded in a text of 1625 with the spelling as now.

Leslie (Fife)

This town northwest of GLENROTHES has a name of Celtic origin meaning 'holly enclosure', from words related to the modern Welsh *llys* (court) (*compare* LISS) and *celyn* (holly). Some instances of the surname Leslie will have originated here, with the modern first name (and its feminine equivalent, Lesley) coming from the surname. The town's name was recorded in a late-twelfth-century document as *Lesslyn*.

Letchworth (Hertfordshire)

This town north of STEVENAGE has the familiar '-worth' for the second half of its name, from the Old English *worth* (enclosure). The first half of the name is less certain, but may represent the conjectural Old English word *lycce*, 'locked place' (related to modern 'lock'), so that the overall sense is 'locked enclosure'. The name was recorded in the Domesday Book as *Leceworde*.

Letterkenny (Donegal)

The chief town of the county, northwest of STRABANE. Letterkenny means 'wet hillside of the O Cannons', from the Irish *leitir* (wet hillside), followed by the personal name. The Irish name of the town is Leitir Ceanainn.

Leuchars (Fife)

A village south of TAYPORT whose name means '(place of) rushes', from the Gaelic *luachar* (rush, rushes), to which a plural English *s* has been added. The name was recorded in 1300 as *Locres*.

Leven (Fife)

A town and resort on the west side of LARGO Bay. It takes its name from the River Leven that enters the sea nearby. The river name means 'elm river', from the same Celtic root that gave the name of LEAMINGTON SPA and LYMPNE. Here, it is the Gaelic *leamhain* (elm). Loch Leven, also in FIFE, is named after the same Leven river, which flows from its southern end. The town's name was recorded as *Levin* in a document of about 1535. *Compare* LENNOXTOWN.

Levenshulme (Greater Manchester)

A district of MANCHESTER whose name means 'Lēofwine's island', with the personal name followed by the Old Norse *holmr* (island, raised ground in marshland). The name was recorded in 1246 as *Lewyneshulm*.

Leverburgh (Western Isles)

A village on the southwest coast of HARRIS that was originaly known as Obbe, with this a name of Gaelic origin meaning 'bay' (*òb: compare* OBAN). In 1918 the name was changed to Leverburgh after William Lever, first Viscount Leverhulme, who bought lands here with the aim of transforming the village into a major fishing port. The name is said to have been proposed by the villagers themselves when Lord Leverhulme expressed his dislike of the name Obbe. For further commercial enterprise by the same man *see* PORT SUNLIGHT.

Lewes (East Sussex)

The county town, situated in a gap of the South Downs northeast of BRIGHTON. Its name could refer to the Downs, as it derives from the plural of the Old English *hlāw* (hill, mound) (as in BASSETLAW). On the other hand, it is perhaps more likely

that the name refers to the many tumuli (burial mounds) found locally. The name was recorded in a document of the mid-tenth century as both *Læwe* and *Læwes*.

Lewis (Western Isles)

The largest and most northerly island of the Outer HEBRIDES; its name is also applied specifically to the northern half of the island, as distinct from HARRIS, which is its southern part. The name may derive from the Gaelic *leoig* (ditch, marsh). This would be appropriate enough, as much of Lewis is a vast tract of peat and moss, with many lochs and streams. The name was recorded as *Leodu* in a text of about 1100.

Lewisham (Greater London)

A borough and town in southeast LONDON whose name means 'Lēofsa's village', with the final element the frequently occurring Old English *hām* (homestead, village). The Domesday Book recorded the name as *Levesham*, while an earlier document of about 1060 has it as *Liofesham*.

Leyburn (North Yorkshire)

A small market town southwest of RICHMOND. The second half of the name is certainly the Old English *burna* (stream), referring to one that runs into the River URE here. The first half of the name is harder to explain; it is almost certainly not the Old English *lēah* (woodland, clearing), which is anyway rarely found as the first element in a name. A possible origin in the Old English *hlīg* (shelter) has been suggested. The name was recorded in the Domesday Book as *Leborne*.

Leyland (Lancashire)

A town south of PRESTON whose name means 'fallow land', 'land that has been allowed to lie untilled', from the Old English *læge* (fallow, unploughed) and *land* (tract of country). No doubt much of the land by the River Lostock here was used for grazing rather than for growing crops. The town's name was recorded in the Domesday Book as *Lailand*.

Leyton (Greater London)
A town in the southern part of the Borough of Waltham Forest (*see* WALTHAM ABBEY). It takes its name from the River Lea, which forms the boundary between Leyton and Clapton to the west (and which was formerly the more important boundary between ESSEX and MIDDLESEX). The name thus means 'farm by the River Lea', whose own name may mean 'bright one', or represent the name of the river god, Lugus. The same river gave its name to LUTON, near which it rises, but the difference between the names of Luton and Leyton has not been explained, although they have exactly the same meaning. *Compare* LEYTONSTONE.

Leytonstone (Greater London)
A district of LEYTON whose name is of identical origin to Leyton, for it too is on the River Lea. However, it has added 'stone' by way of differentiation. The stone in question is the so-called High Stone, said to stand on the site of a Roman milestone. Leytonstone is known to be on the former Roman road from LONDON to EPPING Forest. The district's name was recorded as *Leyton atte Stone* in a document of 1370, showing it to be 'Leyton by the stone'.

Lichfield (Staffordshire)
This cathedral city north of BIRMINGHAM was long thought to have a name that meant 'field of corpses', with the first half of the name supposed to represent the Old English *līc* (body, corpse) and refer to early martyrs or battle victims. But the name is older and of Celtic not English origin. It means 'grey forest', from two words related respectively to the modern Welsh *llwyd* (grey) (*compare* LEATHERHEAD) and *coed* (wood, forest) (*compare* BETWS-Y-COED). The name was recorded in the fourth century as *Letoceto*, although the precise reference then was to the Roman station at Wall, a village two miles southwest of Lichfield (the centre of settlement subsequently shifted from Wall to its present location). Later records of Lichfield's name include *Liccidfeld* in about 730, and *Lichesfeld* in 1130. The second part of the name has thus been wrongly assimilated to the Old English *feld*, modern 'field'.

Liffey (Wicklow/Dublin)
The name of this well-known river on which DUBLIN stands remains unexplained. It is not from the Irish *leath* (broad), nor does it seem to share any element of the name of LIFFORD.

Lifford (Donegal)
A small town just west of the River FOYLE, across the water from STRABANE. The river forms the boundary between the counties of DONEGAL and LONDONDERRY, and so between the Republic of Ireland and Northern Ireland. The name of the town means 'side of the water', with an English *d* added to the Irish name, Leifear, by association with 'ford'.

Limavady (Londonderry)
A small town southwest of COLERAINE whose name represents the Irish Léim an Mhadaidh, 'leap of the dog', with this originally relating to the site of a former castle overhanging a deep glen two miles to the south, in the valley of the River Roe. This may well be a corruption of some earlier name. If not, it presumably refers to a local legend or incident of some kind.

Limerick (Limerick)
The county capital and third largest city in Ireland. Its name means 'bare area of ground', represented by its Irish name of Luimneach. This would have originally applied as a description of land by the lower reaches of the SHANNON, on which the town stands. 'Bare' can perhaps be understood both literally and figuratively, in the latter sense indicating an open or vulnerable location. The county name came from that of the town.

Lincoln (Lincolnshire)

Ptolemy recorded the name of this well-known city as *Lindon* in the second century A D. This represents the Celtic word for 'pool', 'lake', which gave the modern Welsh *llyn*. The reference is to the marshy land and pools of the River WITHAM, on which the city stands, with the original feature still partly preserved as Brayford Pool. The Romans established a station here for veteran legionary soldiers, and to the romanized name of the place, *Lindum*, they added the Latin *colonia*. These two words are thus the basis for the modern name, with 'Lin-' representing the Celtic name, and '-coln' the Latin word. The name is unusual in that it has survived with almost no alteration over the centuries, and also because it never acquired the '-caster' or '-chester' that came to designate many former Roman camps and forts, such as at DONCASTER and MANCHESTER. In the eighth century, the Venerable Bede referred to the settlement as *Lindocolina*, and in the Domesday Book it was *Lincolia*, with the *n* omitted presumably because the Norman scribe found its pronunciation difficult after *l*. The same Celtic origin lies behind the name of LINDSEY. Lincoln gave its name to Lincolnshire, which is recorded in a document of 1016 as *Lincolnescire*.

Lindisfarne (Northumberland)

The former name for and still the alternative name of HOLY ISLAND, five miles off the northeast coast opposite BELFORD. Its name derives from that of LINDSEY, to which has been added the Old English *faran* 'travellers' (compare modern 'farewell'). People from Lindsey, in north Lincolnshire, probably made regular journeys to the island as a place of religious pilgrimage. The Venerable Bede referred to the island several times in his *Ecclesiastical History of the English People*, calling it *insula Lindisfarnenis*, *ecclesia Lindisfaronensis*, and so on, while the actual people from Lindsey he referred to as the *gens Lindisfarorum*.

Lindsey (Lincolnshire)

One of the three former divisions or 'parts' of Lincolnshire, in the north of the county, where it is now represented by the administrative districts of East Lindsey and West Lindsey. The name was that of an Anglo-Saxon kingdom here, and means 'territory of the *Lindenses*', that is, of the people who lived round the Roman *colonia* that had been set up at *Lindum* (*see* LINCOLN). To this, the Old English *ēg* (island) has been added. Lindsey was something like a real island until the FENS beside the River WITHAM were drained. The Venerable Bede referred to Lindsey in the eighth century as *prouincia Lindissi*. Lindsey in turn gave its name to LINDISFARNE.

Lingfield (Surrey)

This village north of EAST GRINSTEAD has a name more complex than it seems, meaning overall 'open land of the people of the forest clearing'; the first half represents a conjectural Old English name *Leahingas*, that is, *lēah* (clearing) followed by the -*ingas* suffix (people of). The second part of the name is simply the Old English *feld* (open land; modern 'field'). So the initial *L-* of the name is all that is left of *lēah*. The name was recorded in the ninth century as *Leangafeld*.

Linlithgow (Lothian)

This historic town west of EDINBURGH takes its name from Linlithgow Loch, by which it stands. The loch's name means 'lake in a moist hollow', with the first element the same as in LINCOLN, the second as in LEITH, and the final part as in GLASGOW. (At one time, the county of West LOTHIAN was known by the alternative name of Linlithgowshire.) The name was recorded in a document of about 1138 as *Linlidcu*.

Linnhe, Loch (Highland/Strathclyde)

A long sea loch whose name means 'loch of the pool' (Gaelic *linn* 'pool'; *compare* KING'S LYNN, LINCOLN, and similar names). The 'pool' referred to is the less turbulent water in the inner part of the loch, by FORT WILLIAM. This was known locally as *an linne sheileach*, 'the brackish pool'. The main name of the loch thus derives from this.

Liphook (Hampshire)

A large village west of HASLEMERE whose name may mean 'corner of land with a deer leap', from the Old English *hlīep* (leap, place where deer leap) and *hōc* (hook, angle, corner of land). The description would seem to suit the locality, as Liphook is on the lower slope of HINDHEAD (the hill, rather than the present town), with the 'deer' connection similarly evident in the latter's name. Liphook was recorded in a fourteenth-century document as *la Leephook*, and a century later as *Liephok*.

Lisburn (Antrim)

This town southwest of BELFAST has the Irish name of Lios na gCearrbhach, which means 'fort of the gamblers'. This refers to the old fort sites northeast and southwest of the town where 'outlaws' used to gamble with cards and dice. There was formerly thick woodland here, which would have concealed their activity. The former English name of Lisburn was Lisnagarvey, based on the Irish name. The present name superseded the earlier one at some stage in the seventeenth century. The new second element of the name has been variously explained as referring to a fire, or relating to the River Lagan (as a stream or 'burn'). But it almost certainly represents an Irish word, so that the present name may be *Lios na Bruidhne*, 'fort of the fairy palace', with the second element the Irish *bruidhne*, genitive of *bruidhean*. The word occurs in other place-names, and was doubtless introduced as an improvement on the 'undesirable' association with gamblers.

Lisdoonvarna (Clare)

A small town northwest of ENNIS with the Irish name Lios Dúin Bhearna, meaning 'fort of the gapped fort'. The first word,

lios, is normally translated as 'ring-fort', but as two forts are involved here, it is perhaps better understood as 'enclosure'. A 'gapped' fort is a broken or dilapidated one. This particular fort is to the left of the road from Lisdoonvarna to Ballyvaughan.

Liskeard (Cornwall)

This town east of BODMIN has a name that certainly begins with the Cornish *lys* (court, palace). Normally such names have a personal name as the second element; here, for example, something like 'Carrad'. However, it is possible that the latter half of this name represents the Cornish *carow* (stag) in its plural form (which has not been recorded, so is unknown). Liskeard may therefore be the 'court at the place where stags are found'. Its name was recorded in the eleventh century as *Lyscerruyt*.

Lismore (Waterford, Strathclyde)

Either of two places: a small town east of FERMOY in Ireland, or a long narrow island in Loch Linnhe, north of OBAN in Scotland. Both names have the same basic meaning: 'big enclosure', from the Irish (*lios mór*) and Gaelic (*lios mòr*) respectively. In the case of the Irish town, however, the 'enclosure' is a historic ring-fort, built round a seventh-century monastery. It can still be seen as a flat-topped mound a mile to the east of the town. The Scottish island is regarded as an 'enclosure' more in the sense of its natural limits, with particular reference to its fertile soil. It is thus more a kind of large 'market garden'.

Liss (Hampshire)

This large village northeast of PETERSFIELD has a Celtic name meaning simply 'court', 'palace', related to the names of LISKEARD and The LIZARD. The name implies that a dwelling-place here was the chief one in the district. The Domesday Book records the name as *Lis*.

Listowel (Kerry)

A market town northeast of TRALEE with the Irish name of Lios Tuathail, 'Tuathal's fort'. A *lios* is a so-called 'ring-fort', which in Irish history was the term for a circular fort built inside a much larger one, known as a *ráth* (*see* RáTH LUIRC for example).

Littleborough (Greater Manchester)

A town northeast of ROCHDALE whose name means virtually what is says, and indicates a small borough. No record for this particular Littleborough has been found earlier than 1577, when it was recorded as *Littlebrough*.

Littlehampton (West Sussex)

This coastal resort west of WORTHING was originally known simply as 'Hampton' (*Hantone* in the Domesday Book), meaning 'homestead', from the Old English *hām-tūn*. Later, it added 'Little-' in order to be distinguished from SOUTHAMPTON, further west along the south coast, which itself was similarly just a 'Hampton' before adding 'South-' (*compare also* NORTHAMPTON). Littlehampton was recorded in a document of 1482 as *Lyttelhampton*.

Littleover (Derbyshire)

This district of DERBY lies to the southwest of the city on a slope, and this is what its name describes, with the basic origin in the Old English *ufer* (slope, ridge). It was originally simply 'Over' (*Ufre*, in the Domesday Book), but then added 'Little-' to be distinguished from nearby MICKLEOVER ('big slope').

Liverpool (Merseyside)

This famous city and port has an interesting name, both linguistically and topographically. The first half derives from a Middle English word *livered*, meaning 'clotted', 'coagulated' (indirectly related to the 'liver' of the body). The latter half means what is says. There was thus formerly a 'clotted pool' here. This was 'The Pool', a former creek of the MERSEY that has now been filled in. 'Clotted' meant that the water was very muddy and no doubt weedy. The name as a whole has thus been recorded in its present form from at least the twelfth century (*Liuerpol* in a text of about 1190). Liverpool's name has produced its own idiosyncratic mythology, with the fabled 'Liver bird' (pronounced like 'diver') even appearing on the city arms and giving the name of the Merseyside office block known as the Royal Liver Building. At the same time, natives of the city are known as Liverpudlians, with a pun on 'pool' and 'puddle'. (They are also known as 'Scouses', but that is another story!)

Liversedge (West Yorkshire)

The name of this town northwest of DEWSBURY is quite unconnected with that of LIVERPOOL. It means 'Lēofhere's edge', and was recorded in the Domesday Book as *Livresec*. Liversedge is on a long low ridge above the River CALDER. *Compare* EDGE HILL.

Livingston (Lothian)

A town (designated a New Town in 1962) west of EDINBURGH whose name means 'Leving's farmstead'. It was recorded in a document of the mid-twelfth century as *Uilla Leuing*, and as *Leiggestun* somewhat later in this same century. The Anglo-Saxon personal name derives from the Old English *lēofing* (dear person, darling), from *lēof* (dear; related to modern 'love' and the archaic 'lief').

Lizard, The (Cornwall)

A well-known peninsula, with its headland of Lizard Point, that is the most southerly point of the English mainland. Its name is a combination of the two conjectural Cornish words *lys* (court) and *arth* (height), referring to an administrative centre ('court') on the 'height' here in medieval times. The name appears in the Domesday Book as *Lisart*. The location of the actual 'court' was doubtless at or near the present village of Lizard here on the peninsula. The Roman name for The Lizard was *Dumnonium Promontorium*, 'promontory of the *Dumnonii*'. The tribal name may be based on that of Dumnonos, their pagan god, whose own name may mean 'mysterious one'. An earlier Roman name for the whole headland was *Ocrinum Promontorium*. The first word of this may mean 'sharp point', and refer to the group of rocks off Lizard Point called The Manacles. These would appear as 'sharp points' when approached from the sea. *See also* DEVON.

Llanberis (Gwynedd)

The name of this town east of CAERNARVON exemplifies many similar Welsh names (see below) beginning with 'Llan-', meaning 'church' (as in the Cornish name of LANHYDROCK). This element is frequently, but not always, followed by the name of the saint to whom the particular church is dedicated. Many such saints are of obscure origin, and for some the only surviving record of them is the place-name (and church dedication, of course). In the case of Llanberis, the reference is to St Peris, who is said to have arrived in Wales as a missionary from Rome in the sixth century.

Llandaff (South Glamorgan)

A district of CARDIFF that takes its name not from a saint, but from the River TAFF on which the city stands. The name thus means 'church on the Taff', and the church in question is the cathedral church of St Teilo, whose name lies behind that of LLANDEILO. Llandaff (Llandaf, in its Welsh spelling) was recorded in a document of the mid-twelfth century as *Lanntaf*.

Llandeilo (Dyfed)

A town east of CARMARTHEN whose name means 'St Teilo's church'. St Teilo, known also in latinized form as St Elidius, was an important sixth-century saint and bishop whose work and cult was centred in South Wales. LLANDAFF Cathedral is dedicated to him, and many other places are named after him. The name of Llandeilo was recorded as *Lanteliau Maur* in a document

of 1130, with the second word meaning 'great' (modern Welsh *mawr*) and distinguishing this Llandeilo from all the others. The town's parish church is dedicated to St Teilo. *See also* LLANBERIS.

Llandovery (Dyfed)

This small town west of BRECON lies at the confluence of the rivers Bran and Gwydderig and just over a mile from the confluence of the Bran and the TOWY. Small wonder, then, that its name means 'church by the stream', from the Welsh *llan am dwfr*. Llandovery is thus an anglicised version of its Welsh name, Llanymddyfri, often shortened to Llanddyfri. This is therefore a 'Llan-' name that does not incorporate the name of a saint (*see* LLANBERIS). Llandovery was recorded as *Llanamdewri* in a twelfth-century text.

Llandrindod Wells (Powys)

The English second word indicates that this town northwest of HEREFORD has a spa, and the natural springs nearby have been exploited from the eighteenth century. The first word means 'Trinity church', from the Welsh *llan* (church) followed by *trindod* (trinity). An earlier name for the place was Llanddwy, 'God's church' (*llan* plus *Duw*), and this is recorded in a document of 1291 as *Lando*. The present name appears in a text of 1535 as *Llandynddod*. Llandrindod Wells became the ecclesiastical capital of Wales, and it now has two churches dedicated to the Holy Trinity, an old one to the south of the town, and a modern one in the centre. *See also* LLANBERIS.

Llandudno (Gwynedd)

This popular coastal resort has a name that means 'St Tudno's church'. Very little is known about the saint to whom the town's St Tudno's Church is dedicated. He may have been active here in the sixth century. *See also* LLANBERIS.

Llandyssul (Dyfed)
A small town north of CARMARTHEN whose name means 'St Tysul's church'. As so often, little is known about this particular saint, who was probably here in the sixth century. The town's parish church is dedicated to him in the spelling of St Tyssel. *See also* LLANBERIS.

Llanelli (Dyfed)
An industrial town northwest of SWANSEA whose name means 'St Elli's church'. She was a woman saint, and is said to have been one of the daughters of the legendary prince, Brychan, who gave his name to BRECON. The name was recorded in a document of about 1173 as *Lan Elli*, and until the fairly recent 'correction' of Welsh place-names it was popularly spelt as Llanelly. Non-Welsh visitors still frequently mispronounce the name as 'Lanelthy', making a gallant attempt at one of the notorious Welsh *ll*s but ignoring the other altogether. *See also* LLANBERIS.

Llanfair Caereinion (Powys)
A small town west of WELSHPOOL whose name means 'St Mary's church by Einion's fort'. 'Llanfair' represents the Welsh *llan* (church) and *Mair* (Mary), here in its 'mutated' form as *Fair* after the feminine singular noun *llan*. Llanfair is such a common name that it frequently needs to have a differentiating addition. Here it is Caereinion, referring to a nearby Roman fort (Welsh *caer*) on the River Einion, which runs through the town. *See also* LLANBERIS.

Llanfairfechan (Gwynedd)
A small resort halfway between BANGOR and CONWY whose name means 'Little St Mary's Church', with '-fechan' representing the Welsh *bychan* (little), added to distinguish this St Mary's church (where all the services are in Welsh) from the larger church of the same name at Conwy (where they are not). (For the origin of Llanfair *see* LLANFAIR CAEREINION.) It has been said that the abundance of St Mary's churches is due to an Anglo-Norman preference for a dedication to the Virgin Mary instead of an obscure Welsh saint, so that many church dedications were changed in this way after the Conquest.

Llanfairpwllgwyngyll (Gwynedd)
This is the shortest postally acceptable version of the notorious lengthy Welsh place-name, that of a village in ANGLESEY. The full, contrived version, artificially devised in the nineteenth century (apparently by a local tailor) is Llanfairpwllgwyngyllgogerychwyrndro-bwllllandysiliogogogoch, and is based on the village's own original name with the names of other villages and parishes added. As it stands it means 'St Mary's church near the pool of the white hazel near the fierce whirlpool and St Tysilio's church by the cave'. Not to be outdone, a Welsh wit has recently concocted an even longer name for a village near BARMOUTH, for details of which the curious reader is referred to the *Guinness Book of Records*. *See also* LLANBERIS.

Llanfyllin (Powys)
A small town northwest of WELSHPOOL whose name means 'St Myllin's church'. Hardly anything is known about the saint to whom the parish church here is dedicated. The name was recorded in 1254 as *Llanvelig*. *See also* LLANBERIS.

Llangammarch Wells (Powys)
As with LLANDRINDOD WELLS, the final word of this name announces it to be a spa, and in fact the village is only four miles from another, LLANWRTYD WELLS. The first word of the name means 'church (by the River) Cammarch', on which the village stands. For further details about 'Llan-' names *see* LLANBERIS.

Llangefni (Gwynedd)
This market town in ANGLESEY takes its name from the River Cefni, on which it stands, with the initial 'Llan-', as in all

similar names, meaning 'church' (*see*
LLANBERIS). The river's name may mean
'stream from the ridge', from the Welsh
cefn (back, ridge). A document of 1254
records the name as *Llangevni*.

Llangollen (Clwyd)

A town, southwest of WREXHAM, whose
name means 'St Collen's church'. The saint
is said to have been a former soldier in the
Roman army who came to Britain in the
seventh century to become Abbot of
GLASTONBURY. The town's parish church
is dedicated to St Collen, as one would
expect, and the name was recorded in 1234
as *Lancollien*. *See also* LLANBERIS for
comments on 'Llan-' names.

Llanidloes (Powys)

This small town southwest of NEWTOWN
has a name that means 'St Idloes' church';
it was recorded in a document of 1254 as
Lanidloes, almost as now. The saint is said
to have been active here in the seventh
century. Local residents quite frequently
refer to the town affectionately as 'Llani'.
See also LLANBERIS.

Llanrwst (Gwynedd)

The name of this small town south of
COLWYN BAY means 'St Grwst's church'.
Little is known about the Celtic saint. In a
document of 1254, the name appears as
Lhannruste. *See also* LLANBERIS.

Llanthony (Gwent)

To non-Welshmen, the name may
suggest a church dedicated to Anthony,
but the name actually relates to the
River Honddu on which the village stands,
north of ABERGAVENNY. The Welsh
name of Llanthony is Llanddewi Nant
Hodni, showing that the church here is
actually dedicated to St David (Welsh
Dewi) and that the *Nant* of the
original name, meaning 'valley', has
been replaced by *Llan-* (church).
The name was recorded in the twelfth
century as *Lanthotheni*. *See also*
LLANBERIS.

Llantrisant (Gwent)

A village south of USK whose name
declares its parish church to be dedicated
to three saints (Welsh *tri*, 'three' and *sant*,
'saint'), who are respectively Illtyd,
Tyfodwg, and Gwynno. Such a name is not
unusual, and resembles that of the hamlet
near CARMARTHEN named Llanpumsaint,
'church of five saints'. Llantrisant was
recorded in a text of 1246 as *Landtrissen*.
See also LLANBERIS.

Llantwit Major (South Glamorgan)

A town west of BARRY whose name has a
first word meaning 'St Illtyd's church', the
named saint having founded a monastery
here in the sixth century. The town is
'Major' by contrast with Llantwit Fardre in
Mid Glamorgan, and Llantwit-juxta-Neath
in West Glamorgan; here the additional
words mean respectively 'by the steward's
house' and 'near NEATH'. The Welsh
names of the three places are: Llanilltud
Fawr; Llanilltud Faertref; and Llanilltud
Fach, the last meaning 'Little Llantwit', or
'Llantwit Minor'. For comments on 'Llan-'
names *see* LLANBERIS.

Llanwrtyd Wells (Powys)

As its name indicates, Llanwrtyd Wells is a
spa with a church dedicated to St Gwrtud.
It is in fact only four miles from a similarly
named place, LLANGAMMARCH WELLS,
itself not far from the larger BUILTH
WELLS; all three places are on the same
River Irfon. The name of Llanwrtyd Wells
properly applies to the nearby much older
village of Llanwrtyd, as the present spa
developed only in the nineteenth century.
It should also be said that the village
church is now dedicated to St David, not St
Gwrtud, about whom nothing is known.
See also LLANBERIS.

Lleyn Peninsula (Gwynedd)

This peninsula, also known as The Lleyn,
lies between CAERNARVON Bay and
CARDIGAN Bay, and has a name of
uncertain origin. It may derive from the
tribal name of Celtic people here, known to

the Romans as the *Lagenii*, with their own name perhaps coming from that of LEINSTER, in Ireland, from where they may have emigrated. The Welsh name of the peninsula is simply Llŷn.

Loanhead (Lothian)
A town south of EDINBURGH whose name indicates its location at the top ('head') of a 'loan', a Scottish word equivalent to 'lane'. No doubt the original 'loan' was one that ran up from the North ESK river here. The name was recorded in a document of 1618 as *Loneheid*.

Lochaber (Highland)
The name of this administrative district in the southwest of the region derives from that of the area here, extending generally east of Glen More (the 'Great Glen'), from Loch LEVEN and Loch Linnhe to Loch LOCHY and Glen Spean. The name means 'lake at the confluence', from the Gaelic *loch* (lake) and the Celtic *aber* (river-mouth, confluence), usually found as the first element in place-names, as in ABERDEEN and ABERNETHY. There is no actual Loch Lochaber here now, but there may once have been, its having now dried up. However, Lochaber Loch southwest of DUNDEE still exists, and its name has exactly the same origin and meaning.

Lochgelly (Fife)
This coal-mining town southwest of GLENROTHES takes its name from the small Loch Gelly to the southeast of it. The loch's name means 'bright', 'shining', from the Gaelic *geal* in this sense. The name was recorded in a document of 1606 as *Lochgellie*.

Lochgilphead (Strathclyde)
A town south of OBAN at the head of Loch Gilp, as its name indicates. The loch's name describes its shape and means 'chisel', from the Gaelic *gilb* in this sense. The name was recorded as *Lochgilpshead* in a text of 1650.

Lochinvar (Dumfries and Galloway)
The name of this loch northeast of DALRY is well known from its association with 'Young Lochinvar', the hero of Sir Walter Scott's *Marmion*, who lived in a castle on a small island in the loch. The name means 'loch on the height', from the Gaelic *loch an bharra* (*compare* BARRHEAD), referring to its location among hills.

Lochinver (Highland)
A small fishing port and resort north of ULLAPOOL at the head of Loch Inver, from which it takes its name. The name describes its location, with the second element, meaning 'river-mouth', more familiar as the first element of a name, as with INVERNESS and other places.

Lochmaben (Dumfries and Galloway)
This small town northeast of DUMFRIES is surrounded by several small lochs, but none of them is called 'Maben'. The town's name must therefore have some other origin, although opinions differ as to what it is. The second part of the name may be a personal name, perhaps that of a pagan god.

Lochnagar (Grampian)
A mountain ridge southeast of BRAEMAR that takes its name from the small loch below it, whose own name means 'loch of the outcrop', Gaelic *loch na gaire*.

Lochy, Loch (Highland)
A loch in Glen More ('the Great Glen') in the LOCHABER district; its name means 'dark one', from the Gaelic *lochaidh*.

Lockerbie (Dumfries and Galloway)
This market town east of DUMFRIES has an Old Norse name meaning 'Locard's farm', with the final element of the name the Old Norse *bý* (farm), more familiar as the final '-by' of many English names. The name was recorded as *Lokardebi* in a document of 1306.

Loddon (Norfolk)
A small town northwest of BECCLES on the

River Chet. The river was formerly called the Loddon; it has the same meaning as that of the River Loddon in Hampshire and Berkshire, which is 'muddy one', from a conjectural British (Celtic) word *lutá*. This also lies behind the original name of Paris, the French capital, which was Lutetia. The River Chet takes its name from the village of Chedgrave, which adjoins Loddon on the other side of the river.

Lomond, Loch (Central/Strathclyde)
One of the best-known lochs in Britain, as well as being the largest inland stretch of water. Its name comes from the nearby mountain of Ben Lomond, itself from a Celtic word meaning 'beacon hill' (*compare* PLYNLIMON). The Lomond Hills on the border of FIFE and TAYSIDE have the same origin for their name.

London (Greater London)
The capital city of the United Kingdom has a name that is internationally famous but unfortunately has no internationally accepted origin, or indeed any reliable explanation at all. It was long held to derive from a conjectural Celtic or pre-Celtic root element *londo-*, said to mean 'bold' and to have possibly given a personal or tribal name, such as *Londinos*. But this theory is now discredited, and the true origin remains unexplained. The Roman name for it was *Londinium*, and some versions of the name with '-chester' (denoting a Roman settlement) have been recorded, such as *Lundenceaster* in about 890. It is clearly a very old name, and the settlement here an ancient one, which no doubt accounts for the obscurity of the name. *See also* LONDONDERRY.

Londonderry (Londonderry)
The Irish name of this well-known city in the north of Northern Ireland is Doire, meaning 'oak wood', with this name found for several other places in Ireland. In the early seventeenth century it acquired its addition, when James I granted a charter authorizing merchants from LONDON to make a settlement here. As well as preserving the 'colonial' link, the addition served to distinguish this Derry from other places of the name. Today the original version of the name is preferred by many, and is postally acceptable. The town gave its name to the county.

Long, Loch (Strathclyde)
This narrow sea loch running north from the Firth of CLYDE does *not* have a name that means 'long loch'! Like the majority of lochs, it has a Gaelic name, meaning 'ship loch' (Gaelic *long* 'ship'). The loch would have been a safe anchorage for ships that had sailed up the Clyde.

Long Eaton (Derbyshire)
This manufacturing town east of DERBY is almost surrounded on three sides by the rivers EREWASH and TRENT, and it is clear that the name relates directly to such a location, with the second and principal word meaning 'island farm', from the Old English *ēg* (island) and *tūn* (farm) (*compare* ETON). 'Long' means that the farm or estate extended further than that at Little Eaton, a village north of Derby. The name was recorded in the Domesday Book as *Aitone*, and in a document of 1288 as *Long Eyton*.

Longford (Longford)
The chief town of the county with the same name, in central Ireland. The name wrongly suggests a 'long ford' here. In fact the name is a rendering of the Irish An Longfort, 'the fortress' (Irish *longphort*). Longford was formerly the site of a fortress of the O Farrels, although no trace of it now exists. The county name derives from that of the town.

Longleat (Wiltshire)
Longleat House is the Renaissance mansion and seat of the Marquess of BATH, west of WARMINSTER. It takes its name from the long water-channel or 'leat' that flowed here and that was flooded to form ornamental lakes when the house was built

in the late sixteenth century. The name was recorded in a document of 1325 as *la Langelete*, with the two component elements ultimately deriving from the Old English *lang* (long) and *gelǣt* (channel, conduit). The latter word is seen also in the name of RADLETT.

Long Melford (Suffolk)

A small town north of SUDBURY on a tributary of the River OUSE. 'Melford' means 'mill ford', and is recorded in the Domesday Book as *Melaforda*. 'Long' means that the ford extended for some distance from one bank to the other, as distinct from one that was 'broad' or wide.

Long Mynd, The (Shropshire)

This range of hills southwest of SHREWSBURY has a half English and half Welsh name (as one might expect in Border country), from the Old English *lang* (long) and the Welsh *mynydd* (hill). The name thus simply means 'the long hill', referring to the central ridge of the hills. The name was recorded in a twelfth-century document as *Longameneda*. *Compare* LONGRIDGE.

Longridge (Lancashire)

A town northeast of PRESTON that takes its name from Longridge Fell, the ridge to the northeast, whose own name is self-explanatory. The name goes back to at least the thirteenth century, when it was recorded as *Longryge*.

Longtown (Cumbria)

This small town north of CARLISLE has a self-explanatory name, relating to its location alongside the River ESK. It was recorded as *Longeton* in a document of 1267. *Compare* the name of LANGHOLM, north of it on the same river.

Looe (Cornwall)

A coastal town south of LISKEARD whose name represents the conjectural Old Cornish word *loch* (pool, creek), ultimately related to the Scottish *loch* and English

lake. The name is properly that of the river here, which divides the town into East Looe and West Looe. The name was recorded in a document of 1301 as now.

Lossiemouth (Grampian)

A fishing port and resort north of ELGIN at the mouth of the River Lossie, as its name indicates. The river name perhaps means 'herbs', 'plants', and is of Gaelic origin. The fact that the name is not 'Inverlossie', as might be expected, shows that Lossiemouth arose relatively recently; it was in fact laid out in the final years of the seventeenth century, when the harbour was built here.

Lostwithiel (Cornwall)

A town on the River FOWEY southeast of BODMIN. Its name consists of three Cornish elements: these are *lost* (tail), *gwyth* (trees), and a conjectural adjectival suffix *-yel*. This means that the town is at the 'tail' end of a district with many trees formerly known as 'Withiel'. Put more simply, this means that Lostwithiel is the 'place at the end of the wood'. The surrounding countryside is still well wooded, especially to the north. The name was recorded in 1194 as *Lostwetell*.

Lothian (Scotland)

An administrative region on the southern flank of the FIRTH OF FORTH. The name's origin remains uncertain. It may be a tribal name, possibly relating to one Leudonus, although nothing is known about him. The name was recorded in the tenth century as *Loonia*. The region is now divided into the districts of East Lothian, Midlothian, West Lothian, and EDINBURGH City.

Loughborough (Leicestershire)

This manufacturing town north of LEICESTER has a name that means 'Luhhede's fortified place', with the personal name followed by the Old English *burg* (fortified place), here occurring as '-borough' instead of the more common '-bury'. The Domesday Book recorded the name with a slight copying error, as *Lucteburne* (with *n* instead of *u*).

Loughor (West Glamorgan)

An industrial location northwest of SWANSEA that takes its name from the river on which it stands, with the river's own name of Celtic origin and meaning 'shining one' (ultimately related to the Latin *lux* and Greek *leukos*, both meaning 'light'). The Welsh name of Loughor is Casllwchwr, 'castle by the (River) Loughor', referring to a former Norman castle here. The Romans called the river by the name of *Leuca*, with the origin as explained. The name is pronounced 'Loocher', with the *ch* as in Scottish 'loch'.

Loughrea (Galway)

This small market town northeast of GORT takes its name from Lough Rea here, whose own name means 'grey lake'. The town's Irish name is Baile Locha Riach.

Loughton (Essex)

A town to the east of EPPING Forest whose name means 'Luca's village'; it was recorded in a document of 1062 as *Lukintone*.

Louth (Louth, Lincolnshire)

Either of two places, one in Ireland, the other in England. The Irish county, in the northeast of the Republic, takes its name from the small village of Louth, southwest of DUNDALK. Its Irish name is Lú, which represents a former much longer name, *Lughmhaigh*. The latter half of this is the Irish *magh* (plain), but the first part of the name remains of uncertain origin. It does not seem to be a personal name. The Lincolnshire town of Louth, south of GRIMSBY, takes its name from the river on which it lies. This is the Lud, whose own name means 'loud one', from the Old English *hlūd*, seen also as the first element in the name of LUDLOW. The site here was referred to in a text of the late eighth century as *Hludensis monasterium*.

Lowestoft (Suffolk)

This coastal town south of Great YARMOUTH has an Old Norse name meaning 'Hlothver's dwelling place', with the personal name followed by the Danish *toft* (originally meaning 'building site') that is found in many village and hamlet names in Yorkshire, the East Midlands, and East Anglia, that is, inside the Danelaw. The Domesday Book recorded Lowestoft as *Lothu Wistoft*.

Lowther Hills (Strathclyde/Dumfries and Galloway)

A range of hills lying between SANQUHAR and MOFFAT. The general name follows that of the names of the range's two highest mountains, respectively Green Lowther and Lowther Hill. The origin of the name remains obscure, and there are no grounds for linking it with LAUDER, as some have sought to do.

Lucan (Dublin)

A small town and former spa west of DUBLIN whose name means 'place of elms', represented in its Irish name of Leamhcán.

Ludgershall (Wiltshire)

This military town northwest of ANDOVER has a name that has been much disputed over the years. The present opinion of many toponymists is that it means 'secluded place of the trapping spear', from the Old English *lūtegār* (trapping spear) and *healh* (nook, secluded place). A 'trapping spear' is a spear set as a trap for impaling wild animals. The name was recorded in the Domesday Book as *Litlegarsele*, a distorted form that caused much of the problem. In a document of 1190, however, the origin is more recognisable in *Lutegareshala*. A 'secluded place' would be a suitable site to set such a trap, and for Ludgershall this may have been one of the valleys that run into the flat-topped hill on which the present town stands, by the remains of the old castle.

Ludlow (Shropshire)

This town southwest of BRIDGNORTH stands on a hill above the River Teme, and its name refers to both these natural features, deriving from the Old English *hlūd* (loud), describing the river as a noisy torrent (*compare* LOUTH), and *hlāw* (hill). Ludlow is thus a place 'on a hill by the loud river'. It was recorded in a document of 1138 as *Ludelawe*.

Lulworth Cove (Dorset)

A circular bay southwest of WAREHAM that derives its name from the village of West Lulworth (or possibly East Lulworth) here; 'Lulworth' means 'Lulla's enclosure'. The name was recorded in the Domesday Book as *Lulvorde*. The actual cove is referred to in a document of 1539 as *the Creke of Lulworthe*.

Lundy (Devon)

This island at the entrance to the BRISTOL Channel is famous for its puffins, and this is what its name means, 'puffin island', from the Old Norse *lundi* (puffin) and *ey* (island). The island was referred to in a text of 1189 as *Insula de Lundeia*.

Lune (Cumbria/Lancashire)

A river that rises north of SEDBURGH and flows southwestward to MORECAMBE Bay. The name is of Celtic origin meaning 'health-giving one' (the root element for this is *lon-*), perhaps referring to its water god, who was invoked to heal the sick. The name lies behind that of KIRKBY LONSDALE, as well as LANCASTER, and is related to the name of the Irish River SLANEY. It was recorded in a document of the mid-twelfth century as *Loin*.

Lurgan (Armagh)

This town immediately north of CRAIGAVON has a name that is found elsewhere in Ireland and means 'strip of land', from the Irish *lorg*, literally 'shin', 'leg'. The implication is of land on a long low 'shin-like' hill.

Luton (Bedfordshire)

This well-known industrial town has a name whose origin and meaning are exactly the same as those of LEYTON; it means 'farm on the River Lea', which rises north of it and flows through it. The reason for the different forms of the name is uncertain. Luton was recorded in the late eighth century as *Lygetun*, in the Domesday Book as *Loitone*, and as both *Lowton* and *Leuton* in the late thirteenth century. For the possible origin of the river name *see* LEYTON. *See also* LUTON HOO.

Luton Hoo (Bedfordshire)

A mansion located two miles southeast of LUTON. Its name is derived from that of the town, with 'Hoo' added to mean 'spur of land', from the Old English *hōh*. This same word lies behind the names of HUGH TOWN and PLYMOUTH Hoe, the elevated tract of land fronting on to Plymouth Sound.

Lutterworth (Leicestershire)

This town northeast of RUGBY has a rather problematical name. It is clearly a '-worth' name, with this element meaning 'enclosure', but the first part of the name presents difficulties. It does not seem to be a personal name, as is frequently the case. An examination of early forms of the name, and a consideration of the topography (the town is on the River Swift) suggests that the first half of the name may derive from an earlier name of the river. This could have been something like *Hlūtre*, meaning 'clean one', originating from the Old English *hlūttor* (clear, bright, clean). The Domesday Book recorded Lutterworth as *Lutresurde*.

Luxulyan (Cornwall)

A village southwest of LOSTWITHIEL whose name is probably based on the conjectural Cornish *loc* (chapel), followed by the personal name Sulian, that of the abbot who founded a monastery here in the sixth century. Rather loosely, therefore, the name can be understood as 'St Sulian's church'. This seems to be the only place in Cornwall with a *loc* name, and the fact that there are many similar names in Brittany suggests that Sulian was a Breton saint in origin. (The Breton names include Locmaria, 'St Mary's church'; Locronan, 'St Ronan's church'; and Loctudy, 'St Tudy's church'. For this last name, compare the Cornish village of St Tudy.) Luxulyan was recorded in a document of 1329 as *Lauxsolian*.

Lydd (Kent)
A town northwest of DUNGENESS whose name represents the Old English *hlid* (slope); more precisely it derives from the dative plural of this noun after the preposition 'at' (Old English *æt thāra hlidum*, 'at the slopes'). Lydd arose on a slight slope above the marsh here. Its name was recorded as *Hlide* in about 1100.

Lydney (Gloucestershire)
A small town northeast of CHEPSTOW whose name probably means 'Lida's island', from the personal name (which happens to be the Old English word for 'sailor') followed by *ēg* (island). The town is situated between two streams which flow into the SEVERN not far from here, hence the 'island'. The name appears in a document of 972 as *Lidaneg*.

Lyme Regis (Dorset)
This small resort takes its name from the River Lyme on which it stands, with the river's own name of British (Celtic) origin, and meaning simply 'flood'. The place, which was simply *Lime* in the Domesday Book, acquired its royal suffix at the end of the thirteenth century, when Edward I declared it a free borough.

Lymington (Hampshire)
A residential town and yachting centre east of BOURNEMOUTH that takes its name from the river on which it stands. Today this is also the Lymington, but originally it may have been something like *Limen*, meaning 'elm river'. (*Compare* the name of

the Leam, which gave the name of LEAMINGTON SPA; *see also* LYMPNE.) In the Domesday Book, Lymington appeared as *Lentune*.

Lymm (Cheshire)
This town east of WARRINGTON stands on a stream that joins the MERSEY to the north, and it seems likely that this stream could have been called something like *Hlimme*, deriving from the Old English *hlimme* (noisy stream, torrent), thus giving the town its name. Lymm appeared in the Domesday Book as *Lime*.

Lympne (Kent)
This village west of HYTHE takes its name from the river on which it stands. Today this is the ROTHER, but its earlier name was the Lympne, which is of Celtic origin, meaning 'elm' and deriving from the same root that gave the names of LEAMINGTON SPA, LYMINGTON, and ASHTON-UNDER-LYNE, among other places. The Roman name of the river was *Lemana*, and the Roman fort here was called *Portus Lemanis*; these names have the same origin.

Lyndhurst (Hampshire)
This small town north of LYMINGTON has a straightforward name that means 'lime-tree wood', from the Old English *lind* (lime) and *hyrst* (copse, wood). The town could hardly have any other name, as the so-called 'capital of the NEW FOREST', although the trees of the Forest are by no means exclusively or even predominantly limes. Lyndhurst was recorded in the Domesday Book as *Linhest*.

Lynmouth (Devon)
A small resort at the mouth of the River Lyn (as its name indicates) beneath the cliff on which LYNTON stands. The river's name probably derives from the Old English *hlynn* (noisy one, torrent). Lynmouth appears in a text dated 1330 as *Lymmouth*.

Lynton (Devon)

A clifftop resort northeast of BARNSTAPLE that takes its name from the River Lyn, which flows through the town to enter the sea at LYNMOUTH below. (For the meaning of the river's name, see the previous entry.) Lynton's name thus originally meant 'farm on the Lyn', and was recorded as *Linton* in the Domesday Book.

Lytham St Anne's (Lancashire)

This coastal resort west of PRESTON has a compound name, resulting from the amalgamation in 1922 of the two separate towns of Lytham and St Anne's. The former name means 'at the slopes', and is exactly the same in origin, even grammatically so, as that of LYDD; the final element of the name (the grammatical ending) is altered to '-ham', although it is not a true '-ham' name. St Anne's is named after its church, which was the first building to be erected in the newly planned town when it began to develop in the late nineteenth century.

M

Mablethorpe (Lincolnshire)

A North Sea resort whose name is popularly associated with 'Mabel'. Its true origin, however, is in the Old French personal name Malbert. The name thus means 'Malbert's outlying settlement', with the second half of the name representing the Old Norse *thorp*, used of secondary or outlying settlements that were dependent on a larger place. The personal name shows that Mablethorpe's name arose after the Norman Conquest. It was recorded in the Domesday Book as *Malbertorp*.

Macclesfield (Cheshire)

A town south of STOCKPORT whose name probably means 'Maccel's open land', with the 'open land' (Old English *feld*) doubtless part of the former forest that was here in the PEAK DISTRICT, to the east of Macclesfield. The name was recorded in the Domesday Book as *Maclesfeld*.

Macduff (Grampian)

A small fishing town east of BANFF that takes its name from James Duff, second Earl of FIFE, who rebuilt the settlement here at the end of the eighteenth century. The Earl claimed to be descended from the semi-mythical Macduff who features in Shakespeare's *Macbeth*, although he named the town directly after his father, William Duff, the first Earl, who had acquired the land here earlier in the century. Scottish 'Mac-' in surnames means 'son of', so the name reflects this tribute from a son to his father.

Macgillycuddy's Reeks (Kerry)

These mountains southwest of KILLARNEY were a place of refuge for the powerful sept (tribal unit) of the MacGillycuddys, whose modern family head still bears the title of 'MacGillicuddy of the Reeks'. This is therefore the origin of the name, with 'Reeks' meaning 'ridges'. The Irish name of the mountains is quite different: Na Cruacha Dubha, 'the black peaks'.

Machynlleth (Powys)

A small market town northeast of ABERYSTWYTH whose name means 'Cynllaith's plain', with the first element of the name representing the British (Celtic) word for 'plain', seen in MAGHERA, among other names. It is not known who Cynllaith was. Some tourist guides say that Machynlleth was the former Roman station of *Maglona*, but there is no historical basis for this. *Maglona* was probably the Roman fort at Old CARLISLE, south of WIGTON in Cumbria. The 'plain' of the name, or part of it, was the tract of open land on the left bank of the River DOVEY here. The name itself was recorded in a document of 1254 as *Machenleyd*.

Macroom (Cork)

A market town west of CORK whose name is a 'smoothing' of its Irish equivalent, which is Maigh Chromtha, 'crooked plain'. This can be understood as a plain that is not level, i.e. one that slopes, as is the case here to the north and east of the town.

Maentwrog (Gwynedd)

A village northeast of PENRHYNDEUDRAETH whose name means 'Twrog's stone', with the personal name said to be that of a sixth-century saint. The actual stone is a plain round block, about four feet high, at the southwest corner of St Twrog's church. The Welsh *maen* means 'stone'.

Maesteg (Mid Glamorgan)

This town east of PORT TALBOT arose only in the nineteenth century, and took its name from the original field site: the Welsh *maes teg* thus means 'fair field'. This very local name was recorded in the sixteenth century as *Maes tege issa*, literally 'lower fair field'. The name thus corresponds to those places in England named Fairfield.

Maghera (Londonderry)

A small town south of COLERAINE whose name means simply 'plain', from the Irish *machaire*. The present Irish name of the town is therefore Machaire, or in a fuller version, Machaire Rátha, 'plain of the fort'. The name is found elsewhere in Ireland. *Compare* MAGHERAFELT.

Magherafelt (Londonderry)

A small town northeast of COOKSTOWN whose name means 'plain of Fíolta', as represented by its Irish equivalent name of Machaire Fíolta. *Compare* MAGHERA.

Maghull (Merseyside)

Maghull (pronounced '*Ma*gull', with the second syllable stressed) is a town north of LIVERPOOL whose name probably means 'mayweed nook', from the Old English *mægthe* (mayweed) and *halh* (nook). There is no obvious 'nook' or secluded site here, and the name may have been influenced by the Old English *hyll* (hill), which suits the topography rather better. The Domesday Book recorded the name as *Magele*.

Maida Vale (Greater London)

This district northwest of CHARING CROSS was developed on a section of WATLING STREET in or around the mid-nineteenth century, and was named commemoratively for the Battle of Maida in 1806 (in Calabria, Italy), when Sir John Stuart defeated the French. The 'vale' of the name arose because the new houses were built at the foot of a hill, which was called Maida Hill. The name *Maida* appears on a large-scale map of LONDON published in 1822. The association with 'maid' (as in MAIDENHEAD) may have helped the name.

Maidenhead (Berkshire)

This town on the THAMES west of SLOUGH has a name that is usually regarded as meaning 'maidens' landing-place', from the Old English *mægden* (maiden, young unmarried woman) and *hÿth* (landing-place) (as in names such as HYTHE and ROTHERHITHE). The second half of the

name is thus not '-head', as can be proved by early records of the name, such as *Maidenhee* in 1202, and *Maydenhith* in 1262. The question remains as to how the 'maidens' were associated with the river in this way. It could simply have been that the 'landing-place' was one where young women gathered regularly, without any suggestion of them actually landing there. A landing-place, after all, is a place where there is activity, and a constant coming and going. The river itself is also a constant attraction in its own right. *Compare* MAIDSTONE.

Maidstone (Kent)

The county town on the River MEDWAY, whose name was recorded in the Domesday Book as *Medestan*, representing the Old English *mægden* (maiden) and *stān* (stone). The name is thus similar to MAIDENHEAD, denoting a meeting-place of young unmarried women and girls. But here, the stone (wherever it was) was probably the focal point for rituals or customs. However, some toponymists prefer a derivation from the Old English *mægth* (folk, people), meaning that the stone was an assembly point for judicial or administrative purposes, so that the name may thus be similar to FOLKESTONE. Support for this theory is provided by Maidstone's long and continuing history as an administrative centre; also, it was the former capital town of western Kent.

Mainland (Orkney, Shetland)

Either of two islands, one in the ORKNEY Islands, the other in the SHETLAND Islands. In each case the name is self-explanatory, applying to the largest or 'main' island in each group. The islands are not simply the largest, but the most important from an administrative point of view. The name, however, is not English in origin, but Old Norse, from *megin* 'main' (as in the phrase 'might and main', implying strength) and *land* 'land'.

Malahide (Dublin)

This small seaside town north of DUBLIN has a difficult name, tradition-ally interpreted as 'Íde's hill-top', representing its Irish name of Mallach Íde. Some, however, derive it from the personal name of John de la Hyde (or some similar spelling), a landowner here in the thirteenth century. The former explanation seems the more plausible.

Maldon (Essex)

A town east of CHELMSFORD whose name means 'hill with a cross', from the Old English *mæl* (cross, crucifix) and *dūn* (hill). Maldon stands in a commanding position above the River BLACKWATER, and it is likely that the Anglo-Saxons erected a cross or crucifix here as a focus for religious services, perhaps on the site now occupied by All Saints Church. The name was recorded in a document of 913 as *Mældun*. *Compare* NEW MALDEN.

Malin Head (Donegal)

Ireland's most northerly point, familiar from radio weather forecasts, has a name that derives from the Irish *malainn* (brow), a suitable name for the headland's 'beetling' cliffs. The Irish name of the headland is simply Malainn.

Mallaig (Highland)

A small fishing port north of ARISAIG with an Old Norse name meaning 'gull bay', from *már* (gull) and *vík* (bay), the latter represented in the name by the Norse-Gaelic *aig*.

Mallow (Cork)

This market town northwest of CORK has a name that represents the Irish *Magh Eala*, 'plain of the Allow', the latter being the former name of the river (now the BLACKWATER) on which the town stands. The origin of the river's name is unknown. The town's current Irish name is Mala.

Malmesbury (Wiltshire)

A town west of SWINDON whose name means 'Mailduf's fortified place', with the Old English *burg* following the personal name. One would have expected the present name to be something like 'Malesbury' if the personal name had not been influenced by that of Bishop Aldhelm, who built a monument and chapel on the site of Mailduf's cell here in the seventh century; Mailduf is said to have been the original founder of the monastery. The blend of the two men's names produced the second *m* in the place-name (from Aldhel*m*). Mailduf is actually an Irish name, meaning 'black chief'. The town's name was recorded in the early eighth century as *Maildufi urbs*, and as *Maldulfes burgh* in the late ninth century.

Malpas (Cheshire)

This town east of WREXHAM has a name of Old French origin meaning literally 'bad pass', that is, referring to a place of difficult passage. There are other places of the name, and in most instances the reference is to marshy terrain or a very muddy track. This Cheshire Malpas replaced an earlier name, which was *Depenbech*, meaning '(place at the) deep valley with a stream'. Its present name was recorded in a document of about 1125 with the spelling as now. The town is not actually in a 'bad pass', but on a hill above it.

Maltby (South Yorkshire)

A town east of ROTHERHAM whose name means 'Malti's farm', with the Scandinavian personal name followed by the Old Norse *bý* (farm, village). It was recorded in the Domesday Book as *Maltebi*.

Malton (North Yorkshire)

This town northeast of YORK has a name that is a Scandinavian version of the English Melton (as for MELTON MOWBRAY); it thus means 'middle farm'. The Domesday Book recorded the name as *Maltune*. There was a Roman fort at

Malton named *Derventio*, deriving from the name of the river on which the town stands, the DERWENT.

Malvern Hills (Hereford and Worcester)
The Malvern Hills have given their name to a modern administrative district (Malvern Hills); to the town of Great Malvern on their eastern slope, southwest of WORCESTER; to the village of Little Malvern, south of Great Malvern; to the village of West Malvern, west of the town; to the smaller location of Malvern Wells, south of the town; and to the district of Great Malvern known as Malvern Link. The basic name is Welsh and means 'bare hill', from *moel* (bare, bald) (*compare* MOEL HEBOG and MOEL SYCH) and *bryn* (hill) (*compare* BRYNMAWR). Great Malvern has a prefix that distinguishes it from Little Malvern. The 'Link' of the last name listed here means 'hill-slope', from the Old English *hlinc* (ridge, bank), as found also in golf 'links' and the name of SHANKLIN. The Domesday Book recorded Malvern as *Malferna*.

Mam Tor (Derbyshire)
A hill west of CASTERTON whose name probably means 'breast-shaped hill', from a British (Celtic) conjectural word *mamma* (related to modern 'mammary' and 'mama') and the Old English *torr* (rocky peak), as found in names in southwest England, such as YES TOR and TORQUAY (*compare also* MANCHESTER). The name was recorded in a document of 1577 as *Manhill*, and in a text of 1630 as *Mantaur*. The hill is also known as Shivering Mountain, because of the frequent landslides on its southern face.

Man, Isle of
The name of this well-known island in the Irish Sea is said to be linked with that of Manannan mac Lir, an Irish god whose own name may perhaps mean 'king of the land of promise'. The Roman name of the island was *Monapia*, and this may well be associated in turn with the Roman name of

ANGLESEY, which was *Mona* and means simply 'mountain' (compare Welsh *mynydd*). It may well be that the sense of 'mountain' lies behind the name of the Isle of Man, no doubt referring to the mountainous mass that culminates in SNAEFELL in the centre of the island. The adjective 'Manx' is of Old Norse origin (*mansk*; compare *norsk* as the Norwegian for 'Norwegian', and *dansk* as the Danish for 'Danish'), and the Scandinavian presence in the island is well reflected in its place-names. The Manx name for the island itself is Ellan Vannan, 'island of Man'.

Manchester (Greater Manchester)
This well-known city in northwest England has an indicator in its name (the '-chester') that it was once a Roman station. The Roman name for it was *Mamucium* (not 'Mancunium', as sometimes stated), which is based on the British (Celtic) word that also provides the 'Man-' of the modern name. This word was probably *mamma* (breast) (*compare* MAM TOR), describing the round hill on which the Roman fort was situated (probably at the confluence of the rivers Irwell and Medlock). Manchester was recorded as *Mameceaster* in a document of 923. The adjective 'Mancunian' seems to have derived from an early miscopying of the Roman name as *Mancunio*. *Compare also* MANSFIELD.

Mangotsfield (Avon)
A town northeast of BRISTOL whose name means 'Mangod's open land', with this recorded in the Domesday Book as *Mangodesfelle*. Many names ending in '-field' (Old English *feld*, 'open land') have a personal name for their first element, even where the place arose after the Norman Conquest (as did PETERSFIELD, for example).

Manningham (West Yorkshire)
A district of BRADFORD whose name means 'homestead of Mægen's people'; it

was recorded in a text of 1249 as *Maningeham*.

Manningtree (Essex)

This town northeast of COLCHESTER has a name that has traditionally been interpreted as 'Manna's tree', with the first element a personal name, as for BRAINTREE, COVENTRY, OSWESTRY, etc. The tree itself could have been one where people met for legal or other assemblies, or else a cross or crucifix erected by the named man. But more recently, it has been suggested that the name may actually mean simply '(place of) many trees', from the Old English *manig* (many). (Contrast the name of AINTREE.) The name was recorded as *Manitre* in a document of 1274.

Mannofield (Grampian)

This district of ABERDEEN apparently received its name from the eighteenth-century estate here of Robert Balmanno, who devised the name for it.

Manorbier (Dyfed)

A village southwest of TENBY whose name means 'Pyr's manor', Pyr being a sixth-century saint who gave his name to the Welsh name of CALDY ISLAND (which lies off the coast here in CARMARTHEN Bay). The Welsh name of Manorbier shows Pyr's name more clearly, as Maenorbyr. The name was recorded in a document of 1188 as *Mansio Pyrri*.

Manorhamilton (Leitrim)

A small town southeast of BUNDORAN whose name derives from that of Sir Frederick Hamilton, to whom lands here were granted by Charles I in the first half of the seventeenth century. (The remains of Sir Frederick's fortified house can still be seen just north of the town.) The Irish name of Manorhamilton is Cluainín, 'little meadow'.

Mansfield (Nottinghamshire)

This manufacturing town near KIRKBY IN ASHFIELD takes its name from the River Maun, on which it stands, with '-field' here meaning 'open land' (Old English *feld*). The river's name comes from a hill, four miles southwest of the town. The hill was formerly called *Mammesheud*, meaning 'headland of Mam'; the latter is not a personal name but that of the hill itself, and doubtless derives from the same Celtic *mamma* (breast) that gave the names of MANCHESTER and MAM TOR. Mansfield was recorded in the Domesday Book as *Mamesfelde*. *See also* MANSFIELD WOODHOUSE.

Mansfield Woodhouse (Nottinghamshire)

A town immediately north of MANSFIELD, after which it takes its basic name. The second word of the name means 'woodland hamlet', 'houses in woodland', and the name overall implies that a separate settlement was established here by people who came from Mansfield. The name was recorded in 1230 simply as *Wodehuse*, but in 1280 as *Mamesfeud Wodehus*.

Marazion (Cornwall)

A small town east of PENZANCE whose name, despite its exotic appearance, simply means 'little market', from the Cornish *marghas* (market) and *byghan* (little); it was recorded in a text dated 1372 as *Marghasbighan*. Presumably the market here was 'little' by comparison with that at Penzance, three miles away. An alternative name of Marazion has long been Market Jew, with this still current as the name of one of the main streets of Penzance, Market Jew Street, leading from the Market Place in the direction of Marazion. It was believed that this name was a corruption of Marazion, but it has now been shown to derive from the Cornish *marghas* (as before) and *yow* (Thursday). This 'Thursday market' would itself have been a contrast to the 'little market'. This alternative name was recorded in 1291 as *Marchadion*. One of the most important industries of Marazion is still market-gardening.

March (Cambridgeshire)

This town east of PETERBOROUGH has a name that simply announces it to be a place on a boundary, from the Old English *mearc* (boundary; modern 'mark', as for a boundary mark). The question is, however, which boundary? March is not on a county boundary, although the old course of the River NENE here could certainly have served as some kind of boundary. It has been suggested that March may have been at the western boundary of the district of ELY (whose name means 'eel district'). March appears in the Domesday Book as *Merce*, and the use of the word occurs elsewhere to denote a borderland or a boundary, as for the Welsh Marches, the border country between England and Wales.

Margam (West Glamorgan)

A district of PORT TALBOT whose name is basically that of Morgan, who gave his name to GLAMORGAN.

Margate (Kent)

The name of this well-known coastal resort on the Isle of THANET northeast of CANTERBURY is usually explained as meaning 'sea gate', from the Old English *mere* (sea) and *geat* (gate, gap). A 'gate' usually leads to some special place, yet here any such gap would have simply led to the sea. It seems likely, therefore, that the other sense of *mere* is intended here, which was 'pool'. The name would then have referred to a gap in the cliffs by a particular pool, doubtless one that has now long dried up. (A further suggestion involves quite another sense, from an identical Old English word that meant 'mare'. 'The Mare' may have been a distinctively shaped rock somewhere on the coast here.) The name was recorded in 1254 as *Meregate*.

Market Bosworth (Leicestershire)

The name of this small town north of HINCKLEY has a first word that occurs in many other place-names (see below). In some cases 'Market' is used to differentiate places of identical name, denoting the one with a regular market. In other cases it simply emphasizes that the named place was a market town. In the case of Market Bosworth, the contrast is with the village of Husbands Bosworth, some twenty miles away, west (as it happens) of MARKET HARBOROUGH. The second word of the name means 'Bār's village'. (Husbands Bosworth suggests a 'husbandmen's village', that is, a rural place with an agrarian market, by contrast with the more 'commercial' market at Market Bosworth.) Market Bosworth was simply *Boseworde* in the Domesday Book.

Market Drayton (Shropshire)

A town northeast of SHREWSBURY. 'Drayton' is derived from the Old English *draeg* (drag) and *tūn* (farm, village); the first of these words is found only in place-names, and describes a place where something can be dragged, such as a portage on a river, or a place where boats can be dragged out of the water, or a 'slipway' where sleds can be dragged. In many cases, and certainly where no river is involved, it will be a place where timber can be dragged from a forest. Market Drayton is on the River Tern, so the 'dragging' must have been done on (or from) this. Many places called Drayton (and also Draycot) have a distinguishing word, and here it is 'Market' to describe the place's dominant commercial activity. The town is still an important agricultural centre. Its name was recorded in the Domesday Book simply as *Draitune*.

Market Harborough (Leicestershire)

This town southeast of LEICESTER has a truly agricultural name, meaning 'market place on the hill where oats are grown'. The second word of the name thus comes from the conjectural Old English *hæfera* (oats) (formerly carried in a *haver*sack) and *beorg* (hill). The first word emphasizes the commercial activity of the place (*see* MARKET BOSWORTH) rather than distinguishing it from any other

Harborough. Its name was recorded in a document of 1177 as *Hauerberga*.

Markethill (Armagh)
A small town southeast of ARMAGH with a self-descriptive name, whose Irish equivalent, Cnoc an Mhargaidh, means 'hill of the market'. Markethill is situated in a fertile district, and the hill referred to may be the one called Draper's Hill in the grounds of Gosford Castle (itself now part of Gosford Forest Park).

Market Rasen (Lincolnshire)
This market town (as its name implies) northeast of LINCOLN must have grown up by a plank bridge, as the second word of its name represents the Old English *ræsn* (plank), and so 'plank bridge'. This would have been over the stream that runs through the town. The name as a whole also differentiates the place from the two villages of Middle Rasen and West Rasen, respectively two and three miles west of it. Market Rasen was recorded in the Domesday Book simply as *Resne*.

Market Weighton (Humberside)
A small town northeast of GOOLE whose main name (Weighton) describes it as having originated by a Roman settlement, what the Romans called a *vicus* (the 'Weigh-' of the name), with '-ton' the Old English *tūn* meaning 'village'. The town lies on a Roman road. 'Market' describes its chief commercial activity, but also distinguishes it from the village of Little Weighton, about nine miles away northwest of HULL. In the Domesday Book, the name of Market Weighton appears as *Wicstun*.

Markinch (Fife)
A small town to the east of GLENROTHES with a Gaelic name meaning 'horse meadow', from *marc* (horse) and *innis* (island, riverside meadow). The town is on the River LEVEN. The name was recorded in 1055 as *Marchinke*.

Markyate (Hertfordshire)
A village southwest of LUTON whose name means '(place by the) boundary gate', from the Old English *mearc* (boundary) (*compare* MARCH) and *geat* (gap, gate) (*compare* MARGATE). Markyate is almost on the Bedfordshire/ Hertfordshire border, and the 'gate' would doubtless have been through the former forest here. The name was recorded in about 1130 as *Mark ate*.

Marlborough (Wiltshire)
The name of this town south of SWINDON undoubtedly ends in the Old English word for 'hill', *beorg*; Marlborough is situated at the foot of the Marlborough Downs. The first part of the name has been interpreted as either a personal name, such as Marl, or as the Old English word *meargealla* (gentian). Perhaps this plant grew here, and was exploited for its medicinal properties. Either way, the name was recorded in the Domesday Book as *Merleberge*.

Marlow (Buckinghamshire)
A town on the THAMES northwest of MAIDENHEAD whose name in modern terms could be understood as 'mere leavings', that is, it was regarded as a place that arose by the remains (Old English *lāf*, 'that which has been left') of a lake (*mere*, modern 'mere', as in WINDERMERE). The former lake would obviously have linked up with the river here. The name was recorded in a document of 1015 as *Merelafan*.

Marple (Greater Manchester)
A town east of STOCKPORT whose name means 'boundary stream', from the Old English *gemǣre* (boundary, border) and *pyll* (pool in a river, stream). The reference is to the River Goyt, on which the town stands and which was the former county boundary between Cheshire and Derbyshire. The name was recorded in the thirteenth century as *Merpille*.

Marsden (West Yorkshire)
A town southwest of HUDDERSFIELD whose name probably means 'boundary valley', from the Old English *mearc* (boundary) (as for MARCH) and *denu* (valley). The town is certainly in a deep valley, through which runs the River COLNE. The boundary would have been that between Yorkshire and Lancashire, two miles southwest of the town. The name appears in a document of 1274 as *Marchesden*.

Marske-by-the-Sea (Cleveland)
A residential town and resort on the North Sea coast east of MIDDLESBROUGH. Its name describes its location, or rather the marshy terrain here, deriving from the Old English *mersc* (marsh). The spelling of the name with *sk* (not *sh*) is doubtless due to Scandinavian influence, as Marske was in the Danelaw. The suffix of the name distinguished this Marske (also previously known as Marske-near-Redcar) from the village of Marske near RICHMOND (which was similarly also known as Marske-near-Richmond). Moreover, New Marske is a village southwest of Marske-by-the-Sea. The suffix also has a commercial use as a seaside designation, of course. The town's name appeared in the Domesday Book as *Mersc*.

Marston Moor (North Yorkshire)
The famous site of the Parliamentarian victory of 1644 in the Civil War takes its name from the nearby village of Long Marston, west of YORK. The common village name means 'marsh farm', with 'Long' denoting a village with a long street. The two basic Old English words behind the name are *mersc* (marsh) (*compare* MARSKE-BY-THE-SEA) and *tūn* (farm, village).

Martock (Somerset)
This small town northwest of YEOVIL derives its name from the two Old English words *mere* (lake) and *stoc* (place); the *s* of the latter word is missing because of

Norman influence (the Domesday Book gives the name as *Mertoch*.) A *stoc* was often a holy place, one where people gathered to worship, and this is probably the sense here. The lake here would have linked with the River Parrett, on which the town stands, and it is tempting to suppose that the original 'holy place' was the site of the present parish church of All Saints.

Maryhill (Strathclyde)
A district of GLASGOW said to be named after a landowner here in the mid-eighteenth century, Mary Hill of Gairbraid.

Marylebone (Greater London)
The name of this district of north central LONDON has been the subject of change and confusion over the years, and is still popularly misunderstood as meaning 'St Mary the Good', as if the '-bone' represented the French *bon*! It is really St Mary's *burn*, that is, it takes its name from the stream here, which was known as St Mary's stream. The stream's original name was Tyburn, however, meaning 'boundary stream', and when this particular name came to be associated with the Tyburn gallows, erected at Marble Arch, the name was changed to the favourable St Mary's, a 'good' name to replace the 'bad' one. Later, in the seventeenth century, the meaningless '-le-' was inserted in the name, possibly by association with St Mary-le-Bow. But in the speech of many people, even today, this did not affect the pronunciation, and local residents or Londoners often talk simply of 'Marybone'. Records of the name thus range from *Tiburne* in the Domesday Book, to *Maryburne* in 1453, and *Tyborne otherwise called Maryborne* in a document of 1490. The '-bone' is therefore the Old English *burna* (stream).

Maryport (Cumbria)
This town on the SOLWAY FIRTH arose as a coal port in the eighteenth century, and took its name from Mary Senhouse, the

wife of the man who developed it, Humphrey Senhouse. There was a Roman fort here, named *Alauna*, this deriving from the name of the River Ellen, at whose mouth Maryport stands. The river's name is identical to that of the Aln, which gave its name to ALNWICK, and similarly means 'great one' or 'holy one'.

Masham (North Yorkshire)

A small town northwest of RIPON whose name means 'Mæssa's homestead', with the frequently found combination of a personal name followed by the Old English *hām* (homestead, village). The town appeared in the Domesday Book as *Massan*.

Matlock (Derbyshire)

An inland resort and spa southwest of CHESTERFIELD whose name means 'assembly oak', from the Old English *mæthel* (assembly) and *āc* (oak). The reference would have been to a special oak tree where meetings were held to discuss legal and administrative matters, in other words a so-called 'moot', where a hundred met. No record has been found, however, of Matlock being such a meeting-place. The name was recorded in the Domesday Book as *Meslach*. There were certainly plenty of oaks locally, for Matlock is in the valley of the River DERWENT, whose own name means 'oak river'.

Mauchline (Strathclyde)

This small town southeast of KILMARNOCK may have a name that derives from the Gaelic *magh linne*, 'plain with a pool'; these two words also occur, respectively, in the names MAGHERA and KING'S LYNN. The description certainly suits the locality here, and Mauchline (pronounced 'Mochlin', with *ch* as in 'loch') lies on low ground between the Cessnock Water to the north and the River AYR to the south. The name was recorded in a document of about 1130 as *Machlind i Cuil*, the last word meaning 'corner'.

May, Isle of (Fife)

An island lying southeast of ANSTRUTHER whose name means 'seagull island', from the Old Norse *már* (seagull) (as in MALLAIG) and *ey* (island). The name appears as *Mai* in a text dated 1143.

Maybole (Strathclyde)

This town south of AYR probably has a name that means 'plain of danger', from the Gaelic *magh* (plain) and *baoghail* (danger). Presumably the open terrain here was regarded as affording little protection or cover. A document of 1275 has the name as *Mayboill*.

Mayfair (Greater London)

This district of central LONDON has a name that means what it says: 'place where an annual May fair is held'. The site of the fair was Brook Field, beside the Tyburn (*see* MARYLEBONE), where Brook Street now is (the street is named after the river). The fortnight-long fair was held here every year until it was suppressed in the middle of the eighteenth century, by which time building had begun on the site.

Maynooth (Kildare)

A town west of DUBLIN whose name means 'Nuadu's plain', with Nuadu said to have been the legendary ancestor of Leinstermen. The Irish name of the town is Maigh Nua.

Mayo (Mayo)

The village that gave its name to the county lies southeast of CASTLEBAR, and has a name that means 'plain of the yew tree', representing its current Irish name of Maigh Eo. The name is really a tribute to the ancient abbey near the village, which was founded in the seventh century and was a centre of learning.

Meath (Ireland)

A county on the east coast of Ireland whose name represents the Irish An Mhí, 'the middle'. Meath was the fifth and final province of Ireland to be established, and the name refers to its location between the provinces of ULSTER to the north, CONNAUGHT to the west, and LEINSTER to the south. The original territory thus covered a much wider area than the present county, and included neighbouring WESTMEATH. The county name emerged in the thirteenth century. The basic Irish word for 'middle' is *mide*.

Medina (Isle of Wight)
An administrative district in the north of the county that takes its name from the River Medina, whose own name means 'middle one', from the Old English *medume* (middle). The river rises near the south coast and flows north across the island, dividing it into two almost equal halves. Its name was recorded in a text of the thirteenth century as *Medeme*.

Medway (East Sussex/Kent)
A river that rises in the WEALD and flows northeastwards to form a broad estuary near CHATHAM. The river has a Celtic name that literally means 'mead way', with 'mead' referring either to the colour of the water or possibly to its sweetness (or even both), and 'way' implying a river that carries boats along in its current (*compare* WEY; WYE). A document of 764 has the name as *Meduuuæian*.

Meirionnydd (Gwynedd)
This administrative district has adopted the original Welsh spelling of MERIONETH, which see for the meaning.

Melbourne (Derbyshire)
The name of this town south of DERBY means 'mill stream', from the Old English *myln* (mill) and *burna* (stream). The stream in question would have been the Carr Brook, which flows north through the town to the TRENT. The Domesday Book recorded the name as *Mileburne*. Melbourne Hall, nearby, was the home of Lord Melbourne, the Prime Minister who died in 1848. He took his title from the

place-name, and in turn gave Melbourne, Australia, its name.

Melksham (Wiltshire)
A town on the AVON south of CHIPPENHAM whose name probably means 'riverside pasture where the cows give much milk', from the Old English *meoluc* (milk) and *hamm* (water meadow, land in the bend of a river) (as in CHIPPENHAM, also on the Avon). One has to say 'probably' as it is unusual for a common noun to take a possessive *s* (representing in the modern name the Old English genitive), although this almost always occurred after a personal name. For example, similar names with 'milk' as the first element have no such *s*, such as the village of Melkridge in Northumberland. But the Domesday Book record of the name clearly incorporates it, as *Melchesham*.

Mellifont Abbey (Louth)
The remains of this twelfth-century abbey, the first Cistercian abbey in Ireland, lie northwest of DROGHEDA. The founders were Irish monks who had been to Clairvaux, France, and both the abbey and its riverside site were modelled on the continental abbey, itself founded by St Bernard in 1115. As was common for the time, the Irish abbey was given a Latin name, in this case meaning 'source of honey', representing the Latin *Fons Mellis*. The name may or may not have been linked to beekeeping carried on by the Irish monks. The Irish name of the abbey is simply An Mhainistir Mhór, 'the great abbey'.

Melrose (Borders)
This small town east of GALASHIELS has a British (Celtic) name meaning 'bare moor', from the root elements *mailo-* (bare) (as in the name Meldrum, 'bare ridge') and *ros-* (as in ROSS). The name was recorded in about 700 as *Mailros*.

Meltham (West Yorkshire)
A town southwest of HUDDERSFIELD

whose name was recorded in the
Domesday Book with a spelling exactly as
now. A document of 1316, however, has it
as *Muletham*, and it has been suggested that
the first half of this represents the Old
English *mylen-gelæt*, 'mill-stream'
(compare the dialect 'mill-leat'), and the
second element the common *hām*
(homestead). Meltham may thus have been
a 'homestead by a mill-stream'.

Melton Mowbray (Leicestershire)
The first word of the name of this town
northeast of LEICESTER means 'middle
farm', and corresponds to the name that
elsewhere is MIDDLETON, but that here
was influenced by the Scandinavians, with
the Old Norse *methal* (middle) instead of
the Old English *middel*. The second word
comes from the name of the Norman owner
of the manor here in the first half of
the twelfth century, Roger de Moubray
(who came from Montbray, Normandy).
The 'middle farm' was obviously so called
to distinguish it from two or more
others, but it is not known where they
were. In the Domesday Book, Melton
Mowbray was just *Medeltone*, but in a
document of 1284 it was *Melton Moubray*,
almost as now.

Menai Bridge (Gwynedd)
This ANGLESEY town is at the end of a road
bridge across the Menai Strait, and takes its
name from both, having arisen here soon
after 1826, when the bridge was built (by
Thomas Telford, who gave his name to
TELFORD). The strait has a name that
probably represents the Welsh root
element *men-*, having a sense of 'going',
'carrying' (*men* itself means 'carriage',
'cart'); it thus refers to the current, which
is swift here. The Welsh name of Menai
Bridge is Porthaethwy, from the tribal
name Daethwy, with the addition of
porth (ferry). Some local Welsh-speakers
still refer to the place simply as Y
Borth, 'the ferry'. The name of the Strait
was recorded in the eleventh century as
Mene.

Mendip Hills (Somerset)
The chain of hills southwest of BRISTOL
that effectively form a ridge some 27 miles
(42 km) long. The first half of the name
represents the Welsh *mynydd* (hill). The
second half is the Old English *hop* (valley).
The name thus (coincidentally) refers to
both the hills and the valleys of the long
ridge. However, some toponymists object
to this explanation on the grounds that the
Old English *hop* is rarely found in the West
Country, and properly belongs much
farther north, where it appears, for
example, in BACUP, GLOSSOP, and
WORKSOP. The Mendips had their name
given in a text of 1185 as *Menedepe*.

Menstrie (Central)
This small town northeast of STIRLING has
a Cumbrian (Celtic) name probably
meaning 'plain dwelling', 'settlement on
the plain', representing *maes* (plain) and
tref (settlement). The name was recorded as
Mestryn in 1261.

Merchiston (Lothian)
A district of EDINBURGH whose name
means 'Merchion's farm', with the
personal name being an Old Welsh one. In
a document of about 1265 the name was
recorded as *Merchinston*.

Merioneth (Wales)
The former Welsh county, also known as
Merionethshire, is now represented by the
administrative district of MEIRIONNYDD,
in the county of GWYNEDD, and this Welsh
spelling of the name represents more
clearly its origin in the personal name
Meirion. The named man was the son (or
possibly grandson) of the fifth-century
ruler Cunedda, whose name lies behind
that of Gwynedd. (His other sons, Ceredig
and Brychan, gave their names respectively to CEREDIGION and BRECON.) The
name Meirionnydd (Merioneth) thus
literally means 'seat of Meirion'.

Mersea Island (Essex)
An island just off the coast south of

COLCHESTER. It has a straightforward name that means simply 'sea island', from the Old English *mere* (sea) and *ēg* (island), with this name recorded in a document of 895 as *Meresig*. The notion 'sea' is thus present in the name, but not in its final '-sea'! This name is in no way related to that of the River MERSEY. *See also* WEST MERSEA.

Mersey (Greater Manchester/Merseyside)
This well-known river of northwestern England has a name that means 'boundary river', from the Old English *gemǣre* (boundary) (as for MARPLE) and *ēa* (river). The Mersey formed the old county boundary between Cheshire and Lancashire, and before that, the boundary between the kingdoms of Mercia and Northumbria. The historic association with the border was broken in 1974 when the new county of MERSEYSIDE was formed. The river's name was recorded in 1002 as *Mærse*.

Merseyside (England)
A county of northwest England formed in 1974 and centred on LIVERPOOL on the MERSEY. Most rivers of note have long added '-side' to indicate the district along their banks (compare 'Thames-side'), and some of these have now become the official names of administrative districts, such as North and South TYNESIDE and TAMESIDE, or of larger units, such as the English county of HUMBERSIDE and the Scottish region of TAYSIDE.

Merthyr Tydfil (Mid Glamorgan)
A town northwest of CARDIFF whose name means 'Tydfil's burial place', with the first word of the name the Welsh for 'martyr', and hence 'place where a martyr is buried'. Tydfil was a woman saint, said to be a daughter of Brychan (who gave his name to BRECON); according to tradition she was murdered by pagans in the fifth century at what is now Merthyr Tydfil, and buried here. As is to be expected, the town's

parish church is dedicated to St Tydfil. The Welsh spelling of the name is Merthyr Tudful, with this recorded in 1254 as *Merthir*, and later the same century as *Merthyr Tutuil*.

Merton (Greater London)
A borough of southwest LONDON whose name means 'farm by a pool', from the Old English *mere* (pool, lake) and *tūn* (farm, village). Local historical evidence shows that the pool was in the River Wandle (*see* WANDSWORTH) in southwest MITCHAM. The name was recorded in 967 as *Mertone*, and in the Domesday Book as *Meretone*.

Mevagissey (Cornwall)
This small town south of ST AUSTELL has an unusual name that means '(church of) Mewa and Ida'; the *d* of the latter name became *s*, and the *-ag-* of the name represents the Cornish *hag* (and). Nothing is known about either saint, although the names are of men. A document of 1410 records the place-name as *Mevagisi*.

Mexborough (South Yorkshire)
A town northeast of ROTHERHAM whose name means 'Meoc's fortified place' with the personal name followed by the Old English *burg* (fort), in its frequently found form of '-borough'. The name appears in the Domesday Book as *Mecheburg*.

Mickleover (Derbyshire)
A district of DERBY whose name means '(place by the) big slope', from the Old English *micel* (big, great) and *ufer* (slope, bank). The district lies southwest of the city centre, and is 'big' by contrast with LITTLEOVER, also here. Mickleover's name was thus originally 'Over', before it was recorded as *Magna Oufra* in a document of about 1113.

Middlesbrough (Cleveland)
This town and port has a name that means 'middle fortified place', or in the original, 'middlemost fortified place', from the Old English *midleste* (middlemost) and *burg*; the

name was recorded in a document of about 1165 as *Midelesburc*. It is not certain what the place was in the 'middle' of, although local historians favour a description of Middlesbrough midway between DURHAM and WHITBY, serving as a sort of 'halfway house' for travellers journeying from the monastery at Durham (St Cuthbert's) to that at Whitby (St Hilda's). Perhaps 'Middle' was simply the name of a district here, with the River TEES, on which the town stands, as its northern boundary.

Middlesex (England)
This former southeastern county of England has a name that means 'territory of the Middle Saxons', these being the ones living between the East Saxons of ESSEX and the West Saxons of WESSEX. The original territory was considerably larger than that of the old county, and probably included SURREY and part of Hertfordshire as well as the whole of LONDON. The greater part of London was still in Middlesex down to 1888, when London was constituted as an administrative county in its own right. In 1964 this county was abolished, and most of Greater London was placed under the jurisdiction of the new Greater London Council (now itself abolished), with certain parts going to Surrey and Hertfordshire. The name 'Middlesex' was recorded in the early eighth century as *Middelseaxan*. The Post Office still recognises the name for postal addresses, thus preserving something of an anomaly.

Middleton (Greater Manchester)
This name is a common and self-explanatory one for a 'middle farm' or 'middle village' in between two others; its best-known instance is perhaps the town north of MANCHESTER, probably so called because it lies midway between Manchester and ROCHDALE. A latish first record of 1194 gives it as *Middelton*.

Middlewich (Cheshire)
This town is situated approximately

halfway between NORTHWICH and NANTWICH, hence its name. The Old English *wīc*, which gives the final element of all these names, often meant 'outlying farm' or 'special premises', and here in Cheshire the 'special premises' were saltworks; salt production was (and still is in Middlewich and Northwich) an important commercial activity in these three places. This particular association is reflected in the name of the former Roman settlement at Middlewich, which was *Salinae*, just as it was at DROITWICH, another town famous for its salt. The Roman name is simply the Latin for 'saltworks'. In the Domesday Book, Middlewich appears as both *Wich* and *Mildestuich*, the latter showing the 'middle' element to be really 'middlemost', as for MIDDLESBROUGH.

Midhurst (West Sussex)
The name of this town north of CHICHESTER does not mean 'middle hurst', that is 'middle wooded hill' (from the Old English *hyrst*), but 'place amid wooded hills'. This is borne out not only by the topography — Midhurst is situated between high woodland to the north and the woods of the South Downs to the south — but by the form of the name, for the Old English *mid* was not an adjective but a preposition (or adverb). The name was recorded in 1186 as *Middeherst*.

Midlands (England)
The general name for the central counties of England, also currently in official use for the county of WEST MIDLANDS, centred on BIRMINGHAM, and for the name of the East Midlands Airport, southwest of NOTTINGHAM. There is no county of 'East Midlands', however. The basic name has been in use since the seventeenth century, with the *Oxford English Dictionary* quoting a text of 1610 from Michael Drayton's *Poly-Olbion*: 'Vpon the Mid-lands now th'industrious Muse doth fall'. ('Industrious' is even today an apt reference to the many industries of the

region.) To some extent, the Midlands correspond geographically to the former kingdom of Mercia.

Midleton (Cork)

A small market town situated roughly halfway between CORK (to the west) and YOUGHAL (to the east), as well as between the villages of Carrigtohill and Castlemartyr. Its Irish name is Mainistir na Corann, 'monastery of the weir', referring to its location at the head of the Owenacurra estuary.

Midlothian (Lothian)

This administrative district in the centre and south of the region has preserved the name of the former county in which EDINBURGH was situated and which lay between East LOTHIAN and West Lothian. In many contexts, too, the name is synonymous with that of the capital itself, so that Sir Walter Scott's novel *The Heart of Midlothian* takes its title from the old Edinburgh Tolbooth, or prison, known as the 'Heart of Midlothian'. As a sporting spin-off it has also given the name of the Heart of Midlothian Football Club, more familiarly known as 'Hearts'.

Midsomer Norton (Avon)

This town southwest of BATH has an attractive name that rightly suggests both 'midsummer' and SOMERSET (its former county). The name refers to an annual festival held here, probably on Midsummer Day (St John's Day, 24 June), represented today by the regular Midsomer Norton Fair, held in May. The same reference to summer (although not specifically midsummer) is present in the name of Somerset, and therefore in the name of SOMERTON, also in the county. The main word of the name, 'Norton', states that the place is a 'northern settlement' (where the midsummer festival was held), by contrast with some other place further south, although it is not certain where this was. The town's name was recorded in 1248 as *Midsomeres*

Norton, and, as is to be expected, its parish church is dedicated to St John the Baptist, hence the festival.

Milborne Port (Somerset)

This small town northeast of SHERBORNE is not on the coast; the second word of the name indicates that it was formerly a borough, with the word deriving from the Old English *port* in the sense of 'town' (as for NEWPORT PAGNELL, for example). The first word of the name means 'mill-stream' (Old English *mylen-burna*). The stream's name was recorded as *Mylenburna*, therefore, in the early tenth century, and the town's name was *Meleburne* in the Domesday Book, and *Milleburnport* in 1249 after it had been declared a borough (in 1225).

Mildenhall (Suffolk, Wiltshire)

Either of two villages, each famous for their Roman remains, but in quite different counties. The Suffolk Mildenhall, northeast of NEWMARKET, is the better known for its hoard of Roman silver, called the 'Mildenhall Treasure', discovered here in 1942. The Wiltshire village, east of MARLBOROUGH, arose on the site of the former Roman station of *Cunetio*. The place-names seem to have a different origin in each case, however. The Suffolk Mildenhall was recorded as *Middelhala* in 1130, and as *Middehala* in 1162, suggesting that the name means '(place at the) middle nook', representing the Old English *æt middelan hale*. The Wiltshire Mildenhall, on the other hand, always appears in a form such as the Domesday Book record of *Mildenhalle*, which means 'Milda's nook', after a personal name. The 'nook' was often a recess or indentation in a hill, and for the Wiltshire village this is clearly one in Mildenhall Hill. The Roman name *Cunetio* has an uncertain origin, although it apparently links up with the name of the KENNET, the river on which Mildenhall stands.

Mile End (Greater London)
A district of TOWER HAMLETS whose name
is found elsewhere in the country. It
denotes a place located a mile from some
other place. This Mile End is a mile from
ALDGATE. The name was recorded in 1441
as *La Mileende*. The route of the 'mile' is
up the present WHITECHAPEL Road (A11).

Milford Haven (Dyfed)
A town and port southwest of
HAVERFORDWEST named after the large
estuary and natural harbour on which it
stands. The harbour name consists of the
Old Norse *melr* (sand) and *fjorthr* (inlet;
fjord), and the English 'haven' was added
later (no doubt when the original name was
no longer understood). The Welsh name of
Milford Haven is Aberdaugleddau,
meaning 'mouth of the two Cleddau', from
the Welsh *aber* (river-mouth) (as for
ABERYSTWYTH), *dau* (two), and the name
of the two rivers that combine in the
estuary here, the Eastern Cleddau and the
Western Cleddau. The river name itself
means 'sword' and is of Celtic origin,
referring to its 'straight bright' course. The
Norse name was recorded in a document of
about 1191 as *de Milverdico portu*.

Milford on Sea (Hampshire)
A resort and residential town southwest of
LYMINGTON whose name means what it
says, that is, 'ford by a mill'; it was
recorded in the Domesday Book as
Melleford. The 'maritime' suffix '-on-Sea'
was added some time in the first part of the
twentieth century when the place began to
develop as a seaside resort. (One of the
original developers wished to resurrect the
historic name, and call the place
'Melleford-on-Sea', but the name was not
liked, and was dropped.) *Compare*
MILFORD HAVEN.

Mill Hill (Greater London)
This district of BARNET had its name
recorded as *Myllehill* in 1547, although
there is no evidence where the mill was,
and the name does not appear to be a

distortion of some other word. Perhaps it
was on the hill now known as Highwood
Hill.

Millom (Cumbria)
A town northwest of BARROW-IN-
FURNESS whose name grammatically
represents the dative plural (*mylnum*) of the
Old English word for 'mill' (*myln*) after a
word such as 'at' (*compare* HIGH
WYCOMBE). The sense is thus '(place at
the) mills'. The mills may have been on or
near the hill where Millom castle now
stands. The name was recorded in about
1180 as *Millum*.

Millport (Strathclyde)
A resort and port (as its name indicates) on
the island of Great CUMBRAE. The 'mill' of
the name was the grain-mill that formerly
stood over the harbour. The present town
developed only in the early nineteenth
century.

Millwall (Greater London)
A district on the Isle of DOGS named after
the mills that existed here until the
eighteenth century. The 'wall' of the name
should be understood more as a riverside
embankment, as in the name of Blackwall
or the street called Wapping Wall. The
wall here was at one time called Marsh
Wall, descriptive of the low-lying ground
here.

Milngavie (Strathclyde)
A town north of GLASGOW whose name
(pronounced 'Mull-*guy*' or 'Mill-*guy*', with
the second syllable stressed) represents the
Gaelic *muileann gaoithe* (windmill). The
exact site of the windmill is uncertain.

Milton Abbas (Dorset)
This almost unnaturally picturesque village
southwest of BLANDFORD has a name that
derives from the former abbey nearby,
founded in the tenth century and today
represented by the (unfinished) church,
dating from the fourteenth and fifteenth
centuries, that is the chapel of Milton

Abbey boys' school. The original village was razed in the eighteenth century, and replaced by the present model village. 'Milton' does not mean 'mill farm' but 'middle farm', from the Old English *middel* and *tūn*. This can be established by the earliest forms of the name, such as the tenth-century record of *Middeltun*. A late-thirteenth-century document has the present name as *Middelton Abbatis*, with the second word Latin for 'of the abbot'.

Milton Keynes (Buckinghamshire)
This New Town (designated in 1967) has an old name, that of the original village of Milton Keynes here south of NEWPORT PAGNELL. The first word of the name means 'middle farm' (*compare* MILTON ABBAS). The second word is a so-called 'manorial' addition, naming the Norman lord of the manor here in the thirteenth century. He was Lucas de Kaynes, from Cahagnes in Normandy. The Domesday Book recorded the name simply as *Middeltone*, therefore, with a document of 1227 giving the present name as *Milton Kaynes*.

Milverton (Somerset)
A small town west of TAUNTON whose name can be understood as 'mill ford town', or in its original Anglo-Saxon sense, 'farm by the mill ford'. The elements of the name are thus the Old English *myln, ford* and *tūn*. The middle word has been 'reduced' because it was not accented when the name was pronounced. Milverton is on a tributary of the River Tone (*see* TAUNTON), and its name was recorded in a text of 917 as *Milferton*.

Minch, The (Highland/Western Isles)
The sea passage between the northwest mainland of Scotland and the HEBRIDES, comprising the Little Minch as its southern section, between the island of SKYE and the Western Isles, and the North Minch as its northern section, between the mainland and the island of HARRIS and LEWIS. The name is probably Scandinavian in origin,

deriving from the Old Norse *megin* (great) and *nes* (headland). The original 'great headland' of the name could perhaps have been either CAPE WRATH, at the northeast end of the passage, or the Butt of Lewis, at the northwest end. Or perhaps the reference was to both of these headlands.

Minehead (Somerset)
A resort on the BRISTOL Channel whose name is half Welsh and half English, representing the Welsh *mynydd* (hill) and the Old English *hēafod* (headland). The town is situated both below and on the face of a hill, which may formerly have been called 'The Myne', and this particular name is preserved in the areas known as East Myne and West Myne, on North Hill, to the west of the town. If this is so, the name of Minehead properly means 'headland on The Myne'. But either way, the ultimate origin is the same. The name was recorded in a document of 1046 as *Myneafdon*, which seems to have added the Old English *dūn* (hill). For a similar half-Welsh, half-English name of this type *see* MENDIP HILLS (also in Somerset).

Minster Lovell (Oxfordshire)
A village northwest of WITNEY whose name basically derives from the Old English *mynster* (monastery), to which has been added the 'manorial' suffix of Lovell, referring to the family of William Luvel (or Lupellus) who held the manor here in the early thirteenth century. (His name means 'wolf cub', and may have originated as a nickname.) Minster Lovell was simply *Minstre* in the Domesday Book, referring to the former Benedictine priory here. In a text of 1391 the present name appears as *Munster Lovell*.

Mirfield (West Yorkshire)
A town southwest of DEWSBURY whose name means 'pleasant open land', from the Old English *myrig* (pleasant) (compare modern 'merry') and *feld* (open land; modern 'field'). The Domesday Book recorded the name as *Mirefeld*. It is itself

pleasant when one finds a name with an 'aesthetic' quality about it like this, instead of a purely factual statement. No doubt the River CALDER here contributed to the pleasing aspect of the site.

Mitcham (Greater London)
A district of MERTON whose name simply means 'large village', from the Old English *micel* (large) (*compare* MICKLEOVER) and *hām* (homestead, village). Perhaps Mitcham was regarded as 'large' by comparison with nearby STREATHAM. Its name appeared in the Domesday Book as *Michelham*.

Mitchelstown (Cork)
This market town north of FERMOY had its name recorded in the late thirteenth century as *Villa Michel*, apparently after its Welsh-Norman owner, one Mitchel Condon. The town's Irish name is Baile Mhistéalai, 'Mitchel's homestead'.

Moelfre (Gwynedd)
A fishing village in ANGLESEY southeast of AMLWCH whose name means 'bare hill', from the Welsh *moel* (bare) and *bre* (hill) (here in its 'mutated' form as *fre*). The name obviously occur elsewhere. *Compare* MOEL HEBOG; MOEL SYCH.

Moel Hebog (Gwynedd)
A mountain west of BEDDGELERT whose name means 'bare hill of the hawk', from the Welsh *moel* (bare, bald) (with 'hill' or 'mountain' understood) and *hebog* (hawk). Most such 'bare hills' have descriptive names, although some are named after rivers and some after people. *Compare* MOEL SYCH.

Moel Sych (Clwyd/Powys)
A mountain southwest of LLANGOLLEN whose name means 'dry bare hill', from the Welsh *moel* (bare, bald) ('mountain' understood) and *sych* (dry). *Compare* MALVERN; MOEL HEBOG.

Moffat (Dumfries and Galloway)
A small town and resort, on the River ANNAN northeast of DUMFRIES, whose name means '(place in the) long plain', from the Gaelic *magh* (here in the locative, *mo*), 'plain' (*compare* MAGHERA) and *fada* (long). The 'long plain' is the valley of the River Annan.

Moher, Cliffs of (Clare)
A range of cliffs extending for about five miles along the Atlantic coast west of ENNISTYMON. Their name means 'cliffs of the ruin', representing the Irish name, Aillte an Mhothair. The 'ruin' would have been an old fort here.

Mold (Clwyd)
This town northwest of WREXHAM unexpectedly turns out to have a Norman-French name, from the Old French *mont hault*, 'high hill', with these two words 'fused' to form the present spelling. A document of 1278 has the name as *Montem Altum*, and one of 1284 as *Moald*, showing the shortening of the name already recorded. The 'high hill' in question is Bailey Hill, northwest of the town, where there was a British and possibly a Roman fort, and later a medieval castle. The Welsh name of Mold is Yr Wyddgrug, 'the burial mound'. (For a similar name *see* SNOWDON.)

Mole Valley (Surrey)
An administrative district that takes its name from the River Mole, which flows through it. The river's name is a 'back formation' from that of Molesey (*see* EAST MOLESEY), through which it also flows to enter the THAMES.

Monaghan (Monaghan)
The county town, southwest of ARMAGH, has a name that means '(place of) little thickets', representing its Irish name of Muineachán. The county took its name from the town in the usual manner.

Monasterevin (Kildare)
A small town west of KILDARE whose
name means 'St Eimhín's monastery'.
Little is known about the saint, although he
may have been a contemporary of St
Patrick. The monastery no longer exists,
but its site is that of the present Moore
Abbey.

Moneymore (Londonderry)
This small town southwest of
MAGHERAFELT has a name commonly
found elsewhere that means 'big grove',
representing the Irish name, Muine Mór.

Monklands (Strathclyde)
An administrative district east of GLASGOW
that takes its name from the former
parishes of Old Monkland and New
Monkland here. These names in turn refer
to the monks of Newbattle Abbey, south of
DALKEITH, who were granted lands here
by Malcolm IV in the twelfth century.

Monmouth (Gwent)
A market town northeast of NEWPORT at
the confluence of the rivers WYE and
Monnow; it takes its name from the latter.
The river's name probably means 'fast-
flowing'. The Welsh name of Monmouth is
Trefynwy, 'homestead on the Mynwy', the
latter being the river's more accurate
Welsh name. The name of Monmouth
appeared in an eleventh-century document
as *Munwi Mutha*, and was in the
Domesday Book as *Monenmvde*. The
second syllable of the river's name
disappeared soon after this. Monmouth
gave its name to the former county of
Monmouthshire, officially in England, but
often claimed by Wales.

Montacute (Somerset)
This village west of YEOVIL arose on what
is now the estate of Montacute House, the
Elizabethan mansion here. Its name was in
the Domesday Book as *Montagud*, this
representing the Old French *mont aigu*,
'pointed hill', a name transferred from
France (there is a Montaigu near Caen) for

Flamdon Hill nearby. The present form of
the English name comes from its Latin
equivalent, *Mons acutus*, with this form recorded in the mid-twelfth century. The Old
English name for Montacute was 'Bishops-
ton' (*Biscopestone* in the Domesday Book).

Montgomery (Powys)
The former county town, now a village, lies
to the south of WELSHPOOL and takes its
name from the Norman who held it, Roger
de Montgomery, with his own name
deriving from Montgommery in Calvados.
No doubt the original use of the name in
Wales was for the castle that Roger built at
the foot of what is now Castle Hill (so
named after a second castle built on top of
it in the thirteenth century). The Welsh
name of Montgomery is Trefaldwyn,
'Baldwin's homestead', after the Norman
who recaptured the first castle after it had
been taken by the Welsh. This was
Baldwyn de Boller. The 'Mont-' of the
name is thus coincidentally appropriate for
Castle Hill. The town (as it was) gave its
name to the former county of
Montgomeryshire, which was known as Sir
Drefaldwyn in Welsh. The Domesday
Book recorded Montgomery as
Montgomeri.

Montrose (Tayside)
This port northeast of DUNDEE does not
have a French name (like the two names
above!) but one that is pure Gaelic,
meaning 'moor of the promontory', from
moine (moor) and *ros* (promontory).
Montrose is on a low peninsula at the
entrance to the tidal expanse of water
known as Montrose Basin. The town's
name was recorded in a text of about 1178
as *Munros*.

Moorgate (Greater London)
This district of east central LONDON has a
self-descriptive name referring to a former
gate here that led on to moorland or
marshland. The gate would have been a
postern gate in the wall that surrounded the
City of London.

Morar (Highland)

A coastal area in the LOCHABER district between Loch Nevis to the north and Loch nan Uamh to the south, with Loch Morar dividing the region into North Morar and South Morar. The Gaelic name means 'big water', ultimately referring to the River Morar that flows into the loch. The name was recorded in 1292 as *Morderer*, showing more clearly the Gaelic component elements of *mór* (big) and *dobhair* (water).

Moray (Grampian)

The name of this administrative district in the northwest of the region comes from that of the former county here, which in turn took its name from the much larger ancient province of Moray. The name means 'sea settlement', from the Old Celtic elements that are related to the modern Welsh *môr* (sea) and *tref* (home, town). The province gave the name of the Moray Firth, the great arm of the North Sea that extends inland to INVERNESS. The name of Moray was recorded in the late tenth century as *Moreb*.

Morden (Greater London)

This district of MERTON has an Old English name derived from *mōr* (marshland) and *dūn* (hill), so can be understood as 'hill by marshland'. There is hardly a hill here in the usual sense, but the ground does rise between Beverley Brook to the west and the River Wandle (*see* WANDSWORTH) to the east. The name was recorded in a document of 969 as *Mordune*.

Morecambe (Lancashire)

This popular coastal resort northwest of LANCASTER takes its name from Morecambe Bay, on which it lies. The bay was given the name in the eighteenth century when it was supposedly identified with a bay or inlet on the coast here named *Morikambe* by Ptolemy in the second century AD. The original name was based on the British (Celtic) root elements *mori-* (sea) and *cambo-* (curved), implying a curved bay or a curved inlet (although a

'curved sea', to take the terms literally, actually describes a bay anyway!). The name happens to be very apt, for not only does it echo other resort names ending in the similar '-combe', such as ILFRACOMBE, but it even suggests 'more come', and so has the commercially attractive overtones that all resorts desire. (Many achieve this by adding '-on-sea'.) The present resort was known as Poulton-le-Sands down to 1870. For the origin of this name *see* POULTON-LE-FYLDE.

Moretonhampstead (Devon)

A small market town west of EXETER on the eastern side of DARTMOOR. Its name indicates this location, as a homestead (like HAMPSTEAD) by a farm (Old English *tūn*) by the moor (*mōr*). In other words, the 'moor farm' came first, and had its name recorded in the Domesday Book as *Mortone*; the homestead with its new dwellings came later, so that the first record we have of the present name is no earlier than 1493 (as *Morton Hampsted*). *Compare* MORETON-IN-MARSH.

Moreton-in-Marsh (Gloucestershire)

The first and main part of the name of this small town northwest of CHIPPING NORTON means 'farm by a moor', allowing for the fact that the Old English *mōr* originally denoted barren waste land (and in the north of England, marshland). The guidebooks like to say that the 'Marsh' of the name is a corruption of 'March', meaning 'boundary', as the town stands near the point where four counties meet. But records of the name show that the place was first simply 'Moreton' (*Mortun* in a document of 714), then 'Moreton in Henmarsh' (*Morton in Hennemersh* in 1253), with 'Henmarsh' meaning more or less what it says, 'marsh where wild birds are found'. So the 'boundary' theory, though outwardly convincing, is not supported by the evidence. There are a number of streams near the town, and the River Evenlode rises nearby.

Morley (West Yorkshire)
A town southwest of LEEDS whose name occurs elsewhere and means 'moorland clearing', from the Old English *mōr* (moor, marshland) and *lēah* (wood, clearing). The region here must have been heavily wooded at one time, and there are many names ending in '-ley' to indicate this (*see* BATLEY for a selection). In the Domesday Book, Morley is recorded as *Moreleia*.

Morningside (Lothian)
A district of EDINBURGH whose name is said to mean 'morning seat', but it seems likely that the first half of the word will represent a personal name of some kind.

Morpeth (Northumberland)
This market town north of NEWCASTLE UPON TYNE has an unusual name meaning literally 'murder path', from the Old English *morth* (murder) and *pæth* (path, way). No doubt the neighbourhood here was regarded as dangerous, with the 'path' being the road (the former Great North Road, now the A1) that crosses the River WANSBECK here. It seems strange that such an unfavourable name has been retained for a town of this size. But no doubt the original sense has been forgotten, or the name is perhaps interpreted as 'moor path'. It was recorded in a document of about 1200 as *Morthpath*.

Mortehoe (Devon)
This coastal village west of ILFRACOMBE takes its name from the nearby promontory of Morte Point, with '-hoe' representing the Old English *hōh* (hill-spur, headland). Morte Point has a name that probably means 'The Stump', representing the dialect word *murt* 'stumpy person'. The name was recorded in the Domesday Book as *Morteho*. *See also* WESTWARD HO!

Mortlake (Greater London)
A district south of the THAMES in RICHMOND whose name may mean either 'Morta's stream' or 'salmon stream', in the latter case from the Old English *mort*

(salmon). If the former origin is true, then 'Morta's stream' could have been an earlier name for Beverley Brook, which flows into the Thames here. The second half of the name is the Old English *lacu* (stream) (not 'lake', which came into English, via French, from the Latin *lacus*, 'basin'). The Domesday Book recorded the name of Mortlake as *Mortelege*.

Moseley (West Midlands)
There are three Moseleys within a few miles of one another; two are districts of WOLVERHAMPTON, one is a district of BIRMINGHAM. The two Wolverhampton Moseleys lie respectively north and east of the city centre, with the latter known as Moseley Village until comparatively recently. The Domesday book recorded the name as *Moleslei*, which must mean 'Moll's clearing', from the personal name. The Birmingham Moseley, south of the city centre, was recorded in the Domesday Book as *Museleie*, so means 'clearing where mice are found', from the Old English *mūs* (mouse). This means that the area would have been infested with field-mice.

Mossley (Greater Manchester)
A town southeast of OLDHAM whose name means 'clearing by mossy land'; it was recorded in 1319 as *Moselegh*. The River Tame runs here, which would contribute to the 'mossiness' or marshy nature of the terrain. *Compare* MOSS SIDE.

Moss Side (Greater Manchester)
A district of MANCHESTER, south of the city centre, whose name means 'edge of the mossy land', recorded in 1530 as *Mossyde*. The name is found elsewhere locally, such as Moss Side east of MAGHULL and Moss Side southwest of WARRINGTON. *Compare* MOSTON.

Moston (Greater Manchester)
A district of MANCHESTER, northeast of the city centre, whose name means 'farm by mossy land'; it was recorded in a document of 1195 as now (*compare*

MOSSLEY; MOSS SIDE). In all three names 'moss' seems to imply 'marsh', rather than simply the name of the plant.

Mostrim (Longford)

The anglicised version of the Irish name of EDGEWORTHSTOWN.

Motherwell (Strathclyde)

This town southeast of GLASGOW has a name that really means what is says, so long as 'mother' is understood as meaning 'Our Lady' ('Mother of God'). The original well dedicated to the Virgin Mary has its site marked by a plaque in Ladywell Road. The name was recorded in a document of the mid-thirteenth century as *Matervelle*.

Mountain Ash (Mid Glamorgan)

This town in the coal-mining district southeast of ABERDARE has a modern name given to the community in the nineteenth century when it began to develop its industry. It probably comes from an inn here, whose own name may be a pun on the name of the rowan tree (otherwise called the mountain ash). The Welsh name of the town is Aberpennar, 'mouth of the Pennardd'. This refers to its location at the confluence of this stream (whose name means 'head of the height') with the River Cynon (itself a tributary of the TAFF).

Mountmellick (Laois)

A small market town northwest of PORT LAOISE whose name represents its Irish name of Mointeach Milic, so there is no question of a 'mount' here! The meaning is 'bogland of the water meadows', referring to the town's location by (and virtually encircled by) the River Owenass.

Mourne Mountains (Down)

A range of mountains in southwest Northern Ireland, not far from the Irish Sea. The name derives from that of the Mughdhorna tribe, with their own name taken from that of their leader, Mughdhorn. The mountains have a quite different Irish name: Beanna Boirche, 'peaks of Boirche'. The named man is said to have been a shepherd who looked after the royal cattle of ULSTER here in the third century.

Mousehole (Cornwall)

A 'cosy' name for a 'cosy' village, on the coast south of PENZANCE. The name means what is says (in a figurative sense), and was probably a name for a cave here originally. It was recorded in a document of 1284 as *Mushal*. Local residents pronounce the name to rhyme with 'tousle'.

Moville (Donegal)

A small market town on the western shore of Lough FOYLE whose name means 'plain of the ancient tree', representing the Irish, Maigh Bhile. Irish *bile* was a word for a sacred or historic tree, especially one in a fort or by a holy well.

Mow Cop (Cheshire/Staffordshire)

This hill northeast of KIDSGROVE has an Old English name meaning literally 'heap hill', from *mūga* (heap) and *copp* (hill). The reference seems to be to a cairn formerly here, marking the county boundary. There now remains only an eighteenth-century artificial ruin, serving as a viewpoint over the CHESHIRE plain. The second word of the name is related to 'The Kop', the bank of terracing for standing spectators at ANFIELD, the home ground of LIVERPOOL Football Club. This was originally known as 'Spion Kop', in turn from the Afrikaans name (meaning 'spy hill') of a hill near Ladysmith, South Africa, where a famous battle was fought in the Boer War. Nearer home, the word is also the second element of the name SIDCUP. Mow Cop was recorded in a document of the late thirteenth century as *Rocha de Mowa*.

Much Hadham (Hertfordshire)

A village west of BISHOP'S STORTFORD whose basic name, Hadham, probably means 'Hæda's homestead'. The first word of the name represents the Middle English *muche* (from the Old English *mycel*), 'great' (giving modern 'much'), so that the village is effectively 'Great Hadham', by comparison with Little Hadham just over two miles away. This will always be the sense of 'Much' in English place-names. Much Hadham was simply *Hadam* in the Domesday Book. *Compare* MUCH WENLOCK.

Much Wenlock (Shropshire)

This small town northwest of BRIDGNORTH lies at the northeast end of WENLOCK EDGE, and takes its name from this hill ridge. It is called 'Much' for the reasons explained for MUCH HADHAM. Little Wenlock, which was probably named after it rather than the other way round, is five miles north of Much Wenlock, on the other side of the SEVERN. Both Much Wenlock and Little Wenlock appear as *Wenloch* in the Domesday Book.

Muck (Highland)

An island in the Inner HEBRIDES, southwest of EIGG, whose name means '(island of) pigs', from the Gaelic *muc* (pig). No doubt pigs must have been pastured here at some time. A document of 1370 records the name as *Helantmok*; the first half of this represents the Gaelic *eilean* (island).

Muckle Flugga (Shetland)

A small rocky island north of UNST with an Old Norse name meaning 'great precipices', from *mikill* (great) (related to the first element of MICKLEOVER) and *flugi* (precipice). The description is appropriate for the island, which is the highest and outermost of three rocks in the sea here.

Mudeford (Dorset)

A seaside district of CHRISTCHURCH, east of the town centre. Its name probably means what it says, 'muddy ford', referring to a crossing over one of the streams here.

The Ordnance Survey map of 1811 gives the name as *Midderford*, as if avoiding the undesirable origin.

Muine Bheag (Carlow)

A small market town south of CARLOW with an Irish name meaning 'little grove'. Its former English name was Bagenalstown, from the Bagenal family who lived here from the sixteenth century, and in particular as a tribute to Walter Bagenal, who founded the present town in the late eighteenth century. (He had intended to design a grand architectural complex and to name it 'Versailles'!) The name is pronounced roughly 'Moneybeg'.

Muirkirk (Strathclyde)

A town northeast of CUMNOCK with a Scandinavian name meaning 'moorland church', from the Old Norse *mór* (moor) and *kirkja* (church). The town is on the River AYR northeast of the tract of barren moorland known as Airds Moss ('marshland of the heights').

Mull (Strathclyde)

This island in the Inner HEBRIDES has a name of doubtful origin. Although the Old Norse *múli* (snout, headland), has been suggested and would suit the topography, a derivation in the Gaelic *meuileach* (dear one) has also been proposed, implying that the island was regarded as 'favourable' in some way. Ptolemy recorded the name as *Malaia* in the second century AD.

Mullingar (Westmeath)

The county town, lying in the centre of WESTMEATH county, has a name that has been explained as 'the wry mill', from the Irish *muileann* (mill) and *cearr* (wrong, left-handed), meaning 'a mill with a wheel that turned in an anticlockwise direction'. The Irish name, which as it stands has this meaning, is An Muileann gCearr.

Mullion Cove (Cornwall)
This popular little seaside resort lies on a small bay ('cove') a mile southwest of the village of Mullion, from which it gets its name. The village name derives from that of the saint to whom its parish church is dedicated, St Melan, said to have been a fourth-century bishop. The saint's name appears in a Latin text of 1262, relating to the Cornish church, as *Sanctus Melanus*. The same saint lies behind the name of St Mellons, now a northeastern suburb of CARDIFF.

Mull of Kintyre (Strathclyde)
'Mull' is a common word in Scotland to designate a cape and itself derives from either the Gaelic *maol* (bald), especially for a bare headland, or the Old Norse *múli*, literally 'snout' (*see also* MULL). The name that follows 'Mull' is of the respective region. Here it is KINTYRE. The Mull of Kintyre, at the southwest end of Kintyre, is one of the most distinctive capes in Scotland, and one of the best known. *See also* MUMBLES.

Mumbles (West Glamorgan)
This district of SWANSEA lies to the west of Mumbles Head and takes its name from it. The headland itself has a name of uncertain origin, but it may well be based on the Old Norse *múli* (snout), a word that sometimes lies behind the name of Scottish headlands named 'Mull of . . .' (*see* MULL OF KINTYRE). The name was recorded in a document of 1549 as *Mommulls*.

Munster (Ireland)
One of the five ancient kingdoms of Ireland, the others being CONNAUGHT, LEINSTER, MEATH, and ULSTER. Munster, in the south of the country, has a name that means 'land of the Mumu people', with the tribal name followed by the Old Norse genitive *s* and the Irish *tír* (land, territory) (as also in the name of TYRONE).

Murrayfield (Lothian)
This district of EDINBURGH is said to derive its name from an eighteenth-century advocate, Archibald Murray, who presumably held land and lived here.

Musselburgh (Lothian)
A town on the FIRTH OF FORTH whose name means what it says and refers to the mussels that have made the town famous for the past eight hundred years or more. The name was recorded in about 1100 as *Muselburge*. Mussels are still gathered at Musselburgh.

Muswell Hill (Greater London)
A district of HARINGEY whose name means 'hill by a mossy spring', from the Old English *mēos* (moss) and *wella* (spring, well). The well is said to have been dedicated to St Mary and to have contained water with medicinal properties. A house in Muswell Road has a plaque showing its original site. The name was recorded in about 1155 as *Mosewella*.

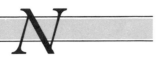

Nass (Kildare)

The county town, southwest of DUBLIN, has a name that means 'the assembly place', representing the Irish name, An Nás. Naas was the residence of the kings of ULSTER until the tenth century, and was a meeting-place for the great state assemblies.

Nailsea (Avon)

A small town west of BRISTOL whose name means 'Nægl's island', with the personal name followed by the Old English *ēg* (island). The reference is to the raised terrain on which Nailsea stands, to the east of the low-lying Nailsea Moor. The same personal name, which is a nickname meaning 'nail', also lies behind NAILSWORTH, although it is not necessarily that of the same man! Nailsea was recorded in a late-twelfth-century document as *Nailsi*.

Nailsworth (Gloucestershire)

A town south of STROUD whose name means 'Nægl's enclosure', with the personal name as for NAILSEA. In a document of the late twelfth century, the name of the town appears as *Nailleswurd*.

Nairn (Highland)

This town and resort takes its name from the river at whose mouth it stands, with the river's own name of Celtic origin meaning something like 'penetrating one'. The town's particular location is reflected in early records of its name as 'Invernairn' (*Inuernaren* in a document of the late twelfth century), with 'Inver-' denoting the river mouth, as for INVERNESS and other places. The town gave its name to the former county of Nairnshire.

Nantwich (Cheshire)

This town southwest of CREWE was once a centre of the salt-mining industry, an activity reflected in its name, which means 'famous saltworks'. The two elements are the Middle English *named* (renowned; literally 'named') and the Old English *wīc* (special place), with the latter applying specifically to saltworks here (and in other towns in Cheshire, such as MIDDLEWICH and NORTHWICH, and, in Hereford and Worcester, DROITWICH). The town's name was recorded in the Domesday Book simply as *Wich*, with the present form of the name found as *Nametwich* in a text of 1194.

Narberth (Dyfed)

A small market town east of HAVERFORDWEST whose name means '(place) by the hedge', from the Welsh words *yn* (in), *ar* (the), and *perth* (hedge) (*compare* PERTH). It is the *n* of the first word here that begins the modern name. The Welsh equivalent is Arberth. The name was recorded in 1220 as *Nethebert*.

Naseby (Northamptonshire)

A village southwest of MARKET HARBOROUGH whose name has gone down in history as that of the battle of 1645 in the Civil War. (The actual battlefield is a mile to the north of the village.) The name itself was originally something like 'Navesbury', or *Navesberie* in the Domesday Book, meaning 'Hnæf's fortified place'. When the Danes arrived, they substituted the Old Norse *bý* (village) for the Old English *burg*, as they quite often did.

Navan (Meath)

The county town, southeast of KELLS, has a name that represents the equivalent Irish name, An Uaimh, and so means 'the cave'. The cave in question was probably a grotto on either of the rivers BOYNE or BLACKWATER, which meet here. In the twentieth century, a poll of local residents showed Navan to be the preferred name.

Nayland (Suffolk)

A small town north of COLCHESTER whose name means '(place) at the island', with the initial *N* representing the final letter of the Middle English *atten* (at the), followed by the Old English *ēg-land* (island). The 'island' is the land here that lies in a bend of the River STOUR. The town's name was simply *Eilanda* in the Domesday Book, that is, 'island'. *Compare* STOKE-BY-NAYLAND.

Naze, The (Essex)
A headland on the east coast south of HARWICH. The word is merely the Old English *næss* (promontory) (compare its Old Norse equivalent, *nes*, in Scottish names like TARBAT NESS). Early records show that The Naze was originally 'Ēadwulf's Ness' — *Eadulfes næsse* in a document of 1052. *See also* WALTON ON THE NAZE, which took its name from it.

Neagh, Lough (Antrim/Armagh/Londonderry)
Ireland's (and Britain's) largest lake, west of BELFAST, has a name that means 'Eochaid's lake', with the named man said to have been a legendary king of MUNSTER who drowned in the lake when it suddenly flooded in the first century AD. The Irish name, with the same meaning, is Loch nEathach.

Neasden (Greater London)
A district of BRENT whose name means 'nose-shaped hill', from the Middle English *nese* (nose) and the Old English *dūn* (hill). The first element of the name suggests that it was given relatively late, and the first record of it is as *Neosdune* in the early eleventh century. It is difficult to say precisely which hill is involved here. Perhaps it was in the area of the present Gladstone Park, towards Dollis Hill, rather than westwards, towards the River Brent.

Neath (West Glamorgan)
A town northeast of SWANSEA on the River Neath, after which it takes its name. The river (in Welsh known as the Nedd) has a name that is of Celtic origin and may mean 'shining one'. The Welsh name of Neath is

Castell-nedd, referring to the Roman fort that was once here. Its name was *Nidum*, deriving from that of the river.

Needham Market (Suffolk)
A town southeast of STOWMARKET whose basic name, Needham, probably means literally 'homestead of need', from the Old English *nēd* (need, poverty) and *hām* (homestead). The implication is that the people here were poor and often went hungry, no doubt because the land bore poor crops. (*Compare* HUNGERFORD). However, the second word of the name appears to contradict this! But 'Market' is not recorded in the name until the sixteenth century, when clearly the agricultural scene had changed. The additional word was given to distinguish this market from STOWMARKET, only four miles away, while also emphasizing that the place had a market (and even that it was no longer 'needy'). The name was recorded in the thirteenth century as *Nedham*, and in 1511 as *Nedeham Markett*.

Needles, The (Isle of Wight)
The striking group of jagged chalk rocks at the western end of the Isle of Wight, where they extend into the English Channel. The name is self-descriptive, referring to the sharp tapering peaks of the rocks. They are referred to in a fourteenth-century text as *les nedeles del Isle de Wight*.

Nelson (Lancashire)
This town north of BURNLEY arose only in the early nineteenth century with the development of the textile industry, and the name is taken from an inn here, the Lord Nelson, around which the town grew. The inn's name, like many others, refers to Nelson's victory at the Battle of Trafalgar in 1805. *Compare* WATERLOOVILLE.

Nenagh (Tipperary)
This market town northeast of LIMERICK has a name meaning 'the assembly place', representing its Irish name, An tAonach. Nenagh has long been a gathering point of

one kind or another, with the former horse fairs now replaced by cattle markets. *Compare* NAAS.

Nene (Northamptonshire/Cambridgeshire/Norfolk)
This river, which rises near DAVENTRY and flows through the above-mentioned counties to enter The WASH, has a name that is of British (Celtic) origin and means 'bright one', from a conjectural root word *nēnā*, which also lies behind the name of the NIDD.

Ness, Loch (Highland)
Perhaps Scotland's best known loch, forming part of the CALEDONIAN CANAL through Glen More. Its name derives from that of the river that flows from it to INVERNESS. The river's own name is of Old Celtic origin and may mean 'roaring one'. (The name is thus not the same as the 'Ness' that means 'headland', in such names as TARBAT NESS and FIFE Ness.)

Neston (Cheshire)
This town on the WIRRAL peninsula west of ELLESMERE PORT has a name that refers to its location here and means 'headland farm', from the Old English *ness* (a Mercian dialect version of *næss*) and *tūn* (farm, village). The suggestion has been made that the whole of the Wirral peninsula may have been called 'Ness' at one time, so that Neston's name really means 'farm in (or on) Ness'. There is a small village just southeast of Neston named simply Ness. Neston's own name appears in the Domesday Book as *Nestone*.

New Alresford (Hampshire)
The official name of the town more usually known, at least locally, as ALRESFORD.

Newark-on-Trent (Nottinghamshire)
A town northeast of NOTTINGHAM whose basic name, Newark, really means 'new work', referring to building work that is 'new' by comparison with buildings, such as fortifications, that already exist. Here

the 'old work' was almost certainly the Roman fort of *Margidunum*, which was located at what is now Castle Hill, East Bridgford (*compare* WEST BRIDGFORD). The Roman fort was actually recorded as *Aldewerke* in medieval times. The fort, some ten miles from modern Newark, was linked with the modern site by the FOSS WAY. *Margidunum* may mean 'marly fort', that is, one built on marl (clayey soil). Newark was recorded as *Newarcha* in a document of about 1060. The '-on-Trent' was added to distinguish it from other Newarks, such as the one that is now a district of PETERBOROUGH (although this is some distance away).

Newbiggin-by-the-Sea (Northumberland)
This fishing town and resort east of ASHINGTON has a basic name, Newbiggin, that means what it says: 'new building', with the second half of the name from the Middle English *bigging* (building). The name simply refers to new building carried out on or near a site of existing buildings. There are many Newbiggins in the north of England and Scotland (Cumbria has at least half a dozen). This particular Newbiggin, now differentiated from others by its maritime suffix, was recorded as *Niwebiginga* as long ago as the twelfth century.

Newbridge (Gwent)
This town on the River Ebbw (*see* EBBW VALE) northwest of NEWPORT has an obvious name referring to a new bridge over the river here. The name is fairly common in south Wales.

New Brighton (Merseyside)
A district of WALLASEY, now a popular resort, that developed in the first half of the nineteenth century and took its name from the existing well-known resort of BRIGHTON in Sussex.

Newburgh (Fife)
This small town on the south bank of the Firth of TAY has a 'new' name that is one of

the oldest in the country. Mention of it occurs in a document of about 1130: *ad Niwanbyrig, id est, ad Novam Civitatem*. The town is a Royal Burgh of long standing, receiving its charter in 1266, when it was referred to as *Novus burgus juxta monasterium de Lindores*, 'the new burgh beside the monastery of Lindores'. (The reference is to Lindores Abbey, founded to the east of Newburgh in 1191).

Newburn (Tyne and Wear)

An industrial suburb on the north side of the River TYNE west of NEWCASTLE UPON TYNE. Its name means 'new stream', from the Old English *nīwe* (new) and *burna* (stream). A 'new stream' is one that has changed its course. The same origin lies behind the name of the Suffolk village of Newbourne, south of WOODBRIDGE. Newburn was recorded as *Neuburna* in a document of about 1121.

Newbury (Berkshire)

This town west of READING has a 'newer' name than many other 'new' places, with the '-bury' of the name (Old English *burg*) better understood as 'market town' than the more common 'fort'. The name was recorded as *Neweburgh* in a document of 1431. The town developed from the earlier settlement here whose name was recorded in the Domesday Book as *Ulvritun*, 'estate of Wulf's people'. This manorial holding in turn arose near the site of the Roman fort called *Spinis*, which was probably located to the west of Speen, now a western suburb of Newbury itself. *Spinis* means '(fort in the) thorn bushes'; Speen has preserved this Roman name. The growth of Newbury as a market town was due to its location at the point where the road from OXFORD to WINCHESTER (now the A34) crossed the River KENNET.

Newcastle (Down)

This seaside resort southwest of DOWNPATRICK had a 'new castle' in the sixteenth century, later demolished (in the nineteenth century) to make way for a hotel

(now itself also demolished). The name is thus self-explanatory, and the Irish name of An Caisleán Nua, 'the new castle', is exactly the same. The name Newcastle is fairly common in both Ireland and Britain generally, and for each place it is a matter of establishing the date when the particular castle could be said to be 'new'. *Compare* NEWCASTLE EMLYN; NEWCASTLE-UNDER-LYME; NEWCASTLE UPON TYNE.

Newcastle Emlyn (Dyfed)

This small town east of CARDIGAN had a 'new castle' in the thirteenth century, and the name was recorded at the time as *Novum Castrum de Emlyn*. It was 'new' by comparison with the existing castle at Cilgerran, some eight miles away downstream on the River Teifi, which flows through both places. The second word of the name means literally 'round the valley' (Welsh *am glyn*), and was the name of the so-called cantref or district here, with Newcastle as its administrative centre. The Welsh name of the town is thus Castellnewydd Emlyn, with the same meaning.

Newcastle-under-Lyme (Staffordshire)

This town immediately west of STOKE-ON-TRENT had a 'new castle' in the twelfth century, of which now very little remains. The second part of the name refers to the ancient Lyme Forest formerly here, with Newcastle close to its southern edge. The name means 'place of elms' (not 'limes'!) with 'Lyme' directly related to the 'Lyne' of ASHTON-UNDER-LYNE. The name as a whole was recorded in a document of 1168 as *Nouum Oppidum sub Lima* (Latin for 'new town under the Lyme [Forest]').

Newcastle upon Tyne (Tyne and Wear)

This well-known city and port on the River TYNE had a 'new castle' built in the eleventh century on the site of the old Roman fort known as *Pons Aelii*. This name actually means 'Hadrian's bridge', referring to the Roman emperor who gave his name to HADRIAN'S WALL, near the eastern end of which Newcastle now stands. (Aelius was the name of the Emperor's *gens* or clan, so that his full name was Publius Aelius Hadrianus.) Newcastle's name was thus recorded in a document of 1130 as *Novum Castrum*, and the restored keep of the castle has been preserved as a museum.

New Forest (Hampshire)

An extensive area of heath and woodland in the southwest of the county that represents the 'new' forest created as a hunting preserve by William the Conqueror in the eleventh century; its name is recorded in the Domesday Book as *Nova Foresta*. The name of the existing forest here prior to this was 'Forest of Andred'; it also is recorded in the Domesday Book (as *Andret*), but occurs in much earlier records too: a late-ninth-century document gives the name in the spelling just quoted. The original name is believed to mean 'great fords', from two Celtic words, the second of which is related to the modern Welsh *rhyd* (ford) (*see* PEVENSEY for further details about this name).

New Galloway (Dumfries and Galloway)

This small Royal Burgh north of KIRKCUDBRIGHT arose in the seventeenth century when its royal charter was granted by Charles I in 1629 to Sir John Gordon, subsequently first Viscount Kenmure and Lord Lochinvar. The particular name was chosen to mark the Gordon family's ties with LOCHINVAR in the then county of GALLOWAY, and the name of the burgh was recorded in a document of 1682 as *The New Town of Galloway*. The name was appropriate as New Galloway was itself not in the county of its name but in Kirkcudbrightshire.

Newham (Greater London)

A borough of east central LONDON created in 1965 as an amalgamation of the two existing towns of EAST HAM and WEST HAM; the name was designed to unite the two as a 'new Ham'. The name was the final selection of ninety proposed for the new borough, and was originally intended to be pronounced as two distinct words, with the *h* clearly sounded. Such a pronunciation is still heard, although many people now say 'Newam', as other places of the same name are pronounced.

Newhaven (East Sussex)

A busy port at the mouth of the River OUSE to the east of BRIGHTON. It arose here in the mid-sixteenth century when local landowners canalized the lower section of the river in an endeavour to drain the Ouse Valley marshes and improve navigation. Prior to this the Ouse had made its main route to the sea further to the east, near SEAFORD, but the barrier of shingle there was constantly breached in storms and a number of different outlets developed in medieval times. Similar problems were caused by drifting shingle after the canal was cut in about 1540, and the 'new haven' or new harbour was continually blocked. The problem was solved only in the mid-nineteenth century, when the western pier was built. The name was recorded in a document of 1563 with the spelling as now. It is perhaps significant that the English name of the French port of Le Havre, across the English Channel from Newhaven, was itself 'Newhaven' for some time after that port was founded by François I in 1517. Le Havre means simply 'the harbour'.

Newington (Greater London)

This district of SOUTHWARK has a somewhat misleading name. It does not contain the '-ington' element as seen in KENSINGTON, for example, but one that arose as a corruption of the original Old English phrase that gave the name: *æt thæt nīwan tūne*, 'at the new farm', with *nīwan* here grammatically the dative form of *nīwe* (new) required after *æt* (at). The present form of the name evolved gradually, therefore, from *Neuton* in about 1200, and *Niwentone* in the thirteenth century, to *Newyngton juxta Suthwerk*, 'Newington by

Southwark' in 1325. For more on the 'Newton' that the name represents *see* NEWTON ABBOT.

New Junction Canal (South Yorkshire/Humberside)

A canal linking the Sheffield and South Yorkshire Navigation with the Aire and Calder Canal. It runs from Bramwith Junction on the former to a point south of Snaith (west of GOOLE) on the latter, a total distance of about six miles. The canal was constructed in 1905 and has a name that reflects the 'new junction' made between the two existing canals.

Newlyn (Cornwall)

A former fishing village, now a southern suburb of PENZANCE, whose name suggests it is 'new', or was so at one time. But the two elements of the name probably derive from the Cornish *lu*, literally 'host', 'army', here meaning 'fleet of boats', and the more certain *lyn* (pool) (*compare* KING'S LYNN). So what might have been 'Lulyn' became 'Newlyn', by association with 'new'. The name would indicate a capacious or safe harbour. This interpretation of the name seems to be confirmed by early records of it as *Lulyn*.

New Malden (Greater London)

A district of KINGSTON UPON THAMES that arose as a northern extension of the existing district of Malden in the first half of the nineteenth century, acquiring its separate local authority in 1866. The original Malden then became known as Old Malden. The basic name has exactly the same origin as that of MALDON, meaning 'hill with a cross' from the Old English *mǽl* (cross) and *dūn* (hill). It is not clear which hill is referred to, but it could well be the small rise on which the present parish church of St John the Baptist stands overlooking Hogsmill River. Old Malden was recorded as *Meldon* in the Domesday Book, and New Malden's name appears on the one-inch Ordnance Survey map published in 1876 (but surveyed ten years earlier).

Newmarket (Suffolk)

This town with its famous racecourse east of CAMBRIDGE has a name that dates back to the thirteenth century, when it was recorded in a medieval Latin text as *Novum Forum*. It denotes not so much a 'new market' as such, but more a new settlement or town that has acquired the right to hold a market. In this respect, the name resembles NEWBURY and NEWPORT.

New Milton (Hampshire)

This urban development west of LYMINGTON arose in the late nineteenth century when the railway station came here in 1888. It 'borrowed' the name of the existing village of Milton, half a mile to the south, itself having a name that means 'middle farm', recorded in the Domesday Book as *Mildeltune*.

Newnham (Cambridgeshire)

A southwestern district of CAMBRIDGE that gave its name to the women's college of Cambridge University. The name means 'new homestead' or 'new enclosure'. The second *n* of the name has the same origin as the *-ing-* of NEWINGTON. Newnham was recorded as *Neuham* in a document of 1195.

Newport (Dyfed, Gwent, Isle of Wight)

Any of various places in Britain, the names of which are a blend of two meanings, depending on the interpretation of 'port'. In the obvious sense, they are 'new ports' in their respective locations: the Dyfed town is at the mouth of the River Nyfer, southwest of CARDIGAN; the Gwent county town is on the River USK; and the Isle of Wight town is at the head of the River MEDINA estuary. But 'port' also has the sense of 'market town', as for NEWPORT PAGNELL (which is not on the coast), and this equally applies to the other three, especially to the Isle of Wight town, which is the commercial capital of the island. The two meanings of 'port' are of course entirely compatible, as the activity of the market is directly linked with the transportation of goods via the port. But historically it was the 'new market town' sense that came first. The Dyfed Newport was recorded as *Nuport* in 1282; the Gwent town as *Novus Burgus* in 1138; and the Isle of Wight town also as *Novus Burgus* in the thirteenth century. The Dyfed Newport has the Welsh name of Trefdraeth, 'town on the shore', from *tref* (town) and *traeth* (strand, shore). The Gwent town is known in Welsh as Casnewydd-ar-Wysg, 'new castle on the Usk'. This is a name similar to the NEWCASTLE ones above, and here the twelfth-century castle (whose ruins remain) was regarded as 'new' by comparison with the Roman fort at CAERLEON, three miles away. *Compare* NEWPORT-ON-TAY; NEWPORT PAGNELL.

Newport-on-Tay (Fife)

This town on the south bank of the Firth of TAY, opposite DUNDEE, arose as a 'new port' in medieval times, and for some eight hundred years was an important ferry port to Dundee, until the railway bridge was built in the nineteenth century and, finally closing the ferry, the road bridge in the twentieth century. *See also* TAYPORT.

Newport Pagnell (Buckinghamshire)

This town north of BLETCHLEY arose as a 'new town' with market rights like the towns mentioned under NEWPORT. So 'port' here does not have its popular sense of 'shipping harbour'. Its name was recorded in the Domesday Book as *Neuport*, and its present name appeared as *Neuport Paynell* in a document of 1220. The second word represents the name of the Norman lord of the manor here in the twelfth century, Fulc Paganel. The name (which arose as a nickname, meaning 'little heathen') also occurs for the Lincolnshire village of Boothby Pagnell, near GRANTHAM, where the owner was Johannes Paynel in the fourteenth century, and for the Wiltshire village of Littleton Panell, near DEVIZES, where the manor was held by William Paynel in the thirteenth century.

Newquay (Cornwall)

A coastal resort north of TRURO whose name dates back to 1439 when Bishop Lacy of EXETER granted an indulgence for a new *Kaye* to be built here, to enable ships to lie at anchor under the protection of its wall, which the original harbour lacked. The present name is first recorded in a document of 1480, and appears as *Newe Kaye* in Richard Carew's *Survey of Cornwall* of 1602. The Cornish name of Newquay is Towan Blistra, with the first word meaning 'sand dune', but with the second word of unknown meaning.

New Quay (Dyfed)

A small coastal resort southwest of ABERYSTWYTH that developed after the construction of the harbour here in 1835, as a 'new quay' to replace an older, smaller one. The Welsh name of New Quay, Ceinewydd, has the same meaning as the English name.

New Radnor (Powys)

This village northwest of KINGTON was the former county town of RADNOR. But it does not take its name from the county but from what is now the hamlet of Old Radnor, three miles east of it. New Radnor thus became 'new' in 1064, when King Harold granted the settlement the right to be the new administrative centre of the region, instead of (Old) Radnor. (For the meaning of the basic name *see* RADNOR.) New Radnor has the Welsh name of Maesyfed, 'field of Hyfaidd', while Old Radnor is Pencraig, 'chief rock'.

New Romney (Kent)

A town southwest of HYTHE that was formerly the administrative centre of the district now known as ROMNEY Marsh. It was one of the original CINQUE PORTS, although alterations in the sea coast over the past century have now left it almost a mile inland. It is 'new' by contrast with the smaller village now known as Old Romney, two miles west of it. The latter's name was recorded as *Old Rumney* in 1575 (and New

Romney's as just *Rumney*), and as *Old Romney* in 1610 (when New Romney was still just Romney). The addition of 'New' is thus relatively recent. For the meaning of the basic name *see* ROMNEY.

New Ross (Wexford)
A small town west of WEXFORD that is 'New' by contrast with the village of Old Ross to the east of it. Its 'newness' relates effectively to its former importance as an inland port on the River Barrow, and historically to its foundation as an Anglo-Norman settlement in the twelfth century. The town's Irish name is Rhos Mhic Thriúin, 'wood of the sons of Treon', while Old Ross is known as An Sean Ros, 'the old wood'.

Newry (Down)
This town and port northwest of CARLINGFORD Lough does not have a 'new' name like the other places mentioned above and below. The name represents its Irish name of An tIúr, 'the yew tree'. Traditionally, the name is said to refer to a yew tree planted by St Patrick at the head of Carlingford Lough when he founded the monastery here in the sixth century. Both monastery and yew are said to have been burned down in the twelfth century.

Newton Abbot (Devon)
This market town northwest of TORQUAY has a basic name, Newton, that is the most common of all British place-names, and simply means 'new farm', 'new village'. The Ordnance Survey *Gazetteer of Great Britain* (1987) lists over 150 plain 'Newtons' and many more with a distin-guishing addition, as Newton Abbot itself has. The town's name was recorded as *Nova Villa* in the late twelfth century, and as *Nyweton Abbatis* in 1270. The second word was added because the place was given to Torre Abbey (*see* TORQUAY) in 1196.

Newton Aycliffe (Durham)
This New Town (designated in 1947) north of DARLINGTON has a name that is a recent

adoption of the old 'Newton' for a specialized usage. The town arose as a residential development for workers on the nearby Aycliffe Industrial Estate, which in turn developed from the Royal Ordnance factory in the village of Aycliffe. The basic name, Aycliffe, which is sometimes used alone for the New Town, means 'oak wood', from the Old English *āc* (oak) and *lēah* (wood). Aycliffe (the village) was frequently also known as Great Aycliffe, by contrast with the much smaller hamlet of School Aycliffe, west of it. The latter seems to have been named after a Scandinavian called Skúli, who was given land in DURHAM in the tenth century. His name means 'skulker' (compare modern 'scowl').

Newton Ferrers (Devon)
This town southeast of PLYMOUTH arose as a 'new farm' (*Niwetone* in the Domesday Book) whose manor came to be held by William de Ferrers in the thirteenth century. Its present name was recorded as *Neweton Ferers* in a document dated 1303.

Newtongrange (Lothian)
A coal-mining town south of DALKEITH whose name is said to have been given to distinguish the place from Prestongrange, the estate near PRESTONPANS; both of these places were granges of the abbots of Newbattle Abbey. A 'grange' was not simply a granary, but the place where an abbey's rates and tithes were paid. (Compare the associated English 'tithe barn', where the agricultural tithe of a village and its parson was stored.)

Newton-le-Willows (Merseyside)
This town east of ST HELENS was originally known as Newton-in-Makerfield, for the second part of which name *see* ASHTON-IN-MAKERFIELD. Its present name, which has the same meaning as that of the identically named village in North Yorkshire, west of BEDALE, means: 'Newton (i.e. 'new farm') among the willow trees'. It is strange that it should have changed a perfectly acceptable

differentiating addition in this way, especially as there is now confusion between this town and the Yorkshire village. Its name was recorded in the Domesday Book simply as *Neweton*, and in 1257 as *Neuton Macreffeld*. The present name was being used as an alternative in the nineteenth century, and may well have been adopted considerably earlier.

Newton Mearns (Strathclyde)
A southwestern suburb of GLASGOW whose name means 'new town in Mearns', the latter being an alternative name (The Mearns) for the former county of KINCARDINE. It represents the Gaelic *An Mahaoirne*, 'the stewartry', with the English plural *s* added (*see also* STEWARTRY). The present name is found in a text of 1609 as *Newtoun de Mernis*.

Newtonmore (Highland)
A holiday and skiing centre west of KINGUSSIE whose name probably represents 'new town on the moor', referring to its location by the River SPEY among hills and mountains.

Newton Stewart (Dumfries and Galloway)
A small town north of WIGTOWN named after William Stewart, son of the second Earl of GALLOWAY, who laid it out here in the seventeenth century. *Compare* NEWTOWNSTEWART.

Newtown (Powys)
This town on the River SEVERN southwest of WELSHPOOL was already a 'new town' or new settlement in the thirteenth century, when its name was recorded as *Newentone*. But in 1967 it was officially designated a New Town! It is thus unique in being the only one of Britain's thirty-two New Towns to have been already called 'new town' when officially designated. The original settlement arose around a place called Llanfair in Cedewain, 'St Mary's church in Cedewain', the latter being the name of the district here, itself said to mean 'territory of Cadaw'. Both this Welsh name

and the English one continued in parallel use down to 1832, when the English name alone was officially adopted, with the current Welsh name of Y Drenewydd translating it ('the new town').

Newtownabbey (Antrim)
The name of this northern suburb of BELFAST derives from a combination of 'Newtown' and the latter half of the name of the nineteenth-century village Whiteabbey. It was given in the present century when several individual communities (of which Whiteabbey was one) were combined administratively as a single unit. Newtownabbey's Irish name is Baile na Mainistreach, 'town of the abbey'.

Newtownards (Down)
A market town situated at the head of STRANGFORD Lough in the ARDS PENINSULA and founded early in the seventeenth century. Both its English name and its Irish name, Baile Nua na hArda, have exactly the same meaning: 'new town in the Ards Peninsula'.

Newtownstewart (Tyrone)
A market town northwest of OMAGH founded by William Stewart in the seventeenth century; it takes its name from him. The Irish name is simply 'the new town', An Baile Nua.

New Tredegar (Mid Glamorgan)
A town north of BARGOED founded as an industrial settlement in the mid-nineteenth century. It was named after the landowner here, Lord Tredegar, whose family name was Morgan and whose title comes from the family seat at Tredegar Park, near NEWPORT, Gwent. It was regarded as 'new' by contrast with TREDEGAR, which had developed a few years earlier.

Neyland (Dyfed)
This small town and former port opposite PEMBROKE DOCK has an Old English name meaning '(place) at the island', with the initial *N*- coming from the Middle

English *atten* (at the). The 'island' is the virtual peninsula on which the town stands east of MILFORD HAVEN. For some time in the nineteenth and first part of the twentieth century Neyland was known by the alternative name of New Milford, as a 'competitive' name (in industrial aspirations) against that of Milford Haven itself. Neyland's present name was recorded as *Nailand* in 1596 and is exactly the same in origin as that of STOKE-BY-NAYLAND.

Nidd (North Yorkshire)
A river that rises in the eastern PENNINES and flows roughly southeastwards to join the OUSE north of YORK. The name is British (Celtic) in origin and means something like 'bright', 'shining', from a conjectural root element *nido-*. It was recorded in a document of about 715 as *Nid*.

Nith (Strathclyde/Dumfries and Galloway)
A river that rises south of AUCHINLECK and flows roughly southeastwards to the SOLWAY FIRTH south of DUMFRIES. The river valley is Nithsdale, with this now the name of an administrative region. The name is of British (Celtic) origin and probably means 'new', possibly referring to its constantly changing course. If this is so, its name is indirectly related to 'new' itself.

Norbiton (Greater London)
The name of this district of KINGSTON UPON THAMES can be regarded as a sort of 'opposite number' to SURBITON, as it means 'northern grange' (literally 'barley farm', Old English *bere-tūn*), as opposed to Surbiton's 'southern grange'. Both granges belonged to the royal manor of Kingston, and the two places are separated from each other by the hill on which BERRYLANDS Farm was situated. Norbiton was recorded in a document of 1205 as *Nortberton*.

Nore, The (Essex/Kent)
The sandbank at the entrance to the estuary of the THAMES between SHOEBURYNESS to the north and SHEERNESS to the south. Its name probably represents the Old Norse *nór* (sea inlet).

Norfolk (England)
The name of this East Anglian county refers to the 'northern folk', that is, those East Angles who lived in this part of the territory, as distinct from the 'southern folk', who lived in SUFFOLK. It is interesting that the names of both territories (now counties) were adopted without any additional '-land', unlike NORTHUMBERLAND and WESTMORLAND. The Domesday Book recorded the name of Norfolk as *Nordfolc*. Names indicating 'north', like this one, often imply a matching 'south' name, although not always (see entries below).

Normanton (West Yorkshire)
A coal-mining town east of WAKEFIELD whose name, like almost all other Normantons in the country, will mean 'farm of the Norsemen', and was given by Anglo-Saxons to Scandinavians in their territory. (Note that they used the Old English *tūn*, 'farm', which will thus differentiate the name from places called Normanby, where the final element is the Old Norse *bý*, 'farm'. In the latter case, the name will have been given to one group of Scandinavians by others, that is, to Norwegians by Danes.) The first element in the name of Normanton is the Old English *Northman*, 'Norseman'. Normanton was recorded in the Domesday Book as *Normantone*.

Northallerton (North Yorkshire)
A town south of DARLINGTON whose name shows it to be a 'northern Allerton', as distinct from other Allertons (*see* ALLERTON). Not all places of the name have the same origin, however, and this Allerton is 'Ælfhcrc's farm', recorded in the Domesday Book as *Aluretune* (and as *North Alverton* in a document of 1293).

Northam (Devon)

A town north of BIDEFORD whose name appeared in the Domesday Book as now and means 'northern homestead', as distinct from one further south (i.e. a 'Southam'), although it is not clear which this was.

Northampton (Northamptonshire)

The county town arose as a 'Hampton' (*Hamtun* in a document of 917), and by the eleventh century it was regarded as a northern one in contrast with the other 'Hampton' — SOUTHAMPTON. 'Hampton' means 'home farm' (*see also* HAMPTON). Northampton was recorded as *Northhamtun* in a text of 1065, and the county name was recorded even before this, as *Hamtunscir* in 1011, and as *Northhamtunscir* in 1114. The county name is abbreviated to 'Northants' for the same reason that HAMPSHIRE is abbreviated to 'Hants'.

Northfleet (Kent)

This industrial town on the THAMES west of GRAVESEND arose on a creek (Old English *flēot*, *see* FLEET) that was regarded as being to the north of another at what is now the village of Southfleet, not far south of it. The name was recorded in the late tenth century as simply *to Flyote*, but as *Norflvet* in the Domesday Book a hundred years later.

Northiam (East Sussex)

A village northwest of RYE whose name describes it as a 'northern hay meadow', from the Old English *hēg* (hay) and *hamm* (meadow), by contrast with the hamlet now called Higham just south of it. The latter's name means 'high meadow', but was re-corded as *Suthyhomme*, 'southern hay meadow' in a document of 1339. Northiam's own name appears in the Domesday Book as *Hiham* in its basic sense, then as *Northeham* in a record of 1288.

Northolt (Greater London)

This district of EALING, where London's main airport used to be, has a name that means 'northern nooks', from the Old English *north* and *healh* (nook, secluded place) (this despite the final *-t* which suggests it was the 'northern holt', i.e. 'wood'). It was 'northern' by contrast with SOUTHALL, whose second element, despite appearances, also derives from *healh*. Northolt was referred to in a document of 960 as *æt northhealum*, with the final '-*um*' representing the dative plural case required after *æt* (at).

North Shields (Tyne and Wear)

This town is situated on the north bank of the TYNE opposite SOUTH SHIELDS, as the first part of its name indicates. The second word of both names means 'sheds', from the Middle English *schele* (shed, cottage) (compare modern 'shieling'). The reference is to fishermen's huts, which formed the nucleus of the settlements that grew into the present towns on both sides of the river. North Shields was simply *Chelis* in a document of 1268, but then *Nortscheles* in 1275.

Northumberland (England)

The northeasternmost county of England, whose name should be interpreted as 'north Humberland', that is, as the 'land' of those people who lived north of the HUMBER. Put another way, Northumberland was the territory of the 'North Humberlanders', who gave their tribal name to the region they inhabited. (It was much more extensive than the present county, whose southern border is far north of the Humber.) The name was recorded in 867 as *Northhymbre*, this being the tribal name, then in its present form as *Northhymbralond* in 895. The county of Northumberland dates from the early twelfth century.

North Walsham (Norfolk)

This market town north of NORWICH is so named to contrast it with the village of South Walsham twelve miles southeast of it, east of Norwich. The basic name probably means 'Walh's homestead'. North Walsham appears as *Northwalsham* in the mid-eleventh century, but in the Domesday Book it was simply *Walsam*.

Northwich (Cheshire)

This town southwest of MANCHESTER has long had a salt industry, which is still active, and the final element of the name indicates this: it is the Old English *wīc*, usually meaning 'special place' and here specifically referring to salt production, as it does in the names of MIDDLEWICH, NANTWICH, and DROITWICH. Northwich is 'north' of Nantwich, therefore, with Middlewich, as its name implies, lying between the two. The Roman fort at Northwich was known as *Condate*, a name of British (Celtic) origin meaning 'confluence', and referring to the rivers Dane and WEAVER that meet at Northwich.

Northwood (Greater London)

This district of HILLINGDON has a self-explanatory name, with the 'northern wood' being to the north of RUISLIP. Its name was recorded in 1435 as *Northwode*. Compare NORWOOD.

Norwich (Norfolk)

The county town has a name that means 'northern specialised place', with the Old English *wīc* here meaning either 'town' or even 'port', as it does for GREENWICH, WOOLWICH, and so on. Norwich was regarded as 'north' by contrast with IPSWICH, which lies to the south of it (and is also a port). The name of the city was recorded as *Northwic* as early as the first half of the tenth century, and in the Domesday Book it was *Noruic*.

Norwood (Greater London)

A south LONDON district whose name shows it to have been a 'north wood', this originally being one to the north of CROYDON, and not entirely cut down until the nineteenth century. (*Cassell's Gazetteer* of 1897 describes Norwood as 'hilly and finely wooded'.) The name was recorded as *Norwude* in a document dated 1176.

Nottingham (Nottinghamshire)

This county town just northeast of DERBY has a name that declares the place to be the 'homestead of Snot's people', with the initial *S-* of the personal name having been (perhaps fortunately) dropped by the Normans, who found the pronunciation of *sn* a troublesome matter. However, the *S-* of the name still exists in the name of SNEINTON, 'farm of Snot's people', now an eastern district of Nottingham. Nottingham was recorded as *Snotengham* in the late ninth century, and as *Snotingeham* in the Domesday Book, but as *Notingeham* in 1130. The county of Nottinghamshire appeared as *Snotingahanscir* in 1016, and in the Domesday Book as *Snotingehamscyre*.

Notting Hill (Greater London)

This district of west LONDON has a name that is still under discussion. It may mean 'hill of the Knotting family', with the surname coming from the village of Knotting in Bedfordshire, near RUSHDEN. Or a conjectural Old English word *cnott* meaning 'hill' may lie behind the name. But the personal name seems the most likely origin, to judge by early records of the name, such as *Knottynghull* in 1346.

Nuneaton (Warwickshire)

A manufacturing town north of COVENTRY whose name means 'nuns' river farm' (*compare* ETON); the *Nun-* was added to the basic name in the twelfth century to refer to the Benedictine nunnery founded here then. The Domesday Book thus has the name of Nuneaton as *Etone*, and the present name is first recorded in a document of 1247 as *Nonne Eton*. Part of the original nunnery is preserved in St Mary's Church. The 'river' of the basic name is the little River Anker.

Nunney (Somerset)

This picturesque village with its moated castle southwest of FROME has a name that probably means 'Nunna's island' rather than 'island of the nuns', as has also been proposed. The 'island' is the land beside the tributary of the River Frome here. Nunney was recorded as *Nonin* in the Domesday Book. If 'nun' does lie behind the name, it will have come from the Old English *nunne*.

O

Oadby (Leicestershire)
A town immediately southeast of
LEICESTER with a Scandinavian name
meaning 'Authi's village', with the
personal name followed by the
characteristic Old Norse element *bý*
(homestead, village), that ends many
names in this part of England. The name
was recorded in a document of 1199 as
Outheby.

Oakham (Leicestershire)
This former county town of RUTLAND has
a name that suggests a connection with
'oaks' but actually means 'Occa's
homestead' or possibly 'Occa's riverside
meadow', depending whether one takes the
second element to be the Old English *hām*
(homestead) or *hamm* (meadow, riverside
pasture). The latter is possibly more likely,
as the town, in the Vale of Catmose, is
situated on a tongue of land between two
streams. The name was recorded in 1067 as
Ocham.

Oban (Strathclyde)
This east coast port and resort, on the bay
of the same name, has a name that really
relates to this bay, as it means 'little bay',
deriving from a full Gaelic name which is
An t-Òban Latharnach, 'the little bay of
Lorn'. Lorn is the name of the territory
here that lies between Loch AWE and the
coast and extends northwards to Loch
LEVEN. The name of Lorn is a tribal one,
that of Loarn's people. Loarn Mór, the
'great fox', was their leader in the sixth
century. For a name related to that of Oban
see LEVERBURGH.

Ochill Hills (Central/Tayside)
A range of hills extending approximately
from STIRLING in the west to the Firth of
TAY in the east. The name is of British
(Celtic) origin meaning simply 'high ones',

from a root word *uxello* related to the
modern Welsh *uchel* (high).

Offaly (Ireland)
A county in the centre of Ireland whose
name represents its Irish name of Uíbh
Fhailí, '(place of the) descendants of
Failghe'. This tribal name refers to Russ
Failghe, the legendary ancestor of the
people who lived here, known as the Uí
Failghe, or Offaly people. The present
county boundary was established in 1556,
when the territory was shired under the
name of King's County, after King Philip
II of Spain, husband of Queen Mary.
(Compare the former name of Queen's
County for LAOIS.) The county reverted to
its Irish name, or the present form of it, in
1920.

Offa's Dyke (Wales/England)
The lengthy entrenchment built in the
eighth century by Offa, King of Mercia, to
mark the boundary between Anglo-Saxon
and Welsh territory. It runs from
PRESTATYN in North Wales to CHEPSTOW
in the south, and is still clearly visible at
various points along its course. Offa is said
to have been buried at the village of Great
Offley, near HITCHIN, Hertfordshire, so
that this name derives from his own. The
present border between England and
Wales only rarely coincides with the line of
Offa's Dyke.

Ogmore (Mid Glamorgan)
The name occurs for several places and
features in the county, such as Ogmore
Vale, the village north of BRIDGEND; the
Ogmore Forest, that extends to the east of
this village; Ogmore-by-Sea, the coastal
village southwest of Bridgend; and above
all the River Ogmore, at whose mouth this
last village stands, so that its Welsh name is
Aberogwr, 'mouth of the Ogwr'. Ogwr, the
Welsh name of the river, is also the name of
an administrative district in the county.
Moreover, the Welsh name of Bridgend,
which is on the river, is Pen-y-Bont ar
Ogwr, 'end of the bridge over the Ogwr'.

The river name itself means 'sharp river' (compare the Welsh *miniog*, 'sharp', 'cutting').

Ogwr (Mid Glamorgan)
An administrative district in the west of the county, and a river that runs through it. *See* OGMORE.

Okehampton (Devon)
A market town below the northern edge of DARTMOOR at the confluence of the rivers East and West Okement, after which it takes its name, with the Old English *tūn* (village) added. The river itself probably has a name of British (Celtic) origin, meaning 'swift one', from a conjectural root element *aku-* related eventually to the English 'acute'. The '-hampton' of the place-name is thus misleading. Okehampton was recorded in a document of about 970 as *Ocmundtun*.

Oldbury (West Midlands)
This district of WARLEY, west of BIRMINGHAM, has a name that is found elsewhere in the country and means 'old fort'. This will usually mean a pre-Anglo-Saxon fort of some kind, such as the Iron Age fort known as Oldbury Camp near CALNE, Wiltshire. In the case of the West Midlands Oldbury, whose name was recorded in the twelfth century as *Aldeberie*, the precise reference is uncertain. But the name clearly indicates that there was some kind of ancient fortification here.

Oldham (Greater Manchester)
A town northeast of MANCHESTER whose name refers to an 'old promontory'. A record of the name dated about 1227 gives it as *Aldholm*, showing the second element to be not the Old English *hām* (homestead) but Old Norse *holmr* (island, promontory), as for DURHAM, where the '-ham' is similarly misleading. Oldham is situated on a spur at the western edge of SADDLEWORTH Moor, hence the promontory' of the name. The exact sense

of 'old' here is uncertain, although the word frequently indicated an ancient site, such as an Iron Age fort (*compare* OLDBURY). The suggestion has been made that 'old' may simply refer to a site that has long been occupied.

Old Sarum (Wiltshire)
A large earthwork immediately north of SALISBURY, and the original site of the city, which was moved down to the valley below from this bleak and exposed location in the thirteenth century. 'Old' refers to the former Iron Age hill-fort and subsequent Roman fort here (*compare* OLDBURY). 'Sarum' is an abbreviated form of the Latin name of Salisbury.

Old Trafford (Greater Manchester)
This district of SALFORD, with its well-known cricket and football grounds, has a name that is a variant of STRETFORD, the town lying to the south. The Norman form of Stratford, without the initial *S-* and with *-tf-* blended as *-ff-*, was given to the manor of Trafford formed out of the township of Stretford. 'Old' Trafford is thus designated by its first word as the original manor here, as opposed to Trafford Park, now a district of Stretford, which evolved later. The name Old Trafford appears on a map of 1786. For the origin of the basic name *see* STRETFORD.

Olney (Buckinghamshire)
A town on the River OUSE north of NEWPORT PAGNELL, whose name means 'Olla's island', with the personal name followed by the Old English *ēg* (island, land partly surrounded by water). Olney lies in a bend of the Ouse, which is joined from the south by several streams at this point. The town's name was recorded as *Ollaneg* in a late-tenth-century document.

Olympia (Greater London)
The exhibition hall and the district surrounding it in HAMMERSMITH. The hall itself was built in 1886 by the National Agricultural Hall Committee and was

given a typical Victorian 'grand and classical' name, regarded as appropriate for an architectural showpiece.

Omagh (Tyrone)

A market town northeast of ENNISKILLEN whose name simply means 'the plain', as is reflected in its equivalent Irish name of An Ómaigh. (The initial Ó- of this, however, remains obscure. The name was recorded as *Oghmaigh* in the fifteenth century, with only *magh* 'plain' as a certain element.) The town, although itself on a slope, stands at the point where three rivers meet.

Openshaw (Greater Manchester)

A district of MANCHESTER whose name means 'open wood', that is, one that is not enclosed. The two Old English elements of the name are *open* (open) (not all that common in place-names) and *sceaga* (wood). The name was recorded in a document of 1282 as *Opinschawe*.

Ordsall (Greater Manchester, Nottinghamshire)

A district of SALFORD and a district of RETFORD. In each case the name almost certainly has the same meaning, which is 'Ord's nook', with the second half of the name representing the Old English *halh* (nook, corner of land). Both places are in a fairly low-lying area, where nevertheless several small valleys are found, any one of which could be the 'nook' in question. The Salford Ordsall was recorded in 1177 as *Ordeshala*, and the Retford one appears in the Domesday Book as *Ordeshale*.

Orford (Suffolk)

This village east of WOODBRIDGE stands on the River Ore, and it might be supposed that it takes its name from it, as a place by a ford over it. But the river takes its name from the village, and the first half of the village's name in fact represents the Old English *ōra* (shore), so that its name means 'ford by the shore'. The village is quite close to the east coast, and gave its name not only to the river but, more obviously,

to the headland of Orford Ness, east of it, and the strip of shingle south of it known as Orford Beach. The name was recorded in 1164 as *Oreford*. For a river with a name that evolved in a similar way *compare* CHELMSFORD.

Orkney (Scotland)

This well-known group of islands north of mainland Scotland (but south of the SHETLAND Islands) has an ancient name recorded as early as the first century AD by the Latin geographer Mela as *Orcades*. The precise origin of the name remains uncertain, but it may mean 'whale', 'sea monster', either from the Greek word *oruga*, which gave the Latin *orca* and English 'orc', or from a Celtic word related to the Irish *orc*, which itself can also mean 'whale' as well as its more common meaning of 'pig' (so that it is indirectly related to English 'pork'). The adjective 'Orcadian' derives from this earliest classical form of the name. The final element of the name, more certainly, is the Old Norse *ey* (island).

Ormes Bay (Gwynedd)

The bay on the North Wales coast, also known as LLANDUDNO Bay. The name of the bay derives from those of the two flanking headlands, GREAT ORMES HEAD to the west, and Little Ormes Head to the east. *See* GREAT ORMES HEAD.

Ormskirk (Lancashire)

A town southeast of STOCKPORT whose name means 'Orm's church', with the personal name followed by the Old Norse *kirkja* as an alteration of the original Old English *cirice* (church). A man named Orm is on record as having held the place in 1203, but he was not necessarily the founder, although the first record we have of the name is not much earlier, and a document of about 1190 has Ormskirk as *Ormeschirche*.

Oronsay (Strathclyde)

The name occurs more than once in

Scotland, and means 'St Oran's island'.
Perhaps the best known island of the name
is the one south of COLONSAY, in the Inner
Hebrides. St Oran, a disciple of St
Columba, founded a monastery here in the
sixth century, perhaps on the site of the
present ruins of the fourteenth-century
Augustinian priory. The chapel here is
dedicated to St Oran. The name was
recorded as *Orvansay* in a document of
1549, with the final element representing
the Old Norse *ey* (island), as frequently
found in island names in this part of
Scotland.

Orpington (Greater London)
This former KENT town, in the Borough of
BROMLEY, has a name that means 'village
of Orped's people', with the Old English
tūn (farm, village) following the common
-ing suffix that means 'people of'. Orped's
own name arose as a nickname meaning
'stout', 'strenuous', 'energetic', from the
Old English *orped*, and this survives in the
modern surname Orpet or Orpett.
Orpington was recorded as *Orpedingtun* in
about 1011.

Orwell (Suffolk)
The name of the tidal part of the River
Gipping from IPSWICH to its confluence
with the STOUR at HARWICH. The name
probably means 'shore river', based on the
Old English *ōra* (shore) (as for ORFORD),
although early-eleventh-century records of
the name give it as *Arewan*, which suggests
some other meaning, unless this is a
miscopying of an earlier name.

Osborne (Isle of Wight)
The name of this house, Queen Victoria's
former home southeast of COWES,
probably means 'sheep stream'. The
second element of the name is certainly the
Old English *burna* (stream), but the first
part is less certain. The name was recorded
in a document of 1316 as *Austeburn*, which
suggests that the first element could be the
Old English *eowestre* (sheepfold) (the word
is itself related to modern English 'ewe').

Ossett (West Yorkshire)
A town west of WAKEFIELD whose name
has been interpreted as either 'Ōsla's fold'
or 'fold where blackbirds gather'. The
second part of the name is certainly the Old
English *geset* (dwelling, camp, stable, fold)
(related to 'settle'), but the first element
could be either the personal name or the
Old English *ōsle* (blackbird) (compare
'ouzel'). The name was recorded in the
Domesday Book as *Osleset*.

Oswaldtwistle (Lancashire)
The name of this town immediately
southwest of ACCRINGTON means
'Oswald's land in a fork between two
streams'. The latter half of the name
represents the Old English *twisla* 'river
fork', 'land between the junction of
streams' (compare 'betwixt' and 'twist' as
something with 'two strands'). Two
streams meet at Oswaldtwistle. It is not
known who Oswald was despite attempts to
identify him with King Oswald of
Northumbria. The name was recorded as
Oswaldthuisel in a thirteenth-century
document. *Compare* HALTWHISTLE.

Oswestry (Shropshire)
A town northwest of SHREWSBURY near
the Welsh border whose name means
'Oswald's tree', with the personal name
followed by the Old English *trēow* (tree).
The name is traditionally supposed to be
that of St Oswald, King of Northumbria
(sometimes also claimed by
OSWALDTWISTLE), whose death at a place
called *Maserfelth*, said to be near here, was
documented by the Venerable Bede in the
eighth century. But Oswestry's name has
not been documented until the thirteenth
century (as *Oswaldestre* in 1272), and this is
so long after the time of Oswald that the
connection seems doubtful. 'Tree',
whether associated with the king and saint
or not, could mean 'cross', 'crucifix', as
well as in the ordinary sense. There is a real
link with the saint in the dedication of the
town's parish church to St Oswald. The
place called *Maserfelth*, usually referred to

as 'Maserfield' in modern reference books and guides, has not been identified.

Otley (West Yorkshire)
A town northwest of LEEDS whose name means 'Otta's clearing', with the latter element of the name the Old English *lēah* (forest clearing), which is found in so many names in this part of Yorkshire, indicating the former extensive woodland here. *See* BATLEY for some examples.

Ottery St Mary (Devon)
A town east of EXETER by the River Otter, after which it takes its name. The river's name, for once, means what it says, 'otter river', from the Old English *oter* (otter) and *ēa* (river), with the final *-y* of Ottery representing this second word. Ottery St Mary has added the dedication of its parish church to be distinguished from the village of Upottery ('up the Otter') some ten miles to the north, and also from Venn Ottery ('fenland village on the Otter') three miles southwest of the town. Ottery St Mary appears in the Domesday Book as *Otri*, and in 1242 is recorded as *Otery Sancte Marie*.

Oughterard (Galway)
This village and angling centre northwest of GALWAY stands a short distance from Lough CORRIB at the foot of rising ground leading to the CONNEMARA mountains. Its name seems appropriate for this location, being a rendering of its Irish name, Uachtar Árd, meaning 'upper height', 'high upper place'.

Oulton Broad (Suffolk)
The second word of the name refers to the lake that is one of The BROADS here. Oulton itself is a northwest suburb of LOWESTOFT, with a name that means 'Āli's farm'; it was recorded in a document dated 1203 as *Aleton*. Oulton Broad is now the name of a western district of Lowestoft as well as that of the lake.

Oundle (Northamptonshire)
The name of this town southwest of

PETERBOROUGH is a tribal one, meaning '(place of the) non-sharing people', from the Old English *un-* (not; the modern prefix 'un-') and *dāl* (share, portion; modern 'dole'), implying that the territory given to these people was left over after the rest of the land had been divided up and duly apportioned elsewhere. A reference to the name appears in a document of about 725 as *in Undolum*, 'in the non-sharers' land', with another text some twenty-five years later showing the tribal name more clearly, *in provincia Undalum*. The Domesday Book recorded the present place-name as *Undele*.

Ouse (England)
Any of three well-known rivers of the name. One, also known as the Great Ouse, rises near TOWCESTER and makes its way circuitously across the country to The WASH; another rises near HORSHAM and makes its way east and south to the sea at NEWHAVEN (which see in this respect); and the third is formed by the confluence of the SWALE and URE and flows generally south to join the TRENT to form the HUMBER. There are also two rivers named Little Ouse in East Anglia. The name always has the same meaning: it is simply 'water' (*compare* AVON). The name comes from a Celtic root seen also in Greek *hydor*, Irish *uisce*, Gaelic *uisge* (and therefore 'whisky'), and, indirectly, English 'wash', and even ultimately in 'water' itself. The name is so common because, as for the many Avons, people simply talked about 'the water' for their nearby river. It should be stated, however, that the Sussex Ouse seems to have got its name from that of LEWES. It was described as *aqua de Lewes* in a document of about 1200, and this seems to have been misunderstood as 'de l'Ouse'.

Oxford (Oxfordshire)
The name of this well-known university city means exactly what it says, 'ox ford', implying that a ford here over the THAMES was used regularly by oxen. The location of the actual ford was probably just south of

Folly Bridge. The town's name was recorded as *Oxnaforda* in a document of about 925, and in the Domesday Book as *Oxeneford*. The county name appears as *Oxenafordscir* in a text of 1010. People with the surname Oxenford will have preserved the older form of the name. (See also the quotation under CLERKENWELL.)

Oxshott (Surrey)

A suburban district northwest of LEATHERHEAD whose name refers not to oxen but means 'Ocga's corner of land'. The personal name is followed by the Old English *scēat*, 'corner of land', 'projecting patch of land', as for ALDERSHOT and similar names. A text of 1180 has Oxshott's name as *Okesetta*.

Oxted (Surrey)

A town west of WESTERHAM whose name refers to oaks, not oxen. It means 'oak-tree place', 'place where oak trees grow', from the Old English *āc* (oak) and *stede* (place, site). This particular origin can be seen in the Domesday Book record of the name as *Acstede*.

Oystermouth (West Glamorgan)

This location in the MUMBLES district of SWANSEA has an English name that means what it says, 'river-mouth with oyster beds' (for a somewhat similar name *compare* MUSSELBURGH). Mumbles Head was formerly well known for its oyster fisheries; the oysters were gathered and brought to this southern end of the bay to 'fatten up' before being harvested. The Welsh name of Oystermouth is Ystumllwynarth, which seems to be an attempt to make a meaningful name from a variant rendering of the English, so that *ystum* means 'bend', *llwyn* is 'grove', and *garth* is 'hill' (or, as takes the fancy, *arth* is 'bear').

P

Paddington (Greater London)

A district of west central LONDON whose name means 'Padda's farm' or 'Padda's estate', with the familiar Old English -*ingtun* suffix not necessarily implying that the named person actually owned the farm, but merely that he was associated with it in some way. A document of about 1045 has the name as *Padington*.

Paddock Wood (Kent)

This small town east of TONBRIDGE has a self-evident name. Early records of it, such as *Parrock* in 1279, seem to show a different origin, but the modern English 'paddock' was originally 'parrock' (a dialect word), and developed in its present spelling with the -*rr*- of the word becoming -*dd*- to give an 'easier' pronunciation. (Compare 'pediment', which was originally *periment*, and associated with 'pyramid'.) The Old English word for 'paddock' was *pearroc*, to which modern 'park' is related. The original meaning of the word was more general than is today's association with horses, and was simply 'small enclosure'. The 'Wood' of the name came relatively late.

Padstow (Cornwall)

This town and resort near the coast northwest of WADEBRIDGE has an English name meaning 'St Petroc's church', with the saint's name, in somewhat distorted form, followed by the Old English *stōw* in its fairly common sense of 'holy place', 'church', as in the name of FELIXSTOWE. Padstow's name is mentioned in a document of the late tenth century as *Sancte Petroces stow*, and its present form began to appear in about the fourteenth century, such as *Padristowe* in 1351 and *Padestou* ten years later. It goes without saying that the town's parish church is dedicated to St Petroc. So is that of

BODMIN, whose name was recorded in early documents in a form virtually identical to that of Padstow, such as *Petrocys stow* in the eleventh century.

Pagham (West Sussex)

A suburban district west of BOGNOR REGIS whose name means 'Pæcga's village'; it was recorded in a document of the late seventh century as *Pecgan ham*.

Paignton (Devon)

A seaside resort southwest of TORQUAY, recorded in the Domesday Book as *Peinton*, a name that means 'village of Pæga's people' (the personal name is basically the same as that behind PAGHAM). Until the middle of the nineteenth century the spelling of the name was regularly 'Paington', and the present spelling, with a reversal of the -*ng*-, seems to have been introduced by the Great Western Railway, possibly under the influence of the name of TEIGNMOUTH, on the same railway line thirteen miles to the north.

Painswick (Gloucestershire)

This town northeast of STROUD was originally 'Wick', meaning 'outlying farm (Old English *wīc*), and so appears in the Domesday Book as *Wiche*. Its present name, recorded in 1265 as *Payneswick*, has added the name of Pain Fitzjohn, who is on record as having held the manor here in the first half of the twelfth century. His name means 'pagan' (*compare* NEWPORT PAGNELL).

Paisley (Strathclyde)

This manufacturing town west of GLASGOW might seem at first sight to have a name of English origin, although it actually means simply 'church', and is of Celtic origin from a word that itself derives from the Latin *basilica* (which in turn comes from the Greek *basilikos*, 'royal'!). An identical name is found in the Welsh village of Bassaleg (or Basaleg), near NEWPORT, Gwent. Paisley's name is of

Irish origin, given by the 'Scots' who came from Ireland to settle in eastern Scotland from the end of the sixth century. Paisley was recorded as *Passeleth* in 1157, and as *Paisleth* the following year. The *t* in these names is probably due to a misreading of the *c* in *baslec*, the Irish form of the word at that time.

Palmers Green (Greater London)
A district of ENFIELD whose name derives from the family of Matthew le Palmere, recorded as living here in 1341. The first record of the name, however, dates from earlier than this, and is *Palmeresfeld* in a text of 1205. The *-feld* ('open land') has become the modern 'Green'.

Pangbourne (Berkshire)
This town on the THAMES northwest of READING is also on the smaller River Pang, which flows into the Thames here, and its name is really the 'full' name of this river — the 'Pang Bourne'. The name of the town was thus referred to in a document of 843 as *æt Peginga burnan*, meaning 'at the stream of Pæga's people', so that the present shorter name of the river is a 'back formation' from that of Pangbourne itself.

Papa Sound (Orkney)
The Channel between the islands of WESTRAY and Papa Westray. It takes its name from the latter, and 'Papa', wherever it occurs in ORKNEY and SHETLAND, represents the Old Norse *pap-ey* (priest island), referring to the 'father' of the monastery on it, otherwise the abbot (a word that also ultimately means 'father', although from the Aramaic and Greek).

Par (Cornwall)
This small resort and port east of ST AUSTELL has a Cornish name that represents the commonly found *porth* (cove, harbour) in such names as PERRANPORTH and (as the first element) POLPERRO and POLRUAN.

Parkeston Quay (Essex)
The second word of the name represents the 'business' side of this western suburb of HARWICH, with its passenger and freight ferry terminal. The main name derives from the surname of Charles H. Parkes, chairman of the Great Eastern Railway, when the railway opened a quayside terminal here in the late nineteenth century to facilitate the transfer from boat to boat-train of passengers arriving at Harwich from the Continent.

Parknasilla (Kerry)
This well-known beauty spot on the estuary of the KENMARE river has an attractive name to match, meaning 'field of the willows', representing its Irish name, Páirc na Saileach.

Partick (Strathclyde)
A district of GLASGOW whose name is of Celtic origin meaning 'bushy place', from the same root word that also gave the names of NARBERTH and PERTH; it is represented by the modern Welsh *perth* (bush). Partick was recorded in about 1136 as *Perdeyc*.

Passage West (Cork)
This former dockyard town east of CORK is situated on the narrow western passage joining the inner division of Cork Harbour with the main outer section, and its name relates to this location, while at the same time differentiating the place from Passage East, the village on the eastern side of the estuary of the River Suir, above WATERFORD Harbour. The Irish name of both places is simply An Pasáiste, 'the passage'.

Peacehaven (East Sussex)
The present suburb of NEWHAVEN, on the coast to the west of the town, arose during the First World War as a 'plotland' development, as happened elsewhere at about this time along the south coast. In 1916 a competition was announced to find a name for the new resort, with

advertisements appearing in national newspapers headed '£2,600 in Prizes for a Name of a NEW SOUTH COAST RESORT' (*The Times*, 10 January 1916). The winning name was *New Anzac-on-Sea*, chosen as a tribute to the Australian and New Zealand Army Corps (ANZAC) who were stationed locally. However, after some dispute about the legality of the competition, and the wartime use of much of the land for agricultural purposes, the original planner of the plotland, Charles Neville, announced a new name for it in 1917. This was Peacehaven, denoting not merely a 'peaceful haven' but a desire for peace to end the war; also the name matched that of nearby Newhaven.

Peak District (Derbyshire/Staffordshire/Cheshire)
An upland region centred on the north Derbyshire High Peak, an area of rocky hills east of HAYFIELD; the highest summit of this area is KINDER SCOUT. 'Peak' therefore does not designate an individual hill or mountain. High Peak, now also the name of an administrative district centred on BUXTON, is so named by contrast with Low Peak, centred on WIRKSWORTH; these are former names of hundreds here. A text of the seventh century refers to the Peak as *Pecsætna lond* ('district of the peak dwellers'), and High Peak appears in a document of 1196 as *Alto Pech*. *See also* PECKHAM.

Peckham (Greater London)
A district of SOUTHWARK whose name means 'hill village', from the Old English *pēac* (hill; modern 'peak') (the word behind the name of the PEAK DISTRICT), and *hām* (homestead, village). There is not much of a hill at Peckham, but the old village is on higher ground immediately west of the area now known as Telegraph Hill (whose own name is significant in this respect). Peckham appears in the Domesday Book as *Pecheham*. *See also* PECKHAM RYE.

Peckham Rye (Greater London)
An area south of PECKHAM proper (which see for the origin of 'Peckham'), typically thought of as Peckham Rye Common and Peckham Rye Park, the open spaces east of East DULWICH. 'Rye' means 'stream', from the Old English *rith*, and the reference is to a stream that formerly flowed through this area, but that has long been covered over. A document of 1512 gives the name exactly as now.

Peebles (Borders)
A town and resort on the River TWEED south of EDINBURGH whose name is of Celtic origin, meaning 'shelters' (compare modern Welsh *pabell*, 'tent', plural *pebyll*, itself derived from the source that gave English 'pavilion'). The reference is to temporary shepherds' huts or shielings used on the summer pastures here. Compare the names of GALASHIELS and (although a different sort of livestock) NORTH SHIELDS and SOUTH SHIELDS. The name was recorded in about 1125 as *Pebles*. The Celtic word has acquired an English plural *-s*. The town gave its name to the former county of Peebles-shire.

Peel (Isle of Man)
A resort on the west coast of the island famous for its ancient (now ruined) castle on St Patrick's Isle; it is to this castle that the town's name refers, deriving from the Middle English *pēl*, literally 'enclosure' (modern 'pale' in 'beyond the pale'). This name was recorded in a charter of Henry IV dated 1399: *Concessimus eidem Comiti Northumbriae Insulam, Castrum, Pelam, et Dominium de Man* ('we grant to the said Earl of Northumberland the island, castle, peel, and lordship of Man'). (The castle included here was Castle Rushen, at CASTLETOWN.) Before the sixteenth century, the name of Peel was regularly 'Holmetown', that is, 'island town'; this name is itself reflected in the Manx name of the town, which is Port-na-Hinsey, 'port of the island'.

Pegwell Bay (Kent)

The traditional site of the Roman landing in Britain in AD 43, of the Saxon landing in 449, and also of St Augustine's arrival in 597. It has given its name to the former village of Pegwell, now a district of RAMSGATE. The name has not been found recorded earlier than 1799, and it appears to mean 'pig spring', 'spring where pigs drink'. If so, it is the same name as that of the location called Pigwell near LYDD, which was recorded as *Pigwell wall* in 1433, and *pyg Well* in 1530.

Pembroke (Dyfed)

A town southwest of CARMARTHEN on a peninsula in the southwest of the county. Its situation is somewhat similar to that of PENZANCE, near LAND'S END, and its name describes this location, meaning 'end of the land', from the British (Celtic) root words that correspond to the modern Welsh *pen* (head, end) (as in PENZANCE also) and *bro* (region, land). (The Welsh name of Pembroke reflects this more clearly, as Penfro.) The name was recorded in the mid-twelfth century as *Pennbro* and as *Pembroch* in 1191. It seems to be no mere coincidence that names of this type are invariably on the west coast, not the east, with Land's End itself having its continental parallels of Finistère and Finisterre on the western coasts of France and Spain respectively. *Compare also* the name of WESTWARD HO! Pembroke gave its name to the former county of Pembrokeshire. *See also* PEMBROKE DOCK.

Pembroke Dock (Dyfed)

A port near the head of MILFORD HAVEN estuary, where it arose in 1814 as the Royal Dockyard, established by the government and soon taking the name of nearby PEMBROKE. Previous to this, the location here was known as the small village of Pater, or Paterchurch, 'St Patrick's Church'; the Welsh name of this hamlet, Llanbadrig, remains for Pembroke Dock today. The Royal Dockyard closed in 1926.

Penarth (South Glamorgan)

This port and resort south of CARDIFF takes its name from the promontory, Penarth Head, on which it is situated, with 'Penarth' meaning 'headland of the hill', from the Welsh *pen* (head) and *garth* (hill)

Pendlebury (Greater Manchester)

This town northwest of MANCHESTER takes its name from a nearby hill that must have been known as Pendle (with the same origin for this name as for PENDLE HILL). The final element of the name is the Old English *burg* (fort). The hill name has now been lost, but is preserved in the town's name. Pendlebury was recorded in a document of 1201 as *Penelbiri*.

Pendle Hill (Lancashire)

A prominent hill east of CLITHEROE is located in the area known as the Forest of Pendle, with 'Pendle' now the name of the administrative district here in the east of the county. Pendle itself is derived from two root words, the first Celtic, the second Old English, that both mean 'hill': respectively, *penno-* (as in modern Welsh *pen*) and *hyll* (modern 'hill'). These can be clearly seen in a record of the name in 1296 as *Pennehille*. No doubt the Anglo-Saxons added their 'hill' to the Celtic one, not understanding that the sense of 'hill' was already there. Finally, the modern 'Hill' was added to 'Pendle' when in turn *it* was no longer understood, so that the complete name effectively says 'hill' three times! This Pendle Hill is not the one behind the name of PENDLEBURY, although the evolution of the name is identical.

Penge (Greater London)

A district of BROMLEY whose name is of British (Celtic) origin and consists of the two root elements meaning 'head' and 'wood', as in the modern Welsh *pen* (in PENARTH) and *coed* (in BETWYS-Y-COED). The sense is thus 'chief wood', with the name recorded in a document of 1067 as *Penceat*. Penge was at one time an important woodland pasture, and until

1888 belonged to the manor and parish of
BATTERSEA. The survival of the Celtic
name shows that there must been a sizeable
number of (Ancient) Britons living here at
the time of the Anglo-Saxon settlement.

Penicuik (Lothian)
This town south of EDINBURGH has a
Celtic name that means 'cuckoo hill', from
root words related to the modern Welsh
pen (hill) and *cog* (cuckoo). The name was
recorded in 1250 as *Penikok*.

Penistone (South Yorkshire)
A town west of BARNSLEY whose name
was recorded in the Domesday Book as
Pengestone; this probably represents the
name of a hill, called 'Penning' (Celtic *pen*
as in PENICUIK etc., plus the Old English
-ing), to which the Old English *tūn* (farm,
estate), was added. The meaning as a whole
is thus perhaps 'estate by Penning Hill',
although no such hill of the name has been
found here. However, the town itself
occupies a lofty site, at least 700 feet above
sea level.

Penmaenmawr (Gwynedd)
This North Wales coastal resort west of
CONWY takes its name from the nearby
mountain of Penmaen Mawr, 'great stony
head', comprising the Welsh *pen* (head),
maen (stone), and *mawr* (big).

Pennines (England)
England's main mountain range, extending
from the PEAK DISTRICT in the south to
the CHEVIOT HILLS in the north. Its name
has not been found in records earlier than
the eighteenth century, and it is said to be
the mock-Celtic invention of the literary
forger Charles Bertram, who wrote an
account of Britain by an imaginary monk
called Richard of Westminster. But it
seems strange that this important chain,
now nicknamed the 'backbone of
England', should not have had an earlier
name, even if no record of it has been
traced. Moreover, it is highly likely that its
name would be based on the Celtic *pen* or

penn, whether in its sense of 'hill' or 'head'
(perhaps even a blend of both, as the 'chief
hills'). But until substantiation of the name
has been made, we will simply have to
accept that it *may* be a modern invention,
but that it could well be a genuinely ancient
name.

Penrhyndeudraeth (Gwynedd)
This large village east of PORTHMADOG
has a self-descriptive name for its location,
'promontory with two beaches', from the
Welsh *penrhyn* (promontory), *dau* (two),
and *traeth* (strand, beach).
Penrhyndeudraeth stands on a ridge of
land (the 'promontory') at the confluence
of two rivers as they flow through Traeth
Bach ('little beach') to create a large
estuary. Part of the estuary, Traeth Mawr
('big beach'), was reclaimed in order to
create the resort of Porthmadog. *Compare*
PENRYN.

Penrith (Cumbria)
A town southeast of CARLISLE whose name
is of British (Celtic) origin meaning 'ford
by a hill', from root words seen in the
modern Welsh *pen* (hill) and *rhyd* (ford).
The hill is Penrith Beacon, to the east of
the town. The ford was probably over the
River Eamont two miles southeast of
Penrith, by Brougham Castle. This was
certainly where the Roman road crossed
the river and was the site of the Roman fort
of *Brocavum*, a name probably meaning
'heathery place'. Brougham's own name
means 'village by the fort', referring to the
Roman fort, from the Old English *burg*
(fort) and *hām* (village). Penrith's name
was recorded as now in a document of
about 1100.

Penryn (Cornwall)
A town northwest of FALMOUTH on a
small promontory at the head of the River
Penryn; its name means simply 'promontory', from the conjectural Cornish
pen-ryn, identical to the Welsh *penrhyn* that
forms the basis of PENRHYNDEUDRAETH.
Its name was recorded in 1259 as *Penrin*.

Penshurst (Kent)
This village west of TONBRIDGE is well
known for the fourteenth-century manor
house of Penshurst Place, named after it.
'Penshurst' means 'Pefen's wooded hill',
with the personal name followed by the
Old English *hyrst* (hillock, wooded hill).
The name was recorded in a document of
1072 as *Peneshurst*. The same personal
name is found in that of PEVENSEY. 'Place'
has been used as a word for a main
dwelling-place or manor house since the
fourteenth century, and occurs in Chaucer
in this sense ('With grene trees shadwed
was his place', *Canterbury Tales*).

Pentland Firth (Scotland)
The sea strait between mainland Scotland
and the ORKNEY Islands. 'Pentland' means
'Pictland' or 'land of the Picts'; this was the
name used by the Vikings for the north of
Scotland generally. 'Firth' means 'sea inlet'
(*see* FIRTH OF FORTH). The name as a
whole was recorded in a text of about 1085
as *Pettaland fjorthr*. This Pentland should
not be confused with the PENTLAND
HILLS, which has a different origin.

Pentland Hills (Strathclyde/Borders/
Lothian)
A chain of hills southwest of EDINBURGH
whose name is of different origin to that of
the PENTLAND FIRTH. Here, the basis is
almost certainly in the Celtic root word
penn (hill, head), found in such names as
PENRITH and (in Cornish form)
PENZANCE. The second element of the
name is the English '-land'.

Penwith (Cornwall)
This administrative district, the most
westerly in the county, includes
PENZANCE and LAND'S END, and has
adopted a former hundred name in this
region. The name was originally the
Cornish name of Land's End itself, and
seems to derive from an unrecorded
Cornish word *penwyth*, meaning 'far end',
'extremity', based on *pen* (head, top, end).
The name was recorded in 1186 as *Penwid*.

Penzance (Cornwall)
This well-known resort and port southwest
of TRURO has a name that means 'holy
headland', from the Cornish *pen*
(headland) and *sans* (holy) (related to
English 'saint'). The name refers to the old
chapel of St Mary, now represented by St
Mary's Parish Church, which stood on the
headland at what is now the bottom end of
Chapel Street. The name was recorded as
Pensans in a document of 1284 and is an
exact Cornish equivalent of the name of
HOLYHEAD.

Perivale (Greater London)
A district of EALING whose name means
'pear-tree valley', recorded in 1508 as
Pyryvale, from the Middle English *perie*
(pear tree) and *vale* (valley). This name
replaced the earlier name of Little
Greenford (*see* GREENFORD), recorded in
1254 as *Greneforde Parva*, as distinct from
Greneforde Magna, which was 'Great
Greenford', or Greenford itself.

Perranporth (Cornwall)
A coastal resort southwest of NEWQUAY
with a Cornish name meaning 'St Perran's
port', with the saint's name that of the
dedication of the parish church. The name
was originally *Porth Perane*, which might
have become 'Polperran', like POLPERRO
and POLRUAN. No doubt the transposition
of the elements of the name took place
when English-speakers realised that the
Cornish *porth* meant 'port' and rearranged
the name as a sort of 'translation', so that
the elements came in the English order (as
for NEWPORT). St Perran (or Piran) was a
fifth-century monk who came from Ireland
or Wales to settle in Cornwall.

Perry Barr (West Midlands)
A district of BIRMINGHAM whose name
means 'pear-tree place near Barr', from the
Old English *pirige* (pear tree) (compare
modern 'perry'). Barr would have been the
name of a hill here, northwest of the city
centre, with its own name of Celtic origin
and meaning simply 'hill', as for Great

Barr, southeast of WALSALL, and the hill there known as Barr Beacon. Perry Barr was simply *Pirio* in the Domesday Book.

Pershore (Hereford and Worcester)

This town west of EVESHAM lies on the River AVON and has a name that means 'osier slope', from a conjectural Old English word *persc* (twig, osier) (surviving as the Gloucestershire dialect word 'persh') and the Old English *ōra* (bank, slope). The reference is no doubt to the land between the river and a slight hill to the west of the town, where once osiers grew, with their twigs used for basket-making. The name was recorded in a document of 972 as *Perscoran*.

Perth (Tayside)

This ancient town on the River TAY north of EDINBURGH has a name of Pictish (pre-Celtic) origin meaning 'bush', 'thicket' (related to Welsh *perth* with this meaning), describing its original location. The name was recorded in about 1128 as *Pert* (*Compare* NARBERTH.) The town gave its name to the former county of Perthshire.

Peterborough (Cambridgeshire)

An industrial and cathedral city originally known as 'Medeshampstead' (*Medeshamstedi* in a document of about 750); this probably means 'homestead by the whirlpool', with the name that of the Anglo-Saxon settlement that arose on the site of a monastery in the seventh century. Two hundred years later, the monastery was destroyed by the Danes, but was rebuilt in the mid-tenth century as a Benedictine centre. Some time after that the place became known simply as 'the town' (*Burg* in the Domesday Book), but the old name was still on record in a document of the twelfth century, which referred to *Medeshamstede qui modo Burg dicitur* ('Medeshampstead which is now only called Burg'). (*Compare* BURY ST EDMUNDS.) By the fourteenth century the name had come to be recorded in its present form, *Petreburgh* in 1333, after the

original dedication of the abbey to St Peter, with the Domesday Book *Burg* now the '-borough' of the longer name. The cathedral, similarly dedicated, stands on the site of the old abbey, where it was built in the twelfth century.

Peterculter (Grampian)

A village and housing development southwest of ABERDEEN. Its basic name, *-culter*, is found elsewhere in Scotland as Culter or Coulter, meaning 'corner land', from the Gaelic *cùil* (corner) and *tìr* (land). Here, Peterculter has added the name of its church, dedicated to St Peter, to be distinguished from Maryculter, south of the River DEE, whose church is dedicated to St Mary. An almost exact parallel exists in the villages of Peter Tavy and Mary Tavy, in Devon, also either side of the river (the Tavy).

Peterhead (Grampian)

A fishing port north of ABERDEEN whose name means 'St Peter's headland', with the first part of the name referring to the dedication of the church. The original name of Peterhead was Inverugie, 'mouth of the Ugie', from its location at the mouth of this river. The remains of the twelfth-century St Peter's Kirk lie by the golf links in the south of the town. The present name was recorded in 1544 as *Petyrheid*, this being the headland (named after the church); the actual town was not founded until 1593 (by George Keith, the fifth Earl Marischal).

Peterlee (Durham)

A New Town (designated in 1948) northwest of HARTLEPOOL, named after the popular local miner and trade union leader Peter Lee, who died in 1935. The name seems to have been chosen, after due consideration, by C.W. Clark, engineer and surveyor to EASINGTON Rural District Council, who explained the background to his choice in the report entitled *Farewell Squalor*, published in 1947. It is fortuitous that the named man's surname serves as an appropriate ending to a place-name, suggesting the commonly found '-ley' or '-leigh'.

Petersfield (Hampshire)

This town northeast of PORTSMOUTH had its name first recorded (as *Peteresfeld*) in a document of 1182, showing that the place arose as a Norman-style 'new town' well after the Conquest. The town took the name of St Peter's church, now its parish church, which already existed when the town was founded as a borough. The second element of the name means 'open land', from the Old English *feld* in this sense, and today a portion of this is represented by the open public space known as Petersfield Heath, to the east of the town centre.

Petts Wood (Greater London)

A district of BROMLEY whose name means 'wood by a hollow', from the Old English *pytt* (pit, hollow) in its Kent variant of *pett*. The word itself implies either a natural hollow or one dug specially for mineral extraction or as a trap for animals. Equally, it could be a grave. The basic word is found in several local names in Kent, such as Pett Farm, Pett Place, Pett Street, and so on.

Petworth (West Sussex)

A small town northeast of CHICHESTER whose name means 'Pēota's enclosure' (Old English *worth*); it is recorded in the Domesday Book as *Peteorde*.

Pevensey (East Sussex)

This village, which gave its name to Pevensey Bay to the south, lies near the coast northeast of EASTBOURNE. Its name means '(place by) Pefen's river', referring to the stream on which it stands, with the final element from the Old English *ēa* (river). There was a Roman fort at Pevensey, named *Anderita*, perhaps meaning 'great fords', and referring to crossings over a sea inlet here. (The coastline has changed considerably over the past centuries, and it would be

impossible to identify the particular site of the 'fords' today.) This Roman name gave the subsequent Anglo-Saxon name *Andred* for the forestland along the south coast, with a section of the NEW FOREST so designated, although some distance west of *Anderita* itself. For a time, Pevensey was known as 'Andredchester' (*Andredesceaster* in the late fifth century, according to the *Anglo-Saxon Chronicle*), but Pevensey's own name appears as *Pefenesea* in 947. The same personal name appears for PENSHURST, Kent.

Pewsey (Wiltshire)

A small town south of MARLBOROUGH on a branch of the River AVON. The name means 'Pefe's island', referring to its riverside location in the more extensive Vale of Pewsey. The name was recorded in a late-ninth-century document as *æt Pefesigge*, with the final element of the name representing the Old English *ēg* (island).

Pickering (North Yorkshire)

This market town, at the foot of the North Yorkshire Moors west of SCARBOROUGH, has a name whose precise origin has not yet been finally established. It may be a tribal name based on the Old English *pīc* (point, pointed hill), perhaps meaning something like '(place of the) hill dwellers', although others regard it as an Old Norse name, but perhaps having a similar meaning (there is a Norwegian dialect word *pik* used to refer to a pointed mountain). Pickering at least has the '-ing' ending that means 'people of', found also in SPALDING and other names. The name was recorded in the Domesday Book as *Picheringa*.

Piddletrenthide (Dorset)

A village north of DORCHESTER on the River Piddle (or Puddle, or Trent, oddly enough), which gives the first element of its name. The remainder of the name means 'thirty hides', from the French *trente* (thirty) and the Old English *hīd* (hide) (the amount of land needed for one family to live on). The Domesday Book has the name simply as *Pidrie*, but in 1212 it appears as *Pidele Trentehydes*, and then as *Pudele thrittyhide* in 1314, with the Old English *thrittig* for 'thirty'. (The French and English words for this number alternate in records of the name over the years, until eventually the French one wins!) The basic river name probably means 'fenland river', from a conjectural Old English word *pidele* (fen). It lies behind many Dorset names, such as PUDDLETOWN, Affpuddle, Bryants Puddle, and TOLPUDDLE, with the change from Piddle to Puddle presumably for reasons of propriety. The alternative name of Trent for the river is curious. It cannot derive from that of the well-known TRENT, although an early-twelfth-century document does refer to the Piddle as the *Terente*. If this latter name is itself not an early 'back formation', no doubt the alternative name of Trent itself derived as a combination of this and of the middle *-trent-* of Piddletrenthide. Or possibly it was influenced by another River Trent in Dorset, the one that gave the name of the village of Trent, northeast of SHERBORNE.

Pilgrims Way (Hampshire/Surrey/Kent)
An ancient track that follows the southern slope of the North Downs, doubtless used by pilgrims journeying to CANTERBURY in medieval times. However, it does not seem to have received its name in this connection until the second half of the eighteenth century, where different sections of it are referred to respectively as *the Upper Pilgrim Road* and simply *Pilgrim Road* in a text of 1778 (Hasting's *History of Kent*). It would be wrong to suppose, therefore, that it was solely used by such pilgrims, as it existed long before their time.

Pimlico (Greater London)
This district of south central LONDON has a curious name with what may be an unusual origin. It was first recorded in 1630, as *Pimplico*, and is said to have derived from the name of a local innkeeper,

Ben Pimlico, or from an inn here named after him. (According to some accounts, he himself came from Hoxton, in northeast London.) But what sort of a surname does he have, and what nationality is it, if not British?

Pinkie (Lothian)
The site of the battle of 1547, southeast of MUSSELBURGH, in which the English defeated the Scots. Here also is Pinkie House, where Prince Charles Edward Stuart (the 'Young Pretender') spent the night after the Battle of PRESTONPANS in 1745. The name was recorded in the twelfth century as *Pontekyn*, showing its origin to be two Celtic words meaning 'wedge-shaped valley' (modern Welsh *pant*, 'valley' and *cŷn*, 'wedge').

Pinner (Greater London)
A district of HARROW whose name means literally 'pin bank', from the Old English *pinn* (pin) and *ōra* (edge, bank). The reference is to the 'pin-shaped' humped ridge that crosses Pinner Park. The name was recorded as *Pinnora* in a document of 1232.

Pitlochry (Tayside)
This resort with its well-known festival theatre, northwest of DUNKELD, has a typical Pictish name with the frequently found 'Pit-' element (seen also in PITTENWEEM) that means 'portion', from a conjectural word *pett* corresponding to the modern Welsh *peth* (part). Pitlochry's name thus means 'portion of the stones'; the latter half of the name is of Gaelic origin, representing *cloichreach*, and almost certainly refers to stepping-stones. This may indicate a crossing-place on the River Tummel, on which Pitlochry stands. It seems likely that the name of the Picts themselves relates to this word, so that they were the 'portion people', 'people who held a piece of land', rather than the 'painted people' (Latin *picti*) as is traditionally stated.

Pittenweem (Fife)
A fishing port, on the FIRTH OF FORTH west of ANSTRUTHER, with a Pictish name containing the *pett* element described for PITLOCHRY and meaning 'cave portion'. The second half of the name represents the Gaelic *na h-uamha*, 'of the cave' (*compare* the Irish An Uaimh; *see* NAVAN).

Plaistow (Greater London)
There are two places of the name in LONDON, one in the Borough of NEWHAM, the other in BROMLEY. In each case the meaning is the same, 'play place', from the Old English *pleg-stōw*, 'sport place', comprising *plega* (play) and *stōw* (place); that is, a place where people gathered for sport and recreation, as well as for meetings of the local community generally. The site would have been an open space corresponding to some extent to the modern village green or common, or a public tract such as HAMPSTEAD Heath.

Plumstead (Greater London)
A district of GREENWICH whose name means 'plum place', 'place where plum-trees grow', it was recorded in about 961 as *Plumstede*. The two Old English elements of the name are *plūme* (plum tree) and *stede* (place).

Plymouth (Devon)
This famous city west of TORQUAY has a name that relates directly to both PLYMPTON and PLYMSTOCK. As it stands, it obviously means '(place at the) mouth of the Plym'. The river, however, got its name from Plympton, although this place is not actually on it. Hence, before the river acquired its name by 'back formation', Plymouth must have had another name. This was Sutton, 'southern village', in which the manor was held by the priory of Plympton. This old name is preserved today in the name of Sutton Pool, one of Plymouth's three main harbours. Plymouth therefore acquired its present name only in about the middle of the fifteenth century, and was referred to in a document of this period: *Sutton Prior vulgariter Plymmouth nuncupatur* ('Sutton Prior is now commonly called Plymouth').

Plympton (Devon)
An eastern district of PLYMOUTH whose name means 'plum-tree village', from the Old English *plūme* (plum tree) (*compare* PLUMSTEAD) and *tūn* (village). Its name was recorded in the early tenth century as *Plymentun*, and it gave the name of the River Plym, although not actually on the river. The adoption of the name no doubt occurred because the western boundaries of the parishes of both Plympton and PLYMSTOCK were actually formed by the river, and it was assumed that they were both named after it. Therefore, the river was assumed to be the Plym!

Plymstock (Devon)
A district of PLYMOUTH southeast of the city centre. Its name means 'outlying farm (Old English *stoc*) belonging to PLYMPTON', which adjoined it to the north, as it still does. For the basic sense of the name *see* PLYMPTON. Plymstock's name was recorded in the Domesday Book as *Plemestocha*. All three names here are interwoven with each other and with that of the River Plym, which flows into Plymouth Sound to the east of Plymouth.

Plynlimon (Dyfed)
This mountain east of ABERYSTWYTH near the Powys border has a name that may mean 'five beacons', as reflected in its Welsh name of Pumlumon, from *pum* (five) and *llumon* (chimney). The mountain certainly has five distinct summits, on one or more of which beacons could have been lit in medieval times. (*Compare* the name of the BRECON BEACONS, also in Wales.)

Pocklington (Humberside)
A town northwest of MARKET WEIGHTON whose name means 'village of Pocel's people', with the personal name followed by the common Old English suffix *-ingtūn*, 'place of the people of' or 'place associated

with'. The name was recorded in the
Domesday Book as *Poclinton*.

Polegate (East Sussex)

A suburb of EASTBOURNE whose name
means 'pool gate', 'gate by a pool'; it was
first recorded only as recently as 1563, as
Powlegate Corner.

Polesden Lacey (Surrey)

The Regency house northwest of DORKING
has a basic name that derives from that of
an earlier settlement here. It means 'Pāl's
valley', with the personal name followed by
the Old English *denu* (valley). This name
was recorded in the late twelfth century as
Polesdene, and as *Pollesdon Lacy* in 1538. It
remains uncertain who the 'Lacey' is, and
it is possible that the name is not a genuine
manorial addition at all, but a spurious
one, especially in view of the late record of
it. The name is duplicated in that of
Camilla Lacey, a country house two miles
east of Polesden Lacey. This was built in
about 1798 by Madame D'Arblay (Fanny
Burney) and originally called 'Camilla',
after her novel of this name published in
1796; the proceeds from the sale of the
novel were used to build the house. 'Lacey'
was subsequently added to match the name
of Polesden Lacey.

Pollok (Strathclyde)

A district in southwest GLASGOW
whose name also occurs in those
of the neighbouring districts of
POLLOKSHAWS and POLLOKSHIELDS (see
below). Pollok is a word of British
(Celtic) origin meaning 'little pool', with
this recorded in a document of 1158 as
Pullock.

Pollokshaws (Strathclyde)

A district of southwest GLASGOW whose
name comprises the basic POLLOK (as
above), with 'shaws' added to distinguish
this particular 'little pool' from
POLLOKSHIELDS (below). The addition
means 'woods' (Old English *sceaga*), as in
the name of WISHAW.

Pollokshields (Strathclyde)

A district of southwest GLASGOW whose
name consists of the basic word POLLOK
(see above), 'little pool', with 'shields'
added to distinguish this place from
POLLOKSHAWS (above). The addition
means 'shielings', 'temporary sheds by
summer pastures' (*compare* GALASHIELS;
NORTH SHIELDS; SOUTH SHIELDS).

Polperro *(Cornwall)*

This coastal resort southwest of LOOE has a
name based on the Cornish *porth* (harbour);
it was recorded in a document of 1303 as
Portpira. The second half of the name is
difficult to establish with certainty: it may
represent a name such as *Pyra*, referring to
the small stream that runs through the
middle of the resort, dividing it into the
two parishes of Lansallos and Talland.

Polruan (Cornwall)

A village opposite FOWEY at the mouth of
the river of this name. It has the Cornish
porth (cove, harbour) for the first element
of its name (rather than the similar *pol*,
'pool', 'cove'), as evidenced by a record of
the name as *Porthruan* in 1284. The second
half of the name is that of the Celtic saint
Ruan or Rumon, whose name is also
present in that of the Devon village of
Romansleigh, near SOUTH MOLTON. Little
is known about Rumon, but he may have
been a sixth-century monk from
GLASTONBURY.

Polzeath (Cornwall)

A village on the east side of PADSTOW Bay
northwest of WADEBRIDGE whose name
derives from the Cornish *pol* (pool, cove)
and *segh* (dry). A 'dry pool' is one that dries
up in summer, like an English
'Winterbourne' (which is a stream flowing
only in winter).

Pomona (Orkney)

The former name of the island now known
as MAINLAND. In classical mythology,
Pomona was the name of the goddess of
fruit trees, but this is not the origin here!

Nor does it mean that Mainland, as the largest island, was regarded as the 'apple' of the group. The name seems to have arisen through a mapmaker's error in medieval times or earlier, perhaps in connection with the fruit trees associated with some other island, real or mythical. A document of the late fourteenth century refers to the Orkneys as *Insulae Pomoniae*.

Ponders End (Greater London)

This district of ENFIELD owes its name to a family called Ponder, who were recorded here in the fourteenth century. The name literally means 'keeper of the pond', although whether a member of this family was ever an actual 'pond-keeper' here seems doubtful. 'End' means 'remote district of the estate'. The name as a whole was recorded in 1593 as *Ponders Ende*.

Pontardawe (West Glamorgan)

This town northwest of NEATH lies in the valley of the River Tawe, and its name indicates this location, meaning 'bridge of the Tawe', comprising the Welsh *pont* (bridge) and *ar* (on, over). *Compare* PONTARDDULAIS.

Pontarddulais (West Glamorgan)

A small town northwest of SWANSEA whose name translates from the Welsh as 'bridge over the Dulais', this river name meaning 'black water'. The Dulais is a small stream that flows into the larger River LOUGHOR on which the town more obviously stands.

Pontefract (West Yorkshire)

This town southeast of LEEDS is famous for its Pontefract (or Pumfret) cakes – round flat liquorice sweets once made from the liquorice plant that was formerly grown here extensively in gardens and nurseries. But the town is also famous for its Latin name, literally 'broken bridge' (*pontus fractus*); the name's modern form represents the ablative singular (*ponte fracto*), denoting 'location'. It is remarkable that the name has survived in this form,

and not in the 'smoothed' Norman French pronunciation and spelling, as preserved in the 'Pumfret' already mentioned. (The name was recorded in a document of the late twelfth century as *Pumfrate*). All that remains is to explain the 'broken bridge'. Where was it, and why was it broken? It is very probable that the bridge of the name was not over the AIRE or the CALDER, although the confluence of these two rivers is near the town, but was over a small stream known as the Wash Dike, with the actual site of the bridge where Bubwith Bridge now is, east of the town near the A645 road to KNOTTINGLEY. The stream is a small one, but the bridge over it would have been an important one, giving access to the Great North Road. A 'broken bridge' at this point would thus have been of considerable significance to an advancing army in medieval times. It is not known precisely why it was broken, and the historic event of its breaking is not recorded. However, the inevitable legends record how William the Conqueror deliberately destroyed it for strategic reasons, besides other similar accounts. Pontefract also had an Old English name, which was 'Taddenshelf' (*Taddenscylf*), meaning 'Tædden's shelf' (i.e. 'shelf of land'). This was then ousted by the French (Latin) name, but not before a Norse name for the town was recorded in the twelfth and thirteenth centuries. This was 'Kirkby' (*Kyrkebi*), otherwise 'church village'. Pontefract is thus a town with a distinctive product (still made today, although using imported liquorice plants), and with a distinctive set of names in no less than four different languages.

Ponteland (Northumberland)

A town northwest of NEWCASTLE UPON TYNE whose name (pronounced 'Pont*ee*land') means 'island by the (River) Pont', otherwise 'riverside land' by this river. The second half of the name thus represents the Old English *ēa-land*, 'river land', perhaps referring to newly cultivated land by the river. The name of the river on

which the town stands, the Pont, is of
Celtic origin, and means simply 'valley
(river)' (compare Welsh *pant* 'valley' in
many names). Ponteland was recorded
simply as *Eland* in a document of 1242, but
in an earlier text of 1202 it was *Punteland*,
as now.

Pontycymer (West Glamorgan)

A coal-mining town north of BRIDGEND
whose name means 'bridge at the
confluence', from the Welsh *pont* (bridge),
y (the), and *cymer* (confluence). This refers
to its location at a point where two streams
meet.

Pontypool (Gwent)

This town north of NEWPORT has a half-
Welsh, half-English name, meaning
'bridge by the pool', from the Welsh *pont*
(bridge) and the English 'pool'. (The
Welsh name of the town translates this
fully, as Pont-y-pwl.) Pontypool is on the
River Llwyd, and no doubt this was the
original 'pool' of the name. The origin is
thus not in 'Pont-ap-Howell', understood
as 'Howell's bridge', as sometimes stated,
and the name is a quite recent one,
recorded in 1617 as *Pont y Poole*.

Pontypridd (Mid Glamorgan)

A town standing at the confluence of the
rivers RHONDDA and TAFF, northwest of
CARDIFF. Its original name, recorded in a
document of about 1700, was *Pont y Ty
Pridd*, 'bridge by the earthen house', from
the Welsh *pont* (bridge), *y* (the), *tŷ* (house),
and *pridd* (earth). There must have been
such a house by the river here. Later, the *tŷ*
or 'house' element disappeared from the
name, as the two letters that comprised it
were already present in *pont y*, the first two
words of the name, and were thus felt to be
unnecessarily duplicated. For a time, the
town was known as Newbridge, after a
'new bridge' was built over the river here
in 1755. This English name was finally
abandoned, however, in order to avoid
confusion with NEWBRIDGE in
Gwent.

Poole (Dorset)

This port and manufacturing town west of
BOURNEMOUTH has a straightforward
name that refers to its 'pool' or harbour.
The town's name was recorded in a
document of 1194 as *Pole*.

Pooley Bridge (Cumbria)

A village at the northeastern end of
ULLSWATER whose basic name, 'Pooley',
means 'pool mound', 'mound by the pool',
from the Old English *pōl* (pool) and the
Old Norse *haugr* (mound, hill). The 'pool'
would be the lower end of Ullswater, and
the 'mound' the ancient camp site on the
round hill known as Bowerbank to the west
of the village. The bridge of the name is
over the River Eamont, which leaves
Ullswater here to flow northeast towards
PENRITH. In a document of 1252 Pooley
Bridge was recorded as *Pulhoue*.

Poplar (Greater London)

A district of east LONDON, in the Borough
of TOWER HAMLETS, whose name means
what it says, and refers to a poplar tree or
trees formerly here. The name has been
recorded in a document of 1327 as *Popler*,
which is earlier than the earliest record of
the actual tree-name in the *Oxford English
Dictionary* (where it is first quoted in a
record of 1382).

Porlock (Somerset)

This small resort lies at the foot of a steep
hill not far from the coast, and its name
refers to its location there as an 'enclosure
by a harbour', from the Old English *port*
(harbour) and *loca* (enclosure). The name
was recorded in 918 as *Portloca*.

Portadown (Armagh)

An ancient town on the River Bann
southwest of LURGAN whose name means
'landing-place of the little fort', with the
English version of the name representing
the Irish, Port an Dúnáin. Irish *port* could
mean not only 'port' but 'fort', especially one
by a river. Here, the fort would have guar-
ded a strategic crossing-place over the river.

Portaferry (Down)
A small seaside town and port on the east
side of the entrance to STRANGFORD
Lough whose name means 'port of the
ferry', that is, port of the crossing-place
over the entrance to the lough. There is still
a ferry-crossing from Portaferry over to
STRANGFORD here today.

Portarlington (Laois)
The name of this town northeast of
MOUNTMELLICK derives from that of Lord
Arlington (Sir Henry Bennet), who was the
landowner here in the seventeenth century.
The Irish name of the town is Cúil an
tSúdaire, 'secluded place of the tanner'.

Port Bannatyne (Strathclyde)
A large village and resort on the east coast
of BUTE that takes its name from the
Bannatyne family, who came to the island
of Bute from Ayrshire in the early
thirteenth century and made their home at
Kames Castle, immediately northwest of
the village.

Port Charlotte (Strathclyde)
This coastal village in southwest ISLAY was
given its name after Lady Charlotte
Campbell, mother of W.F. Campbell who
planned the settlement in 1828. *Compare*
PORT ELLEN.

Portchester (Hampshire)
A town on the north shore of
PORTSMOUTH Harbour whose name refers
to its location there, meaning 'Roman fort
by Port' (i.e. by the harbour). The Roman
name of the fort here was *Portus Ardaoni*
(rather than *Portus Adurni*, as usually
given), with the second word of the name
deriving from the British (Celtic) root
element *ardu-* (height) (seen in such names
as ARDGLASS and NEWTOWNARDS). This
means that the overall name has the sense
'fort of the height', with the particular
reference to the hill known as Portsdown,
below which Portchester lies. The town's
name was recorded as *Porteceaster* in a
document of about 960. *See also* ADUR.

Port Dinorwic (Gwynedd)
This small town on the MENAI Strait
southwest of BANGOR was formerly the
port for the slate quarry at the village of
Dinorwic (Dinorwig), near LLANBERIS,
with the latter now familiar for its
hydroelectric pump storage station. The
basic name means 'fort of the Ordovices',
these being an ancient tribe of North
Wales, mentioned by such classical writers
as Tacitus and Ptolemy. Their own name
probably means 'hammer-fighters', and is
based on a British (Celtic) root element
ordo- that gave the modern Welsh *gordd*
(hammer). (This meant that they either
fought with hammers or possibly adopted
the hammer as their symbol.)

Port Dundas (Strathclyde)
This district of GLASGOW takes its name
from Sir Lawrence Dundas of Kerse, who
laid it out in the late eighteenth century as a
port at the eastern end of the FORTH and
CLYDE Canal.

Port Ellen (Strathclyde)
This small town is the chief port of ISLAY
and takes its name from Lady Ellenor
Campbell of Islay, wife of W.F. Campbell,
Gaelic scholar and the man who planned
the settlement in 1821. His mother, Lady
Charlotte Campbell, gave her name to
PORT CHARLOTTE.

Port Glasgow (Strathclyde)
This industrial town on the Firth of CLYDE
east of GREENOCK arose in the 1660s on
the site of a fishing village known as
Newark, with the aim of developing as a
main port and harbour for GLASGOW,
some seventeen miles away. The deepening
of the Clyde, however, prevented this, so
the town instead concentrated on
shipbuilding, with Glasgow itself becoming
a port in the late eighteenth century.

Porth (Mid Glamorgan)
A town at the confluence of the rivers
RHONDDA and Little Rhondda, west of
PONTYPRIDD, whose name is the Welsh

for 'gateway' (masculine *porth*, from Latin *porta*; as distinct from feminine *porth*, 'harbour', from Latin *portus*). The reference is to the confluence itself, which serves as a navigable 'gateway' to places further south in the Rhondda valley.

Porthcawl (Mid Glamorgan)
A coastal resort west of BRIDGEND with a name meaning 'sea-kale harbour', from the Welsh *porth* (harbour; *see* PORTH) and *cawl* (kale). No doubt this plant, cultivated for its edible asparagus-like shoots, grew here at one time. The town's name was recorded as *Portcall* in a document of 1632.

Porthcurno (Cornwall)
This village southeast of LAND'S END is named after the bay here, whose own name means 'cove of the corners', from the Cornish *porth* (cove) and *corn* (horn, corner). The reference is to the two prominent headlands to the west and east of the bay.

Porthleven (Cornwall)
A small town and harbour southwest of HELSTON whose name means 'smooth cove', from the Cornish *porth* (cove, harbour) and *leven* (smooth, even). But 'Leven' may have originally been the name of the stream here, descriptively referring to its smooth waters or current, in which case the present name simply means 'harbour on the Leven'.

Porthmadog (Gwynedd)
This resort on the estuary of the River Glaslyn was formerly the port for the region's slate industry, hence the first element of the name, which overall means 'port of Madocks'. The reference is to the Member of Parliament, William Alexander Madocks (1772–1828), who in 1821 constructed a harbour here for the shipping of locally quarried slate. The name has a Welsh word order, but is not genuinely Welsh, as this would be 'Porthfadog', with the appropriate alteration of *M*- to *F*- after *porth*. Locally, Porthmadog (formerly

known in a more anglicised form as Portmadoc) is known simply as Port. *Compare* TREMADOC BAY.

Port Isaac (Cornwall)
This north coast village with its harbour north of WADEBRIDGE has a misleading name that seems to suggest the personal name Isaac. In fact the meaning is probably 'chaff harbour', from the Cornish *porth* (cove, harbour) and a conjectural adjective *usek* deriving from the Old Cornish *usion* (chaff). Presumably chaff was shipped from here for use as animal fodder elsewhere.

Portishead (Avon)
A small port and residential town west of BRISTOL whose name means 'ridge of the harbour', from the Old English *port* (harbour) and *hēafod* (head, hill, ridge). The reference is to the ridge of hills that run along the estuary of the SEVERN here, with Portishead to the north of them, below Portishead Down.

Portland, Isle of (Dorset)
This peninsula south of WEYMOUTH has a name that basically means 'land by the port', the latter referring to Portland Harbour, between the Isle of Portland and Weymouth. (Compare the use of the name 'Port' for a harbour in the names of PORTCHESTER and PORTSMOUTH.) Portland was referred to simply as *Port* in a document of 837.

Port Laoise (Laois)
The county town of LAOIS in central Ireland has a name that means 'fort of Lugaid', with this personal name the same as that represented by the name Laois itself. From 1556 to 1920, Port Laoise was known as Maryborough, after Queen Mary, just as Laois was known as Queen's County. The Irish name of Port Laoise is identical.

Portmahomack (Highland)
A village, southwest of TARBAT NESS on

the south shore of DORNOCH Firth, whose name means 'harbour of Machalmac', that is, of 'my little Colman', with the saint's name being in the affectionate or 'reverential' form. Colman was a common Celtic saint's name, with over three hundred alone featuring in Irish martyrologies. (The name is a diminutive of Columb, 'dove', which gave the name of the well-known St Columba, active in both Ireland and Scotland.) Portmahomack was recorded in a document of 1678 with its name as *Portmachalmok*. *Compare* PORTMARNOCK.

Portmarnock (Dublin)

This small seaside resort northeast of DUBLIN has a name that means 'harbour of my little Eirnín', with the saint's name in the affectionate form (*compare* PORTMAHOMACK). *Compare* similarly KILMARNOCK, featuring the same saint in its name. The Irish name of Portmarnock is Port Mearnóg, with the same meaning.

Portmeirion (Gwynedd)

This small resort southwest of PENRHYNDEUDRAETH has a name of twentieth-century origin, devised by the architect Clough William-Ellis in the 1920s for his Mediterranean-style creation here. 'Port' denotes the coastal location of the resort, and 'Meirion' indicates its situation in the former county of MERIONETH (the modern administrative district of MEIRIONNYDD).

Portobello (Lothian)

An eastern district of EDINBURGH, on the FIRTH OF FORTH, that derives its name from that of a house here in the mid-eighteenth century, Portobello Hut, itself said to have been named commemoratively by a sailor who had been present at the capture of Portobello, Panama, in 1739. In its own right, the name happens to mean 'fine port', which is appropriate for the district, with its extensive sands and coastal attractions. The name was recorded in a document of 1753 as *Porto-Bello*.

Portpatrick (Dumfries and Galloway)

A small resort and harbour southwest of STRANRAER whose name means 'St Patrick's harbour', with the saint's name that of the dedication of a chapel here. The name of this particular saint is doubtless no coincidence for a place that was formerly the main crossing-point to Ireland, before it was superseded by Stranraer.

Portree (Highland)

The port and chief town of SKYE whose name is traditionally explained as meaning 'royal harbour' (Gaelic *port righe*), referring to the visit of James V here in 1540. But local pronunciation of the name shows that its origin is really *Port-righeadh*, 'harbour of the slope', implying a shieling (summer pasture) on the sloping ground nearby. The name was recorded as *Portri* in 1549.

Portrush (Antrim)

This coastal resort north of COLERAINE has a descriptive name meaning 'harbour of the headland', referring to the peninsula known as Ramore Head here. The Irish name of Portrush, with the same meaning, is Port Rois, the latter word representing the Irish *ros* (headland).

Port St Mary (Isle of Man)

This small resort to the west of CASTLETOWN is named after the dedication of its parish church, with the first word of the name referring to its harbour, that of the fishing village it originally was.

Portsea Island (Hampshire)

The island on which most of PORTSMOUTH is situated. Its name means 'island by Port', with the latter referring to what is now known as Portsmouth Harbour. The '-sea' of the name is thus misleading, and the second part of the name really represents the Old English *ēg* (island), after 'Port' and a possessive *-s*. A document of about 1125 recorded the name as *Porteseia*.

Port Seton (Lothian)

Together with COCKENZIE, Port Seaton
forms a single town on the FIRTH OF
FORTH northeast of MUSSELBURGH. Its
name derives from that of the Seton family,
whose residence was at the former Seton
Palace, on the site of the present Seton
Castle.

Portslade-by-Sea (East Sussex)

A town west of BRIGHTON whose basic
name, Portslade, probably represents the
Old English *port* (harbour) and *gelād* (river-
crossing) (rather than simply *lād*,
'watercourse'). The implication is that
there may at one time have been inlets of
the sea here, which had to be crossed with
special causeways. The name as a whole
applies to the resort that has developed by
the coast, as distinct from Portslade
proper, which is now an inland (and older)
district of the town. The name was
recorded in the Domesday Book as
Porteslage.

Portsmouth (Hampshire)

This well-known port and naval base has a
name that refers to its own harbour, 'Port',
so that it arose as a place at the mouth of
the harbour. The name 'Port' was
doubtless borrowed from the Roman name
of the harbour as *Portus*, or even as a short
form of the Roman name of
PORTCHESTER, which stands on the north
shore of Portsmouth Harbour and which
was probably known as *Portus Ardaoni*. A
document of about 900 refers to
Portsmouth as *Portesmutha*.

Portstewart (Londonderry)

This small resort west of PORTRUSH takes
its name from the Stewart family, who were
landowners here in the mid-eighteenth
century. The Irish name, with the same
meaning, is Port Stiobhaird.

Port Sunlight (Merseyside)

An industrial complex on the WIRRAL
peninsula beside the estuary of the
MERSEY. It arose in 1888 as a residential
estate laid out by William Hesketh Lever
(later Lord Leverhulme) for workers
making Sunlight soap at his factory here.
As such, the name is unusual in deriving
from that of a commercial product.
Compare LEVERBURGH.

Port Talbot (West Glamorgan)

This town and port east of SWANSEA arose
in 1836 when docks were built here, and
the new settlement was named after the
Talbot family of MARGAM Abbey nearby,
who owned much of the land and
sponsored the enterprise. The Talbots,
who came from LACOCK, Wiltshire, had
inherited Margam Abbey and the
surrounding land in the mid-eighteenth
century.

Port William (Dumfries and Galloway)

A small resort southwest of WIGTOWN that
takes its name from Sir William Maxwell of
Monreith, who founded the town here in
1770.

Postbridge (Devon)

A small village on DARTMOOR southwest
of MORETONHAMPSTEAD, which has an
old 'clapper' bridge believed to date from
the thirteenth century. This must have
been the forerunner of the later 'post
bridge', recorded in a document of 1675 as
*a stone bridge of three arches called Post
Bridg*, which was so named as it took the
post road from EXETER to PLYMOUTH
across the East Dart river here.

Potterne (Wiltshire)

A village south of DEVIZES whose name
means either 'pottery' or 'potters' house',
from the Old English *pott* (pot) and *ærn*
(house, building). The local clayey soil
would have been suitable for the making of
earthenware pottery. The name was
recorded as *Poterne* in the Domesday
Book.

Potters Bar (Hertfordshire)

A town north of LONDON whose name
almost certainly refers to a man named

Potter who kept a gate or 'bar' here, probably leading into ENFIELD Chase. The name was recorded in a text of 1509 as *Potterys Barre*. This despite the fact that the town's official guide suggests that the reference is to local potteries.

Potton (Bedfordshire)
A small town northeast of BIGGLESWADE whose name may mean 'village where pots are made' from the Old English *pott* (pot) and *tūn* (village). The name was recorded in about 960 as *Pottune*.

Poulton-le-Fylde (Lancashire)
A town northeast of BLACKPOOL whose basic name, Poulton, means 'village with a pool', from the Old English *pōl* (pool) and *tūn* (village). The Domesday Book recorded this as *Poltun*. Later, the second part of the name was added to distinguish this Poulton from Poulton-le-Sands, the former name of MORECAMBE. 'Fylde' means 'plain': *see* FYLDE.

Powys (Wales)
A county in central Wales that adopted the name of a former kingdom here, whose own name means 'provincial', from the Latin *pagensis*, the adjective of *pagus* (province, district). The implication is that the people who lived here were 'country folk', inhabiting an open tract of upland that was not protected in the same way that the regions to the north and south were, where hills and valleys provided shelter.

Poynton (Cheshire)
This town south of STOCKPORT has a name of tribal origin, meaning 'village of Pūn's people', with the personal name perhaps meaning 'pounder', from the Old English *pūnian* (to pound). The present name thus really represents 'Punington', as shown in a record of it for 1248 as *Poninton*. The same name lies behind that of the West Sussex village of Poynings, near BRIGHTON.

Prescot (Merseyside)
A town southwest of ST HELENS whose name means 'priests' cottage', 'parsonage'; it has been suggested that the name indicates an endowment for the church at nearby Eccleston. The name was recorded in 1178 as *Prestecota*. *Compare* PRESTATYN, PRESTEIGNE, and PRESTON, all of which involved priests (Old English *prēost*).

Preseli (Dyfed)
This administrative district in the west of the county takes its name from the hill ridge known as Mynydd Preseli, south of NEWPORT, whose own name is probably based on *prys* (wood, grove), or on some dialect form of this Welsh word. ('Mynydd' means 'mountain'. *Compare* LONG MYND; MENDIP HILLS; MINEHEAD.)

Prestatyn (Clwyd)
A coastal resort east of RHYL whose name means 'priests' village'; it is actually a 'welshified' form of the English PRESTON. Thus the expected '-ton' has become '-tyn', and the stress on the Old English *prēosta* in the compound *prēosta-tūn* has moved from the first syllable to the second, so that it falls on the penultimate syllable, as is common in Welsh words and names (such as LLANELLI, MACHYNLLETH, CAERNARVON, and so on). The Domesday Book recorded the name as *Prestetone*.

Presteigne (Powys)
This small town south of KNIGHTON has an English name that means 'priests' household', from the Old English *prēost* (priest) and *hǣmed* (household, society). The exact sense of the name is uncertain, but it probably denoted a religious community here. The Welsh name of the town is Llanandras, 'St Andrew's church' (compare names such as Llanfair, 'St Mary's church'). A mid-thirteenth-century document records the name of Presteigne as *Prestehemede*.

Preston (Lancashire)

The name of this large town northwest of
MANCHESTER is found in several other
places in the country, and means 'priests'
village', 'parsonage'. The name does not
necessarily imply that several priests lived
here, but that the place was an endowment
for priests who actually served a church
somewhere else. The name was recorded as
Prestvne in the Domesday Book. *Compare*
the names above and below beginning with
the element 'Pres-'.

Prestonpans (Lothian)

A town on the FIRTH OF FORTH northeast
of MUSSELBURGH whose name refers to
salt pans here at the 'priests' village'
(*compare* PRESTON). The priests referred to
were the monks of Newbattle Abbey, who
laid out the salt pans in the early thirteenth
century. The town's name was recorded in
a document of 1587 as *Saltprestoun*, and as
now in a text dated 1654.

Prestwich (Greater Manchester)

A town northwest of MANCHESTER whose
name means 'priests' outlying farm' (Old
English *wīc*); it was recorded as *Prestwich*
in a document of 1194. The farm was no
doubt an endowment to support a religious
house elsewhere, as for PRESTON. *Compare*
PRESTWICK.

Prestwick (Strathclyde)

This town and resort on the Firth of CLYDE
has a name that is exactly the same as that
of PRESTWICH, and so means 'priests'
outlying farm'. The name was recorded in
a document of about 1170 as *Prestwic*.

Primrose Hill (Greater London)

This district of Camden (*see* CAMDEN
TOWN) has a self-explanatory name
meaning 'hill where primroses grow'. The
name was first recorded in a song title of
1586, *A Sweete and Courtly Songe of the
Flowers that grow on Prymrose Hyll*.

Princes Risborough (Buckinghamshire)

This town south of AYLESBURY has a
rather impressive name. The basic name,
Risborough, means 'hill where brushwood
grows', from the Old English conjectural
hrīsen, 'growing with brushwood' (from
hrīs, 'brushwood') and *beorg*, 'hill'. The
first word of the name refers to the Black
Prince, no less, the eldest son of Edward
III, who held the tenure of the place in the
fourteenth century. The name was thus
recorded as *Risenbeorgas* in a document of
1004, but as *Pryns Rysburgh* in a text dated
1433. The royal prefix was added to
distinguish this Risborough from Monks
Risborough, which lies immediately to the
north of the town. (The monks here were
from CANTERBURY.)

Princetown (Devon)

A town in the middle of DARTMOOR, east
of TAVISTOCK, that arose in the first half of
the nineteenth century around a prison
built (1806–13) to accommodate French
and American prisoners taken in the
Napoleonic Wars. The town was named
after the Prince of Wales, the future George
IV, who owned Dartmoor as part of his
Duchy of CORNWALL.

Prudhoe (Northumberland)

An industrial town west of GATESHEAD
whose name means 'Prūda's hill-spur',
with the personal name (meaning 'proud
one') followed by the Old English *hōh*
(heel, spur of land). The spur referred to is
almost certainly the elevated site above the
River TYNE here on which Prudhoe Castle
stands. The town's name was recorded as
Prudho in a document of 1173.

Puddletown (Dorset)

This village northeast of DORCHESTER
takes its name from the River Piddle or
Puddle on which it stands, with the
Domesday Book recording it as *Pitretone*.
In 1956 there was some controversy
concerning the name, and Dorset County
Council wanted to change it to
'Piddletown' to make it conform with the
names of other places in the river valley,
such as Piddlehinton and

PIDDLETRENTHIDE. There was keen opposition to the proposal, however, mainly on the grounds of the expense involved, but also because Puddletown sounded 'nicer' as a name. *Compare also* TOLPUDDLE.

Pudsey (West Yorkshire)

A town east of BRADFORD whose name probably means 'Pudoc's island land', with the personal name followed by the Old English *ēg* (island, raised land in marshland or moorland). The latter description could suit Pudsey, whose name was recorded in the Domesday Book as *Podechesaie*.

Puffin Island (Gwynedd)

An island off the east coast of ANGLESEY with a self-descriptive name, similar to that of LUNDY. It is also known as Priestholm, 'priests' island', referring to the monastery founded here in the sixth century by St Seriol. The saint's name forms the basis of the Welsh name of the island, which is Ynys Seiriol, 'Seriol's island'. Puffins still nest on the island, although in decreasing numbers. The '-holm' of the alternative name represents the Old Norse *holmr* (island), also found in the names of other islands around the Welsh coast, such as GRASSHOLM and SKOKHOLM.

Pulborough (West Sussex)

A town northwest of WORTHING whose name means 'mound by the pools', from the Old English *pōl* (pool) and *beorg* (hill, mound). The 'pools' would have been formed by the bend on the River ARUN on which the town stands, and the 'mound' is the hill on which the older part of Pulborough is situated, including its parish church. The name was recorded in the Domesday Book as *Puleberge*.

Punchestown (Kildare)

Punchestown, famous for its racecourse, lies southeast of NAAS and has a name that means 'Punch's homestead', as represented also by the Irish name, Baile Phúinse.

Punch is a family name of Norman origin, related to the name Pontius.

Purbeck (Dorset)

This name applies not only to an administrative district but also to the Isle of Purbeck, a peninsula crossed by the Purbeck Hills. The Isle of Purbeck was recorded in a document of 948 as *tellus Purbicinga*, the former word being Latin for 'land', 'district'; the Domesday Book gives the basic name as *Porbi* and (as the name of a hundred) *Porbiche*. The name Purbeck has been interpreted as meaning 'bittern point', from the Old English *pur* (bittern, snipe) and a conjectural word *bīc* (point). The reference would be not to the Isle of Purbeck but to the Purbeck Hills, which form a conspicuous 'pointed' range here, with the outline of the range suggesting a bittern's long pointed bill. If this is the correct origin, it is presumably simply a coincidence that only a few miles away lies Portland Bill, the southern 'beak-like' tip of the Isle of PORTLAND.

Purfleet (Essex)

An industrial complex on the north bank of the THAMES west of GRAYS. It has a name that means 'Purta's creek', with the second half of the name representing the Old English *flēot* (inlet, creek) (*compare* FLEET). Purfleet was recorded in a document of 1285 as *Purteflyete*. The 'creek' would have been the River Mar Dyke, which flows into the Thames here just west of Purfleet.

Purley (Greater London)

This former SURREY town in the Borough of CROYDON has a name that means 'pear-tree wood', from the Old English *pyrige* (pear tree) and *lēah* (wood). The name was recorded in 1200 as *Pirlee*. This is a notably 'arboreal' region, with many names relating to trees and woods, such as WOODMANSTERNE and Woodcote to the west of Purley, WHYTELEAFE to the south, and Forestdale and Farleigh ('woodland clearing with ferns') to the east. There are still many individually named woods locally.

Putney (Greater London)
A district of WANDSWORTH, south of the THAMES, whose name means 'Putta's landing-place', with the personal name followed by the Old English *hȳth* (landing-place, port), as in ROTHERHITHE and (on its own) HYTHE. The landing-place in question would have been on the Thames. The Domesday Book recorded the name of Putney as *Putelei*, with *l* substituted for *n*, possibly by confusion.

Pwllheli (Gwynedd)
A market town and harbour on TREMADOC BAY whose name means 'brine pool', 'pool of salt water', from the Welsh *pwll* (pool) and *heli* (brine, salt water). The latter part of the name emphasises that the pool is near the sea (*compare* English SALTBURN), as distinct from an inland pool, as at WELSHPOOL. The town was recorded as *Pwllhely* in a late-thirteenth-century text.

Quantock Hills (Somerset)

The Quantocks, west of BRIDGWATER, had their name recorded in a document dated 682 as *Cantucuudu*. This is a combination of a British (Celtic) element *canto-*, found also in the name of KENT and meaning 'edge', 'rim', and the Old English *wudu* (wood). The 'edge' would probably have referred to a section of the hills, not necessarily the whole chain. The hills are in effect a series of ridges extending for some eight miles towards TAUNTON.

Queenborough (Kent)

This industrial area at the western end of the Isle of SHEPPEY arose as a chartered town ('borough') named after Queen Philippa of Hainault, wife of Edward III. She died shortly after the town received its charter in 1367, and nine years later the name was recorded as *Queneburgh*.

Queensbury (West Yorkshire, Greater London)

The Yorkshire town north of HALIFAX was originally a village named after an inn here, the Queen's Head. In 1863, however, its name was changed to Queensbury as a result of a vote taken at a public meeting, with the new name intended as a compliment to Queen Victoria. (The name change was itself celebrated on Whit Tuesday that same year by the inauguration of an elaborate mock-Gothic drinking-fountain known as the Albert Memorial. Prince Albert, Victoria's consort, had died only two years previously, and this Yorkshire Albert Memorial thus predates the more famous London one.) London's Queensbury, in the Borough of BRENT, takes its name from that of the Underground station here, which was itself given the name on its opening in 1934, simply to 'match' KINGSBURY, the next station south on the Metropolitan line.

Queensferry (Clwyd)

A town on the south bank of the River DEE west of CHESTER. It was originally known as King's Ferry, with this name recorded in 1835, but when Queen Victoria came to the throne in 1837 the name was changed to Queensferry. Neither name seems to relate to any direct royal connection with the place. *Compare* SOUTH QUEENSFERRY.

Quorndon (Leicestershire)

A village southeast of LOUGHBOROUGH, also known as Quorn, which gave its name to the Quorn hunt founded here. The longer name means 'hill of millstones', from the Old English *cweorn* (hand-mill; compare the modern 'quern') and *dūn* (hill). The name implies that millstones were obtained locally. A document of about 1225 has the name of the village as *Querendon*.

R

Raasay (Highland)

An island off the east coast of SKYE with an Old Norse name meaning 'roe ridge island', from *rár* (roe deer), *áss* (ridge), and *ey* (island). The 'ridge' is the chain of mountains in the southern part of the long island; red deer are still found here.

Radcliffe (Greater Manchester, Nottinghamshire)

The town southwest of BURY has a name that refers to the red sandstone cliff beside the River Irwell here. The Nottinghamshire town, east of NOTTINGHAM, has a similar name, describing the red loamy clay that slopes down to the River TRENT. The latter town is formally known as Radcliffe on Trent in order to be distinguished from the village of Ratcliffe on Soar, northwest of LOUGHBOROUGH. The two Radcliffes were recorded in the Domesday Book as *Radclieu* and *Radeclive* respectively.

Radlett (Hertfordshire)

A residential town south of ST ALBANS whose name means 'road junction', from the Old English *rād* (road) and *gelæt* (junction). The name was recorded in 1453 as *Radelett*, showing that the junction or crossroads was important here in medieval times. Radlett lies northwest of LONDON at a point where the road from WATFORD joins WATLING STREET.

Radnor (Powys)

The present administrative district preserves the former name of Radnorshire, as well as that of Radnor Forest here, in central east Wales. The basic name means '(place at the) red bank', referring to the red loamy soil found on the hill-slopes. The two Old English words that gave the name are *rēad* (red) and *ofer* (bank, slope), and the Domesday Book recorded the name as *Raddrenoue*. See also NEW RADNOR. Compare REDHILL.

Radstock (Avon)

This town southwest of BATH was recorded in the Domesday Book simply as *Stoche*, with this representing the first element of STOCKTON and many other names, from the Old English *stoc* (place, farm). Later, a document of 1221 gives the name in its present form as *Radestok*. The first element of this is the Old English *rād* (road) (as for RADLETT), so that the name as a whole means 'farm by the road', 'roadside settlement'. The road here is the ancient FOSS WAY, and doubtless the first element was added to distinguish this Stoke from another nearby, such as the village of South Stoke immediately south of Bath.

Raglan (Gwent)

A village southwest of MONMOUTH whose name means 'rampart', from the Welsh *rhag* (before) and *glan* (bank). The reference is to the former castle here; the present remains to the north of the town are those of a fifteenth-century castle built on the site of an earlier motte-and-bailey structure dating back to the eleventh century. The Welsh spelling of the name, as Rhaglan, shows its origin more accurately. The name was recorded as *Raghelan* in a document of 1254.

Rainham (Greater London)

A town south of ROMFORD whose name means 'village of the Roegings', with this tribal name recorded only here and in the identically named village (now a district of GILLINGHAM) in Kent. The name itself may mean 'prevailing ones'. The Domesday Book recorded the name as *Renaham*, which has almost lost the Old English *-ingas* suffix that means 'people of'.

Ramsbottom (Greater Manchester)

This town north of BURY has a name that probably means 'rams' valley', from the Old English *ramm* (ram) and *botm* (valley). However, some toponymists interpret the name as 'wild-garlic valley', with the first element representing the Old English *hramsa*. A record of the name of 1324 is inconclusive in this respect, giving it as *Romesbothum*. If 'ram' does lie behind the name, the reference need not necessarily be to the animal, but to a rock formation that resembled a ram or a ram's head. Alternatively, wild garlic may once have grown here in the valley of the River Irwell. *Compare* RAMSEY.

Ramsey (Cambridgeshire, Isle of Man)
The small town southeast of PETERBOROUGH and the coastal resort on the Isle of Man have names that are nearly but not quite the same in origin. The first element of each is the Old English (and Old Norse) *hramsa* (wild garlic) (*compare* RAMSBOTTOM). But the Cambridgeshire town's second element is the Old English *ēg* (island), while the Isle of Man resort has the Old Norse *á* (river). The difference is apparent in early records of the name: *Rameseia* in the Domesday Book for the former town, and *Ramsa* in a document of 1257 for the Manx resort. 'Island' has its frequent sense of 'dry land in marshland' for the Cambridgeshire Ramsey, which is a fenland town. Although the Manx town is at the mouth of the River Sulby, it is also near the mouth of a small stream, by which wild garlic must have grown. *Compare also* RAMSEY ISLAND.

Ramsey Island (Dyfed)
An island lying to the southwest of ST DAVID'S, hence its Welsh name of Ynys Dewi, '(St) David's island'. Its 'English' name is actually Old Norse, and means 'wild-garlic island', from the Old Norse *hramsa* (as in RAMSEY) and *ey* (island). Ramsey Island was noted for its abundance of the plant until as recently as the nineteenth century. Its name was recorded as *Ramesey* in a document dated 1326.

Ramsgate (Kent)
This well-known resort on the Isle of THANET east of CANTERBURY has a name

that can be translated as 'Raven's gap', from the Old English *hræfn* (raven) and *geat* (gap), the latter being a gap in the cliffs, as at MARGATE. But the first part of the name has not yet been satisfactorily explained. It could refer to a rock here, named The Raven because of its resemblance to this bird. Or possibly it is a personal name, Hræfn, originating as a nickname for the named person. It could even refer to the birds themselves, which were perhaps once frequent visitors here. The name was recorded as *Remmesgate* in 1275, which unfortunately does not reveal who or what the 'raven' was.

Randalstown (Antrim)
A small market town south of BALLYMENA that derives its name from Randal MacDonell, first Marquis of Antrim, to whose wife the manor of Edenduffcarrick (Shane's Castle) was granted by Charles II in 1683. Previous names of the settlement here were Mainwater (after the River Main that flows through the town) and Ironworks (for the forges and furnaces that smelted the local iron-ore here). The Irish name of the town, with the same meaning, is Baile Raghnaill.

Rannoch (Highland/Strathclyde/Tayside)
A name that applies to several features in the GRAMPIANS, notably Rannoch Moor, Rannock Forest, and Loch Rannoch. The name represents the Gaelic *raineach* 'bracken (place)'.

Rathlin Island (Antrim)
This island off the coast of Northern Ireland has an ancient name, recorded by Ptolemy in the second century AD as *Rikini*. Its exact meaning is still obscure, but it may derive from a Celtic root word represented by the modern Welsh *rhygnu* (to rub, to scrape), referring to the manner in which the island has been eroded by the sea and the wind over the centuries.

Ráth Luirc (Cork)
A town south of LIMERICK with an Irish

name meaning 'Lorc's fort', from *ráth*
(ring-fort) and the personal name in the
genitive case. (The present Irish name is
simply An Ráth, 'the fort'.) From the mid-
seventeenth century to the 1920s the town
was known as Charleville, after Charles II.

Rathmines (Dublin)
A southern district of DUBLIN whose name
means 'De Moenes' fort'. The personal
name is that of the Norman family who
became owners of the land here in the first
half of the fourteenth century. The Irish
name, with the same meaning, is Ráth
Maonais.

Rathmullan (Donegal)
A small resort on the western shore of
Lough SWILLY whose name means
'Maolán's fort'; the Irish name, with the
same meaning, is Ráth Maoláin.

Rattray (Tayside)
A town lying on the River Ericht opposite
BLAIRGOWRIE. Its name makes no
reference to this riverside location,
however, and means 'farm by the fort',
from the Gaelic *ràth* (fort) (as for the three
Irish names above), and a conjectural
British (Celtic) word *treb* that gave the
modern Welsh *tref* (farm) (as in TREFRIW
and other names). A late-thirteenth-
century document gives the name of
Rattray as *Rotrefe*.

Raunds (Northamptonshire)
A small manufacturing town whose name
represents the plural of the Old English
rand (border, edge, boundary). Raunds is
situated not far from the point where three
counties meet: Northamptonshire,
Cambridgeshire (formerly
Huntingdonshire here), and Bedfordshire;
the name describes this location 'at the
boundaries', or *æt Randan*, as it was
referred to in a late-tenth-century text.

Ravenglass (Cumbria)
This village on the estuary of the River ESK
southeast of SEASCALE has a name that

means 'Glas's share', with the first element
of the name of Celtic origin related to the
modern Gaelic *rann* and Welsh *rhan* (part,
portion). There was a Roman fort here,
named *Glannoventa*, meaning 'place at the
bank', from Celtic root words represented
by the modern Welsh *glan* (bank, shore) (as
for RAGLAN) and *venta* (as in GWENT and
WINCHESTER). The 'bank' or 'shore' is
that of the estuary here. Ravenglass was
recorded as *Rengles* in a document of about
1170.

Rawtenstall (Lancashire)
This town on the River Irwell south of
BURNLEY is also on the edge of high
moorland, and its name alludes to this,
meaning 'rough cow-pasture', from the
Old English *rūh* (rough) and the
conjectural *tūn-stall*, literally 'farm site'.
The latter term took on a specialised sense
to refer to buildings used when cattle were
pastured on higher ground, as here. The
name was recorded as *Routonstall* in a
document of 1324.

Rayleigh (Essex)
A town northwest of SOUTHEND-ON-SEA
whose name means 'doe clearing', 'clearing
where does are found', from the Old
English *ræge* (doe) and *lēah* (forest
clearing). The Domesday Book recorded
the name as *Ragheleia*.

Reading (Berkshire)
This well-known county town west of
LONDON has a name that means 'place of
Rēad's people', with the personal name
meaning 'red one'. The name was recorded
as *Readingum* in about 900, and as *Redinges*
in the Domesday Book. The latter
preserves the full Old English *-ingas* suffix
that means 'people of' (the named person).

Reculver (Kent)
This coastal village east of HERNE BAY has
a name that preserves that of the Roman
fort here, which was *Regulbium*. This is of
British (Celtic) origin and means 'great
headland', from the prefix *ro-* (great) and a

root element *gulbio-*, meaning literally 'beak' (as in modern Welsh *gylfin*) but here understood metaphorically as 'headland'. (Compare the 'bill' of PORTLAND Bill; see PURBECK.) There is no obvious headland here, but Reculver is immediately west of the Isle of THANET, which could certainly be regarded as a 'great headland'.

Redbridge (Greater London)
This borough of northeast LONDON has a name that refers to a former 'red bridge' that crossed the River Roding (*see* The RODINGS) at a point formerly known as Redbridge Lane, where Eastern Avenue now crosses the river just west of Redbridge Underground station. The bridge was formerly on the boundary between the boroughs of WANSTEAD and ILFORD, and was so named because it was made of red brick and was designed to carry wheeled transport, unlike the nearby White Bridge, which was for pedestrians only. The name is found on a map of 1746, but probably dates back a good hundred years earlier. The modern borough of Redbridge was created in 1965.

Redcar (Cleveland)
This town and resort on the North Sea coast northeast of MIDDLESBROUGH has a part-English, part-Norse name, consisting of the Old English *hrēod* (reed) and the Old Norse *kjarr* (marsh). The 'reedy marshland' is the low-lying land by the sea on which the town stands. Its name was recorded in about 1170 as *Redker*.

Redditch (Hereford and Worcester)
A town south of BIRMINGHAM whose name could mean either 'reedy ditch' or 'red ditch', depending whether the first half of the name represents the Old English *hrēod* (reed) (as for REDCAR) or *rēad* (red) (as for RADCLIFFE). The second element is certainly *dīc* (ditch; compare modern 'dyke'). The fact that the name was recorded in a Latin text of about 1200 as *Rubeo Fossato*, however, seems to settle the matter, with 'red ditch' winning the day. A

document of 1247 has the name as *La Rededich*, suggesting that the original name was that of an actual ditch ('the red ditch'), rather than that of a place by it. 'Red' would have applied to the colour of the soil, rather than of the water. Presumably the ditch itself linked with the River Arrow, on which the town stands.

Redhill (Surrey)
A district of REIGATE whose name was recorded in a document of 1301 as *Redehelde*, showing that its origin lies in 'red slope' (Old English *helde*) rather than 'red hill' (*hyll*), although the overall sense is much the same. There was nothing like a town here until the mid-nineteenth century, with the coming of the railway. The slope of the name is probably the hill now known as Redstone Hill, the road (A25) that leads east out of Redhill. The 'red' colour would have been that of the soil.

Redruth (Cornwall)
A town west of TRURO whose name means 'red ford', although it is the second element, the Cornish *ruth*, that means 'red', not the first, which is the Cornish *rid* (ford) (similar to the Welsh name, Rhydaman, of AMMANFORD). The order of the words, with the adjective following the noun, is characteristic of Celtic languages. There is no river at Redruth, so the 'red ford' must have been over the small stream on which Redruth Church stands to the west of the town. The soil or bed of the stream would thus have been red-coloured. Redruth was recorded in a document of 1259 as *Ridruthe*.

Reigate (Surrey)
A town north of CRAWLEY whose name means 'doe gate', from the Old English *rǣge* (doe) and *geat* (gate, gap) (*compare* RAMSGATE; MARGATE). A 'doe gate' would have been an entrance to a deer park, or a gap in a boundary fence where a doe could pass with her young. A similar name, but referring to a male deer, is that

of the West Sussex village of Rogate, near
PETERSFIELD. If there was a deer park at
Reigate, it would have been to the south of
the present town, where Reigate Park is
today. The name was recorded as *Reigata*
in a text of 1170.

Renfrew (Strathclyde)
A town west of GLASGOW on the River
CLYDE at the point where it is joined by the
Gryfe. The name refers to this location,
and derives from two British (Celtic) words
meaning respectively 'point' and 'current'
(Welsh *rhyn* and *ffrwyd*), so that the 'point
of current' is the confluence. The name was
recorded as *Reinfry* in a document of about
1128. The town gave its name to the former
county of Renfrewshire.

Renton (Strathclyde)
This town north of DUMBARTON has a
relatively modern name, derived from that
of Cecilia Renton, daughter of John
Renton of Blackadder and daughter-in-law
of Jean Telfer, sister of Tobias Smollett,
the eighteenth-century novelist. The name
dates from the 1780s, when bleaching and
other industrial enterprises developed here
by the River LEVEN.

Repton (Derbyshire)
This small town northeast of BURTON-
UPON-TRENT has a name that should
really end in '-don', not '-ton'; it means
'hill of the Hreope people', with the tribal
name followed by the Old English *dūn*
(hill). The same folk name occurs for
RIPON. There is hardly a hill in the normal
sense at Repton, but the ground does rise
gradually from the River TRENT, near
which the town stands. Repton's name
occurs in a mid-eighth-century document
as *Hreopandune*, and in the Domesday
Book as *Rependuna*.

Restormel (Cornwall)
The locality, famous for its medieval (but
ruined) castle north of LOSTWITHIEL, has
now given its name to an administrative
district of Cornwall. The name itself

probably means 'moorland by the bald
hill', from the Cornish *ros* (moor) (as in the
many places named ROSS), *tor* (hill;
literally 'belly'), and *moyl* (bald, bare) (as
in the names of Welsh mountains, such as
MOEL HEBOG). There may thus have been
a hill near Restormel called something like
'Tor Moyl', although it has not been
identified. No doubt it was on the headland
on which Restormel Castle stands, or was
even a name for the headland itself. A
document of 1310 has the name as
Rostormel.

Retford (Nottinghamshire)
A town northeast of NOTTINGHAM whose
name is a variant on the more familiar
Radford; it thus means 'red ford', from the
Old English *rēad* and *ford*. The 'red ford'
would have been one with red soil over the
River Idle, on which Retford stands. The
town is often known as East Retford, to
distinguish it from the location of West
Retford immediately northwest of it across
the river. The basic name was recorded as
Redford in the Domesday Book.

Rhayader (Powys)
The name of Rhayader, the small market
town on the River WYE north of BUILTH
WELLS, means simply 'waterfall', from the
Welsh *rhaeadr*, as also seen in the Welsh
name of the town, which is Rhaeadr Gwy,
meaning 'Rhyader on the Wye' (as distinct
from the many other waterfalls on other
rivers). The particular waterfall was
prominent on the river here until the
bridge was built in 1780. A document
dated 1191 has the name as *Raidergoe*, as a
version of the Welsh name.

Rhondda (Mid Glamorgan)
This town northwest of PONTYPRIDD takes
its name from the river on which it stands,
the Afon Rhondda Fawr, 'great River
Rhondda'. 'Rhondda' means 'noisy one',
from the Welsh *rhoddni* (with the middle
consonants changing places). The river
name was recorded as *Rotheni* in a twelfth-
century text, and the name then passed to

that of the valley (*Glenrotheny* in a document of 1268) before becoming that of the present town, which arose only in the mid-nineteenth century, when the coal mines here were first exploited.

Rhosllanerchrugog (Clwyd)

This urban area southwest of WREXHAM has a fully Welsh descriptive name that means 'moor of the heather glade', from *rhos* (moor, heath), *llannerch* (glade, clearing), and *grugog*, the adjective of *grug* (heather). The name appears in a document of 1544 as *Rose lane aghregog*, suggesting a transcription by an English writer who did not understand the sense of the Welsh words.

Rhos-on-Sea (Clwyd)

A small resort immediately northwest of COLWYN BAY whose basic name, Rhos, means 'headland', referring to the small promontory here. (This sense of Welsh *rhos* is secondary to its main meaning of 'moor'.) The second part of the name is not only a commercial attraction but serves to distinguish this Rhos from the many other places of the name, especially in North Wales.

Rhuddlan (Clwyd)

A suburb of RHYL whose name means 'red bank', from the Welsh *rhudd* (red) and *glan* (bank), referring to the red-coloured soil on the banks of the River CLWYD here. The Domesday Book recorded the name as *Roelend*.

Rhum *See* Rum.

Rhyl (Clwyd)

This resort on the North Wales coast has a name of mixed Welsh and English origin, with the Welsh *yr* (the) prefixed to the Old English *hyll* (hill). There is hardly a hill here in the accepted sense, but the ground does rise gradually to the south of the town. Early records of the name include *Ryhull* in 1301, and simply *Hull* in 1351.

Rhymney (Mid Glamorgan)

A town east of MERTHYR TYDFIL that takes its name from that of the river on which it stands, with the river's own name meaning literally 'auger', 'borer', from the Welsh *rhwmp* with the suffix *-ni*. The Welsh spelling of the name is Rhymni, and this was recorded in the late thirteenth century as *Rempney*. *Compare* RIBBLE.

Ribble (North Yorkshire/Lancashire)

A river that rises in the PENNINES north of SETTLE and curves south and west to its estuary west of PRESTON. The name means 'tearing one', from the conjectural Old English *ripel* 'strip'. The reference is to the scouring action of the river, just as that of the RHYMNEY relates to its 'piercing' action. A document of about 715 records the name as *Rippel*. *See also* RIBCHESTER.

Ribchester (Lancashire)

A village north of BLACKBURN whose name declares it to be a former Roman fort ('-chester', from the Old English *ceaster*) on the River RIBBLE, which gives the first part of its name. The Roman name of the fort was *Bremetenacum Veteranorum*: the first word is of Celtic origin and means 'roaring one', referring to the Ribble (whose own Roman name seems to have been *Belisama*, probably meaning 'most shining one'); the second word refers to the 'old soldiers', the Sarmatians, who were brought to Britain from Central Europe in the second half of the second century AD, and who settled here to cultivate the land. The Ribble, true to its (Old English) name, has now torn away or eroded about a third of the Roman fort. Ribchester was recorded in the Domesday Book as *Ribelcastre*.

Richborough Castle (Kent)

The well-known remains of a Roman fort on the Kent coast, midway between RAMSGATE and SANDWICH. Its name consists of the original British (Celtic) element that gave the Roman name of *Rutupiae* for the fort, with the Old English *burg* (fort) added. The root stem of the name is probably the Celtic *rutu-* (mud), with this referring to the muddy streams of Richborough Creek, which flow around the fort. The present name is thus a corruption of the original, perhaps developed by association with 'rich' rather than 'rat', as the name might otherwise have become (a document of 1197 has Richborough as *Ratteburg*). Even in the eighth century, the Venerable Bede commented on the way the name had become corrupted: *ciuitas quae dicitur Rutubi portus a gente Anglorum nunc corrupte Reptacaestir* ('the township which is called Rutubi harbour now corruptly by the English [called] Reptacaestir').

Richmond (Greater London, North Yorkshire)
It is more than convenient to have England's two main Richmonds in the same entry, as the former Surrey town was given the name of the Yorkshire one! The southern Richmond was originally known as Sheen, meaning 'shelters', with this name preserved locally in Sheen Road and elsewhere. Edward I built a palace here in the thirteenth century, and this was rebuilt and enlarged by Henry VII in the late fifteenth century. When the palace was destroyed by fire in 1501, however, Henry renamed it Richmond, after his previous title of Earl of Richmond (Yorkshire). No doubt he felt that this was a worthier name than one meaning simply 'shelters', especially for a royal seat. 'Richmond' basically means 'strong hill', and the northern Richmond was so named by Norman settlers there, either as a directly descriptive name for its high location (although not obviously on a hill), or using a name 'exported' from France (as Richemont). The Yorkshire name was thus recorded as *Richemund* in a text of about 1112, and the London Richmond appeared in print in 1502 as *Richemount*. French *riche* certainly now means 'rich', but the word itself is Germanic in origin, and has the basic sense of 'strong', 'powerful', as is

appropriate for a fort (compare modern German *Reich*).

Rickmansworth (Hertfordshire)
A town northwest of LONDON whose name means 'Ricmar's enclosure', with the personal name (meaning 'famous might') followed by the Old English *worth* (enclosure). The Domesday Book recorded the name as *Prichemaresworde*, with an erroneously added *P-*. The *r* of the personal name subsequently became *n*, no doubt because the first part of the name was wrongly associated with the now obsolete word *richman*, meaning 'wealthy man'.

Rievaulx (North Yorkshire)
This village, with its famous ruined Cistercian abbey dating from the twelfth and thirteenth centuries, lies west of HELMSLEY and has a name that means 'valley of the Rye', this being the river here. The second half of the name thus represents the Norman French *val* (valley). The name was recorded as *Rieuall* in a document of about 1149. *Compare* JERVAULX ABBEY, which has this same French word.

Ringwood (Hampshire)
A town northeast of BOURNEMOUTH whose name probably means 'boundary wood', referring to its location near the edge of the NEW FOREST. The Old English words behind the name are thus likely to be the conjectural *rimuc* (boundary) (compare modern 'rim') and *wudu* (wood). The name was recorded as *Rincvede* in the Domesday Book, but earlier texts spell out the precise origin (*to rimuc wude* in 917).

Rinns of Galloway (Dumfries and Galloway)
The extreme southwestern peninsula of mainland Scotland south of STRANRAER, with GALLOWAY its precise region of location. 'Rinns', found elsewhere in Scottish place-names, represents the Gaelic *roinn* (point, promontory), to which an English plural *s* has been added. This

particular promontory was recorded in a document of 1460 as *Le Rynnys*. *Compare* RINNS OF ISLAY.

Rinns of Islay (Strathclyde)
Although the name is that of a peninsula on the western side of the island of ISLAY, the 'Rinns' here differs from that of the previous entry. Here it represents the Gaelic *rann* (division), and thus is one of the three districts into which the island was at one time divided. But by confusion with *roinn* (point), the name has come to apply not only to this headland, but to that of Rinns Point, at the southern end of the island.

Ripley (Derbyshire)
A town north of DERBY whose name means 'strip-shaped clearing', from the Old English *ripel* (strip) (*compare* RIBBLE) and *lēah* (forest clearing). The name Ripley occurs elsewhere in the country, but this particular one was recorded as *Ripelie* in the Domesday Book.

Ripon (North Yorkshire)
A town north of HARROGATE whose name is based on that of the tribe known as the Hreope people, who gave their name also to REPTON. (The '-on' of the name represents the grammatical ending required after a preposition such as 'in'. Compare the similar endings of names such as HIGH WYCOMBE and HITCHIN.) Nothing is known about the tribe except their name, although it seems likely that the people moved from Ripon to settle in Repton rather than the other way round. Ripon was recorded as *in Hrypis* in a document of about 715, and as *Rypum* in about 1030.

Risca (Gwent)
A town northwest of NEWPORT whose name represents the Welsh *rhisga* (as in the Welsh spelling of the name), meaning 'bank'. Risca stands on rising ('banking') ground to the north of the EBBW river.

Rishton (Lancashire)
A town northeast of BLACKBURN whose name means 'rush farm', 'farm where rushes grow', from the Old English *risc* (rush) and *tūn* (farm). There are several streams and rivers in the region, suitable for rushes, as is testified by the names of such neighbouring places as Blackburn, BURNLEY, and OSWALDTWISTLE. Rishton was recorded as *Riston* in a document of about 1200. Elsewhere the name is found as Rushton.

Robin Hood's Bay (North Yorkshire)
A small resort and fishing village named after and sited on the bay of the same name; this bay was recorded in the mid-sixteenth century as *Robyn Huddes Bay*. This is the most northerly instance of place-names given in honour of the English folk hero Robin Hood, whose deeds feature in ballads at least as early as the fourteenth century. He was especially associated with Nottinghamshire and Yorkshire.

Roby (Merseyside)
A town east of LIVERPOOL whose name was recorded in the Domesday Book as *Rabil*, where possibly the influence of the Old English *hyll* (hill) has affected the basic name, which is Old Norse in origin and means 'settlement by a boundary-mark', from *rá* (landmark, boundary-mark) and *bý* (farm, settlement). The boundary was presumably that of a hundred here.

Rochdale (Greater Manchester)
This town on the River Roch northeast of MANCHESTER does not take its name from this river, but gave its name to it. It originated as something like 'Rachedham', from the Old English *ræced* (building, hall) and *hām* (homestead), with this 'homestead by a hall' recorded in the Domesday Book as *Recedham*. The river here took its name from this form, and was originally the *Rached*. Later, the river valley came to be known as the *Rached-dale*, and this name then superseded 'Rachedham', the settlement name eventually evolving to its

present spelling as Rochdale. A rather complex evolution!

Roche Abbey (South Yorkshire)
This twelfth-century Cistercian abbey southeast of MALTBY has a basic name, Roche, that simply means 'rock', from the Middle English *roche*, itself from the French. The abbey ruins are well known for the limestone rocks in the form of a cross here, formerly an object of pilgrimage.

Rochester (Kent)
This ancient city and port on the River MEDWAY has a name that announces it to be a former Roman fortress ('-chester', as in WINCHESTER and many other names). The first element of the name is a 'smoothed' and abbreviated form of the Roman name of the fort, which was *Durobrivae* (accented on the second syllable). This name itself means 'bridge fort', from the two British (Celtic) root elements *duro-* (fort) and *briua-* (bridge). Remains of the Roman bridge over the Medway have been found here. The present form of the city's name took some time to evolve, and proceeded from *Hrofæscæstræ* in the early eighth century (with the initial *H-* indicating the strongly 'aspirated' *r*), to *Rovescestre* in the Domesday Book, before assuming its present spelling subsequently. *Compare* the identical Roman name of CHESTERTON.

Rochford (Essex)
This town north of SOUTHEND-ON-SEA has a name that somewhat surprisingly turns out to mean 'ford of the hunting dog', from the Old English *ræcc* (hunting-dog) and *ford*. There was no doubt a regular crossing-point for hunting-dogs over the River Roach here (with the river's own name deriving from that of Rochford itself). The present spelling of the name is probably due to an association with the French 'Rochefort', which began with the Domesday Book's record of it (written by

Norman clerks) as *Rochefort*. The word 'rache' for a hunting-dog was in regular use down to the sixteenth century, and continued in Scottish use after that, being found even today.

Rockall (Western Isles)
This small uninhabited island almost two hundred miles west of ST KILDA has a name that is probably of Old Norse origin, deriving from conjectural *rok*, 'stormy sea', and *kollr*, 'bald head', giving an overall sense 'bald island in a rough sea'. *Compare* COLL.

Rockingham Forest (Northamptonshire)
A former royal hunting preserve that takes its name from the village of Rockingham to the west; the village name means 'homestead of Hrōc's people'. Rockingham was recorded in the Domesday Book as *Rochingeham*.

Rodings, The (Essex)
The general name for that area of Essex between CHELMSFORD and BISHOP'S STORTFORD through which the River Roding flows. The basic name means 'Hrōtha's people', and this family occupied a wide territory here, having given their names to eight different places, all of which have been prefixed by a necessary distinguishing word. These are (with origin of addition in brackets): Abbess Roding (held by the Abbess of BARKING); Aythorpe Roding (held by Aitrop, son of Hugh, in the twelfth century); Beauchamp Roding (held by the De Beauchamp family); Berners Roding (held by Hugh de Berners in the eleventh century); High Roding (for its higher location); Leaden Roding (for the leaden roof of its church); Margaret Roding (for the dedication of its church to St Margaret); and White Roding (for the white walls of the church). The Domesday Book recorded the general name as *Roinges*. Until relatively recently, 'Roding' was pronounced 'Roothing' (as 'soothing').

Roehampton (Greater London)

This district of WANDSWORTH was originally known simply as Hampton (or East Hampton), meaning 'farmstead'. Later, the Middle English *roke* (rook) was added, probably to distinguish this place from HAMPTON near KINGSTON UPON THAMES. The present name thus really amounts to 'rook farm', 'farmstead where rooks gather regularly', and the name was recorded as *Rokehampton* in a document of 1350.

Rollright Stones (Oxfordshire)

This famous Bronze Age stone circle north of CHIPPING NORTON takes its name from the village of (Great) Rollright here, whose own name was recorded in the Domesday Book as *Rollandri major*. This probably represents a personal name followed by a form of the Old English *land-riht* (land-rights), referring to an estate where special local legal rights applied. No doubt in the popular mind, the name Rollright has come to be associated specifically with the stones themselves, as has happened (with greater justification) for STONEHENGE.

Romford (Greater London)

A former ESSEX town whose name simply means 'broad ford', from the Old English *rūm* (broad) (as it were, 'roomy') and *ford*. The ford so described would have been over the River Rom here, which takes its name by 'back formation' from Romford. A document of 1177 gives the name as *Romfort*. Compare ROMILEY.

Romiley (Greater Manchester)

A town east of STOCKPORT whose name means 'broad clearing', for the Old English *rūm* (broad) (as for ROMFORD) and *lēah* (clearing). The Domesday Book recorded the name as *Rumelie*. Compare ROMNEY MARSH.

Romney Marsh (Kent)

An area of marshland west of DYMCHURCH that was apparently once known simply as Romney, with the name representing the Old English phrase *æt thǣre rūman ē*, 'at the broad river' (*compare* the names based on *rūm* i.e. ROMFORD, ROMILEY). The area is now well drained, and used for sheep grazing, but originally there were doubtless many streams here, giving the impression in places of a single 'broad river'. The people who lived here were known as the *merscware*, or 'marsh people', with their name recorded as *Merscuuare* in a document of 774. The present town of NEW ROMNEY and village of Old Romney arose much later (see the town's name for details).

Romsey (Hampshire)

A town on the River TEST northwest of SOUTHAMPTON whose name means 'Rūm's island', with the personal name followed by the Old English *ēg* (island). The 'island' is the somewhat higher land away from the river around Romsey Abbey, in the vicinity of which the town arose in the early tenth century. The name was recorded in the mid-tenth century as *Romeseye*. The name Rūm is a short form of some longer personal name, such as Rūmwald ('glorious ruler').

Rona (Highland)

A small island between northern SKYE and the mainland. It has a Scandinavian name meaning 'rough island', from the Old Norse *hraun* (rough, rocky) and *ey* (island). This unpropitious sense does not seem to have stopped the name being adopted (or adapted) for the girl's name Rhona or Rona!

Roscommon (Roscommon)

A county and county town in central Ireland whose name means 'St Comán's wood', with this sense better seen in the Irish equivalent name, Ros Comáin. The Dominican friary here is said to stand on the site of the original foundation of St Comán in the eighth century.

Roscrea (Tipperary)

A market town north of THURLES whose name means 'Cré's wood'. The Irish name

of the town is Ros Cré. It is not certain who
Cré was.

Ross (Highland)

Today the name of Ross is familiar from
the administrative district of Ross and
CROMARTY, while formerly it was well
known as that of the county of Ross-shire.
The basic name is also found in the two
districts of Easter Ross and Wester Ross,
respectively in the eastern and western
regions of the territory. 'Ross' has the
prime sense of 'moorland', from the Gaelic
ros, although the secondary meaning of
'promontory' and even 'wood' cannot be
ruled out as being equally or alternatively
applicable for this large region. Perhaps the
name really blends all three senses, as
appropriate.

Rossendale (Lancashire)

One would expect a name like this
to be that of a valley of a 'River
Rossen'. However, Rossendale is actually
the valley of the Irwell, or the section
of it between BACUP and RAWTENSTALL.
The name doubtless derives from that of
the Forest of Rossendale, the moorland
area to the north, so that the name
effectively blends the moorland and the
valley ('dale'). Most 'Ross' names are in
obviously Celtic regions, such as
Scotland (ROSS) and Wales (ROSS-ON-
WYE, almost in Wales), so the presence
of this prominent Celtic name in
Lancashire is unusual. It was recorded
as *Rocendal* in 1242; unfortunately
this is the earliest known record,
making interpretation somewhat
tentative.

Rosslare (Wexford)

This well-known seaside resort and
its nearby passenger port of Rosslare
Harbour take their name from the
headland here, known in Irish as Ros Láir,
'middle headland'. This lies between
The Raven Point to the north and
Greenore Point to the south. Hence its
name.

Ross-on-Wye (Hereford and Worcester)

This market town on the River WYE
northeast of MONMOUTH is close enough to
Wales to have a Welsh name, from *rhos*
(moor, raised plain). The latter of these two
senses well suits the town, which is on a
steep hill overlooking the Wye. The Welsh
name of Ross-on-Wye, Rossan-ar-Wy, has
the same meaning. Ross appeared in the
Domesday Book as *Rosse*.

Rostrevor (Down)

A small resort on the northern shore of
CARLINGFORD Lough whose name means
'Trevor's wood', as better seen in the Irish
name, Ros Treabhair. No doubt the forest
nature-reserve here, with its ancient oaks,
would have been at least part of the wood of
the name.

Rosyth (Fife)

This town immediately northwest of
INVERKEITHING has a name of uncertain
origin. It seems to be based on the Gaelic
ros (headland), which could refer to the
rock by the River FORTH on which the
ruins of the town's castle stand. The latter
half of the name suggests the Old English
hȳth (landing-place), which would
similarly suit a waterside location. But a
combination of both these elements seems
unlikely. Early records of the name offer
no alternative proposal for the origin, and
are much as now (*Rossyth* in the late twelfth
century, for example, and *Westir Rossith* in
1363).

Rothbury (Northumberland)

A small market town southwest of
ALNWICK whose name means 'Hrotha's
fortified place' (with the Old English *burg*,
'fort'); it was recorded as *Routhebiria* in a
document of about 1125.

Rother (East Sussex)

An administrative district in the east of the
county that takes its name from the River
Rother that flows through it. The river's
own name derives as a 'back formation'
from that of Rotherbridge, a former

hundred here, with its own name meaning 'bridge for oxen' (Old English *hrīther*, 'ox'; *compare* OXFORD), and recorded in the Domesday Book as *Redrebrige*. The Rother thus had an earlier, different name, and this was Shire, meaning 'bright one' (Old English *scīr*, 'bright', as for SHEERNESS). The River Rother in Yorkshire has a name of quite a different origin (*see* ROTHERHAM). *See also* ROTHERHITHE for a name related to this Sussex Rother.

Rotherham (South Yorkshire)
An industrial town northeast of SHEFFIELD at the confluence of the rivers DON and Rother; it takes its name from the latter river, with *hām* as the Old English for 'homestead'. This Yorkshire Rother has a name of different origin to the Sussex ROTHER. Its name means 'main river', and is of British (Celtic) origin. The first element is the British *ro-* (main, principal), as also found in *Regulbium*, the Roman name of RECULVER. The second element is *dubro-* (river), as found in the name of DOVER. The river's name was recorded as *Roder* in a document of about 1200, while Rotherham appears in the Domesday Book as *Rodreham*.

Rotherhithe (Greater London)
A district of east LONDON by the THAMES in the Borough of SOUTHWARK. It has a name that means 'landing-place for cattle', from the Old English *hrȳther* (ox, cattle) (*compare* ROTHER), and *hȳth* (landing-place) (as also found disguised in CHELSEA, LAMBETH, PUTNEY, and STEPNEY, all on the Thames in London). The name of Rotherhithe was recorded in a document of about 1105 as *Rederheia*, and an alternative version of the name — Redriff — was current down to at least the eighteenth century.

Rothes (Grampian)
A small town southeast of ELGIN whose name is based on the Gaelic *ràth* (circular fort), as for the many Irish names that contain a virtually identical word (RÁTH LUIRC, RATHMINES, and so on). *See also* GLENROTHES.

Rothesay (Strathclyde)
The chief town and port of the island of BUTE. Its name means 'Rother's island', the reference being to Roderick, the son of Reginald, to whom Bute was granted in the early thirteenth century. The Gaelic name of Rothesay alludes to the status of the town, and is Baile Bhoid, 'town of Bute'.

Rothwell (Northamptonshire)
A small town northwest of KETTERING whose name means 'spring by a clearing', from the conjectural Old English *roth* (clearing) and the fairly common *wella* (spring, well). Rothwell was recorded as *Rodewelle* in the Domesday Book.

Rottingdean (East Sussex)
A coastal village east of BRIGHTON whose name means 'valley of Rōta's people', with the same personal name (but hardly the same person!) as found in the name of RUTLAND. The Domesday Book recorded the name as *Rotingedene*.

Rough Tor (Cornwall)
A granite tor (rocky hill) on BODMIN Moor, southeast of CAMELFORD. Despite the pronunciation of the name as 'Row Tor' (rhyming with 'cow') there seems little doubt that the meaning is the obvious one, and that the name is thus of basically English origin, unlike that of its near neighbour, the Cornish-named BROWN WILLY.

Roundstone (Galway)
A coastal village in the south of CONNEMARA whose name is an English distortion of the Irish name, which is Cloch na Rón, 'rock of the seals'; the English 'stone' translates the Irish *cloch*.

Roundwood (Wicklow)
This village northwest of WICKLOW has an English self-descriptive name that is quite different from the Irish name, An Tóchar,

'the causeway'. Roundwood lies in the wooded valley of the River Vartry.

Roxburgh (Borders)
This village southwest of KELSO gave its name to the former county of Roxburghshire, now represented by the administrative district of Roxburgh. The name means 'Hroc's fortress', and is Old English in origin, with a document of 1127 giving it as *Rokisburc*.

Royal Canal (Ireland)
This now disused canal, extending from the River LIFFEY near DUBLIN to the SHANNON west of LONGFORD, was built over the period 1789–1802 and was named after the reigning monarch, George III. The Irish name of the canal, with the same meaning as the English, is An Chanail Rioga. *Compare* ROYAL MILITARY CANAL.

Royal Military Canal (Kent/East Sussex)
A (now disused) canal that ran from just east of HYTHE to near HASTINGS. It was built in the early nineteenth century to form part of the land defences here in conjunction with the Martello towers constructed on the coast during the Napoleonic War. Like the ROYAL CANAL it was named in honour of the reigning monarch, George III.

Royston (Hertfordshire, South Yorkshire)
Either of two towns, with names of different origin. The Hertfordshire Royston, southwest of CAMBRIDGE, had its name recorded in a document of 1184 as *Crux Roaisie*, 'Rohesia's cross'. This refers to a stone cross erected at the junction of the ICKNIELD WAY and ERMINE STREET here in medieval times by a lady named Rohesia (or some similar spelling). This Latin version of the name was then contracted as *Cruceroys*, and finally shortened to simply *Roys*, with the Old English *tūn* (village) (or possibly *stān*, 'stone') then added. The cross no longer exists. The Yorkshire Royston, north of BARNSLEY, has a name that means 'Hror's

village', with this recorded in the Domesday Book as *Rorestone*.

Royton (Greater Manchester)
Both the name of this town, north of OLDHAM, and that of RYTON have the same origin, which is 'rye farm', from the Old English *rȳge* (rye) and the common *tūn* (farm). Royton appears as *Ritton* in a document of 1226.

Ruabon (Clwyd)
This industrial town southwest of WREXHAM has a name that means 'Mabon's hill', with the initial *M-* of the personal name originally modified to *F-*, then lost altogether in the final version of the name, even in its more authentic Welsh spelling as Rhiwabon (Welsh *rhiw* means 'hill slope'). Mabon was a Celtic god of youth, said to have been the father of St Teilo (who gave his name to LLANDEILO). Ruabon appears as *Rywuabon* in a document dated 1291.

Rugby (Warwickshire)
This well-known town east of COVENTRY was originally 'Rockbury' (or something similar), as the Domesday Book record of the name shows (*Rocheberie*). This means 'Hroca's fortified place', with the personal name followed by the Old English *burg* (fort). Subsequently, the Scandinavians substituted *bý* (settlement) for *burg*, as sometimes happened, to give the present form of the name.

Rugeley (Staffordshire)
A town southeast of STAFFORD whose name means 'clearing on a ridge', from the Old English *hrycg* (ridge) and *lēah* (woodland clearing). The Domesday Book recorded the name as *Rugelie*. There is no obvious ridge at Rugeley, but the town lies close to the northeastern edge of CANNOCK CHASE.

Ruislip (Greater London)
This district of HILLINGDON has a name that probably means 'rushy leaping-place',

from the Old English *rysc* (rush) and *hlȳp* (leap). The reference would have been to a point on the River Pinn that could serve as such a crossing for agile travellers. (It is still possible to leap the Pinn in this way in places!) The name was recorded as *Rislepe* in the Domesday Book.

Rum (Highland)

A mountainous island south of SKYE in the Inner HEBRIDES. It has a Gaelic name that means 'room' (Gaelic *rùim*) referring to its relative spaciousness, especially by comparison with neighbouring EIGG and MUCK. The name is commonly but mistakenly spelt 'Rhum', and this spelling was introduced by the island's English owners, the Bulloughs, between 1888 and 1957. Perhaps they were influenced by such alternative spellings as 'Rinns' and 'Rhinns' (as for RINNS OF GALLOWAY). Rum was recorded as *Ruim* in a document of 677.

Runcorn (Cheshire)

This New Town, designated in 1964, stands on the southern bank of the MERSEY south of WIDNES. Its name, meaning 'roomy cove', refers to this location, or more specifically to the former spacious bay that existed between Widnes and Castle Rock. A document of about 1000 refers to the site as being *æt Rūm cofan*, 'at the roomy cove'. The two component Old English words are thus *rūm* (spacious) (as for ROMFORD) and *cofa* (cover, bay) (originally 'chamber').

Runnymede (Surrey)

The historic meadows northwest of EGHAM, where King John negotiated with the barons and subsequently drew up the Magna Charta in 1215. The site has an appropriate name for this transaction, meaning 'council island meadow', from the Old English *run* (secret, council) (compare 'runes'), *ēg* (island), and *mǣd* (meadow). The 'island', or land by the River THAMES (which does have an actual island here named Magna Charta Island), would thus already have been a meeting-place for royal or other assemblies. The name was recorded as *Ronimede* in the text of the Magna Charta itself, with the meadow referred to as the Latin *pratum*.

Rushcliffe (Nottinghamshire)

An administrative district, formed in the south of the county in 1974, that took the name of a former hundred here, itself meaning 'brushwood hill'.

Rushden (Northamptonshire)

A manufacturing town east of WELLINGBOROUGH whose name means 'rushy valley', from the Old English *riscen* (rushy) and *denu* (valley). The land is generally low-lying here, and Rushden is only two miles from the River NENE. The name was recorded as *Risden* in the Domesday Book.

Rushmoor (Hampshire)

An administrative district, set up in 1974 in the extreme northeast of the county, that takes its name from that of Rushmoor Bottom, a natural feature to the west of ALDERSHOT. The name means what it says, 'waste land overgrown with rushes'.

Rustington (West Sussex)

A coastal town east of LITTLEHAMPTON whose name perhaps means 'Rusta's farm', with the personal name being the equivalent of 'Rusty', applied as a nickname to a red-haired person. The name was recorded as *Rustincton'* in a document of 1185.

Rutherglen (Strathclyde)

A town on the south bank of the CLYDE immediately southeast of GLASGOW whose name is of Gaelic origin and means 'red valley', from *ruadh* (red) and *gleann* (glen, valley). The reference is to the reddish-coloured soil here. The name was recorded as *Ruthirglen* in about 1160, and until comparatively recently had an alternative version as 'Ruglen'.

Ruthin (Clwyd)

This town on a hill above the River CLWYD west of WREXHAM has a Welsh name meaning 'red fort', from *rhudd* (red) and *din* (fort), with these words perceived more obviously in the Welsh version of the name, Rhuthun. The thirteenth-century castle here was at one time known as *Y Castell Coch yng gwernfor*, 'the red castle in the great marsh'. It is now in ruins, but fragments of the original red sandstone can still be discerned. The town's 'redness' is also evident in its brickworks. Its name appears as *Ruthun* in a text of 1253.

Rutland (Leicestershire)

The name of Britain's former smallest county is preserved in that of the modern administrative district in east Leicestershire, as well as in that of Rutland Water, the large reservoir west of STAMFORD. The name means 'Rōta's estate', with the Old English *land* having the special sense of a defined estate of relatively small extent, unlike the '-land' of the other county names, such as CUMBERLAND and NORTHUMBERLAND, where the reference is to a large tract of sizeable extent. Rutland was in fact originally a 'soke' (Old English *sōcn*), a district over which special rights were exercised. (Until fairly recently, the Soke of PETERBOROUGH was a specific administrative entity.) Rutland became a county in the thirteenth century. Its name was recorded in a document of about 1060 as *Roteland*.

Rydal Water (Cumbria)

One of the central lakes of the Lake District, located north of WINDERMERE. 'Rydal' means 'rye valley', from the Old English *rȳge* (rye) and *dæl* (valley), with this the name of the hamlet at its eastern end. This name is fairly recent, and the lake was originally known as Routhmere, so named after the River Rothay that flows through it. (The river's own name means 'trout stream'.) Perhaps the new name, first recorded in the sixteenth century, was

adopted because it was felt to be more meaningful than the earlier name, which is in fact of Old Norse origin. The new name would thus fall in line with other 'transparent' names of lakes in the district, such as BUTTERMERE and GRASMERE. A thirteenth-century document thus records the lake as *Routhemere*, and one of 1576 as *Rydal Water*, its present form.

Ryde (Isle of Wight)

A coastal resort on the northeast side of the island whose name simply means 'stream', from a local dialect word ('ride'), which comes from the Old English *rith* (stream). The stream in question is Monktonmead Brook, which flows through the town to the sea. Ryde was recorded as *La Ride* in a document of 1257.

Rye (East Sussex)

This town and former port (one of the CINQUE PORTS) now lies some two miles from the sea northeast of HASTINGS. Its name has nothing to do with rye, but represents the Old English phrase *æt thǣre īege*, 'at the island'; the initial *R-* of the name is all that remains of the second word. (The phrase was 'smoothed' to *atter ie*, and then wrongly divided as *atte Rie*, on the basis that *atte*, 'at the' is found in other names, for example, even now in HAVERING-atte-Bower.) Rye was actually built on an island in the flooded marshes here, and was an important port down to the time of Shakespeare. Its name was recorded as *Ria* in a document of 1130.

Ryhope (Tyne and Wear)

A district of SUNDERLAND whose name probably means 'rough valley', from the Old English *hrēof* (rough, rugged) and *hop* (valley) (as for BACUP). Its name was recorded in about 1050 as *Reofhoppas*.

Ryton (Tyne and Wear)

As mentioned for ROYTON, the name of this town by the TYNE west of NEWCASTLE UPON TYNE means 'rye farm'. It was recorded as *Ritona* in a document dated 1183.

S

Saddleworth (Greater Manchester)
An area of moorland on the edge of the
PEAK DISTRICT east of OLDHAM. Its name
means 'enclosure on a saddle-shaped
ridge'. The Old English *sadol* frequently
occurs in medieval charters to denote a
saddle-shaped ridge in its own right. A text
of about 1230 mentions Saddleworth as
Sadelword.

Saffron Walden (Essex)
This ancient town north of BISHOP'S
STORTFORD was originally known simply
as Walden, meaning 'valley of the Britons',
from the Old English *walh*, literally
'foreigner' (as the Ancient Britons were
regarded by the occupying Anglo-Saxons)
and *denu* (valley). Later, 'Saffron' was
added to distinguish this Walden from the
many others in the region, such as King's
Walden southwest of HITCHIN and St
Paul's Walden west of STEVENAGE. The
added word referred to the fields of saffron
crocus grown here from the fourteenth
century. (This is not the common crocus,
but *Crocus sativus*, cultivated for the
medicinal properties of its orange-coloured
stigmas when dried.) In the Domesday
Book, Saffron Walden was thus simply
Waledana, but in 1582 it was recorded as
Saffornewalden.

St Abb's Head (Borders)
Both the headland northwest of
EYEMOUTH and the village of St Abbs just
south of it take their name from St Æbba or
Ebbe, the seventh-century Abbess of
Coldingham, nearby, herself the sister of
King (and Saint) Oswald of Northumbria.

St Agnes (Isles of Scilly)
Whereas two of the five inhabited islands
are named after recognisable and genuine
saints (ST MARY'S and ST MARTIN'S), St
Agnes is almost certainly a 'bogus' name,
actually deriving from the Cornish *enys*
(island), but modelled after these other
two. Significantly, local residents refer to
the island simply as 'Agnes', without the
'St'.

St Albans (Hertfordshire)
This well-known cathedral city takes its
name from the third-century saint and
martyr Alban, to whom the abbey here is
dedicated. The Roman station here was
known as *Verulamium*, a name perhaps
based on a Celtic root element *uero-*
meaning 'broad', although in what precise
sense is still obscure. This name, and two
subsequent ones, are referred to by the
Venerable Bede in his eighth-century
Ecclesiastical History of the English People,
where he talks of the *ciuitatem Uerolamium
quae nunc a gente Anglorum Uerlamacaestir
siue Uaeclingacaestir appellatur* ('town of
Verulamium which is now called
Verlamacaestir or Waeclingacaestir by the
English'). The first of these two names is
based on the Roman name, with the Old
English *ceaster* ('-caster') added to denote
the fort. The second derives from the tribe
known as the Wæclings, who gave their
name to WATLING STREET, the Roman
road that runs from LONDON to St Albans.
But for St Alban, therefore, the city might
today be called something like
'Werchester' or 'Watchester'. The city is
on the River Ver, which took its name as a
'back formation' from the Roman name, or
more precisely from the first of Bede's
recorded names, or a later variant of it.
(The Domesday Book gives the river name
as *Wearlame*.) The earliest record
of the present name is the eighth-century
one of *Æcclesia sancti Albani*, 'St
Alban's church'; at this time the original
Benedictine abbey was founded on the site
where St Alban was executed, the location
also of the present cathedral. The
Roman city was on the west side of modern
St Albans, across the river, and the
pagan location has been duly 'sanctified'
by the erection of St Michael's Church
there.

St Andrews (Fife)
This historic university town takes its name from St Andrew, Scotland's patron saint, whose relics were said to have been brought here in the eighth century but were 'lost' in the sixteenth century, when the great cathedral of St Andrew, built two hundred years earlier to commemorate him, was destroyed (it has never been rebuilt). The name is not a possessive, and the final *-s* is part of the personal name *Androis*, the Scottish name of Andrew. A document of about 1158 has the name as *Sancti Andree*, but one of about 1139, only a few years earlier, refers to the place as *Chilrimunt*. This represents a previous name, 'Kilrimont', meaning 'church of the royal hill', from the Gaelic *cill* (church) and words corresponding to the modern Gaelic *righ* (king) and *monadh* (hill).

St Anthony-in-Roseland (Cornwall)
Although a mere hamlet, St Anthony-in-Roseland, on the River Percuil opposite ST MAWES, has a name of memorable attractiveness. The latter word of the name, however, is not what it seems — the first half of it represents the conjectural Cornish *ros* (moor, promontory), otherwise the same basic Celtic word behind the names of ROSS and ROSS-ON-WYE, among other places. The name thus means '(village of the church dedicated to) St Anthony in the moorland region'. The long name differentiates this hamlet from nearby St Anthony-in-Meneage ('monks' enclosure', from the Cornish *manach*, 'monk').

St Asaph (Clwyd)
This village with its small cathedral south of RHYL takes its name from the sixth-century saint and bishop to whom the cathedral is dedicated. The Welsh name of St Asaph, however, is Llanelwy, 'church on the (River) Elwy'. The river's own name means 'driving one'.

St Austell (Cornwall)
A town northeast of TRURO that takes its name from the sixth-century saint and monk to whom its church is dedicated. Austell was a disciple of St Mewan, who gave his name to the village of St Mewan, immediately west of St Austell. The two later went to Brittany, and are buried in the same tomb at the village of St Méen, also named after Mewan.

St Bees Head (Cumbria)
Both the headland and the nearby village of St Bees, south of WHITEHAVEN, are named after St Bega, a seventh-century Irish (female) saint about whom little is known. The village was recorded under the name of *Cherchebi*, i.e. Kirkby, in a document of about 1125, and the saint's name seems to have been added to this before 'Kirkby' was dropped leaving the saint's name alone for the place.

St Blazey (Cornwall)
A town northeast of ST AUSTELL named after St Blaise, a fourth-century martyr under the Roman Empire, and believed to have been a bishop in Armenia. The dedication here proves that not all Cornish saint-names derive from Celtic saints!

St Brides Bay (Dyfed)
A prominent bay on the west coast of Wales that takes its name from the small village of St Brides near its southern end. St Bride is better known as St Brigid of Ireland, the sixth-century Abbess of KILDARE about whom many legendary tales are told. Many places are dedicated to her in both Ireland and Wales, and this particular St Brides emphasises the close link between Irish and Welsh Christianity, with the coastal location one where missionaries could land and depart by sea. The Welsh name of the village is Sain Ffred, short for *Llansanffraid*, 'St Bride's church', a name commonly found elsewhere in Wales in its own right.

St Budeaux (Devon)
A district of PLYMOUTH, northwest of the city centre, that derives its name from St

Budoc, to whom the church here is
dedicated. Budoc was a sixth-century
Celtic saint whose name is the masculine
equivalent of Boudicca (better known as
Boadicea, although she was no saint!). The
Domesday Book recorded the name of St
Budeaux as *Bucheside*, which in modern
terms would be 'Budshead', otherwise
'Budoc's headland' (on the estuary of
the River TAMAR). This was therefore
the earlier name of St Budeaux, and its
present name seems to have settled
relatively late, as the following many
alternative names indicate, recorded in a
deed dated 1671 (*al.* meaning 'alias'):
*Butshead al. Boxhead al. Budocoshide al. St
Budeax.*

St Columb Major (Cornwall)

A village east of NEWQUAY whose
name shows that its church is dedicated
to St Columba, although this is probably
not the well-known Columba, the Abbot of
IONA, but a much more obscure virgin
martyr, usually known as Columba the
Virgin. The churches of both St Columb
Major and nearby St Columb Minor are
dedicated to her. The place-name was
recorded as *Sancte Columbe* in a document
of 1266, with 'Major' and 'Minor' added
about this time to differentiate the two
parishes.

St David's (Dyfed)

This village, with its small St David's
Cathedral, southeast of St David's Head,
has a self-explanatory name, with the
dedication being to the patron saint of
Wales. The village's Welsh name is
Tyddewi, literally 'David's house', while
the headland is Penmaen Dewi, 'David's
head or rock'. The Roman name of St
David's Head was *Octapitarum
Promontorium*, with the first word perhaps
based on a root Celtic word meaning
'eight'. If so, the reference may be to the
group of small rocky islands (actually over
twenty in number) off St David's Head,
where they are known as the Bishops and
Clerks.

St Edmundsbury (Suffolk)

An administrative district in the west
central region of the county that takes its
name from the Domesday Book record of
the name of its chief town, BURY ST
EDMUNDS (which see for details).

St George's Channel (Ireland/Wales)

It is difficult to say precisely when this
well-known sea channel between Ireland
and Great Britain was named, or by whom.
Mention of it is made, however, in the
journal of the English navigator, Martin
Frobisher, describing his second voyage of
1577 to search for gold in the northern
regions of Canada. Undoubtedly the name
was given in honour of England's patron
saint. It is interesting that the Channel runs
directly past ST DAVID'S Head, which was
certainly already named then. Perhaps this
name prompted the English namer,
whoever he was, to respond in like fashion?

St Helens (Merseyside)

This industrial town east of LIVERPOOL
acquired its name relatively late, with the
first record of a chapel dedicated to St
Helen here dated 1552. This was probably
a medieval chapel-of-ease, and stood at the
junction of the WARRINGTON-to-
ORMSKIRK road and the PRESCOT-to-
ASHTON-UNDER-LYNE road. There have
been four churches on this site
subsequently, with the third (from
1816 to 1916) dedicated to St Mary. The
present town arose only in the seventeenth
century.

St Helier (Channel Islands)

The chief town of JERSEY derives its
name from the sixth-century martyr who
was Jersey's first saint. He was a Belgian
monk, said to have lived in a cave above
the town that now bears his name. The
small island on which Elizabeth Castle was
built in the mid-sixteenth century was
also originally named after the saint, and
was known as *l'îlet de St Helier*. The
town itself effectively also dates from this
time.

St Ives (Cambridgeshire, Cornwall)

Either of two towns, dedicated to different saints, respectively male and female. St Ives in Cambridgeshire (formerly Huntingdonshire), on the River OUSE east of HUNTINGDON, takes its name from St Ivo (or Ives, or Yves), whose bones were discovered here at the end of the tenth century, when the place was then known as Slepe, 'slippery place' (for its riverside location). Its name was thus recorded as *Slæpi* in a document of 672, and as *S. Ivo de Selepe* in one of 1110. The parish church is dedicated to All Saints, however, not to St Ivo. The Cornish resort, northeast of PENZANCE, derives its name from St Ia, who according to local legend was an Irish virgin who was wafted across the sea from Ireland on a leaf to land here at some time in the sixth or seventh century. Hence the former Cornish name of St Ives as Porthia, 'Ia's landing-place'. The place-name was recorded as *St Ya* in a document of 1283, and the following year as *Porthya*. At least the parish church is dedicated to her, as one would expect in a Celtic land.

St John's Wood (Greater London)

This district of northwest central LONDON has a name that refers to the Knights Hospitallers of St John, to whom the land here was transferred from the Knights Templars when the latter were suppressed in the early fourteenth century. The name was recorded as *Boscum Prioris Sci Johannis* in a text of 1294, and as *Seynt Johns Woode* in one of 1524. There is now no trace of the former wood, although Lord's Cricket Ground perhaps represents something of the original greenery.

St Just (Cornwall)

A town north of LAND'S END, formally known as St Just in PENWITH to distinguish it from the village of St Just in Roseland, north of ST MAWES (*see* ST ANTHONY-IN-ROSELAND). The town may not be dedicated to the relatively well-known Justus of Beauvais, the third-century boy martyr, but to another, much more obscure Justus, who is described as a martyr in a document of 1140. Either way, both places have parish churches dedicated to St Just, and are recorded respectively as *Sancti Justi in Penwithe* in a document of 1334, and as *Sancti Justi in Roslonde* in one of 1282.

St Kilda (Western Isles)

This steep rocky island some distance to the west of HARRIS appears to have a name dedicated to a St Kilda, duly entered in *The Oxford Dictionary of Saints* (1978) as a 'virtually unknown saint who has given his (or her) name to the remote island to the west of the Outer Hebrides in the Atlantic Ocean'. However, St Kilda is not simply 'virtually unknown' but is actually non-existent! The Old Norse name of the island, *Skildar*, was misread on charts and as a result a spurious saint was born. The name means 'shields', and may have been intended to describe the shield-like outline of the island group, seen from the sea. It seems likely that some saintly recluse may have lived on St Kilda at some time, and a holy well can be found there, but the recluse was not St Kilda. An alternative name was Hirta, another Norse name that may mean 'herd island', from the Old Norse *hjǫrth* (herd) and *ey* (island).

St Leonards (East Sussex)

This coastal town immediately west of HASTINGS is named after the original parish church here, dedicated to St Leonard, and mentioned in a document of 1279 as *ecclesia Leonardi de Hastynges*. This church was washed away by the sea in about 1430, and was replaced by another to be superseded in turn in the 1830s by the present parish church, similarly dedicated. The present resort developed soon after this date, when the London builder James Burton bought land here with the aim of establishing a fashionable watering place similar to BRIGHTON, further west along the coast. The formal name of the town is St Leonards on Sea, with the familiar 'commercial' suffix, designed to attract residents and holiday-makers.

St Martin's (Isles of Scilly)

The third largest of the five inhabited islands in the group (after ST MARY'S and TRESCO). St Martin's is named after the dedication of its parish church to St Martin of Tours, and the small but attractive stained-glass window in the church shows the traditional scene of St Martin cutting his cloak in half to clothe a beggar. This saint is associated with the establishment of churches and places of worship in remote districts, away from urban areas, and it is perhaps fitting that the island, itself dependent to a large extent on St Mary's, should bear his name.

St Mary's (Isles of Scilly)

The largest and main island of the five inhabited islands in the group. It takes its name from the Virgin Mary, to whom the parish church at HUGH TOWN is dedicated. No doubt the particular association of St Mary with the sea (one of her titles is *Stella Maris*, 'star of the sea') influenced her adoption as the island's main patron saint.

St Mawes (Cornwall)

This town, at the eastern side of the entrance to the CARRICK Roads, south of TRURO, has a name deriving from that of its patron saint, Mawdeth, a rather obscure Celtic monk and missionary who was a companion of St Budoc (*see* ST BUDEAUX); their two names are associated in Brittany as they are here. The church is mentioned in a document of 1345 as being dedicated to *Sanctus Maudetus*.

St Michael's Mount (Cornwall)

This well-known island in Mounts Bay, opposite MARAZION, takes its name from the dedication of its chapel to St Michael the Archangel; the place-name was recorded in the Domesday Book as *Sanctus Michael*. According to an old Cornish legend, St Michael appeared to some fishermen on the western side of the island

in about AD 500. The Mount has a direct link with its French namesake and lookalike, Mont St Michel in Normandy, off the northwest coast of France; the abbot of the abbey there came to Cornwall to build a similar priory where the chapel now stands in the early twelfth century, and it was consecrated by the Bishop of EXETER in 1144. In a sense, therefore, this particular dedication is an 'import'.

St Monance (Fife)

A small fishing and boat-building town on the FIRTH OF FORTH that takes its name from Monans, the sixth-century Bishop of Clonfert, Ireland, to whom its church is dedicated. For some time the alternative name of St Monance (now often spelt St Monans) was Abercrombie, 'mouth of the bent stream', referring to the winding St Monans Burn that flows through the town to the sea.

St Neots (Cambridgeshire)

This town on the River OUSE southwest of HUNTINGDON grew up around a monastery built in the tenth century to commemorate the Cornish saint, Neot. His relics were brought here from the village of St Neot, near LISKEARD, where he had died a hundred years previously, to be buried at nearby Eynesbury (now a district of the town). St Neots was recorded as *S' Neod* in a document of 1132, while the Cornish village appeared as *Nietestov* (i.e. 'Neotstow') in the Domesday Book.

St Pancras (Greater London)

This district of Camden (*see* CAMDEN TOWN) takes its name from the dedication of its parish church to St Pancras, an early-fourth-century martyr in Rome. The Domesday Book recorded the dedication here as *Sanctum Pancratiu*. The saint's own name is Greek, meaning 'all strength'.

St Peter Port (Channel Islands)

This town is the capital of GUERNSEY, and takes its name from the dedication of its fine church, which dates back to the twelfth century. The addition of 'Port' to the name (unlike the name of ST HELIER, the capital of JERSEY) emphasises the island's historic commercial activity, by comparison with the tourist trade of Jersey, and the climatic conditions on Guernsey are still more favourable for dairy farming and market-gardening than they are on Jersey. The associations of St Peter with fishing make his dedication especially appropriate for a town that is also a seaport and (formerly) a fishing port.

Salcombe (Devon)

A resort south of KINGSBRIDGE whose name means 'salt valley', from the Old English *sealt* (salt) and *cumb* (valley). The reference is to the production of salt here (as at BUDLEIGH SALTERTON, further up the coast), rather than simply to the salt water of the Kingsbridge Estuary. The name was recorded as *Saltecumbe* in a document of 1244.

Sale (Greater Manchester)

A town southwest of MANCHESTER whose name is derived directly from the Old English *salh* 'willow tree' (compare modern 'sallow'), referring to the location of the original place among willows by the River MERSEY. Sale is only five miles from SALFORD (see below), whose own name is of similar meaning, showing that willows must have been abundant in this region of what was formerly LANCASHIRE. Sale was recorded as *Sala* in a document of about 1205.

Salford (Greater Manchester)

This large town to the west of MANCHESTER is only a short distance from SALE (see above), and like it has a name that refers to willow trees. The name thus means 'willow-tree ford' or 'ford where willows grow', with the ford being over the River Irwell. Salford's name was recorded exactly as now in the Domesday Book.

Salisbury (Wiltshire)

The Roman name for the settlement here was *Sorviodunum*. It was located at the site of the Roman fort, not where the present city stands (at the confluence of the AVON and the Nadder, northwest of SOUTHAMPTON), but at OLD SARUM, two miles to the north. The second half of this Roman name refers to the fort itself, from the same Celtic element (*dunos-*) that occurs in many other Roman names, such as *Camulodunum* for COLCHESTER and *Moridunum* for CARMARTHEN. The first half of the name, as frequently, is the more difficult to interpret. It cannot derive from a river name, as there is no river at Old Sarum. It is undoubtedly British (Celtic) in origin, but still defies attempts to interpret it. Whatever the *sorvio-* meant, the Anglo-Saxons seem to have associated it with their own word *searu* (trick), and when they substituted their own *burg* (fort) for the Roman -*dunum*, they accordingly modified the first half of the name. It was thus recorded as *Sarisberie* in the Domesday Book. This version of the name, in an abbreviated form of its latinised version as *Sarisburiensis*, then produced the 'Sarum' of Old Sarum, with the '-um' simply a conventional ending. Meanwhile, the Normans found it easier to pronounce the name with an *l* rather than with an *r*, and so came to spell the name in something like the modern version; this is apparent in a record of 1227 as *Salesbury*. Interestingly, the modern pronunciation of the name ignores the second vowel altogether, so that it sounds as 'Salsbury', somewhat similar to SALFORD. The modern town arose in the thirteenth century, when the former dry bleak site on Old Sarum was abandoned and a new Salisbury was built, with a new cathedral, in the valley below beside the lush fertile meadows of the rivers mentioned. The name of 'New Sarum' is now thus officially used for the modern city, by contrast with the abandoned Old Sarum.

Salop (Shropshire)

The long-established abbreviated form of
the name of SHROPSHIRE, and the official
name of the county from 1974 to 1980. It
arose as a contraction of the Norman
version of the county name, which was
recorded as *Salopescira* in a document of
1094. This itself represents a much
'smoother' version of the original Anglo-
Saxon (*see* SHROPSHIRE). Shropshire has
always been the form of the county name
preferred by its inhabitants, and the
change to 'Salop' was resented by many.
It was particularly unpopular with the
European Member of Parliament for Salop
and Staffordshire, who discovered when
attending political debates on the
Continent that 'Salop' bore an unfortunate
resemblance to the French *salope* (slut)!
Even so, the name continues to be used, as
'Hants' is for Hampshire, or 'Oxon' for
Oxfordshire, and the adjective 'Salopian' is
still used in a number of respectable
contexts, such as for members of
SHREWSBURY School.

Saltash (Cornwall)

A town immediately west of PLYMOUTH
over the TAMAR estuary. Its name means
what it says: 'salt ash', that is, referring to
an ash tree that grew by saltworks, or by
salt water (the former seems more likely).
Originally Saltash was simply 'Ash' (*Aysh*
in a record of 1284), with 'salt' added later
(*Saltesh* in 1337). For similar 'salt' names
in the neighbouring county of Devon,
compare SALCOMBE and BUDLEIGH
SALTERTON. *Compare also* SALTBURN-
BY-THE-SEA; SALTCOATS; SALTDEAN.

Saltburn-by-the-Sea (Cleveland)

This coastal resort to the east of
MIDDLESBROUGH has a name that means
'salt stream'. It probably refers not simply
to a salt-water stream here, but more likely
indicates the nearby brine wells, whose
brine was regularly transported to Saltburn
for use in the brine-baths opened in the
1890s. The name was recorded as
Salteburnam in about 1185. The addition of

'-by-the-Sea' is partly for commercial
reasons, but it does also distinguish this
Saltburn from the Scottish village of the
name near INVERGORDON.

Saltcoats (Strathclyde)

A town and resort immediately southeast of
ARDROSSAN on the Firth of CLYDE. Its
name refers to the saltworks established
here in the sixteenth century by James V.
The precise meaning is 'salt sheds'
(compare 'cottage'), denoting the buildings
in which the salt was prepared or stored.
The name was recorded as *Saltcoates* in a
document dated 1548. The production of
salt from saltpans in the region was
recorded at various periods before this,
however, and James V was essentially
taking advantage of the place's natural
potential.

Saltdean (East Sussex)

An urban location east of BRIGHTON
whose name means 'salt valley', referring
to a gap or cleft in the sea cliffs here. Such
'deans' are a feature of this region of the
Sussex coast, and are incorporated in the
names of Ovingdean, ROTTINGDEAN, and
Roedean, among others. A reference to this
particular 'salt dean' is recorded in the
latter half of the sixteenth century.

Samson (Isles of Scilly)

The largest of the group's uninhabited
islands, south of BRYHER. It is said (on
doubtful grounds) to have a name whose
first element is the Cornish *sans* (saint), as
if matching the names of ST MARY'S, ST
MARTIN'S, and ST AGNES (although this
last is almost certainly not a saint's name).
If this is so, it is uncertain what the name of
the saint could be. The name as a whole is
similarly associated with St Samson, who is
said to have given his name to the Cornish
village of St Sampson, near FOWEY. But
this origin is similarly not convincingly
attested.

Sanday (Highland, Orkney)

Any of at least two islands of the name,

with the ones here respectively northwest of RUM and northeast of MAINLAND in the ORKNEYS. In each case the name has the same meaning, which is simply 'sand island', from the Old Norse *sand* (sand) and *ey* (island).

Sandbach (Cheshire)

This town northeast of CREWE has a name that means 'sandy stream', from the Old English *sand* (sand) and *bæce* (stream in a valley). Sandbach is on a small tributary of the River Wheelock. The name was recorded in the Domesday Book as *Sandbec*.

Sanderstead (Greater London)

A district of CROYDON whose name means 'sandy place', from the Old English conjectural *sanden* (sandy; the adjective of *sand*) and *stede* (place). The name should thus really be 'Sandenstead', but the Normans altered the final -*n* of *sanden* to -*r* for ease of pronunciation. (Compare similar adjectives, such as 'golden', 'oaken', and 'wooden', still in use.) The name was thus recorded in the late ninth century as *Sondenstede*, and in the Domesday Book two hundred years later as *Sandestede*. The soil is noticeably sandy at Sanderstead.

Sandhurst (Berkshire)

This town with its well-known Royal Military Academy, west of CAMBERLEY, has a straightforward name meaning 'sandy wooded hill', from the Old English *sand* (sand) and *hyrst* (hillock, wooded hill). The name was recorded as *Sandherst* in a document of 1175. The soil is markedly sandy at Sandhurst.

Sandown (Isle of Wight)

This resort south of RYDE has a somewhat misleading name, suggesting 'down' (or 'dune'). It was recorded as simply *Sande* in the Domesday Book, and as *Sandham* in 1271, showing that it consists of the two Old English words *sand* (sand) and either *hām* (homestead) or *hamm* (riverside land).

The latter is more likely, and would refer to the flat ground between the upper reaches of the River Yar (*see* YARMOUTH) and the sea. So Sandown is really the place of 'sandy riverside land'.

Sandringham (Norfolk)

This estate village with its royal residence of Sandringham House, northeast of KING'S LYNN, has a name that was recorded in the Domesday Book as *Santdersincham*, which gives a somewhat clearer concept of the origin. The meaning is 'sandy (part of) Dersingham', the latter being the name of the village immediately north of Sandringham. Dersingham itself means 'homestead of Dēorsige's people'. The deep sandy soil at Sandringham is noteworthy even today.

Sandwich (Kent)

This port east of CANTERBURY was one of the original CINQUE PORTS but is now two miles from the sea due to changes in the coastline (as at RYE). Its name means 'sandy landing-place', with the second element of the name the Old English *wīc*, here having its 'specialised' sense of 'port', as it has for NORWICH, IPSWICH, and elsewhere. The name was recorded as *Sondwic* in a document of 851. The sand is not that of the seashore but of the soil here, a rich sandy loam, conducive for the local market-gardening.

Sandy (Bedfordshire)

A town east of BEDFORD whose name is rather more than it seems. It means 'sandy island', from the Old English *sand* (sand) and *ēg* (island), and this particular origin can be better made out in the Domesday Book record of the name as *Sandeia*. The 'island' is the slightly higher ground immediately east of the River Ivel, on which Sandy stands. The rich sandy soil in the district is suitable for market-gardening, as it is at SANDWICH.

Sanquhar (Dumfries and Galloway)

A town on the River Noth northwest of

THORNHILL whose name (pronounced 'Sanker') means 'old fort', from the Gaelic *sean* (old) and *cathair* (fort). The fort in question is the ancient earthwork called the Devil's Dyke, to the west of the town. A mid-twelfth-century text records the name as *Sanchar*.

Sark (Channel Islands)

The fourth largest of the five main islands of the group, Sark has a name that has been tentatively derived from the Old Norse *serkr* (shirt), referring to its outline, presumably with the 'top' at the northeastern end. Recent research has established that the Roman name of Sark was *Caesarea*, a name formerly associated with JERSEY. This suggests a derivation in the name of Julius Caesar, but the name is probably a latinised form of some earlier name, with the present spelling developing by false association with that of the emperor.

Sarn Helen (Wales)

The name given to various sections of the Roman road that may at one time have linked CAERNARVON and CARMARTHEN, respectively in the north and south of the principality. The name represents the Welsh *sarn hoelen*, 'paved causeway'.

Saundersfoot (Dyfed)

A small coastal resort north of TENBY whose name probably refers to a location at the foot of a hill owned by a man named Saunders or Alexander; it was recorded as *Sannders foot* in a document dated 1602. The present town has grown up only since the 1820s. Its site suits the name, and it is situated at a point where two valleys meet in an opening in the cliffs to the west of CARMARTHEN Bay.

Savernake Forest (Wiltshire)

An extensive woodland area to the southeast of MARLBOROUGH whose name probably derives from a river here once known as the Sabrina. This could be the River Bedwyn or some other nearby, such

as the eastern branch of the East AVON. If this origin is correct, the name of the forest is directly related to that of the River SEVERN, which was also formerly known as the Sabrina. The name Savernake was recorded as *Safernoc* in a document of 934, with the final element of this representing the British (Celtic) root element *-aco-* (district).

Sawbridgeworth (Hertfordshire)

A town northeast of HARLOW whose name means 'Sæbeorht's enclosure'. Not surprisingly, the Norman clerks had some difficulty in transcribing the Anglo-Saxon name, and Sawbridgeworth appears in the Domesday Book as *Sabrixteworde*. The modern spelling of the name attempts to make it meaningful by rendering the second half of the personal name (which means 'sea bright') as 'bridge'. This happens to be suitable for the town, which lies on the west bank of the River Stort (*see* BISHOP'S STORTFORD), crossed by a bridge.

Sawston (Cambridgeshire)

A southeastern suburb of CAMBRIDGE whose name means 'estate of Salsa's people'. The present form of the name thus really represents a fuller 'Salsington', or *Salsingetune*, as it was recorded in a document of 970. This shows the Old English suffix *-ingtūn* that meant 'estate of the people of' or 'estate associated with' (the named person).

Saxmundham (Suffolk)

A small town northeast of IPSWICH whose name means 'Seaxmund's homestead', with the Domesday Book record of it as *Sasmundesham*. The personal name, meaning either 'protector of the Saxons' or 'stone protection' (probably the former), has not been recorded elsewhere.

Scafell Pike (Cumbria)

England's highest mountain, in the Lake District, has a name that is of Scandinavian origin and means 'hill with a summer pasture', from the Old Norse *skáli* (temporary hut, shieling) and *fjall* (hill, mountain) ('fell'). 'Pike' means 'peak'. Sca Fell is the name of a separate mountain here, just under half a mile from Scafell Pike.

Scalloway (Shetland)
A small town on the west coast of MAINLAND whose name means 'bay by the shielings', from the Old Norse *skáli* (shieling, temporary shed) (*compare* SCAFELL PIKE) and *vágr* (bay). Shielings were sheds set up for shepherds in the summer months.

Scapa Flow (Orkney)
The large natural anchorage between MAINLAND (to the north), HOY (to the west), and the PENTLAND FIRTH (to the south). It has a name that means 'sea-bay of the boat isthmus', from the Old Norse *skalpr* (boat), *eith* (isthmus), and *flóa* (flood; related to English 'flow'). The 'isthmus' is the stretch of land south of KIRKWALL on the eastern side of Scapa Bay, as the northeastern part of Scapa Flow is called.

Scarborough (North Yorkshire)
This fishing port and resort south of WHITBY is traditionally said to have been founded by a Norseman named Thorgils Skarthi. If this is so, the name can be understood as meaning 'Skarthi's fort', although he is said to have been here in the second half of the tenth century, which predates the earliest known record of the place-name: *Scardeburg* in 1158. This need not invalidate the account, however. Alternatively, the first part of the name may represent the Old Norse *skarth* (gap). If this is so, the second element of the name may not be *borg* but *berg* (hill), so that the town is effectively on a 'hill by a gap'. This description suits the topography, with the 'gap' being the valley through which the present A64 road approaches the town from the south. It could well be that this second origin is the true one, but that the

skarth became associated with the personal name of Skarthi (actually a nickname, meaning 'hare-lipped').

Scilly Isles (Isles of Scilly)
The origin of the basic name of this island group southwest of CORNWALL is still rather obscure. It was recorded in about 400 in a Latin text as *Sylinancim* (*insulam, quae ultra Britannias sita est*, 'an island that is situated beyond Britain'). This curious name may be a miscopying of a simpler name such as *Silina*, which could conceivably link up with the name of the Roman god Sulis, occurring in the Roman name of BATH, *Aquae Sulis*. But despite studies of the name as recorded at other dates and in other languages (such as French *Sorlingues*), the ultimate origin remains elusive. It seems clear, however, that the name originally referred to a single island. This could well be because the present island group represents the partly submerged remains of what would at one time, and certainly in the Roman period, have been just one fairly large island, with a few very small outlying isles and rocks.

Scone (Tayside)
The name is familiar as that of Scone Palace, the nineteenth-century mansion on the site of a medieval mansion and palace, across the River TAY from PERTH, with the villages of Old Scone and New Scone nearby. The basic name means 'lump', 'mass of rock', from the Gaelic *sgonn*, with this referring to the Mote Hill here, the traditional ritual site of Scottish kings. The name thus does not relate to the famous Stone of Scone, as is sometimes thought, despite the sense of the Gaelic word. (Nor does it relate to the type of cakes known as scones, whose origin lies in the Dutch *schoonbrood*, 'pure bread', despite their association with Scotland!) The place-name was recorded as *Sgoinde* in a document of 1020.

Scotch Corner (North Yorkshire)
This well-known road junction on the A1

northeast of RICHMOND is so named
because the road (now the A66) that
branches off to the northwest here follows
the established shortest route to Scotland
from this point, that is, via PENRITH and
CARLISLE to GRETNA GREEN. The
Scottish border is about 60 miles further
south at its western end than it is at
the eastern end (at BERWICK-UPON-
TWEED).

Scotland (Britain)

A country occupying the northern part of
Great BRITAIN; the name (obviously)
means 'land of the Scots'. The Scots were
the Celtic raiders from northern Ireland
who crossed over to settle in what was then
known as Caledonia in the fifth and sixth
centuries AD. By about the middle of the
ninth century, the name *Scotia* had become
established for the earlier *Caledonia* and
Pictavia, as they were named in Latin
texts. The ultimate meaning of their own
name is not known. For the meaning of
Caledonia see CALEDONIAN CANAL.
Pictavia was the 'land of the Picts' (*see*
PITLOCHRY).

Scrabster (Highland)

A village and small port northwest of
THURSO with a Scandinavian name
meaning 'rocky homestead', from the Old
Norse *skjære* (rocky) and *bólstathr*
(homestead). The name was recorded as
Skarabolstad in 1201.

Scunthorpe (Humberside)

This iron and steel manufacturing town
east of DONCASTER has a Danish name (it
was well inside the Danelaw) meaning
'Skúma's outlying settlement', with the
personal name followed by the Old Norse
thorp, 'outlying farm depending on a larger
one' (in some ways corresponding to the
Old English *stoc*, as in BASINGSTOKE).
Most places with *thorp* in their name have
remained as small villages, but Scunthorpe
has gained its present size and importance
thanks to the iron-ore deposits discovered
here in the nineteenth century. The name

was recorded as *Escumetorp* in the
Domesday Book, with a typical 'French'
treatment of the initial *Sk-* to make it
pronounceable.

Seaford (East Sussex)

This residential town and resort southeast
of NEWHAVEN has a straightforward name
that means what it says, referring to a ford
over a river near the sea. However, there is
no river at Seaford now, because it has
been diverted to enter the sea at Newhaven
(see NEWHAVEN for the history). Seaford
was recorded as *Saford* in the mid-twelfth
century.

Seaham (Durham)

This coal port south of SUNDERLAND has a
name meaning 'homestead by the sea',
from the Old English *sæ* (sea) and *hām*
(homestead). The name appeared as
Sæham in a document of the mid-twelfth
century.

Seahouses (Northumberland)

A resort and former fishing port on the
North Sea coast northeast of BAMBURGH.
Its name means what it says: 'houses by the
sea', and is of relatively recent appearance.
In the nineteenth century the name was
usually recorded as *Sea Houses*.

Seascale (Cumbria)

A small town and resort south
of WHITEHAVEN that has a Scandinavian
name meaning 'temporary huts by the
sea', from the Old Norse *sær* (sea)
and *skáli* (temporary shelter, shieling)
(*see* SCALLOWAY). The name was
recorded as *Sescales* in about 1165.

Seaton (Devon)

A small resort at the mouth of the River
AXE southwest of AXMINSTER. It has a
name meaning 'village by the sea', from the
Old English *sæ* (sea) and *tūn* (farm,
village). In a document of 1244 the name
appears as *Seton*. Many Seatons
acquired distinguishing additions (see
below).

Seaton Carew (Cleveland)
A coastal locality south of HARTLEPOOL.
It has the basic name SEATON (as above)
followed by the family name of Peter
Carou, who held the manor here in the
second half of the twelfth century. A
document of 1345 records the name as
Seton Carrowe.

Seaton Delaval (Northumberland)
A town south of BLYTH. It has the basic
name SEATON (as above), for its site not far
from the sea, followed by the family name
of the De La Vals, who were here in the
thirteenth century, possibly earlier. They
came from Le Val, in Normandy. The
name was recorded as *Seton de la Val* in a
document of 1270. *See also* SEATON
SLUICE.

Seaton Sluice (Northumberland)
A coastal locality northeast of WHITLEY
BAY at the mouth of the Seaton Burn, five
miles east of SEATON DELAVAL. It has the
basic name SEATON, describing its
location. The second word of the name
refers to the sluice built across the river
mouth in the eighteenth century by
the landowners here, the Delaval family.
The aim was to stop up the water of the
river before releasing it to sluice out the
silt and sand of the harbour. It was a
good idea in theory, but in practice did
not work. Instead, therefore, a great
cut was made through the rock to reach
the sea, forming a sort of canal.
This then became the harbour. Now it
in turn has been abandoned, and the
channel is blocked by large boulders.
So Seaton Sluice never really had a
sluice.

Seaview (Isle of Wight)
This popular village resort on the northeast
coast has an obvious name for a place of
this kind, designed to attract holiday-
makers. It is a recent name, originating
from a lodging house built here in the early
nineteenth century.

Sedbergh (Cumbria)
This small town east of KENDAL has a
descriptive name relating to the hill on
whose slope it stands in the valley of the
River Rawther. It is Scandinavian in
origin, and means 'flat-topped hill', from
the Old Norse *setberg* (itself a compound
of *set* 'seat' and *berg* 'hill'). There are
identically named places (Setberg) in
Iceland and Norway. Sedbergh was
recorded in the Domesday Book as
Sedbergt.

Sedgefield (Durham)
An administrative district in the east of the
county that takes its name from the village
of Sedgefield, northwest of STOCKTON-
ON-TEES. The village's name does not
mean what it says, but is 'Cedd's open
land'. This origin can be deduced from a
record of about 1050, where the name
appears as *Ceddesfeld*.

Sedgemoor (Somerset)
An administrative district in the northwest
of the county that takes its name from the
area of marshland between BRIDGWATER
(in the west) and STREET (in the east).
Sedgemoor means what it says: 'tract of
moorland where sedge grows'. The name is
thus true to its nature, unlike that of
SEDGEFIELD. Sedgemoor was recorded as
Seggemore in a document of 1263.

Sedgley (West Midlands)
This northwest district of DUDLEY has a
name that means 'Secg's clearing', with the
personal name followed by the Old English
lēah (forest clearing). The name was
recorded in the late tenth century as
Secgesleage, and in the Domesday Book (a
hundred years later) it was *Segleslei*.

Sefton (Merseyside)
An administrative district in the northwest
of the county that takes its name from the
village north of LIVERPOOL. The name
means 'farm where rushes grow', from the
Old Norse *sef* (sedge, rush) and the Old
English *tūn* (farm). The Domesday Book

record of the name is slightly incorrect, as *Sextone*. No doubt the written *f* was taken to be an *x*.

Selborne (Hampshire)

A village southeast of ALTON, famous for being the setting of Gilbert White's *Natural History of Selborne*. The name was originally that of Oakhanger Stream here, meaning 'willow-tree stream', from the Old English *sealh* (willow, sallow) and *burna* (stream). The name was recorded as *Seleborne* in a document of 903. 'Oakhanger' means 'slope where oak trees grow'. It seems strange that the stream should have had one 'tree-name' substituted for another. *Compare* SELBY.

Selby (North Yorkshire)

A town on the River OUSE south of YORK whose name means 'village by the willows', from the Old English conjectural *sele* (willow copse) (related to *salh* 'willow') and the Old Norse *bý* (village). Although the name was recorded as *Seleby* in a document of about 1030, it seems likely that the second element of the name replaced the Old English *tūn*, so that the name was originally entirely Old English, something like 'Selton'.

Selhurst (Greater London)

A district of CROYDON whose name means 'willow-tree wood', from the Old English *sealh* (willow, sallow) and *hyrst* (wood). The name was recorded as *Selherst* in a text dated 1229. There is little evidence here now of the willow wood that existed down to the eighteenth century, when the common land in the area was enclosed.

Selkirk (Borders)

A manufacturing town north of HAWICK whose name means 'church by the hall', from the Old English *sele* (dwelling, house, hall) and either the Old English *cirice* or the Old Norse *kirkja*, both meaning 'church'. The name was recorded as *Selechirche* in about 1120, suggesting that the name is entirely Old English in origin. The town

gave its name to the former county of Selkirkshire.

Selly Oak (West Midlands)

This southwest district of BIRMINGHAM was originally known simply as Selly, meaning literally 'ledge clearing', 'clearing on a shelf of land', from the Old English *scelf* (ledge, shelf, projecting rock) and *lēah* (forest clearing). This name was recorded as *Escelie* in the Domesday Book (for the spelling here *compare* SCUNTHORPE). 'Oak' was added to the village name comparatively recently, referring to a prominent tree formerly here.

Selsey (West Sussex)

A seaside resort south of CHICHESTER, well known for the nearby headland of Selsey Bill. Its name means 'seal island', from the Old English *seolh* (seal) and *ēg* (island). This was recorded in about 710 as *Seolesiae*, and refers to the peninsula (rather than 'island' in the common sense) on whose beaches seals were seen. There is a tradition that the name actually derives from the Old English *selig* (holy), referring to the monastery that was founded here in the late seventh century by St Wilfred. But records of the name do not support this account, and indeed the Venerable Bede spells out the meaning in his eighth-century *Ecclesiastical History of the English People*, when he refers to Selsey as *Selaeseu quod dicitur Latine Insula uituli marini*, 'Selsey, which is called in Latin the Island of the sea calf [i.e. seal]'. The monastery has now long been submerged by the sea.

Sennen (Cornwall)

This village east of LAND'S END, with its nearby Sennen Cove on the coast, has a name derived directly from St Senan, about whom next to nothing is known apart from his (or even her) name. The name was recorded as *St Senane* in a document dated 1327, while Sennen Cove, formerly an active fishing port, appears as *Portsenen* in 1370. The parish church at Sennen is dedicated to the saint.

Settle (North Yorkshire)

A town on the River RIBBLE northwest of SKIPTON whose name directly represents the Old English *setl* (seat, dwelling-place). The name was recorded in the Domesday Book as *Setel*.

Sevenoaks (Kent)

A residential town southeast of LONDON whose name means what it says: 'seven oaks', recorded as *Sevenac* in a document of about 1200. There was probably a legendary story behind the name, now forgotten. The 'magic' number seven is fairly frequent in place-names, for example in SEVEN SISTERS, which is more recent than most. The phenomenon is not confined to Britain; around half a dozen places named Siebeneich ('seven oaks', again) occur in Germany. There may well have been seven actual oaks in Sevenoaks in medieval times, although these have long since gone. However, the townsfolk have always been conscious of their rather unusual name, and in 1955 planted seven oak trees (from nearby Knole Park) on a cricket ground in the eastern part of the town. In the autumn storms of 1987 six of them were blown down, but within a matter of weeks were replaced so as to preserve the symbol of the town's name.

Seven Sisters (East Sussex)

The seven chalk cliffs that extend along the coast to the west of BEACHY HEAD. They all have individual names (such as Baily's Brow or Flagstaff Point), and were recorded in a document of 1588 as *the Seven Cliffes*. The present name is thus relatively recent. In classical mythology, the Seven Sisters were the seven daughters of Atlas and Pleione, with their name collectively used for the cluster of stars known as the Pleiades.

Severn (Wales/England)

Britain's longest river, which rises in mid Wales and flows initially north and east before turning south to its estuary, opening into the BRISTOL CHANNEL. The name

remains of uncertain origin. It was recorded by the Roman writer Tacitus in the second century AD as *Sabrina*, and although this would appear to be of Celtic origin, no similar word or name has been recorded that can make it meaningful. The Welsh name of the river is Hafren, and the present English name is essentially based on this, while retaining the initial *S*- of the Roman name. *See also* SAVERNAKE FOREST.

Shaftesbury (Dorset)

This small town west of SALISBURY has a name that probably derives from a combination of a personal name and the Old English *burg*, thus meaning 'Sceaft's fortified place'. But an alternative derivation has been proposed from the Old English *sceaft* (shaft, pole) as the first element. If this is so, the reference could be to the steep hill on which the town is situated, with this either having a pole as a landmark or boundary post (Shaftesbury is close to the border with WILTSHIRE), or the word being a figurative description of the hill itself. The first interpretation above seems more likely, however, especially in view of the grammatical forms of early records of the name, such as *Sceaftesburi* in about 871, and *Sceptesberie* (with a miscopying) in the Domesday Book.

Shaldon (Devon)

This small resort south of TEIGNMOUTH appears to have a name that means 'shallow valley', from the Old English conjectural *sceald* (shallow) and *denu* (valley). Shaldon is on the southern side of the entrance to the estuary of the River Teign, and presumably the name refers to an inland valley here, not that of the river. Or perhaps the situation of Shaldon was regarded as a low-lying valley by contrast with the hills that rise immediately behind Teignmouth on the other side of the estuary.

Shankill (Dublin)

A village southeast of DUBLIN whose

name, found elsewhere in the country, means 'old church', usually rendered in Irish as Seanchill. The two components of the name are the Irish *sean* (old) and *cill* (church).

Shanklin (Isle of Wight)

The name of this resort on SANDOWN Bay means 'cup ridge', from the Old English *scenc* (cup) and *hlinc* (ridge). This was recorded by the Domesday Book as *Sencliz*. The first half of the name refers to the waterfall at Shanklin Chine, with the water seen as falling from a drinking-cup. The name may originally have been that of the stream itself here. The 'ridge' is more difficult to pinpoint, but possibly it is or was a feature of the waterfall itself, such as one of the 'shelves' that cause the water to descend in a series of cascades.

Shannon (Limerick/Clare)

Ireland's longest river, rising north of LEITRIM in northwest county CAVAN and flowing south through LIMERICK to the Atlantic coast. The name probably means something like 'old one' ('Old Man River', in effect), with a basis in a root word that is now the Irish *sean* (old) (*compare* SHANKILL). The suggestion is of an ancient water god personified by the flowing waters of the river. Ptolemy recorded the river's name in the second century AD as *Senos*.

Shap (Cumbria)

This small town south of PENRITH is well known to railway travellers for Shap Summit, three miles south of it and the highest point on the LONDON-to-CARLISLE line. The basic name means simply 'heap', and 'shap' is actually this same word, or a version of its Old English original, *hēap*. The reference is to the remains of an ancient stone circle by the main road (the present A6) south of the town. Shap was recorded as *Hep* in a twelfth-century document.

Sheerness (Kent)

A port and resort at the northwest point of the Isle of SHEPPEY whose name means 'bright headland', from the Old English *scīr* (bright, clear) (compare modern 'sheer silk') and *næss* (headland). The 'brightness' of the headland here was probably that of its open spacious character, overlooking the estuary of both the THAMES and the MEDWAY. The name was recorded as *Shernesse* in 1221.

Sheffield (South Yorkshire)

This well-known city on the River DON has a name that means 'open land by the River Sheaf'. The latter, smaller river flows through the middle of Sheffield to enter the Don here. The river's own name means 'boundary', literally 'dividing one', from the Old English *scēath* (sheath), and the Sheaf formed the boundary between Derbyshire and the former West Riding of Yorkshire. The second element of the name is the Old English *feld* (open land; modern 'field'). Sheffield was recorded in the Domesday Book as *Scafeld*. There are other places of the name, but they will usually have another meaning. (*See* SHEFFIELD PARK for an example).

Sheffield Park (East Sussex)

The country house of this name east of HAYWARDS HEATH is not named after SHEFFIELD (above)! It has a name in its own right that means 'open land where sheep graze', from the Old English *scēap* (sheep) and *feld* (open land; modern 'field'). The Domesday Book recorded this as *Sifelle*, in a 'smoothed' (and somewhat distorted) version of the Anglo-Saxon name. The modern 'Park' was added in much more recent times.

Shefford (Bedfordshire)

A small town southeast of BEDFORD whose name means 'sheep ford' (Old English *scēap* and *ford*), referring to a ford over the River Ivel here where a Roman road (now represented by the A600) crossed it. This would therefore have been the regular crossing-point for the sheep, as it was for the oxen at OXFORD. The name was recorded as *Sepford* in a document of 1220.

Shepherds Bush (Greater London)

A district of HAMMERSMITH whose name almost certainly derives from a family name, such as Shepherd or Sheppard, with the 'Bush' being a bushy area of land owned by the family. The name was recorded as *Sheppards Bush Green* in a document of 1635. Of course, a reference to shepherds need not be altogether ruled out, but names of this type, with a natural feature such as 'Green' or 'Fields' added, usually derive from a personal name.

Shepperton (Surrey)

An urban location, on the north bank of the THAMES opposite WALTON-ON-THAMES, whose name means 'shepherds' village', from the Old English *scēaphierde* (shepherd) and *tun* (farm, village). The place would have been a site where shepherds gathered or lived on pastures by the Thames. There are still meadows, if not sheep, here today. The name was recorded as *Scepertun* in a text of 959.

Sheppey, Isle of (Kent)

An island off the north coast of KENT, linked to the mainland only by a single road and rail bridge. Its name means 'sheep island', 'island where sheep are kept', such a location being ideal for the purpose, with its good grazing and natural boundary. (Islands have always been favoured for sheep farming: *compare* the name of FAIR ISLE, and see the reference there to the Faroes.) Sheppey was recorded as *Scepeig* in 696; the two component Old English words are *scēap* (sheep) and *ēg* (island).

Shepshed (Leicestershire)

A town west of LOUGHBOROUGH whose name means literally 'sheep's head', with the latter half of the name (Old English *hēafod*) denoting either a headland or a place where sheep were sacrificed and the

heads impaled. There is no evidence of the latter custom, although it cannot be ruled out; the fairly high location of Shepshed seems to favour the first derivation. Shepshed appeared in the Domesday Book as *Scepeshefde*.

Shepton Mallet (Somerset)

A town south of BRISTOL whose basic name, Shepton, means 'sheep farm', from the Old English *scēap* (sheep) and *tūn* (farm). The second word of the name was added to distinguish this Shepton from others in the area, such as West Shepton, now a district of Shepton Mallet, and Shepton Montague, nine miles southeast of the town. It represents the name of the Malet family from Normandy, who held the manor here in the early part of the twelfth century. The town's name was recorded in a document of about 1227 as *Sheopton Malet*. *Compare* the names of SHIPTON UNDER WYCHWOOD and SKIPTON.

Shepway (Kent)

An administrative district in the southeast of the county that takes its name from the former so-called 'lathe' of Shepway here, this being one of the five administrative districts into which Kent was divided in Anglo-Saxon times. It means 'sheep way', from the Old English *scēap* (sheep) and *weg* (way), referring to a regular route used by sheep. One such 'way' might have been the route now followed by the Roman road known as Stone Street, which leads across the North Downs towards CANTERBURY, with the Romans adopting the 'sheep way' for their road. The name was recorded as *Shepweye* in 1227.

Sherborne (Dorset)

This town east of YEOVIL has a name (found elsewhere in the country, sometimes as Sherburn), meaning 'bright stream', 'clear stream', from the Old English *scīr* (bright, clear) and *burna* (stream). In many cases the stream or river of the named place is itself called the

Sherborne, although in the Dorset town the river is the Yeo. Even so, this could once have been known as the Sherborne, and the record of the name as *æt Scireburnan* in a document of 864 certainly refers to the river, not to a settlement. The Domesday Book record of the name, however, refers to the original settlement here, as *Scireburne*.

Sheringham (Norfolk)

A coastal resort north of NORWICH whose name means 'homestead of Scīra's people', with this recorded in the Domesday Book as (rather wrongly) *Silingeham*. (The Normans frequently found *l* easier in a name than *r*; *compare* SALISBURY, where the *l* has remained.) The final element of the name is the Old English *hām* (homestead), with this preceded by the '-ing-' that usually means 'people of (the named person)'.

Sherwood Forest (Nottinghamshire)

An ancient royal forest between NOTTINGHAM and WORKSOP, associated most famously with Robin Hood. Its name denotes its special status, meaning 'shire wood', that is, a wood owned by the shire or county, either as a hunting-ground or as a common pastureland. If the latter, it would have been for pigs, who would have fed on the acorns of the oaks that dominated the forest. The name was recorded as *Scirwuda* in a document of 955.

Shetland (Scotland)

This northernmost group of Scottish islands has a rather difficult name; it probably derives, however, from the Old Norse *hjalt* (hilt) and *land* (land). 'Hiltland' could thus refer to the sword-shaped outline of the group, or of MAINLAND, its largest island. (A glance at the map will illustrate this. *Compare also* the name of ST KILDA.) The name was recorded as *Haltland* in the early twelfth century. An alternative name of Shetland is Zetland, formerly used as a county name. The initial Z- of this represents the medieval letter (ʒ),

used to express the sound of Old Norse *hj* at the beginning of *hjalt* (something like a combined *h* and *y* sound).

Shifnal (Shropshire)

A small town east of TELFORD whose name means 'Scuffa's corner of land', with the personal name, unrecorded elsewhere, followed by the Old English *halh* (nook, corner). The name appears as *Scuffanhalch* in a document dated 664.

Shildon (Durham)

A town southeast of BISHOP AUCKLAND whose name means 'shelf hill', from the Old English *scelf* (shelf, sloping ground) and *dūn* (hill). The name is appropriate for Shildon, which is surrounded by hills. It was recorded in a document of 1214 as *Sciluedon*.

Shillelagh (Wicklow)

A village northwest of GOREY with the Irish name of Síol Éalaigh, meaning '(place of the) descendants of Éláthach'. The named person was a ninth-century folk hero. The cudgel called the 'shillelagh' is said to have been originally made from the wood of oaks here.

Shin, Loch (Highland)

A loch extending for some seventeen miles northwest of Lairg. Its name derives from that of the River Shin flowing from it. The origin of the river name is uncertain; it may mean simply 'river', or it may relate to the name of the SHANNON, in which case it could similarly mean 'old one'. But it is more likely to be of pre-Celtic than Celtic origin.

Shipley (West Yorkshire)

An industrial town northwest of BRADFORD whose name (found elsewhere in the country) means 'sheep clearing', 'woodland glade where sheep graze'. This particular Shipley was recorded in the Domesday Book as *Scipeleia*. The two Old English words that comprise the name are thus *scēap* (sheep) and *lēah* (forest, clearing).

Shipston on Stour (Warwickshire)
This small town west of BANBURY has a basic name, Shipston, that means 'sheepwash farm', that is, a farm by a place called Sheepwash, this being a location where there was a sheep dip. The 'wash' element of the name has now been reduced to the single -s-, but it can be seen in the record of the name dating from about 770, which was *Scepuuæisctune*. Not surprisingly, this long name was subsequently shortened to its present form. The three Old English words that comprise the original are thus *scēap* (sheep), *wæsce* (wash), and *tūn* (farm). The '-on-Stour' addition of the modern name was no doubt to distinguish this place from the many similarly (but not identically) named places called Shipton, such as SHIPTON UNDER WYCHWOOD. *See also* STOUR.

Shipton under Wychwood (Oxfordshire)
This village northeast of BURFORD has a basic name, Shipton, that is common elsewhere, especially in central and southern England. Hence the frequent need for a distinguishing addition, as here. The basic sense is 'sheep farm', from the Old English *scēap* (sheep) and *tūn* (farm). The addition in this case refers to a nearby forest that belonged to the people called Hwicce, lying either on the boundary of their territory, or actually inside it. The Hwicce were a well-known tribe who occupied an area corresponding to much of the present counties of Hereford and Worcester, Gloucestershire, and Warwickshire. The 'under' of the place-name denotes that the original farm was on the edge of the forest, which was itself at the eastern extremity of the tribal territory. The name was thus basically *Sciptone* in the Domesday Book, then *Shupton under Wycchewode* in a document of 1391.

Shirebrook (Derbyshire)
A town north of MANSFIELD whose name means 'bright stream', from the Old English *scīr* (bright, clear) and *brōc* (brook, stream). The name thus virtually corresponds to that of SHERBORNE. Shirebrook appears as *Scirebroc* in a document of 1202.

Shirley (Greater London)
A district of CROYDON whose name probably means 'bright wood', from the Old English *scīr* (bright) and *lēah* (wood), a 'bright' wood being a sparse one, as distinct from the more usual shady wood. The name is found elsewhere, and in many cases has an alternative meaning of 'shire wood' or 'shire clearing', referring to a place held in common by landowners in a particular shire or county. The Shirley mentioned here was recorded as *Shirleye* in a document of 1314, and it happens to be the Shirley that gave its name to the Shirley poppy, which was first grown here in a vicarage garden.

Shoeburyness (Essex)
A district of SOUTHEND-ON-SEA whose name means 'headland by Shoebury', that is, by a place that was a 'sheltering fortification' (either a natural or a man-made one). The three Old English words that make up the complete name are thus: the conjectural *scēo* (shelter) (probably related to Sheen, the original name of RICHMOND, Surrey); *burg* (fortified place); and *næss* (headland). The headland here is one at the mouth of the THAMES estuary. The 'sheltering fortification' is difficult to locate in such a predominantly flat area, but it may have been the ancient camp whose remains can still be seen here east of Southend. The basic name was recorded as *Sceobyrig* in a document of 894.

Shoreditch (Greater London)
This district of HACKNEY has a name that looks straightforward but is still of uncertain origin. The meaning seems to be 'ditch draining a slope', although the precise location of the ditch and the nature of the bank are obscure. It can hardly have been the bank of the THAMES, as Shoreditch lies some way north of the river, with the City of London in between.

The name was recorded as *Soredich* in about 1148.

Shoreham-by-Sea (West Sussex)
A container port west of BRIGHTON whose basic name, Shoreham, means 'homestead by a bank', from the conjectural Old English *scora* (shore, bank) and *hām* (homestead). The reference is not to the seashore, however, but to the steep slope of the downs east of the River ADUR, at the mouth of which Shoreham is situated. There are in fact two Shorehams here, with Old Shoreham about a mile north of Shoreham-by-Sea. This original Shoreham was recorded as *Sorham* in a text dated 1073, while Shoreham-by-Sea was known for a time as 'New Shoreham' (*Noua Sorham* in 1235) before acquiring its present distinguishing (and commercial) addition. A document of 1457 refers to the harbour here as *port of Hulkesmouth alias Shorham*, with 'Hulkesmouth' presumably referring to a wreck thay lay here long enough for the place to be named after it.

Shotton (Clwyd, Durham)
Either of two places, one a town next to QUEENSFERRY, the other a well-known colliery near PETERLEE. Both have names that probably mean 'Scots' village', although an alternative sense 'farm by the steep slope' is also possible for some places called by this name. There are no obvious steep slopes by either of these Shottons, however, so the first meaning is more likely. The Old English words behind the name are thus the (conjectural) *Scot* and *tūn*, rather than (also conjectural) *scēot*. The Durham Shotton was recorded as *Sottun* in a document of about 1165.

Shrewsbury (Shropshire)
The well-known county town whose name was recorded in a document of 1016 as *Scrobbesbyrig*, showing it to be really 'Scrubsbury' and referring to a fortified place (Old English *burg*) by scrubland (conjectural *scrubb*). The evolution of the present name can be traced through the

different records of it, among them *Sciropesberie* in the Domesday Book, *Salopesberia* in 1156, *Shrobesbury* in 1327, and *Shrovesbury* in 1346. The current spelling of the name developed because words like 'shrew' and 'shrewd' were formerly often pronounced to rhyme with 'show' and 'showed'. Hence the present pronunciation of the name, 'Shrowsbury'. *See also* SALOP; SHROPSHIRE.

Shrivenham (Oxfordshire)
A village northeast of SWINDON, well known for its Royal Military Academy of Science. It has an interesting name that seems to mean 'riverside land allotted by decree'. The Old English words behind the name are *scrifen* (allotted) and *hamm* (riverside land). The interpretation is that land beside the River Cole here was disputed, so it was allotted, impartially (but officially), by a third person. The name of the village was recorded as *Scriuenham* in a text of 821.

Shropshire (England)
A county in the western Midlands, bordering Wales. The name developed directly from that of its chief town and administrative centre, SHREWSBURY, so it is in essence 'Shrewsburyshire'. A record of the name as *Scrobbesbyrigscir* in 1006 should be compared with the first record of the town's name quoted above. The Domesday Book then entered the name as *Sciropescire*, with a further record of it about ten years later as *Salopescira*. This shows the typical Norman 'easing' of *Sc-* to *S-* and of *r* to *l*, as for SALISBURY. It also gave the alternative name, SALOP, for the county.

Shugborough (Staffordshire)
The seventeenth-century house of this name east of STAFFORD has a name that means 'goblin hill', from the Old English *scucca* (demon, evil spirit), and *beorg* (hill). The implication is that the hill was haunted.

Sidcup (Greater London)
A district of Bexley whose name probably means 'flat-topped hill', or more literally 'seat-shaped hill', from the conjectural Old English *set-copp*, with the first element of this as for SEDBERGH, and the second as for MOW COP. The implication is that Sidcup arose as a place 'seated' on a hilltop. This seems difficult to envisage now, but the ground does fall away to the north and south of the High Street, and street names such as High View Road testify to the high location here. The name was recorded as *Cetecopp'* in 1254.

Sidlaw Hills (Tayside)
A range of hills stretching from PERTH to near FORFAR. The name seems to be a combination of the Gaelic *suidhe* (seat) and the Old English *hlāw* (hill). The 'seat' would thus refer to the flat tops that are found at various points in the range. A text dated 1799 refers to the hills as the *Seedlaws*.

Sidmouth (Devon)
A coastal resort east of EXETER at the mouth of the River Sid, after which it takes its name. The river name means 'broad one', from the Old English *sīd* (spacious, extensive). A text of about 1085 refers to the river-mouth here as *Sidemutha*.

Silbury Hill (Wiltshire)
An ancient earthwork south of AVEBURY whose name most probably ends in the Old English *beorg* (hill), but whose first element remains uncertain. It could represent the Old English *sele* (dwelling, hall), giving a full meaning of 'hill by a hall'. An alternative explanation, however, suggests that the second element may not be *beorg* but *burg*, 'fortified place', which seems appropriate for a hill site like this. The name was recorded in about 1235 as *Selleboruwe*, and as *Seleburgh* in 1281.

Silchester (Hampshire)
This village north of BASINGSTOKE has the '-chester' element showing it to have been a former Roman camp. The first element of the name probably represents the first element of the Roman name of Silchester which was *Calleva Atrebatum*, with the first word of this deriving from a Celtic root word meaning 'wood' (compare modern Irish *coill* and Welsh *celli*). The second word is the name of the tribe, the Atrebates, who had their capital here. Their own name simply means 'inhabitants', 'settlers', from a Celtic root related to the modern Welsh *tref* (home, town). Until recently, the first element (Sil-) of Silchester was traditionally derived from conjectural Old English *siele* (willow copse). But Silchester is on a hill spur, and there are oaks, not willows.

Silloth (Cumbria)
A town and small port northwest of WIGTON whose name means 'sea barn', 'barn by the sea', from a combination of the Old English *sǣ* (sea) and the Old Norse *hlatha* (barn, storehouse) (related to modern English 'load'). A document of 1299 has the name as *Selathe*.

Silsden (West Yorkshire)
A town north of KEIGHLEY whose name means something like 'valley of the Sigol', with the latter being the original name of the stream on which the town is located, itself meaning 'moving one', from the Old English *sīgan* (to sink, to move). The second half of the town's name is the Old English *denu* (valley). The name was recorded as *Siglesdene* in the Domesday Book.

Silverstone (Northamptonshire)
A village southwest of TOWCESTER, famous for its motor-racing circuit. Its name has nothing to do with silver or stone but means 'Sǣwulf's village' or 'Sigewulf's village'. (The personal names respectively

mean 'sea wolf' and 'victory wolf'.)
Silverstone was recorded in a document of
942 as *Sulueston*.

Silvertown (Greater London)
This district of NEWHAM has a modern
name that derives from the firm of S.W.
Silver & Co., who opened a factory here in
the mid-nineteenth century to produce
rubber goods.

Sissinghurst (Kent)
A village northeast of CRANBROOK,
famous for nearby Sissinghurst Castle, the
Tudor house with a noted garden. The
name means 'wooded hill of Seaxa's
people', with the personal name followed
by the Old English *-ingas* suffix that
means 'people of'; this in turn is followed
by *hyrst* (wooded hill). One would have
expected the present name to be something
like 'Saxinghurst', therefore, as in a
record of about 1180, which has it as
Saxingherste. But no doubt the *x* became
ss under the 'softening' influence of the
Normans.

Sittingbourne (Kent)
An industrial town east of GILLINGHAM
whose name means 'stream of the slope-
dwellers', with the folk name (Old English
sīdingas) derived from *sīde* (slope), and
followed by *burna* (stream). Sittingbourne
is situated on the lower slope of a ridge by
Milton Creek, a tributary of the River
Swale. The name was recorded as
Sidingeburn in a document of about 1200.

Sizewell (Suffolk)
This coastal location, with its nuclear
power station east of LEISTON, has a name
that means 'Sighere's spring', with the
personal name followed by the Old English
wella (spring, well). The name was
recorded in 1240 as *Syreswell*.

Skara Brae (Orkney)
The remains of this Neolithic settlement on
the west coast of MAINLAND have a name
that almost certainly means 'steep bank by

the shore', from the Old Norse *skari*
(shore) and Scottish *brae* (bank, as in
Robert Burns's 'Ye banks and braes o'
bonny Doon'). The name describes the
location accurately enough.

Skegness (Lincolnshire)
This popular coastal resort south of
MABLETHORPE has a name that means
'Skeggi's promontory', with the
Scandinavian personal name followed by
the Old Norse *nes* (headland, promontory).
There is no obvious promontory at
Skegness, although there is a hook-like
projection at Gibraltar Point, four miles
south of the town, and the reference could
be to this. Skeggi, which means 'bearded
one', is still used as an affectionate
nickname for the resort. The place-name
was recorded as *Shegenesse* in a text of
1166.

Skelligs, The (Kerry)
The three small islands that lie southwest
of VALENTIA. The name means 'the
splinters', representing their Irish name,
Na Scealaga. The name is descriptive of the
sharp slate rock of which the islands are
composed.

Skelmersdale (Lancashire)
The present New Town, designated in
1961, developed from a former mining
village here, west of WIGAN, whose name
was recorded in the Domesday Book as
Schelmeresdele. This means 'Skelmer's
valley', with the Scandinavian personal
name, perhaps meaning 'horse shield',
followed by the Old Norse *dalr* (valley,
dale). Most '-dale' names have a river name
for the first element, so Skelmersdale is
exceptional in this respect (compare
Weardale, Teesdale, Wharfedale, and so
on; *see* WEAR; TEES; WHARFE). *Compare
also* WENSLEYDALE!

Skelmorlie (Strathclyde)
A resort on the Firth of CLYDE north of
LARGS whose name seems to mean
'Scealdamer's clearing', with the Old

English personal name followed by *lēah* (forest, clearing). The name was recorded as *Skelmorley* in a document of about 1400, and is currently pronounced with the first syllable accented.

Skerries, The (Gwynedd, Dublin, Shetland)
Wales, Ireland, and Scotland all have a distinctive group of rocky islands called The Skerries: the Welsh Skerries are off the northwest coast of ANGLESEY; the Irish isles lie just off the coast southeast of BALBRIGGAN, where they have given their name to the seaside resort of Skerries; and the Scottish rocks, also known as Out Skerries, lie to the east of MAINLAND (Shetland). In each case the meaning is 'the reefs', from the relevant language, such as the Irish *sceir*, Gaelic *sgeir*, or Old Norse *sker* (the source of English 'skerry'). The Welsh name of The Skerries is Ynysoedd y Moelrhoniaid, 'islands of the seals'. The Irish name of the seaside resort is Na Sceirí, 'the skerries'.

Skiddaw (Cumbria)
The mountain in the Lake District, to the east of BASSENTHWAITE Lake, whose name could mean either 'ski height' or 'crag height', from the Old Norse *skíth* (ski, snow-shoe) or *skýti* (crag), and *haugr* (height, hill, mound). 'Ski height' would refer to the outline of the mountain, not to the act of skiing down it! The name was recorded as *Skithoc* in a document of 1230.

Skipton (North Yorkshire)
A market and industrial town northwest of BRADFORD whose name is the Scandinavian version of Shipton (*see* SHIPTON UNDER WYCHWOOD), and so means 'sheep village'. The elements are Old English, however, as *scēap* and *tūn*, but with Norse-style spelling (*Sk-* instead of *Sh-*). The Domesday Book recorded Skipton as *Scipton*. The town was for long well known for its sheep markets.

Skokholm (Dyfed)
This island off the southwest coast of WALES, south of SKOMER, has a Scandinavian name meaning 'block island', from the Old Norse *stokkr* (trunk, log), presumably referring to its shape, and *holmr* (island). The spelling of the present name with *Sk-* instead of the expected *St-* is probably due to the influence of the name of nearby Skomer. However, a record of 1275 does give the name as *Stokholm* to support the origin quoted. (The island thus happens to have a name identical to Stockholm, the Swedish capital, although there the 'log' reference is different, and probably refers to landmarks or wooden structures.)

Skomer (Dyfed)
An island north of SKOKHOLM, larger than its neighbour, whose name means 'cloven island', from the Old Norse *skalm* (split, cloven) and *ey* (island). The reference is to the marked narrowing at the eastern end of the island, where the inlets of North Haven and South Haven almost meet at a narrow isthmus known as The Neck. A text of 1324 has the name as *Skalmey*.

Skye (Highland)
The largest island of the HEBRIDES whose name represents the Gaelic *sgiath* (wing), referring to the 'winged' or 'divided' appearance of the island from the mainland, with its two mountain masses in the north and south of the island rising as 'wings' either side of the central lower terrain. Written records of the name date back to the second century AD, when Ptolemy noted it as *Sketis nesos*, 'island of Scitis'.

Slaney (Wicklow/Carlow/Wexford)
An Irish river that rises in the WICKLOW Mountains and enters the sea at WEXFORD Harbour. Its name means 'healthy one', from the Old Irish word *slán* (the same in Modern Irish) 'healthy'. (Compare the traditional Irish and Gaelic toast, *Sláinte!* 'Your Health!') The name of the river is thus identical in nature to that of the LUNE.

Sleaford (Lincolnshire)

This town northeast of GRANTHAM takes its name from the River Slea, which flows through it. The river's own name means 'slimy one', 'muddy river', from a root element related to the Old English *slīm* (slime), and so to modern words such as 'slink', 'slick', and 'slime' itself (and even SLOUGH). The ford across the river could have been where the modern A15 road crosses it today, more or less in the centre of the town. The name was recorded as *Slioford* in a document of 852.

Slieve Donard (Down)

The highest peak of the MOURNE MOUNTAINS, whose name means 'Donart's mountain', representing the Irish name, Sliabh Dónairt. (Many mountain names begin with the Irish *sliabh*, 'mountain', 'range', 'upland'.) Donart, or Domhanghart, is said to have been a disciple of St Patrick who built his church on the mountain's summit.

Sligo (Sligo)

This cathedral town in northwest Ireland, which gave its name to the county, has a name that means 'shelly place', as indicated by the Irish name, Sligeach (from Irish *slige* 'shell'). The name refers to the stony bed of the River Garavogue that flows through the town.

Slimbridge (Gloucestershire)

This village with its Wildfowl Trust nature reserve near the SEVERN estuary has a name that literally means 'slime bridge', that is, 'bridge at a slippery place'. The sense of 'bridge' here may perhaps be understood more as 'causeway' (across the muddy terrain) rather than denoting an actual bridge. The name was recorded in a rather distorted form by the Domesday Book clerks as *Heslinbruge*, this being a Normanised attempt to deal with the initial *Sl-* of the name. The Old English words behind the name are thus *slīm* (slime, mud) (*compare* SLEAFORD) and *brycg* (bridge).

Slough (Berkshire)

This well-known industrial town has a name that refers to the low-lying marshy terrain or 'slough' formerly here (the Old English word was *slōh*). The land by the THAMES here is very flat, and the town owes its development on such an unpromising site to commercial and 'logistical' considerations — it is near LONDON and has easy access to routes to the west and south. Modern Slough developed only after the First World War, when an industrial estate was established on the site of a former army depot. The name was recorded as *Slo* in a document of 1195.

Smethwick (West Midlands)

A town west of BIRMINGHAM whose name means 'smiths' place of work', from the Old English *smith* (smith, metalworker) and *wīc* in the sense of 'special place', denoting a particular occupation or product. The Domesday Book recorded the name as *Smedeuuich*.

Smoo Cave (Highland)

A large cavern near the north coast of the SUTHERLAND district. It has a Scandinavian name related directly to the Icelandic *smuga* (hiding-place) and indirectly to modern English 'smuggle'. The name is thus self-descriptive of the activity, real or potential, that was carried on here!

Snaefell (Isle of Man)

The island's highest mountain has a straightforward Old Norse name meaning 'snow mountain', from *snær* (snow) and *fjall* (mountain). Snaefell is often snow-topped, although not permanently. *Compare* SNOWDON.

Snake Pass (Derbyshire)

The winding pass over the PENNINES north of KINDER SCOUT. It has a modern and self-explanatory name that describes its course.

Sneem (Kerry)

An attractive village on the estuary of the
river of the same name, west of KENMARE,
whose name means 'the knot' (Irish
snaidhm 'knot', 'junction'). Many roads
and rivers meet at Sneem, with two other
rivers joining the River Sneem. The Irish
name is An tSnaidhm, 'the knot'.

Sneinton (Nottinghamshire)

This eastern district of NOTTINGHAM has a
name meaning 'village of Snot's people',
with Snot being the person whose name lies
behind that of Nottingham itself. In the
case of Sneinton, however, the initial *S-*
of the personal name has been retained,
whereas in Nottingham it has been lost.
It nearly disappeared for Sneinton, too,
which was recorded in the Domesday Book
as *Notintone* (but in 1165 as *Snotintone*).
What *has* been almost lost from Sneinton
is the *-ing-* that Nottingham still has.
Sneinton is really 'Snottington' in modern
terms, therefore.

Snodland (Kent)

An industrial location on the MEDWAY
northwest of MAIDSTONE whose name
means 'land of Snodd's people', with the
'land' here probably newly worked
agricultural land by the river, as the Old
English *land* sometimes denotes (*compare*
PONTELAND). The name was recorded as
Snoddingland in a document of 838,
showing that the modern version of the
name has lost the middle element *-ing-* that
means 'people of' (the named person).

Snowdon (Gwynedd)

Wales's highest mountain, and one of the
best known in Britain, situated in the
northwest of the principality. Its name
means 'snow hill', from the Old English
snāw (snow) and *dūn* (hill). The name was
recorded as early as 1095 (earlier than for
many English mountains) as *Snawdune*.
The Welsh name of Snowdon is Yr
Wyddfa, 'the cairn place', from *gwyddfa*
(mound, tumulus); many mountains have
served as burial places in historic times. A

general name for the mountainous area
around Snowdon is Snowdonia, known in
Welsh as Eryri, 'abode of eagles' (Welsh
eryr 'eagle'). The name Snowdonia is
recent, and does not seem to date from
much before the nineteenth century.
Snowdon is not permanently snow-capped,
but its heights retain snow for much of the
year.

Soham (Cambridgeshire)

A village southeast of ELY whose name
means 'lake homestead', 'homestead by a
lake', from the Old English *sǣ* (sea, lake)
and *hām* (homestead). There is no lake here
now, as it was drained in medieval times.
The name was recorded as *Sægham* in a
document of the late twelfth century.

Soho (Greater London)

This district of the City of WESTMINSTER
has a name that may well originate from the
traditional hunting cry, 'So-ho!', which
was used for hare hunting just as 'Tally-
ho!' was (and is?) used for fox hunting.
There were fields in Soho before the region
was built over in the eighteenth century,
and it is on record that hunting took place
here in the mid-sixteenth century. The
name is first found in a text of 1632 as
So Ho.

Solent, The (Hampshire/Isle of Wight)

The sea channel that separates the Isle of
Wight from the mainland. It has a name of
rather obscure origin, although a meaning
'place of cliffs', from the Phoenician (or
Punic), has recently been proposed. The
Venerable Bede recorded the name as
Soluente in the eighth century, but
unfortunately added no commentary (as he
sometimes did) to explain its meaning. No
doubt he simply did not know! The Roman
name for the whole area between the Isle of
Wight and the mainland, including both
The Solent and SOUTHAMPTON Water,
was *Magnus Portus*, 'the great harbour'.

Solihull (West Midlands)

An industrial town to the southeast of

BIRMINGHAM whose name probably means 'muddy hill', from the conjectural Old English *sylig* (muddy) (from *sol*, 'mud', related to modern 'soil') and *hyll* (hill). The 'muddy hill' in question is probably the one south of St Alphege's Church, where the road runs through thick red clayey soil. The name was recorded in a document of 1242 as *Sulihull*.

Solway Firth (England/Scotland)

The arm of the Irish Sea that extends between the coasts of CUMBRIA (England) and DUMFRIES and GALLOWAY (Scotland). Its name means 'inlet of the pillar ford', from the Old Norse *súl* (pillar), *vath* (ford) and, as for other inlets, *fjorthr* (firth). The 'pillar' was probably the Lochmaben Stone, a granite boulder that marked the end of the ford on the Scottish side. A document of 1229 has the name as *Sulewad. Compare* SOLWAY MOSS.

Solway Moss (Cumbria)

A marshy tract of land east of GRETNA GREEN, close to the Scottish-English border. It was the scene of the battle of 1542 in which the Scots were defeated by the English. The name means 'moss (in its old sense of 'swamp', 'marsh') at the muddy place', with the first word representing the dative plural (*solum*) of the Old English *sol* (mud, wallowing-place). No doubt the ending of this became '-way' by association with nearby SOLWAY FIRTH. The name was recorded as *Solum* in a document of 1246.

Somerset (England)

A county in southwest England whose name means 'SOMERTON settlers', 'people who have come to live around Somerton'. The first part of the name represents the name of this town, and the final element is the Old English *sæte* (settlers, dwellers). The additional element '-shire' has been added to denote the county status of Somerset, but is now conventionally omitted, as it is for DORSET. Even so, it occurs in a record of the name for 1122, as

Sumersetescir. Earlier records do not have it, however, such as *Sumers ton* in 1015. *See also* SOMERTON.

Somerton (Somerset)

A small market town northwest of ILCHESTER whose name means 'summer dwelling', from the Old English *sumor* (summer) and *tūn* (farm, dwelling, village). A 'summer' dwelling is one by pastures that are usable only in summer, being too wet or marshy in winter. The region around Somerton has now been drained, so there is no longer marshland here in the winter. Even so, local names, such as King's Sedge Moor, Thorney ('thorn island'), and Low Ham, show that originally the district was a wet one, with 'islands' of higher, drier land. The fact that Somerton itself is on slightly raised land, combined with the good summer pasturage here, must have attracted the settlers who came to dwell in the district, and who thus gave their name to SOMERSET. Somerton was recorded as *Sumertone* in the Domesday Book.

Sompting (West Sussex)

A residential area northeast of WORTHING whose name means 'dwellers by the swamp', with the conjectural Old English *sumpt* (swamp, marsh; compare modern 'sump') suffixed by the '-ing' ending that means 'people of'. The name was recorded as *Suntinga gemære* (the latter word meaning 'boundary') in a document of 956, and as *Sultinges* in the Domesday Book, with the expected Norman difficulty over the consonant cluster *-mpt-*. The terrain is not obviously marshy here, but the land is low-lying and, of course, not far from the sea.

Southam (Warwickshire)

A small town southeast of LEAMINGTON SPA whose name simply means 'southern homestead', from the Old English *sūth* (south) and *hām* (homestead). The name must have been given to contrast with a 'Northam' or 'northern homestead', or some other *hām*, but it is not clear which this was. Southam was recorded as *Suthham* in a document of 965, and as *Sucham* in the Domesday Book.

Southampton (Hampshire)

This well-known city and port has a name that declares it to be 'southern Hampton', by contrast with a 'northern Hampton'. The latter was NORTHAMPTON, and the two towns were connected by a north-south route in medieval times, despite the sizeable distance between them. However, the 'Hampton' of Southampton is a *hamm-tūn*, 'waterside farm', as distinct from Northampton, which was a *hām-tūn*, 'home farm'. The location of Southampton at the confluence of the rivers ITCHEN and TEST confirms this origin. But both places were originally just 'Hampton' before they added 'North' and 'South' respectively; Southampton was *Homtun* in a document of 825, and then *Suthhamtun* in one of 962. It was Southampton that gave the name of its county, HAMPSHIRE.

Southborough (Kent)

This town immediately north of TUNBRIDGE WELLS was originally a 'southern borough' or 'southern manor', by contrast with TONBRIDGE, to the north of it, to which it belonged. Its name was recorded as simply *bo. de Suth'* in a document of 1270, then as *la South Burgh* in 1450.

Southbourne (Dorset)

This seaside district of BOURNEMOUTH has a name that was originally used for a terrace of shops near The Square in the town, and as such it was selected for a seaside development planned in the 1870s to the east of the town centre. Logically, its name should have been 'Eastbourne', therefore, but this name was already in use for EASTBOURNE itself. Therefore the name remained unaltered, although it could be argued that the district is a *south*erly one, near the River *Bourne*, with its name reflecting these two aspects.

Southend-on-Sea (Essex)

This resort on the north side of the THAMES estuary acquired its name from its location at the *south end* of Prittlewell (now itself a district of Southend), with this name recorded in 1481 as *Southende*. But this was long before the present resort began to develop, which was at the turn of the nineteenth century. The addition '-on-Sea' is largely for commercial purposes, although it does distinguish this resort from other places of the name that are not resorts (such as Southend in LEWISHAM, Greater London).

Southgate (Greater London)

A district of ENFIELD that takes its name from the gate formerly here that gave access from the south to Enfield Chase. The name was recorded as *Suthgate* in 1370.

Southminster (Essex)

A village north of BURNHAM-ON-CROUCH whose name defines it as a 'southern church' by contrast with a northern one, or at least another one. This can hardly be UPMINSTER, which is over 25 miles west of Southminster. Perhaps the contrasting 'minster' was that of the village of Steeple, two miles north of Southminster. The name was recorded as *Suthmynster* in a document of about 1000.

South Molton (Devon)

A market town southeast of BARNSTAPLE whose basic name, Molton, seems to relate to that of the village of Molland, on the southern slopes of EXMOOR, east of the town. The main name of the small village of North Molton, just to the north, is similarly derived. The 'Mol-' of the names may represent a former Celtic name for one or more of the hills of Exmoor here, with the meaning being 'bald one' (*compare* MOEL HEBOG in Wales). If this theory is correct, then Molland means 'land by the bald hill' and (North) Molton 'farm by the bare hill'. South Molton, which is not actually on the slopes of Exmoor, then

derived its name in contrast to North
Molton. The two places are recorded in the
Domesday Book as *Nortmoltone* and
Sudmoltone, so they had already been
differentiated by the eleventh century.

South Ockendon (Essex)

A northwest suburb of GRAYS whose basic
name, Ockendon, means 'Wocca's hill',
recorded as *Wokendune* in a document
dated 1067. Its prefix distinguishes it from
the district of HAVERING known as North
Ockendon, a mile to the north and just
inside the boundary of Greater London.

Southport (Merseyside)

This coastal resort north of LIVERPOOL has
a modern name given to the development
around a hotel here at the end of the
eighteenth century, when the name itself
was given by a Dr Barton of Hoole. The
question is: 'south' of where? Possible
explanations include the following: (1) a
port south of PRESTON; (2) a modification
of the original name of the location, which
was South Hawes; (3) a port south of
BLACKPOOL; (4) a generally favourable
name suggesting (in the north of England)
a place that was actually in the south, such
as SOUTHSEA; and (5) a tribute to the
builder of the first hotel here, William
Sutton, whose surname could be
understood as 'south town', with 'port'
substituted for greater precision.

South Queensferry (Lothian)

Both South Queensferry, at the southern
end of the FORTH bridges, and North
Queensferry, at their northern end (in Fife),
have a basic name that commemorates
Queen Margaret of Scotland, who in the
eleventh century regularly crossed the
river here on her way from EDINBURGH to
her residence at DUNFERMLINE. The
crossing-place is specifically referred to in
a text of 1183: *Passagium S. Marg.
Regine*. A ferry operated between the
two places for hundreds of years, until
the Forth Road Bridge was opened in
1964.

Southsea (Hampshire)

This residential and holiday district of
PORTSMOUTH derives its name from the
'goodlie and warlyk castill' that Henry VIII
planned here in 1538 to be a 'south sea
castle' at the entrance to Portsmouth
Harbour. The castle was originally called
Chaderton Castle, after its first governor,
but the simpler name Southsea prevailed
for the castle and for the district that arose
around it. A text of 1535 refers to the castle
as *le South Castell of Portesmouth*. The
name happens to be an agreeable and
suitable one for a holiday resort, with its
suggestion of 'South Seas' (i.e. the South
Pacific).

South Shields (Tyne and Wear)

This port with its many docks on the south
side of the River TYNE stands opposite
NORTH SHIELDS; its basic name 'Shields',
has exactly the same origin (*see* NORTH
SHIELDS). Like its 'twin', it was originally
simply 'Shields' (*Scheles* in a document of
1235), with its present, differentiated name
following later. The two towns were in
different counties until the reorganisation
of local government boundaries in 1974:
North Shields was in Northumberland,
and South Shields in Durham.

Southwark (Greater London)

This borough on the south side of the
THAMES has a name that means 'southern
work', that is, a defensive post on the south
side of the river forming an outpost of the
City of LONDON. The 'south' of the name
also relates to the 'south' contained in the
name of SURREY, as shown in a tenth-
century reference to Southwark as
Suthringa Geweorche, 'fort of the men of
Surrey'. The Domesday Book recorded the
name as *Sudwerca*. Southwark is still
known by its alernative name of 'The
Borough', a title that dates from the middle
of the sixteenth century, when it became
the city ward of Bridge Without (i.e.
beyond the bridge over the Thames).
'Borough' as used here strictly means
'suburbs'.

Southwell (Nottinghamshire)

The name of this town west of NEWARK-ON-TRENT means 'southern spring', as distinct from the 'northern spring' at the village of Norwell, seven miles northeast of it. The 'southern spring' itself is the Lady Well by the minster church. Southwell was referred to as *æt Suthwellan* in a document of 958.

Southwick (West Sussex)

A town on the coast to the east of SHOREHAM-BY-SEA whose name means 'southern farm', with the latter half of the name representing the Old English *wīc* in its sense of 'outlying farm'. Southwick was dependent on the manor of Kingston. Its name was recorded as *Sudewic* in 1073.

Southwold (Suffolk)

A small coastal resort east of HALESWORTH whose name means 'southern wood'. It was probably not 'south' of the village of Northwold in Norfolk, as this is much too distant to be associated by name. It was possibly regarded as being a wood south of LOWESTOFT. Its name appears in the Domesday Book as *Sudwolda*.

Sowerby Bridge (West Yorkshire)

A town on the River CALDER southwest of HALIFAX whose basic name, Sowerby, is derived from the village of Sowerby, a mile west of it. The meaning is 'swampy place', from the Old Norse *saurr* (mud, dirt, marshland) and *bý* (place, village). The district here is low-lying and the soil liable to be waterlogged. The village was recorded as *Sorebi* in the Domesday Book, and Sowerby Bridge as *Soureby Brygge* in a document of 1478.

Spalding (Lincolnshire)

This town southwest of BOSTON has the '-ing' suffix that means 'people of'. The first part of the name is not a personal name, however, but that of a district. The problem is that it has not been located, and 'Spald' could have been anywhere, perhaps even on the Continent; its meaning is unknown. The name was recorded as *Spaldyng* in 1051.

Speke (Merseyside)

A district of LIVERPOOL whose name means '(place by) brushwood', from the Old English *spǣc* (small branch) (probably related to modern 'spoke' and 'spike'). The name was in the Domesday Book as *Spec*.

Spelthorne (Surrey)

An administrative district in the north of the county that adopted the name of a former hundred of Middlesex when it was established in 1974. The hundred name means 'speech thorn-tree', denoting a tree where assemblies took place and where speeches were made. The two elements of the name are the Old English *spell* (speech) (as in modern 'spell' meaning 'spoken magic formula') and *thorn* (thorn tree).

Spennymoor (Durham)

This town northeast of BISHOP AUCKLAND has a difficult name (apart from the 'moor'); the first element may be the conjectural Old English *spenne*, literally meaning 'clasp', 'buckle' (compare 'span' in the sense of 'joining'), but with some other sense still uncertain in place-names. Perhaps it means 'hedge', 'fence', or something similar. It occurs in the fourteenth-century alliterative poem *Sir Gawain and the Green Knight*, written in Middle English, in which, for example, a hunted fox doubles through groves and listens at hedges and *At the last bi a littel dich he lepeth ouer a spenne, steleth out ful stilly by a strothe rande, Went haf wylt of the wode*, etc. ('at last by a little ditch he leaps over a *spenne*, steals out quietly by the edge of a plantation, he intended to have escaped from the wood'). So if the fox jumps over a *spenne*, a meaning like 'fence' or 'hurdle' seems the most appropriate. Spennymoor thus may mean 'moor with fences', and its name was recorded as *Spendingmor* in about 1336 (even if this contains *spenning*, it seems to have the same basic sense as *spenne*).

Spey (Highland/Grampian)
The name of this river is an ancient one, probably pre-Celtic in origin, but as yet it defies meaningful interpretation.

Spilsby (Lincolnshire)
A small town west of SKEGNESS with a Scandinavian name meaning 'Spilli's village'. The personal name probably means 'waster', from an Old Norse word related to modern English 'spill'. The place-name was recorded as *Spilesbi* in the Domesday Book.

Spitalfields (Greater London)
A district in the Borough of TOWER HAMLETS whose name can be understood as meaning 'hospital fields'. The land here was the property of the Priory of St Mary Spital, founded in 1197, and a record of the name in 1394 gives it as *Seintmariespitel in Shordich*. The word 'spital' or 'spittle' was formerly current in English for a 'low-class' hospital or hospice, i.e. one that catered for beggars and the poor.

Spithead (Hampshire)
The roadstead (sheltered water) off the entrance to PORTSMOUTH Harbour, although the name is sometimes applied to an area greater than this, extending to the Isle of WIGHT, and so including part of The SOLENT. The name derives from that of a sandbank on the HAMPSHIRE coast called Spit Sand, now built over and represented by the strip of land that runs from Haslar Royal Naval Hospital to HMS Dolphin. (The name survives in that of Spit Sand Fort, at the entrance to Portsmouth Harbour.) The name of the sandbank then extended to apply to the whole of the roadstead as described, so that it covered the area from the 'head' or end of Spit Sand. 'Spit' in the original name means 'narrow tongue of land or sand that extends into the sea' (the same 'spit' as for a pointed rod used for roasting meat). The

name has been recorded no earlier than the seventeenth century, and the document of 1653 that mentions *Spithead* is one of the earliest instances we have in English of the use of 'spit' in this particular sense.

Spofforth (North Yorkshire)
A village northwest of WETHERBY with its ruined fourteenth-century house known as Spofforth Castle. Its name may mean 'ford by a spot of land', from the Old English conjectural *spot* (small piece, bit; modern 'spot') and *ford*. The reference would be to a small piece of land. The name was recorded as *Spoford* in the Domesday Book, and as *Spotford* in a document of 1218. The ford would have been over the stream here, a tributary of the NIDD.

Spurn Head (Humberside)
The headland at the end of the long spit of land on the north side of the mouth of the HUMBER. Its name refers to the spur-like outline of the headland. (The word is related to modern English 'spurn' as well as 'spur'.) When Henry IV landed here in the early fifteenth century, the site was known as either Ravenspurn or Ravensburgh (*Ravenserespourne* in a document of 1399). Ravenspurn represents the earlier name of Ravenser for the location, with this meaning 'Hrafn's gravel bank'; the Scandinavian personal name (meaning 'raven') is followed by the Old Norse *eyrr* (gravel bank). The headland at that time was known as Ravenser Odd, with the latter word being the Old Norse *oddr* (point of land). But in the early years of the fifteenth century both Ravenser and Ravenser Odd were submerged by the sea, leaving Spurn Head in their place.

Staffa (Strathclyde)
This uninhabited island in the Inner HEBRIDES, famous for its columns of basaltic rock, has a name that refers to this feature; it thus means 'pillar island', from the Old Norse *stafr* (pillar, rod) (related to English 'staff') and *ey* (island).

Stafford (Staffordshire)

This town south of STOKE-ON-TRENT has a name that means 'landing-place ford', from the Old English *stæth* (landing-place) (later, 'river-bank', 'shore', as in modern 'staithe' meaning 'wharf') and *ford*. Stafford is on the River Sow, and no doubt the ford was located at the river's limit of navigation, which was thus a landing-place. (Perhaps it was at or near the point where Bridge Street now crosses the river. The Sow narrows considerably just here.) Stafford was recorded as both *Stæth* and *Stæffod* in the tenth century, (as *Stæfford* in a document of 913). The county of Staffordshire was recorded as *Stæffordscir* in 1016. *Compare* STAITHES.

Staines (Surrey)

A town on the THAMES west of LONDON whose name simply means 'stone', from the Old English *stān*; a deceptive plural *-s* had been added by the time the name came to be recorded in the Domesday Book, as *Stanes*. But an earlier record of about 1050, as *Stane*, shows the name to be really singular. The stone in question is said to have been a Roman milestone on the road from London to SILCHESTER, which crossed the Thames at Staines. However, no such stone has been found, and the reference may have been to a natural glacial boulder here, although there was a Roman settlement here, called *Pontibus*, '(at) the bridges'. The English name should really have become STONE, as for the town of this name.

Staithes (North Yorkshire)

This fishing village on the North Sea coast has a name that means 'landing-place', from the Old English *stæth* (as for STAFFORD). The fact that the name was recorded as *Setonstathes* in a document of 1415 shows that the particular landing-place was designed to serve nearby SEATON.

Stalybridge (Greater Manchester)

This town east of MANCHESTER was originally simply Stayley or Staveley, meaning 'clearing where staves are got', from the Old English *stæf* (staff, stave) and *lēah* (clearing), with the present name that of a hamlet across the River TAME here. In the eighteenth century the name extended from this place, in Lancashire, to the present site, in Cheshire, so replacing the original 'Stayley' and coming into use for the whole town. The present name thus implies 'bridge over the Tame at a place formerly called Stayley'. *Compare* STAVELEY.

Stamford (Lincolnshire)

This ancient town on the River WELLAND has a name that means simply 'stone ford', implying a ford where stones had been laid on the river bed for ease of crossing. ERMINE STREET passed through Stamford, and other long-established roads converged here, with the Great North Road (the present A1) passing through the town until relatively recently, when a bypass was built. The site of the actual ford, which was levelled only in the present century, can still be made out just below the Town Bridge. This was not where the Roman road crossed the river, however, and the Romans' ford was about half a mile further downstream, on a route now followed by the streets named Water Furlong and Roman Bank. The name was recorded as *Steanford* in a document of 922, and it corresponds to the much more common name of Stanford. *Compare also* STAMFORD BRIDGE; STANFORD LE HOPE.

Stamford Bridge (Humberside)

A village at the crossing of the River DERWENT east of YORK. It was the site of the famous battle of 1066 in which King Harold of England defeated Harald Hardrada of Norway. The name means 'bridge by the stone ford', with the original 'stone ford' as described for STAMFORD. The bridge had been built (to replace the ford) by the date of the battle, however, and the name is recorded in a contemporary account that same year as *Stanfordbrycg*, although three hundred years earlier the site was referred to simply as *Stanford*. Stamford Bridge nearly acquired quite a different name, as a record of 1251 shows, naming it as *Pundelabataille*, Norman French for 'battle bridge'. *Compare* the name of BATTLE, which commemorates a similarly famous early battle.

Stanford le Hope (Essex)

This town northeast of TILBURY stands on a stream near the north bank of the THAMES. 'Stanford' means 'stone ford', as for STAMFORD. The common name of Stanford frequently acquired a distinguishing addition, as here; the 'Hope' refers to the nearby location of Broad Hope, by the Thames, which makes a broad curve here, known as Lower Hope Reach. 'Hope' represents the Old English *hop*, which basically means 'valley', but can extend to other senses, such as 'inlet', 'bay', with the latter sense something like its use here. Stanford le Hope was simply *Stanford* in a document of 1068.

Stanhope (Durham)

A small town on the River WEAR west of WOLSINGHAM whose name means 'stone valley', referring to a valley that is full of stones or that has stony soil. The Old English *hop* often specifically denotes an enclosed or sheltered place, and Stanhope, which is protected by hills and moorland, is a good illustration of the term. Its name was recorded as *Stanhopa* in 1183.

Stanley (Durham)

This coal-mining town west of CHESTER-LE-STREET has a name that is fairly common elsewhere, especially in the Midlands and north of England. It means simply 'stone clearing', denoting a woodland glade or clearing with stony or rocky soil. This particular Stanley was recorded as *Stanlei* in the Domesday Book. The two Old English words that comprise the name are *stān* (stone) and *lēah* (clearing).

Stanmore (Greater London)

A district of HARROW whose name means 'stone pool', from the Old English *stān* (stone) and *mere* (pool, lake). The reference is probably to a former gravelly pond here. The name was recorded in the Domesday Book as *Stanmere*.

Stansted (Essex)

This village northeast of BISHOP'S STORTFORD, with its nearby airport, has a name that means 'stone place', from the Old English *stān* (stone) and *stede* (place, site). The reference was probably to a prominent stone building here, and the name was recorded in the Domesday Book as *Stanesteda*. As the name is common, a distinguishing addition is often made; in full, Stansted is called Stansted Mountfitchet. The latter word derives from the family name of Richard de Muntfichet, who held the manor here in the late twelfth century. His family came from Montfiquet, in Normandy.

Stanwell (Surrey)

An urban district northeast of STAINES whose name means 'stone stream' or 'stone well', that is, a stony one. No doubt the reference is to the stream that still flows through Stanwell. The name was recorded as *Stanwelle* in the Domesday Book.

Stapleford (Nottinghamshire)

A town west of BEESTON whose name is found elsewhere and means 'ford marked by posts', from the Old English *stapol* (post, pillar) (of wood or stone) and *ford* (ford). Places so named would have had either dangerous fords, where the crossing needed to be marked, or fords situated some distance from a main route, that needed to be pointed out. This Stapleford was a crossing over the River EREWASH; its name was recorded as now in the Domesday Book.

Starcross (Devon)

A village on the west side of the estuary of the EXE, opposite EXMOUTH. Its name seems to refer to some kind of cross here, presumably a star-shaped one. On the other hand, the reference may well be to the river-crossing to Exmouth, with 'Star' the name of a former inn here. The name is fairly recent, and the earliest record of it is *Star Crosse* in 1689.

Start Point (Devon, Orkney)
It is simply a coincidence that the same name belongs to two headlands at virtually opposite ends of Britain. The Devon Start Point is on Start Bay, extending south of DARTMOUTH. The Orkney headland is at the eastern end of the island of SANDAY. In both cases the name has the same meaning, literally 'tail point', but with the English name representing the Old English *steort*, and the Scottish one deriving from the Old Norse *stertr*. The reference is to the shape of the headland. (Compare the name of the redstart, a bird with a pinkish tail.)

Staveley (Derbyshire)
A town northeast of CHESTERFIELD whose name means 'clearing where staves were got' from the Old English *stæf* (staff, stave) and *lēah* (clearing). The name was recorded in the Domesday Book as *Stavelie*. *Compare* STALYBRIDGE.

Stechford (West Midlands)
An eastern district of BIRMINGHAM whose name means 'sticky ford', implying one that was clayey or muddy. The origin lies in the Old English *sticce* (sticky) and *ford*. The ford in question would have been over the River Cole. The name was recorded as *Stichesford* in a document of 1267.

Steeple Bumpstead (Essex)
A village east of HAVERHILL whose main name, Bumpstead, may originally have been something like 'Bunhampstead', with the first element of this perhaps being, as 'Bune', the former name of the stream on which the village stands. The meaning would be 'reedy one', from the Old English *bune* (reeds). The rest of the word would mean simply 'homestead', as for

HAMPSTEAD. The first word of the present name refers to the steeple of the parish church here, and distinguishes this village from nearby Helion Bumpstead (where the first word refers to Helléan, in Brittany, from where the holder of the manor here in the eleventh century had come). Steeple Bumpstead was recorded in the Domesday Book simply as *Bunsteda*, with the present name appearing as *Stepilbumstede* in a text of 1261.

Stenhousemuir (Central)
A town northwest of FALKIRK whose name straightforwardly means 'moorland by the stone house'; it was recorded as *de Stan House* in about 1200, and as *Stenhous* in 1601. The elements of the word are all Old English, respectively *stān*, *hūs*, and *mōr*.

Stepney (Greater London)
A district of east LONDON whose name means 'Stybba's landing-place', with the personal name followed by a well-disguised Old English *hȳth* (landing-place), as seen much more clearly in ROTHERHITHE. There are other places by the THAMES with this element, including CHELSEA and PUTNEY. Stepney is similar to the latter, which also has a personal name followed by an identical altered ending. Stepney was recorded as *Stybbanhythe* in about 1000, and as *Stibenhede* in the Domesday Book. A document of 1542 refers to the place as *Stebenheth al. Stepney*.

Stevenage (Hertfordshire)
Although a New Town, designated in 1946, Stevenage has an old name. It means '(place at) the firm oak', from the Old English *stīth* (stiff, strong), an element not often found in place-names, and *āc* (oak). The reference seems to have been to a particularly robust oak tree formerly here. The name thus has nothing to do with a person named Steven, and was recorded in a document of about 1060 as *Stithenæce*. The *-th-* of this later became the *-v-* of the present name.

Stevenston (Strathclyde)

This town east of ARDROSSAN appears to be named after a Steven or Stephen who owned land here in medieval times. The name was recorded as *Stevenstoun* in a document of 1246. The name means 'Steven's farm', although the identity of the owner is not known.

Stewarton (Strathclyde)

A small town north of KILMARNOCK whose name means 'steward's estate'; it refers to Walter, Seneschal (High Steward) to King David I in the mid-twelfth century. The name was recorded as *Stewartoun* in a document dated 1201.

Stewartry (Dumfries and Galloway)

This administrative district in the central area of the region adopted the ancient name for the district as a 'stewardship' of KIRKCUDBRIGHT, its capital. The term corresponded to the more common 'county'. The actual 'steward' of Stewartry was the Earl of DOUGLAS. The role and status of steward have historically assumed much greater importance in Scotland than for the same title in England; hence the common Scottish surname Stewart or Stuart.

Stewartstown (Tyrone)

A village west of Lough NEAGH that takes its name from the English Stewart family who owned land and lived here from the seventeenth century. Sir Andrew Stewart built Roughan Castle nearby in 1618; Stuart Hall, the residence of Lord Castlestewart, was built by John Stewart in the mid-eighteenth century. The Irish name of the village is An Chraobh, 'the mansion' (a figurative sense of *craobh*, which is literally 'branch', 'tree').

Steyning (West Sussex)

A town northwest of SHOREHAM-BY-SEA whose name means either '(place of) Stān's people' or '(place of) the dwellers by a stone'. The Old English *stān* (stone) could thus be either a personal name or the common noun. Most '-ing' names of this type in Sussex (and there are many) are based on a personal name. But this need not necessarily rule out the 'stone' origin, which could perhaps have applied to a stony place, rather than to a single stone. The name was recorded as *æt Stæningum* in about 880, and in the Domesday Book it was *Staninges*, showing the Old English suffix *-ingas* that meant 'people of'.

Stilton (Cambridgeshire)

This village southwest of PETERBOROUGH is famous for the cheese of its name (although made in Leicestershire) that was distributed from the Bell Inn here. Its name means literally 'stile farm', from the Old English *stigel* (stile) and *tūn* (farm). It may be significant that Stilton is on ERMINE STREET, and that there was a point here where a fence had to be climbed to continue a northward journey to Peterborough, as Ermine Street deviates to the northwest just here, taking potential travellers to Peterborough away from that town. Alternatively, as Stilton is at the foot of a hill, the 'stile' could have the sense 'ascent', denoting a 'climb'. The name was recorded as *Stichiltone* in the Domesday Book.

Stirling (Central)

A historic town on the slope of a rocky hill above the River FORTH. Its seemingly simple name has never been satisfactorily explained. The origin may lie in a former name of the Forth here; the Gaelic *sruth* (river, stream) has been mentioned in this connection. A document of about 1124 has the name as *Strevelin*. The county name, Stirlingshire, came from that of the town.

Stockbridge (Hampshire)

A village on the River TEST south of ANDOVER whose name means 'bridge made of tree-trunks', from the Old English *stocc* (stock, tree-trunk) and *brycg* (bridge). The village is quite far up the river, and it would have been no great problem to bridge it in this way. Perhaps the bridge was where the present A30 road crosses the Test here. The name was recorded as *Stocbrigge* in 1227. *Compare* TROWBRIDGE.

Stockport (Greater Manchester)

A town southeast of MANCHESTER whose name is found fairly widely elsewhere and means 'market-place at a dependent settlement', from the Old English *stoc* (place) (often implying a secondary settlement dependent on another, among other meanings) and *port* (town, market-place) (the latter as in GOSPORT and LANGPORT). The name was recorded as *Stokeport* in about 1165. *Compare* the STOKE names below.

Stocksbridge (South Yorkshire)

This steel-manufacturing town on the Little DON northwest of SHEFFIELD has a name identical to that of STOCKBRIDGE, and so has the same sense. Here the 'tree-trunk bridge' would have been over the Little Don, probably where the minor road leaves the present A616.

Stockton-on-Tees (Cleveland)

A town on the left bank of the TEES, where it is part of the TEESSIDE urban complex. 'Stockton' means 'farm at a dependent settlement', with the Old English *stoc* (place) having the same sense as described for STOCKPORT, here followed by *tūn* (farm). The name is a common one, and frequently has distinguishing additions, as here. The name was recorded as *Stocton* in a document of 1196.

Stoke-by-Nayland (Suffolk)

This village southwest of HADLEIGH has the very common basic name, Stoke, representing the Old English *stoc*. The meaning is 'place', but the word acquired the two special senses of 'religious place' (such as a place of worship or a monastery) and 'secondary settlement' (as mentioned for STOCKPORT). In the case of Stoke-by-Nayland, the name has the first sense, as a monastery was known to exist here. The rest of the name is the typical addition

found with many 'Stoke' names and refers to the nearby town of NAYLAND. The village was recorded exactly as now in a document of the mid-tenth century.

Stoke Newington (Greater London)

This district of HACKNEY has a rather different 'Stoke' name than most. The main name is the second word, which represents the Old English *nīwe* (new) and *tūn* (farm), so that originally the place was 'Newton' (*Neutone* in the Domesday Book). The first word of the name is the Old English *stocc* (tree-trunk) (as for STOCKBRIDGE), and was added to distinguish this place from HIGHBURY, which was formerly the manor of Newton Barrow. So, overall the present name means 'new farm by the tree-stumps', and is recorded in this form in a text of 1274 (*Neweton Stoken*).

Stoke-on-Trent (Staffordshire)

This well-known city has a basic name derived from the Old English *stoc* (place), as considered for STOKE-BY-NAYLAND. It is more likely that the meaning here is 'dependent settlement' rather than 'religious place', as there is no evidence for the latter sense. The addition of the river name distinguishes this Stoke from the hundreds of others. The name of this city, perhaps the best-known example, was recorded as *Stoche* in the Domesday Book.

Stoke Poges (Buckinghamshire)

A suburban area north of SLOUGH with the same basic 'Stoke' origin as considered for STOKE-BY-NAYLAND. Despite the fame of the church here, or rather the churchyard (with which Gray's *Elegy* is popularly identified, as the poet is buried here), the meaning is likely to be 'secondary settlement' rather than 'religious place'. The second word of the name, which is a distinguishing addition, is that of the family of le Pugeis, a member of whom is known to have held the manor in the mid-thirteenth century. Stoke Poges was thus *Stoches* in the Domesday

Book, and *Stokepogeis* in a document of 1292.

Stokesay Castle (Shropshire)

This thirteenth-century manor house takes its name from the village of Stokesay, south of CRAVEN ARMS. The settlement here was originally known as 'Stoke' (*Stoches* in the Domesday Book), probably in the sense of 'dependent settlement' (*see* STOKE-BY-NAYLAND). The latter part of the name is a distinguishing addition, derived from the de Sei family who held the manor here. The present name was recorded as *Stoksay* in 1256. No doubt the personal name blended with the main name partly because of its brevity, and partly because it happens to resemble the second element (often meaning 'island') in such names as RAMSEY and LINDSEY.

Stone (Staffordshire)

A town on the River TRENT north of STAFFORD whose name means what it says. It is often extremely difficult, however, to establish what kind of 'stone' gave the name. It could have been a natural boulder, for example, or a man-made boundary marker, or in some cases even a stone building. Sometimes the meaning is 'stones', not 'stone', as seems to be the case here, with the name recorded in 1187 as *Stanes*. Many places of the name, like this town, are on a river, although this does not necessarily make interpretation of the name any easier. *Compare* STAINES.

Stone Bassett (Oxfordshire)

A proposed new country town east of OXFORD, designed in 1987 to ease the pressure of housing on that city. Its name appears to be specifically devised for the purpose, with the first word no doubt referring to the predominant construction materials, and the second matching the Norman family name already existing in such names as Thorpe Bassett, Berwick Bassett, WOOTTON BASSETT, Drayton Bassett, and Colston Bassett. ('Bassett', too, may have some special significance for the construction company.)

Stonehaven (Grampian)

A fishing port south of ABERDEEN whose name probably means what it says: 'stone landing-place', from the Old English *stān* (stone) and *hȳth* (landing-place), despite the fact that the place is in Scotland and that early records of the name vary and date from only the late sixteenth century. Thus a document of 1587 has the name as *Stanehyve*, and one of 1629 as *Steanhyve*. The latter half of these is rather far removed from the modern '-haven'. Even so, the derivation given here is probably the likely one, and one must allow for variations in the Scottish spelling of the English name, and in the Scottish pronunciation, too, which is often 'Stain-high', matching the earliest records of the name.

Stonehenge (Wiltshire)

The famous ancient earthwork and stone circle on SALISBURY Plain. Its name basically means 'stone-hanging', describing the stone circle, in which the top lintel stones 'hang' over the two uprights. The name was recorded in a document of about 1130 as *Stanenges*.

Stonehouse (Gloucestershire)

A district of STROUD whose name means '(place by a) stone house'; it was recorded in the Domesday Book as *Stanhus*, which happens to represent exactly the two Old English words (*stān* and *hūs*) that gave the name. *Compare* STENHOUSEMUIR.

Stony Stratford (Buckinghamshire)

A small town on the River OUSE in the northwest part of MILTON KEYNES. Its basic name means, like all Stratfords, 'ford by a Roman road', from the Old English *strǣt* (road, street) and *ford*; Stony Stratford lies on WATLING STREET. The first word of the name, added to distinguish this Stratford from the several others, refers to the stony or gravelly nature of the crossing over the Ouse. The name was recorded as *Stani Stratford* in a document dated 1202. *See also* STRATFORD.

Stormont (Down)

A district of BELFAST that has given its name to the Northern Ireland parliament. It probably derives its name from the Irish *starr* (projection) and *muineach* (back, hill, ridge), or some similar words. Stormont is some five miles east of the city centre at the foot of what could be regarded as a 'projecting hill' to the north of it.

Stornoway (Western Isles)

The port and chief town of LEWIS whose name probably means 'steerage bay' or 'rudder bay', from the Old Norse *stjǫrn* (steerage, rudder) and *vágr* (bay), although the precise sense of this is not clear. Possibly the original harbour here required special manoeuvring. The name was recorded as *Stornochway* in a document of 1511. The Gaelic rendering of the name is *Steornabhagh*.

Storrington (West Sussex)

A small town southeast of PULBOROUGH whose name has been explained as meaning 'stork farm', from the Old English *storc* (stork) and *tūn* (farm). The name was recorded as both *Storgetune* and (with greater difficulty) *Estorchetone* in the Domesday Book. The derivation is acceptable in view of the nearby marshes of the ARUN valley, although storks do not seem to occur in any other place-name. Possibly the deceptive '-ington' of the name arose by association with the many villages nearby that contain this ending, such as Sullington, Washington, Chiltington, and Ashington.

Stour (England)

There are several rivers of this name up and down the country, including others such as the Great Stour and Little Stour in Kent. The following three place-names (see below) all take their names from a Stour.

Wherever it occurs, the name represents a conjectural British (Celtic) root element *stur-* meaning 'strong', referring to the force or power of the current.

Stourbridge (West Midlands)

An industrial town west of BIRMINGHAM that obviously takes its name from the River STOUR on which it stands. The name was recorded as *Sturbrug* in a text of 1255. The bridge was probably where the present High Street crosses the Stour to the north of the town centre. The river is bridged again in the east of the town by Stamford Street, suggesting that there was formerly a stony ford there (*see* STAMFORD).

Stourhead (Wiltshire)

An attractive house with pleasure-gardens northwest of WINCANTON. The name is taken from the River STOUR, which rises near here and then flows south to pass through (and give its name to) STURMINSTER NEWTON before eventually flowing into the sea at CHRISTCHURCH.

Stourport-on-Severn (Hereford and Worcester)

A town whose name tells all: it is a port at the confluence of the rivers STOUR and SEVERN, southwest of KIDDERMINSTER. The name is a recent one, as the town itself arose only in the mid-eighteenth century when the Staffordshire and Worcestershire Canal opened, linking the Trent and Mersey Canal with the Severn here. Before this, the site here was known as Little Mitton; Upper Mitton is now a northern district of Stourport. Basic 'Mitton' means 'farm at the junction of streams', appropriately enough, from the Old English *gemȳthe*, 'mouth of a river where it runs into another' (i.e. confluence), and *tūn* (farm). The name of Stourport was recorded as now in about 1775. For another name with this special 'canal' association of 'port', *compare* ELLESMERE PORT.

Stowmarket (Suffolk)

A market and industrial town northwest of IPSWICH whose name was originally just 'Stow' (*Stou* in the Domesday Book). This represents the Old English *stōw*, which basically means 'place', but which also had the narrower senses of 'place of assembly' or 'holy place'. Here, it seems to have been the latter, as the Domesday Book's full reference is to the *ecclesia de Stou*. On the other hand, the name of the hundred here was also *Stou*, and could therefore have been an assembly-place of that hundred. When 'Stow' came to be associated with its market, it then added the latter half of the name, first recorded with a spelling as now in a document of 1268.

Stow-on-the-Wold (Gloucestershire)

A small town west of CHIPPING NORTON whose basic name (from the Old English *stōw* 'place') could mean either 'place of assembly' or, perhaps as here, 'holy place', with the Norman parish church, on its hilltop site, doubtless representing an even earlier building. The addition to the basic name distinguishes this Stow from the many others. 'Wold' means 'upland wood' (Old English *wald*) (*compare* The WEALD). The name was recorded as *Edwardestowe* in a document of about 1107, deriving from the dedication of the parish church, which even today is to St Edward.

Strabane (Tyrone)

A large market town to the south of LONDONDERRY whose name means 'the white riverside land', as shown more clearly in the Irish name, An Srath Bán. Strabane is on the River Mourne.

Strandhill (Sligo)

This small resort west of SLIGO has an English name that refers to its location at the foot of a hill by the coast. Its Irish name is An Leathros, 'the half headland', describing the peninsula here in more general terms.

Strangeways (Greater Manchester)

A district of MANCHESTER, known for its prison, whose name means literally 'strong washing', from the Old English *strang* (strong) and *gewæsc* (washing, flood). The reference is to the location of the place on a tongue of land between two rivers north of the city centre, with this site formerly subjected to flooding from the strong currents of the rivers. The name was recorded as *Strangwas* in 1322, and the present form of the name is an attempt to make it meaningful.

Strangford (Down)

The village of Strangford is on the western side of the entrance to Strangford Lough, opposite PORTAFERRY, and takes its name from the lake. Strangford is an Old Norse name, from *strangr* (strong, violent) and *fjǫrthr* (inlet; 'fjord'), describing the powerful current in the Narrows between the lough and the sea. The Irish name of the lough is Loch Cuan, 'haven lake', almost by contrast with the Norse name. The Irish name of the village is Baile Loch Cuan, 'town on Loch Cuan'.

Stranraer (Dumfries and Galloway)

A port and resort west of WIGTOWN whose name means literally 'fat peninsula', from the Gaelic *sròn* (peninsula) and *reamhar* (fat, plump). This seems to refer to the broad peninsula at the northern end of the RINNS OF GALLOWAY, west of the town. The name was recorded as *Stranrever* in a document of 1320. There was a Roman fort at or near Stranraer (its precise location has not been established), under the name of *Rerigonium*. This is Celtic in origin and means 'very royal (place)', with the initial *Re-* having the same sense as in the Roman name of RECULVER, *Regulbium*. The second part of the name relates to such Celtic words as the Gaelic *righ* (king), and so ultimately to the Latin *rex* (genitive *regis*) and to English 'royal' itself.

Strata Florida (Dyfed)

A hamlet northeast of TREGARON that

derives its Latin name from the twelfth-century abbey formerly here. The meaning is 'flowery road', a partly descriptive, partly pleasant name for the road here where the original Cistercian community was founded. The Welsh name of Strata Florida, with a slightly different meaning, is Ystrad-fflur. In this, the first word actually means 'valley', while the second element is meaningless. The name as a whole is thus a partly meaningful recasting in Welsh of the Latin original.

Stratford (Greater London)
Wherever this name occurs, it means 'ford by a Roman road', from the Old English *strǣt* (road), i.e. 'Roman road' (adopted from the Latin *via strata* 'paved way', and giving the modern English 'street'), and *ford*. This Stratford, in the Borough of NEWHAM, with Stratford New Town immediately north of it, stands by the Roman road that ran from LONDON to COLCHESTER and that crossed the River Lea here. On the other side of the river is BOW, formerly known as Stratford-at-Bow (*see* BOW). Stratford was recorded as STRATFORDE in 1066. *Compare* STRATFORD-ON-AVON.

Stratford-on-Avon (Warwickshire)
This town, southwest of WARWICK and famous as Shakespeare's birthplace, has a name that is identical to that of STRATFORD, and so means 'ford by a Roman road', in this case one over the AVON. The Roman road here joined the Roman settlements at ALCESTER and Tiddington, east of the town, and the ford was probably at or near the point where Bridgefoot crosses the river now. The name was recorded as *Stretford* as long ago as about 700, while the Domesday Book entered the name as *Stradforde*. The full name of the town today is frequently given with '-upon-' rather than '-on-', almost as if to emphasise the importance or status of the town.

Strathaven (Strathclyde)
A town south of HAMILTON whose name denotes its location in the valley (Gaelic *srath*) of the AVON water. Strathaven was recorded as *Strathouen* in a document of about 1190. *Compare* the other 'Strath-' names below.

Strathclyde (Scotland)
An administrative region of western Scotland that encompasses the whole of the basin of the River CLYDE, hence its name, meaning 'valley of the Clyde' (from the Gaelic *srath* and the river name). The present region was established only in 1975, but the name is at least a thousand years older! It was recorded as *Stratcluddenses* in a document of about 900. *See* CLYDE for the origin of this early name.

Strathmiglo (Fife)
A small town to the southwest of AUCHTERMUCHTY whose name means 'valley of the Miglo', although the town is actually in the valley of the EDEN. Miglo was thus an earlier name of the river, meaning 'marshy lake', from Celtic words related to the modern Welsh *mign* (bog, quagmire) and *llwch* (loch). The area here is low-lying but is not as obviously marshy as it must once have been. The town's name was recorded as *Scradimigglolk* in about 1200.

Strathmore (Scotland)
'The great valley' — the extensive fertile valley that basically separates the HIGHLANDS, to the north, from the Central Lowlands, to the south. Its name is thus self-descriptive, from the Gaelic *srath* (valley) and *mór* (great).

Strathpeffer (Highland)
A village and resort west of DINGWALL whose name describes its location in the valley (Gaelic *srath*) of the River Peffery, whose own name is of Pictish origin and means 'radiant one', from a root word *pevr* (related to the modern Welsh *pefr* 'radiant',

'beautiful'). The Gaelic name of Dingwall is Inbhir-pheofharain, otherwise Inverpefferon, denoting its location at the mouth of the Peffery east of Strathpeffer.

Stratton (Cornwall)

This town near the north coast forms one half of the resort now known as BUDE-Stratton. Many places named Stratton were on or near a Roman road, and so have a name like STRATFORD. But here the name is quite different, as can be seen from a record of it dating from about 880, as *Strætneat on Triconscire*. The first word of this means 'valley of the Neat', from the conjectural Cornish *stras* (valley) (related to the 'Strath-' of the Scottish names above) and *neth*, a word of uncertain meaning that gave the former name of the river here. But now the river is called the Strat, with the word that actually meant 'valley' taken to be the name of the river. (The second part of the early name is a tribal name, corresponding to the *Tricorii*, or 'three-army people', of Roman Gaul.) The Domesday Book recorded the name of this place as *Stratone*, based on the present river name (possibly with the Old English *tūn* 'farm', 'village' added or assumed). And thus this exceptional Stratton evolved!

Streatham (Greater London)

A district of LAMBETH whose name means 'homestead by a Roman road', with the same Old English *strǣt* (Roman road), that gave such names as STRATFORD and STREET. Here the word is followed by *hām* (homestead). The Roman road here lay along the course now followed by Streatham High Road (the A23). The name was recorded as *Estreham* in the Domesday Book, with the usual Norman solution for names beginning with *St-* or *Sc-* (*compare* the equivalent process for SCUNTHORPE).

Street (Somerset)

This shoe-making town to the west of GLASTONBURY has a straightforward name representing the Old English *strǣt* (Roman road), with no further addition (unlike STRATFORD or STREATHAM, for example). The Roman road here was the one from ILCHESTER to the BRISTOL Channel coast. Street was *Stret* in a document of 725.

Stretford (Greater Manchester)

A town southwest of MANCHESTER whose name is simply a variant of STRATFORD, and so means '(place by a) ford on a Roman road'. The town is on the Roman road that ran from CHESTER to Manchester, at the point where it crossed the MERSEY. The site of the ford is that of the present (appropriately named) Crossford Bridge. The name of Stretford was recorded in a document dated 1212 exactly as now.

Strokestown (Roscommon)

A market town northeast of ROSCOMMON whose English name is a literal translation of the Irish name, Béal na mBuillí, meaning 'ford-mouth of the strokes' (although Irish *béal*, representing *béal átha*, 'ford-mouth', may be an alteration of *baile*, 'town', as there is no river here). The 'strokes' may well refer to a historic battle here, as the basic sense of the Irish *buille* is 'blow', as well as 'stroke' in various shades of meaning (such as 'touch').

Stroma (Highland)

An island in the PENTLAND FIRTH off the coast by JOHN O'GROATS whose name means 'stream island', from the Old Norse *straumr* (stream, current) and *ey* (island). The name is thus descriptive of the sea currents here. A document of the mid-twelfth century has the island as *Straumsey*. *Compare* STROMNESS.

Stromness (Orkney)

A small town and fishing port on MAINLAND whose name means 'stream headland', from the Old Norse *straumr* (stream, current) (as for STROMA), and *nes* (headland). The name is thus properly that of the peninsula here, and describes the strong current off it. A document of 1150 refers to Stromness as *Straumsness*.

Strood (Kent)

An industrial and residential district northwest of ROCHESTER whose name derives from the Old English *strōd*, a word that meant 'marshy land overgrown with brushwood'. Most such places are low-lying, as Strood is, beside the MEDWAY. Its name was recorded as *Strod* in 889. *Compare* STROUD.

Stroud (Gloucestershire)

This town south of GLOUCESTER has a name of exactly the same origin as that of STROOD, and so also denotes a marshy place with brushwood. Although on a hill slope, Stroud lies behind the River FROME, and the name would have applied to this lower-lying area in the south of the town. Its name was recorded as *La Strode* in a document of 1221. A good contemporary example of an Old English *strōd* can be seen today at and near the village of Stroud, west of PETERSFIELD, where there are many streams and springs interspersed with clumps of trees and bushes.

Strumble Head (Dyfed)

The name of this headland northwest of FISHGUARD remains of uncertain origin, and no records of it have been traced earlier than the seventeenth century (as *Strumble headde* in 1602). It may be Scandinavian, perhaps based on some word meaning 'stump' related to the modern German *Strunk* (trunk, stump), referring to trees or tree-stumps here.

Studland Bay (Dorset)

A bay south of POOLE Bay that takes its name from the village of Studland on its shore, with this in turn meaning more or less what it says, 'tract of land with a horse stud', from the Old English *stōd* (stud, herd of horses) and *land* (land). The village name was recorded in the Domesday Book as *Stollant*. *Compare* STUDLEY.

Studley (Warwickshire)

A suburb of REDDITCH with a name similar to that of STUDLAND BAY; it means 'horse pasture', from the Old English *stōd* (herd of horses) and *lēah* (clearing, pasture). The Domesday Book recorded the name as *Stodlei*.

Sturminster Newton (Dorset)

A small town on the River STOUR northwest of BLANDFORD whose basic name, Sturminster, means 'church on the Stour', from the Old English *mynster* (church, minster) and the name of the river. The second word of the name ('new estate') distinguishes it from that of Sturminster Marshall, some seventeen miles southeast of it, also on the Stour. Strictly speaking, Newton is a place in its own right, on the opposite side of the river, and this name was added to that of Sturminster when the distinction became necessary. Sturminster Newton is thus simply *Newentone* in the Domesday Book, while Sturminster Marshall is *Sturminstre*. The former was then recorded as *Sturministr' Nyweton* in a document of 1291, while Sturminster Marshall was *Sturmenystr' Mareschal* (after the Marshal family) a few years earlier.

Sudbury (Suffolk)

A town on the River STOUR northwest of COLCHESTER whose name means 'southern fortified place', from the Old English *sūth* (south) and *burg* (fortified place). Presumably the matching 'northern fortified place' was BURY ST EDMUNDS, to the north. Sudbury was *Sudberi* as early as 798, however, whereas Bury St Edmunds did not receive its 'Bury' name until the eleventh century. Before this, the site of the latter was known as *Beadriceswyrth*, a name not incorporating *burg* at all. Even so, there is no reason to suppose that the location could not have been a fortified place of one sort or another, and other English cathedral towns and cities have arisen on the site of a historic or ancient fort.

Suffolk (England)
A county in eastern England whose name matches that of its northern neighbour, NORFOLK. It thus derives from the 'south folk', the southern group of East Anglian tribes, whose name, as in Norfolk, became a place-name without the addition of any other word. Suffolk was recorded as *Suthfolci* in a document of 895.

Sugar Loaf (Gwent)
A conical hill in the BLACK MOUNTAINS northwest of ABERGAVENNY, whose name refers to its shape. The Welsh name of the mountain is Mynydd Pen-y-Fâl, or 'top of the summit mountain'.

Sulgrave Manor (Northamptonshire)
This country house is famed for being the home of George Washington's great-grandfather. It takes its name from the nearby village of Sulgrave, north of BRACKLEY. The meaning of this name is 'gully grove', from the Old English *sulh* (literally 'ploughland', but by extension 'gully') and *grāf* (grove). This could suit the location of Sulgrave, at the source of the River Tove. The name was recorded as *Solegreue* in a text of about 1240.

Sullom Voe (Shetland)
This inlet or 'voe' (Old Norse *vágr*, 'bay'), in the north of MAINLAND, has a name probably derived from the Old Norse *súla* (gannet) (rendered in English as 'solan' or 'soland goose'), referring to the presence of these seabirds here. 'Voe' is found in the names of other Shetland inlets, but this one, because of its sheltered site for shipping, and now for its oil terminal, is probably the best known.

Sumburgh (Shetland)
Both Sumburgh Head, at the southern extremity of MAINLAND, and Sumburgh Airport there, have a name of uncertain origin; it appears as *Swynbrocht* in a document of 1506. The first half of this may be a Scandinavian personal name, while the latter half seems to represent the Old Norse *borg* (fort, stronghold).

Summer Isles, The (Highland)
A group of uninhabited islands off the northwest coast of the ROSS and CROMARTY district. The name indicates that sheep were put to pasture here in the summer months. The group seems to have no overall Gaelic name, although the individual islands do.

Sunbury (Surrey)
This town east of CHERTSEY is also known as Sunbury-on-Thames, for its location on this river. Its basic name means 'Sunna's fortified place', with the personal name followed by the Old English *burg* (fortified place). The same personal name lies behind that of Sonning, Berkshire, whose name means 'Sunna's people', and also SUNNINGDALE and Sunninghill, also in Berkshire. Sunbury was referred to as *æt Sunnanbyrg* in a document of about 960.

Sunderland (Tyne and Wear)
An industrial town and seaport southeast of NEWCASTLE-UPON-TYNE, whose name can literally be understood as 'sundered land', that is, territory that was at one time separated from a main estate. The term seems to have had some technical sense, perhaps indicating territory that was private land. The name was recorded as now in a document of about 1168.

Sunningdale (Berkshire)
This residential district of STAINES has a relatively modern name, devised in the mid-nineteenth century for a parish formed from parts of Old WINDSOR and Sunninghill. It can be understood as meaning 'dale of Sunninghill', with the 'dale' alluding to this low-lying region south of VIRGINIA WATER. 'Sunning-' means 'Sunna's people'. *Compare* SUNBURY.

Surbiton (Greater London)
A district of KINGSTON UPON THAMES whose name means 'southern barley farm',

from the Old English *sūth* (south) and *bere-tūn* (barley farm). This farm was 'south' by contrast with NORBITON, 'northern barley farm', the other side of the hill on which BERRYLANDS Farm was located. Both these farms or granges were dependent on the royal manor of Kingston. Surbiton was recorded as *Suberton* in a document of 1179.

Surrey (England)
A county of southeastern England whose name means 'southerly district', from the Old English *sūther* (southerly) and the conjectural *gē* (district) that is also found in ELY ('eel district'). The name applied to the district inhabited by the Saxons of the middle THAMES valley. North of the river they were the 'Middle Saxons' of MIDDLESEX, between ESSEX ('East Saxons') and WESSEX ('West Saxons'). South of the river a new, distinctive name was needed for the Saxons here, and this was it, midway between the Jutes of KENT to the east and the Sunnings of Sonning (*see* SUNBURY) of BERKSHIRE. South of the 'southerly district' were the South Saxons of SUSSEX. The name is recorded as *Suthrige* in 722.

Sussex (England)
A county of southern England, administratively divided into the two separate counties of East Sussex and West Sussex. 'Sussex' means 'South Saxons'; it was recorded as *Suth Seaxe* in 722. The name resembles that of SUFFOLK in that no additional word was added to denote 'land' or 'territory' (unlike CUMBERLAND or SURREY, for instance).

Sutherland (Highland)
An administrative district whose name was formerly that of the most northerly but one (CAITHNESS) county of mainland Scotland (even occurring as Sutherlandshire). It is surprising to find that the name means 'southern territory', from the Old Norse *súthr* (south) and *land* (land, territory). But the name is of Viking origin,

and to the Norsemen, who settled in ORKNEY and SHETLAND, this was indeed the 'southern territory' on the mainland. Equally, the Norsemen named the HEBRIDES as *Suthreyar*, 'southern islands', as they were also south of Orkney and Shetland. This last Norse name gave modern English Sodor, still in use today as the title of the Bishop of Sodor and MAN, whose jurisdiction extends to the respective islands. Sutherland was recorded as *Suthernelande* in a document of the mid-thirteenth century.

Sutton (Greater London)
This former SURREY town, west of CROYDON, has a common name meaning 'southern farm', from the Old English *sūth* (south) and *tūn* (farm). The name usually presupposes a 'northern farm', or at least some more northerly place to be distinguished from the Sutton. This particular Sutton was south of ACTON. Its name was recorded as *Suthtona* in a document of 1181. *Compare* the following SUTTON entries.

Sutton Bridge (Lincolnshire)
A town west of KING'S LYNN whose basic name is the same as that of SUTTON and so means 'southern farm'. The second word of the name refers to the River NENE on which the town stands. It is 'south' (or more precisely southeast) by contrast with Long Sutton, only two miles away.

Sutton Coldfield (West Midlands)
A town northeast of BIRMINGHAM with the same basic name, meaning 'southern farm', as for SUTTON. The second word of the name not only distinguishes it from other Suttons, but refers to its location on a 'coalfield', that is, a region where charcoal was worked. It is said to be 'south' by comparison with LICHFIELD, although the distance between the two places is so great that it should perhaps more realistically be contrasted with Shenstone, three miles south of Lichfield. Sutton Coldfield was recorded simply as *Sutone* in the Domesday

Book, with the present name found in a document of 1289 as *Sutton Colfeld* and also *Sutton in le Colfeld*.

Sutton Hoo (Suffolk)

The famous ancient ship-burial site, east of WOODBRIDGE. It has the same basic name as the places above and so means 'southern farm'. 'Hoo' means 'spur of land' (*compare* LUTON HOO), probably not referring to the tumuli here where the ships were buried, but to a natural rise in the ground. It is difficult to say with certainty with what other place it was contrasted as being 'southern'. Perhaps it was Woodbridge itself, on the other side of the River Deben.

Sutton in Ashfield (Nottinghamshire)

This town southwest of MANSFIELD has the basic name, Sutton, meaning 'southern farm', like the other Suttons above. This one is distinguished by being in the region known as Ashfield, for the origin of which *see* KIRKBY IN ASHFIELD. It was called Sutton perhaps because it was south of the village of Teversal, two miles north of it. Its name was recorded as *Sutone* in the Domesday Book, and as *Sutton in Essefeld* in a document of 1276.

Sutton on Sea (Lincolnshire)

A coastal resort with the name, Sutton, meaning 'southern farm' (*see* SUTTON). It lies immediately south of MABLETHORPE, although it is hardly likely to have been regarded as the 'southern farm' in relation to it, as the town's name is of later origin. In fact, Sutton on Sea is virtually surrounded by places with names ending in '-thorpe' and '-by', so it is difficult to determine where its northern counterpart could have been. It was formerly known simply as Sutton, with its maritime addition designed to help it compete as a resort with Mablethorpe.

Swadlincote (Derbyshire)

A town southeast of BURTON-UPON-TRENT whose name means 'Swartling's cottage', with the personal name (which is probably English rather than Norse) followed by the Old English *cot* (cottage). The Domesday Book recorded the name rather differently, as *Sivardingescotes*, but the derivation of the name given here is supported by later records, such as *Suartlincote* in 1208, and *Swertlyngcote* in 1410.

Swaffham (Norfolk)

This old market town southeast of KING'S LYNN has a name meaning 'homestead of the Swæfas', this being the Old English rendering of the tribal name more commonly known as 'Swabians', from Swabia, the former duchy that is now a district of southwest West Germany. The name was recorded as *Suafham* in the Domesday Book.

Swale (North Yorkshire)

This river, which joins with the URE to form the OUSE east of BOROUGHBRIDGE, has an Old English name, from the conjectural *swalwe*, meaning 'rushing one', 'swirling one'. Its name was recorded as *fluuio Sualua* in about 730.

Swanage (Dorset)

A coastal resort southeast of WAREHAM whose name probably means 'dairy farm of the herdsmen', from the Old English *swān* (herdsman) (compare the rustic 'swain') and *wīc* (special premises) (here a dairy farm). But it is also just possible that the name means 'swannery', as it is difficult to tell the Old English *swān* (herdsman) from *swan* (swan) in place-names. A dairy farm seems more likely, however, if only because of the pastures beside the sea here, which were probably used by inland farmers in the summer months. The name was recorded as *æt Swanawic* in 877, and as various forms of 'Sandwich' from the sixteenth century, by false association with SANDWICH, much further along the coast in Kent. (One deed of 1828 dutifully supplies a whole reel of alternative spellings, referring to *Swan otherwise Swanage otherwise*

Sandwythe otherwise Swanythe otherwise Swanwyche.)

Swanley (Kent)

A town south of DARTFORD whose name probably means 'herdsmen's clearing', from the Old English *swān* (herdsman) and *lēah* (clearing), although 'swans' clearing' is also theoretically possible (*compare* SWANAGE). The name was recorded as *Swanle* in 1334.

Swanscombe (Kent)

An industrial town west of GRAVESEND whose name means 'herdsmen's field', from the Old English *swān* (herdsman) (as for SWANAGE, SWANLEY) and *camp* (field, enclosed piece of land) (adopted from the Latin *campus* 'field' and giving in turn modern English 'camp'). A document of 695 has the name as *Suanescamp*, showing that the apparent '-combe' of the name is misleading.

Swansea (West Glamorgan)

A large town at the mouth of the River Tawe with a Scandinavian name meaning 'Sveinn's sea (place)', with the personal name (meaning 'servant', and related to the Old English *swān* of SWANAGE, etc.) followed by the Old Norse *sǽr* (sea). The name was recorded as *Sweynesse* in about 1165. The Welsh name of Swansea is Abertawe, 'mouth of the Tawe', referring to its location. The river's own name may mean 'dark one' or simply 'water', and be related to that of the THAMES.

Sway (Hampshire)

A small town southwest of BROCKENHURST whose name was recorded in the Domesday Book as *Sveia*; it may represent an earlier name of the Little AVON, the river on which Sway is situated. If so, it could derive from some Old English word related to modern 'sway' that meant 'move', 'go'.

Swilly, Lough (Donegal)

This sea lough, in the north of the county,

takes its name from the river that flows into it, with the river's own name deriving from the Irish *súil* (eye). The sense is probably 'river full of bubbles' (like 'eyes'). The Irish name of the lough is Loch Súilí, with the same meaning.

Swindon (Wiltshire)

This industrial town in the north of the county, north of MARLBOROUGH, has a name that means literally 'pig hill' (or 'swine down', to get nearer the original Old English *swīn* and *dūn*), denoting a hill that was a pasture for swine. Old Swindon, the oldest part of the town, is on a noticeable hill as one approaches it from the south, and in early records it is referred to as *Higheswindon* or, more classically, *Swyndon super montem*. The basic name appears in the Domesday Book as *Suindune*. *Compare* the name of the administrative district in which Swindon is located, THAMESDOWN.

Swinford (Mayo)

A market town east of CASTLEBAR whose name means 'swine ford', translating the Irish name, Béal Átha na Muice, 'ford-mouth of the pigs'. There is no actual ford-mouth here, so the name must have referred to the nearby stream where pigs regularly crossed, or where a pig market was held.

Swinton (Greater Manchester)

A town northwest of MANCHESTER whose name is related to those of SWINDON and SWINFORD, and means 'pig farm', from the Old English *swīn* (pig) and *tūn* (farm). The name was recorded as *Suinton* in a document of 1258.

Swiss Cottage (Greater London)

This district of Camden (*see* CAMDEN TOWN) takes its name from a former inn in the style of an Alpine chalet, called the Swiss Tavern, built here in the early years of the nineteenth century on the site of a tollkeeper's cottage. The inn name was subsequently changed to Swiss Cottage, and the building was reconstructed in 1965. The local Underground station, called Swiss Cottage, has promoted the district name in the region.

Swords (Dublin)
This ancient village north of DUBLIN has a misleading English name that has nothing to do with 'swords'. It probably derives from the Irish *sord* (sward), and is traditionally said to refer to St Columba's well here, so that the full Irish name is Sord Colaim Chille, 'Columba's sward'. A plural English -*s* has been added to the Irish name, apparently by analogy with names such as FERNS.

Sydenham (Greater London)
A district of LEWISHAM whose name is virtually an exact parallel to that of CHIPPENHAM and thus means 'Cippa's village', with the personal name followed by the Old English *hām* (homestead, village). This was recorded as *Chipeham* in a document of 1206, and as *Shippenham* in 1315. However, a text of 1690 has the name as *Sidenham*, and the present spelling of the name preserves the copyist's error in transcribing the *p* of the original name as *d*.

Symonds Yat (Hereford and Worcester)
A well-known beauty spot on the River WYE north of MONMOUTH whose name means 'Sigemund's gap', with the personal name (meaning 'victory protection') followed by the Old English *geat* (gap; modern 'gate'). The latter word refers to the pass through the hills here in the river valley. The site is a strategic one, on the English-Welsh border.

Syon House (Greater London)
An eighteenth-century house by the THAMES, opposite the Royal Botanic Gardens at KEW. Its name derives from a former monastery here, founded by Henry V in the early fifteenth century. Its official name was the Monastery of the Holy Saviour and St Brigid, to which 'of Zion' was added later for reasons that are not clear. This latter word then came to be regarded as the 'official' name of the religious house, and persisted after the monastery was suppressed in the sixteenth century. A document of 1564 records the name as *Istelworth Syon*, with the first word here being ISLEWORTH.

T

Tadcaster (North Yorkshire)

The name of this town on the River WHARFE northwest of YORK has the '-caster' element that declares the town to have arisen on the site of a former Roman settlement (Old English *ceaster*, 'Roman fort'). As it now stands, the name thus means 'Tata's Roman station'. The Roman name of the settlement here was *Calcaria*, 'lime works', from the Latin *calx*, genitive *calcis* (chalk, lime). The present name could well have developed from this, and have been something like 'Calcaster', and indeed this nearly happened, as is shown by the Venerable Bede's reference to Tadcaster. In his eighth-century *Ecclesiastical History of the English People* he refers to the settlement as *civitatem Calcariam, quae a gente Anglorum Kaelcacaestir appellatur*, 'the settlement of *Calcaria*, which is called by the English *Calcacaster*'. It is also rather surprising that the Roman name of the river (the Wharfe) has not survived as an element of the present name, as has happened in the case of many Roman camps.

Tadworth (Surrey)

A suburban district southwest of BANSTEAD whose name probably means 'Dæda's enclosure', although there is some uncertainty about the personal name. The name was recorded as *Theddewurth* in a document of 675, as *Thæddeuurde* in 1062, and as *Tadeorde* in the Domesday Book. The *Th-* of the second text quoted here represents the Old English letter (*Đ*) that was very similar to *D*, and it is possible that the Domesday Book clerk took the former letter as the latter. The second element of the name is the fairly common Old English *worth* (enclosure).

Taff (Wales)

This river, known in Welsh as the Taf, rises as the two rivers, Great Taff (Taf Fawr) and Little Taff (Taf Fechan), by the BRECON BEACONS, and then flows generally south (as two rivers until MERTHYR TYDFIL) to enter the SEVERN Estuary at CARDIFF (which see in this respect). The name is of British (Celtic) origin and derives from the same basic word *tamos* that lies behind the names of many other rivers, such as the THAMES; it probably means simply 'water', although some consider the sense to be 'dark one'. Its name was recorded as *Taf* in an early-twelfth-century text. *See also* TAFF-ELY.

Taff-Ely (Mid Glamorgan)

An administrative district, in the south of the county, that takes its name from two of the rivers that flow through it — the TAFF and the Ely (Elai, in Welsh). The latter's name probably derives from the same Celtic root that lies behind the name of the WYE and thus means 'carrier', 'transporting one'.

Tain (Highland)

This small town northeast of INVERGORDON probably has a pre-Celtic name referring to a stream here that flows into the DORNOCH Firth and meaning 'water', 'river'. The Gaelic *tain* means 'water', which seems to support this origin. The name was recorded as *Tene* in a document of 1226, and as *Thayn* in 1257.

Talgarth (Powys)

A small town southwest of HAY-ON-WYE with a Welsh name meaning 'end of the hill', from the Welsh *tâl* (end) and *garth* (hill, promontory). Talgarth lies at the foot of the BLACK MOUNTAINS.

Tallaght (Dublin)

A village southwest of DUBLIN whose name means 'plague burial-ground', said to refer to a large number of plague victims buried here in prehistoric times. The Irish version of the name is Tamhlacht.

Tallow (Waterford)
This small town southwest of LISMORE has the Irish name Tulach an Iarainn, with the present name representing the first word of this. The full meaning is 'little hill of the iron', the specific reference being to former iron workings here.

Talybont (Dyfed)
A village northeast of ABERYSTWYTH whose name means '(place at the) end of the bridge', from the Welsh *tâl* (end), *y* (the), and *pont* (bridge), here in its 'mutated' form as *bont*. The name thus corresponds to that of BRIDGEND, and is found in a number of other places in Wales, where there will be a bridge over a stream or river. This Talybont is on the River Leri.

Tamar (Cornwall/Devon)
The river that forms the boundary between Devon and Cornwall for most of its length, before flowing into PLYMOUTH Sound. Its name is of British (Celtic) origin, and as for the TAFF, THAMES, and other rivers, has a sense that may mean simply 'water' or else more specifically 'dark one'. The root element is the conjectural *tamos*. The Romans knew the Tamar as the *Tamarus*, and there appears to have been a Roman fort at some point on it called *Tamara*. Its site has not been established, but one suggestion is of a settlement lying buried beneath modern LAUNCESTON.

Tame (England)
Any of at least three rivers in central and northern England, with the best known being that which gave its name to TAMWORTH. The name itself falls into the extensive group of similar names, such as the THAMES and TAMAR (see above), that may mean 'river' or more specifically 'dark one' and are of Celtic, if not pre-Celtic, origin. The Roman name of the Tame that is a tributary of the TRENT seems to have been *Tamus*.

Tameside (Greater Manchester)
An administrative district in the east of the county that takes its name from the particular River TAME that rises here and flows south to join the Goyt near STOCKPORT, forming the MERSEY.

Tamworth (Staffordshire)
A town northeast of BIRMINGHAM that takes its name from the River TAME on which it is situated, with the latter half of the name deriving from the Old English *worthig*, which has the same meaning as *worth* (enclosure). Tamworth was referred to as *Tamouuorthi* in a document of 781.

Tandridge (Surrey)
This administrative district in the east of the county takes its name from the village of Tandridge here, whose own name may mean 'swine pasture ridge', from the Old English *denn* (woodland pasture) (especially one for pigs) and *hrycg* (ridge). The village lies close to Tandridge Hill, which could represent the 'ridge', or a section of it. The name was recorded as *Tenhric* in a document of about 960, and this probably represents a lost spelling *Dennhrycg*.

Taplow (Buckinghamshire)
A village in the THAMES valley west of SLOUGH whose name means 'Tæppa's mound', with the personal name followed by the Old English *hlāw* (mound, tumulus). The actual mound has been identified, and is a barrow in the churchyard in which burial treasure has been found. The name was recorded in the Domesday Book as *Thapeslav*.

Tara (Meath)
This ancient royal site southeast of NAVAN has a name that represents the Irish *teamhair* (elevated place, assembly hill). Recent researchers have, however, associated the name with that of the earth goddess Temair, whose name may mean 'dark one' (and may thus link up with the name of the THAMES and other similarly

named rivers). This is the Tara of the Irish poet Thomas Moore's famous line, 'The harp that once in Tara's halls', from his *Irish Melodies*.

Tarbat Ness (Highland)
The name of this headland on the south side of DORNOCH Firth is directly related to TARBERT and TARBET (see below), and all three represent the Gaelic *tairbeart* (isthmus, portage), as a site on a narrow promontory or neck of land between lochs where boats and their contents could be carried or dragged from one waterway to the next. The headland (Ness) is not itself the portage, but is named after it, and lies to the west of it.

Tarbert (Strathclyde, Western Isles)
Either of several places, including the village at the head of Loch Tarbert, at the north end of KINTYRE; and the village and port of HARRIS, on the isthmus between East and West Loch Tarbert, among other similarly named places. As mentioned for TARBAT NESS, the name indicates a narrow stretch of land over which a portage could be made. The Strathclyde Tarbert has an isthmus two miles wide, over which Magnus Barefoot of Norway is said to have been dragged in a galley in 1093. *Compare* TARBET.

Tarbet (Strathclyde)
A village and resort on the western shore of Loch LOMOND whose name corresponds in meaning (isthmus, portage) to TARBAT NESS and TARBERT. King Haakon of Norway dragged his ships from this Tarbet across the narrow strip of land to Arrochar in 1263 when laying waste the countryside here.

Tarporley (Cheshire)
A village northwest of NANTWICH whose name has been traditionally explained as meaning 'pear-tree clearing by a hill', from the Old English *torr* (hill, rocky peak) (as in the names of Devon hills, such as YES TOR) and *per-lēah* (pear-tree clearing). But recent

research has suggested that the name may actually mean 'peasants' clearing', with the first part of the name representing a conjectural Old English word *thorpere* (peasant), related to the Old Norse *thorpari* (villager; from *thorp*), followed by *lēah* (clearing) as mentioned. The Domesday Book recorded the name as *Torpelei*.

Taunton (Somerset)
The county town takes its name from the River Tone, on which it is situated, with the river's own name meaning 'roaring one', from a British (Celtic) root element *tan-*. Taunton is thus 'farm by the Tone', and the name was recorded as *Tantun* in 722. The town lies in the Vale of Taunton Deane, a tautologous name, as 'Deane' (Old English *denu*) already means 'valley'. However, it serves for the name of the administrative district of Taunton Deane in this southwestern region of the county.

Tavistock (Devon)
This market town on the western edge of DARTMOOR takes its name from the River Tavy, on which it is located. The river's name may mean 'dark one', as it belongs to the large family of similarly named rivers (including the THAMES, TAME, and TAFF) that have a common origin. Tavistock is thus 'secondary settlement by the Tavy', with the latter half of the name the Old English *stoc* (secondary settlement). Tavistock may have originated as a dependent settlement of Mary Tavy and Peter Tavy, now two villages northeast of the town on either side of the river, where they were originally known simply as 'Tavy'. (The distinguishing additions are from the dedications of their respective churches to St Mary and St Peter.) Tavistock was recorded as *Tauistoce* in a document of 981.

Tay (Central/Tayside)
Scotland's longest river, which flows generally eastwards across the country to enter the North Sea at the Firth of Tay, south of DUNDEE. The name may mean

either 'strong one' or 'silent one', from a conjectural British (Celtic) root name *Tausos*. Not far from its source it flows through, and gives its name to, Loch Tay. *Compare* TAYPORT; TAYSIDE.

Tayport (Fife)

This town with its small harbour stands opposite BROUGHTY FERRY on the southern side of the Firth of TAY, and takes its name from this river. However, it has had different names in the past, including Scotscraig (thirteenth century), South Ferry of Portincraig (sixteenth century), Port-on-Craig (seventeenth century), and South Ferry (nineteenth century). This last name distinguished the port from Broughty Ferry, on the northern side of the river. The 'Craig' of the earlier names is the rock or crag on which Tayport is situated. The present name dates from only 1888, by which time the Tay Bridge had been built (and rebuilt after its collapse), so that the importance of the place as a ferry port began to decline.

Tayside (Scotland)

An administrative region in central and eastern Scotland whose name dates officially only from 1975, with the alteration in local government administration and the abolition of the former counties. However, the name has long been given to the land by the River TAY, which flows through the region, although it is not as old as Strath Tay, the name of the Tay Valley above DUNKELD. More specifically, Tayside, before 1975, was the name of the local government planning region that comprised DUNDEE, the county of ANGUS, much of the county of PERTH, and part of FIFE, in other words the 'business' end of the river.

Teddington (Greater London)

The name of this district of RICHMOND, on the left bank of the THAMES, is memorable from Kipling's line about 'Tide-end-town, which is Teddington', in his poem about the Thames entitled *The River's Tale*.

Unfortunately, this is not the true origin of the name, although it *is* certainly true that the Thames is tidal only as far as Teddington. The name actually means 'farm of Tudda's people', and hence is a name like that of PADDINGTON. It was recorded as *Tudintun* in a document of 969.

Tees (Cumbria/Durham/Cleveland)

A river in northern England that rises in the northern PENNINES and enters the North Sea south of HARTLEPOOL. Its name is probably of Celtic origin related to modern Welsh *tes* (heat), and therefore means (figuratively) 'boiling one', 'seething one' with reference to the many waterfalls and rapids along the course of the river, and to its strong current. *Compare* TEESDALE; TEESPORT; TEESSIDE.

Teesdale (Durham)

This administrative district, in the southwestern quarter of the county, takes its name from the valley of the TEES here that crosses it, with the valley name dating back at least eight hundred years; it was recorded as *Tesedale* in about 1130.

Teesport (Cleveland)

This port and oil refinery near the mouth of the TEES has an obvious name, if a recent one. The port, and therefore the name, arose only in the first half of the twentieth century.

Teesside (Cleveland)

A self-descriptive name for the industrial conurbation lying either side of the TEES estuary, embracing STOCKTON-ON-TEES, MIDDLESBROUGH, BILLINGHAM, and REDCAR, and forming a county borough in the North Riding of YORKSHIRE from 1969 to 1974. The name itself obviously dates back much earlier than this.

Teignmouth (Devon)

This resort south of DAWLISH takes its name from the River Teign, at whose mouth it is situated, with the river's own name of British (Celtic) origin, and probably meaning simply 'river'. The name was recorded as *Tengemutha* in a document of 1044, while the river itself was *Teng* in a text of the early eighth century. The administrative district of Teignbridge in this part of the county also takes its name from the river, and alludes to the many bridges over it, especially at places similarly named after it, such as Bishopsteignton, Kingsteignton, and Drewsteignton, as well as Teignmouth itself.

Telford (Shropshire)

This New Town, designated in 1963 and lying northwest of WOLVERHAMPTON, is one of the few New Towns in Britain to have a new name. It derives from that of the Scottish civil engineer, Thomas Telford (1757–1834), who was appointed surveyor of Shropshire in 1786 and who was responsible for many famous engineering projects, including the Ellesmere Canal (*see* ELLESMERE PORT), and, outside the county, the CALEDONIAN CANAL and the suspension bridge at MENAI BRIDGE. His surname happens to provide a genuine-seeming place-name, suggesting a ford over a stream or river, although it is almost certainly a name of Norman origin, meaning 'iron-cutter' (appropriately enough for Telford), from the French *taille-fer*. Telford himself is on record as saying, 'When I was ignorant of Latin, I did not suspect that Telfor, my true name, might be translated "I bear arms" (*tela fero*), and, thinking it unmeaning, adopted Telford'.

Templecombe (Somerset)

A village south of WINCANTON whose name means 'narrow valley held by the Knights Templar', the reference being to the former military religious order, suppressed in the fourteenth century, that held large estates in many countries, including Britain. The second element of the name is the Old English *cumb* (narrow valley), found in many names in the West

of England. Templecombe was simply *Come* in the Domesday Book, but *Cumbe Templer* in 1291. It is known that the settlement here came to the Templars before 1185. Villages with similar 'temple' names elsewhere are likely to have been also held by the Knights Templar, or by the Knights Hospitallers who succeeded them.

Templemore (Tipperary)

A market town north of THURLES whose name, common elsewhere in Ireland, means simply 'big church', from the Irish *teampall* (adopted from Latin *templum*), usually applied to a post-twelfth-century church, and *mór* (big, great). In the case of this town, the name also ties in with that of the Knights Templar (*see* TEMPLECOMBE), who had their castle and monastery on the site that is now the Town Park, where the remains of their original 'big church' can be seen. The Irish name of the town is An Teampall Mór, 'the big church'.

Tempo (Fermanagh)

A village northeast of ENNISKILLEN whose name represents the central element of the Irish name, An tIompú Deiseal. This means 'the right-hand turn', and may refer to some former pagan ritual involving a turn made clockwise towards the sun.

Tenbury Wells (Hereford and Worcester)

This small town northeast of LEOMINSTER takes its basic name, Tenbury, from the River Teme, on which it stands. The river's own name perhaps means 'dark one', as it is almost certainly in the same group as the THAMES, TAMAR, TAFF, and others, which may have this sense. The second element of the first word is the Old English *burg* (fortified place), with this said to refer to the mound known as Castle Tump, just over the river in Shropshire. The second word of the name refers to the saline springs that were discovered here in about 1840, and that led to the development of the town as a spa. The name was recorded as

Temedebyrig in a document of the eleventh century.

Tenby (Dyfed)

A resort on CARMARTHEN Bay east of PEMBROKE whose name is identical to that of DENBIGH, although in a spelling apparently influenced by the Scandinavians. The elements behind the name are the same: Welsh *din* (fort) and *bych* (little) (modern *dinas* and *bychan*). The 'little fortress' stood on Castle Hill, the rocky headland where the ruins of the thirteenth-century Tenby Castle stand today. The Welsh name of Tenby is Dinbych-y-pysgod, 'little fort by the fish'; the additional word is an unusual way of distinguishing this fortress, i.e. by the sea and its fish.

Tendring (Essex)

An administrative district in the east of the county that takes its name from that of the former hundred here, preserved also in the name of the village of Tendring, northwest of CLACTON. The name may be a folk name in origin, and refer to the 'dwellers by the beacon', from an Old English conjectural element that is related to modern 'tinder'. The Domesday Book recorded the name as *Tendringa*.

Tenterden (Kent)

A town southwest of ASHFORD whose name means 'swine pasture for the Thanet dwellers', referring to the area of woodland here that must have been granted to a community of people from the Isle of THANET, some distance east of Tenterden. The final element here is the Old English *denn* (woodland pasture; especially one for pigs), found in many names in Kent and East Sussex, such as Benenden, Chillenden, Cowden, and Pinden. In this part of the country, therefore, a name ending in 'den' is likely to represent this word rather than the more common *denu* (valley) found widely elsewhere. The *-er-* of the name represents the Old English *ware* (dwellers), just as it does in CANTERBURY

(also in Kent). A document of 1179 has the name as *Tentwardene*.

Test (Hampshire)

This river, which flows into SOUTHAMPTON Water, has a name that may derive from a British (Celtic) conjectural root element *trest-* meaning 'strong one', 'runner', related to the modern Welsh *treio* (to ebb). The reference would be to the speed of the current. The name was recorded as *Terstan* in a document dated 877.

Tetbury (Gloucestershire)

A small town northwest of MALMESBURY whose name means 'Tetta's manor'. It is known that Tetta was a sister of King Ine of WESSEX, and an abbess of WIMBORNE. A record of the name as *Tettan monasterium* in a document of 681 reveals that there must have been a monastery at Tetbury. The second element of the name is the Old English *burg* (fortified place, manor).

Teviot (Borders)

The Scottish river, which joins the TWEED at KELSO, almost certainly has a name that brackets it with the TAFF, TAMAR, THAMES, and others, and thus means either 'dark one' or simply 'river'. A document of about 700 gives its name as *Tesgeta*, with the *s* here a miscopying for an *f* (the two letters looked similar when handwritten).

Tewkesbury (Gloucestershire)

A town at the confluence of the SEVERN and AVON, northwest of CHELTENHAM. Its name means 'Tēodec's fort', with the personal name followed by the Old English *burg* (fortified place). The name was recorded as *Teodechesberie* in the Domesday Book.

Thame (Oxfordshire)

A town southwest of AYLESBURY that takes its name from the river on which it stands, with the river's own name being directly related to that of the TAME, the TAMAR, and the THAMES, and so of Celtic origin and probably meaning simply 'river' or 'dark one'. The town's name was recorded as *Tamu* in the second half of the seventh century. The *h* in the name is not pronounced (as in 'Thames').

Thames (England)

England's best known river rises in the COTSWOLD HILLS near CIRENCESTER and flows east, through the country's capital, to its estuary on the east coast. Its name derives from a conjectural British (Celtic) root element *teme-*, meaning either simply 'river', or else more specifically 'dark one'. Experts are still disputing (and studying) the source of this and related names, such as TAFF, TAMAR, TEVIOT, and many others. Those who favour the 'dark' interpretation point to words in different ancient languages that have this sense, such as the Sanskrit *tamisra* (dark), Latin *tenebrae* (darkness, shadows), Irish *teimhe* (darkness), Russian *tëmnyy* (dark), and so on. The Roman name of the Thames was *Tamesa* or *Tamesis*. The very frequency of the name in its different variants suggests that a meaning 'river' is more likely. *Compare* THAMES DITTON; THAMESDOWN; THAMESMEAD.

Thames Ditton (Surrey)

This urban area by the THAMES west of SURBITON has a basic name, Ditton, that means 'village by a ditch', from the Old English *dīc* (ditch, dike) and *tūn* (farm, village), with the ditch here being one that was excavated to drain the land and channel the standing water into the Thames. The first word of the name serves to differentiate this Ditton from Long Ditton, immediately east of it. The name was recorded as *Ditune* in the Domesday Book, and as *Temes Ditton* in a document of 1235.

Thamesdown (Wiltshire)

An administrative district in the northeast of the county, centred on SWINDON ('swine down'), so that the second half of the name echoes this as well as referring to the Wiltshire Downs, which form the southern boundary of the district. The first half of the name refers to the THAMES, which forms its northern boundary.

Thamesmead (Greater London)

This large residential development on the southeast edge of ERITH Marshes, along the southern bank of the THAMES, has a modern name, referring to the river and the former marshland here, now reclaimed and redesignated as a 'mead'. The development is in effect a new town, and the work here was inaugurated only in 1967.

Thanet, Isle of (Kent)

The easternmost peninsula of Kent, with the towns of MARGATE, RAMSGATE, and BROADSTAIRS. Thanet is now the name of the corresponding administrative district here. The name is an ancient one, known to the Romans (at a time when it actually was an island) as *Tanatis* or *Tanatus*. The name is of British (Celtic) origin from a conjectural root element *tan-* meaning 'bright', 'fire', related to the modern Welsh *tân* (fire). If 'fire' is the sense, the reference may have been to a beacon on the island. If 'bright', the reference may have been to the island's exposed location, with the North Sea on one side and the English Channel on the other; the western coast of the island would have been separated from the mainland by the Wantsum Channel. If 'bright' is the preferred sense, then the name of Thanet duplicates the meaning of SHEERNESS, the headland further west along the north Kent coast.

Thatcham (Berkshire)

A suburb of NEWBURY whose name is similar to that of THAXTED. It means 'riverside meadow where thatch is obtained', from the Old English *thæc* (thatch) and *hamm* (riverside land). Thatcham is by the River KENNET. The name was recorded as *Thæcham* in a document of the mid-tenth century.

Thaxted (Essex)
A small town southeast of SAFFRON
WALDEN whose name, similar to that of
THATCHAM, means 'place where thatch is
obtained', from the Old English *thæc*
(thatch) and *stede* (place, locality). The
name was recorded as *Tachesteda* in the
Domesday Book.

Thetford (Norfolk)
A town on the confluence of the rivers Thet
and the Little OUSE whose name means
'people's ford', from the Old English *thēod*
(people, tribe) and *ford* (ford). The
reference was probably to a public ford or
an important one, that many people used.
The ford would probably have been over
the Little Ouse, rather than the Thet,
perhaps just below the present Bridge
Street, where the river divides into two and
has narrower channels. The Thet takes its
name from Thetford. The town's name was
recorded as *Theodford* in a document of
870, and as *Tedfort* in the Domesday Book
(with the Normans avoiding the un-French
Th-).

Thirlmere (Cumbria)
A lake southeast of KESWICK, now used as
a reservoir, whose name has not been
traced in any early records; it may mean
'hollow lake', from the Old English *thyrel*
(hole, opening, something pierced) (related
to modern 'thrill' and 'nostril'), followed
by *mere* (lake). The 'hollow' may have been
the narrow strip of water that was formerly
the 'waist' of the lake, before the water
level rose following damming of the lake to
form a reservoir. There was a wooden
bridge over this central part of the lake as
recently as the nineteenth century. The
earliest record of the name to date is one of
1574, as *Thyrlemere*.

Thirsk (North Yorkshire)
A town southeast of NORTHALLERTON
whose name represents the conjectural Old
Norse *thresk* (fen, lake; modern Swedish
träsk), with this recorded in the Domesday
Book as *Tresch*. Thirsk is on low-lying land

in the Vale of Mowbray on the Cod Beck, a
tributary of the SWALE.

Thornaby-on-Tees (Cleveland)
An urban area on the right bank of the
TEES, in the STOCKTON-ON-TEES district
of the county. 'Thornaby' means
'Thormōth's village', with the
Scandinavian personal name followed by
the Old Norse *bý* (village). Before
incorporation as a borough in 1892,
Thornaby was officially known as South
Stockton, from its location opposite
Stockton-on-Tees on the north side of the
river. But the present name is an old one,
and was recorded in the Domesday Book as
Tormozbi. *Compare* THURMASTON.

Thorne (South Yorkshire)
A town northeast of DONCASTER with a
straightforward name meaning '(place by a)
thorn bush', meaning either a place by a
single prominent bush, or one by many
such bushes. The name was recorded as
Torne in the Domesday Book. The
commonness of the Old English *thorn* in
place-names is partly due to its widespread
use in hedges or enclosures. *Compare*
THORNEY ISLAND; THORNHILL;
THORNTON HEATH.

Thorney Island (West Sussex)
An 'island' in CHICHESTER Harbour,
joined to the mainland by two narrow
strips of land and a road bridge. 'Thorney'
in effect makes the second word
redundant, as it means 'island overgrown
by thorn bushes', from the Old English
thorn (thorn bush) and *ēg* (island). But the
name is properly that of the village of West
Thorney here, from which it passed to the
present Thorney Island. The village's
name was recorded as *Tornei* in the
Domesday Book, with 'West' added later
to distinguish it from Thorney Farm at
East Wittering, across the entrance to
Chichester Harbour.

Thornhill (Dumfries and Galloway)
There seems little reason to doubt that the

name of this small town northwest of DUMFRIES has the same meaning as any place of the name in England, which is 'hill covered with thorn bushes'.

Thornton Heath (Greater London)
A district of CROYDON whose name means 'heath by (a place called) Thornton', with the latter name probably meaning 'thorn-tree farm' (Old English *thorn* and *tūn*), or else 'thorn-tree hill' (*thorn* and *dūn*). Unfortunately no early forms of the name have been found to establish the exact origin with any certainty. The earliest record of the name is one of 1511, giving the place as *Thorneton Hethe*. The Grangewood Recreation Ground to the east of Grange Road (the A212) can be regarded as a remnant of the common land that was part of the original heath.

Thorpe-le-Soken (Essex)
The Old Norse *thorp* and the less common Old English *throp* usually have the sense 'outlying village', 'secondary settlement', with most such names in the Danelaw, that is, in northern, central, or eastern England. For purposes of distinction, many Thorpes add a further word, as for this village north of CLACTON. 'Soken' is a form of 'Soke' (Old English *sōcn*), as for the formerly familiar Soke of PETERBOROUGH (*see* RUTLAND for a further consideration of the word). Thorpe-le-Soken was thus an 'outlying village in an area of special jurisdiction', with the addition also found in nearby Kirby-le-Soken, east of the village. The name was recorded as simply *Torp* in a document of 1181.

Thorpeness (Suffolk)
This coastal resort north of ALDEBURGH takes its name from the nearby headland of Thorpe Ness, but was originally known simply as Thorpe to the nineteenth century, thus giving its name to the headland. The basic meaning of the name is 'outlying village', well illustrated here by the still apparent isolation of the place. Thorpeness developed as a resort only in the present century, with its starting point in the artificial lake known as The Meare, immediately west of the village. This was created only in 1910.

Three Bridges (West Sussex)
A district of CRAWLEY that arose as a residential development from the middle of the nineteenth century, after the railway line to BRIGHTON was opened here in 1841. Earlier records of the name can be found in a document of 1534, which referred to *two bridges called the Three bridges leading from Charlewood to Crawley* (although the present Three Bridges is east of Crawley, not northwest of it, as this text implies). The bridges concerned would have been over the River Mole (*see* MOLE VALLEY), which rises at Crawley.

Thruxton (Hampshire)
This village west of ANDOVER, with its nearby motor-racing circuit, has a name that means 'Thurkil's farm', with the personal name apparently a Scandinavian one, found also for the Yorkshire village of Thirkleby, near THIRSK. The name of Thruxton was recorded as *Turkilleston* in a document of 1167.

Thundersley (Essex)
A town east of BASILDON whose name means 'Thunor's clearing', meaning that the clearing was sacred to the pagan god Thunor, otherwise Thor (who gave his name to Thursday). The second element of the name is the Old English *lēah* (clearing). The name was recorded in the Domesday book as *Thunreslea*. *Compare* WEDNESBURY.

Thurles (Tipperary)
A market town north of CASHEL whose name is a corruption of its Irish name, Durlas, itself representing the Irish *dur* (hard) and *lios* (fort), in other words, a stronghold. Thurles had a strategic importance in medieval times, when it was surrounded by several castles.

Thurmaston (Leicestershire)
A suburb of LEICESTER whose name means 'Thormōth's farm', with this same personal name also apparent in the name of THORNABY-ON-TEES. The name was recorded in the Domesday Book as *Turmodestone*.

Thurrock (Essex)
An administrative district in the southwest of the county. It has a name derived from Thurrock Marshes here, also represented in the villages of Little Thurrock and West Thurrock. For the origin of the name *see* GRAYS.

Thurso (Highland)
A town and port northwest of WICK at the mouth of the River Thurso, from which it takes its name. The Gaelic form of the name is *Inbhir Thorsa* ('Inverthurso'), indicating its location, as for similar 'Inver-' names of places at river-mouths, such as INVERNESS. The river's own name probably means 'bull river', from a conjectural Celtic root element *tarvo-* (bull) (related to Greek *tauros* and Latin *taurus*) and Old Norse *á* (river). The name was recorded as *Thorsa* in a document of 1152. A 'bull river' is one that 'roars' and is 'headstrong'.

Tideswell (Derbyshire)
A small town east of BUXTON whose name means 'Tīdi's stream', with the personal name followed by the Old English *wella* (stream, well). The name was recorded as *Tidesueela* in the Domesday Book, and is still pronounced locally as 'Tiddzle' by some people.

Tidworth (Wiltshire/Hampshire)
This military town on the eastern edge of SALISBURY Plain is properly divided into North Tidworth, in Wiltshire, on the western side of the River Bourne, and South Tidworth, in Hampshire, on the eastern side. The basic name means 'Tuda's enclosure', with the personal name followed by the Old English *worth*

(enclosure). South Tidworth was recorded as *Tudanwyrth* in a document of 975, and as *Todeorde* in the Domesday Book, in which North Tidworth appears as *Todeworde*. A common nineteenth-century spelling of the name, especially of South Tidworth, was 'Tedworth', although the one-inch Ordnance Survey map of 1817 has both villages with the 'i' spelling as now. The 'e' spelling reflects the current local pronunciation of the name (it is surprising, however, to find this spelling entered in Eilert Ekwall's *Concise Oxford Dictionary of English Place-names*, as recently as the book's fourth edition of 1960).

Tighnabruaich (Strathclyde)
This village and resort on the western shore of the KYLES OF BUTE has a Gaelic name that translates as 'house on the bank' (*taigh na bruaich*), describing the location of the solitary house that formerly stood here over the water.

Tilbury (Essex)
An industrial town and passenger port on the THAMES east of LONDON. Its name means 'Tila's fortified place', the final element being the Old English *burg* (fort). The name was recorded in the Domesday Book as *Tilaburg*.

Tillicoultry (Central)
A town northeast of ALLOA whose name represents the Gaelic *tulach cùl tìr*, 'hillock of the back land', describing its location and its topography, at the foot of the main ridge of the OCHILL HILLS.

Timoleague (Cork)
This village, with its extensive monastic ruins east of CLONAKILTY, has a name that means 'St Molaga's house', representing the Irish name with this same meaning, Tigh Molaige. The monastery here was founded in the sixth century by St Molaga of Templemolaga. 'House', Irish *teach*, should be understood here as 'monastic house'.

Timperley (Greater Manchester)
A district of ALTRINCHAM whose
name probably means 'timber wood',
'wood where timber is obtained', from
the Old English *timber* (timber) and
lēah (wood, clearing). The name was
recorded as now in a thirteenth-century
document.

Tintagel (Cornwall)
A village northwest of CAMELFORD,
famous for Tintagel Castle, the legendary
stronghold of King Arthur. Its name
probably derives from the two conjectural
Cornish words *dyn* (fort) and *tagell* (throat,
constriction), the former being the historic
ruins of the castle on the peninsula known
as Tintagel Island, and the latter the rocky
gorge that separates it from the mainland,
where there are other ancient remains. The
name was recorded as *Tintaieol* in a
document of 1205. *Compare* the name of
TENBY, where Welsh *din* (fort) has
similarly produced *Ten-* (*see also* TINTERN
ABBEY).

Tintern Abbey (Gwent)
This ruined medieval abbey by the
River WYE north of CHEPSTOW has a
name that means 'king's fortress', from
Celtic words related to the modern Welsh
dinas (fort, city) and *teyrn* (monarch,
sovereign). The Welsh name of Tintern,
with the same meaning, is Tyndyrn. The
name was recorded as both *Dindyrn* and
Tindyrn in a document of the mid-
twelfth century, and the *din* of the original
has become *Tin-*, as happened for
TINTAGEL.

Tipperary (Tipperary)
The well-known name of this town, and its
county in central southern Ireland, derives
from its Irish name, Tiobraid Árann, 'well
of (the River) Ara', the latter being the
river on which the town stands. The river's
name is that of the territory here, and
means 'ridged place', as for the ARAN
Islands. The original well was in Main
Street, but has now been covered over.

Tipton (West Midlands)
A district of WEST BROMWICH whose name
means 'Tibba's farm', it was recorded in
the Domesday Book as *Tibintone*. The
personal name is followed by the Old
English *tūn* (farm).

Tiptree (Essex)
A town southwest of COLCHESTER whose
name means 'Tippa's tree', so matching
similar names where a personal name is
followed by the Old English *trēow* (tree),
such as BRAINTREE, COVENTRY, and
OSWESTRY. The 'tree' could have been a
prominent actual tree or a man-made cross
or crucifix. Tiptree was recorded as
Typpetre in a document of about 1225.

Tiree (Strathclyde)
An island in the Inner HEBRIDES,
southwest of COLL, whose name was
recorded in the mid-ninth century as *Tir
Iath*. This means 'land of Ith', a person
who has not been identified. The first part
of the name thus represents the Gaelic *tir*
(land).

Tiverton (Devon)
A market and manufacturing town on the
River EXE north of EXETER whose name
means 'farm at the double ford', referring
to the location of the town at the confluence
of the Exe and its tributary, the Loman. A
'double ford' is either one with two tracks
or two fords close together over different
rivers. The latter is probably the sense
here. Places named TWYFORD also denote
a 'double ford' of one kind or the other.
Tiverton was recorded as *Twyfyrede* in a
document of about 885, but in the
Domesday Book is rather less recognisable
as *Tovretone*. For an identical name to
Tiverton *see* TWERTON.

Tobermory (Strathclyde)
This resort and chief town of the island of
MULL has a name that is the Gaelic for 'St
Mary's well', from *tiobar* (well) (*compare*
TIPPERARY) and *Moire* (Mary), that is, the
Virgin Mary. The well of the name is

located by the ruins of the old chapel to the west of the modern town of Tobermory, which was founded in the eighteenth century by the British Fisheries Society. A document of 1540 refers to Tobermory as *Tibbermore*.

Todmorden (West Yorkshire)
A town on the River CALDER northeast of ROCHDALE whose name probably means 'Totta's boundary valley', with the personal name followed by a word that is a compound of the Old English *gemǣre* (boundary) and *denu* (valley). Names formed from a personal name prefixed to a compound like this are rare. The 'boundary valley' of the name is probably the one that runs to the northwest of the town, with the boundary here being the county one between West Yorkshire and Lancashire. The name was recorded as *Tottemerden* in a document of 1246.

Tolpuddle (Dorset)
This village west of BERE REGIS is famous for its 'Tolpuddle Martyrs', the agricultural workers deported to Australia in 1834 for opposing a decrease in their wages. Its name means 'Tola's manor on the Puddle', the latter being the river also known as the Piddle, on which the village is situated (*compare* PIDDLETRENTHIDE and PUDDLETOWN in this respect). Tola was the widow of Urc, the royal bodyguard or *huscarl*, of Edward the Confessor; between 1058 and 1066 she got Edward's permission to give her lands to Abbotsbury Abbey, northwest of WEYMOUTH. Tolpuddle belonged to Abbotsbury at the time of the Domesday Book survey, and it is entered in that record as simply *Pidele*. The present name is first recorded in a document of 1210, as *Tollepidele*.

Tomintoul (Grampian)
A village and resort southeast of GRANTOWN-ON-SPEY whose name represents the Gaelic *tom an t'sabhail*, 'knoll of the little barn', describing its location. The word *tom*, meaning 'little

hill', 'knoll', is found in a number of place-names in the central Highlands.

Tonbridge (Kent)
The name of this industrial and residential town on the MEDWAY means 'village bridge', referring to a bridge that led to the original village here from some other part of the manor. The name was recorded as *Tonebrige* in the Domesday Book, and the two Old English words that compose the name are *tūn* (farm, village) and *brycg* (bridge). *Compare* TUNBRIDGE WELLS.

Tonypandy (Mid Glamorgan)
A town in the RHONDDA Valley southeast of Rhondda. It has a Welsh name meaning 'grassland of the fulling mill', from *ton* (grassland), *y* (the), and *pandy* (fulling mill). Unlike other towns in the Rhondda Valley, Tonypandy had its origins in the woollen industry, not in coal.

Tooting (Greater London)
A district of WANDSWORTH whose name means '(place of) Tōta's people'. In medieval times there were two manors here, Upper Tooting (or Tooting Bec, held by the abbey of Bec-Hellouin in Normandy), and Lower Tooting (or Tooting Graveney, held by the Gravenel family in the twelfth century). The basic name was recorded as *Totinge* in a document of 675.

Torbay (Devon)
An administrative district that takes its name from the urban area of Torbay, which includes the towns of TORQUAY, PAIGNTON, and BRIXHAM and which gets its own name from Tor Bay, on which it is situated. The bay's name derives from the hill called Torre that gave its name to Torquay.

Torcross (Devon)
A coastal village north of START POINT that seems to get its name from a hill or 'tor' near here, with the first half of the name thus derived from the Old English

torr (rock, rocky peak), with 'cross' presumably referring to a cross or crossing here.

Torfaen (Gwent)

An administrative district in the centre of the county that takes its name from a former region here, with the Welsh words translating as 'stone gap', from *tor* (gap, break) and *maen* (stone).

Torpoint (Cornwall)

A town beside the TAMAR estuary (where it is known as the Hamoaze) that takes its name from the peninsula on which it is situated, which is thus a 'hill headland'. *Compare* TORQUAY.

Torquay (Devon)

This well-known coastal resort is the chief town of TORBAY district. Its name means 'Torre quay', 'quay at (the place called) Torre'. The quay here was built by monks from Torre Abbey nearby, with the abbey itself named after the hill (Old English *torr*) at whose foot it lay. It was founded at the end of the twelfth century in the parish of Tormoham ('Mohun's manor by the hill'), and the present name of Torquay perhaps owes as much to this name (recorded itself in the Domesday Book as *Torre*) as it does to that of Torre Abbey. Torquay itself is first recorded only in 1591, as *Torrekay*.

Torridge (Devon)

An administrative district in the west of the county that takes its name from the River Torridge that flows through it, with its own name meaning 'rough one', from a Celtic word related to the modern Welsh *terig* (rough). *Compare* TORRINGTON.

Torrington (Devon)

This town, on a hill above the River TORRIDGE southeast of BIDEFORD, takes its name from this river and so means 'farm by the Torridge'. The name was recorded as *Torintona* in the Domesday Book. Officially the town is known as Great Torrington, as distinct from the nearby villages of Black Torrington and Little Torrington.

Tory Island (Donegal)

An island off northwest Ireland whose name means 'place of towers', from the Irish *tor* (tower). The 'towers' are the high cliffs and isolated rocky hills ('tors') in many parts of the island, whose Irish name is Toraigh.

Totnes (Devon)

A town at the head of the tidal estuary of the River Dart (*see* DARTFORD), west of TORQUAY. Its name means 'Totta's headland', referring to the promontory, just north of Butterwalk, on which the ruins of the twelfth-century castle stand. The name was recorded as *Totanæs* in a document of about 1000, and the second element of the name is the Old English *næss* (headland).

Tottenham (Greater London)

A district of HARINGEY whose name means 'Totta's village', with the personal name followed by the Old English *hām* (homestead, village). The name appeared in the Domesday Book as *Toteham*. LONDON's Tottenham Court Road is not named after this Tottenham; its name is actually a corruption of 'Tottenhale', meaning 'Totta's corner of land' (Old English *healh*), with this Totta almost certainly a different person. The direct source of the street name is Tottenham Manor, formerly near the present site of EUSTON Station, to which the road led.

Totton (Hampshire)

This town at the head of the TEST estuary west of SOUTHAMPTON had its name recorded in the Domesday Book as *Totintone*, so that it is really 'Tottington'. This means 'farm of Tota's people'. The central -*ing*- of the name, representing the Old English -*ingas* (people of), has now disappeared from the name.

Towcester (Northamptonshire)
This small town southwest of
NORTHAMPTON takes its name from the
River Tove on which it stands, with its own
name meaning 'slow one', from a
conjectural Old English word *tōf* (slow).
The latter half of the town's name
represents the Old English *ceaster*, 'Roman
fort', and the Roman town here stood on
WATLING STREET (now the A5 through
Towcester). The name of the Roman
settlement was *Lactodurum*, which may
mean literally 'milk fort', from a British
(Celtic) conjectural root element *lacto-*
(milk), related to the modern Welsh *llaeth*,
Latin *lac*, genitive *lactis*, and the English
words derived from this. (The latter half of
the name is the *duro-* element, meaning
'fort', 'walled town', usually found as the
first element of a Roman name, such as
Durobrivae for ROCHESTER.) It seems
likely that the 'milk' of this name may
represent an early name of the River Tove,
referring to its milky water. Towcester was
recorded as *Tofeceaster* in a document of
921, and in the Domesday Book was
Tovecestre.

Tower Hamlets (Greater London)
A borough north of the THAMES
immediately east of the City of LONDON.
Its name more or less means what it says,
and refers to the many former hamlets here
that adjoined the Tower of London. The
name dates back to the sixteenth century,
and there were at one time over twenty
such hamlets, all under the jurisdiction of
the Tower. They have since gradually
merged and unified. The present single
borough was formed in 1964 when the
Metropolitan Boroughs of BETHNAL
GREEN, POPLAR, and STEPNEY were
amalgamated.

Tow Law (Durham)
A town northwest of BISHOP AUCKLAND
whose name means 'lookout mound', from
the Old English conjectural *tōt* (lookout)
and *hlāw* (mound). Tow Law stands on
rising land east of WOLSINGHAM Moor. Its

name was recorded as *Tollawe* in a
document of 1423.

Towy (Wales)
A river, called the Tywi in Welsh, that
rises on the borders of Dyfed and Powys
and then flows generally south and west
to enter the sea with the TAFF at
CARMARTHEN Bay. Its name may mean
'rocky one', from a Celtic root element *tob-*
or *teb-*. The Romans knew it as *Tovius*.

Toxteth (Merseyside)
This district of LIVERPOOL has a
Scandinavian name meaning 'Toki's
landing-place', with the personal name
followed by the Old Norse *stǫth* (landing-
place, jetty), related to the Old English
stæth in the sense that occurs in names such
as STAITHES and STAFFORD. At Toxteth,
to the south of the city centre, the landing-
place was probably on the bank of the
MERSEY, perhaps at or near the point
where Toxteth Docks are located. The
Domesday Book recorded the name as
Stochestede, with an unnecessary (especially
for the Normans) *St-*. *Compare* the name of
CROXTETH, to the east of the city centre.

Tralee (Kerry)
The main town of the county at the head of
Tralee Bay in southwest Ireland, has a
name that means 'strand of the Lee',
referring to the river of this name that runs
into the sea just south of the town. The
Irish name is thus Trá Lí, with the first
word of this the Irish *traigh* (strand, beach,
shore). The 'strand' here is probably the
seashore by the river-mouth.

Tramore (Waterford)
A coastal resort south of WATERFORD
whose name aptly describes its three-mile
strand, as it means 'big strand', from the
Irish *traigh* (as for TRALEE) and *mór* (big).
Its Irish name is Trá Mhór.

Tranmere (Merseyside)
A district of BIRKENHEAD whose name is
Scandinavian and means 'cranes'

sandbank', from the Old Norse *trani* (crane) and *melr* (sandbank). Cranes must have frequented the former sands here by the MERSEY at one time. The name was recorded as *Tranemor* in a document of 1220.

Trawsfynydd (Gwynedd)
A village on the eastern side of the lake of the same name, southeast of MAENTWROG. Its name means 'cross mountain', even (more closely) 'transmontane', from the Welsh *traws* (cross, trans-) and *mynydd* (mountain). The somewhat isolated location of the village can be regarded as 'across the mountain' from almost any direction. The lake is a man-made reservoir created in 1926 to supply hydroelectric power to the Maentwrog Power Station. *Compare* The TROSSACHS.

Trearddur Bay (Gwynedd)
A small resort on the coast of HOLY ISLAND, ANGLESEY, whose basic name means 'ploughmen's village', from the Welsh *tref* (homestead, village) and *arddwr* (ploughman). No doubt ploughmen lived or gathered here at one time. The bay here took its name from the village, which then took it back, partly to denote its seaside location.

Tredegar (Gwent)
This town north of CARDIFF arose only in the nineteenth century, taking its name from Baron Tredegar, the landowner here, who took his title from the family seat at Tredegar near NEWPORT; its original meaning is 'farm of Tegyr'. For a further transfer of the name *see* NEW TREDEGAR.

Trefriw (Gwynedd)
The village northwest of LLANRWST, and the spa of Trefriw Wells north of it, have a Welsh name that means 'farm on the hill', from *tref* (farm) and *rhiw* (hill). The name is descriptive of the steep hill in the village, by which the original farm was built. A record of 1254 has the name as *Treffruu*.

Tregaron (Dyfed)
A small town northeast of LAMPETER whose name means 'village of Caron', with the Welsh *tref* (village) followed by the name of the saint to whom the parish church is dedicated. The same man lies behind the name of Llangarron, the village northwest of MONMOUTH.

Tremadoc Bay (Gwynedd)
A large bay on the south side of the LLEYN PENINSULA that takes its name from the village of Tremadoc, a short distance inland on the northern shore, north of PORTHMADOG. The name, more correctly spelt Tremadog, derives from the same man who gave his name to Porthmadog, William Madocks. He developed Tremadoc soon after creating the other village. The name thus means 'village of Madocks', with the Welsh *tref* (village) followed by the surname.

Trent (England)
This major river rises in Staffordshire and flows through many important towns and cities, including STOKE-ON-TRENT, BURTON-UPON-TRENT, NOTTINGHAM, and NEWARK-ON-TRENT, before joining the OUSE to form the HUMBER. Its name means 'trespasser', that is, it is a river that is liable to flooding. The name is of British (Celtic) origin, from a root element *sento-* (path) represented by the modern Welsh *hynt* (way), Latin *semita* (footpath), and French *sentier* (path). The Roman name for the Trent was *Trisantona*, also with this meaning, with the initial *Tri-* the British 'intensive' prefix. (This is the same Roman name as for the River ARUN, which was originally the Tarrant. *See also* ARUNDEL.) The earliest record of the name is this Roman one, found in the *Annals* of Tacitus in the second century AD. The present spelling of the name is a 'worn-down' version of the original. The famous Council of Trent has nothing to do with this river: the council (of the Roman Catholic Church) met in the mid-sixteenth century at Trento (Roman name *Tridentum*,

German name Trent), the city in northern Italy. *See also* PIDDLETRENTHIDE for another river of this name.

Treorchy (Mid Glamorgan)
A town in the RHONDDA Valley, northwest of PONTYPRIDD. Its name means 'village on the Orci', the latter being the stream, a tributary of the Rhondda, on which it is situated. The stream's own name is of uncertain origin. The Welsh spelling of the town's name is Treorci.

Tresco (Isles of Scilly)
The second largest of the Scilly Isles, whose name means 'elder-tree farm', from the Cornish *tre* (farm) and *scawen* (elder tree). This was originally the name not of the whole island but of a farm where Tresco Abbey now is. The sixteenth-century antiquarian John Leland recorded the name of the island rather differently in his *Itinerary* (the record of his journey through England made between 1535 and 1543), referring to it as *Inisschawe*, 'that ys to sej, the Isle of Elder, by cawse yt bereth stynkkyng elders'. An earlier record dated 1305, however, has the name as *Trescau*.

Trim (Meath)
A market town southwest of NAVAN whose name represents the final word of its Irish name, Baile Átha Troim, 'town of the ford of the elder tree' (Irish *trom* 'elder tree'). The elders would have grown by the ford over the River BOYNE here.

Tring (Hertfordshire)
This town northwest of BERKHAMSTED had its name recorded in the Domesday Book as *Tredung*, and in a later document of 1265 as *Trehangre*. From these and similar records it is possible to deduce an origin in the Old English *trēow* (tree) and *hangra* (wooded hillside) (the 'hanger', in such names as Oakhanger, related to modern English 'hang'). The name thus means 'tree-covered hillside', which describes the town's location among hills and beech woods. The Domesday Book

record of the name seems to have confused *h* with *d*.

Troon (Strathclyde)
This port and resort on the FIRTH OF CLYDE has a Celtic name meaning 'the headland', either from the Gaelic *an t-sròn* (*sròn* 'headland') or from a word related to the modern Welsh *trwyn* (nose, cape). The name was recorded as *le Trone* in a document of 1371. Either way, the name describes the prominent promontory on which the town is located.

Trossachs, The (Central)
The attractive area surrounding the wooded gorge between Lochs Achray and KATRINE. It means 'transverse hills', and is said to be a Gaelic adaptation (*Tròsaichean*) of Wales's TRAWSFYNYDD, or at any rate of the first part of this. The reference is to the hills that divide the two lochs.

Trowbridge (Wiltshire)
A town southeast of BATH whose name means 'tree bridge', 'bridge made of tree-trunks', from the Old English *trēow* (tree) and *brycg* (bridge). The original such bridge was probably one crossing the little River Biss to the west of the town centre, where Trowle Bridge is now. (This bridge name seems to reinforce the interpretation and original siting of the location.) In the Domesday Book, Trowbridge is recorded as *Straburg*, which appears to be a serious distortion or miscopying of the original name, especially in view of the quite uncharacteristic initial *Str-*, which the Normans would normally have avoided at all costs. Perhaps the clerk was attempting to restore what he took to be a missing initial *S-*, by comparison with such names as STRATFORD. The latter half of the name may have arisen by a confusion between the Old English *burg* (fort) (the '-bury' of many names) and *brycg*, which words have three letters in common. For similar names *compare* STOCKBRIDGE and WOODBRIDGE.

Trumpington (Cambridgeshire)
A suburb of CAMBRIDGE whose name means 'village of Trump's people', with the personal name perhaps related to the modern English 'tramp' and meaning 'surly one'. The name was recorded as *Trumpintune* in a document of the mid-eleventh century.

Truro (Cornwall)
The county town lying inland north of FALMOUTH, has a name that is probably based on the conjectural Cornish *try-* (three, triple), sometimes with simply an 'intensive' sense meaning 'very'. (Compare the Roman name *Trisantona* discussed for TRENT.) Unfortunately, the second part of the name, which is the important element, is still obscure, although a word *erow*, 'unit of land' (something like a 'hide') has been suggested. The name was recorded as *Triueru* in a document of 1176.

Tuam (Galway)
A small market town northeast of GALWAY whose name means 'burial mound', with this seen in the Irish name, Tuaim. The full original Irish name was Tuaim an Dá Ghualainn, 'burial mound of the two shoulders', referring to its shape. The mound in question must have been at or near the ancient sixth-century monastery here. Tuam has always been an important religious centre.

Tullamore (Offaly)
This county town located in central Ireland, has a name that simply means 'big hill', as seen more clearly in its Irish name, Tulach Mhór. The town was planned and built only in the eighteenth century, so before that the name would have been purely a hill name. The 'big hill' itself is the prominent one nearby on which St Catherine's (Church of Ireland) Church now stands, just east of the town. *Compare* TULLIBODY; TULLOW.

Tullibody (Central)
This town northwest of ALLOA has a Gaelic name meaning 'hill of the hut', from *tulach* (small hill) and *both*, genitive *botha* (hut, cottage) (compare English 'bothy'). The name would have originally applied to an isolated hut or cottage here on the higher ground north of the River FORTH.

Tullow (Carlow)
A market town east of CARLOW whose name, found elsewhere in the country, simply means 'the hill', as in its Irish equivalent, An Tulach. The terrain is not obviously hilly here by the River SLANEY, but the land is not entirely level and 'the hill' could have been any of the eminences in this region.

Tunbridge Wells (Kent)
This well-known residential town arose round the springs ('Wells') discovered here in the seventeenth century, and took its name from TONBRIDGE, five miles to the north. The name thus means 'springs near Tonbridge'. Although Tonbridge was *Tonebrige* in the Domesday Book, later records of the name spell it with *u* instead of *o* (as *Tunbridge* in 1610), reflecting the pronunciation. With the development of Tunbridge Wells, however, Tonbridge reverted to the earlier spelling with *o*. The difference of vowel, as well as the additional 'Wells', now serves to distinguish the towns, although the basic names are pronounced identically.

Tunstall (Staffordshire)
One of the constituent towns of STOKE-ON-TRENT, Tunstall has a name that means 'farm place', from a conjectural Old English combination *tūn-stall* comprising *tūn* (farm) and *stall* (place; modern 'stall'). The name is found fairly widely elsewhere in the country, and also occurs as a residence name, such as Tunstall House, Tunstall Farm, and so on. This particular Tunstall was recorded as *Tunstal* in a document of 1212.

Turnhouse (Lothian)
The location of EDINBURGH Airport, west

of the city centre. It presumably has a name that refers to a house by a turnpike or some similar kind of 'turn' object.

Turriff (Grampian)

This town south of BANFF has a difficult name that may be based on the Gaelic *torr* (hill, mound). The second part of the name is obscure. No doubt the present spelling of the name has altered considerably from the original, which was probably Gaelic.

Tweed (Scotland/England)

This well-known river rises in Scotland and flows into the North Sea at BERWICK-UPON-TWEED in England. Its name may mean 'strong one', from a British (Celtic) root element *teu-* related to Sanskrit *tavás* (powerful). The name was recorded as *Tuuide* in a text of about 700.

Twerton (Avon)

A district of BATH whose name means 'farm at the double ford'; it is exactly the same in origin as TIVERTON (which see for a consideration of the elements). Twerton is west of the city centre, and the main river involved for the 'double ford' here is the AVON. The name was recorded as *Twertone* in the Domesday Book. *See also* TWYFORD.

Twickenham (Greater London)

A district of RICHMOND whose name may mean either 'Twicca's riverside land' or 'riverside land at the confluence', with the final element of the name almost certainly the Old English *hamm* (riverside land, land in the bend of a river), which described the situation of Twickenham by the THAMES. If the second derivation is correct, the first element will be the conjectural Old English *twicce* (confluence), from *twi-* (two), and perhaps refer to the point where the River Crane joins the Thames. The name was recorded as *Tuican hom* in a document of about 700.

Twyford (Berkshire)

A town east of READING whose name

means 'double ford', in the sense considered for TIVERTON ('farm at the double ford'). The two rivers involved at Twyford are the Loddon and the THAMES. The name was recorded as *Tuiford* in a document of 1170. *Compare* TWERTON.

Tyldesley (Greater Manchester)

A town southwest of BOLTON whose name means 'Tilwald's clearing', with the personal name followed by the Old English *lēah* (woodland, clearing). The name was recorded as *Tildesleia* in a document of about 1210.

Tyne (Northumberland/Tyne and Wear)

This well-known river flows through NEWCASTLE UPON TYNE to enter the North Sea at TYNEMOUTH. Its name means simply 'water', 'river', from a root British (Celtic) element *ti-* meaning 'to flow'. The Romans knew the Tyne as *Tinea*.

Tyne and Wear (England)

A county formed in northeast England in 1974 and centred on NEWCASTLE UPON TYNE and the surrounding urban area. It takes its name from the two main rivers here, the TYNE and the WEAR. The county name is the only one in Britain to comprise two river names.

Tynemouth (Tyne and Wear)

This town and resort at the mouth of the TYNE obviously takes its name from this river. The resort developed in relatively modern times on what was originally the site of a seventh-century monastery. The name is recorded as *Tinanmuthe* in a document of about 1121.

Tyneside (Tyne and Wear)

The general name for the urban and industrial complex on either side of the lower reaches of the TYNE. It has now received official recognition in the names of the two administrative districts of North Tyneside and South Tyneside, respectively north and south of the river in the east of the county.

Tynwald Hill (Isle of Man)
The artificial mound at St Johns, east of
PEEL, that is famous as the site where new
laws of the island are promulgated. Its
name is that of the Tynwald, the Manx
Parliament, itself a word of Scandinavian
origin, from the Old Norse *thing*
(assembly) and *vǫllr* (field). As such, it is
exactly the same in origin as DINGWALL.

Tyrone (Northern Ireland)
This county in the west of the province has
a name that represents the Irish name, Tír
Eoghain, 'Eoghan's land', referring to
Eoghan (Owen), the semi-legendary ruler
whose descendants are said to have
possessed this territory.

Tywyn (Gwynedd)
A resort on CARDIGAN Bay, west of
MACHYNLLETH, whose name translates as
'seashore', 'strand' (Welsh *tywyn*). The
name was recorded as *Thewyn* in a
document of 1254.

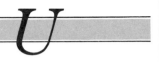

U

Uckfield (East Sussex)
A town northeast of LEWES whose name means 'Ucca's open land', with the personal name followed by the Old English *feld* (open land; modern 'field'). The name was recorded as *Uckefeld* in a document of 1820.

Uddingston (Strathclyde)
A town southwest of COATBRIDGE whose name probably means 'Oda's farm', with the personal name followed by the Old English *tūn* (farm). The '-ing-' of the name is thus misleading. The name was recorded in a document of 1296 as *Odistoun*.

Uist (Western Isles)
Either of two islands, North Uist and South Uist, respectively north and south of BENBECULA in the Outer HEBRIDES. The basic name has been traditionally interpreted to mean 'abode', literally 'in-dwelling', from the Old Norse *í* (in) and *vist* (dwelling), but it is almost certainly pre-Norse in origin.

Ullapool (Highland)
A small fishing port and resort, on the eastern shore of Loch Broom, whose name is of Scandinavian origin and means 'Olaf's dwelling', with the personal name followed by the Old Norse *bólstathr*, as in the name of SCRABSTER. However, the second half of this word has been lost from the name, and the remaining first half has been altered to suggest English 'pool'. The name was recorded as *Ullabill* in a text dated 1610. The association with 'pool' is all the readier for a place by the water, as Ullapool is.

Ullswater (Cumbria)
The second largest lake in the Lake District, lying southwest of PENRITH. The name means 'Ulf's water', and so is based on a personal name, as is that of the largest lake, WINDERMERE. The name was recorded as *Ulueswater* in a document of about 1235.

Ulster (Northern Ireland)
The name of the ancient province means 'place of the Ulaid (tribe)'. As for LEINSTER and MUNSTER, the name consists of the tribal name followed by the Old Norse genitive (possessive) -*s* with the Irish *tír* (district) added. The Norse record of the name was as *Uladztir*.

Ulverston (Cumbria)
A town northeast of BARROW-IN-FURNESS whose name means 'Wulfhere's estate', with the Old English personal name (meaning 'wolf army') having lost its initial *W*- because of Scandinavian influence. The final element of the name is the common Old English *tūn* (farm, estate). The name was recorded as *Vlureston* in the Domesday Book.

Unst (Shetland)
The most northerly of the main SHETLAND islands. It has a Scandinavian name meaning 'eagles' abode', from the Old Norse *orn* (eagle) and *vist* (dwelling) (*compare* UIST). This was recorded as *Ornyst* in a document of about 1200. Compare the Welsh name for Snowdonia, *Eryri* (*see* SNOWDON).

Up Holland (Lancashire)
An urban area west of WIGAN name means '(a place by the) upper hill-spur land', with the basic part of the name the same as for HOLLAND. The lower area, by contrast, is known as Down Holland. Up Holland is on a hillside, with the land falling away to the northeast and southwest. The Domesday Book record of the name was *Hoiland*.

Upminster (Greater London)
This former ESSEX town has a name that means 'higher church', from the Old

English *upp* (upper, higher) and *mynster* (minster, church). The ground rises slightly at Upminster. The name was recorded as *Upmynster* in a document of 1062.

Uppingham (Leicestershire)

A small town north of CORBY whose name means 'homestead of the upland people'. The actual 'homestead' was probably on Castle Hill, one mile west of the town centre, by the present A47 road to LEICESTER. The site here would have made a good lookout point. The name was recorded as *Yppingeham* in a document of 1067.

Ure (North Yorkshire)

A river that rises northwest of HAWES and joins the Swale near BOROUGHBRIDGE to form the OUSE. It has a name of doubtful origin; it may represent a Celtic root element *isura* meaning 'holy one' or 'strong one'. Whatever the origin was, it gave the Roman name of *Isurium* for the Roman city of Aldborough, near Boroughbridge, and also the first half of the name of JERVAULX ABBEY.

Urlingford (Kilkenny)

This small town west of KILKENNY has the Irish name Áth na nUrlainn, which translates as 'ford of the forecourts'. If this is correct, the reference may be to the courts of the many (now ruined) castles in the region. But an alternative origin has been given in *Áth na nDoirling*, said to mean 'ford of the big stones', and to refer to the ruined castles themselves.

Urmston (Greater Manchester)

A town southwest of MANCHESTER whose name means 'Urm's estate', with the Danish personal name followed by the Old English *tūn* (farm, estate). The personal name represents the Old Norse *ormr* (snake, serpent), as for GREAT ORMES HEAD. Urmston was recorded as *Wermeston* in a document of 1194.

Usk (Gwent)

This small market town east of PONTYPOOL takes its name from the River Usk on which it stands. The river's own name probably means 'fish river', from a Celtic root word reflected in the Latin *piscis* (fish) and in the English word itself, rather than simply 'water', like the similarly named River EXE. Some however, equate all these similar river names (others are AXE and ESK) as meaning 'water'. The Roman name for the river was *Isca*, also from this same Celtic source. The Roman name of the town of Usk, however, was *Burrium*, with this perhaps deriving from a personal name such as *Burros*, meaning 'strong one' (compare modern Welsh *bwr* 'big', 'fat', 'strong').

Uttlesford (Essex)

An administrative district in the northwest of the county that takes its name from a former hundred name here, meaning 'Udel's ford'.

Uttoxeter (Staffordshire)

This market town northeast of STAFFORD appears at first sight to have a *ceaster* name, like EXETER or WROXETER, and so to refer to a former Roman fort here. But early records of the name show this not to be the origin; in the Domesday Book, for example, the name is given as *Wottocheshede*. The meaning is therefore 'Wuttuc's heath', with the personal name followed by the conjectural Old English *hǣddre* (heather), implying 'heath'. The original name gradually evolved to the present spelling by association with the Roman names mentioned.

Uxbridge (Greater London)

This former MIDDLESEX town has a name that means 'bridge of the Wixan (tribe)', these being a people who had come to settle here from elsewhere in England, perhaps from the Midlands. The bridge of the name would have been over the River Colne here. The name was recorded as *Oxebruge* in a document of about 1145.

V

Vale of (the) White Horse (Oxfordshire)

An administrative district in the southwest of the county. Primarily, however, the name is that of the valley of the River Ock north of the Berkshire Downs, and refers specifically to White Horse Hill, six miles west of WANTAGE, in which the figure of a horse was cut from the turf to expose the white chalk beneath. The valley name was recorded as *Vale of Whithorse* in a document dated 1368. The horse figure is much older than this, however, and may even date back to the Iron Age.

Valentia (Kerry)

The name of this island off the southwest coast of the county is sometimes spelt 'Valencia', but it is purely a coincidence that it closely resembles that of the Spanish town and province, even though the names of both places are pronounced identically by most English people. The name of the Irish island represents the Irish *Béal Inse*, 'estuary of the island', referring to the sound that separates Valentia from the mainland. The current Irish name of Valentia, however, is Dairbhre, meaning 'place of oaks'.

Vauxhall (Greater London)

A district of LAMBETH whose name means 'Vaux's manor', with the personal name followed by the Old English *hall* (hall, manor house). 'Vaux' was Falkes (or Faukes) de Bréauté, who built a manor house here in the early thirteenth century. The name was recorded as *Faukeshale* in a document of 1279. Vauxhall was the site of celebrated (and also notorious) pleasure gardens from the seventeenth century to the nineteenth, as a result of which its name was adopted for similar pleasure gardens elsewhere in Europe. One of these was at Pavlovsk, near St Petersburg in Russia, where the name (or word) became specially associated with a pleasure garden near a railway station. As a result of this, the current standard word in Russian for a railway station is *vokzal*, an adoption of the original English place-name.

Ventnor (Isle of Wight)

A coastal resort and residential town southwest of SHANKLIN whose name probably derives from a family called Vintner, who owned a farm here, with this name first recorded (in this spelling) in a document of 1617. Before their time the name of the place was 'Holeway' or 'Holloway' (*Holeway* seems the preferred spelling), meaning 'hollow way', as for HOLLOWAY.

Virginia (Cavan)

This small market town southeast of CAVAN was founded by James I during the English colonisation of Ulster, and was named in honour of his predecessor, Elizabeth I, the 'Virgin Queen' (as was the American state of the same name). The town's Irish name is Achadh an Iúir, 'field of the yew tree'.

Virginia Water (Surrey)

A residential district southwest of STAINES whose name was originally given to the large artificial lake constructed here in the mid-eighteenth century by the Duke of Cumberland, when he was appointed Ranger of WINDSOR Great Park. He gave his topological enterprise the name 'Virginia' to commemorate the pioneers who founded and settled the American colony. This is therefore one example of an American place-name being exported to Britain, a reversal of the usual pattern.

Vyrnwy (Powys)

The river that flows into Lake Vyrnwy, the large reservoir northwest of WELSHPOOL. In its present spelling, the name represents the Welsh Fyrnwy, which comes from Y Fyrnwy, 'the Fyrnwy', from a misdivision of the true Welsh name of both river and lake, Efyrnwy. This in turn derives from a form of Havren, the Welsh name of the River SEVERN, so that its ultimate meaning will be the same, which as explained is still very uncertain (*see* SEVERN).

Wadebridge (Cornwall)
This town on the River Camel (*see*
CAMELFORD) northwest of BODMIN was
originally simply *Wade*, as recorded in a
document of 1382. This means 'ford',
'place where you can wade across', from
the Old English *gewæd* (ford). (Old English
wadan meant generally 'to go', and modern
'wade' developed from it later in a
narrower sense). To this, 'bridge' was
added later, so that the present name can
be understood as 'place by the bridge at the
ford', with the implication that the bridge
replaced the ford. For a somewhat similar
name (of a place with a many-arched
bridge like the one at Wadebridge),
compare FORDINGBRIDGE.

Wadhurst (East Sussex)
A large village southeast of TUNBRIDGE
WELLS whose name probably means
'Wada's wooded hill', with the personal
name followed by the Old English *hyrst*
(hillock, copse, wooded hill). The name
was recorded as *Wadehurst* in a document
of 1253.

Wakefield (West Yorkshire)
This county town and cathedral city south
of LEEDS has a name that almost means
what it says, if one takes 'wake' in its
northern sense of 'holiday'. (Many North
of England towns still have a 'Wakes
Week', when local factories close and there
is a public holiday, perhaps with various
types of entertainment.) Wakefield's name
thus means 'open land where festivities are
held', from the Old English *wacu* (watch,
wake) and *feld* (open land; modern 'field').
Wakefield would have been an ideal site for
such festivities, with the 'open land' being
the region between the River CALDER in
the south and the extensive wood of
Outwood in the north. Wakefield has long

been the traditional capital of the (former)
West Riding of Yorkshire, and the
festivities would have been those of this
region, or at any rate of the southern part of
it; Wakefield still has a twice-yearly fair, at
Christmas and Whitsun. The name was
recorded as *Wachefeld* in the Domesday
Book.

Wales (Britain)
This principality in western BRITAIN takes
its name from the Old English *walh*, which
meant (generally) 'foreigner' and
(specifically) 'Briton', 'Celt' (in this case
'Welshman'), before acquiring the
additional sense of 'slave'. The term was
thus used by the Anglo-Saxons of the Celts,
indicating their (to them) 'alien' nature,
speaking a different language and leading a
different way of life in many respects. The
'foreign' sense of *walh* has been preserved
in some words, such as 'walnut', which is a
'foreign nut' (an Asian import to Britain).
Compare also the name of CORNWALL,
where the *walh* forms the second half of the
name. The same word is also apparent in
the name of the Walloons, the people of
Gaulish (i.e. Celtic) origin who came to
inhabit what is now northeastern France
and southern Belgium; they are distinct
from, i.e. 'foreign' to, the Germanic-based
Flemings (the equivalent of the Anglo-
Saxons in Britain). A related name is that
of the Celtic tribe known by the Romans as
the *Volcae*. *Walh* is also found in other
place-names in Britain, such as
WALLASEY, WALMER, SAFFRON
WALDEN, and some of the places (but not
all) called WALTON. The name 'Wales'
represents the plural of *walh*, which was
walas, while the final *-sh* of 'Welsh' is the
equivalent of the *-ch* in 'French' and
'Dutch', as well as (more obviously) the
-ish of 'English', 'Scottish', and 'Irish'.
Although it seems demeaning, even
insulting, to be called 'foreigner' in one's
native land, one should accept that the
Anglo-Saxons applied the term more or
less factually, to a people who differed
from themselves.

Walkerburn (Borders)

A village on the River TWEED east of INNERLEITHEN. It has a descriptive name that refers to the 'walking' (fulling or dressing of cloth) that took place in the waters of the 'burn' (river). The name is thus English, from the Old English *walcere* (fuller, cloth-dresser) and *burna* (stream).

Wallasey (Merseyside)

An industrial town and resort at the northern end of the WIRRAL peninsula. Its name originally applied to the whole region here, which became an 'island' at high tide and was cut off from the rest of the peninsula. The meaning is thus 'island of the Welsh', from the Old English *wala*, genitive plural of *walh* (Welshman) (*see* WALES) and *ēg* (island). The latter word was in fact added twice to the 'Welsh' root, so that the present name really represents 'Waley' ('island of the Welsh') to which a possessive -*s* and another 'island' (*eg*) has been added, as if it was 'Waley's island'. The Domesday Book recorded the name as *Walea*, but a document of 1351 shows the further addition, with the name as *Waleysegh*. A glance at the map will show the proximity of the Wirral to Wales, and enable one to see that the Welsh did not have far to go to settle there.

Wallingford (Oxfordshire)

A town on the THAMES southeast of OXFORD whose name means 'the ford of Wealh's people', with the personal name followed by the Old English suffix -*ingas* that meant 'people of' (the named person) and *ford* added. The ford would obviously have been over the Thames. The name was recorded as *Wælingford* in a document of 821, and was *Walingeford* in the Domesday Book. The personal name probably indicates a Briton.

Wallington (Greater London)

A district of SUTTON whose name means 'farm of the Britons', from the Old English *walh* (Briton) (as considered above for WALES) and *tūn* (farm). The name of Wallington was originally 'Walton', and was recorded as such in the Domesday Book, for example, as *Waletone*. The middle -*ing*- is thus misleading, and may have been artificially introduced in order to distinguish this 'Walton' from WALTON-ON-THAMES, fifteen miles west of Wallington. The early records of Walton are very similar to those of Wallington.

Wallsend (Tyne and Wear)

This engineering town east of NEWCASTLE UPON TYNE has a self-descriptive name, indicating its location at the eastern end of HADRIAN'S WALL. The name looks modern, but this is simply because the modern English words have remained close to their Old English originals, *wall* and *ende*. There was a Roman fort at Wallsend, named *Segedunum*. This means 'strong fort', from British (Celtic) words related respectively to the Irish *seagh* (strength) (also German *Sieg* 'victory') and the Irish *dūn* (fort) (as in DONEGAL).

Walmer (Kent)

This district of DEAL is well known for Walmer Castle, the official residence of the Lord Warden of the CINQUE PORTS. Its name means 'lake of the Britons', from the Old English *walh* (Briton, Celt) (*see* WALES) and *mere* (lake, pool). There is no lake at Walmer now, but there obviously was once, and doubtless it was used more or less exclusively by the Britons who farmed the Anglo-Saxon settlements in the region. The name was recorded as *Wealemere* in the eleventh century.

Walney Island (Cumbria)

The long narrow island that runs from north to south opposite BARROW-IN-FURNESS. The name has been explained as meaning 'grampus island', from the Old Norse *vǫgn* (grampus) and the Old English *ēg* (island). However, a more likely derivation is from the conjectural Old English *wagen* (quicksands) and *ēg*, with the first word altered to the present *Wal*- of the name by association with names such as

WALSALL and WALTON. The name was first recorded as *Wagneiam* in a Latin text of 1127.

Walsall (West Midlands)

A town northwest of BIRMINGHAM whose name means 'Walh's little valley', with the personal name (probably denoting a Briton, as for WALLINGFORD) followed by the Old English *halh* (corner of land, slight valley). It is thought that the earliest settlement at Walsall was on low ground here. The name was recorded as *Waleshale* in a text of 1163.

Walsingham (Norfolk)

Either of two villages, Great Walsingham and Little Walsingham, south of WELLS-NEXT-THE-SEA, with the latter a former place of religious pilgrimage. The name means 'village of Wæls's people', and was recorded as *Walsingaham* in a document of about 1035. The '-ingham' of the name is the same as in such names as BIRMINGHAM.

Waltham Abbey (Essex)

This town southwest of HARLOW has a name whose first word occurs (with differing additions) for various other places in this region north of LONDON (see below). 'Waltham' means 'homestead by a wood', from the Old English *wald* or *weald* (wood) (*compare* The WEALD) and *hām* (homestead). The 'wood' of the name is today represented by what is left of Waltham Forest. The second word of the name refers to the abbey built by Henry II in the second half of the twelfth century. Waltham Abbey (the town) was formerly often known as Waltham Holy Cross, referring to the dedication of the abbey (to The Holy Cross and St Lawrence), and the Domesday Book refers to the original church on the site of the abbey by mentioning the *canonici sancte Crucis de Waltham*, 'rules ['canons'] of the Holy Cross of Waltham'. *Compare* WALTHAM CROSS; WALTHAMSTOW.

Waltham Cross (Hertfordshire)

This district of CHESHUNT has the basic name as explained for WALTHAM ABBEY. Here, the additional word refers to the Eleanor cross set up here by Edward I to mark the point where the body of his queen rested for the night on its journey south to LONDON, with this being the penultimate cross (the final one was at CHARING CROSS, which see for further details). The much restored Eleanor cross is still here, at the junction of Eleanor Cross Road with the High Street. Like the other Walthams, Waltham Cross was recorded in the Domesday Book as *Waltham*.

Walthamstow (Greater London)

A district of LONDON, north of LEYTON, that appears to have a name directly related to WALTHAM ABBEY or some other 'Waltham'. However, it was recorded in a document of about 1067 as *Wilcumestouue*, showing that its actual origin is as 'Wilcume's place'. The personal name is followed by the Old English *stōw* (place), here almost certainly in its special sense of 'holy place'. Some have interpreted the personal name as the Old English common noun *wilcuma* (guest) (compare modern 'welcome'), so that the name as a whole refers to a religious house where guests were welcome. But Wilcume is well documented as the name of the abbess here. Even so, the present form of the name has developed by association with that of Waltham Abbey.

Walton-le-Dale (Lancashire)

A suburb of PRESTON whose basic name, Walton, means 'village of the Britons', from the Old English *walh* (as for WALES) and *tūn* (farm, village). The addition to the name denotes the location of this particular Walton in Ribblesdale, the valley of the RIBBLE, with the suburb standing on a steep bank above this river. The name was recorded as *Waletune* in the Domesday Book. *Compare* WALTON-ON-THAMES; WALTON ON THE NAZE.

Walton-on-Thames (Surrey)
A town on the north bank of the THAMES southwest of LONDON. It has the same basic name as for WALTON-LE-DALE, and so means 'village of the Britons'. The Domesday Book recorded the name as *Waletone*, and the differentiating addition was added subsequently (*Waleton super Thamis*' in a document of 1279). Not all Waltons have this basic sense, and many mean 'village by a wood', from *weald*, not *walh*.

Walton on the Naze (Essex)
This coastal resort northeast of CLACTON has the same basic name as WALTON-LE-DALE and so means 'village of the Britons'. Its distinguishing addition refers to its location just south of The NAZE. The name was recorded as *Waletuna* in the twelfth century.

Walworth (Greater London)
A district of SOUTHWARK whose name means 'enclosure of the Britons', from the Old English *walh* (*see* WALES) and *worth* (enclosure). The name was recorded as *Wealawyrth* in a document dated 1006.

Wandsworth (Greater London)
A borough of south LONDON whose name means 'Wændel's enclosure', with the same personal name (but not the same person!) as found for WELLINGBOROUGH. Wandsworth is on the River Wandle, which took its name from the settlement as a 'back formation'. The name is recorded as *Wendeleswurthe* in a document of about 1000.

Wansbeck (Northumberland)
An administrative district in the east of the county that takes its name from the River Wansbeck, whose own name remains of uncertain origin. It was recorded as *Wenspic* in a document of 1137, and the latter half of this has produced the more readily meaningful '-beck', as found in several northern river and stream names, such as Borrow Beck. It is just possible that the latter half of the name may represent an unrecorded Old English word *spic*, meaning something like 'brushwood' (compare modern 'spike'). But the first part of the name has so far defied any interpretation.

Wansdyke (England)
An ancient earthwork that was probably constructed for defensive purposes and that ran from BERKSHIRE to the BRISTOL Channel at PORTISHEAD. Little of it now remains, however. Its name means 'Woden's embankment', with the name of this well-known war god followed by the Old English *dīc* (ditch, dike). Either the embankment was supposed to have been built by Woden, or he 'presided' over it. A document of 903 refers to Wansdyke as *Wodnes dic*. Compare WEDNESBURY.

Wanstead (Greater London)
This district of REDBRIDGE derives its name from the Old English *wænn* (hillock) (compare modern 'wen') and *stede* (place). Wanstead thus arose as a dwelling-place by a slight hill, although admittedly hardly a noticeable one in modern terms. Its name was recorded as *Wænstede* in a document of the mid-eleventh century.

Wantage (Oxfordshire)
A town southwest of OXFORD that takes its name from the stream that flows through it (a tributary of the Ock). It means 'diminishing one', from the Old English *wanian* (to decrease; modern 'wane'). The present '-age' of the name is thus really '-ing', as shown in a record of the late ninth century, which refers to the stream as being *æt Waneting*. Even the Domesday Book had the name as *Wanetinz*. The '-ing' thus became '-inge' or '-enge' and finally '-age'.

Wapping (Greater London)
A district of east central LONDON whose name means '(place of) Wæppa's people', with the personal name followed by the Old English *-ingas* suffix that meant

'people of' (the named person) without any further addition. The name was recorded as *Wapping* in a document of about 1220.

Wardle (Greater Manchester)
A town northeast of ROCHDALE whose name means 'watch hill', from the Old English *weard* (watch, look-out; modern 'ward') and *hyll* (hill). The reference is probably to the high Brown Wardle Hill immediately northwest of the town. The name was recorded as *Wardhill* in 1218, so that the present name has reduced the 'hill' to the final '-le'. *Compare* WARDOUR CASTLE.

Wardour Castle (Wiltshire)
There are two Wardour Castles within a mile of each other west of WILTON: the older is called Wardour Old Castle, a now ruined fourteenth-century castle; the other is Wardour Castle, an eighteenth-century mansion and now a girls' school. The latter took its name from the former, with the basic name meaning 'watch slope', from the Old English *weard* (watch) (as for WARDLE) and *ōra* (bank, slope) (as for PERSHORE). There would thus have been an Anglo-Saxon 'lookout post' here on the banks of the River Nadder. The name was recorded as *Weardora* in the early tenth century, and as *Werdore* in the Domesday Book.

Ware (Hertfordshire)
A town on the River Lea northeast of HERTFORD whose name means 'weir' (Old English *wer*), apparently referring to the frequent blockages on the river in the past. The name was recorded as *Waras* in the Domesday Book. *Compare* WAREHAM.

Wareham (Dorset)
A town at the head of the River Frome estuary west of POOLE. Its name means 'homestead by a weir', from the Old English *wer* (weir) (as for WARE) and *hām* (homestead). There was a fishery above the weir on the Frome as early as the fourteenth century, when it was referred to

(rendered in modern English) as 'Elizabeth de Burgo's free fishery at Wareham'. The name was recorded as *Werham* in a text of 784. (The river is not the same Frome that gave the town of FROME its name, although the meaning of the name is the same.)

Warkworth (Northumberland)
A village with a fine castle near the North Sea coast northwest of AMBLE. Its name is said to derive from the conjectural Old English *wæferce* (spider) (literally 'weaver') and more certain *worth* (enclosure). But what is a 'spider's enclosure'? Perhaps more likely would be an origin in the conjectural *wēfer* (winding stream), referring to the winding course of the River Coquet, on which Warkworth is situated. (*Compare* WEAVER as a river name.) Warkworth was recorded as *Wauercuurt* in a document of 1153.

Warley (West Midlands)
A town west of BIRMINGHAM whose name means 'cattle pasture', from the Old English *weorf* (draught cattle) and *lēah* (clearing, pasture). The name was recorded as *Werwelie* in the Domesday Book.

Warlingham (Surrey)
A town southeast of CROYDON whose name means 'village of Wærla's people', with the personal name followed by the common combination of Old English *-ingas* (people of) and *hām* (homestead, village). A document of the mid-twelfth century recorded the name as *Warlyngham*.

Warminster (Wiltshire)
The name of this town south of TROWBRIDGE has nothing to do with 'war', despite its close association with the army camps on the outskirts of the town. The meaning is 'church on the Were', the latter being the river that flows through the town. Its own name probably means 'wandering one', from the Old English *worian* (to wander). No doubt the present parish church of St Denys stands on the

site of the original *mynster*. The name was recorded as *Worgemynster* in a document of about 910.

Warrenpoint (Down)
A town and resort on the north shore of CARLINGFORD Lough, southeast of NEWRY. Its name is said to derive from the extensive rabbit warren formerly here, although there is hardly a 'point' or headland in the accepted sense. The Irish name is An Pointe, 'the point'. The present town arose only in the early nineteenth century.

Warrington (Cheshire)
This large industrial town on the MERSEY southwest of MANCHESTER has a name that means 'weir farm', 'farm by the weir', based on the conjectural Old English *wæring* (weir), related to the *wer* seen in WARE and WAREHAM (*compare* WARWICK). Warrington was recorded as *Walintune* in the Domesday Book, with the Norman substitution of *l* for *r* seen in such names as SALISBURY (where, however, it persisted).

Warsop (Nottinghamshire)
The name of this town northeast of MANSFIELD means 'Wær's little valley', with the personal name followed by the Old English *hop* (valley), as for BACUP. The reference may be to the valley known as Warsop Vale, just over a mile west of the town. The name was recorded in the Domesday Book as *Wareshope*.

Warwick (Warwickshire)
This well-known town on the AVON southwest of COVENTRY has a name that means 'weir dwellings', 'premises by a weir', from the Old English *wering* (weir), related to the words quoted for WARE, WAREHAM, and WARRINGTON, and *wīc*, here in its sense of 'special place'. Here, the weir or dam would, of course, have been over the Avon. The name was recorded as *in Wærinc wicum* in a document of 1001, and in the Domesday Book as *Warvic*. The

town gave its name to the county, recorded as *Wærincwicscir* in 1016.

Wash, The (Lincolnshire/Norfolk)
This wide shallow North Sea inlet on the east coast of England was originally known as *The Washes*, referring to the sandbanks of land that were alternately covered and exposed or 'washed' by the sea, thus forming two fords across the region between Lincolnshire and Norfolk. This form of the name (in the spelling *the wasshes*) is recorded before 1548, and also occurs in Shakespeare's *King John* (1590s), where Philip the Bastard says that (in modern spelling):

> . . . half my power this night
> Passing these flats, are taken by the tide;
> These Lincoln Washes have devoured them.

The plural form of the name was still in use in the eighteenth century, and occurs, for example, in Defoe's *Colonel Jack* (1722): 'There was no way now left, but that by the washes into Lincolnshire'.

Washington (Tyne and Wear)
This New Town west of SUNDERLAND, designated in 1964, has an old name, as is often the case. It was recorded as *Wassyngtona* in the Domesday Book, and probably (although not certainly) means 'farm at a muddy place', from the Old English *wāse* (mud). However, the first element of the name could also be a personal name, giving an overall meaning 'village of Wassa's people'. Washington Old Hall is a (now restored and altered) medieval building that was the home of George Washington's ancestors. The place-name is not unique to the New Town; there is a Sussex village of the name, for example, north of WORTHING. Its name will have an identical origin.

Wast Water (Cumbria)
This lake in the Lake District is in the valley known as Wasdale, and gets its name from it. Wasdale is a Scandinavian name,

from the Old Norse *vatn* (lake) (related to English 'water') and *dalr* (valley). But the lake referred to is Wast Water itself, so the two names are interconnected; Wast Water can be considered as really 'Wasdale Water'.

Watchet (Somerset)

A town and harbour northwest of BRIDGWATER that has a Celtic name meaning 'under the wood', from words related respectively to the Welsh *gwas* (servant) and *coêd* (wood), with 'Wa-' representing the first of these, and '-tchet' the second. The reference would have been to the cliffs behind the town, which were doubtless more thickly wooded in the past than now. The name was recorded as *Wæced* in a text of 918.

Waterford (Waterford)

The name of this city and port in the southeast of the country is not what it seems, despite the location of Waterford on the south bank of the River Suir. It is Scandinavian in origin, and means 'wether inlet', from the Old Norse *vethr* (wether, ram) and *fjǫrthr* (inlet; 'fjord'), referring to the point on the river where wethers (castrated rams) were loaded onto boats for transportation to other ports. It was the Vikings who established a settlement here in the ninth century. The Irish name of Waterford is Port Láirge, 'port of the haunch', referring to the contour of the river or its bank here. The standard Norse spelling of the name was *Vadrefjord*.

Waterlooville (Hampshire)

This town northeast of PORTSMOUTH derives its name from the inn here, called the Heroes of Waterloo, around which it grew in the nineteenth century. The inn itself, now called The Heroes and no longer the original building, was named for the soldiers and sailors (especially the latter) who had fought at the Battle of Waterloo in 1815 and who had disembarked at Portsmouth on their return to England. The inn is on the main London road (now

the A3). The '-ville' suffix, meaning 'town', is typical of places that developed in this period (*compare* BOURNVILLE, CLIFTONVILLE, and COALVILLE). The various other places named Waterloo in the country will also have directly or indirectly commemorated the British victory, or its hero, Wellington. Fortunately, the name of the Belgian town near which the battle was fought is an easy one for English tongues. What if the battle had been fought near Denderleeuw or Ecaussinnes?

Waterville (Kerry)

A small coastal resort on the peninsula south of DINGLE Bay whose name derives from Waterville House here, with its own name referring to its situation (as a 'villa') near the Finglas river, not far from its confluence with the large Currane. The Irish name of Waterville is An Coireán, 'the little whirlpool'. This refers to the swirling of the waters at the confluence mentioned.

Watford (Hertfordshire)

This well-known town northwest of LONDON has a name that means 'hunter's ford', from the Old English *wāth* (hunting) and *ford* (ford). The reference is to a ford over the River Colne, on which Watford is situated, although the exact site of the ford is uncertain. The name was recorded as *Wathford* in a document of about 1180. *Compare* WATFORD GAP.

Watford Gap (Northamptonshire)

A location north of DAVENTRY, sometimes confused with WATFORD (especially in the phrase 'north of Watford', which is sometimes heard as 'north of the Watford Gap'). Watford Gap is familiar today as the name of a service station on the M1 motorway. The basic name probably has the same sense as that of its southern namesake, so means 'ford where hunters pass', with the 'Gap' referring to the break in the chain of hills known as the Northamptonshire Uplands. (This is used not only by the M1, but by the nearby A5, which follows the course of WATLING STREET, the GRAND UNION CANAL, and one of England's main rail routes, from LONDON to RUGBY and the north.) Watford itself is a small hamlet immediately east of the Gap. Its name was recorded in the Domesday Book as now.

Watling Street (England)
A Roman military road that ran from KENT through the southeast and centre of England to North Wales; its course is still largely followed by the A2 and A5 roads (*see* WATFORD GAP). The name derives from ST ALBANS, one of the towns on its route. St Albans was formerly known as *Wætlingceaster* (as it were, 'Watlingchester'), with this based on a tribal name (see the town's name for details). A late-ninth-century text refers to Watling Street as *Wætlingstræt*.

Watlington (Oxfordshire)
A small town south of THAME whose name means 'village of Wæcel's people', with the personal name meaning 'watchful one' (Old English *wacol*). The name was recorded as *Wæclinctun* in a document of 880.

Waveney (Suffolk)
This administrative district, in the east of the county, takes its name from the River Waveney that forms its northern border, as well as the county boundary between Suffolk and Norfolk. The river's name probably means simply 'moving river', from the Old English *wagian* (to move) and *ēa* (river). It was recorded as *Wahenhe* in a document of 1275.

Waverley (Surrey)
The name is familiar as that of Waverley Abbey, the ruins of the oldest Cistercian house in England, south east of FARNHAM beside the River WEY. The name probably means 'clearing by the swampy pool', from the Old English *wæfre* (unstable, restless) (compare modern 'wavering') and *lēah* (clearing). This would refer to the low-lying site of the abbey by the river. Sir Walter Scott is said to have adopted the name of the abbey for his *Waverley* novels, and these in turn gave the name of Waverley Station, the main railway station at EDINBURGH, Scott's birthplace, as well as of the more recent Waverley Market Shopping Centre next to it. The abbey's name was recorded as *Wauerleia* in a document of 1147. *Compare also* WAVERTREE.

Wavertree (Merseyside)
A district of LIVERPOOL whose name means '(place by the) swaying tree', from the Old English *wæfre* (unstable, restless) (as for WAVERLEY) and *trēow* (tree). It has been suggested that the tree in question was an aspen; these trees still grow in the district. The name was recorded as *Wauretreu* in the Domesday Book. (For other Liverpool district names derived from trees *compare* AINTREE and KNOTTY ASH.)

Weald, The (England)
The region of southeast England, in south KENT and north SUSSEX, that is bounded by the North and South Downs. The name derives from the Old English *wald* or (in its Kentish dialect form) *weald*, meaning basically 'woodland' (compare German *Wald*), but also acquiring a more specific sense 'upland wood'. The name is thus virtually generic, and the 'true' name of much of The Weald was formerly *Andredeswald*, at least in Sussex (*see* NEW FOREST, PEVENSEY). The Weald was recorded as *le Walde* in a document of 1330. The word is also related to The Wolds, the two separate regions of chalk hills respectively in north Humberside (formerly 'The Yorkshire Wolds') and northeast Lincolnshire ('The Lincolnshire Wolds'), as well as to the second part of the name of the COTSWOLDS. Both 'Weald' and 'Wold' are probably related to 'wild', but not to 'wood', which is a word of a different origin (Old English *wudu*). *Compare* WEALDSTONE.

Wealdstone (Greater London)
A district of HARROW whose name probably refers to a boundary *stone* that separated Harrow *Weald* from the rest of the parish of Harrow. Harrow Weald itself derives its name from the woodland near it (*see* WEALD). Wealdstone developed as a district only in the nineteenth century, with the coming of the railway.

Wear (Durham, Tyne and Wear)
A river that rises near the village of Wearhead, west of STANHOPE, and then flows generally east to enter the North Sea at SUNDERLAND. It has a name that simply means 'water', with its name deriving from the same Indo-European root element that gave not only English 'water' and 'wet', but also Greek *hudor*, Russian *voda*, German *Wasser*, and so on, all meaning 'water'. The Roman name for the Wear was *Vedra*, from the same root.

Weaver (Cheshire)
This river is a tributary of the MERSEY and has a name that means 'winding one', almost 'weaving one', describing its meandering course. The direct source of the name is the conjectural Old English *wefer* (winding stream), with this in turn indirectly related to words such as 'wave' and 'vibrate'. A document of 1113 refers to the river as the *Weever*.

Wednesbury (West Midlands)
This district of WEST BROMWICH has a name that means 'Woden's fortified place', implying either that the great pagan war god had actually made the place, or that he 'reigned' there and protected it (*compare* WANSDYKE and WEDNESFIELD). Wednesbury, which ends in the Old English *burg* (fort), was recorded in the Domesday Book as *Wadnesberie*.

Wednesfield (West Midlands)
A district of WOLVERHAMPTON with a name similar to WEDNESBURY, except that here it means 'Woden's open land'. The pagan war god, who gave his name also to

WANSDYKE (and 'Wednesday'), was held to have favoured this land and to have been its 'patron'. The name was recorded as *Wodnesfeld* in a document of 996. (This preserves the *o* of the god's name, which later became *e* in the place-name. The Old English for 'Wednesday' was similarly *wodnesdæg*.) In Scandinavian mythology, Woden's son was Thor, the god of thunder, who gave his name to THUNDERSLEY (among other places) and also 'Thursday'.

Welbeck (Nottinghamshire)
This name is familiar as that of Welbeck Abbey, the mainly Victorian mansion southwest of WORKSOP. The name derives from that of a stream here, whose own name seems to have been originally something like 'Wella', from the Old English *wella* (stream, well), to which an unnecessary explanatory 'beck' was added, the latter representing the Old English *bæce* (stream, valley), or possibly the Old Norse *bekkr* (stream, beck). The name was recorded as *Wellebec* in a document of 1179.

Welland (Leicestershire/Lincolnshire)
A river that rises near MARKET HARBOROUGH and then flows generally northeast to enter The WASH. Its name may mean 'good stream', from a British (Celtic) root word related to modern Welsh *gwiw* (fit, worthy) to which a word meaning 'river' was added, the latter probably related to the Old English *flēot* (creek, river) (*compare* FLEET). The name was recorded as *Weolud* in a document of 921, showing that the latter half of the present name seems to have been associated with 'land', as if the name meant 'well land'.

Wellingborough (Northamptonshire)
A town northeast of NORTHAMPTON whose name means 'fortified place of Wændel's people', with the personal name the same as that found in WANDSWORTH. The 'fortified place' (Old English *burg*) is

not evident at Wellingborough, however, and there is no obvious Iron Age or other ancient fort, as there is in other places with similar names. The name was recorded in the Domesday Book as *Wendlesberie*, and if this modification of the original had been adopted, we might today have had a name something like 'Wendlebury' instead of Wellingborough.

Wellington (Shropshire, Somerset)
Either of two towns of the name — the first east of SHREWSBURY, where it forms part of TELFORD; the second west of TAUNTON. There are also villages of the name elsewhere in the country. It seems likely that both towns, and indeed all Wellingtons, have the same origin. The difficulty is knowing what it is. The name could mean 'farm of Wēola's people', but no such personal name has been recorded, and it seems unlikely that this single instance of it should have occurred in at least two places at different locations in the country. Another interpretation could be 'farm of the shrine people', from the Old English *wēoh* (idol, shrine), referring to a heathen temple, perhaps with *lēah* (grove) added. Another general difficulty is that names derived from the Old English -*ingas* (people of) are not common in Shropshire and Somerset. The Shropshire Wellington was recorded as *Welintona* in a document of 1220, and the Somerset one as *Weolingtun* in 904. The famous Duke of Wellington (who gave 'Wellington boots') took his title from the Somerset town. Wellington College, the pubic school at CROWTHORNE, Berkshire, took its name from his title, as it was founded in his honour as a school for the sons of army officers who had died in combat. But Wellington School, the other public school of the name, is at the Somerset town.

Wells (Somerset)
This small cathedral city south of BRISTOL has a self-explanatory name, referring to the natural springs or wells here that have long been known to exist, and that were located near what is now the east end of the cathedral. A document of 766 refers to Wells monastery as *monasterium quod situm est juxta fontem magnum quem vocitant Wielea*, 'the monastery which is situated here next to the large spring that they call *Wielea*'. (The Old English name here should have been spelt *Wiella*.) The 'large spring' referred to is the one now known as St Andrew's Well, in the gardens of the Bishop's Palace. *Compare* WELLS-NEXT-THE-SEA.

Wells-next-the-Sea (Norfolk)
This small port and yachting centre north of FAKENHAM has a name that is identical to that of WELLS, and refers to its springs (Old English *wella* 'spring', 'well'), with the name recorded as *Guella* in the Domesday Book. (This has the typical French *gu*- corresponding to English *w*-, as found in modern French and English *guêpe* 'wasp'; *guerre*, 'war'.) The town is often simply known as Wells, although the suffix does denote its coastal location, and serves as a commercial lure.

Welshpool (Powys)
This market town on the left bank of the SEVERN west of SHREWSBURY has a name that means what it says, referring to the 'pool' at the point where the Lledin brook joins the Severn here. The Welsh name of Welshpool is simply Y Trallwng, 'the pool'. The name was recorded as *Pola* in a document of 1253. Why 'Welsh', though, when the town is obviously in Wales? The adjective was added to show that the pool (and the settlement) were on the Welsh, not English side of the border; Welshpool is less than three miles from the boundary. A brief glance at the map will show similar names elsewhere for places near the border, such as Welsh Frankton and English Frankton, Welsh Bicknor and English Bicknor. There does not seem to be an 'English pool', however, to correspond to Welshpool.

Welwyn (Hertfordshire)
A town south of STEVENAGE whose name means '(place) at the willows', from the Old English *welig* (willow), with the spelling of the name representing an Old English dative plural, used after 'at' to denote location. This can be seen in an early record of the name in about 945 as *ad Welingum*. The willows would have grown beside the small River Mimram that flows through the town. *Compare* WELWYN GARDEN CITY.

Welwyn Garden City (Hertfordshire)
This New Town, designated in 1948, takes its name from the old town of WELWYN, immediately north of it. It is the only New Town in Britain to incorporate the title 'Garden City' in its name, and it is well known for its combination of parkland and flower beds as a blend of 'town and country'. The concept of a 'garden city' had evolved several years earlier, however, and the term was imported to Britain from America. Even so, plans to build an English 'garden city' near an existing town date back to the turn of the century, and *The Times* of 29 August 1903 carried an item about a company called the 'Garden City Pioneer Company (Limited)' which had 'acquired about 4,000 acres of land near Hitchin on which to build the first garden city'. This was to have been at LETCHWORTH, and although some progress was made in the project, the scheme as a whole lacked the necessary financial support. The company instead turned its attention to Welwyn Garden City, which it planned in 1920, but which came to fruition, as the first 'overspill' town for London's increasing population, only after the Second World War.

Wem (Shropshire)
This small town north of SHREWSBURY has a name derived directly from the Old English *wemm* (spot, filth), here probably meaning 'marshy place', in view of the marshy nature of much of the terrain at Wem. The name was recorded as *Weme* in the Domesday Book. There was a standard word 'wem' in use in English down to at least the sixteenth century to mean 'stain', 'disfigurement', and the like. ('There appeered in his head the signes and prints of ten wounds or more: all the which were growne into one wem', Holinshed, *Chronicles*, 1577.)

Wembley (Greater London)
A district of BRENT whose name means 'Wemba's clearing', with the personal name followed by the Old English *lēah* (grove, clearing). The name was recorded as *æt Wemba lea* in a document of 825.

Wemyss Bay (Strathclyde)
A village on the Firth of CLYDE, on the bay of the same name southwest of GREENOCK. Its basic name means 'cave', from the Gaelic *uaimh* (cave), with the English plural -*s* added (*compare* PITTENWEEM). The villages of East and West Wemyss on the FIRTH OF FORTH in Fife have the same origin.

Wendover (Buckinghamshire)
A town at the northern edge of the CHILTERN HILLS, southeast of AYLESBURY. It takes its name from the stream that flows through it, with its own name of Celtic origin meaning 'white stream', from words related to the modern Welsh *gwyn* (white) and *dwfr* (water) (as for DOVER). The soil here is chalky. The name was recorded as *æt Wændofron* in a document of about 970.

Wenlock Edge (Shropshire)
A hill ridge that runs from CRAVEN ARMS to MUCH WENLOCK; it gave its name to the latter place, and also to Little Wenlock. The basic meaning is 'white monastery', from Celtic words related to the modern Welsh *gwyn* (white) (*compare* WENDOVER) and the Old English *loc*, literally 'lock' but here in a specialised sense of the more general 'place' (*compare* 'location'), to denote a religious enclosure. A Cluniac Benedictine abbey was founded at Much

Wenlock in the seventh century, and the ruins of the present priory stand on its site. The name was recorded as *Wenloca* in a document of about 1000, and as *Wenloch* in the Domesday Book. Wenlock Edge is thus 'hill ridge by the white monastery', and its own name was recorded as simply *Egge* in a document of 1227.

Wensleydale (North Yorkshire)
Wensleydale is not the name for the valley of the 'Wensley', as there is no such river. It is in fact the name for the valley of the River URE above MASHAM, and takes its name from the village of Wensley at its lower (eastern) end. The village name means 'Wændel's clearing', with the same personal name as found in both WANDSWORTH and WELLINGBOROUGH. The final element of the name is the Old English *lēah* (forest, clearing). The village name was recorded as *Wendreslaga* in the Domesday Book, while Wensleydale appears as *Wandesleydale* in a text of the mid-eleventh century.

Wensum (Norfolk)
A river that flows through NORWICH to join the Yare (*see* YARMOUTH). Its name effectively means what it says — 'wendsome' or winding. There is no current word 'wendsome' in English, but its existence in Old English can be deduced (as *wendsum*) from the evidence of this very name. A glance at the map will show that the river follows a meandering course as it 'wends' its way generally southeast from its source south of FAKENHAM. Its name was recorded as *Wenson* in a document of 1096.

Wentworth (Surrey)
A residential district with its well-known golf course west of VIRGINIA WATER. It derives its name from a house called Wentworth House (now the clubhouse of the golf club), owned in the early nineteenth century by a Mrs Elizabeth Wentworth. The house was built in about 1800 on ground owned by Mrs Wentworth, which was known locally as

'Wentworth's Waste', and the spelling *Wentworth's* was used for the house until about 1855, when the present district began to develop and the final *s* was dropped. Wentworth is a place-name in its own right (it means 'Wintra's enclosure'), and there are villages called Wentworth in both Cambridgeshire (near ELY) and Yorkshire (near ROTHERHAM), with the latter giving the names of the mansions of Wentworth Castle and Wentworth Woodhouse.

Wessex (England)
The former Anglo-Saxon kingdom in south and southwest England. Its name shows the territory to have been the district of the West Saxons, as distinct from the South Saxons of SUSSEX and the East Saxons of ESSEX. It never became a county name as these other kingdoms did, however, although it was 'resurrected' by Thomas Hardy for his novels, which were set in this region of England, especially Dorset. Hardy did much to promote the name, and in the Preface to *Far From the Madding Crowd*, when first published in book form in 1874, he explained: 'It was in the chapters of *Far From the Madding Crowd*, as they appeared month by month in a popular magazine, that I first ventured to adopt the word "Wessex" from the pages of early history, and give it a fictitious significance as the existing name of the district once included in that extinct kingdom. [. . .] Finding that the area of a single county did not afford a canvas large enough for this purpose, and that there were objections to an invented name, I disinterred the old one'. Today, the name is used by commercial firms and tourist boards as a neater and more historical equivalent to 'the West of England' or 'the West Country', which are two somewhat vague names for approximately the same region. The name proper was recorded as *West Seaxna lond* in a document of 709.

West Bridgford (Nottinghamshire)
A town on the south side of NOTTINGHAM

across the River TRENT. Its basic name, Bridgford, means 'ford by the bridge' (not 'bridge by the ford'), implying that there was a quite lengthy period during which both the ford and the bridge over the Trent were used by travellers to or from Nottingham. The first word of the name distinguishes this 'Bridgford' from East Bridgford, a village about seven miles northeast of the town. In the Domesday Book, West Bridgford was recorded simply as *Brigeforde*, with the present name appearing in a document of 1572 as *Westburgeforde*.

West Bromwich (West Midlands)

A town northwest of BIRMINGHAM whose basic name, Bromwich, means 'broom farm' (for details of which *see* CASTLE BROMWICH). The 'West' differentiates it from Castle Bromwich, about eight miles to the east. The name was recorded as *Bromwic* in the Domesday Book, and as *Westbromwich* in a document dated 1322.

Westbury (Wiltshire)

This town at the foot of SALISBURY Plain, south of TROWBRIDGE, has a name that means 'western fortified place' from the Old English *west* and *burg*. The 'fortified place' is the Iron Age camp on the hill above Westbury, where a spectacular 'white horse' is cut out of the chalk on the hillside. This camp was no doubt regarded as being the 'westernmost' of any others on Salisbury Plain. The name was recorded as *Westberie* in the Domesday Book.

Westcliff-on-Sea (Essex)

This district of SOUTHEND-ON-SEA has a self-descriptive name referring to the cliffs that lie to the west (more precisely, southwest) of Southend proper. The name appears on the one-inch Ordnance Survey map of 1843 simply as *Cliff*. The 'Sea' of the name, added later to advertise the place as a seaside resort, is actually the estuary of the THAMES.

West Drayton (Greater London)

A district of HILLINGDON whose basic name, Drayton, means 'portage farm', 'farm by a portage place', meaning that the original farm here was at a point on the River Colne where boats could be dragged from the water, or where loads could be dragged down to it (*see* MARKET DRAYTON for the Old English origin). This Drayton is 'West' of Drayton Green in EALING. The name was recorded as *Drægtun* in a document of 939, and as *Draitone* in the Domesday Book.

West End (Greater London)

The general name for the 'superior' district of LONDON, defined by the *Oxford English Dictionary* as 'that part of London lying westward of Charing Cross and Regent Street and including the fashionable shopping district, Mayfair, and the Parks'. It is first recorded by this same dictionary in 1776, when a newspaper refers to 'a certain coffeehouse at the Westend of town'. ('East End', by contrast, as a term for the former densely populated and poorer quarter of London, east of the City, it records only in the 1880s.) Why should the West End have been the 'fashionable' one? Various theories, both geographical and economic, have been proposed to account for this, but undoubtedly one factor that determined the development in this way was the weather. England has a prevailing southwesterly wind. Before modern times, and the introduction of 'smokeless zones', the smoke would generally have been blown towards the eastern region of a town or city. Hence, the western district was the more favourable, and the eastern the least favourable. But in the case of London, the West End would also have been away from the docks and the unwholesome waters of the Thames, as well as nearer the 'country'.

Westerham (Kent)

A small town west of SEVENOAKS whose name means 'western homestead', from the conjectural Old English *wester* (westerly)

and *hām* (homestead). The name refers to
the location of Westerham in the west of
the county, not far from the Surrey border.
The name was recorded as *Westarham* in a
document of 871, and as *Oistreham* in the
Domesday Book. The latter spelling shows
one French method of coping with the
unfamiliar *W-* (compare modern French
ouest and English 'west').

Western Isles (Scotland)
This name is obviously self-descriptive for
the Outer HEBRIDES, which is the most
westerly island chain in Scotland, off the
west coast of the mainland. The name
seems to have arisen some time in the
seventeenth or eighteenth century,
possibly earlier, and it was certainly well
established enough for Dr Johnson to use it
(in a slightly different form) for his *Journey
to the Western Islands of Scotland*, published
in 1775.

Westgate-on-Sea (Kent)
A district of MARGATE whose name
means 'western gap in the cliffs to the sea';
the second half of the basic name,
Westgate, is the same Old English *geat*
(gap; modern 'gate') that is found in
other names of coastal places in Kent,
such as Margate and RAMSGATE.
Westgate-on-Sea is west of Margate
proper, and its name was recorded as
Westgata in a document of 1168; the
addition denoting its seaside location was
made much more recently.

West Ham (Greater London)
A town in the Borough of NEWHAM
whose name is the western counterpart to
EAST HAM; the whole of the region here
on the northern bank of the THAMES
was originally a single *hamm*, or
'riverside pasture', until the two parts
were differentiated. This must have
been some time before 1186, when West
Ham is first recorded (as *Westhamma*).
A century earlier, the Domesday
Book had entered the name simply as
Hame.

West Kilbride (Strathclyde)
This town northwest of ARDROSSAN has
the same basic name as EAST KILBRIDE,
which see for the origin. West Kilbride,
however, is separated from its namesake by
almost thirty miles.

West Kirby (Merseyside)
A town and resort on the WIRRAL
peninsula whose basic name, Kirby, means
'village with a church', from the Old Norse
kirkju-bý, as for most of the places named
KIRKBY. It was originally simply 'Kirby'
(*Kircheby* in a document of about 1154),
but had become *Westkirkeby* in 1289. It
may have come to be called 'West' simply
because of its location near the northwest
extremity of the peninsula, rather than by
contrast with any other specific Kirby,
many of which are in Yorkshire. It is
virtually a 'westernmost' Kirby by
comparison with other places of the name.

Westmeath (Ireland)
A county in central Ireland whose name
indicates its situation to the west of
MEATH. It was created in 1542, later than
the other county. Its Irish name, with the
same meaning, is An Iarmhí, from the
Irish *iar-* (west) and *Mhí* (Meath).

West Mersea (Essex)
A town whose name indicates its location at
the western end of MERSEA ISLAND. It was
recorded as *Westmeresheye* in a document of
1238.

Westminster (Greater London)
This district and borough (City of
Westminster) of central LONDON has a
name that refers directly to Westminster
Abbey — the abbey was built in the
thirteenth century on the site of a pre-
eighth-century monastery or *mynster* that
lay to the west of London; the name was
first recorded as *Westmunster* in 785. The
original name of the site here was
'Thorney' (*Thorney* in 969), meaning
'thorn island' (*compare* THORNEY
ISLAND), the island being the land

between the Tyburn (*see* MARYLEBONE) and the THAMES.

Westmorland (England)
A former county of northwest England whose name means what it says, referring to the people who lived on the 'west moorland', that is, those who were to the west of the PENNINES, or this section of them. The name originally applied only to the barony of APPLEBY, in the north of the county, and was recorded as *Westmoringaland* in the mid-tenth century. Later, it came to apply to the whole county, recorded as *Westmeringland* in the twelfth century. The name is thus properly 'Westmooringland', with the middle -*ing*-meaning 'people of'. This element later disappeared from the name. Westmorland has now been swallowed up by the new county of CUMBRIA, and it is perhaps regrettable that its name has not been preserved for one of the new administrative districts established in 1974, as happened elsewhere in Britain when an old county ceased to exist.

Weston-super-Mare (Somerset)
A resort on the BRISTOL Channel southwest of Bristol. Its basic name, Weston, simply means 'western farm', with the Latin addition (meaning '-on-Sea') made to distinguish this place from Westonzoyland, some distance southeast of it, or simply to denote its location by this stretch of the western shore. The name was recorded as *Weston* in a document of 1266, and as now in one of 1349. The additional words, which now serve to give the name a 'classy' status, are not all that common in English place-names; in many cases the original medieval Latin has been translated into English. The village of Newton-on-the-Moor, in Northumberland, for example, was originally *Neuton super Moram*; and in an even closer parallel, Newton-by-the-Sea, in the same county, was *Neuton super Mare*. So Weston-super-Mare is fortunate to have kept its Latin addition.

Westport (Mayo)
This small town and fishing resort, west of CASTLEBAR, has a self-descriptive name for its location on the west coast. Its Irish name is Cathair na Mart, 'stone fort of the beef oxen', from the Irish *mart*, meaning a cow or ox that has been fattened for the butcher. No doubt such stock were pastured here on the rich meadows near the mouth of a small river.

Westray (Orkney)
This island, one of the most northerly in the ORKNEY group, has a Scandinavian name that means 'western island', from the Old Norse *vestr* (western) and *ey* (island). This describes its situation compared to other islands in this northern region of the group, such as SANDAY, although there is no actual 'Austrey' or 'eastern island' as such.

Westward Ho! (Devon)
The exclamation mark of this place-name denotes it as something out of the ordinary, and the village resort northwest of BIDEFORD takes its name directly from Charles Kingsley's novel *Westward Ho!*, published in 1855 and mainly set in this area of the county, around Bideford. The name was thus deliberately given as a tribute to the author and his novel; the present village arose as a commercial development from the early 1870s, with the church being the first building erected, in 1870. The name was of course intended to act as a lure to tourists and holiday-makers, who would travel 'westward ho!' to visit it. It so happens that the name blends in reasonably well with that of MORTEHOE, the resort just over ten miles further up the coast.

West Wickham (Greater London)
A district of BROMLEY whose basic name, Wickham, means little more than 'settlement', from the conjectural Old English compound *wīc-hām*, comprising *wīc* (farm; or 'dairy farm' or 'special site') and *hām* (homestead, estate). In some

instances, a place named Wickham appears to denote a nearby *vicus*, or Romano-British settlement, although this is not always so, and no such site is known near West Wickham. The name added 'West' to distinguish it from East Wickham, in the Borough of Bexley. West Wickham was simply *Wicheham* in the Domesday Book, and is recorded as *W. Wickham* in a text dated 1610.

West Wittering (West Sussex)
This village northwest of SELSEY is essentially the residential equivalent of the coastal resort of nearby East Wittering, with 'West' and 'East' additionally having the connotations that they have for London's WEST END and East End. The basic name means '(place of) Wihthere's people', and was recorded as *Wihttringes* in a document of 683. The division into East and West Wittering occurred in the late thirteenth or early fourteenth century.

Wetherby (West Yorkshire)
A small market town southeast of HARROGATE whose name is of Scandinavian origin, meaning 'wether farm', 'farm where wethers are bred', from the Old Norse *vethr* (wether) and *bý* (farm, village). A wether is a castrated ram (*compare* WATERFORD). The name was recorded as *Wedrebi* in the Domesday Book.

Wetwang (Humberside)
This village west of GREAT DRIFFIELD has a name that means 'wet fields', from the Old English *wēt* and the rather rare *wang* (meadowland, field). (Here the name may conceivably, however, be Scandinavian, as *vétt-vangr*, an Old Norse term for a field where a legal case was tried.) There was a Roman settlement at Wetwang, whose name was probably *Delgovicia*, perhaps deriving from the unrecorded tribal name *Delgovices*, meaning 'spear-fighters'. (Compare the *Longovices* or 'ship-fighters' of LANCHESTER.) The name of Wetwang was recorded in the Domesday Book as *Wetwangham*.

Wexford (Wexford)
A town near the southeast coast of Ireland at the mouth of the River SLANEY. Its name denotes its Viking origin: the meaning is 'inlet by the sandbank', or more literally 'esker fjord', a combination of the Old Irish *escir* (ridge) and Old Norse *fjorthr* (inlet). The Irish name of Wexford, however, is Loch Garman, 'lake of (the River) Garma'. This refers to a pool at the mouth of the Slaney, whose earlier name, at least for this stretch of the river, was Garma, from the Irish *garma* (headland), perhaps referring to the same sandbank denoted by the Norse name, that is, the spit of land to the north of the narrow approach to Wexford Harbour. The town gave its name to the county.

Wey (Hampshire/Surrey)
A river in southern England that gave its name to WEYBRIDGE and the ford at GUILDFORD, and has a name that simply means 'moving one', 'conveyor'; it is basically the same as WYE. The origin is in fact Indo-European, but the direct link is with the Celtic element rather than the English 'way', which is nevertheless related. The name was recorded as *Waie* in a document of 675.

Weybridge (Surrey)
This residential town, just southwest of WALTON-ON-THAMES, fairly obviously takes its name from the River WEY, on which it is located, at a point near the confluence of this river with the THAMES. The name was recorded as *Waiebrugge* as early as 675. The original bridge may perhaps have been at or near the point where Bridge Road crosses the Wey today.

Weymouth (Dorset)
A town and port west of BOURNEMOUTH that takes its name from the River Wey, near whose mouth it stands. The river name has the same origin as that of the WEY above. The name was recorded as *Waimouthe* (referring to the river-mouth) in a text of 939.

Whaley Bridge (Derbyshire)
A town northwest of BUXTON whose basic name, Whaley, probably derives from the conjectural Old English *hwæl* (hill) and *lēah* (forest, clearing), although some researchers feel that the first word could equally be the Old English *weg* (way). 'Bridge' was added to distinguish this Whaley from others in the region. The town is on the River Goyt. The name was recorded as *Walley* in a document of 1230. *Compare* WHALLEY.

Whalley (Lancashire)
A small town northeast of BLACKBURN whose name is essentially the same as that of WHALEY BRIDGE, although here the combination is probably of *hwæl* and *lēah*, as Whalley is in a gap between Clerk Hill, the southern spur of PENDLE HILL, and the hill known as Whalley Nab (from the Old Norse *nabbi* 'knoll', 'hill'). The name was recorded as *Hwælleage* in 798, and appeared in the Domesday Book as *Wallei*.

Whalsay (Shetland)
This island off the east coast of MAINLAND has a Scandinavian name that means 'whale island', from the Old Norse *hvalr* (whale) and *ey* (island). The name almost certainly refers to the general appearance and outline of the island, which resembles a whale (even on the map), rather than having a direct association with the mammal. (Compare the identically named Whale Island at the other end of the country, in PORTSMOUTH Harbour, where the 'whale-like' contour is similarly apparent.) A document of the mid-thirteenth century recorded the name of the island as *Hvalsey*.

Wharfe (North Yorkshire)
A tributary of the OUSE with a Celtic name, meaning 'winding one', that derives from a root element to which the English 'wharf' is indirectly related, as is the German *werfen* (to throw). Another related word, more surprisingly, is 'verbena', and this can be seen more clearly in the Roman name of the Wharfe, which was *Verbeia*,

with this also probably being the name of the Roman fort at ILKLEY. Latin *verbena*, which gives the plant name, was the word for the sacred branch of myrtle or olive carried at religious ceremonies. The link is the 'winding' one, as the branches were curved, not straight.

Wheathampstead (Hertfordshire)
This village east of HARPENDEN has a straightforward name that means 'wheat homestead', 'homestead where wheat is grown' (*compare* HAMPSTEAD). The name was recorded as *Huuæthamstede* in a document of 1065, and as *Watamestede* in the Domesday Book.

Whetstone (Greater London)
A district of BARNET whose name, perhaps unexpectedly, means what it says, referring either to a single whetstone (sharpening-stone) large enough to have been a prominent landmark, or to a place with a number of small stones that could be used for sharpening. The Old English word behind the name is *hwet-stān*, and the name itself was recorded in a document of 1417 as *Wheston*, which might have given a misleading 'Weston' if other records had not retained the true elements of the name.

Whickham (Tyne and Wear)
This town west of GATESHEAD has a name that at first sight appears to be a 'Wickham', like that described for WEST WICKHAM. But the name was recorded as *Quicham* in a late-twelfth-century text, showing that the origin lies elsewhere. The name means 'homestead with a quickset hedge', from the Old English *cwic* (quickset hedge) (compare modern 'quick' as in the 'quick and the dead') and *hām* (homestead).

Whimple (Devon)
This village, famous for its cider and lying northwest of OTTERY ST MARY, has a name that originally was that of a stream here, meaning 'white pool', from Celtic words related to the modern Welsh *gwyn* (white)

and *pwll* (pool, stream). (*Compare* WENDOVER.) The name was recorded as *Winple* in the Domesday Book.

Whippingham (Isle of Wight)
A village southeast of COWES whose name means 'village of Wippa's people', with the personal name followed by the Old English suffix *-ingas* (people of) and *hām* (homestead, village). The name was recorded in the Domesday Book as *Wipingeham*.

Whipsnade (Bedfordshire)
This village south of DUNSTABLE, famous for its zoo at Whipsnade Park, has a name meaning 'Wibba's detached piece of ground', with the personal name followed by the Old English *snǣd* (something cut off), related to German *schneiden* (to cut). (This is the word that gave the modern surname Snoad.) The reference is usually to a portion of woodland that had been 'cut off' or apportioned in this way. Whipsnade was recorded as *Wibsnede* in a document of 1202.

Whiston (Merseyside)
A town immediately southeast of PRESCOT whose name simply means 'white stone', referring to a local feature recorded in early texts. The name appears as *Quistan* in a document of 1190.

Whitburn (Lothian, Tyne and Wear)
Both the Scottish town, southwest of BATHGATE, and the English one, on the North Sea coast southeast of SOUTH SHIELDS, have identical names with the same meaning — 'white stream', from the Old English *hwīt* (white) and *burna* (stream) ('burn' in the North of England and Scotland). The names were thus originally those of streams at the places mentioned. The Scottish town was recorded as *Whiteburne* in 1296, and the English one as *Hwiteberne* in about 1190.

Whitby (North Yorkshire)
This resort and port, on the North Sea coast north of SCARBOROUGH, has a Scandinavian name that does not mean 'white village', as is sometimes supposed, but 'Hvíti's village'. This particular origin can be determined from a Norse record of the name in the twelfth century as *Hvítabýr*. The Domesday Book entered the name somewhat earlier as *Witeby*. However, the Whitby that is now a district of ELLESMERE PORT, Cheshire, *does* have a name that means 'white village', and here the Scandinavians substituted the Old Norse *bý* (village) for the earlier Old English *burg* (fortified place).

Whitchurch (Hampshire, Shropshire)
The name of both the small town east of ANDOVER and the larger town north of SHREWSBURY means 'white church', from Old English words (*hwīt* and *cirice*) that have remained clearly identifiable in their correct sense today. A 'white church' was a stone-built one, with white limestone in the fabric, as distinct from one made of wood. The Hampshire Whitchurch had its name recorded as *Hwitan cyrice* in a document of 909, and the Shropshire one was entered as *Album Monasterium* in a text of 1199. The latter Whitchurch arose on the site of the former Roman town of *Mediolanum*, a name found fairly widely on the continent (for example, as that of modern Milan), meaning '(place in the) middle of a plain', from Celtic root words that are nevertheless related to more readily recognisable European words, such as English 'middle' and 'plain'. However, the 'middle' element may equally be understood as 'central', meaning that the town was important to the local community. It is interesting, but may be purely a coincidence, that the Shropshire Whitchurch is at a point where major roads meet (today the A41 to CHESTER, A49 to the north and south, and A525 to the west and east) near the junction of three county boundaries (Shropshire, Cheshire, and Clwyd, the last formerly Flintshire), and moreover near the border between England and Wales.

Whitechapel (Greater London)
This district of east central LONDON has a
self-explanatory name similar to that of
WHITCHURCH, referring to the original
white-coloured and stone-built chapel
here. The chapel that gave the name was
built in the thirteenth century and in the
following century became the parish
church of St Mary Whitechapel. The name
was recorded as *St Mary de Mattefelon* in a
document of 1282 (the latter word of this
probably being the name of a benefactor of
the chapel, or even possibly of its founder),
and *New Chapel without Aldgate* in 1295,
with the present name emerging as
Whitechapele by Aldgate in a document of
1340 and, in its full glory, *Parish of the
Blessed Mary Matfelon of White Chapell* in
1452.

Whitehall (Greater London)
London's 'centre of government' adjoins
the street of the name that runs from
Trafalgar Square to the Houses of
Parliament by the THAMES. It takes its
name from the former Whitehall Palace
here, of which only the Banqueting House
survives. The palace itself, destroyed by
fire in the late seventeenth century, was
probably so named because of the light
colour of the stonework of the new
buildings added to the original York House
by Henry VIII in the sixteenth century,
when he also changed its name. The name
was recorded as *Whytehale al. Yorke Place*
in a document of 1530.

Whitehaven (Cumbria)
A port on the Irish Sea coast south of
WORKINGTON whose Scandinavian name
was originally more complex than it is now.
A record of about 1135, for example,
names the place as *Qwithofhavene*. This
represents 'Whitehead Haven', from the
Old Norse *hvitr* (white), *hofuth* (head) and
hafn (haven, harbour), and ultimately
refers to the hill of white stone which forms
one side of the harbour and which was
called *Hvithofuth*, 'White Head'. The
middle word of the long name was then

dropped, for ease of pronunciation, so that
the present name has no reference to the
white rock that gave the original name.

Whithorn (Dumfries and Galloway)
A small town south of WIGTOWN whose
name means 'white building', from the Old
English *hwīt* (white) and *ærn* (building).
The Venerable Bede referred to the
original site as *æt Hwitan ærne*, 'at the
white building', and added that it was so
called because it was made of stone (*Vulgo
vocatur Ad Candidam Casam eo quod ibi
ecclesiam de lapide, insolito Brettonibus more,
fecerit*, 'popularly called the [place] at the
White Building, because the church
there will have been made out of stone,
according to the strange custom of the
British').

Whitland Abbey (Dyfed)
This twelfth-century Cistercian house is
now in ruins, but it took its name from
the village of Whitland here, east of
NARBERTH, with the name itself meaning
'white glade', from the Old English *hwīt*
(white) and Old French *launde* (forest
glade) (the latter word is indirectly related
to English 'land' and to the Landes, the
district of sand-dunes and pines in
southwest France). An equivalent to this
name, with both words French in origin, is
that of Blanchland, the village near
HEXHAM, Northumberland. The Welsh
name of Whitland is Hendy-gwyn, 'old
white house', from the Welsh *hen* (old), *tŷ*
(house), and *gwyn* (white). Whitland's
present name was recorded in Latin form
as *Alba Landa* in a document of 1214, but
as now in one dated 1309. The Welsh name
probably refers to an earlier abbey on the
site, so is similar to names such as
WHITCHURCH and WHITECHAPEL.
Whitland Abbey was the first Cistercian
abbey in Wales, and was the mother house
of STRATA FLORIDA.

Whitley Bay (Tyne and Wear)
This North Sea resort to the north of
TYNEMOUTH takes its name from the bay

on which it stands, which itself was named after the original settlement of Whitley here, recorded as *Wyteleya* in the twelfth century, it means 'white wood' or 'white forest-clearing', from the Old English *hwīt* (white) and *lēah* (wood, clearing). A 'white wood' is probably a sparse one, as distinct from a 'Blackwood', which is a dark dense one.

Whitstable (Kent)

A coastal resort northwest of CANTERBURY whose name means 'white post', from the Old English *hwīt* (white) and *stapol* (post) (*compare* BARNSTAPLE). The name is first recorded (as *Witenstapel*) in the Domesday Book as the name of a hundred, and it therefore seems likely that the original 'white post' would have been a marker where the court of the hundred met. The exact site of this is not known. At the same time it may be significant that Whitstable is by the sea, as Barnstaple is, and the 'white post' could in that case have marked a landing-place. Perhaps it served for both purposes?

Whitworth (Lancashire)

A town north of ROCHDALE whose name probably means 'white enclosure', from the Old English *hwīt* (white) and *worth* (enclosure), although the first part of the name could possibly be a personal name, so that the meaning is 'Hwīta's enclosure'. The name was recorded as *Whiteword* in the thirteenth century.

Whyteleafe (Surrey)

The 'Olde Tea Shoppe' spelling of the name betrays its bogus origin, and this suburban district southeast of PURLEY has a modern name, given in the mid-nineteenth century to the residential area that grew up here after the coming of the railway. However, the name is not entirely fanciful, and a record of 1839 mentions a *White Leaf Field* here, apparently so named because of the aspens that grew there. The present spelling of the name is an 'embroidered' variant of this.

Wick (Highland)

This fishing port near the tip of northeastern mainland Scotland has a Scandinavian name simply meaning 'bay', from the Old Norse *vík* (as for LERWICK, even further north). The reference is to Wick Bay, on which the town stands, at the mouth of the River Wick, named after the bay. The name was recorded as *Vik* in a document of 1140.

Wicken Fen (Cambridgeshire)

This nature reserve in the FENS, southwest of SOHAM, takes its name from the nearby village of Wicken, whose own name means '(place) at the outlying farms', from the dative plural (required after 'at') of the Old English *wīc* (outlying farm, special place), exactly as in the name of HIGH WYCOMBE. The original word would have been *wīcum*, and the final -*m* of this has changed to -*n* as sometimes happened, especially in the southeast Midlands, as here. Wicken's name was recorded as *Wikes* in a document of 1203.

Wickford (Essex)

A town northeast of BASILDON whose name may mean 'ford by an outlying farm', from the Old English *wīc* (outlying farm, special place) and *ford* (ford). However, the precise reference may be to a *vicus*, or a Romano-British settlement, as considered under WEST WICKHAM. The name was recorded as *Wicford* in the late tenth century. *Compare also* WICKHAM MARKET.

Wickham Market (Suffolk)

This small town to the northeast of WOODBRIDGE has a basic name, Wickham, that probably means 'homestead by a *vicus*', that is, by a Romano-British settlement, as mentioned under WEST WICKHAM. The Domesday Book recorded the name as *Wikham*. Later, the town acquired a market, as the second word of the name indicates. At the same time, the addition distinguishes this market from the one at STOWMARKET, sixteen miles west of Wickham Market. The town was formerly more important than now, and was granted two annual fairs by Henry VI in 1440, as well as having a weekly market of some size.

Wicklow (Wicklow)

This town on the east coast of Ireland has a Scandinavian name meaning 'vikings' meadow', from the Old Norse *víkingr* (viking) and *ló* (meadow) (related to English 'lea'). The meadows could have been those by the mouth of the River Vartry here. The Irish name of Wicklow is Cill Mhantáin, 'St Mantán's church'. Mantán is said to have been a disciple of St Patrick. The town gave its name to this eastern county of Ireland.

Widecombe in the Moor (Devon)

This DARTMOOR village northwest of ASHBURTON has a basic name, Widecombe, that means 'willow valley', from the Old English *wīthig* (willow; compare 'withy') and *cumb* (hollow, valley). The village may be high on the moor in a general sense, but locally it is in a shallow dip, by the East Webburn. The name was recorded as *Widecumba* in a document of 1270, and as *Wydecomb yn the More* in 1461. The additional phrase perhaps serves to indicate the isolated situation of the village, rather than distinguishing it from other 'willow valleys'. The name is still sometimes spelt with a double *d*, perhaps from the familiar reference to 'Widdicombe Fair' in the old ballad about 'Old Uncle Tom Cobbleigh and all' (spelling here as in the *Oxford Dictionary of Quotations*).

Widnes (Cheshire)

This industrial town on the north side of the MERSEY has a self-descriptive name ('wide ness', or 'wide promontory') referring to the rounded headland on which it is located by the Mersey. The name was recorded as *Wydnes* in a text dating from about 1200.

Wigan (Greater Manchester)

An industrial town northwest of MANCHESTER whose name is simply a personal name without any addition, such as 'town' (in whatever form). The suggestion has been made that a Celtic word related to the modern Welsh *tref* (town) may be missing, as the name is certainly Celtic, and there is a Wigan on ANGLESEY that was *Tref Wigan* originally. So the most that can be said of the name is that it means something like 'Wigan's place'. The name was recorded as now in a document of 1199.

Wight, Isle of (Isle of Wight)

This familiar chalk island (and county) off the south coast of mainland England has a name of Celtic origin, from a word that probably meant 'division', related to the modern Welsh *gwaith* (work, time), and referring to the way in which the waters divide to the north and south of the island, so that ships have to alter course. Perhaps the best concept is as a sort of 'watershed' or 'parting of the waters', involving any ship that is sailing along the south coast. The decision will always have to be made: whether to steer closer to the coast, and pass through The SOLENT, or whether to head more out to sea in the English Channel. The Roman name for the island was *Vectis*, having the same origin. (This name is widely used on the island for commercial purposes; the main bus company is Southern Vectis, for example.) A document of about 890 records the name as *Wiht*. Unfortunately the association of the island with chalk, and the resemblance of its name to 'white', frequently result in the popular supposition that 'white' is its actual meaning.

Wigston (Leicestershire)

A town immediately south of LEICESTER, also known as Wigston Magna, whose name means 'Vikings' farm', from the Old English *wīcing* (pirate, Viking), a word already in use before the Vikings invaded Britain, and *tūn* (farm). The name was recorded in the Domesday Book as *Wichingestone*. Later, 'Magna' was added to distinguish this Wigston from the small village of Wigston Parva, eleven miles southwest of the town. But the latter's name has quite a different origin, and means 'rocking-stone', 'logan stone', from the Old English *wigga*, literally 'beetle', but when associated with *stān* means 'moving' (compare modern 'wiggle'). The Domesday Book recorded this Wigston as *Wicestan*. But the similarity of the name, and the subsequent identity of their forms, obviously required the distinguishing additions of Magna and Parva, or 'Big' and 'Little'. The rocking-stone at Wigston Parva was doubtless associated with its location, on WATLING STREET and by the county boundary.

Wigton (Cumbria)

A market town southwest of CARLISLE whose name means 'Wicga's farm', with the personal name followed by the common Old English *tūn* (farm). The name was recorded as *Wiggeton* in a document of 1163. *Compare* WIGTOWN.

Wigtown (Dumfries and Galloway)

This small town south of NEWTON STEWART has a name that is exactly the same in origin and meaning as that of WIGTON, and so means 'Wicga's farm', with the same Old English name and word. It was recorded as *Wigeton* in a document of 1266, and gave its name to the former county of Wigtownshire.

Willenhall (West Midlands)

The two Willenhalls of note in the West Midlands are the districts of WALSALL and COVENTRY. Their names may have the same origin, and mean 'Willa's nook of land', with the personal name followed by the Old English *halh* (corner, nook). It is possible, however, that the Coventry Willenhall may mean 'willow nook', 'corner of land where willows grow', as there is a slight difference in the historical records of the names. The Walsall

Willenhall appears as *Willanhalch* in a text of about 732, while its namesake is as now, without *a*, in a document of 1167. The Old English word that would give the latter's origin is the conjectural *wiligen* (growing with willows, willowy).

Willesden (Greater London)

A district of BRENT whose name means 'hill by a spring', from the Old English *wiella* (spring, well) and *dūn* (hill), with this recorded in the Domesday Book as *Wellesdone*. The present name should really be something like 'Welsdon', or at least 'Wilsdon', but the spelling was altered to its present form in about 1840 by the railway company, apparently to 'match' it with neighbouring NEASDEN (to the north) and HARLESDEN (to the south). The one-inch Ordnance Survey map of 1822, reissued in 1891 to include railways, shows *Wilsdon* as the name of the village (as it then was), but *Willesden Junction* for the station south of it.

Willington (Durham)

A town north of BISHOP AUCKLAND whose name means 'willow farm', 'farm among willow trees', from the Old English conjectural *wilign* (willow copse) and *tūn* (farm). The name was recorded as *Willetune* in the Domesday Book. Not all Willingtons will have this origin, and others are derived from personal names.

Wilmington (East Sussex)

A village northeast of SEAFORD, famous for the Long Man of Wilmington, the figure cut in the chalk of the South Downs. The name means either 'farm of Wilhelm's people' or 'Wilma's farm'. The latter interpretation is based on the Domesday Book record of it as both *Wineltone* and *Wilminte*, lacking the -ing- element that means 'people of', although this has now appeared in the name, perhaps by association with other Wilmingtons. But if the first interpretation is correct, this element will have always been present, and was simply overlooked or unrecorded by the Domesday Book clerk.

Wilmslow (Cheshire)
A mainly residential town south of MANCHESTER whose name means 'Wīghelm's burial mound', with the personal name followed by the Old English *hlāw* (mound, tumulus). The name does not necessarily imply that Wīghelm was himself buried in the mound, and it may simply have been a way of indicating his estate, i.e. naming it after a burial mound located on it. The name was recorded as *Wilmesloe* in a thirteenth-century text.

Wilton (Wiltshire)
A small town west of SALISBURY that takes its name from the River Wylye, on which it is located, and so means 'farm on the Wylye'. The river's own name is of Celtic origin and comes from a word that is ultimately related to English 'guile' and 'wily'. This means 'tricky', and refers to the river's habit of flooding unpredictably. It was Wilton that gave the name of WILTSHIRE, its county. Its own name was recorded as *Uuiltun* in a document of 838, and as *Wiltune* in the Domesday Book.

Wiltshire (England)
A county in southern England whose name derives from that of WILTON, in the sense 'shire dependent on Wilton', although the town is no longer the county town. The name was recorded as *Wiltunscir* in a document of 870; in another text of the same period, the inhabitants of the region are referred to as the *Wilsætan*, meaning 'dwellers on the Wylye'. If it had not been for Wilton, therefore, the county name today might have been 'Wilset' like its western neighbours of SOMERSET and DORSET.

Wimbledon (Greater London)
The name of this district of MERTON means 'Wynnman's hill', with the final element of the name as the Old English *dūn* (hill). The present form of the name has altered somewhat from the original, which was recorded in a mid-tenth-century text as *Wunemannedun*. The alteration is due to the Normans, who changed the second *n* to *l*, then inserted a *b* between the *m* and this *l* to make it easier to pronounce. Similar changes occurred elsewhere, so that Boulogne, in France, was originally *Bononia*, for example, and the Normans also referred to LINCOLN as *Nicol*. A reminder of the hill of the name still exists in the street called Wimbledon Hill (the A219).

Wimborne Minster (Dorset)
A town on the River STOUR, northwest of BOURNEMOUTH, whose basic name, Wimbourne (by which it is still commonly known), means 'meadow stream', from the Old English conjectural *winn* (pasture) (deduced from place-names like this one) and *burna* (stream). This was a former name of the River Allen, which joins the Stour here. The 'minster' of the name was the nunnery founded here by Queen Cuthburh at the beginning of the eighth century, described as being *æt Winburnan* in the *Anglo-Saxon Chronicle*. The fuller form of the name is recorded as *Winburnan monasterium* in 893.

Wincanton (Somerset)
A small market town northeast of YEOVIL that derives its name from the River Cale, on which it is situated. The river's name was recorded as both *Cawel* and *Wincawel* in a document of 956, and it is the longer word, containing a Celtic element meaning 'white' (compare Welsh *gwyn*), that gave the present name of the town, with *tūn* (farm) added. The Domesday Book thus recorded the name as a whole as *Wincaletone*.

Winchcombe (Gloucestershire)
This town northeast of CHELTENHAM has a name derived from the conjectural Old English *wincel* (corner) (related to modern 'winch', used for turning or 'cornering') and *cumb* (valley). The sense is thus really

'valley round the corner', 'remote valley', referring to the location of Winchcombe in a deep valley of the River Isbourne, near the northeastern foot of the COTSWOLD HILLS. The name was recorded as *Wincelcumba* in a document of 811.

Winchelsea (East Sussex)

This ancient town on a hill southwest of RYE has a name that probably means 'Wincel's river', although 'corner island' has also been proposed. The former interpretation is based on the personal name being followed by the Old English *ēa* (river); the latter would derive from *wincel* (as for WINCHCOMBE) and *ēg* (island). Either way, the original name would have applied to a Winchelsea quite different from the present town, for much of the old town was swept away by the sea in the late thirteenth century, and 'New' Winchelsea arose on a nearby promontory, becoming in due course one of the favoured CINQUE PORTS. The 'river' suggested for the first account of the name would thus have flowed in a region now covered by the sea. The name was recorded as *Winceleseia* in 1130.

Winchester (Hampshire)

This ancient cathedral city and former capital of WESSEX has a name that immediately declares it to have arisen on the site of a Roman settlement; the latter's name forms the 'Win-' of the present name, and the Old English *ceaster* (Roman camp) forms the '-chester'. The full name of the former Roman city was *Venta Belgarum*, with *Venta* of Celtic origin and meaning effectively 'favoured place'. It lies behind a number of other Roman names, such as *Venta Silurum* (CAERWENT) and *Venta Icenorum* (Caistor St Edmund; *compare* CAISTOR), and also forms the basis of GWENT. The second word of the name refers to the *Belgae*, the tribe whose capital it was. The tribal name means 'proud ones', from a Celtic root element *belg-* related to modern English 'bulge' (as if they were 'swelling with pride'), and came

to give the name of Belgium. In the eighth century, the Venerable Bede referred to the settlement here *in civitate Venta, quae a gente Saxorum Uintancaestir appellatur* ('in the city of Venta, which is called Wintancaster by the Saxon people'). If it had not been for the tribal name, it is possible that the former Roman name, and therefore the present one, could have been derived from that of the River ITCHEN on which the city stands.

Windermere (Cumbria)

The largest lake in the Lake District; it has a name that means 'Vinand's lake', with the Swedish personal name (a rarity in English place-names) followed by the Old English *mere* (lake). The name was recorded as *Winendermer* in a text of about 1170.

Windrush (Gloucestershire/Oxfordshire)

A river that rises near WINCHCOMBE and flows southeast to the THAMES. Its name is better understood in Celtic terms rather than English; it is British in origin, and means 'white marsh', from two conjectural elements related to modern Welsh *gwyn* (white) and modern Irish *riasc* (marsh). No doubt the modern name developed by association with 'wind' and 'rushes', both in turn associated with rivers. The name was recorded as *Uuenrisc* in a document of 779. Much of the course of the river is through low-lying land, if not exactly marshland.

Windsor (Berkshire)

This famous town on the banks of the THAMES south of SLOUGH has a name that means 'windlass shore', from the Old English *windels* (winding-gear, windlass) and *ōra* (shore, bank). This probably refers to a mechanism used for assisting carts up the muddy hill from the river's edge, rather than for actually hauling boats out of the water. The 'shore' is thus not the actual edge of the river, but a bank or hillslope higher up. Support for this relatively recent interpretation of the name is given by the same name at Broadwindsor, the Dorset village near BEAMINSTER, where the river is so small that it is not even navigable, and where the 'windlass' would have been used for carts, not boats. It is possible that the original winding-mechanism may have been on or near the site where River Street runs down to the Thames today. The name was recorded as *Windlesora* in a document of about 1060. The Old English word *windels* has been deduced from this and identical place-names; the English word 'windlass' is not recorded until much later, in about 1400.

Winsford (Cheshire)

A town on the River WEAVER south of NORTHWICH whose name means 'Wine's ford', with the personal name followed by the Old English *ford*, much as in the name of BEDFORD. The ford would have taken the road from CHESTER to MIDDLEWICH (now represented by the A54) over the Weaver (now bridged). The name was recorded as *Wyneford bridge* in about 1334, and as *Wynsfurth brygge* in 1475. *Compare* WINSLOW.

Winslow (Buckinghamshire)

This small town southeast of BUCKINGHAM has a name that means 'Wine's burial-mound', with the personal name (identical to the one in WINSFORD) followed by the Old English *hlāw* (burial-mound, tumulus). For a comment on this sort of name, *compare* WILMSLOW. Winslow was recorded as *Wineshlauu* in a text of 795.

Winterton (Norfolk)

This resort north of YARMOUTH has a name that means what it says — 'winter farm' — and seems to be so named by comparison with East or West (or both) Somerton, immediately west of it. It was thus a farm used in the winter months. A site by the sea can often be higher and so drier than one a short distance island, which is frequently lower and certainly damper in the winter months. Winterton

(now also called Winterton-on-Sea) was recorded as *Wintertun* in the mid-eleventh century.

Wirksworth (Derbyshire)

A town south of MATLOCK whose name means 'Weorc's enclosure', with the same personal name as found in WORKSOP but here followed by the Old English *worth* (enclosure). The name was recorded as *Wyrcesuuyrthe* in a text of 835.

Wirral (Merseyside/Cheshire)

This well-known peninsula between the estuaries of the DEE (to the west) and the MERSEY (to the east) (and formerly entirely in Cheshire) has a name that has been explained as meaning 'bog-myrtle nook', from the Old English *wīr* (bog-myrtle) and *halh* (nook). But this interpretation poses some problems. First, the peninsula is hardly a 'nook', even if one extends the sense to mean something like 'land by a river'. The Wirral is too extensive an area, and the rivers too wide to provide a 'nook' by their shore. Second, bog-myrtle, as its name implies, grows in damp locations. Yet the Wirral is largely a high dry ridge. Perhaps, therefore, some other origin lies behind the name, which was recorded as *Wirhealum* (moreover, suggesting a plural, 'nooks') in a document of 984.

Wisbech (Cambridgeshire)

A town in the FENS southwest of KING'S LYNN on the River Nene; however, its name means 'low ridge by the OUSE'. The first half of the name is the river name, and the latter half is the Old English *bæc*, literally 'back'. The apparent anomaly is explained by the fact that the Ouse once flowed to Wisbech, but has since altered its course, as have other fenland rivers and streams. The 'back' would then have been the higher ridge of land on which Wisbech stands. The same word can be seen behind the names of the two Cambridgeshire rivers of Landbeach and Waterbeach, respectively 'land ridge' and 'water ridge', or 'place on a ridge away from a river' and 'place on a ridge by a river' (the Cam). Wisbech was recorded as *Wisbece* in the Domesday Book.

Wishaw (Strathclyde)
A town southeast of MOTHERWELL whose name means either 'willow wood' or 'wood on a bend'. The second half of the name represents the Old English *sceaga* (wood; 'shaw'). The first could be either *wīthig* (willow) or the conjectural *wiht* (bend, river bend, winding valley). The name was recorded as *Witscaga* in the Domesday Book. Perhaps the 'bend' is that of the hillside on which the town is situated.

Witham (Essex, Leicestershire/Lincolnshire)
Either a town northeast of CHELMSFORD or a river in eastern England. The town's name may mean 'village on a bend', with the same Old English *wiht* (bend) as considered for WISHAW. This would then be followed by *hām* (village). There is a bend in the River Brain to the south of the town, so the derivation suggested is suitable. The name was recorded both in a document of 913 and in the Domesday Book exactly as now, which unfortunately does not help with an interpretation of the name, as alternative spellings and forms are lacking. The River Witham, however, has a name of quite a different origin, perhaps meaning 'forest river', from a Celtic word related to the Welsh *gwydd* (forest) plus either a mere suffix or an element actually meaning 'river'. The name was recorded as *Withma* in a document of about 1000.

Withernsea (Humberside)
A coastal resort east of HULL whose name was recorded as *Widfornessei* in the Domesday Book, and that is almost certainly Scandinavian in origin. The components of the name seem to be the Old Norse *vith* (against; i.e. 'near'), *thorn* (thorn tree), and *sær* (sea, lake). The whole sense would then be '(place by a) lake near a thorn tree' (or near several thorn trees). The 'sea' of the name is thus really a lake.

This explanation of the name is not conclusive, however, and a personal name may be involved (perhaps it is Forni, as for FORMBY).

Witney (Oxfordshire)
A town on the River WINDRUSH west of OXFORD whose name means 'Witta's island', with the personal name followed by the Old English *ēg* (island). Witney is on land that is relatively high by comparison with the surrounding terrain, where the river divides into several branches and where much of the land is marshy. This is therefore the 'island'. The name was recorded as *æt Wyttanige* in a document of 969.

Wiveliscombe (Somerset)
A small town west of TAUNTON whose name means 'Wifel's valley'; it was recorded in a document of 854 as *Wifelescumb*. The personal name is followed by the frequently found West Country *cumb*, Old English 'valley'. The town is in a marked valley between high hills here. The name is still sometimes pronounced 'Wilscombe', especially locally.

Wivenhoe (Essex)
A town on the River Colne southeast of COLCHESTER whose name means 'Wifa's spur of land', with the personal name followed by the Old English *hōh* (spur). The Domesday Book recorded the name as *Wiunhov*. The spur referred to is to the north of the town.

Woburn Abbey (Bedfordshire)
This well-known eighteenth-century house, with its large park, takes its name from the nearby village of Woburn, whose own name means 'crooked stream' and is really the name of the stream here. The two Old English words that give the name are *wōh* (crooked) and *burna* (stream). The name was recorded as *Woburninga gemæru* ('boundary of the Woburn people') in a document of 969. *Compare* WOMBOURNE.

Woking (Surrey)
The name of this residential town north of GUILDFORD is interrelated and interdependent with that of WOKINGHAM. Woking's name means '(territory of) Wocc's people', with the personal name followed by the Old English -*ingas* suffix that means 'people of' (the named person). This was recorded as *Uuocchingas* in a document of about 710.

Wokingham (Berkshire)
The name of this town southeast of READING means 'homestead of Wocc's people', almost certainly referring to the same man who gave his name to WOKING. The two towns are only about fifteen miles apart. Wokingham was recorded as *Wokingeham* in a text of 1146.

Wollaton (Nottinghamshire)
A district of NOTTINGHAM whose name means 'Wulflāf's village', with this appearing in the Domesday Book as *Olavestone*, a typical Norman 'easing' of the name. The personal name (which means 'wolf bequest', literally 'one who has been left by a wolf') is followed by the common Old English *tūn* (farm, village).

Wolsingham (Durham)
A town northwest of BISHOP AUCKLAND whose name means 'homestead of Wulfsige's people', with the personal name (meaning 'wolf victory') followed by the Old English -*ingas* ('people of') and the common *hām* (homestead). The name was recorded as *Wlsingham* (*sic*) in a document of the mid-twelfth century. *Compare* WOLSTANTON.

Wolstanton (Staffordshire)
A district of NEWCASTLE-UNDER-LYME whose name means 'Wulfstān's village', with the personal name (meaning 'wolf rock') followed by the frequently found Old English *tūn* (farm, village). The name was recorded in the Domesday Book as *Wlstantone* (*sic*). *Compare* WOLSINGHAM.

Wolvercote (Oxfordshire)
A district of OXFORD whose name means 'dwelling-place of Wulfgār's people', with the personal name (meaning 'wolf spear') followed by the Old English -*ingas* (people of) (not apparent in the modern form of the name) and *cot* (cottage, dwelling-place). The name was recorded as *Ulfgarcote* in the Domesday Book.

Wolverhampton (West Midlands)
This large industrial town has a name that means 'Wulfrūn's high farm'; the second half of the name is not the same 'Hampton' as in names such as NORTHAMPTON and SOUTHAMPTON, where the 'ham' is either the Old English *hām* or *hamm*, but is the dative form (*hēan*) of *hēah* (high). This can be deduced from early records of the name (such as *æt Heantune* in 985) and is supported by the topography. Wolverhampton stands on ground that is higher than the surrounding terrain to the north, east, and west. The personal name, meaning 'wolf council', is that of the lady to whom the manor was given in 985, and eleven years later she gave a number of local estates to the monastery founded by her at Wolverhampton. Her name was not added to the 'Hampton' ('high farm') until it became necessary to distinguish this Hampton from others. A record of about 1080 has Wolverhampton as *Wolvrenehamptonia*. Today Wolverhampton has both a Wulfruna Street and a Wulfrun Shopping Centre. *Compare* WOLVERTON.

Wolverton (Buckinghamshire)
A town in the northwest part of MILTON KEYNES whose name could mean either 'Wulfrūn's farm', with the same personal name as for WOLVERHAMPTON, or else 'village of Wulfhere's people', with the personal name (meaning 'wolf army') followed by the Old English -*ingas* (people of); in each case the final element is *tūn* (farm, village). The name was recorded as *Wluerintone* in the Domesday Book, where the -*in*- could represent either the

second half of Wulfrūn's name, or the
-*ingas* suffix.

Wombourne (Staffordshire)
The name of this town southwest of
WOLVERHAMPTON is sometimes spelt
without the final -*e*, but this does not alter
its meaning, which is '(place at the)
winding stream', so is exactly the same as
the name of WOBURN ABBEY. The
Domesday Book recorded the name as
Wamburne. The 'winding stream' that
flows through Wombourne actually is the
Wombourne.

Wombwell (South Yorkshire)
A town southeast of BARNSLEY whose
name probably means what it says, with
'womb' (the same word in Old English)
used to denote a hollow, and 'well' (Old
English *wella*) a spring. The sense would
thus be 'spring in a hollow'. Wombwell is
on two rivers, the DOVE and the Dearne,
and the spring would doubtless have been
close to one of them. The name appears in
the Domesday Book as *Wanbuella*.

Woodbridge (Suffolk)
A town east of IPSWICH whose name could
mean either 'bridge by a wood' or, more
probably, 'wooden bridge', denoting a
former wooden bridge over the River
Deben here. The name was recorded as
Oddebruge in a document of the mid-
eleventh century, while the Domesday
Book entered it as *Wudebrige*.

Woodchester (Gloucestershire)
This village south of STROUD has a name
that immediately points to a former Roman
settlement (Old English *caester*) by a wood,
or even built of wood. The remains of the
Roman villa can still be seen to the north of
the village. The name was recorded as
Uuduceastir in the first half of the eighth
century, and as *Widecestre* in the
Domesday Book.

Woodford Green (Greater London)
A district of REDBRIDGE whose basic name

means 'ford by a wood', recorded as
Wodeforda in a document of 1062, and as
Wdefort in the Domesday Book. Later,
'green' was added to distinguish this
Woodford from Woodford Bridge, east of
it, and South Woodford, south of it. The
'wood' of the name is EPPING FOREST,
and Woodford Green still has a grassy
enclosure named The Green, although this
can be only a partial representation of the
original 'village green'. *Compare* WOOD
GREEN.

Wood Green (Greater London)
A district of HARINGEY whose name means
what it says, 'green place near a wood'. The
'wood' here is ENFIELD Chase, and a
remnant of the original green exists in the
form of the smallish enclosed area called
Wood Green Common. The name was
recorded as *Wodegrene* in a text of 1502.

Woodhall Spa (Lincolnshire)
This spa town southwest of HORNCASTLE
has a name that can be understood as
'manor house by a wood', with this
recorded in the twelfth century as
Wudehalle.

Woodhouse (South Yorkshire, West
Yorkshire)
Either of two places, respectively districts
of SHEFFIELD and LEEDS, as well as other
Woodhouses; the name means what it says,
'house by a wood' (not 'wooden house').
The two Woodhouses mentioned here were
recorded respectively as *Wdehus* and
Wodehus in early-thirteenth-century
documents.

Woodmansterne (Surrey)
This suburban district east of BANSTEAD
has an unusually long name, without the
inclusion of any personal name. The
meaning is 'thorn tree by the boundary of
the wood', with the component Old
English words being *wudu* (wood), *gemǣre*
(boundary) and *thorn* (thorn tree). The
name was recorded in the Domesday Book
as *Odemerestor*, with a distortion of some of

the original elements. However, they appear more clearly in a document of 1242, as *Wudemeresthorn*. The 'boundary' element has now become '-man-', no doubt by association with 'wood'.

Woodstock (Oxfordshire)

A historic town northwest of OXFORD whose name means simply 'place in the woods', from the Old English *wudu* (wood) and *stoc* (place); it was translated into medieval Latin by Simeon of Durham, a twelfth-century monk, as *silvarum locus*. The trees and woods around Woodstock are still abundant today. The name was recorded in about 1000 as *Wudustoc*.

Wookey Hole (Somerset)

A village with its famous (floodlit) limestone cave, northwest of WELLS. Its basic name, Wookey, means 'snare', from the Old English *wōcig* (related to the *wōh*, 'crooked' that gave the names of WOBURN ABBEY and WOMBOURNE). There must have been a noose or snare set here as a trap for animals. The location here, at the foot of the MENDIP HILLS, would have been a suitable one for such traps (*compare* LUDGERSHALL). The 'Hole' is of course the well-known cave. There is a separate village of Wookey a mile southwest of Wookey Hole. This village was recorded as *Woky* in a document of 1065, while Wookey Hole appears as *Wokyhole* in the same document.

Wool (Dorset)

A village west of WAREHAM whose name does not mean what it says, but means 'spring', 'well', or more precisely, '(place at) the wells', from the Old English *wella*. The springs or wells concerned are just south of the village, and the eighteenth-century Dorset vicar and topographer John Hutchins, in his vast work, *History and Antiquities of the County of Dorset*, was careful to explain of Wool that the name was said to derive 'from the springs that abound there', and in particular 'from a beautiful stream of water, which rises or

wells up in a body, at the head of a small meadow [. . .] on the south side'. (He also mentions that 'Wool and Woolbridge are indifferently used, but among the poor it generally goes by the latter name'.) The reference to the springs is preserved today by such names as Spring Street, Springfield Cottage, and Well Head Close, the latter being the name of a field. Wool was recorded as *Wille* in the Domesday Book.

Woolacombe (Devon)

A resort southwest of ILFRACOMBE whose name means 'valley by a spring', from the Old English *wella* (spring, well) and *cumb* (valley). Woolacombe lies in a characteristic West Country 'coomb'. The name was recorded as *Wellecome* in the Domesday Book.

Wooler (Northumberland)

A small town northwest of ALNWICK whose name means 'spring hill', from the Old English *wella* (spring, well) and *ofer* (hill). Here, the 'hill' is better understood as 'height', describing the location of the town on highish ground overlooking the River Till to the east. The name was recorded as *Wulloure* in a document of 1187.

Woolwich (Greater London)

A district on the south bank of the THAMES in the Borough of GREENWICH. Its name means 'place where wool was loaded or unloaded' from the Old English *wull* (wool) and *wīc* (outlying farm, special place). The name is a good example of a *wīc* that was the site of a particular commercial activity, here defined by the *wull* (*compare* CHISWICK; *contrast* GREENWICH!). Woolwich was recorded as *Uuluuich* in a document of 918, with the double *us* representing modern *w*.

Wootton Bassett (Wiltshire)

This small town west of SWINDON has a common basic name, Wootton, meaning 'farm by a wood', from the Old English *wudu* (wood) and *tun* (farm). Here the distinguishing second word refers to the Basset family, who held the manor here in the thirteenth century (*compare* STONE BASSETT). The name was recorded as *Wdetun* in a document of the late seventh century, and as *Wotton Basset* in 1271. *Compare* WOOTTON WAWEN.

Wootton Wawen (Warwickshire)
This village south of HENLEY-IN-ARDEN has the same basic name as WOOTTON BASSETT, and so means 'farm by a wood'. The addition here is the personal name of the owner of the local manor in the eleventh century. His name is Scandinavian in origin, and means 'cart' (Old Norse *vagn*). The name was recorded as *Uuidutuun* in a document of the early eighth century (showing Old English *widu*, the earlier form of *wudu*), and as *Waghnes Wotton* in 1285.

Worcester (Hereford and Worcester)
The second half of the name of this well-known cathedral city, southwest of DROITWICH, is a reminder that Worcester arose on the site of a former Roman settlement (Old English *ceaster*). The first part of the name is probably a tribal name, referring to the *Weogaran*, or 'dwellers by the winding river', from the same Celtic root word that gave the name of both WYRE and Wyre Forest, now an administrative district of the county. It is not certain which river was the 'winding' one. Worcester is on the SEVERN, but it does not necessarily mean that this was the river so designated. The *Weogoran* came from an area much wider than that of Worcester itself. The Roman name of the fort at Worcester may have been *Vertis*, which although it seems to suggest a sense 'winding' (from a Celtic root related to Latin *vertere* 'to turn'), is almost certainly a corruption of some other name. Worcester was recorded as *Uueogorna civitate* in a text of 691, and the county of Worcestershire, which took its name from it, appears as *Wireceastrescir* in a document of about 1040.

Worcester Park (Greater London)
A district of SUTTON that derives its name from that of Worcester House, the residence of the Earl of WORCESTER, who was Keeper of the Great Park of Nonsuch in the seventeenth century. The house no longer exists.

Workington (Cumbria)
A port on the SOLWAY FIRTH west of KESWICK whose name means 'estate of Weorc's people', with the personal name the same as for WORKSOP, although almost certainly not the same person. The name was recorded as *Wirkynton* in a document of about 1125. The '-ington' element represents, as frequently, the Old English suffix *-ingas* (people of) followed by *tūn* (farm, estate).

Worksop (Nottinghamshire)
A town north of NOTTINGHAM whose name means 'Weorc's valley', with the personal name (the same as for WORKINGTON) followed by the Old English *hop* (valley) (as for BACUP). It is not certain which particular valley gave the name of Worksop, which was recorded in the Domesday Book as *Warchesoppe*.

Worms Head (West Glamorgan)
A headland at the western extremity of the GOWER PENINSULA. Its name means what it says, 'worm's head' (that is, in the historic sense of 'dragon's head'), describing its shape. The origin thus lies in the Old English *wyrm* (snake, dragon) and *hēafod* (head, headland). The name is an exact parallel to that of GREAT ORMES HEAD, on the north coast of Wales. The Welsh name of Worms Head in Pen Pyrod, with the same meaning.

Wormwood Scrubs (Greater London)
This area of HAMMERSMITH, well-known for its prison, has an unpleasant-seeming name with scarcely a more pleasant meaning, although 'wormwood' is not involved. A record of the late twelfth

century gives the name as *Wormeholte*, deriving from the Old English *wyrm* (snake) (*compare* WORMS HEAD) and *holt* (wood). This refers to a former woodland here that was infested with snakes. At some stage, the name was miscopied or misheard, so producing the present Wormwood. The 'Scrubs' refers to the scrubland or land covered with brushwood formerly here. The name was correctly recorded down to the nineteenth century (as *Wormholt Scrubbs* in 1819), so the alteration is quite recent.

Worsbrough (South Yorkshire)
This coal-mining area immediately south of BARNSLEY has a name that means either 'Weorc's fortified place' or 'Wirc's fortified place', with the personal name followed by the Old English *burg* (fort). If Weorc is correct, it is the same as for WIRKSWORTH, WORKINGTON, and WORKSOP. The name was recorded as *Wircesburg* in the Domesday Book.

Worsley (Greater Manchester)
A town west of MANCHESTER whose name probably means 'Weorcgȳth's clearing', although the personal name is in some doubt, owing to conflicting spellings in early records of the name. A text of 1196 has the name as *Werkesleia*, but one of 1212 has *Wyrkedele*, without the possessive *-es* ending that should be present for a personal name. The final part of the name is the Old English *lēah* (woodland, clearing).

Worthing (West Sussex)
A well-known residential town and seaside resort whose name means '(place of) Wurth's people'; it is typical of the many '-ing' names of Sussex, this element representing the Old English *-ingas*, 'people of' (the person named). The Domesday Book recorded the name of Worthing as *Ordinges*, showing the full suffix, but losing the initial *W-* of the personal name.

Wotton-under-Edge (Gloucestershire)
A small town southwest of STROUD whose basic name, Wotton, is the exact equivalent of the 'Wootton' of WOOTTON BASSETT and other Woottons, and so means 'farm by a wood'. The 'Edge' is the hill at the foot of which the town lies in the COTSWOLD HILLS. The name was recorded as *æt Wudetune* in a text of 940, as *Vutune* in the Domesday Book, and as *Wotton under Egge* in a document of 1466.

Wragby (Lincolnshire)
This small town south of MARKET RASEN has a typical Scandinavian name, meaning 'Wraghi's farm'. The personal name is a Danish one, here followed by the Old Norse *bý* (farm). The name was recorded as *Waragebi* in the Domesday Book.

Wrekin, The (Shropshire)
A rocky hill southwest of WELLINGTON whose name represents the same Celtic element that lies behind the name of WROXETER, only four miles away. Unfortunately, the precise origin remains uncertain. The Roman name of Wroxeter, *Viroconium*, presumably applied originally to The Wrekin, which has an ancient hill-fort on its summit. A document of 975 refers to The Wrekin as *Wrocene*. Wrekin is now also the name of an administrative district of the county. *See* WROXETER.

Wrexham (Clwyd)
A town southwest of CHESTER whose name is of English origin and means 'Wryhtel's pasture', with the personal name (meaning 'workman', compare 'wright') followed by the Old English *hamm* (riverside land, water meadow). There is no obvious river at Wrexham now, but clearly there once was some kind of watercourse, as testified in the street-names Watery Road, Watery Lane, Brook Street, and Rivulet Road, with the last but one of these ending at Bridge Street. The original form of the name was probably something like 'Wrightham', in the spelling of its time (*Wristlesham* in 1161); the present spelling

is due to Welsh influence (*Gwregsam* in 1291, and now Wrecsam). *See also* WREXHAM MAELOR.

Wrexham Maelor (Clwyd)
This administrative district, in the east of the county, has a name that partly derives from WREXHAM, its main town, and partly from Maelor, an ancient territorial name, said to derive from *mael* (prince) and *llawr* (level valley floor).

Wroxeter (Shropshire)
This village on the River SEVERN southeast of SHREWSBURY has a name (like that of EXETER) that denotes it to be the site of a former Roman settlement, with the second half of the name thus representing the Old English *ceaster* (Roman camp). The first part of the name derives from the Roman name of the city, *Viroconium*, also recorded as *Viriconium*. This is almost certainly of Celtic origin, but the root element on which it is based remains obscure, despite attempts to link it with Latin *vir* (man). Another version of the name was *Uiroconium* or (perhaps) *Uriconium*, which led to 'Uricon' as a poetic name for Wroxeter, as in A.E. Housman's poem, *A Shropshire Lad*:

> To-day the Roman and his trouble
> Are ashes under Uricon.

The present name of the village almost certainly applied originally to The WREKIN, four miles from Wroxeter. Later historic records of the village's name are *Rochestre* in the Domesday Book (which might have resulted in another ROCHESTER) and *Wroxcestre* in 1155. Wroxeter was originally the capital of the *Cornovii* tribe, who gave their name to CORNWALL.

Wychavon (Hereford and Worcester)
An administrative district, in the east of the county, whose name was devised when the district was established in 1974. It is a combination of the latter half of the name of DROITWICH, in which one of its historic

spellings with *-wych* (as *Drihtwych* in 1347, and *Dirtewych* in 1460), and the River AVON. Droitwich is in the north of the district, and the Avon flows through the southern part. (But might not 'Avonwich' have been a better and more authentic combination, in modern terms?)

Wye (Wales/England; Kent)
There are at least three rivers of the name, with probably the best known the one that rises in Wales and flows generally east then south through HEREFORD, ROSS-ON-WYE, MONMOUTH and CHEPSTOW to enter the SEVERN. This Wye, and the Derbyshire one that flows into the DERWENT, have a name that is identical to that of the WEY, and thus means 'conveyor', 'mover'. The Wye that rises near HIGH WYCOMBE as a tributary of the THAMES has a name that is derived as a 'back formation' from that of the town. The old market town of Wye northeast of ASHFORD in Kent has a name of quite a different origin, meaning '(place by a) shrine', from the Old English *wēoh* (idol, shrine). The reference is to an ancient heathen temple here. (For a name of different origin but identical meaning *compare* HARROW.) The Kent town was recorded as *an Uuaæ* in a document of 839, and in the Domesday Book was *Wi*.

Wymondham (Norfolk)
A small town southwest of NORWICH whose name means 'Wīgmund's homestead', with the personal name followed by the frequently occurring Old English *hām* (homestead). The name was recorded as *Wimundham* in the Domesday Book.

Wyre (Lancashire; Hereford and Worcester/ Shropshire)
This name applies to various geographical features in England. The administrative district of Lancashire, in the northwest of the county, derives its name from the River Wyre that flows through it to the Irish Sea. Further south, the same name is found for

the ancient wooded area (and modern administrative district) of Wyre Forest; the woodland is on the borders of Hereford and Worcester and Shropshire, and the administrative district is in the north of the former county. Both occurrences of the name probably derive from a single origin, and are based on a British (Celtic) conjectural root word *uigora* that means 'winding one'. For the Lancashire river, this is obviously descriptive. For Wyre Forest, it is not certain which river is so designated, although it may be the AVON, which certainly follows a winding course before it joins the SEVERN at

TEWKESBURY. But the name is better known for giving the tribal name *Weogoran*, which in turn gave the name of WORCESTER (which see). The northern Wyre was recorded as *Wir* in a document of about 1180, and Wyre Forest appeared as *in Weogorena leage* ('in the forest of the *Weogoran* tribe') in 816, but as *foresta de Wira* in 1177.

Wythenshawe (Greater Manchester)
A residential district of MANCHESTER whose name means 'willow wood', from the conjectural Old English *wīthegn* (willow) and *sceaga* (small wood).

Y

Yarm (Cleveland)

This town south of STOCKTON-ON-TEES has a name that grammatically represents the dative plural (used to denote location) of the conjectural Old English *gear* (dam; dialect 'yair'), referring to a dam or enclosure arranged to catch fish in a river. Yarm lies in a loop of the TEES, an ideal location for such dams. The name was recorded in the Domesday Book as *Iarun*.

Yarmouth (Norfolk, Isle of Wight)

Either of two places — a Norfolk port and resort, or a coastal resort on the Isle of Wight. The former is officially known as Great Yarmouth (as distinct from Little Yarmouth, now a southern district of Great Yarmouth, and known as Southtown), and takes its name from the River Yare that flows into the North Sea at GORLESTON-ON-SEA, immediately south of Yarmouth. However, the present name of the river derives as a 'back formation' from that of Yarmouth itself, so that the town more precisely takes its name from the earlier name of the Yare, which was *Gerne*, so recorded in a document of the mid-twelfth century. This comes from a British (Celtic) conjectural root element *gar-* or *ger-* meaning 'to shout', 'to talk', so that for the river this can be understood as meaning 'babbler'. The Roman name of the river was *Gariennus*, from the same source, and the Roman name of the fort here (at what is now Burgh Castle, three miles southwest of Great Yarmouth, and also on the Yare) was *Gariannum*, similarly from this Celtic source. In the Domesday Book, Great Yarmouth was recorded as *Gernemwa*, showing the old river name. Down in the Isle of Wight, the coastal resort of Yarmouth west of NEWPORT is also on a River Yare, which also derives its name as a 'back formation' from that of the town at its mouth. But here, the town's name does not derive from that of the river but means 'gravel estuary', from the Old English *ēar* (gravel) and *mūtha* (mouth, river-mouth, estuary). This means that the river must have had some earlier name, and it was probably FRESHWATER, which is now the name of the village resort on the Yar (as distinct from the Yare, whose name is also confusingly spelt as Yar). The southern Yarmouth was recorded in the Domesday Book as *Ermud*. There are thus two distinct Yarmouths and two different rivers called Yar (or Yare). (The Yar that does not flow into the SOLENT at Yarmouth rises near the south coast and enters the sea west of BEMBRIDGE.)

Yeadon (West Yorkshire)

A town northwest of LEEDS whose name probably means 'high hill', from the Old English *hēah* (high) and *dūn* (hill). This would suit the location of Yeadon — on one of the spurs of the hill ridge known as The Chevin. The name was recorded as *Iadun* in the Domesday Book.

Yell (Shetland)

The island between MAINLAND and UNST whose name is said to derive from the Old Norse *geldr*, meaning 'barren' (compare 'gelding' as a castrated horse). A document of the mid-thirteenth century gives the name as *Jala*.

Yelverton (Devon)

A small town on the western edge of DARTMOOR southeast of TAVISTOCK. Its name is recorded on the one-inch Ordnance Survey map of 1809 as *Elfordtown*, with this perhaps representing a basic name of Elford, meaning 'Ella's ford' or 'elder tree ford'. The present form of the name, with *Y-*, was introduced by the Great Western Railway in 1859 to reflect the local pronunciation.

Yeo (England)

There are at least half a dozen rivers of this

name, most of them in Devon, but one is in Avon, and another rises in Dorset and then flows through YEOVIL to join the River Parrett in Somerset. Most of the Devon Yeos have a name that simply represents the Old English *ēa* (river). However, the one that is joined by the Creedy southeast of CREDITON has a name that comes from the Old English *ēow* (yew). The Yeo that flows through Yeovil, and gave its name to the town, was earlier known as the *Gifle* (so recorded in a document of 933); this name is identical to that of the Ivel, the river that joins the OUSE in Bedfordshire, and gives this Yeo another derivation, from a conjectural British (Celtic) root element *gablo-*meaning 'forked' (the Bedfordshire river was also recorded as *Gifle* in the mid-tenth century).

Yeovil (Somerset)

A manufacturing town east of TAUNTON on the River YEO, which as explained (above) was originally known as the *Gifle*. It is this early form of the name that gave that of the town, so that the '-vil' is misleading, and is not related to the '-ville' of such names as WATERLOOVILLE or BOURNVILLE. Yeovil was therefore itself recorded as *Gifle* in the mid-tenth century, and in the Domesday Book was *Givele*. The town's association with the Yeo, and the association of *Gifle* with the River Ivel (*see* YEO), came to give the trade name 'St Ivel' for the dairy products now manufactured by Unigate, but originally by the firm of Aplin and Barrett, of Yeovil. This firm's managing director created an imaginary medieval monk named St Ivel who lived by the Yeo in or near Yeovil.

Yeovilton (Somerset)

This village with its airfield east of ILCHESTER is on the River YEO, which also flows through YEOVIL. As explained above (*see* YEO) its earlier name was *Gifle*. This gave the name of Yeovilton, which is thus 'farm by the *Gifle*'. The name was recorded as *Geveltone* in the Domesday Book.

Yes Tor (Devon)

A famous hill on DARTMOOR, south of OKEHAMPTON, whose name means 'eagle's hill', from the Old English *earn* (eagle) and *torr* (hill, tor). The -*s* of 'Yes' is thus the posessive one. The name was recorded as *Ernestorre* in a document of 1240. Compare the Welsh name for Snowdonia (*see* SNOWDON).

Yiewsley (Greater London)

A district of HILLINGDON whose name means 'Wifel's clearing' (or perhaps 'Wifel's wood'), with the personal name followed by the Old English *lēah* (wood, clearing). The name was recorded as *Wivesleg* in a document of 1235.

York (North Yorkshire)

The present name of this famous city northeast of LEEDS, is a complex distortion of the original! It is best to take the developments and alterations chronologically. In the second century AD Ptolemy recorded the name as *Eborakon*, and the subsequent Roman name of the legionary fortress here was *Eburacum*. Both these names derive from a British (Celtic) personal name, Eburos, probably meaning 'yew man', no doubt referring to his estate among yew trees or containing yew trees. To the Anglo-Saxons, such a name was meaningless (as *Sorviodunum* was at SALISBURY), so they took it as *Eofor*, based on the Old English *eofor* (wild boar), and added *wīc* (dwelling-place) to give a name *Eoforwic*, so recorded in about 1060. The Vikings then came here, and altered the final *wic* of the name to the similar-sounding *vík*, although this meant 'bay', and was hardly suitable for inland York. The first part of the name was in turn now meaningless to them, and so gradually became 'smoothed' to what is now the first three letters of 'York', while the fourth letter represents the final letter of *vík*. The present spelling of the name is recorded as early as the thirteenth century. The tenth-century Viking name, however, is preserved today in that of the Jorvik Viking

Centre, an impressive museum of Viking artefacts opened in 1984 on the important archaeological site in the city. As a former Roman settlement, York had the name of *Eoforwicceaster*, with the Old English '-caster' element (*ceaster*) that meant 'Roman camp'. If this had prevailed, we might today have had a name for York something like 'Evercaster' (one assumes that the *wic* would have been dropped from the name). The town gave its name to the county of Yorkshire, which was recorded as *Eoferwicscir* in a text of the mid-eleventh century, and as *Euruicscire* in the Domesday Book. The original county was so large, that it had to be divided into three parts, called 'Ridings', that is, 'thirdings' (from the Old Norse *thrith-jungr* 'third part').

Youghal (Cork)
A market town east of CORK whose name means 'yew wood', representing the Irish name, Eochaill. Yew trees are still found in the town.

Z

Zennor (Cornwall)
A village near the coast west of ST IVES whose name was recorded in a document of 1291 as *ecclesia Sancte Senare*, so that it is named after St Senara. We have no information about this saint, except that she was a woman. The parish church is dedicated to her, as one would expect.

GUIDE TO FURTHER READING

There are a number of books and sources that anyone interested in place-names and their origins can consult with interest and profit. Some of the best are rather formidably academic; others may be more readable but some can be unreliable or downright wrong. A good rule of thumb for books on place-names is, 'The earlier the book the less reliable it is likely to be'. This is because place-name study has made rapid advances only in recent years, especially from 1960 onwards, and anything before this date *may* be helpful but may equally be inaccurate or out of date. Also to be avoided on the whole, are locally based publications by keen amateurs, who can sometimes have their own misguided notions as to the etymology of place-names. One such book that I treasure is a privately published booklet on the place-names of Lincolnshire. It would be best to grant its well-meaning author discreet anonymity, if only for his interpretation of the Old English name of Stamford ('stone ford') as a Celtic one meaning 'a way out of a smoothly flowing river' and, even better, of the name of Spalding ('the Spald people') as comprising the 'Celtic' elements *s* (out of), *pal* (marsh), *de* (worship), *lyn* (pool) and *ge* (enclosure), so that the overall name nicely reads as 'place out of a marsh by the enclosure of the worship pool'. This book was published in 1945.

Similarly to be avoided are those works by Celtic authors who refuse to acknowledge that any place-names in their land can be of English origin. The author of a work entitled *Gaelic Place Names of the Lothians*, published in 1912, thus derives Musselburgh ('mussel town') from the Gaelic *mas coill bruch* (round-hill hill); Berwick ('barley farm') from *bear uig* (sharp point at a nook); and Haddington ('farm associated with Hada') from a Gaelic root word *chuidan* meaning 'small fold'. Edinburgh, in his book, is even 'brae of the hill', from the Gaelic *aodann* (brae) and *bruch* (hill). And as if this was not enough, he gilds the Scottish lily even further by interpreting the nickname of Edinburgh, Auld Reekie ('old smoky'), as 'high place', from *alt* (high) and *ruighe* (slope)! (Some of the supposedly Celtic words here should be treated with caution.)

For English place-names, easily the best works to consult are the volumes, by counties, published by the English Place-Name Society. Here, as elsewhere, the earlier volumes are liable to be less accurate or detailed than the more recent, but at least they have the information. The various volumes present the material historically, grouping the names by the relevant 'hundred' in its county (and moreover using the pre-1974 county names), with copious examples of early records of a particular place-name from the first known occurrence of it. The volumes cover not merely towns, villages, rivers, hills, and the usual expected features, but anything that can be regarded as having a place-name distinctive of it, such as a street, a farm, a field, or an individual house. They also group all the personal names in a particular county in a single section, dividing them according to their language of origin (Old English, Old Scandinavian, for the most part). There is also a section, sometimes a substantial one, giving all the recorded elements of the place names in the county. As these will frequently often be found in other counties, the listing of such elements can have a more general application than it might seem. One of the most recent such listings, for example, is that of the volumes devoted to the place-names of Cheshire, published in 1981. (A more recent and more specialised volume, published in 1985, is devoted exclusively to Cornish place-name elements.)

The English Place-Name Society was founded in 1923, and has been slowly but surely producing volumes on the different English counties ever since. It has not completed its task, however, and there are still no volumes (as of 1988) on Hampshire, Kent, Leicestershire and Rutland, Lincolnshire, the City of London, Shropshire, or Staffordshire. However, some of the names in these counties are covered in other works, mentioned below.

Two volumes devoted entirely to English place-name elements were published by the Society in 1956, and were reprinted in 1970. 'English' here means 'of England', and the books thus list all recorded elements in whatever language they are found, including not only Old English and Old Norse (the majority), but French, Latin, and Celtic. Particularly valuable are the comments on each element, and the examples of place-names containing them that are quoted. And although research subsequent to 1956 has clarified and corrected some of the material, the two volumes remain both helpful and informative. The title of the work is: *English Place-Name Elements*, by A.H. Smith, English Place-Name Society, Volumes XXV and XXVI, Cambridge University Press, 1956.

Mention should be made at this point of the best-known standard work on English place-names and their origins. This is Eilert Ekwall's *Concise Oxford Dictionary of English Place-Names*, published by the Oxford University Press in its final, fourth edition in 1960. Many of the names in this book are still accounted for accurately, despite the advance in toponymical studies since this date. The work explains the origins of many minor names, such as those of small villages and hamlets, as well as the better known ones, and is particularly detailed in its recording of personal names, where they are involved. The author goes to some pains, for example, to identify the Norman families and their place of origin in the 'double-barrelled' names, where they occur. In short, the book superseded any earlier comprehensive study of English place-names, and remains a milestone to this day.

Exactly ten years later, the British place-name field was opened wider by the publication of John Field's *Place Names of Great Britain and Ireland* (David & Charles, Newton Abbot, 1970). The book is selective, and includes both familiar and unfamiliar names, but it is readable, up-to-date (for its time), and most importantly deals with the whole of the British Isles, not just England. The entries, too, though brief, are usually clear and readable, although some are more in the form of condensed (and abbreviated) annotations than 'spelt out' accounts.

That same year was also published a book by three place-name experts, W.F.H. Nicolaisen, Margaret Gelling, and Melville Richards, entitled *The Names of Towns and Cities in Britain*. The three authors are respectively authorities on the place-names of Scotland, England, and Wales, and the book itself contains readable entries, not mere annotations, on many of the names of well-known towns in Britain, as the title implies, as well as a section devoted to the names of London districts. The book was published by Batsford in a hardback edition, but is now also available in paperback.

Dr Gelling has herself published two scholarly accounts of the place-naming process in England, entitled respectively *Signposts to the Past* (Dent, 1978, new edition 1988) and *Place-Names in the Landscape* (Dent, 1984). The first of these has the self-explanatory subtitle of 'Place-names and the history of England', and concentrates on the linguistic and archaeological side of place-name study. The second book is a study of the way place-names relate to the natural features of the landscape, such as hills, valleys, rivers, streams, marshes, moors, trees, and forests. Basically, Dr Gelling provides a series of articles, each devoted to a single element, such as *hȳth* (landing-place), or *dūn* (hill), and discusses the way these elements appear in place-names.

Of other general books on English place-names, a work not to be overlooked is Kenneth Cameron's *English Place-Names*, first published by Batsford in 1961. In a way, Professor Cameron's book is the best and most readable general study of English place-names that there is, and is wonderfully succinct and informative. For background information to English place-names, the reader should consult this one book, if none other.

But what about Scotland, Wales, and Ireland? English place-names are certainly the most thoroughly researched, but the other countries also have literature devoted to them, even if on a more modest scale. For specifically Scottish names, the reader would do best to consult W.F.H. Nicolaisen's *Scottish Place-Names*, published by Batsford in 1976. However, it is selective in its treatment, and its essentially scholarly approach may deter some readers who seek quick information on a particular name. For that, recourse can be had, with due reservations for certain of its etymologies, some of which are purely fanciful, to James B. Johnston's *Place-Names of Scotland*, first published in 1892, with a third edition in 1934, but since reprinted (in 1970) by S.R. Publishers. It is recommended here chiefly because of its comprehensiveness. For a much more limited account of Scottish names, but also a much more up-to-date and readable one, David Dorward's small book *Scotland's Place-Names*, published by William Blackwood in 1979, is useful. There is also a little paperback with very brief derivations, but for many more names, entitled simply *Place-Names*. The author is Fiona Johnstone, and the booklet appeared in the 'Introducing Scotland' series, published by Spurbooks, in 1982.

For Wales, unfortunately, there is no overall comprehensive place-name dictionary available as yet, although there are local publications of varied worth and value, and for Ireland there was only P.W. Joyce's *The Origin and History of Irish Names of Places*, published in 1875 (although since reprinted), until my own more modest *Dictionary of Irish Place-Names* appeared in 1986, published by the Appletree Press of Belfast. However, there is also a booklet on the same lines as Fiona Johnstone's for Scotland, entitled *The Meaning of Irish Place Names*, which was compiled by James O'Connell and published by the Blackstaff Press, also of Belfast, in 1979; readers who wish bald definitions and an entire absence of comment or historic detail may find this sufficient for their needs.

Cornwall, the fourth Celtic constituent of the British Isles, merits a mention here. The best and most up-to-date study of its names is the one already referred to: *Cornish Place-Name Elements*, by O.J. Padel, English Place-Name Society, Volume LVI/LVII, Cambridge University Press, 1985. This is not a place-name dictionary, however, but an annotated dictionary of Cornish place-name elements. Even so, it enables the names of many places in Cornwall to be interpreted — so long as they are Cornish in origin! The book does not deal with English names in Cornwall, and for a more general guide to the names of the county, the reader is left with no choice but to refer to T.F.G. Dexter's not entirely reliable *Cornish Names*, published locally in Truro in 1968 as a reprint of the original edition of 1926 published by Longman, Green. But a better source, if limited geographically, is P.A.S. Pool's *The Place-Names of West Penwith*, published by the Federation of Old Cornwall Societies in 1973. As its name indicates, however, the book deals only with the place-names of the Land's End peninsula.

A good and handy guide to the Welsh, Scottish (Gaelic), and Scandinavian elements that appear in British names is the small booklet *Place names on maps of Scotland and Wales*, issued by the Ordnance Survey, and first published in 1968, but with a number of successive editions, with additions and corrections.

Readers specifically interested in recent place-names in Britain, such as those of the new administrative counties, may find my own *Concise Dictionary of Modern Place-Names in Great Britain and Ireland* useful. This was first published by Oxford University Press in 1983, with a subsequent corrected paperback edition.

The place-names of Greater London make an important study, especially now that the area covered is so much larger than it used to be, taking in many places that were formerly in Surrey, Kent, Essex, and other counties (including late lamented Middlesex), and the standard work to consult here is that by John Field, *Place-Names of Greater London*, published by Batsford in 1970, the same year as his other work already mentioned. The entries are in the same style, part annotative, part discursive.

John Field is also the author of a third book on place-names, the definitive *English Field Names*, published by David and Charles of Newton Abbot in 1972. This specialist but important field had never been covered before in such depth, so that the book is a 'first' of its kind in its own particular area of study.

For river names, the reader will still find much of value in Eilert Ekwall's *English River-Names*, published by the Clarendon Press, Oxford, in 1928, although some of the author's conclusions have subsequently been corrected and expanded on by more recent research. Ekwall was a firm believer in the value and importance of first-hand groundwork, and he visited many rivers in person in the four years it took him to compile material for the book.

Readers particularly interested in Roman sites and their names could do no better than to consult A.L.F. Rivet and Colin Smith's scholarly but fascinating work, *The Place-Names of Roman Britain*, published by Batsford in 1979, and a milestone of its kind.

Street names, another absorbing speciality, have not been covered comprehensively in Britain, although

Kenneth Cameron's book, mentioned above, has a section devoted to them, as does John Field's Greater London book on London street-names. For a fuller book devoted to the names of London's streets, the reader should consult Sheila Fairfield's *The Streets of London* (subtitled 'A dictionary of the names and their origins'), published by Macmillan as a paperback in 1983.

There appears to be no individual study of any substance on the names of country houses, although books on standard house names exist, such as Leslie Dunkling's booklet *English House Names*, published by The Names Society in 1971, and Joyce Miles's somewhat skimpy and superficial but nevertheless relevant paperback, *The House Names Book*, published by Unwin in 1982.

A paperback that ties in with both district names, street names, and house names is Cyril M. Harris's *What's In a Name?* (a title that normally conceals frivolity or flights of fancy). This deals with the names of London Underground stations, and so combines toponymy with stathmology (the study of stations).

Gazetteers provide a useful adjunct to place-name study, if only for identifying the location of a place, or for examining the distribution or frequency of a particular place-name. For general use, the *Bartholomew Gazetteer of Places in Britain* is ideal, because it combines a comprehensive listing of over 40,000 places, defined and briefly described with an atlas of Britain. The latest edition of this work is the one published in 1986, compiled by Oliver Mason. But for a truly comprehensive volume of this type, recourse should be had to the vast Ordnance Survey *Gazetteer of Great Britain*, published in 1987. This contains all names from the Ordnance Survey's 'Landranger' series of maps, which have a scale of 1:50,000, or two centimetres to the kilometre (approximately $1\frac{3}{4}$ inches to the mile, and so the modern successor to the old 'inch-to-a-mile' maps). The work contains around a quarter of a million names, from rivers and cities down to long-distance footpaths and stately homes, even individual farms, churches, and schools, as well as many other features that appear on the Ordnance Survey 'Landranger' maps.

The Ordnance Survey maps themselves are undoubtedly one of the best and most useful guides to the place-names of a particular local area, and are a valuable substitute for a personal visit to a place. Indeed, in some ways they are better than a personal visit, for they enable the contours and general topography of an area to be noted accurately almost at a glance; the course of rivers; the extent of woods, moors and other natural regions; the course of Roman roads. They can serve as a visual guide to the origin of a particular place-name, too, so that one can instantly see why a place named Lowford, for example, is so called, or to appreciate why the district of a town named Newtown is located where it is: the town has expanded in a particular direction to be nearer to a railway, coast or other significant location.

The 'Landranger' maps have a scale of 1:50,000, which is 2 centimetres for every kilometre on the ground, or about 1¼ inches to the mile. They therefore correspond metrically to the old 'inch-to-a-mile' maps, and offer sufficient detail for a whole number of named objects to be noted, from towns and districts to small hamlets, footpaths and the individual buildings already mentioned above for the *Gazetteer*. They also mark the locations of common or unnamed features, which can be significant for a nearby place-name. For example, Map 196 in the series (The Solent) shows the exact site of the 'Remains of Roman fort' at Portchester, or the 'Nature Trail' on the River Beaulieu.

'Discover the Hidden Treasures of Britain with an Ordnance Survey Map', says the advertising literature. This invitation could well be modified to read 'Discover the Place-Names of Britain with an Ordnance Survey Map', and it is a reminder that the range of maps issued by the Ordnance Survey is wider than often supposed. Most people are interested in the place-names of their immediate neighbourhood, for example,

and for this reason alone the purchase of the relevant large-scale map is a 'must'. The best map for this purpose is the one with a scale of 1:10,000, which is one centimetre to 100 metres on the ground, or six inches to the mile. Maps on this scale have been issued to cover the whole country, from the densest urban area to the remotest moorland and forest, and they enable local place-names and features to be studied in satisfying detail. One can begin to appreciate, for instance, why Hartley Farm ('stag meadow farm') is where it is: *there* is the wood where the stags will have lived, and *there* are the meadows of the farm today, below the hill but near the pond (where the stags will have come to drink). Or, in the heart of the city, consider the names of those tower blocks: Canberra Towers, Rotterdam Towers, Copenhagen Towers, Oslo Towers, all by the street called International Way! In addition, the Ordnance Survey has published maps for cities and significant urban areas on a scale of 1:1,250 (50 inches to the mile), which give not only the street names of the mapped area but individual house names.

Nor should old Ordnance Survey maps be overlooked. Not only are they historically more valuable for place-name study in many cases, especially those a hundred years old or more, but the names themselves appear in a contemporary form and spelling which can be significant, even in the nineteenth century. Modern reprints of old Ordnance Survey maps are now available from various sources, the chief being the ones of England and Wales published by David and Charles of Newton Abbot, and those of Scotland published by Caledonian Books of Collieston, Aberdeenshire. Both publishers issue the maps as 'Victorian Ordnance Survey Maps', with respective sets of 97 maps for England and Wales, and 94 for Scotland. The maps can be purchased singly or in quantity: either way, they are cheaper than current Ordnance Survey maps, which is to the advantage of the toponymist's purse or pocket! The English and Welsh maps are reprints of those issued between 1805 and

1873, while the Scottish ones all date from the edition of 1896 — later, but equally (and increasingly) valuable.

It will no doubt be helpful to give the addresses of the three publishers mentioned here in this connection, so that readers can obtain further particulars if they wish to: Ordnance Survey, Romsey Road, Maybush, Southampton SO9 4DH (tel. 0703–792000); David & Charles Publishers plc, Brunel House, Newton Abbot, Devon TQ12 4PU (tel. 0626–61121); Caledonian Books, Collieston, Ellon, Aberdeenshire AB4 9RT (tel. 035887–288/275).

Finally, in a sort of full circle, the reader who is interested in the *historical* background to Britain's place-names could do no better than to dip into the *Historical Atlas of Britain*, edited by Malcolm Falkus and John Gillingham, published (in a revised edition) by Kingfisher Books, London, in 1987. This gives an informed and clearly illustrated and mapped account of 'the making of Britain' from the Ancient Britons to the present century, as well as affording an insight into the way in which many of Britain's place-names have gone on to live a new life in other countries of the world. That, however, is a subject outside the scope of the present Dictionary!